Points of Truth

By

John L. Orr

INFINITY
PUBLISHING

Copyright © 2012 by John L. Orr

ISBN 978-0-7414-4192-8

Printed in the United States of America

Published November 2012

INFINITY PUBLISHING

Toll-free (877) BUY BOOK
Local Phone (610) 941-9999
Fax (610) 941-9959
Info@buybooksontheweb.com
www.buybooksontheweb.com

TABLE OF CONTENTS

Dedication

For P.K. Spooner, Elmer Spraker, Lt. Al Hunt, Lt. Russ Pierce and Detective Dennis Wilson; mentors all, despite a few kinks in the hoseline in the early years. I have not let you down…and to C. Molnar – you know why.

PREFACE

I have been called "the most prolific serial arsonist of the twentieth century." I learned of the slur while perusing documents related to my case in 1997, five years after a wrongful conviction of federal arson charges. I sat in the Los Angeles County Jail in a cold, dank 9'-by-6' concrete and metal cell, awaiting a state trial on arson and murder charges.

The reference to "the most prolific..." appeared in a handwritten margin note of a case clearance sheet filled out by L.A. City Fire Department arson investigator Glen Lucero. The scratchings seemed to match Lucero's handwriting, but there were eight investigators assigned to the task force prosecuting me, and all had access to the files I examined. In mid-2007, I confirmed Lucero as the originator of the affront.

The top sheet was followed by no less than twelve reports of arson fires occurring in the Hollywood, California area in the mid-to-late 1980s. Lucero closed these cold cases a month before his retirement, arbitrarily blaming me for setting the fires — some of them ten years after the fact. There was no evidence that I set any of the blazes; no witnesses placed me at or near the scenes, and Lucero never queried me about any of the arsons. Most were set in carports or garages in the shabbier areas of Hollywood; actually, in the mid-80s, all of Tinsel Town looked seedy. Had Lucero ever bothered asking me if I appeared at any of the fire scenes, my answer might have resulted in 8–10 additional felony charges. My answer would have been yes.

Lucero, like most of the federal, state, and local investigators assigned to the task force, was a dedicated, honest law enforcer. Glen attended classes I taught. I shared cocktails and meals with him. He and his lovely wife came to a 1989 Christmas party at my home.

Closing cold cases and blaming the felonies on a suspect without evidence is called *Clearing by Exception* (CBE). CBE is law enforcement's equivalent of giving away a 15-year-old derelict car sitting in your backyard through a newspaper ad: pretty the beast up cosmetically and peddle it like it's a cream puff. CBE requires only the barest of statements to hang the crime on your designated suspect, similar to the used car blurb, "Like new, runs great!" really means, "When you can get the beast started..." Lucero's margin notes declaring me "the most prolific serial arsonist" were as useless as the CBE sheet's statement, "This fire attributed to convicted serial arsonist John L. Orr due to

1

similar M.O." The declaration is meaningless, the conclusion unsupported, but you managed to move the dilapidated Gremlin out of the back yard. Unfortunately, many police agencies pad their annual clearance statistics using the CBE method. I suppose Lucero looked pretty good the year he CBE'd his inbox by blaming me for a collection of unsolved cases and at the same time starting the "most prolific" theory.

My appearance at one of Lucero's Hollywood fire scenes is explained and documented in the vast repository of my case. Lucero had access to the documents. He might have read that a private investigator I lived with asked me to run down to a Hollywood fire scene and do an investigation for him. I agreed to $250 for a thirty-minute scene check, a few photos and a report. That was pretty good money in 1985. My files also revealed that I was on an all-night surveillance with a partner at the time of that Hollywood fire; a verifiable, documented alibi. While at that scene, I spoke with a resident who told me of several similar fires in Hollywood. I later incorporated this information in my fact-based - fictional novel, *Points of Origin*. I believe Lucero read my manuscript and decided I set all his Hollywood fires based on my inclusion of actual incidents.

What existed as a hypothesis became accepted fact when best-selling author Joseph Wambaugh published a true-crime book about my case in 2002. Wambaugh interviewed less than 20 percent of the 100+ witnesses quoted in his book. His confirmation of the "most prolific serial arsonist of the twentieth century" assumption came from a referenced Behavioral Science Unit criminal profiler who Wambaugh did not name. Wambaugh's book, advertising, reviews, TV and newspaper interviews perpetuated the baseless speculation. I even wrote to Wambaugh and asked for the criminal profiler's name. After three attempts to get a copy of the profile or communicate with its author through a supervisor, I gave up. Serial criminal profilers jump at the chance to talk with their subjects. I do not believe the profile exists beyond a handwritten submission form I found in the case files in 1997.

Convicted serial killer David Berkowitz, known as Son of Sam, admitted to setting 800–1000 fires before his arrest in the late 1970s. As a full-time arson/explosives investigator, I did not have enough time in my business day to keep up with workload, let alone trying to post fire-setting records. I had to prioritize my caseload to keep up productivity. If I set fires in my own jurisdiction, the arson remained stagnant in my books as unsolved. Why would I jeopardize my unit's clearance rate by adding unsolved cases? From 1981-1991, my unit had the highest clearance rate in southern California, possibly the whole state.

Sentenced to thirty years for arson in September 1992, I was paroled from federal custody in 2002. My conduct during the 10 years I spent in custody was exemplary. My 2002 stroll out the gate of Lompoc Penitentiary ended on a California Department of Corrections bus; my freedom-walk lasting about thirty ankle-shackled steps. Convicted of murder in 1998, my sentence now is life without parole. I have little hope of release. I maintain my innocence; an act that can be done, but what's the point? Telling anyone I am innocent after conviction by two juries makes no sense. Convicted criminals are not believable, but my innocence is valid.

I balked at producing a memoir until several television documentaries examined my case from the investigator's viewpoint. One, narrated by actor Stacy Keach, began, "Captain Orr came from a troubled family life, and his wanton recklessness took its toll on department vehicles..." My "troubled" life? My parents separated when I was 16 years old, divorcing a year later. Destroying fire equipment? I never crashed an engine or ladder truck, but two four-door sedan "narc" cars I operated sustained minor damage to the tune of about $900. One was my responsibility, the other a no-fault bumper car experience. I drove fire department vehicles for over eighteen years, and at least 100,000 miles. Stacy Keach got his conjectural, scripted information from case investigators and prosecutors. My troubled life began when they focused on me as a suspect.

Typical case histories in true-crime, non-fiction books and shows like *Forensic Files*, *American Justice*, and *Investigative Reports* expose all the warts from a convicted criminals' past. There seems to always be a history of some form of child abuse, petty criminal behavior, broken homes, rebellion, or early and continuing alcohol and drug offenses. I did not fit any criminal profile, and no aberrations were found in my background by investigators. This should have been a clue.

I do not imagine myself a great writer. I am adequate; I can tell a story. With minimal creative writing training, I have drawn on my only source of experience: report writing. I penned *Points of Origin* with good intentions, trying to incorporate character development, plot, and solid dialogue. These tactics, typical of every successful writer, did not really work. *Points of Origin* was written like police reports; fact and fiction put down on paper in chronological order with minimal description. Once I put the fact-based fiction on paper, the tale took off like my real-life pursuit of a good case.

I once took a class in creative writing and experimented in a brief report of an accidental garage fire in the early 1990s. Expecting nobody to read the benign account, Sergeant Russ Pierce examined the document, looking for a police DR number. The investigation narration read, "As I arrived at the blazing two-car garage, I noted yellow-orange flames leaping upward from the partially-open overhead door, pushing an oily

3

black, pulsing cloud of smoke to sully a clear, Santa Ana-swept cerulean sky." Russ perused it and sent a copy back to me with a Post-it note attached. "Orr: Are you on drugs?"

I spent twelve of my 22 smoke-eating years as an arson/explosives investigator for the Glendale (CA) Fire and Police Departments. I arrested twenty serial fire-setters during my 12-year law enforcement career, apprehending over 25 more serial arsonists, mostly juveniles. Of the twenty arrested, only four were kids. I usually diverted underage pyromaniacs to counseling programs and ordered restitution in some. I guess serial arson was my specialty. No other investigator I am aware of can match this degree of success apprehending serial firesetters. In a 1995 meeting of task force investigators and my prosecutor, one of the attendees ventured a pompous statement: "Orr caught a bunch of serial arsonists. How did he capture so many? Because he was one and knew how they thought and what their next move was?" Why was I able to arrest twenty-eight residential and commercial burglars in my career? Was I a burglar? No. I simply absorbed training and real-life experience through exposure to these crimes during the course of my employment.

After viewing two of the factual crime shows about my case on television, I decided to write this memoir. If nothing else, my life story may fill in a few blanks for my family, friends, co-workers, case investigators and prosecutors, since they never interviewed me on this topic. My story may also enable me to instruct investigators and firefighters that have little experience with fire-setters of all varieties. My book, *Points of Truth*, is a way of defending myself. I try to keep the effort factual and free of the impression of vanity. Some will use the book to examine my psychology. "A need for attention and self-aggrandizement," they might say. Guilty as charged. I do need attention; always have. I married four times and love relationships and people. A philanderer, yes. A misogynist, no. In some ways I am a loner, typically when co-workers and fellow investigators did not meet my standards and work ethics. These paradoxical traits do fall within the parameters of a serial arsonist profile. I will let the reader decide.

Like in the pre-execution fiasco of convicted Oklahoma City bomber Timothy McVeigh, federal investigators and U.S. attorneys in my case repeatedly conspired to block justice instead of ensuring it. I have found notes from a meeting in early 1992 where I believe the plot hatched. I will hoard this evidence until I can get a confirmation from an attendee or substantiate the scheme through documents I have yet to locate. Maybe an appeals court will listen.

Ironically, an ongoing theme in my life and career, as well as in my fictional novel, *Points of Origin*, is exposure of the poor working relationship between fire department investigators, police officers, and detectives. In my years of service as a fire sleuth, I tried to appease these anomalies and enhance our professional connections; at least locally. Later in my career, I offered specialized training sessions, bringing representatives from these fields together to further eradicate jealousies. I succeeded for the most part, but firefighters and cops always tangle. Coexistence is possible, but not without confrontations, altercations and, occasionally, a little spilled professional blood.

I use several aliases in this text because musings about shortcomings of some of my former partners, and other associates, might cause some embarrassment. All the faults described and tales told are verifiable, or facts known by individuals involved in these amusing anecdotes. Some events I expose here for the first time, primarily because my career has ended and some of the players are reasonably free from retribution by their superiors because they near retirement or are already gone, or just do not care. Walter Beatty, Tom Rickles, and Lance Heiger are aliases. Joe Lopez is a real person, and one of the finest people I have ever met. Several other pseudonyms were necessary because I have so little material available to me for evaluation and verification. Any date/time inaccuracies are for the same reasons, but everything in this work is true; some dialogue engineered by memory.

Arrested in December 1991, the media blared, "Nationally-known fire captain arrested..." I never considered myself famous. I had ten articles published in the *American Fire Journal*, but its subscriber base was less than 15,000 in the early 1990s. Several of my articles were reprinted in related law enforcement and fire service periodicals. I trained over 1200 police officers, firefighters, crime scene analysts, private investigators, and insurance personnel in my career. People traveled from as far away as Hawaii, Washington, and Alaska to attend my training sessions. The rest hailed from closer to my southern California home-base. I marketed myself by hosting about 30 training sessions, but teaching less than a third of them. My skill came in selecting quality, qualified instructors with proven abilities to staff the seminars I moderated. I was recognized by simply offering timely training not covered extensively anywhere else.

Since incarceration, I have never been asked what I miss most. My answer may reveal a lot about who I am. I would answer, "Pink Floyd in the Rose Bowl in 1994, and the Johannes Vermeer exhibition at the National Gallery in Washington, D.C." I long for a good porterhouse, a burger from Tommy's in Eagle Rock, and also crave the thrill of a whodunit case; the pursuit, capture, and arrest of a suspect, but a revelation such as this is not healthy for a former cop in a prison surrounded by a thousand felons. Nevertheless, my combination fire service and law enforcement career was a hell of a ride. How many detectives can say they arrested someone for bigamy? Is there a fire department investigator who can say he worked an obscene bomb threat case? How many bagged a serial arsonist based on the questionable and odiferous evidence of dog feces and muddy footprints? This unusual text provides insight to the minds of serial arsonists I apprehended, the wildly successful operation of an eleven-man arson/explosives unit, and my personal life.

    John L. Orr

CHAPTER ONE
FIREPROOF

April 17, 1991, 1:21 p.m.

I did not hear the explosion or feel the concussion from the blast. Cruising along the residential eastern edge of Glendale, six miles from the detonation, I pondered a foray over the nearby city limits to my home. The day was a crisp sixty degrees with cool offshore breezes sweeping the L.A. basin's blue skies clear of clouds and smog.

Not officially off-duty for several hours, I felt reasonably secure of my decision to drop by home, only five blocks away, since my fire and police radios transmitted only routine emergencies for the past few hours. First responders frequently fall into the complacency trap. I was no different even if I worked in plainclothes and drove an unmarked car. My first novel's completion neared and I occasionally squeezed a few minutes writing time into my normally busy schedule; a benefit of living less than a half-mile from my employer's jurisdiction. The trek was not going to happen today. Three quick beeps from the fire radio got my attention like a bedside telephone jangling at 4 a.m. The tones preceded every emergency fire and paramedic call and this broadcast included the dispatcher keying her microphone immediately instead of allowing a few seconds dead air time for fire crews to get to the rigs. I heard a frenzied telephonic voice on a speakerphone in the background of the comm. center, as well as several other 9-1-1 lines ringing in before she spoke. I held my breath and swung my unmarked Ford Crown Victoria to the curb of east Broadway in front of sprawling Glendale High School, scanning the horizon for smoke. I expected a fire call. The dispatcher's voice cleared up any confusion. "Engine 28, unknown type explosion, many calls." The police radio speaker emitted two short beeps, indicating a rare exigency on their frequency, too. My heart rate jumped another few beats. Glendale PD received all 9-1-1 calls and eavesdropped on those passed off for fire and paramedic crews, dispatching their own units accordingly. "Car 15-Boy, 14 assist, unknown type of explosion..." I did not catch the address, but the assigned districts of Engine 28 and the primary police unit, 15-Boy, narrowed down my destination. The two broadcasts blended into a singular plea for help I knew would ultimately end up in my lap. I was the on-call arson/explosives investigator for the Glendale Fire and Police Departments for April 17, 1991. Bomb crime scenes and smoldering, debris-strewn arson site investigations are similar. Pyromaniacs, serial arsonists and explosive freaks share characteristics and techniques. Consequently, many law enforcement and fire agencies combine investigators with these skills and responsibilities into a team or task force. Glendale created such a fusion of talents successfully in 1980. Monterey County, California Sheriffs Department arson investigators also handle bomb/explosion cases, and cattle rustling in their semi-rural jurisdiction.

Equipped with a red spotlight, rear yellow winker, wig-wag headlights, and a siren, I activated them all and headed for the nearby northbound Glendale Freeway on-ramp. Radio chatter from multiple units kept me from advising the communications centers that I was responding, too. While concentrating on surface street traffic, I jotted down the location of my response notification for my report. After hitting 85 mph on the freeway, I scanned the foothill area of the La Crescenta section of Glendale and saw no telltale signs from the explosion or subsequent fire. I did hear 15-Boy radio in he was "97 the area." He was close to the incident. I slowed to seventy, still 5-6 minutes out myself. Seconds later, 15-Boy gave an exact location, reporting a blown-up residential mailbox. He added, "No need for fire department, no fire..." I seethed. The uniformed officer's statement was typical of a cop response to a "nuisance" call. If an engine did not show up on-scene, or I had not monitored the radio call, the result was a two-to-three day late notification to my unit. Fire captains always called out an arson/explosives investigator; one less report to write. The investigator generated the follow-up. A typical cop's attitude revealed no need for some wannabe-cop like me onsite to tell him how to handle a crime scene. If I did show up, the uniforms expected me to write the original crime report. I had a little difficulty breeching the blue wall of "real" law enforcers. To many of them, I was just a hose-jockey, albeit one with a .45 auto on my hip and a department-issued Mossberg 12-gauge shotgun in my trunk.

The blown-up mailbox, destroyed by common fireworks, an RPG, bazooka, or an IED, was illegal and the resulting crime report and statistics were assigned to my unit. A one- or two-day delay for my notification gave me a cold case, poorly handled or missing evidence, no photos, and limited, if any, follow-up possibilities. An unsolved case dropped my unit's clearance rate. The Glendale Fire/Police Department Arson/Explosives Unit enjoyed the highest clearance rate of any southern California jurisdiction since 1982. Before the police comm. center cancelled Engine 28, the rig and three-man crew arrived on-scene. A quick meeting resulted and, within seconds, both police and fire representatives pleasured me with stereophonic requests over the dual speakers in my car, "request arson investigator on-scene."

Close enough now to pick up the mobile unit broadcasts clearly, I recognized the voices of Officer John Riggs and Fire Captain Marv Owen. Captain Owen had an excellent history of following procedure and calling me out when policy dictated. Officer Riggs did not and, on several occasions, I had sent him a copy of the arson/explosives investigator call-out procedures as a not-so-subtle reminder of his "routine" incident analysis. He jeopardized my unit's efficiency and I out-ranked him considerably. We cleared over thirty percent of our assigned criminal cases when an instant request for an investigator came in. As with any crime, the sooner an experienced detective arrives to evaluate a scene, the better the chance of clearing the crime. Officer Riggs pleased me with his independent request.

Clearing the freeway, I left the lights and siren off and drove into the quiet, well-kept residential neighborhood as just another rubbernecker chasing police cars and a fire engine after an explosion. Many citizens and most criminals recognize the plain-wrapped, four-door sedan I drove as a "narc" car or detective unit. Still, it amazed me how stealthy the unit appeared to some. At fire scenes, I had uniformed officers scream at me for trying to drive around vehicle barricades and roadblocks in a car with so many antennas it looked like the H.M.S. Bounty. I existed in a real world where full-time arson investigators functioned as peace officers, sanctioned by California Penal Code section 830.3. Uniformed police as well as arson investigators from fire agencies can arrest, write and serve search warrants, and legitimately carry a concealed handgun.

Through a pair of powerful Zeiss binoculars I kept under my front seat for occasions like this, I surveyed the recently-rattled neighborhood from a block away. The mailbox topped a three-foot-tall brick base. The repository also rested on a bed of ivy 30 feet away, and a portion leaned against the rear tire of a Toyota Tercel 75 feet up the street from its original location. I could tell several things from my early observations. First, the box was an open-in-front style rectangular, heavy-metal receptacle. Second, whatever destroyed the thing did more damage than a common M-80 or similar device. An M-80 blows the door, bows a mailbox out on the sides and top, but does not send the pieces flying like saucering chunks from the *Challenger* shuttle explosion.

I focused the binoculars on the largest piece of the mailbox and saw it rounded—no longer square—and almost flat. Substantial outward wrenching and rending forces from within the receptacle were evident. From 50 yards away, I knew immediately what caused the blast. A few neighbors eyed me suspiciously, but I stayed put, evaluating my surroundings. The damage to the mailbox came to maybe thirty bucks. My concern surrounded a three-pound chunk of metal sailing through the air with substantial force. The back panel and door spiraled and twisted end-over-end like metallic UFOs. This delay-detonated prank had potential for serious injury.

Arsonists and bombers have one peculiarity not shared by other criminal types: they are compelled to view the results of their felonious actions. An armed robber or burglar does the dirty deed, then flees the scene, distancing themselves from the victims and police. Not the firebug or bomber. The old saying, "Like a moth drawn to a flame" could be no more appropriate. These criminals cannot stay away, and this consistency kept my clearance stats high. I loved ambushing them.

Only inches away from the curb-less roadway, the mailbox was accessible for easy placement of the explosive from a passing car, a bicycle, or a casual walker. Fortunately, a firefighter from Engine 28 guarded the narrow dirt border surrounding the used brick pedestal. It appeared that my training sessions with our fire crews paid off. I always counseled the troops, "A criminal can cover his hands with latex, or a sock, and leave no fingerprints, but can't wear gloves on their feet!" Footprint analysis played a major role in many of my arrests from 1979 to 1991. One culprit, a firefighter trainee, committed such a faux pas. His muddy boot prints and two piles of dog feces told a story he thought was his secret. Result: one in custody; case closed.

None of the onlookers appeared suspicious to me so I drove to the scene, parking on the wrong side of the street despite sufficient room to park legally, a stupid habit I picked up from the officers who partnered with me over the years. I guess it was a form of marking territory. After some investigative chitchat with the officer and firefighters, I asked the engine captain and police officer to clear the scene and leave. I wanted the cop to take basic information from the victim while I collected the destroyed box remnants and get everyone gone quickly. Knowing the culprits responsible were somewhere nearby, I wanted all official vehicles off the street while I set up blocks away with binoculars.

Telltale scraps of accordion-ribbon strips of green plastic littered the crime scene and further confirmed my theory. A larger piece revealed the bomb container: a two-liter soft drink bottle. Putting a bit of dry ice and ounce or two of water inside, tightening the cap, then placing the device and hauling ass was all it took. A dry-ice bomb. The reaction of dry ice with water creates a vapor like that used in movie special effects to simulate a low-lying fog or miasma from a witch's cauldron. The pressure within a container builds for anywhere from a minute or two, or more, depending on the amounts of the mixtures. When the device detonates, the release of pressure sounds like a howitzer firing off a round. No wonder there were so many calls reporting the blast.

I threw all the evidence into several heavy-duty paper bags to preserve fingerprints. We usually used plastic bags that tended to sweat when sealed and potentially neutralized some latents. Nearby, Officer Riggs got what information he needed from the 40-year-old housewife/victim. Tempted to talk with her, I felt it essential to clear the area. Cops, firefighters, and victims sometimes mistook this action as a lackadaisical attitude. In reality, the action was a formula for success. As I knelt to examine the now-unguarded mailbox base, Officer Riggs shouted at me from his idling car. Another blown-up mailbox report came in from a half-mile away. I had again not heard the blast and told him I would meet him there. He roared off.

One quick glance at the dirt by the pedestal gave me another clue. Engine 28's firefighter guarded shoe prints, but he did not tell me before departure. Two distinct sneaker-type impressions, side-by-side next to the brick base, were fresh and at a 45-degree angle to the street. The prints looked strangely like two people spooning in the road as the bomb entered the mailbox. Not sufficiently deep to make casts, the patterns were distinct enough to compare with the actual shoes. The sneakers waited for me a half-mile away. I jumped into my unit and left a pair of short black stripes on the pavement, going to the hot call instead of my original plan to lay in wait.

Unknown to me, at the exact moment I raced off to the second blast and twelve miles away in downtown Los Angeles, federal agent Mike Matassa waited by the L.A. County Sheriff's Automated Fingerprint I.D. System computer. Glen Lucero of the L.A. Fire Department stood next to him. Moments earlier, fingerprint expert Ron George fed a latent into the massive storage system. The fingerprint, recovered from a small fire at a retail store in Bakersfield, California in 1987, had nine identification points originally. The impression contained incomplete whorls and ridges so George joined gaps together and added about four additional "identifiers" before he fed it to the AFIS computer. Now the print had thirteen points; an excellent print. I personally knew all three of these investigators for years. I can only imagine what was said as my name slithered out as the top match of ten names offered by the computer. Also unknown to me, the same impression, analyzed in 1987, found no match by federal technicians. In 1989, the print examiners again closely examined the latent along with 11 suspects fingerprint cards, me included. In that year, the latent appeared as a clear, identifiable impression. There was no match to anyone in 1989. It surely was not mine. The supervisor of the original print examiner in 1989 also examined the eleven comparisons and signed off as "no match." Today, April 17, 1991, the latent was identified as my left ring finger impression, supposedly left on a piece of burned yellow legal pad paper found at the Bakersfield fire scene in 1987. I was now a felony suspect in a string of fires numbering over 30, and later more than 100.

Still several blocks from the second mailbox caper, I heard Officer Riggs' status report to his dispatcher that the call was "cold." The resident returned home to find the battered box with thin strips of green soft drink container still inside and scattered about the street; nobody bothered to report the blast when it went off. Riggs said he would collect the evidence, freeing me to return to the original location. Before arrival, the police comm. center told me the first victim, now indignant, demanded to talk to an officer or investigator. She was no doubt irritated that we took her now-op-art mailbox as just another "nothing" case. I parked legally this time, a Freudian statement now that no other uniforms or spectators were around. Pulling the unit just beyond the scene, I intended to photograph and examine the footprints to help placate the victim.

I covered my premature-departure faux pas with the distraught woman and, at the same time, heard the tinny exhaust notes of a small motorbike laboring up the barely inclined residential street. She queried me about our lackadaisical attitude. It appeared we would write off her $30 loss as a prank. I handed her my business card and said I handled the follow-up investigation. Looking over my shoulder, I glanced at the under-powered moped struggling into view, straining to haul two burly teenaged passengers. The bike continued to slow, chased by a thin blue line of exhaust. Neither kid looked our way. They were fixated on the mailbox stand. I guess the narc car with a government plate was not obvious enough to them. Just short of my unit, they stalled.

I again abandoned the victim and, concealed behind a four-foot-tall hedge, watched both riders put down their feet to steady the no-longer-moving bike. Their sneakered feet, just inches apart, were like I had seen in the dirt area below the pedestal a few minutes before. I stooped low next to the hedge and tuned in my police radio, shouting out for 15-Boy. The kids ran and pedaled to re-start their machine. If I pulled the suspects over and they decided to rabbit on me, Officer Riggs could give chase better than I. He was young, appeared physically fit, and could easily take half of the foot pursuit. At 42 years old, I was good for short sprints, but a hedge-hurdling, backyard obstacle course chase was out of the question.

Riggs called back saying he was with the victim developing suspect information and was unavailable due to my earlier blunder with leaving the first victim. He recommended placing an order for the next nearest available unit three miles away. His statement made no sense. I had excellent suspects, they were fleeing, albeit on a moped, but I needed backup. Then I remembered his past resentment of the "nothing" cases. By the time I reached my car, 14-Adam confirmed he was en route, but the culprits were over a block up the street turning onto a busy thorough-fare, headed downhill.

When I reached the intersection, a string of cars blocked my turn so I popped the siren and forced my way onto the cross street. Screeching tires and a forest of extended middle digits accompanied my pursuit, but a rear yellow winker flashed a warning and quieted the followers. The fleeing moped was not visible as I passed several cars, and the telltale exhaust phlegm I tracked suddenly disappeared from the roadway. A light haze drifted along a narrow residential side street like a traffic arrow flashing *TURN HERE*! I did. The new neighborhood was in the Tujunga district of L.A., so I had a fresh problem. I updated the police dispatcher to my direction of travel, leaving it up to them to advise LAPD of my presence, almost missing the exhaust smoke's disappearance from the new street. Slamming on the brakes, I backed up, adding a few ounces of transmission gear to the pan.

Judging the smoke drift by the prevailing breeze, I stopped in front of a driveway running between two single-family dwellings. A fresh black stripe on the pavement in front of a closed garage door gave the crooks strike one. A hint of blue smoke drifting out a roof vent was strike two. I spun my tires, blasted off for about fifty feet, then parked and ran back to the edge of the driveway next to a large cypress tree. Curiosity caught the criminals. In less than thirty seconds I saw the garage door lift and four juveniles sprint up the driveway. The tree concealed me so I listened to a chorus of giggles and guffaws approach, followed by a collective, "Oh shit...," when they saw my car with a flashing yellow light winking at them next door. No badge needed. They assumed my identity as I stepped out.

Instead of using that error against them, I opted for an old arson investigator tactic: "I'm just a fireman, guys. The cops are on the way. I can cancel them and we keep it a fire department matter. Just tell me what you know and we can work something out..." The group looked like a mob of meerkats, heads swiveling, meekly looking at their feet and each other; anywhere but at me. The leader sealed it. "We did all three. Don't call the cops. Please, man." My ploy worked. I advised the police comm. center. "51 Frank, station, I'm code four. Four in custody. Cancel 14-Adam and LAPD. No 10-15 at this time."

It was not my intention to arrest the kids. One of them appeared to be over 18 and an explosives-related case filed against a youngster his age would follow him forever. I was not quite sure of the involvement of the two new suspects anyway. I also had jurisdictional problems being in L.A. city limits, as well as potential Miranda Rights difficulties since I gained a confession prior to advising the boys of their rights. The key to a Miranda admonition requirement: If a suspect is in custody and not free to go, reading of the Miranda Rights is required. My verbal ploy about not being the police, and calling off the "real" cops, dangling a carrot in front of them in exchange for a confession, was legal and even ethical. Creative interviewing is an acceptable practice; a verbal lie is, too. Outright chicanery in reports is not.

The boys' spooned sneaker imprints, interest in the mailbox pedestal, and their earlier evasive driving established probable cause to pull them over. Coupled with the skid mark on the driveway, exhaust smoke from the garage roof vent and sudden appearance of the suspects seen on the moped earlier, it established more than enough probable cause to detain and arrest. When I first spoke to them, they were detained and required a Miranda admonition. Many police officers simply exercise their creative writing abilities and generate aberrant reports. I did not work that way and never considered it. Witnessing my law enforcement colleagues stretching the truth in reports and on the witness stand was commonplace in the 1980s. Creative arrests, however, inevitably backfired. Such disasters were infrequent, but I heard the horror stories. All it took to unravel a case was a zealous, or lucky, defense attorney and a credible witness to refute an officer or investigator's testimony. An entire case may collapse, but worse, the believability of the officer's future court statements disappears.

In my situation, an arson and explosives investigator is considered an expert witness and able to render opinions on the stand. Any other witness must state only facts: what they see, hear, touch, or smell. An expert witness can say, "I think..," or, "In my training and experience, I believe..." Only an expert witness can speculate in court. Once caught stretching the truth, an investigator may as well start checking the classified ads for a new occupation and career.

The four boys involved in this case paid for their misdemeanors. The exercise cost them just over $600 in investigation time, fire and police unit costs, and the replacement of three mailboxes. They confessed to a third unreported incident nearby. I did not arrest any of the boys. Conceivably, arrest of all four loomed. The two new faces were present during the first unreported incident, and while the remaining devices were planned, constructed, tested, and discussed. A grand conspiracy, but an unnecessary burden on the local juvenile justice system. The older-looking boy was also a juvenile, I determined. Two had previous minor police contacts, three were in high school sports, and all four intended to stay in school and graduate. If I arrested the quartet, solidifying my case required processing all the evidence for fingerprints, impounding the moped, transporting the four for booking procedures, and brief detention. All evidence needed photographs taken and my report writing easily involved 3-4 hours, including duplication (five full sets for each defendant) and presentation/review by juvenile authorities. Also required were appearances of several witnesses at four different juvenile hearings, and the related costs of police lab processing, jailers' and property clerks' time, as well as my own costs. The tab for the arrest easily approached $10,000. Without an arrest, the expenses amounted to less than $1000.

All the parents were involved and demands for a few face-to-face apologies were satisfied; a reasonable outcome for my money. Not driven by arrest/conviction ratios, my unit's clearance rates relied only on identity of the perpetrator and acceptance of responsibility to prove our successes. Robbery/Homicide sergeants in charge of the arson/explosives unit always gave us the freedom to handle our cases however we wanted, and allowed complete latitude in making these choices. Restitution, counseling, and apologies, instead of arrests, took place in about 30 percent of my criminal cases. My logical concepts, however, were more than economics. An arrest to most law enforcers is second nature and, to some, a form of validation. Arrest quotas in some agencies are not unheard of as a measure of an officer's abilities. The effect of a first-time arrest on anybody, his family, and the rest of his or her life causes immeasurable damage. I did not take the final step unless I felt it completely necessary. The second-time offender received less flexibility. At 42 years old, I did not feel the overwhelming need to flash a badge or gun to show who I was or to validate my profession. A business card was more discreet and usually adequate.

Early in my law enforcement career, I did experience the "Dirty Harry" syndrome. The symptoms were a need for validation and acceptance, and usually resulted in bad choices due to a lack of training and experience. In my situation, I had no training and minimal experience when given the task to investigate and enforce fire laws. In no time, accusations of using excessive force, profanity, attempting to seduce a witness and pulling a gun unnecessarily cropped up. A realtor sued me, along with my employer, when I punched him in the mouth. Some of the excessive force was actual, my profanity profuse, and I drew a gun once when I did not need it but because I was frightened. I threw the first punch in my life at the realtor when I was 29-years-old. Fortunately, my first police partner, Tom Rickles, provided the training I needed and arranged for the rest through law enforcement classes and seminars. He reined me in like a marine drill instructor does a recalcitrant 18-year-old recruit, and with the same finesse. His example set the tone for my advancement into the world of law enforcement in the early 1980s.

On April 17, 1991, I had the best job in this city of 180,000 people. No police or fire uniform to wear, no roll calls to attend, a four-day work week, a take-home car, unlimited overtime, command of a 10-man unit, and over $85,000 a year. Respect from my peers in the fire service gratified me. Even more valuable was a degree of esteem from most Glendale police personnel, and many in outside agencies we worked with regularly. These benefits minimized when compared with the affect of the unit's successful operation to the public and other agencies. An abundance of solid arrests over the years, and our consistent high clearance stats during the 1980s and early 1990s helped get me over the wannabe-a-cop shadow that shrouded me for several years. Though I did not achieve total approval, I did not need it. A fire department arson investigator strayed from the typical firefighter job description and was an aberration in the law enforcement field. We were the bastard children, but the money and benefits were good.

On this day, I drove home with overtime coins dancing in my head, a solid case clearance to balance my monthly statistics, a happy homeowner/victim, and plans for a wine-soaked spa dip in my backyard hot tub. Wanda, my wife of five years, met me at the door. Our Dalmatian, Domino, stuck his head through a now-ripped panel in the screen door in his excitement to get to me. His body followed. He looked like a polka-dotted jack-in-the-box popping through the door he always managed to breech even after I reinforced it. Wanda handed me a chilled glass of J. Lohr Riesling and stood by my side on the porch while we watched Domino make the rounds of his trees, bushes, and my unit's tire. This was, after all, his front yard.

I explained to Wanda why I was late and we discussed my lack of progress on an arson/insurance fraud case troubling me since January. A surveillance was necessary to find the crook since he skipped out when I focused on him the month before. A series of nuisance fires without a suspect warmed up as he set more fires along our local freeways, in alleys, and vacant lots. Wanda knew my job was a mistress and, although an unsolved case was not a threat to our marriage, the after-hours requirements and absences could jeopardize some couples; not us. Wanda endured my week-long nocturnal surveillance, call-outs to emergencies two and three times a night, interrupted holiday festivities, as well as many dry-docked spa soaks, without complaint. Unlike characters in every cop movie ever made, I did not have a nagging wife fed up with the impositions of my demanding job, nor did I endure a gruff supervisor constantly badgering me for spending limited overtime money, wrecking city vehicles, or shooting at suspects in high-speed chases through the local flea market. This was a real world. My investigative unit was low maintenance, productive, and high-profile, bringing credit to both fire and police departments. With arrests of more than 20 serial arsonists, identification of over 25 more, and at least 80 other felony arrests, there was a good probability of our solving the open cases troubling me. Glendale did not have more serial arsonists than other southern California city. We simply recognized serial crimes, many overlapping from adjacent and far away jurisdictions, and focused on the potentially disastrous series cases. Over 70 percent of our arson crimes were revenge-motivated and a suspect was named quickly, making these incidents easy to solve. A firebug was more elusive, difficult to ID and capture, but my successes spoke for themselves.

Wanda fooled around with a potted plant on the porch while I bent down and removed an ankle holster holding my Walther PPKS .380 automatic. Domino scampered up to see what I was doing. Scratching his ears, I gave him the gun. He chomped lightly on the rugged Cordura holster liked a good bird dog carries a dead duck. Merrily trotting around in circles, he waited for me to open the screen. Minutes ago, he penetrated it coming outside, now he obediently stalled until I opened the entrance and let him in. He loped in like a gazelle. I spied a couple of gnawed rawhide bones on the carpet just inside the door. A T-bone-shaped plastic chew toy, prime rib remnant, and several wadded up tug-of-war socks littered our normally well-kept living room. The entryway looked like crime scene photos of Jeffrey Dahmer's apartment. Domino looked right at home surrounded by his artifacts.

Wanda chatted with me as I drained the crisp Riesling and asked about my upcoming week-long Officer Safety and Field Tactics class I signed up for. I had a ton of work pending at home and in the office, and she knew I preferred the chase; not a professional vacation. She slipped her arm around my waist and suggested I take a break from the city responsibilities and go north. The training, held in the lush, emerald-green hills outside San Luis Obispo, California, was a bi-annual event I truly enjoyed. Intimating a train trip to meet me at the end of the training got my attention. She added we could hit the local wineries and just fool around all weekend. The proposal sounded good to me.

Domino's muffled woof behind us broke our shameless nuzzling on the porch. He still had the drool-covered Walther in his mouth. We both bent down and shared attention with our only child. Seven months later, on December 4, 1991, all three of us stood on this porch as 11 law enforcement officers, guns drawn, assaulted our home and our lives. The men arrested me for crimes I did not commit, based solely on the fingerprint identified just hours before on April 17, 1991.

CHAPTER TWO
BACKFIRE

The U.S. Air Force granted me an honorable discharge in 1971. Staying in the military made sense but I did not like the idea of uprooting my growing family every three to four years. Civilian jobs were plentiful upon my release so I immediately applied for a position with the Los Angeles City Fire Department and the militaristic LAPD. Looking like a Star Wars movie opening, lines for fire department job vacancies strung out for blocks. LAPD recruiters solicited applicants for employment in 7-11 parking lots and at the unemployment office lobby.

I qualified for the LAPD by passing the written, physical, and background checks in late 1971. At the final stage of the pre-employment phase, I sat down with an elderly police psychologist. He asked me, "Describe your family life..." Not one for long dissertations, I replied, "Ozzie and Harriet..." Apparently satisfied, we moved on to other queries. Ozzie and Harriet were the kindly parents in an idealized American family of two boys depicted in a hit sitcom on 1950s television. Over the years, two pre-employment psychological examiners presented the same query. Again, my abbreviated responses, referring to the sitcom family, satisfied the interviewers. After arrest, conviction, and imprisonment at Terminal Island, a court-ordered psychological exam began the same way: "What was your early family life like...?" The 26-year-old intern had her pen ready as I answered, "Ozzie and Harriet." Her jaw dropped, she lowered her pen, tilted her head and queried, "Ozzie Osborne?" I felt ancient. Only 43-years-old and my future hinged on the perceptions of this intern who thought I grew up in an environment of bat-head-eating rock stars.

Now 51, I am not sure how to approach writing this memoir. Most true-crime texts I have read expose the subject's life and all its blemishes. My memoir should tell all. Tensions, conflict and turmoil are what sell fiction and I suppose non-fiction as well. Fortunately, my life contains little of these difficulties until arrested in 1991. The 1950s and 60s were filled with tragedy, transition, wars, disasters, and calamities, but our home was Ozzie-and-Harriet-land. My father, Joe, and mother, Lee, met during World War II at Lockheed Aircraft in Burbank, California. Working on various components of P-38 fighters, they met when Mom ran a drill bit through her thumb and Dad helped her to the infirmary for first aid. Michael Joseph and Patrick Lee Orr were born in

1945 and '46. I came along in 1949. We all missed being war babies by just months. My dad opened a sporting goods store in 1945 on York Boulevard in Highland Park; a sleepy suburb northeast of downtown Los Angeles. With a $700 investment, he stocked the shelves and brought my Uncle John on board upon his discharge from the military. Other returning G.I.'s kept their store shelves empty during the golden post-war years, at least until a minor recession in 1950. Dad, always the entrepreneur, joined a friend in a fishing tackle business and did well for a while. One of Dad's perks was a new 1953 Ford station wagon. The Ford looked like a NASCAR racer with all the advertising painted on its sides, doors and hood. I was embarrassed to ride in the monstrosity. Lucky Lady Fishing Tackle Company turned out to be an oxymoron and went belly-up in 1956. Uncle John kept the sporting goods store running and Dad moved on to Mitchell Cameras manufacturing.

My earliest memories are of pre-school play and activities at our wood-framed two-bedroom home in Highland Park. One of the oldest sections in the city, our primarily residential neighborhood bordered a busy cross-town thoroughfare. Our home was set back about fifty feet from the street, just behind my grandparent's larger house. The Orr family lived within a 10-block radius of this location for over 40 years. Three events stand out in my memory from my early years in Highland Park. Two of these incidents involved fire. The third was a birdcage tumbling from my older brother's grasp atop a fig tree. Actually, I do not recall the tumbling; just the crash of the cage onto my 1950s-style crew cut-topped head. Three stitches were required and the accident made great fodder for storytelling about my new scar. The fire-related incidents of my childhood are not indicative of any aberrations, just significant events in my early years, among many normal situations.

The mother of one of my closest friends died in her sleep at just 34 years old. A neighboring family moved to Indiana. These two episodes are memories, but had no bearing on the focus of this memoir. When I was five or six years old, three children attending my elementary school were lucky to escape with their lives when one of them set fire to a couch. My brothers and I ran the two blocks to their house in the pouring rain to watch the small wood-framed house collapse into itself as the L.A. Fire Department battled to save adjoining structures.

Not long after the house fire, a companion and I ran out the back door of my home and used the alley as a shortcut to his place on the corner; from the top of the rear porch stairs, we stopped and stared, open-mouthed, at a small blaze in the alleyway. The flames consumed several stacked cardboard boxes and rapidly crawled up the sides of a creosote-covered telephone pole. I do not recall who called the fire department, but the adult directed me to the nearest corner. My friend Clifford stayed behind to assist while I waited for Engine 55 at the intersection. I heard 55 coming from a mile away, but Station 12's engine and ladder roared around a corner one block from me. When 55's bullet-nosed Seagrave engine arrived seconds later, I jumped up and down, pointing toward the obvious fire emitting thick black smoke from the phone pole and boxes. The fire crew idled at the intersection, red lights winking and ancient growler siren winding down, but they did not move. I jumped up and down and shouted some more. Still, they remained stationary. I ran a few yards, pointed at the alley entrance, and jogged back to the intersection. I felt like Lassie with my tongue hanging out, "Come on, Timmy! This way! I need your help!" Engine 55 simply waited for Engine 12's report of whether help was required. I did not know this at 6 years old. I expected the cavalry to roar down the alley and attack. TV firefighters did it that way.

When I launched my firefighting career, I recalled this incident many times as my own assigned engine or ladder truck arrived second-in at a blaze and citizens shouted at us and pointed to the obvious location of the smoking structure. We patiently waited for a first report before committing our resources. If the second rig is available, the crew calls dispatchers and announces they are available to take any other calls for the now-working engine company. I put this scenario in my first novel, *Points of Origin*, because the event happens so often.

For years, I gave no thought to that alleyway fire. After receiving fire investigation training during my rookie year, I figured out the probable cause of the long-ago blaze. Mentally, I pictured the cardboard containers, assorted trash cans, and the base of the flames emanating from the box resting on the alley's surface. In the mid-1950s, backyard incinerators were the most common way to destroy trash. There were no regular trash pick-ups and recycling was unheard of. When a firebox filled with ashy buildup, the remains then cooled before the detritus was shoveled into cardboard boxes for pickup. Apparently, live embers still smoldered in this box and the added weight from the containers on top allowed the insulated heat to eat its way through the sides. I recalled seeing a thin cascade of ash leaking out while the flames enlarged the breech and engulfed everything above.

In the 1950s, my family occasionally visited Dad's childhood friend "Uncle Roy" Mihld. Roy worked for the L.A. City Fire Department and had two sons my brothers' ages. As the youngest, I was an outcast to the older boys, and relegated to sit with the parents. I remember Roy regaling us with stories about the fires he fought and other calamities he helped mitigate. For a while, as he approached retirement, Roy was the standby driver for a Division Chief. On call at home, he parked a 1956 fire-department-issue four-door Buick in his driveway. The car was not fire engine red, but black like a FBI agent's car, with a red spotlight and an under-hood growler siren. It impressed me.

From these seeds, I suppose my career aspirations grew. I never hung out at fire stations nor did I have any toy fire trucks. My older brother did, but not I. I never played with matches, either. Like many young boys, I often said I wanted a firefighting career when I grew up. Uncle Roy had a lot of time off, his friends were primarily firemen, and all were campers, hunters, or fishermen. Our family fit right in with the group. A career choice in my 'tween years was easy to make. My law enforcement aspirations and propensities were not as pronounced.

Another "Uncle," Bill Staffer, worked as a police officer and we only saw him once or twice a year. Dad's family informally adopted him, saving him from a questionable family life. Bill towered over me at six feet and his gruff manner showed his intolerance for kids and most other human beings. Years later, I saw similar mannerisms in several of my own police officer friends and firefighters. Civil servants tend to look at "citizens" as only an unavoidable necessity. The law enforcement lifestyle and idiosyncrasies did not appeal to me until years later. Slightly introverted until my late teenage years, criticism hurt, but I liked people. Even Uncle Bill had good qualities. I honored the fact he enforced the law and had the courage to be a cop. I admired him.

I enjoyed our family and felt comfortable at gatherings, and when we frequently visited our relatives. A 1971 LAPD psychological evaluation later confirmed these characteristics. I took a 600-question MMPI self-analysis and gave my honest impressions of the Rorschach inkblots. Silently I questioned the sanity of the originator of the Rorschach, but I followed directions well. The 1971 tests revealed that I was not police officer material. I saw too many butterflies, boats anchored in sleepy lagoons, and birds in the ink spatters. My observations evaluated as evidence of passivity and responses should have included a few spiders, battleships, and attacking eagles; maybe a few lightning bolts. Something aggressive and macho was the acceptable response. Less than a year later, I repeated these identical tests and passed. I applied for a firefighter position.

Elementary school posed no problem for me. Mom and Dad both worked. Mom was not PTA material because she devoted herself totally to our family, took care of our home life, and did double duty as breadwinner. Dad nurtured his three sons' interests, helped us with projects, put in his eight hours at work and countless time spent keeping the house in good shape. We went camping as a family frequently and on hunting expeditions with just Dad 3-4 times a year. Friday night visits to my Uncle John's sporting goods store kept me interested in the outdoors as Dad and his brother discussed guns, fishing, and how best to repair a rifle stock or firing pin. I chatted with customers who browsed in the small store and felt a bit superior over boys my age that came in; I was behind the counter and I belonged. I was a smug little shit. Dad's Friday night sojourns to the store tapered off as I started junior high school but I continued dropping by, walking the two miles from home with my neighborhood friends.

Hal Collier and Gary McDonough were both ardent hunters and outdoorsmen, as were their fathers. Gary, a redheaded giant by our standards, was an aggressive type-A but we remained close despite the difference in personalities. I recall a youthful touch football game at the top of Barryknoll Drive. Gary's position was blocking my frequently successful sacks of his quarterback. Fun for me, Gary took the game seriously, spectacularly knocking me over. I surprised myself when I shoved him as he got into my space. His block was excessive for our Saturday morning informal games. Neighborhood girls sometimes played. At 10 or 11 years old, we were getting into a pecking order. Gary established himself with the incident. I never took sports seriously. From that point, I never allowed anyone to bully me. I despised harassing or threatening behavior. I did not want anyone within three feet of me to violate my space. Only twice did I strike out. When bullied on the way home from middle school by myself, three older kids harassed me, one grabbing me from behind in a bear hug. I stomped on his toes. When he released me and turned around to nurse his aching foot, I laid a hard, closed fist across his back. With the wind out of him, he dropped to his knees while his companions stepped back. A nearby motorist honked and shouted, "Leave him alone!" I assumed she meant the bully; not me. I walked away without further incident. Only many years later did I strike another person.

Hal Collier was my closest childhood friend. His father, a gruff, bull-like sports fanatic, was a former hunter and customer at my dad's sporting goods store. By the time we were in our teens, Hal's dad no longer hunted, but insisted we spend much of our weekends camped out in his wood-paneled den watching college and professional football games. Hal adored his father despite the heavy-handed manner of the old bear. He belittled my friend, but Hal accepted the treatment like a faithful puppy. The old guy's voice alone scared the hell out of me and I cowered when the big guy picked on us. At 250 pounds, he could bully me all he wanted. I recall he asked me to get him a beer while I was up using the phone. After retrieving the cold one from the kitchen, I dropped it on the way into the den. I picked it up, put it down on the end table next to him, and resumed my position on the carpeted floor. He smiled widely and said, "You're a left-hander, aren't you?" Hal cracked up and rolled around the floor. I did not understand the reference. I am a right-hander.

Hal later told me his dad referred to poor drivers, ineffective quarterbacks and women as "left-handers." Years later, I realized Hal's dad treated the youngsters this way to toughen us up. Even Hal's two beautiful sisters, Gail and Claudia, endured the strategy. Despite the tactics, we all loved the old guy. Hanging out in the testosterone-laden den attracted me back week after week during football season, even though sports were like a foreign country to me.

My friendship with Hal evolved from our similar backgrounds. We lived two blocks apart but we played on Hal's street, Barryknoll Drive, or in the uninhabited canyon at the end of his block. The canyon provided room for our archery hunting forays and target practice as well as bike riding and cardboard sledding down the steep slopes of dry, straw-like grass in the summer. The only live game to hunt in the canyon was an occasional gopher, birds and skunks. A neighbor put a bounty on the destructive, odiferous, annoying striped mammals. While target practicing with our bows one winter evening, I spotted a familiar black - and white rodent waddling along a game trail below a grape stake fence. Reacting instinctively to the movement in the grass, I drew back and let an arrow fly. Hal protested loudly. My range was clear and the hillside protected the background so I did not understand Hal's tirade — not until the projectile struck the skunk's neck, killing him instantly. The stench drifted down-slope like a stream of fetid lava. Hal covered his mouth and nose and laughed his ass off.

I now had to retrieve my expensive arrow, still burrowed in the unmoving animal's neck. We waited until the stench subsided. I ran up the slope, grabbed the arrow, and slid back down, hoping I could outrun the reek. Seemingly successful, I went home and rinsed off my equipment outside the house. I walked through the living room to get to my bedroom, and my trophy followed me like a malodorous ghost. Mom and Dad, watching TV as I slinked through, guided me directly to a bathtub filled with tomato juice and hot water. I do not think my clothes survived the encounter. Maybe Hal's dad was correct; I was an occasional left-hander.

Hal and I attended Washington Irving Junior High School from 1961-64. Over a quarter of the school population was Mexican-American. I recall no discrimination of any kind. Hal and I befriended several Mexican kids and there was no intimidation by the gang members who also attended. We just did not hang with them, and John Garcia, our closest friend, did not either. John's closest buddy was Andy Hoyos, son of the famous 1950s and 60s actor, Rudolpho Hoyos. Hal frequently joined my family on camping and hunting trips in the Mojave Desert. When only 15-years-old and too young to drive, we discussed riding our bikes the seventy miles to the nearest sagebrush to chase down jackrabbits. Planning a four-day biking foray carrying .22 rifles strapped to the frames, seemed normal to us. Dad gave his okay and nothing in the early 1960's prohibited us from such an unsupervised trek. We could not get enough hunting. Hal and I performed well in school. We did not do homework together since projects got completed in study hall or homeroom. Such efficiency gave us time to explore the canyon, play baseball, go to James Bond movies, or just hang out.

On Wednesday, November 22, 1963, I worked on stage crew in the auditorium, helping ready the facility for an assembly. The teacher suddenly tuned the AM radio to the hall speakers. The news report told of the President's attempted assassination. Students and teachers sat stunned, until the updates confirmed John F. Kennedy was dead. School was closed for the next few days. I recall watching the killing of Kennedy's assassin live on TV as well as the funeral procession and burial. I grew up in those few days.

High school was right ahead and Hal and I chose different districts. On the border, we could go wherever we wanted. Franklin's football team successfully beat Eagle Rock regularly, so Hal went there for the sports program. I opted for the track team and closer location of the Eagle Rock Eagles. Still, we went hunting together when we could. Desperate as we were to go to the desert, an offer to hunt with Hal's sister's boyfriend, Johnny, caught us off guard. Neither of us liked Johnny, but he had a car and an offer to take us out. We blindly grabbed it, unsure why the boyfriend, three years our senior, wanted to hunt with us. We finally figured out Johnny needed some positive character development with the Collier family. They did not much care for his rebel-without-a-cause appearance and demeanor. Being nice to the kid brother bought him some credibility. Johnny mirrored the Eddie Haskell character in the 60s TV show, Leave It to Beaver; a two-faced miscreant. After a rainy 100-mile-per-hour ride to the Antelope Valley, we got out, loaded our .22 rifles, and began our stalk. Johnny was loud, boisterous and shot anything moving or not moving, scaring off quarry well in advance of our approach. Cresting a small sand dune, we spooked a black-tailed jackrabbit. Johnny did not see the hare initially. I did, and raised my Mossberg and started swinging in an arc that started behind the loping target, sights settling on the furry body, then into a lead just in front of the rabbit. It was a perfect performance. Hal could not shoot from behind me without his muzzle blast hitting me so he watched, in horror, as Johnny saw the rabbit, took two steps forward and raised his gun. With my left eye closed to aim, and sights moving ahead of the jack, I applied pressure to the trigger to fire. Johnny's head suddenly appeared in front of my barrel. I was a four-pound pull away from sending an 85-grain hollow-point .22 magnum into his skull at 2,000 feet-per-second.

The simpleton blasted away, ignorant of the near-tragedy. Hal's hand was on my right forearm and we looked at each other with dropping jaws. I felt like hugging Hal and smacking Johnny with the butt of my rifle. I did neither.

The aggressive extrovert, Gary McDonough, later became a Captain in the L.A. Fire Department. Passive, compassionate Hal Collier joined the LAPD in 1970. Both my friends attended college after high school, avoiding the draft and military service and opting for education and building families of their own. My firefighting career started immediately upon entry into the U.S. Air Force. I followed my friend's civil service lead, becoming a firefighter in 1974 and starting my law enforcement career in 1979. Only one incident in my childhood demonstrated an aptitude for investigations or analysis. When about seven years old at my Uncle Leonard's home with Mom and Dad, the adults scanned unmarked photographs of past family camping trips. They argued over the location of one picture showing several of us sitting at a folding camp table. A slightly blurred image of a range of mountains appeared in the background and nothing else revealed the location of the photo. As they quibbled, I noticed one of my brothers in the frame held a fork with a sausage skewered on the tines. The sausage indicated morning breakfast. The shadows on the table, ground, and cast by someone out of the frame, revealed similar shading on the barely discernable canyons in the background. The sun rose in the east and cast the shadows. Protected by sun-drenched westerly-facing ridges, the canyons darkened. The adults narrowed the location to two or three possibilities. Before the adults settled the argument, I figured Red Rock Canyon, California. The argument continued and I remained mute. I recalled Dad telling me the mountains near Red Rock Canyon ran west to east and the other locations theorized had north to south ranges. The accomplishment seemed simple to me and not until 20 years later did I again realize the ability to analyze.

High school posed no challenge to me. Studying sufficiently to pass with a B average, print shop was my refuge. Working on a huge 1930s-era linotype machine, setting type for the school newspaper, *The Eagle's Scream*, I found the challenge of mastering the intricacies of the brute satisfying. The temperamental instrument was notorious for squirting molten lead if the operator did not follow proper sequencing. Not very mechanically-inclined, and having no desire for a stream of 600° silvery lava in my lap, I babied the monster and we got along well; so well the teacher asked me to work after school for pay, setting type for the *Scream* and on special projects like football and track programs.

At fifteen years old, I planned to own a car the day I turned sixteen. Dad taught me how to drive our 1962 Chevy truck with a three-speed column shift, and Mom frequently let me practice when we shopped or ran errands. Independence loomed. Both older brothers owned cars. Mike drove an immaculate '53 Ford and Pat a 1960 Ford Starliner. To get closer to my goal of buying a car, I started a small business. I printed business cards at school and distributed advertisements in mailboxes over a wide area. I promoted myself as a "jack-of-all trades", available to do gardening, trimming, car washing, and anything else. For eight months I hustled, working after school and on weekends for several regular customers; one, a 40-year-old divorcée with a desire for my body. Unfortunately, extreme manual labors were the only thing she wanted. For weeks I uprooted tree and bush stumps, cleared brush and bamboo, and washed windows for the woman. Before we started, the yard appeared like an Amazonian refuge, but our labors produced a gratifying open area she planned to enhance with grass. The pleasure of the result gave me more satisfaction than the one-dollar an hour she paid me.

When I turned fifteen, Eagle Rock High School issued a work permit, allowing me to obtain a real job. Giving up my side business, I hired on at the local Jack-in-the Box, keeping my print shop position. Starting at $1.05 an hour—considerably less than the coveted supermarket box-boy jobs—I worked 18-20 hours each week at the fast-food joint. Looking back now, working the Jack-in-the-Box franchise with the owner, Roger Swift, was as valuable as the paycheck. Swift ran an efficient, clean, successful store and he allowed no goldbrickers. Work was fun. Speed and productivity were vital, but he took the time to teach us how make a 29¢ hamburger palatable. McDonald's, still in its infancy, presented our only competition at the time. Our menu was limited, but we kept trying to draw the clown's customers. Swift gave regular raises and bonuses to favored, productive employees and ensured his dedicated charges got the hours they wanted and as many as we could handle. Determined to stay on his good side, I volunteered to take hours when someone called in sick or to go with him on supply runs.

As sarcastic as a marine drill instructor, Swift never held back when correcting an employee's poor performance. More than once I ducked to avoid a flying bagged order. If you put ice in a requested no-ice soda or added pickles when contrary to an order on a burger, the packaged error flew in your direction. Once you knew Mr. Swift, his mannerisms revealed him simply as a conscientious businessperson as concerned with the employee's development as with profit. He consulted with our school by providing progress reports to the work experience office and we received credit towards graduation based on his evaluations. I wanted to please him.

Any turmoil during a rush period quickly dissipated during the next lull. The ultimate goal in the 1960s fast-food business was to run a $100 sales hour. Our store reached the objective many times. After the successes, Roger motivated us to prepare for the expected follow-up rush by wiping down all dirty surfaces, re-stocking supplies, and organizing depleted shelves so product was near the front, accessible and fresh. We separated and re-stacked sliced cheese to make it easier to grab in a rush. I absorbed his tutoring and the traits followed me to other jobs, the military, and into adulthood. Before I ever flipped a burger, I realized I enjoyed work and the recognition of performing well more than the paycheck and bonuses. I needed to do a good job and stand out from those who just punched the time clock and cashed a paycheck.

Mimicking Roger Swift, I applied all he imparted, especially as a firefighter and investigator. As a rookie fireman, I worked for several supervisors with a similar work ethic, only the stakes higher. Lives, not quality burgers were at risk. If a fire crew puttered around after an emergency and did not put hose away or refill the water tank immediately, inevitably another call came in elsewhere in the district. If the crew and equipment were not prepared and the rig not available, a substitute crew was required. The fill-in crew could be miles away. Long responses of 6-8 minutes closed the door on survivability if a victim was not breathing. I saw too many instances where a captain allowed his men a smoke break after knocking down a blaze. The crew should have organized their resources and been available for the next emergency. Often, necessity required us to rest after a vigorous attack on a structure or brush fire, but frequently I worked for lackadaisical captains who neglected their jobs. I tried to avoid similar traits when I supervised a crew in the Air Force and later as a Glendale firefighter and investigator.

If a "Guide for Adolescent Brothers" manual existed, Pat and Mike, my siblings, followed its tenets. As the youngest, dunking at the swimming pool was common, exclusion from group conversations with their friends frequent, and the brothers begrudgingly provided me rides when Mom and Dad were busy. The eldest, Mike, started work while still in high school, in a similar work-experience program as I entered. Hired by a classmate's parents at the Dragon Pearl Chinese Restaurant in nearby Highland Park, my brother Pat joined the ranks of dishwashers and busboys at the same location a few months later. I never heard either brother complain about hard work. Judging by their exhausted, sweaty appearance when they came home, they endured plenty. The benefits of productive employment, under the tutelage of the Lees', seemed to instill in Pat and Mike the same lessons I learned from Roger Swift. My siblings both bought cars within months of starting work. Mike tired of the restaurant after about a year and secured a position at Pacific Telephone, staying with the company until retirement. Pat, a muscle car and drag racing enthusiast and participant, later worked at a muffler shop and gas stations to keep him near cars. Mike moved out of our home when I was about 14-years-old, leaving Pat in charge as senior brother.

Not yet driving age, still on foot, my friends and I caught rides with Pat. He dropped us off at school or the movies. Walking was not a problem but riding in his awesome Ford with a 406-cubic-inch dual carburetor engine seemed an easy choice when offered. Pat's closest friend, Jim Mehl, owned a new red Ford Fairlane with a high performance motor, too. I accepted rides with Jim frequently on my way to work or school. Our schedules coincided though at different locations. Jim treated me like a brother; not a brother, like _my_ brother. He, too, reminded me of the transparent Eddie Haskell character from the 60s TV sitcom, _Leave it to Beaver._ Jim was the perfect prim teenaged guy when around adults, but a prankster when beyond parental influence. Early one Saturday evening as I left Jack-in-the Box on my mile-long walk home, Jim cruised by on the opposite side of the street. At the next cross-street he hung a U-turn and his fire-engine red Ford noisily idled to the curb, purring at a high rpm. Jim smiled, revved the car once and waved me over. Unusual for him to pick me up on my way home, his questionable smile reminded me of a teenager caught smoking in the boy's room; lungs full of Marlboro, and the principal slips in. Climbing in, Jim roared off, setting me back in the seat with a surge of power, chirping the rear tires in all four gears. I did not care what he was up to—he had me hooked.

"You doing anything tonight?" he asked.

"Yeah, big plans tonight," I replied. "Me and Hal are goin' over to the canyon and hunt skunks with our bows and arrows." Jim chuckled. He recalled our infamous foray just 50 yards from his home. The odor of the decaying skunk carcass drifted to Jim's house for days until the city picked up the body.

"You wanna hang out with us tonight? I'm supposed to take on a guy in Monrovia and...uh...mess around with somethin' else later."

"Yeah, I can go. How soon?" I replied nonchalantly.

"Uh, after dark...about seven-thirty or so. Pat doesn't get off work until seven."

"Does Pat know I'm going?"

"Yeah, it was his idea." Right. They did this to me before on a weekend night between their every-two-weeks paychecks. They were broke. Paid weekly, I always had a stack of cash in my sock drawer and I was a willing accomplice under the right circumstances. The previous experience was a brief trip to the local drive-in for burgers and a required contribution for gasoline. After an hour, they dropped me off at home but the thrill of cruising—however brief—was worthy of the $3–$4 contribution for fuel. Gasoline in 1964 only cost about 30¢ a gallon.

With a promise of a trip to Monrovia and to "mess around with something else," as Jim mentioned, we would be gone for several hours.

"Okay," I replied, "I'll pop for a tank of gas." I already noticed Jim's fuel gauge was just below a half tank and figured I would be out only about four dollars. On a clear, cloudless, cool October night, I got into the uniform of the day: Levi jeans, high-top Keds, and a multicolored plaid short-sleeved shirt. Jim picked us up, discretely idling away from Dad's presence until we reached the first intersection. The roar of Jim's 300 horsepower engine no doubt reached Dad's ears, echoing up from the mouth of the narrow canyon we lived in as the Ford slammed through the gears. Suspiciously included in the front seat conversations, it gratified me to be part of the trio; not just a teenaged gasoline credit card on the back seat. Ritually dining at another racer's hangout, the Pasadena Bob's Big Boy, home of the "Little Old Lady From..." fame, Pat and Jim never discussed the pending race. My skepticism rode next to me on the back seat.

We moved on to Monrovia at about 8:30 p.m. and ran into unexpected competition on a residential stretch of Foothill Boulevard. A Chrysler 300 daddy's car idled next to us occupied by four male teenagers. When the light flashed green, smoke boiled from the rear tires of the Chrysler, while Jim's smaller car leaped forward. Within an eighth mile, we were even, but Jim hit fourth gear and had to shut down as we approached another red light. The next long block, filled with small businesses and more traffic, caused Jim to turn right and avoid temptation. The race was not always about the winner, but the simple thrill of competition—the teenaged equivalent of an adult's forbidden extramarital affair. As wild as their reputations were, my companions stayed out of trouble with the law and were usually sensible guys. Meandering around Pasadena, we ended up in the extreme south side of sleepy South Pasadena on Fair Oaks Boulevard. Entering a residential area, Jim, without a word, pulled onto a side street, turned out the lights, got out and went to the trunk. Returning in seconds, he handed Pat a small canvas bag the size of a meat loaf. The pouch clanked like grabbing a handful of silverware. It was a tool kit. I did not have time to query them when we returned to Fair Oaks and stopped at a red light at Huntington Drive. Without a cue, Pat and Jim's heads swiveled simultaneously to the left. Jim's returned 180° to look at Pat, then they both glanced back at me and smiled. Again, the smoking-in-the-boy's-room gapes. I peered to the left, expecting to see teenaged girls, but all I saw was the local Ford dealer's darkened, unfenced storage lot filled with LTDs, Galaxies, and across the front row, Fairlanes like Jim's.

We completed our left turn, cruised by the lot and what I now knew was a target. Pat and Jim discussed "midnight auto supply" discounts before but I was unaware my companions shopped there until now. Hanging a U-turn at the next intersection, we encountered no other traffic and pulled up in front of the lot. Jim turned off his lights, backed into the opening and shut off his engine. Successfully camouflaged as another dealer car, my heart thumped ponderously in my chest. I was a co-conspirator. Pat whispered back to me, "Watch out for cops or people walking this way. Keep your head down." They slipped into the moonless night, the telltale clanging of the tools following like a chained pit bull approaching the end of his leash. Peering out the back window, I made out their dim forms as the hood of a new Fairlane popped open about twelve inches.

Seconds later I heard the rumble of an idling motorcycle and the muted chatter of a police radio. In the left-turn bay we occupied minutes before, a blue light shone from the tip of the antenna mounted on the back of the Harley while the officer waited for the light to change. My heart and breathing stopped. What was I expected to do? Pop the horn once to warn my brother? Tap the brake so the taillights would warn them? Frozen low in the back seat, my heart raced as I watched the police officer complete his turn and pass just 100 feet in front of me. I sweated and waited another five minutes before I heard our trunk pop open and felt the thud of a manifold and carburetor deposited inside. Pat and Jim's smell preceded them. Their hands and clothes, oil and gasoline-soaked, reminded me of a repair garage. Giggling like girls at a slumber party, they jumped back in and we took off as Pat turned around and said, "Good job with that cop..."

I never went cruising with them again, but my displeasure quickly dissipated. Pat was my brother and this aberration did not stop me from admiring him as my older sibling. He soon settled in with his long-time girlfriend, Cathy, married, and joined the U.S. Navy. He always worked hard, and his rough-edged teenaged years grew to manhood. He remained close to our family, especially after Dad divorced in 1966. While I went off to the U.S. Air Force, Pat visited Dad often. The pair went camping and out to dinner frequently. Pat went on to a career as a mechanic, then a regional supervisor for the Metropolitan Transit Authority bus company.

In late summer of 1991, the last time I saw my brother Pat, he sat atop a metal stool in front of a cluttered workbench in Dad's equally littered garage. An hour before, I arrested an alcoholic woman for setting a small fire in her apartment. Her stale stench still clung to my hands and clothes but I had earlier promised Dad I would drop by after work for a beer. I slipped out of Glendale and, when pulling in front of the open garage door, spied Pat inside. Before I could shut off the motor, my pager beeped. I picked up the radio microphone and contacted my comm.

center. Pat remained perched on his stool, waiting for Dad to bring a fresh brew from the house. The dispatcher advised me my female lunatic was not able to stay at the city jail facility. The woman was "a threat to herself and others," according to the Watch Commander. She qualified for transport to Olive View Sanitarium, the L.A. County warehouse for the mentally disabled. With all city police units busy, the arresting officer must transport. I was elected. Hanging up the mic, I shouted over the rumble of my car's V-8, "Hey, bro, gotta go."

"What?" Pat shouted, cupping a hand to his ear.

"Gotta go...," I yelled, "...Olive View..."

Pat smiled broadly and shook his head, "...I love you, too."

I never saw my brother Pat again.

CHAPTER THREE
FIRE FLY

Shortly after I started work at Jack-in-the Box, our family took a hit. My mother left home. I had no idea separation loomed. Neither did Dad, apparently. There were occasional arguments but whatever problems existed were below the radar. I remember arriving home late from school one weekday and found Dad at the dining room table. He arrived home only a short while before I to find a note from Mom. She left without telling anyone and Dad did not know where she fled. Her note said little about her plans except to expect a call in a few days. Dad told me the basics. I did not read the note. Devastated, Dad went to his bedroom after reassuring me everything would be okay. Closer to my mother when a teenager, I knew she was confident enough to survive; Dad, not so much. He depended on her to handle the infrastructure of the family. At least my early perceptions of our family hierarchy gave me this impression. After thirty minutes in his room, Dad came back out and made us supper. I recalled how many times he came home from work and launched into dinner preparation, made phone calls regarding family business, and did home maintenance. The team efficiently kept our home operating.

Mom did call several days later, telling us she was in her childhood hometown in Missouri. I do not recall how affected I was by Mom's excursion but do remember hurt and fear of what lay ahead. Dad's stepping up and Mom's staying in touch helped us both through a rough spot. I also inherited Mom's transportation; a 1962 Chevy pickup with a camper shell. I would not need to buy a car for a while. The split did cause me to realize I rapidly approached adulthood and with it all the complications. Mom was gone and I had only Dad, and my boss Swifty to guide me.

Vietnam war raging, the military sucked up so many young men, our neighborhoods looked like ghost towns. Two years from draft age, I actually looked forward to fulfilling my military requirement. School became secondary to me; work first. Family now a distant third because of the subconscious source of pain our new family created. I went home to sleep and not much else. In 1966, in the 11th grade, I accepted the school's 4/4 plan. Attending classes for four hours in the morning, I left at about noon and the program allowed me to work four hours per day as credit towards graduation. Roger Swift acted as my afternoon and evening instructor, providing the school with weekly progress reports and evaluations. My major in high school was technical but I changed it to general to enable going on the 4/4 plan and still graduating with my class. I also stayed on the track team and did well in my second year. I only weighed 135 pounds in 1966 and ran the 100- and 220-yard sprints, but my specialty was the long jump. Not fast enough to make the first team in the short distance events, I filled in for injured or absent runners, never finishing better than fourth place. In the long jump competition I shined. After a mediocre first year, I came back in 1966 to win the event four times. In the league finals I fouled out on my final leap. I fouled 1/4 inch but the effort was my best jump: 19 feet, 8 inches. Instead of advancing to the city finals, I headed for the showers. As I plodded back to the gym, Coach Oden said my winning jump made me the 'Most Improved' for the season, but the foul ended my year. I did not return to competition. Not much for team sports, track presented solitary performance opportunities.

Without sports to cloud my mind, I discovered girls and met my future wife, Jody DiLieto. Actually pursuing Jody's cute French friend, Teresa, Jody's coyness captivated me. The dark-haired, buxom beauty overwhelmed me. Of pure Italian parentage, she was as cute as a pair of infant Reeboks. We were soon inseparable. Teresa paired up with my friend, Hal Collier, and we double-dated frequently. Hal was a football star at our cross-town rival, Franklin High School, but the rivalry did not affect us. After dating Jody for several months, we found a truck with a camper too tempting so I bought my first vehicle, a 1958 Ford Ranchero with a healthy 352 cubic inch V-8. With an aberrant reversed three-speed stick shift pattern, the beast had to be pushed off the lot to get it started. A true left-hander's car.

By mid-1966 I made $1.50 an hour at Jack-in-the-Box and found myself a shift leader working ten hours a week more than the school regulations allowed. The late night and early morning hours cut into my time with Jody so I took a box boy job at the independent Empire Market in Eagle Rock. The position paid $1.80 to start and I worked no later than 9 p.m. With Sunday off, I toiled for the Saenz brothers, using skills I learned from Jack-in-the-Box. Nearby upper-class residents drove their Cadillacs and Lincolns onto our lot and the walk-in itinerants from the nearby fleabag motel were as welcome. I swept floors, bagged groceries, and performed general clean-up and maintenance duties. Business was brisk and I soon found myself assisting the cashiers with the upkeep and stocking of the walk-in coolers. Like Jack-in-the-Box, after a busy period, I re-stocked the check-outs with bags, then straightened the cooler merchandise. Pulling forward the dairy products, soft drinks and beer, I ensured the perishables were rotated to the front. Partial six-packs were filled, leaky milk cartons removed, and everything wiped down. In a month, the cooler became my entire responsibility, right down to letting the brothers know what to order each week. Swifty taught me to always look busy, even if the effort was a sham. Have a wet cloth in hand and keep moving. I kept active, always wiping down even clean surfaces, picking up and moving items to other locations, and re-stocking supplies. The boss must see you bustling and at least appear like you are doing something constructive when on the clock. Life was good, but Vietnam ever present. In 1966, an Eagle Rock graduate I knew was killed in Southeast Asia. Richard Karger was engaged to one of my oldest friends from school, Judy Sander. As one of the boys, Judy remained part of our group until she started dating Richard. I only met him a few times and he was a year or two ahead of us in school. His death was an unnecessary reminder that I neared a very adult world. My high school grades qualified me for college but I gave advanced education little thought. Avoiding the draft by enrolling in college never occurred to me. I was through with school. With my sitcom-based adolescence training, I obeyed my parents, the law, and intended to do my time in the military. Rebelling or protesting the war seemed sacrilegious. I felt my decisions were sound. Required military service loomed and I did not question the need. At career day in high school, I talked with a Los Angeles Fire Department Captain and he convinced me that a fire service career was the way to go. He added actual firefighting experience in the military was equal to a college degree in fire science. The pep talk assuaged any guilty feelings about not going to college. I visited an air force recruiter at the same time the U.S. military draft went to a lottery system based on a random drawing of birthdates. In the middle section of the list, I had less than a year to join or expect the selective service to get me. I wanted a choice of job and the branch of service. The draft gave you up to the army and infantry with only one destination: Southeast Asia. I gave some thought to taking an infantry assignment but how my military decisions affected those around me was a consideration. I did not want anyone thinking I feared infantry service and the dangers Vietnam presented. If the draft got me, I would go, but I needed practical fire fighting experience to reach my goal when I returned home. The decision was mine and Dad supported whatever I wanted. He seemed a bit empty-nest-anxious about my pending departure. With brother Pat away in the navy and older sibling Mike married and on his own, Dad would be totally alone. The air force recruiter indicated no problem becoming a firefighter if I signed up with him. Friends told me a recruiter's promises were as believable as a used car salesman's spiel. Unable to swim well left the navy out, and I did not care for the "oohrah" marine persona so my choice was easy. In February 1967, two days after winter graduation, I entered the U.S Air Force Delayed Enlistment Program, shipping out on my 18th birthday on April 26, 1967. Dad drove me to the induction center in downtown Los Angeles and dropped me off at 5 a.m. With a full day of testing and physicals, I ended the day at Amarillo Air Force Base, Texas at 11 p.m. The basic training experience mimicked every war movie ever made. I cannot say I enjoyed loud, foul-mouthed drill instructors in my face 18 hours a day, but tolerated the situation. I did experience a twinge of homesickness and the loss of choices. Everything occurred at the whims of the D.I. assigned to my flight. Determined not to be one of their toys, I allowed the sergeants to become my surrogate parents. Mom and Dad raised me to be obedient.

Near the end of basic training we qualified with the M-16 on the firing range. I scored second highest in the flight of 35 recruits, qualifying me for my first military award: the marksmanship ribbon. Dad still displays my tattered, bullet-riddled target in his garage. He taught me how to shoot when five-years-old, plinking at tin cans and rocks. The air force targets were man-shaped and full-body sized. A senior recruit warned his minions not to shoot too well or assignment to the air police resulted and Vietnam your only destination. By this time I realized almost nobody graduated from basic with the job assignment their recruiter promised. I had no assurances of firefighting school and a military policeman assignment sounded pretty good so I fired as well as I could. Several days before graduation, the First Sergeant called me into his office. Used to acting like a robot or a wind-up toy for seven weeks, the gruff sergeant started off our meeting with scary words, "You have a choice." I almost laughed but kept my smart mouth shut and listened to him. He went on to tell me I scored well on writing skills and comprehension testing. He offered me an opportunity to attend language skills training at the military school at the Presidio in San Francisco. The 18-month assignment allowed me to live off-base, but an extension on my enlistment was possible, too. He gave me a moment to make a decision and added the language skill training currently offered was—no surprise here—Vietnamese and Laotian. This menacing addendum did not influence my decision but added military time did. I told the sergeant, "No," and explained my desire to obtain practical firefighting training and experience instead. He chuckled and said I wasted my time and abilities on an air force job not much more useful than a bulldozer jockey. I thanked him for the flattering offer to go to the Presidio, but again declined. The sergeant had my post-graduation job assignment and destination in front of him but he refused to tell me anything about the documents. It seems now he should have told me I was not going to firefighting school since three days later, I received my orders and the assignment was not as a hose handler. If my orders were for my desired job, the vengeful sergeant had them changed after my declination. On graduation day, job and destination assignments ended up in our calloused hands. My base assignment: Chanute, Illinois. My technical school: "Jet, over two." My aptitude showed a latent talent as a jet engine wrench turner on aircraft with more than two engines: B-52s, B-58s, both bombers; or the lumbering C-141 cargo haulers, possibly KC-135 refuelers. The largest mechanical challenge of my young life was rebuilding a 750 cfm Holley carburetor on my Ranchero. When I completed the project I had three pieces left over. Brother Pat had to help me out. Changing the sparkplug on my 3-horsepower mini-bike resulted in a shattered insulator and a nasty gash on a finger. Now the air force wanted me to take responsibility for multi-million-dollar jets. Fifteen of us departed Amarillo on a two-day rail trek to Chicago where we changed trains and rode 125 miles south to Chanute Air Force Base. Illinois was as flat as Texas, but greener. After settling into our World War II-vintage two-story wooden barracks, drill instructors said technical training started in 3-6 weeks. The two weeks before school started required a recruit's assignment to KP at the massive base chow hall. I survived the 4 a.m.-to-noon schedule for eight days. On the ninth, while at a noon formation in front of our barracks, the First Sergeant made an announcement: "The firefighting technical school needs volunteers. Anybody interested fall out and report to my office." The only volunteer, I dropped "Jet, over two" school and enrolled in firefighting training. The class started in three weeks and required an additional two weeks KP. I gladly made the change. The eight-week firefighter school accepted fifteen of us and we learned basic fire sciences then moved rapidly into fire service history and apparatus/equipment operation. In the third week, operation of the rigs consisted of running the pump and hose lines but the instructors actually drove the behemoths. We arrived at blazing pools of 800-1000 gallons of waste jet fuel, or piled wooden pallets fires, and operated pumps, pulled hose lines, and sprayed foam from roof-mounted turrets on the crash trucks. The equipment was old; much of it manufactured in the early 1950s. Looking like huge red jeeps, the structural fire rigs were 530B, 6X6 military-chassis vehicles or the boxy, cumbersome 750A apparatus. The 750's transmissions were so sloppy finding any gear was like sticking a metal rod into a box of tin cans and expecting forward movement. The monstrous crash trucks were of a similar vintage with the exception of the newer P-2 rig. Powered by two six cylinder, in-line engines the size of a CEO's desk, the P-2's carried over 3300 gallons of water and foam. Despite their size, the automatic transmission allowed the trucks to accelerate from 0-60 mph in less than 50 seconds.

On graduation day I received orders for the Morôn/San Pablo Air Base complex in southern Spain. My first two choices were southern California bases and the third selection Vietnam. I also received a surprise along with my diploma—an honor graduate certificate. Granted a 30-day leave after tech training, I returned to Los Angeles and asked Jody to marry me. Only eighteen-years-old, Jody agreed and so did our parents; hers reluctantly. I planned to return in March 1968 for the wedding. After my leave ended, I managed to catch a military hop from Dover Air Force Base, Delaware directly to Madrid, Spain and pocketed the travel allowance difference. A shuttle south to Sevilla put me down directly across the airport from the San Pablo Air Base complex I was assigned to. A military van picked me up and the driver explained that Morôn/San Pablo was actually two separate bases. San Pablo was the administrative complex for the main base at Morôn, 40 miles southwest of the city. Assigned initially to San Pablo's structural fire station, we had no aircraft so no crash trucks in quarters. The base contained several office buildings, a commissary, base housing, a bakery, Bachelor Officer Quarters, NCO barracks, and a bowling alley. I stayed in a three-story concrete barracks. The San Pablo Fire Department housed two of the 1954-vintage 530B engines. Four men were assigned to one rig and one to the second. We worked a 24-on/24-off schedule with a three-day break every two weeks. Several civilian firefighters, Spanish nationals, worked with us and our mascot, Bootsie, a Spanish sheepdog. San Pablo's slow pace was the perfect atmosphere to work in since I still had additional probationary training and testing to complete. Practical firefighting experience at the small base consisted of two small grass fires and periodic hot-fire training next to the firehouse. I learned more about the intricacies of poker than I did the fire service.

In March 1968 I returned to L.A. and married Jody. The wedding was a typical Italian/Catholic fête. We honeymooned in Dana Point, California. Hal Collier was my best man and the lovely Teresa, maid-of-honor. Hal and Terry had already married, too. Upon return to Spain, I found a new crew member assigned. Sergeant Wally Merrell from Massachusetts rotated into San Pablo after doing time at Morôn. Wally drove the engine and passed the staff sergeant exam, due to promote in months. Wally became another role model for me. Like Roger Swift, sergeant Merrell's characteristics enhanced the learning atmosphere at San Pablo. Wally came on as Kevin Costner-with-an-education. His vocabulary immense and general knowledge broad, Wally did not flaunt his abilities; he just spoke well and treated us as his pliable charges. Eager to learn from him, our young crew found Scrabble supplanted the daily poker fest. Sergeant Merrell taught English to our Spanish crewmembers. I received my airman second-class stripes in mid-1968 and Wally made staff sergeant at about the same time. I looked forward to working with the man and absorbed all I could from him. He made me his engineer, responsible for driving and maintaining the lead engine company.

After Jody's departure in early 1969, I transferred to Morôn. She missed home and family and my assignment changed from three years to just two. Morôn was much larger than San Pablo and contained a 10,000-foot runway. A wing of RF-4C Phantom jets kept us busy with fuel spills and miscellaneous in-flight emergency calls. I loved the powerful twin-engined aircraft. These recon jets, with their green/brown camouflage color scheme and full after-burner takeoffs, carried no weapons. With four crash trucks, two structural engines, and a near-new GMC 2500-gallon tanker, I rotated through assignments on the crash rigs since I had no experience on them except in tech school. Tooling around the flight line in the new P-2's invigorated me. The boxy 011-A's were slow, cumbersome and had stick shifts much like the 750's. The shifter flopped around like a geriatrics walking cane. Finding any gear other than second was pure luck. Ironically, the 0-11's did not go any faster than 25 miles-per-hour anyway so second was all we needed. Low on manpower, the shift chief assigned me as the only fireman on a P-2, occasionally. Quickly proficient in crash rig operation, I also volunteered frequently for tanker duty since the truck went on both crash and structural responses, as well as wash-downs of fuel spills from the leaky F-4s. I never enjoyed sitting around the firehouse. Keeping busy made time go faster and I gained more experience in all phases of the fire service; even the mundane. Sergeant Merrell reinforced the need for a worker to stay active and productive, and also encouraged me to capitalize on my writing abilities and generate reports and memos whenever possible. He found many senior air force NCOs were almost illiterate and required to write frequently. Offering to write the reports for the experience gave the NCOs a way to turn in a better product. My supervisors plagiarized my reports shamelessly but everybody was happy.

I experienced two crashes while assigned to Morón. On a hot summer afternoon we found ourselves lounging in the air-conditioned dayroom when a long-ring came in from the bells scattered around the station. One long bell signaled an aircraft emergency. The dispatcher announced the nature of the call immediately instead of delaying long enough for the crews to get into the rigs and listen over the radios. The unusual chronology sent my heart racing. Static from the speakers added to the tensions. I heard excited radio chatter in Spanish in the background of the dispatch center while airman Diaz spoke. He monitored the pilot's frequency. "Attention all responding units. In-flight emergency, F-86, flame-out directly over the base, on final approach, runway 2-1..." The F-86, a Korean-war era single-pilot, one-engine jet could not expect to travel too far with his only propulsion gone. Like an egg in the hands of a three-year-old, a silvery glider like the F-86 would inevitably meet a hard, flat surface. The Spanish Air Force maintained a covey of the aging aircraft at Morón and half our in-flight emergencies were for these ailing birds. Less than thirty seconds after the bell, I hit the tarmac in my assigned P-2. In-flight-emergency policy designated us to advance to assigned taxiways parallel to the runway. I scanned the sky instead, searching for the glider as my rig idled on the ramp. I saw it almost immediately. About 2,000 feet up, he whooshed over and, like a toy at the end of a string, swept around so close I read the numbers on his wings. The plane made no in-line approach to the runway but continued dropping and, as he hit the bottom of his arc, met the concrete threshold. It appeared the engine-less plane traveled at over 250 mph and I expected a spectacular impact from his drop rate. I held my breath and braked to a stop when he hit on his nose wheel, curling it back like a finger, then bounced hard on the two main gears and left the ground. The next bounce on a three-point hit was not as hard, and the pilot instantly raised the nose as he slowed, protecting the damaged gear. By the halfway mark he allowed the nose wheel to gently touch down, throwing a spectacular shower of sparks as he rolled to a stop. I found myself sailing across the ramp followed by a string of crash rigs, structural engines and a variety of ramp-tramp vehicles. By the time we arrived at the smoking aircraft, the pilot opened his canopy and straddled the windshield, waiting for a ladder. Only a short drop, I believe he waited because his legs could not hold up his own weight after the near-fatal experience.

My other F-86 incident did not end as successfully. Off-duty and driving to my apartment, a Sevilla city fire engine sailed by me, headed out of town. A column of thick, black smoke rose about five miles north. I followed. After we traveled several miles, I saw two Spanish F-86's circling the small village ahead. They looked like distraught bird parents hovering over a chick fallen from their nest. I parked just off the main town plaza and saw a blazing carpentry shop and F-86 parts, not actually recognizable as one of the small jets, scattered across the plaza itself. A bright orange and white parachute lay across the red-tiled roof of a pension. At the end of the parachute's shroud line were half the remains of the pilot still strapped to his ejection seat. The other half of the body lay among gleaming aluminum plane parts on the ground. Several local officials recovered the body parts, sans gloves, in their hands. Later, back at work, I learned the young pilot buzzed his fiancée's home and dropped too low, striking a small hill with his tail and pancaked onto the carpentry shop.

In mid-1969 I received notice that I made sergeant and was promoting in September. Only twenty years old, my elevation made me the youngest NCO on base. I had Wally Merrell to thank for his encouragement and guidance. With my rotation back to the states nearing, I expected a choice assignment in California. I asked for Edwards and March AFBs near Los Angeles. The orders arrived in November 1969. I departed sunny southern Spain for Great Falls, Montana in the dead of winter. In the military, Murphy's Law rules. Pleased to leave Spain, I viewed my stay as only passing through on my way to bigger things. I caught an air force mail plane to Torrejón Air Base in Madrid and found a gaggle of military school-aged kids also vying for my standby space back to the U.S. They had priority since their parents were lifers. A friendly base operations clerk went out of his way to accommodate me and located a hop directly to California, but I would have to get to Frankfurt, Germany in less than 10 hours. I made the deadline and found the KC-135 air refueling tanker with just the flight crew and no air force brats on board. The 12-hour, non-stop trip took the polar route. A noisy, cold trip, the freebie enabled me to again pocket my remaining travel allowance. The crew allowed me to wander around the cockpit and the NCO crew chief let me tread on the thick, clear Plexiglas panels where the refueling boom dropped down to gas up aircraft in flight. The exhilarating sight of snow-covered mountains 35,000 feet below my feet, cruising at 550 miles per hour will stay with me forever.

After a brief stay at home over the holidays, Jody and I rolled into Great Falls, Montana. Our new Volkswagen hatchback did well on snowy roads in the flatland city of 40,000 people. Cold, stormy and icy streets greeted us and stayed for several months while we settled in. After a few weeks of sub-zero temperatures, a sunny day warmed to 45° and presented short-sleeved weather to these strange folks we called neighbors. I took a crew chief's position as soon as I arrived at Malmstrom AFB, just north of town. With only a few F-106 fighters assigned, the complex served as the mother base for several hundred nuclear-tipped ICBMs, housed in underground silos scattered around central Montana. Huey helicopters outnumbered airplanes on the base. The lumbering Hueys ferried relief crews to the distant ICBM sites. With a large tract of base housing, structural fire calls were sporadic, usually for smoke investigations but no real fires. The only fire ground experience I gained at Malmstrom was another off-duty incident. I stopped off at the firehouse to pick up my paycheck and, as I started to leave, a staff sergeant flagged me down and said to get my firefighting gear and meet him at our 1956 vintage 2000-gallon tanker. A small house just off-base reportedly burned on the no-man's land between Malmstrom and the city limits. The base fire chief approved our mutual aid response to do what we could until a distant volunteer department arrived from eight miles away. The tiny wood-frame house was only a quarter-mile off the base boundaries and as we pulled up, several neighbors mingled around the open front door as smoke pulsed out. We saw no flames. The tanker was not equipped with breathing apparatus so I dragged a hose line in as the sarge ran up the pump pressure. Dropping to my knees, I crawled around searching for victims, sucking in vast quantities of thick, brownish smoke. Some visibility near the floor helped verify that nobody was inside. The sarge broke out a few windows and his actions cleared the air, allowing the smoke to escape and I found the fire. Inside a closet I found a smoldering cardboard shoebox, its contents emitting the smelly phlegm. The sides of the box burned through and fire extended up the thin wooden wall inside the closet, but died down from lack of oxygen. I removed the smoldering box, set it behind me, and sprayed a small amount of water onto the closet wall. I also pulled apart the damaged wood to get at any deep-seated fire and sprayed again. I struggled to crawl back outside and leaned over a hose bib, coughing up the nasty chunks accumulated in my lungs. When recovered, I told the sarge the fire was out. A minute or two passed and the sergeant said I should go back in and check. The smoke was increasing. I looked at the front door and, sure enough, more smoke than before pushed out. A siren howled in the distance and we did not want to give up our fire to another company so I dragged my line back inside. I re-traced my steps and found the closet damage still cold to the touch. I backed up to ponder this discovery and put my gloved hand into a flaming hot mass. The blazing shoe box spread to a low-slung cotton and foam-stuffed sofa I inadvertently placed it on. A cushion, armrest, and adjacent ottoman blazed away, oozing a cloud so thick I tasted chunks of it. Extinguishing the new fire, I backed out again, hacking and coughing, but pleased we were able to knock the thing down with just a few gallons of water. The volunteer's antiquated engine rolled onto the block with 6-7 citizens hanging onto its sides and tailboard. Fortunately, my second foray succeeded in killing the fire. We turned the scene over to the volunteers after I sheepishly advised them there were now two points of origin to the fire. I caused the secondary blaze.

As a crew chief/supervisor, policy required me to provide at least two hours of training to my subordinates each shift. As the new guy, four other crew chiefs forced me to train their men, too. In the shift chief's office, a pigeon-hole wall unit contained standard training forms already filled in with various daily training topics. Instead of actually conducting a class, the supervisor typically filled in his crew members' names, the date, and time of the session, and filed the bogus reports, rotating the categories so the scam did not seem too contrived. I never used the standard forms. The setup exposed laziness to me, and I elected to actually educate the men. Each shift I developed a unique, seldom-taught procedure or created a relevant topic to teach. I wanted my guys to learn, and want to acquire knowledge used in our field. At least once per shift, a fuel leak from an aircraft required a wash down. If the pool of flammable AVGAS exceeded 25 gallons, the incident ungraded to a major fuel spill and a full station response was necessary instead of just the tanker with one man. Larger spills were more susceptible to ignition by static electricity and even an open-air pool of flaming AVGAS created aircraft visibility problems and dangerous distractions. Properly estimating the size of a fuel spill by a firefighter was important. A supervisor was blamed if an estimate turned out wrong. The reaming occurred to me twice. My training involved filling several containers with varying amounts of water, and spilling the control samples along a stretch of taxiway. I had each crew drive by the 5-6 pools and write down their estimates of spill size. The tower personnel thought me a bit touched when they saw my activities, but the crews loved the simple class. The session got them out of the station and solved a real problem. In my later years as an investigator for Glendale, I set up similar, unique training not offered or only covered briefly in available classes. The activities made my years on the California Conference of Arson Investigators and Fire Investigation Regional Strike Team training committees worthwhile.

With little I could do to gain practical firefighting experience in the air force, I studied various fire service topics in my spare time; particularly fire prevention. Air force bases were kept immaculate and all buildings inspected frequently for fire safety. After talking to colleagues in the local civilian fire departments, I found my counterparts in the same situation. The typical firefighter spends over 25 percent of the on-duty schedule training for what might happen and much of the rest preventing the fire from occurring. This made sense to me. The real worth of firefighters is in the fire prevention efforts. Prevention is the mission of all fire departments. We are employed to save lives and protect property but if the fire never occurs, no lives are jeopardized and no possessions lost. After this revelation, I volunteered for more fire patrol and inspection work while voraciously reading available fire service manuals and textbooks. With all the competition for civilian fire service jobs, I prepared. My discharge date loomed. By mid-1970, Jody and I agreed to take military discharge and leave service life. Nothing could alter our thinking. Both close to our families, we missed L.A. and our friends. In September 1970 we found out Jody was pregnant. The baby was due 50 days after my discharge date. We considered a 6-month extension to have the baby at the base hospital. The base reenlistment officer resolved our dilemma. He said the child was conceived while I was on active duty and it was the air force's responsibility to cover the costs of birth and after-care. We were in the clear. Jody again left for home early. I finished my last four months of military service living off-base and working a second job at a Circle K store until honorably discharged on my 22nd birthday on April 26, 1971. As much as I enjoyed my service time, I felt I was released from prison upon discharge, reaching my limit of others telling me where to go, when, and for how long. I wanted to make my own choices and thus developed a negative attitude. Cocky, resentful of authority, and generally rebellious, this posture apparently came from my own insecurities. I had a family to provide for now. We lived with Jody's parents after my discharge. Competition for firefighter jobs was worse than I expected so I applied to take tests for several agencies, including L.A. City and County Fire Departments as well as LAPD and the county sheriff's department. Later, I lined up entrance exams for Glendale and Burbank. Testing for the larger agencies was months away. The civil service tests came around every two years with the established lists longevity the same length of time. I planned to accept a law enforcement job and later transfer to the fire department when my name came up on their list—a common practice in the 1970s and 80s. Within weeks of discharge, my old friend from school, Gary McDonough, hired me for his crew at Sparkletts Bottled Water Company near my home. Gary married another old friend, Judy Sander, the girl who lost her fiancée to the Vietnam War. My Uncle Leonard also worked days at Sparkletts. I labored on the 3-11 p.m. shift loading trucks with 5-gallon bottles of water and coolers. My other close friend, Hal Collier, already worked for the LAPD Both Gary and Hal went to college instead of going into military service. Hal worked Hollywood Division and met me several times under the Hyperion bridge on the extreme northern edge of Hollywood territory. He told me stories of his exploits while he smoked cigars and exhibited an image unfamiliar to me. I looked forward to possibly joining the LAPD and working with my old friend. Unfortunately, I absorbed his cocky attitude and the new traits added more arrogance and selfishness to my demeanor. Our daughter, Carrie Lyn, was born June 10, 1971. Jody's obstetrician arranged for her to have Carrie at a home for unwed mothers where he donated some of his time. With a caesarean section necessary, we only had to schedule date and time of delivery. Carrie was beautiful. Seeing her for the first time literally took my breath away. If allowed, I would have taken my new baby home with me while Jody recovered.

Carrie's birth probably saved our marriage. After discharge from the air force, I regressed to post-high school antics guys pursued during those formative periods. Getting off work at 11 p.m., I went to bars and night spots with the crew from Sparkletts several times each week. Occasionally I went street racing in my newly-acquired 1963 Dodge

Polara. The 413-cubic-inch V-8 was a monster and I found myself cruising after work, looking for races. With a new baby and the responsibilities of maintaining our apartment, I still lived a single-like existence. An arrogance I was not cognizant of took over and I thought only of myself. I brought home the paycheck and fulfilled my requirements in an Ozzie and Harriet world, but I never saw Ozzie shoot pool on a weeknight or drag race down Ventura Boulevard in a Dodge. Nevertheless, we had no parenting or similar classes in high school in the 1960s. Without further guidance, I ignored reality. My focus was on advancement of a career and better-paying job while Jody took care of the home and paid the bills. I failed to consider how Jody suffered in my absences. I came to a self-serving conclusion on one of the rare mornings I rose early to allow Jody to sleep in. I wandered out to the backyard with my new baby and chatted with her. Overjoyed with her laughing and gurgling, I pointed out flora and fauna in our jungle-like hillside enclosure. Settling on a low retaining wall, I thought about how intensely I loved her, how much I wanted to protect and nurture my daughter. This love was far stronger than my feelings for her mother. I did not feel I loved or could love my wife as much as I did Carrie Lyn. My caring for Jody lessened and, instead of working on the existing problems, I selfishly ignored them. I had no prior training or experience to apply to the difficulties. Simplistic as it sounds, I operated with the only relationship education from my past: Mom resolved her marriage enigma by leaving. I had no concept of how much time Mom and Dad spent debating before Mom left, but considered this my easiest option so pondered when to accomplish the act.

In the meantime, the LAPD processed me through the written exam, physical agility, oral interview, and the final step before hiring; the medical. I thought I had it made when given a start date for the LAPD academy. The medical exam included psychological testing. The psych exams included the 550-question MMPI self-inventory. The MMPI was comical to me, with its inane true-or-false queries such as, "I enjoy the ballet more than loading a truck," or "I'd rather take dance lessons than commit suicide." The Rorschach inkblot series I verbally resisted since all I saw were pieces of cardboard stained with pools of dried symmetrical ink. I was not a real insightful guy but continued, trying to be mature about the tests. After the first two or three displays I started seeing some pretty cool images. Dancers, native drummers around a bonfire, a ship moored in a foggy lagoon, and some butterflies. Then the examiner held up the "sex" card. Its images bear resemblance to female genitalia and internal reproductive organs I had seen in biology and anatomy books in school. Afraid to be labeled as sex-obsessed, I revealed I saw a map of Italy or an outline of a flying bat. Fortunately, my sex-

44

related anxiety was common, as were my actual responses. I left the testing room bewildered. Still, I felt confident of hiring with my firm start date and accompanying pre- hire brochure. Several weeks later I received a rejection letter from the LAPD based on the psychological evaluations. There was no reason provided and no further explanation, the wording vague, saying I was not "suitable" for police work. The news devastated me, not so much at the LAPD rejection, but for the down-the-road affect. The L.A. Fire Department used the same psychological testing. The rejection letter outlined an appeal procedure. Pursuing an appeal required an independent evaluation by a privately retained psychologist or psychiatrist. I followed the procedure and had two sessions with a Glendale doctor I found in the Yellow Pages. He said he saw no reason to exclude me as a police candidate and made a plea for my reinstatement. A month later I had an appointment to see the LAPD psychologist. He informed me I still remained on the rejection list and he was not allowed to discuss the test results but he would see me anyway. When I arrived, he was cordial and understood my dismay for the lack of specific reasons for rejection. The kindly doctor said standard procedure did not allow him to reveal exact findings so the candidate would not "learn" the tests and return later to skew his answers to conform to test standards. He said some candidates read psychology texts and taught themselves how to pass the exams. Naïvely I responded, "But that's not right; it's cheating." He told me, "That's a pretty good response, young man. Pretty much as your test results revealed, you have the basics, but..." The doctor said I showed some passivity and a police candidate required aggressiveness. We chatted a bit more and he frequently referred to my file, open in front of him. He emphasized his statements by pointing to sections of the form on his desk, apparently the "Conclusion" section of the complete report. Then he surprised me and stood up, pointing at the form, and said, "I'm going to get a cup of coffee...I'll be back in about five minutes..." Then he left. I peeked, but read the form as it lay upside down, careful not to move it around in case he tested my trust. Scanning the top sheet I picked up the name of one of the guys I used as a reference. A current supervisor at Sparkletts, the man replaced Gary McDonough when he was hired by the L.A.F.D. several months before. I competed with him for Gary's vacant position, but with my short tenure of less than one year, he promoted and I understandably remained a subordinate. For months we worked side-by-side, hefting 5-gallon water bottles, loading 38 trucks per night and driving forklifts, but I found him a bit priggish and rigid. He tried too hard. We joked around and he joined his crew at the cantina occasionally after work, but he found me immature. At that time I was, but did not realize it until I read his perceptions of me. He told the LAPD researcher I resented his promotion over me and that I was lazy. I have never been lazy and Sparkletts supervisors made the right choice by promoting my antagonist. I never voiced otherwise. I was disappointed but not openly resentful as stated. He truthfully said I was late on two occasions and thought adapting to the rigidity of the police department posed potential problems. My four successful years in the military apparently were not considered. The psychological report further discussed my shortcomings in my honest revelation I once stole a six-pack of beer from my employer at the Empire Market. Peer pressure. I did not tell the background investigator I had later paid for the six-pack by leaving three dollars on a cash register. To me, I stole the beer so revealed the error in judgment because I knew a polygraph exam was on the horizon so I showed all my warts. The final evaluation stated I needed a few years to "mature before re-applying." That, at least, encouraged me. Less than a month later I quit Sparkletts and entered the Jack-in-the-Box management program. Restaurant management paid more than my night loader position at the water company but I had to work over 50 hours per week. I applied all I learned from Roger Swift and progressed rapidly once I started on the management side of the food service industry. Not flipping burgers anymore, I hired and fired employees, scheduled the work shifts and ordered supplies under the watchful eyes of several different managers around Glendale and Los Angeles. As a floating manager, I filled in for managers on vacation as well as a long stint at two stores when the managers left or were fired. Close to getting my own store, I found an ad for a manager position with a nearby Kentucky Fried Chicken outlet in affluent La Canada/Flintridge. An interview proved successful and I started immediately, at $100 a week more than Jack-in-the-Box paid. If a fire or police job did not come up soon, my paychecks at least equaled the civil service positions. A mentor, Martin, guided me briefly then gave me full reign over one of his three KFC outlets. I still labored over 50 hours per week but the bonuses compensated me for the absences from home. Martin gave me several days off with pay when our beautiful daughter, Lori Leigh was born on August 20, 1973. My baby girls meant the world to me. Lori was a doll, a Gerber baby look-alike and personality like that of her sibling. Both laughed and gurgled contentedly despite short bouts with colic. A proud father, I was a miserable husband. I tried to temporarily smooth over my home life without really realizing I was the problem; not Jody. Continuing to focus on work and ignoring the family situation, I still kept late hours but made some effort to break the chain of neglect by selling my Dodge. I had at least some insight but still did not communicate well with my wife. In September 1973 Martin gave me both a nice raise and a big bonus for our successful summer months' performance. I had an excellent crew, mostly children of the affluent living in the La Canada/Flintridge area. One of my best employees, Dave Kubly, let me know his KFC job was only temporary. He longed to join the LAPD and later did. While working alone in Hollywood Division in 1977, he got into a vehicle pursuit, crashing with the fleeing suspect. The criminal was quicker getting out of the mangled wreckage, and killed Dave with one shot. Retirement approached for Martin and he voiced his desire to seek a general manager for his three franchises. The offer was so lucrative I considered applying for the position. Jody insisted I stay, too, giving up civil service for a much higher-paying career. After working for Martin a short time, I felt his presence constantly and could not imagine him not showing up for work. Another manager had more seniority than I and my selection was not guaranteed. The L.A.F.D. gave me a hiring date in November. I had to make a decision, but Martin held off on announcing his retirement. He could sell the operation outright and retire, leaving me high and dry as I was ready to do to him if I chose the L.A.F.D. As usual, my career desires and job satisfaction hinged on performance; not money. I looked forward going to my jobs to put forth a good effort and do a better-than-average job. I wanted recognition as an employee who did not just punch the clock twice a day. I allowed myself to get off-track at Sparkletts but my work virtues improved vastly in the last eight months. Over Jody's protests, I gave Martin thirty days' notice in October 1973. I ignored Jody more and more instead of working on the relationship. Still cocky from L.A.F.D. acceptance, I strutted around figuring I had it made. Everything was "I" and "me." The rejection of LAPD had devastated me. I knew I was suited for law enforcement, and acceptance by the L.A.F.D. revealed I was a promising candidate for a critical civil service position. So wrapped up in myself I prepared minimally for the upcoming eight-week academy. In good physical shape from my active jobs, I also had four solid years firefighting experience. Two days before scheduled start on the L.A.F.D. recruit academy, I accepted an offer to play racquetball with Bob Turner, another recruit at L.A. fire station 55 where Bob's dad worked. I played tennis but this was my first experience with racquetball. Bob beat me soundly and I walked away with painful blisters on both feet from wearing ill-fitting sneakers, a stupid thing to do two days before a new job. My stamina and strength were excellent but I did not plan on the amount of twisting, turning and stooping the vigorous game required. On Friday, November 13, 1973, I was called in to the Training Captain's Office at the L.A.F.D. academy in North Hollywood. The education, while strict and regimented, fell short of military basic training's intensity. Captain Metz, the supervisor of the 40 recruits, was kindly and supportive. He informed me I was not cutting it as a recruit; I scored poorly on a written test and two critical rope and ladder exams. My sore feet tortured me and limited my movements so took it easy during the first two weeks, hoping to improve later. Metz asked me what was wrong and listened intently to my explanation. He gave me a choice of resigning or waiting for the results of the day's exams and risk firing Monday. Confident of the day's work, I told him how much the job meant to me. I opted to wait for Monday.

Bob Turner and several other rookies held study groups on our off-duty days, practicing ladder carries, tying rescue knots, and quizzing each other on the contents of the huge textbooks and manuals issued. I attended few of these sessions, preferring to study at home; confident I could tie knots and throw ladders against buildings. I was wrong. I did not absorb enough of the texts and my cocky attitude was, "I've been a firefighter for four years. I already know this stuff. Experience should count for something." I ignored the obvious: the instructors taught us to be a well-oiled team and how to operate automatically as everyone else operated in the frenzy of an emergency. Placing fingers in the wrong position or missing a mark in ladder placement resulted in injury to oneself, a citizen, or a member of the team. The L.A.F.D. expected us to carry a 24-foot extension ladder at a 45 degree angle and stab the base into the ground at a prescribed distance from the target based on the building's height. If carried too high, the butt end spears a comrade or fleeing citizen in the face. Place the base too close to the objective and the climbing angle is dangerously steep for hauling bulky equipment up or struggling victims down. I did not pay attention. My mind elsewhere, I convinced myself experience carried the day. After all, I had four years' training and experience. I recall walking into our living room and giving the news to Jody. She cried. I wept. She sat down on the couch while our infants napped and said, "What am I going to do now?" Not "we", but "I." What could I expect after my treatment of our family?

CHAPTER FOUR
FIREFIGHT

Fifteen wild-eyed young men started the first formal Glendale Fire Department Recruit Academy on March 1, 1974. I was one of the optimists. Prior to 1974, Glendale fire rookies were immediately assigned to a company and learned the fire business on the job, hanging from a tailboard with one hand and textbooks in the other.

The academy training sessions were a breeze compared to the L.A.F.D. I graduated and found myself at Glendale Station Six. Just north of downtown, the district was primarily residential with a few small businesses and a half-mile square of industry and manufacturing structures. I was assigned to Truck Six, a rig that was built before I was born and purchased by Glendale about the time of my first diaper change 25 years before. The beast looked like it belonged in an early Three Stooges comedy. With seating for only two men, the rest of us hung onto brass rails on the sides of the aerial's trailer; one hand locked onto our helmets to keep them on in the wind. I worked for Captain Ed Meese, a 30-year veteran approaching retirement. My first run was a box alarm in Engine Seven's district. We were cancelled after only a half-mile but the thrilling experience was like a teenaged make-out session. Sensational, but without climax. We returned to quarters.

Also assigned to the station was a 1954 GMC brush fire rig and an engine. The ladder truck crew manned the 400-gallon tanker when a wildland fire call rang in. We caught a few brush blazes during the summer, but otherwise, my first quarter assignment was quiet. Three months after I started at Six, I moved to adjoining Station Seven's district, an engine-only house on the extreme west side of town, bordering Burbank. Captain Bill Dodson, my new supervisor, also neared retirement but was the polar opposite of Captain Meese. Bill saw to it that his crew stayed busy helping me complete probationary written and practical exams. The new district's business and manufacturing areas equaled the upper and lower income residential turf. There seemed to be no middle income section. The north and southbound lanes of Interstate Five kept us busy with vehicle accidents and fires as well as frequent alarm malfunctions in the industrial district. I did make two rescues while working at Seven. At about 3:30 a.m. on September 25, I crawled on the floor of a small three-bedroom home while the living room couch blazed away. No occupants were located in the balance of the house so I passed the couch a second time while the captain and a firefighter dragged a hose line in from the driveway. With the smoke down to knee level, I spied a pair of bare legs at a table. The drunken homeowner sat reading a newspaper despite the fire in the next room. Conscious, but groggy, I convinced the staggering man to drop to the floor and half-dragged him outside where we revived him. Three months later, to the day and almost the same hour, we again responded to the house of the drunken man. Heavy smoke pouring out, we repeated our search/extinguishment patterns. I located him collapsed against the service porch door. I struggled with the 280-pound unconscious figure while the heat line dropped down to my ear level. I could not stand up to move him and had to slide him back into the kitchen, then reach up into the heat for the door knob. I dragged the man to the driveway. Our attempts to revive him were unsuccessful this time.

I spent my final probationary period at Station Nine in the northern part of town nestled in a modern brick firehouse in the shadows of the San Gabriel Mountains. Assigned, again, to the ladder truck, I worked with a friend from the recruit class, Jim Fitzpatrick. Also on his final probationary assignment, we held study groups and constantly practiced tying knots and raising ladders. Jim became a life-long buddy and helped me through the final phases of our one-year probation despite a serious training accident. The mishap put a threaded gash in my helmet from an out-of-control, flailing high-pressure 2½-inch hose line. We were reprimanded for the incident but laughed it off; injuries are part of the job. Held in February 1975, our final written exam caused our crews to run short. As we sat scribbling away, the radio blared with an urgent emergency broadcast. "Engine seven, engine six...a truck fire, north-bound 1-5 at Alameda off-ramp...be advised CHP reports explosives placards on the truck..." The missed incident ended benignly and both of us passed our tests.

As full-time firefighters, the major change we saw immediately was the fact we could now watch television. Not every waking moment required a textbook or rope in hand. I welcomed the opportunity to sit in the dayroom as part of the crew. The TV rooms reminded me of my friend Hal Collier's den. This was now home-away-from-home. However, the station became more of a home than my residing with Jody. Now able to work overtime, I grabbed the opportunities constantly and I was able to work the stations I missed during probation. The extra shifts enabled me to meet the rest of the department's personnel and train with the different rigs and equipment.

Shortly after probation ended, our fire chief, Allan R. Stone, bought into the fire service's newest trend: painting the traditional red fire equipment an ugly—but reportedly safer—lime-green. Stone was an excellent administrator but this act did not endear him with any of the men. Citizens complained of the concept, along with my recruit academy graduates. We were assigned at least six hours of each shift to sand off the red paint in preparation of application of the new paint scheme. Glendale is still the only L.A.-area department preserving the antiquated concept.

Jody and I weathered the tension of my first year with GFD. To me, the end of the marriage was inevitable, but I did not communicate this to my wife. Still catching up with my post-high school years, I felt smothered by Jody and the responsibility of a full-time father. I loved my daughters unequivocally but found anything outside the house infinitely more intriguing. I took another job at 7-11, working days and some graveyard shifts when no overtime was available at the stations. The extra money enabled me to buy my first truck, a 1965 Ford ½-ton with a camper shell. Jody drove our 1971 Datsun station wagon. Working two jobs kept me busy and the money helped placate Jody over my absences. One of my co-workers, Sheila, also experienced problems in her marriage. Three years younger than I, she was on her second husband. Neither of us could afford to move out on our own so we made a spur-of-the-moment decision to take an apartment together to save money. I gave Jody no notice. The only experience I had with separation was my mom's leaving Dad. I moved out one weekday morning while Jody was at work and the kids at daycare. I explained my exit in a note, just like Mom. I left the checkbook with Jody and the next day went to the Department of Public Social Services. I had them compute my income, circumstances, and tell me how much child support I should pay. I masked my true feelings and guilt over the abandonment and selfishly thought the efforts at child support would make the impact on Jody easier. Cognizant only of my desire to leave, I wanted money to be the least of my family's worries. Sheila and I moved into our one-bedroom apartment in Glendale the same day I left Jody. Our platonic relationship lasted about twenty minutes. Maintaining two residences—mine and Jody's—created hardship all around both emotionally and fiscally. Fortunately, I still had my G.I. Bill education allowance available, and I also needed college to ensure advancement in the department. Going back to school was a no-brainer. I enrolled in two classes per week the first semester at Glendale Community College. Textbooks and supplies were inexpensive and I was able to channel 90 percent of the allowance to Jody and my girls. I enjoyed returning to school. I attended all the fire science classes available and, when done with those, signed up in administration of justice courses.

I could not understand the enigma of the poor professional relationship between firefighters and local police. We provide basically the same service to the community. I wanted to explore both sides of the conflicts so I enrolled in basic police organization class as well as police report writing. Firemen did not write many reports in the 1970s, but I found the efforts worthy through my air force experience. If my original report was not forwarded beyond my supervisor, they generally ended up plagiarized and passed up the chain of command. With no fire service-related report-writing sessions available, I attended one taught by a Glendale police detective. While working at 7-11 in 1975, I discovered a knack for catching shop-lifters. Observations started with elementary-aged youngsters stopping by the store on their way home from school when I began the 3-11 p.m. shift. The kids gave themselves away by eye movements and exaggerated casualness and body language. Once I mastered these key elements, I read the same, but more subtle, moves of the older kids and adult thieves. I was amazed at how often we were hit. The store had to lose hundreds of dollars each month before I began my quest. When it was busy, I deterred the potential thieves by shouting out to them from the cash booth, "Hey! You need some help back there?" The crooks generally either made their purchase or left the store. Identifying shoplifters became a challenge and seemed the only reason to go to work. The store owner appreciated the efforts and my recoveries made the normally boring job tolerable. I always documented the successful apprehensions by taking names and addresses. I never called the police while at 7-11. Again, writing a "report" helped advance me in my job.

Eventually, I saw shoplifters and thieves everywhere, even when not at 7-11; in department stores, markets, and driving along the street. The criminal element seemed to share the pre-crime characteristics. Was there a class for crooks? On a warm summer morning I walked into a grab-and-run at a Montgomery Ward store in Eagle Rock. The bad guy left the store with an armload of men's suits while a diminutive store agent attempted to capture him. Together we wrestled the man to the ground and recovered the goods. That same day, a theft of tools went down in front of me at the Glendale Sears outlet. Notifying and assisting the security manager and his Wayne Newton look-alike partner, Chuck Mesrobian, I capitalized on the opportunity and applied for a job. With store security staff primarily off-duty Glendale cops, Chuck said he needed someone to work days and a few nights. I gave notice at 7-11 and started at Sears the following week. Chuck gave me a walk-around orientation and quizzed me about basic search and seizure, laws of arrest, and detention issues. These areas were part of my fire training since firefighters have limited peace officer powers when on-duty. The rest I picked up in college courses. Orientation lasted about an hour, then

Chuck sent me out on my own to apprehend shoplifters, stolen credit card users and light-fingered employees.

Sheila was sympathetic of the time I spent working two jobs and still attending college. She worked for the Bank of America and we both had at least one or two weekends per month off where our time off coincided. We spent this time camping, shooting and prowling around old mining claims. I divorced Jody in early 1976. The child support arrangement gave my girls 10 percent of my fire department paycheck with built-in raises. Every time Glendale gave me a 6 percent raise, the child support went up a like amount. I kicked in occasional bonuses for school clothes, supplies, and paid for Jody's car upkeep. I was an asshole for the abandonment but tried also to be a positive presence. Working in plainclothes during my first few months at Sears, I arrested over 30 people, apprehended another 20 I chose not to arrest, and bagged two car burglars in the Sears underground parking structure, and one employee thief. Statistically, employees were responsible for most of Sears' losses than walk-ins, but the in-house crooks were cagier. At shift change one evening at Sears, I initiated a take-down of a family using their children to steal boys' jeans. The father, waiting in the van just outside the store doors, decided to fight us. Assisted by the aging police Chief's second-in-command, Pete Hamilton, we jumped into the van and dragged the man onto busy Central Avenue and succeeded in handcuffing him. The arrests ended up with over $30,000 worth of the pants recovered in a search warrant on the family compound. Pete and I were battered and bloody but the end result satisfying to all of us. Reports and follow-up kept me at the store past closing and Pete asked me to join him for drinks. We met the rest of the night security crew: Dave Calame, Dave O'Connor, and Jim Peterson. All were GPD detectives. Several years later I worked cases alongside this elite group. Calame was a juvenile investigator I frequently referred child fire-setter cases to; O'Connor and Peterson worked robbery/homicide and co-investigated fires when an injury or fatality occurred. After several months of exposure to law enforcement with Sears, I noticed more crime both on- and off-duty from my two jobs. Developing the sixth sense that says something is "not quite right" about a person or situation, my arrest/apprehension stats soared. For the cops, Sears was just an off-duty way to pick up a few dollars; for me, a kick. I loved going to work despite a few vicious take-downs and suffering my share of bumps and bruises. It seemed to me I created more work for the security crew to back me up and help with my apprehensions and standby with report-writing and booking procedures. Jim Peterson summed the feelings up one evening when he said, "John, I come to work at Sears to rest! Slow down..." He related this good-naturedly and he later said he enjoyed a good arrest or foot pursuit, too, but he was "getting too old for this."

Many of my arrests were heroin addicts with a pronounced aversion to apprehension. We recovered a few with knives and I chased one of these guys for over two blocks through downtown Glendale before he tired out behind a music store. Exhausted, he still pulled a four-inch knife and confronted me. Out of breath myself, I heard sirens approaching and told him I was armed and if I drew my .357 there were no witnesses in the area. The bluff worked. He tossed the blade into a dumpster and I took him into custody. After several similar foot pursuits, taking me blocks away from Sears without ready backup, Pete Hamilton suggested that I submit a request for a concealed weapons permit. As the police chief's assistant, the request routed through Pete for approval. Less than a week later, I found myself one of only six CCW permit holders in a city of 160,000 people.

On-duty at the fire department, we rotated station assignments annually. In 1977, I requested assignment to the Fire Patrol unit out of my favorite station, Firehouse Six on north Brand Boulevard. As one of the busiest houses in the city, the assigned men were older, experienced and easy-going. The eight-man, three-unit Station went out on all second alarms in the city, were first on out-of-city mutual aid runs and responded to most of Glendale's wildland fires. The patrol ran out of Six's quarters as a fourth unit, but, during the daylight hours, was assigned to the entire city. On January 1, 1977, I started my first shift as a patrolman. The unit, a 1974 Chevy ½-ton pickup, had a small capacity pump and carried 150 gallons of water and an assortment of heavy tools and equipment. The overloaded Chevy drove like a Yugo with an elephant in the trunk. My responsibilities included fire inspection and prevention work from 8-5 and, upon return to quarters, I was assigned as a fifth man on our 1975 American LaFrance rear-mount 100-foot aerial truck. I wanted fire ground experience and Station Six was the place to get it without having to sit around the station all day waiting for the alarm bells to ring. Very few men volunteered for the patrol unit. No one on 'B' shift showed any interest so I asked to change shifts to guarantee the position, and got it. On New Year's morning I met with Captain Joe Algiers, my new supervisor. Joe, a 25-year fire service veteran, reminded me of actor Peter Graves, albeit buffed-out. Over six-feet-tall with white hair and a George Hamilton tan, Algiers was a weightlifter. A genuine man, he used his rookie like a new toy, but that is what I wanted. We checked out the LaFrance and I familiarized myself with equipment locations, then we took the traditional 8:15 coffee break. I hopped into the patrol rig and headed downtown to meet with the battalion chief to get my daily assignments. I hoped for a slow New Year's Day, still sore from an incident at a small garage fire two days before. The owner of the burning structure opened her back door and an 80-pound German Shepard zeroed in on me. Attacking silently from behind, he made two 10-foot leaps from the porch and chomped several times on my left butt cheek.

Just five minutes out of Station Six, the radio beeped twice, followed by a dispatch, "Engine 6, Engine 7, Truck 6, Battalion 2...a structure fire, PD reports heavy smoke from Toll Junior High School, 700 Glenwood Road, Toll Junior High..." I responded from downtown and arrived simultaneously with my station's rigs. Thick, grayish-brown clouds drifted out of every window of the two-story main school building, but primarily from the office area near the main entrance. Engine six stretched a supply line to a nearby hydrant while I donned my breathing apparatus. I heard Captain Algiers ask for a second alarm when I joined him at the front of the building. We could see some flames from a broken basement window, but none from the first floor where we forced entry. The truck company's job was to check for victims, fire extension, and to ventilate the structure so crews entering the basement could find the source of the fire. Once we entered, visibility was limited to inches above the floor only. We could not see our hands in front of our faces anywhere above knee height. After opening a few windows, I felt Captain Algiers grab my coattail and he dragged me into a hot, smoke-filled office. I only knew it was an office by the credenza my knee crashed into. Joe shouted for me to help firefighter John Wray—another rookie I came on the job with—in moving furniture out of the office. I could barely make out John's skinny 150-pound frame, and stepped towards him. Suddenly there was no floor. The fire originated directly below us in a storage closet, and ate away the underside of the deck we stood on. The tongue-and-groove gave way. As I dropped, I instinctively sat down and smacked onto the remaining surface, but my weight caused it to fail. I felt the tremendous heat below me. The flames and embers traveled up my pants legs and I felt the dog bite wounds rip open. Before I tumbled into the fire pit I felt a grip on my collar. John Wray, all 150-pounds of him, jerked my bulk out of the hole and threw me backwards. We did not take time to recover, and automatically went back to what Algiers told us to do; move furniture. We knocked out the blaze quickly and, during a break, I thanked John for saving my ass. I do not know how he managed to pull my 180 pounds like he did but I was grateful. For the next 18 years he kept reminding me I owed him. I still owe him.

I fell into the routine of the new position as patrolman and Sears job for several months, then Sheila and I took a vacation. We fooled around the Mojave Desert for a few days and ended up in Las Vegas. On a whim, we married. A crazy move but we enjoyed life together so we solidified the relationship. My mom and dad loved Sheila and treated her like a daughter. She was not afraid of rolling around in the sand and sage brush, even when she stepped on a four-foot-long rattlesnake that same year near Lake Isabella, California.

On a return trip to the same area with my dad along this time, we spotted a column of smoke and followed it to a developing forest fire in Kelso Valley. A 10-year-old and his sister, left alone in camp while their off-duty sheriff's deputy father puttered around in a nearby canyon, decided to play in the campfire. They managed to ignite dry grass and a light breeze spread it quickly. As we arrived, the blaze covered about 1000 square feet and looked uncontrollable. Dad, Sheila and I grabbed shovels, blankets, canteens, and attacked the flames. We concentrated on extinguishing the light grass, ignoring the fiery sagebrush. Two other cars appeared out of nowhere and, in about ten minutes, we had the blaze stopped. The father showed up, too. He did not seem grateful, and basically wanted us to go away. He was truly embarrassed. We had a hell of a good time, and this event capped a sensational trip.

In the mid-1970's, a rash of arson-caused fires ripped through Glendale. A series of three destructive fires struck the 4-story Webb's department store in the downtown area. The first blaze started around noon in a shoe storage area, trapping a salesman and burning him badly. A group of police and fire department investigators from Glendale and outside agencies descended on the damaged building and attempted an investigation. Petty professional jealousies flared when fire department sleuths wanted to assist in pursuing leads. I was not close to the investigation but heard about the difficulties. Local media also picked up on the problem and broadcast the crisis. The investigation stalled and, several weeks later, a second fire occurred while the store was open for business. The minor blaze renewed the investigation but it again bogged down. On a Friday night, a month after the second fire, I punched out from an evening shift at Sears and strolled onto the loading dock to the sound of sirens and a smell of smoke. Webb's, just one block south, again blazed away, on two floors this time. I jogged down to the scene and found a helmet and turnout coat to wear. I fought fire for two hours but the building was gutted this time. The final arson originated in a pile of stacked luggage or boxed items right at closing time. Fortunately, all customers and employees escaped. Again the task force came together and clashed. I could not understand why these people could not get it together. Several possible suspects were developed but no pursuit resulted. I only received bits and pieces from second-hand sources.

Years later, in 1991, a Glendale police motorcycle officer stopped me and we discussed the Webb's fires. He surprised me when he said, "You know who set that fire, don't you?" I told him I was not involved in the Webb's investigation and did not know they had ID-ed anybody as a good suspect. He laughed and said, "My family thinks it was my dad. He worked there." I later located the Webb's file in the archives and found the officer's tale was true. His dad was listed as interviewed, but the fire department's file was obviously incomplete, probably because the police did not share it all with us. The statute of limitations ran out on the Webb's fires and the man could not be prosecuted even if he came forward. The Webb's fiasco and other arsons convinced the city they needed to pay more attention to investigating and preventing arson fires; however, little was done to improve the situation.

My experience at Sears and the few busts of burglars while on the fire patrol irritated a few uniformed Glendale officers. I still had my detective advocates at Sears with whom I got along just fine. I did not want to perpetuate the police/fire conflict; I wanted to resolve it. I wanted to be accepted by all of the Glendale police personnel. Still, I was an outsider and my continuing exposure to law enforcement enhanced my job on the patrol, so I ignored criticism.

Shortly after the Webb's fires, I met another firefighter while running the evening mail to the outside stations. Walter Beatty, about ten years my senior, was also an avid hunter and outdoorsman. We swapped stories about travels and hunting, as well as good-natured joking about my escapades at Sears. A life-long bachelor, Walt lived in a small one-bedroom cabin in the Angeles National Forest, eight miles up a canyon above Glendale, near a public campground. We shared a few beers off-duty and he introduced me to several unique area cantinas. Filled with interesting facts on anything from binoculars to wheel lugs, Walt was pleasant to hang out with for limited amounts of time. As gregarious as he was with me, he preferred anonymity. His skill at seeking out or attracting women was legendary. At times, I felt he only tolerated me because he had few close friends and those friends were much like him—loners. Many firefighters refused to work with the man. Today I would describe him as a Type-A minus personality. He was aggressively successful, but in a malevolent way. Walt asked me about working at Sears and, after a short interview, he was hired. At the firehouse, our reputations as eccentrics blossomed. The Sears job paid well, filled up hours normally spent wasting money to keep busy, granted tremendous employee discounts and, of course, provided a variety of women for Walt to stalk. Sheila was not too crazy about my association with Walt, stating that she thought he was a bad influence on me. He was and, as a result, Sheila and I lost faith in each other and drifted. Still good friends, we divorced. I never worked a fire station assignment with Walt. Exposure to him 24-hours at a time was not feasible. Although we traveled to the desert and mountains for a few days exploring and hunting, I adjusted to his quirks.

From the time of my first divorce to the late 1970s, I saw my daughters on the average of one weekend per month, and several Saturdays or Sundays when not toiling at Sears or the firehouse. I wanted to be with them more often but dropping the girls off with Jody and leaving were the most trying episodes of my life. The events were difficult for my daughters, Jody, and me. This was the primary reason I did not spend more time with them. I was the bad guy and the continuing guilt plagued me, particularly when I had to drive away and watch them cry in my rearview mirror.

By 1978, I moved into a 800-square foot, 2-bedroom house on a quiet alley in Glendale. I lived in Engine Six's district and rode my bike to work if I wanted and many times drove the patrol home to have lunch, do my paperwork, or nap. As long as I had my radio on and available for response, I felt perfectly safe hanging out at my remote home to write reports on-duty. The abode was also within stumbling-home distance from two of my favorite bars. My patrol duties included maintaining fire roads, gates, water storage facilities and hydrants in the 10-square-miles of our city covered by brush land. My two-wheel drive, overloaded Chevy pickup truck deteriorated due to other two shifts failing to maintain the truck and its appearance. It was dangerous to drive, particularly on code-three runs. It cornered like a furniture truck and tended to tip on fire road grades when water sloshed around in the unbaffled tank. In 1977, I exercised my report-writing skills and penned a recommendation to my supervisors to replace the current patrol with a four-wheel drive truck with at least a one-ton rating. At the same time, I revised the patrol procedures manual for the unit since the existing one was produced twenty years before and did not reflect the current responsibilities of the job. I submitted the procedures manual just prior to the truck upgrade request, knowing from past experience how to work the bureaucracy. As expected, my manual was adopted and immediately implemented to the dismay of my counterparts on the other shifts. Specific duties of the patrol personnel created work they did not do, and which I accomplished on my shift. Now they were accountable for the shared responsibilities. I made more work for them, but actually lessened mine. Not a bad tradeoff, but the effort perpetuated my image as an eccentric. Small price to pay because my new Chevy 4X4 patrol unit was great compensation for my report-writing skills. It was the first patrol unit to have air conditioning. Unfortunately, the new rig shined in all its ugly lime-green splendor.

Being single gave me the ability to come and go as I pleased and work as much or as little as needed, but I hated the solitude. I enjoyed marriage and the stability of a relationship but was not quite ready. I opted to work more and save as much as possible towards the purchase of a home. However, nightlife, dating, a new Chevy Blazer, and child support kept me strapped.

My patrol functions during the wildland fire season increased tremendously. The patrol was responsible for inspecting about 1000 vacant flatland and hillside lots with required clearance dates falling in late May. The vacant lot inspection duty increased by citizen complaints of dry grass and weeds and unsecured vacant buildings around town. A drive-by inspection determined the hazard existed, we researched current ownership, wrote warning notices, and met with or phoned the recalcitrant owners. Twenty to thirty inspections per shift was not unusual, but eliminating such hazards was a priority and the results measurable. Occurrence of fires in these areas went down. However, we still had brush fires every year. Many originated on un-cleared, vacant city property. Several serial arsonists worked the Glendale hillsides and canyons, as well as in neighboring communities. I knew little about fire cause and origin investigation in the 1970s but assumed the responsibility even though the detail was not in my manual of operations. I attended a fire cause class at Glendale Community College with Walter Beatty. Armed with this limited knowledge, I looked closer at the origins of our hillside and canyon fires. One of several fire prevention inspectors from the department was called to suspicious fires but their primary job was checking building plans, fire extinguishing and sprinkler systems. Fire investigation was a sideline. The four inspectors rotated call-outs and I worked alongside all of them at one time or another. I absorbed little training from them since three out of the four never attended a formal fire investigation class. They seemed to appreciate my assistance, especially when I found evidence, turned it over to them, and wrote a report. The discoveries made us all look good.

Glendale still had street corner fire alarm boxes in the late 1970s, and false pulls accounted for 98 percent of the alarms. When the boxes were installed in the 1920s, telephones were almost a novelty and the only place to turn in an alarm of fire effectively was through the boxes. Firefighters, too, used the alarm boxes to communicate, since mobile radios were years away early in the century. Several alarm boxes activated regularly near schools or major intersections. I mapped the repeat alarms and tried to pattern activations. Using my Sears stealth skills, I parked my lime-yellow, Christmas-tree-like patrol rig to blend in with surroundings and bagged more than ten kids who pulled the boxes. Half-hiding behind buildings, parking bumper-to-bumper with parked trucks, and sometimes in plain sight, I watched. Chasing down and capturing the juvenile offenders became easy. A few nighttime pull problems got resolved when I asked Captain Algiers for permission to trek out in the evening hours for surveillance of the troublesome devices. I picked up the sobriquet "Officer Orr" for my successful forays. I did not mind a bit and, I believe, the men on all three shifts were happy to have the false box alarm responses cut substantially.

Catching a serial arsonist was another matter. Their efforts are random and as unpredictable as the crimes of a serial killer. I did bag several juvenile fire-setters after small blazes in vacant lots and trash cans, and while I did not always catch them in-the-act, I used my interviewing skills from Sears to gain confessions. Both cops and firemen played down capturing shoplifters as a usable or valuable skill. They were unaware of several characteristics of this work I capitalized on to train myself as an investigator. Shoplifters, like most criminals, give themselves away before and sometimes after they commit the act. Exaggerated eye movement, body language and positioning after the act can be a dead giveaway. Recognizing these traits takes time, and thousands of hours of doing it prepared me for my future career. I learned early to cruise or patrol the surveillance area in order to increase the chance of running into someone displaying the pre- or post-crime posturing. Most security agents chose stationary concealment sites to watch activities via see-through mirrors. The same holds true for many police officers choosing to sit in a Winchell's donut shop parking lot to wait for calls instead of patrolling. This laying-in-wait tactic works well in Sears high-crime areas like hardware, where high-value items are small and easily concealed. Cops, too, enjoy parking near a popular bar at closing time to fill their ticket quotas. I preferred constant movement until I spotted a likely suspect or my sixth sense said something was not quite right. Once I spotted a potential, taking a position of visible concealment sealed the deal. Standing half behind a rack of clothing provided a way to discretely watch a shoplifter while giving the appearance of just another customer to the crook and other shoppers. At times, visible concealment required me to get down on my hands and knees or, at least, stoop down to get out of the suspect's line of sight. A shoplifter frequently scans the area at eye level but does not take the time to look below plain sight. Typically a quick-look-see is followed by a nonchalance attitude. Hiding in plain sight at floor level became a great tactic. Parking behind a large truck in my multi-colored patrol pickup allowed for blending in. These spying tactics prepared me for thousands of hours of surveillance I later spent capturing arsonists, burglars, and car thieves. The skills I developed from work at Sears helped give the Glendale Fire Department the highest clearance rate in the state in the 1980s. Much later, after arrest, prosecutors cited my propensity to appear in the area of so many fires as beyond coincidence. In their eyes, the knack spelled guilt. Prior to my trial for murder and arson in 1998, I examined documents related to my response to all incidents between 1980-1991. I needed to defend myself from the expected prosecutorial tactic citing my "knack." I found my responses to emergencies during those years when I arrived before or with first-arriving fire units, amounted to about 60 occasions. Many times I was with my partners at the time of the call. The prosecutors ventured my early arrivals indicated I set the "early arrival" fires and stayed in the area to watch "my" fires; typical behavior of pyromaniacs. In reality, those 60-plus early arrivals confirmed successful patrol tactics I learned at Sears and on the fire patrol assignment. Sitting in a third-story office at the civic center with my car parked five minutes down the road precluded my getting to fire scenes quickly. Something the prosecutor never calculated.

During slow periods, my partners and I left the office to cruise or conduct interviews in person, rather than the lazy over-the-phone method. When with my partner, I obviously could not set fires we actually responded to. Thus, of the 60 I found, 21 of the early arrivals occurred when I was with my cop or fireman partner. Of the remaining 40 or so, I found 20 cases where I captured or apprehended the suspect in arson fires. Case clearance in about 30 percent of the 60-plus incidents is a very impressive figure and validates my methodology. The remaining "early-arrival" responses turned out accidental fires and about 11 where the fire was arson, but no apprehension made. No other crime reveals the perpetrator sticking around after the dirty deed is done. Burglars, robbers, rapists and thieves commit their crime and distance themselves from the scene. Arsonists do not; they stay and watch or leave and come back as an innocent bystander, blending into the crowd. I learned this early in my law enforcement career by staying in the field rather than camping out behind a desk waiting for something to happen. Arrests of residential and commercial burglars, as well as recognizing and acting in instances of car thefts in-progress and even assault with a deadly weapon, were common for me from 1977 to 1991. All these cases are well-documented. Unfortunately my lawyer in the murder case, Peter Giannini, chose to ignore the prosecutor's "consciousness of guilt" theory about my early-arrival cases. Giannini set the pattern early in my representation, citing the issue as "not important," only to have the prosecutors spring the trap in closing arguments, stating, "The defense never defended the early-arrival accusations, so they must be true. John Orr set fires, waited around the corner and arrived early at his fires." The jury was left with the impression I got to fire scene quickly because I did the typical arsonist thing; returned to the fire scene. The prosecutors never researched my emergency call histories or, if they did, came to the same conclusion as I. Since we never challenged the issue pre-trial, the prosecutor, Michael Cabral, felt safe offering the theory. My own lawyer ignored my protestations of my obvious, provable alibi.

Many of my early apprehensions at Sears were juveniles. Kids generally provided exaggerated signals of their intent to steal and were easy catches. Many denied guilt even after apprehension, before I retrieved the concealed merchandise. Knowing unequivocally a suspect was guilty, I frequently prolonged the revelation of the location or type of contraband so I could gauge body language and types of evasion and denial displayed by a known guilty subject. I honed this tool because I observed customers revealing the profile of a shoplifter without actually witnessing a theft. Fear of a false arrest or detention lawsuit caused me to let possible thieves go without contact on many occasions during my first few months at Sears. After dozens of post-arrest interviews, I developed a standard pre-detention dialogue when approaching shoppers I suspected of theft. A store agent could not just stop a customer and ask, "Hey, what did you steal?" or "Did you forget to pay for something while in our store?" Lawsuit was written all over these statements. I could not simply demand to examine a purse or a Sears' bag if I did not actually see the theft. If my detainee resisted, the subject was released. Instead I chose to introduce the phantom witness: "Excuse me, I'm with store security. A customer pointed you out and...Well...should we talk before you leave? My partner is reviewing the videotapes right now." Sears did not introduce video cameras until years after I quit. I used several variations of the approach and, if the individual was guilty, body language and subtle statements generally confirmed my suspicions. I found the biggest giveaway, initially in juveniles: a hung head, eyes to the ground in shame. Some fought the urge to look down and, instead, their shoulders started to shrug as if to cover their head. The technique was not foolproof but my mini-investigations never resulted in a complaint or lawsuit, either, but many times ended up with a recovery of merchandise. I did not arrest in a case when the theft was not actually witnessed. I relished the gift of the sixth sense and the opportunity to use the new skills. I applied the phantom witness scenario on juveniles and moved up to adults. Similar responses revealed themselves and I had a few failures. A particularly adamant denial resulted in release of the subject. I did not take any chances. Since I bagged so many shoplifters, my observations of the truly guilty helped perfect the whodunit case. I gained confidence in variations of the phantom witness and found the results wildly successful. On the patrol, I found that juvenile fire-setters always gravitated back to fires they set, like 95 percent of all arsonists, and the interviewing skills I perfected bagged me many of the pyromaniacs. The hunching shoulders and cast-down eyes gave the culprits away even if there were 30 kids watching the fire. It seemed all it took was to walk, in uniform, towards the crowd and focus on whose shoulders hunched up and eyes dropped to the ground. Generally I would take the posturing kid aside and say, "Son, the lady in the Chevy down the street says you were near that trash can when the fire started. You didn't burn your hands trying to put it out, did you? Are your fingers okay? Let me see." The staccato presentation did not give them time to think of an excuse and required immediate answers. I launched into the next phase: "Did you maybe drop a match that struck the edge of the trash can? I know you didn't mean to start it." The formula worked spectacularly. Confessions erupted spontaneously with the harmless ignition offered. I later used the technique on adults and even seasoned criminals fell into the routine of the seemingly inoffensive line of questioning.

In mid-1978 I had a whodunit fire in a boarded up vacant house in Engine Two's district. A huge pile of discarded furniture, trash, and palm fronds ignited in the living room on a weekday afternoon. By the time I wandered down to the call and had a peek at the damage, an hour passed since the fire's discovery. Nobody was around except the last engine crew taking a smoke break, and a woman walking her dog. I casually asked the woman how long the vacant house had been unsecured. She told me about four weeks and pointed to a house on the other side of the street. She said, "I think the man in that house did some cleanup there for the owners when it was occupied. He may know who owns it." I thanked her and started to walk to the small wood-framed house. Before I crossed the street I spied two 10-year-old boys, jaws dropped, behind the screen door. Sure enough, as soon as I hit their walkway one of them hunched up his shoulders and turned sideways as if to walk away. The other stood there frozen, eyes cast to the floor. I had to strain to keep from smiling; this was too easy. When I got to the door I simply said, "I just talked to that lady with the dog. Don't you think it's time we discussed that house?" I didn't have to toy with them any further. They copped to starting the fire that caused over $20,000 damage. One of them lit a palm frond for a torch to provide light as they rummaged through the darkened structure. Apparently, burning embers dropped from the flaming frond as they inched their way along. After they moved to a back bedroom, the trash pile in the living room behind them lit up. In seconds the pile flared, blocking their only exit. It chilled me to listen to the tale of their confronting the flames, and backing into the bedroom only to find the bedroom windows boarded up with nails. They decided running by the growing fire was the only way out so they hot-footed it back through the inferno and escaped through the kitchen door to the backyard. While explaining the scenario to me, the storyteller raised his left arm up to demonstrate how he protected himself from the heat emanating from the pile of flaming debris. I peered closer and found both suffered first degree burns to the left forearms and sides of their faces. They were extremely lucky.

My years with Sears readied me for a career in fire law enforcement. In the late 1970s, I saw a tremendous need for better follow-up in fire investigations in Glendale. The shoplifter was too easy. I wanted bigger game. I did not care about promotional exams or higher pay. I took the tests but gained job satisfaction through measurable results and preventing future fires by capturing fire-setters. By early 1979 the patrol became an 8-hour day, 5-day workweek position. I applied for the new job even though I hated the thought of leaving the 24-on/24-off firefighter schedule. There were rumors about the fire department hiring a full-time arson investigator and I wanted more involvement with the people already functioning in that capacity even if not chosen. The new patrol was a one-man operation and worked directly under the Fire Prevention Bureau's head, the fire marshal. In some parts of the country a fire marshal is the title of an arson investigator. On the west coast, a fire marshal is usually a Battalion Chief who oversees fire prevention and investigation activities. Nobody else applied for the 8-hour position; I got the job. With the patrol came the ability to issue citations. No longer required to fool around with repeated warning letters to offenders, and then refer the reticent to the City Attorney's Office, a citation went directly to the city lawyers. The citation process cut my clearance rate time by at least one-half. After I was issued the concealed weapons permit, a penal code requirement forced me to take a 12-hour firearms handling course. The sessions were the same as those required to arm security guards. The course included an eight-hour day in the classroom covering topics like weapon choice, maintenance, and shoot-don't-shoot scenarios. The following day we spent on the range firing our weapons for qualification. The man standing to my right on the firing line was a Glendale/Burbank-area freelance security guard. He later became a suspect in a series of fires involving several million dollars loss. His qualification weapon was an ancient .38 caliber English revolver appearing to date to World War I. The first rounds he fired caused me and his other firing line neighbor to drop our weapons on the bench and flee. The poor mating between the barrel and cylinder allowed the exploding bullet to shear off pieces of hot lead and spatter them on both sides of the gun as the rest of the bullet went downrange as designed. He really got our attention and I remembered him for years. He was given a range gun to qualify with. I passed the weapons courses and also attended similar sessions in the police science classes at Glendale College. I paid attention to the shoot-don't-shoot sessions in particular. News reports frequently cast doubts on police-involved shootings when citizen witnesses countered the officer's versions of the incident. I frequently played over such scenarios of shoot-don't-shoot and studied Glendale PD's policies, too. Carrying a concealed weapon at Sears related in no way to the Glendale Fire or Police Departments, but I found the policy sources enlightening. In my early "carry" days I only drew my weapon a few times. As I chased a thief on the first occasion, my ankle holster strap broke and I had to grab the .38 before it bounced onto the street. I held it as I ran, scaring the man into surrender. In mid-1978, all my weapons training came into play when I walked into a car-theft-in-progress. Again, my patrol tactics succeeded and put me near an incident when it went down.

My new schedule precluded my working at Sears weekdays so I lost a little income from the change and worked nights instead. By then, Walt Beatty was available to pick up the loose hours. A new manager controlled Sears' security, Ron Spelic, and he was a pleasure to work with when I could.

The Sears automotive garage complex sat on a corner across a small side street from the main-store and parking structure. I occasionally walked over to the auto parts sales floor to scope out potential shoplifters. As I left Sears' main store, I heard my agent code on the loudspeakers and stopped at a locksmith kiosk in the parking lot to use the phone and see what was up. The caller was a clerk across the street at automotive. Mary, the clerk, related a guy tried to pick up a Buick from the battery shop. He had no work order and the car was not his, she said. Mary described the guy and I saw her wave at me from the nearby sales floor phone. Since we were in sight of each other, she pointed and said, "That's him getting into the blue Mustang on your left, John." I saw him, too, just two parking stalls away. I asked Mary to page my partner Ron Spelic to back me up until I could determine what was going on with the man. Maybe the Buick was his wife's car. But then why was he getting into the Mustang? As I approached, the 25-year-old disheveled-looking guy sat in the driver's seat bent under the dashboard. He fooled around with something I could not see. Identifying myself as store security, I asked what was going on with the Buick. He continued playing around with something under the dashboard. Then I saw a short length of wire in one hand, heard the sound of an electrical arc, and the crank of the starter. The guy hot-wired the car right in front of me. I looked over my shoulder for Ron Spelic and saw only an elderly couple walking by the key shop. The car started, I screamed at him and he slammed the Mustang into gear and roared backwards. He turned the wheel and struck me with the left front fender. I allowed the fender to push me sideways and rolled when I hit the ground. He crunched into a parked pickup, shoving it into a Chevy. As I rolled, I grabbed the .45 Colt Combat Commander automatic I carried that day and jumped towards the now-stalled Mustang. The felon tried to restart the car. Without taking my eyes off the crook, I imagined the elderly couple was about in the middle of the lane behind me. They, too, were in imminent jeopardy of this maniac. I stuck the Colt to within inches of his face and screamed directions at him. The car started again and I told him I would drop the hammer on him if the car moved even an inch. For emphasis, I actually cocked the hammer. The motor revved but the Mustang was not in gear. In the second it took him to decide, I saw a Glendale motor officer, Skip Crill, across the street sipping coffee at an open-air hamburger stand about 300 feet away. Ron Spelic approached behind me, gun in hand, and the guy decided to give up. Within a six-pound trigger pull of death, this was a wise decision. If Ron had not shown up when he did, I do not know what course I would have taken. I could have shot, but not all the shoot-don't-shoot parameters existed to qualify the shooting, so I probably would not have fired. In the split second it took me to analyze the scenario, I imagined the elderly couple had enough sense to take refuge somewhere rather than standing in the lane so the "threat-to-others" part of the equation was eliminated also, in my mind. I feel most cops would have fired and the shooting was justifiable. The guy committed a felony hitting me, along with the theft itself. Almost enough justification to dump him as a dangerous fleeing felon. A small turn of the steering wheel could have put me in danger again, too. The thief looked at the end of the .45's barrel just a foot from his face, and told me he intended to shut the car off; and he did. Ron and I dragged him out to the ground and handcuffed him. I glanced at Officer Crill and he continued to nonchalantly sip his coffee. Apparently traffic noise on the busy side street and music at the stand covered the racket created by our apprehending the car thief. Fifteen minutes after we called for the police, Skip came into our office, mumbling that he does not take charge of shoplifters since he could not transport them on a motorcycle, but the dispatcher made our call seem urgent. He wanted to see what was up. He heard my loud profanity confronting the crook but Skip thought he was just a shoplifter. He did not hear the crash of the cars coming together, or else chose to ignore it. He imagined it was another Orr-the-wannabe shoplifter caper. He was angry he'd missed the chance to roll around on the ground with a crook and grabbed the handcuffed man, threw him to the office floor, and traded handcuffs with us. The bad guy had a bail receipt in his wallet from another auto theft arrest.

Skip became a friend and advocate, sharing a few drinks with me over the years before his life ended abruptly in 1987. After qualifying for the weapons handling guard card, I practiced with the Glendale Fire Department's Firefighter's Olympics shooting team. Not officially a member, I used their time on the police pistol range. Pete Hamilton obtained permission for me to use the indoor range at the police station, but my few negative encounters with some GPD officers caused me to avoid the facility. I did not want to further fuel the wannabe image by using "their" range. I also discretely dated the part-time girlfriend of one of these troublesome, and married, officers. Sharon was serious about him but she was one of several of his girlfriends I was aware of. I met Sharon after I arrested a shoplifter at Sears and found other contraband belonging to a department store employing Sharon at the Glendale Galleria. Sharon was an undercover security agent at the Ohrbach's and came to Sears to retrieve her employer's merchandise. We had drinks that night and started a friendship lasting to this day. We still talk on the phone and write several times a year.

My new boss on the patrol, the Fire Marshal, knew of my interest in the pending arson investigator hire and he also processed many of the juvenile arson and box alarm pull reports I generated. The chief gave me free rein in patrol operations and procedures, enjoying the credit I brought to his realm. He gave me specific permission to practice at the police ranges while on-duty. The department's shooting team generally practiced weekday afternoons. Departmental regulations forbade me to carry a weapon in a fire vehicle but I assumed the Fire Marshal recognized the fact traveling to and from the range necessitated carrying my guns in the patrol pick-up. Later, I wished the approval were in writing.

CHAPTER FIVE
FIREBRAND

In January 1979, I managed to run into an apartment burglary in-progress while on duty. In the patrol pickup, I cruised by an alley in Engine 7's district and saw two suspicious-looking guys loitering near a garage. One cast his eyes to the ground and hunched his shoulders, the other man's jaw dropped. Killing time before an afternoon appointment to practice with the department's shooting team, I set up two blocks west, broke out my binoculars, and spied on the pair. They nonchalantly crammed a TV, stereo and paper bags into their trunk. Trying to get a license number, I idled down the alleyway, hoping the lime-green monster I drove appeared benign to the criminal duo. My ruse did not work. They hopped in and sped off, running me into a curb as they split. Pursuing, I tried to surreptitiously get dispatcher Gary Oldham to mask my chase while getting police into the area during their 2 p.m. shift change. After a few wild blocks, the Toyota doubled back and, as they flew by, I looked down and saw the passenger had a ten-inch kitchen knife in his hand. The driver flipped me off with a smile on his face, overriding my consideration to let the police handle it. The car had no license plates. I stayed with them and considered my plan if they bailed out. I had an unloaded .357 next to me for the upcoming practice. A .380 nestled beside it in my briefcase, a fully-loaded clip next to it. Steering with one hand, I slid the clip into the Walther. A block later it looked like a bomb went off in the Toyota. The car had slowed when both doors blew open and the crooks leaped out and ran. The car continued and crashed into a brick planter. Updating the dispatcher to my plight, I parked and took off after the guy with the knife. I chased him down and he gave up after two blocks. Holding him at gunpoint, a Burbank motor officer arrived before Glendale police and handcuffed the man. The other got away clean. One week later the Fire Marshal called me into his office where he gave me a pat on the back and a commendation from the city council for the arrest. He shook my hand and said I would receive 30 "atta-boy" points in my personnel record. The fact I actually went into a pursuit never came up. Gary Oldham, my pal the dispatcher, covered for me after the half-assed chase. A rare secret was kept in the fire department. Chatting briefly with the Fire Marshal, he maneuvered me down a hallway to meet with Fire Chief Allan Stone. The Chief gave me an "atta-boy" and slapped me on the back. Then he hit me with 50 demerits for carrying a firearm in a fire department vehicle. I stared at my boss and informed the Chief I was en route to practice with the department's shooting team at the time of the incident. I expected the Fire Marshal to back me up since he gave me verbal permission to transport the guns to the range. Instead, he cast his eyes down and slightly hunched his shoulders. Chief Stone reiterated the offense was clear cut. My boss stayed silent and both the commendation and the disciplinary action remained in my personnel file. I never discussed the session with the Fire Marshal. Subconsciously I said, "You owe me one." Ironically, just over two years later, an identical situation presented itself just a few blocks from my other burglary arrest. I watched two creeps case a house across the street from a city park while I got to a position to watch. I observed as they took a screen off a window and climbed in. I used my portable radio to advise incoming police units where to set up until the burglars came out. I hid in the middle of a jasmine bush while coordinating the cavalry to remain concealed on both sides of the house. One of the arriving motorcycle officers impetuously parked right in front and scared the crooks out the back window. Seconds later they found themselves surrounded by a mob of police officers, prone out on the ground. I was an officially appointed arson investigator this time and carried a gun legally. No "atta-boys" were forthcoming for this incident. I was a peace officer and such actions were expected. The homeowner called me later that day and said he appreciated the effort and offered me a bottle of Jack Daniels. I declined and he asked for me to drop by after work to shake hands. I did so and as I chatted with him in the living room, his wife slipped out and returned seconds later. When I departed I found a half-gallon bottle in a paper bag on my front seat.

In 1979 and 1980, Walter Beatty, Detective Tom Rickles and I attended two fire investigation courses. Fire Investigation II and III were week-long sessions and taught by a variety of arson experts. Beatty and I hung out after the classes and drank with Rickles, one of the few police detectives at the classes. Rickles was assigned arson cases for the Glendale Police Department and performed follow-up investigations after the fire department investigators determined the fires were intentionally set. Assigned to the General Detail, Rickles handled thefts that were not burglaries, missing property cases and anything not classified as a righteous crime. He frequently referred to his assignment as the "garbage detail." Not as glamorous as robbery or homicide but just as busy, the unit was still a detective position. Everyone had to start somewhere. The arson cases referred to him and his effective partner, Mark Stocks, had a low priority until Rickles attended a few fire related classes. I got along moderately well with these two men even though I had little contact with them professionally. My partners at Sears worked with Tom and I imagined Tom's perception of me was enhanced by these advocates. The Investigation II and III classes spent a lot of time on arson crime scene evaluation and the criminal case follow-up aspects of this uncommon crime. Arson accounted for less than 10 percent of Glendale's crime statistics. We also watched staged fires set and allowed to burn in vehicles, structures and wildland. Seeing a furnished room before it burns, watching how it ignites and progresses, and examining the aftermath was fascinating. Firefighters never get the privilege to view before and after aspects of a fire scene. We were always too busy putting the blaze out after arrival. The training provided a better understanding of fire behavior and exposure to Rickles gave me an idea of the police end of arson follow-up.

In early 1980 I managed to arrange for fire dispatchers to call me out to after-hours and weekend fires. Gary Oldham, my old buddy, and several other dispatchers already knew of my interest and took the initiative to call me when we had an unusual fire. The Fire Marshal approved, this time in writing. While 1979 and 1980 were a positive training period and I looked forward to a future as an arson investigator, I hit a few potholes along this road. The magical citation book gave me some grief. I arrested minor crooks and a few felons at Sears and, when in plain-clothes and you flash a badge, it is assumed you are in law enforcement. Few suspects give you any problems. When you receive a citation or traffic ticket, you expect the transaction accomplished by a six- foot cop wearing a distinctive blue or black uniform, carrying a six-inch Smith & Wesson .357 magnum, wearing mirrored sunglasses and driving a black and white vehicle. Not wearing a light blue shirt like a car wash towel guy and tooling around in a lime-green pickup truck like I did. My citations were designed for issuance to property owners who neglected to clean up, care for, or secure their real estate. Generally business people, not petty thieves or felons, contact with them provoked ire when there was a potential for costing hundreds or thousands of dollars. My only instructions, given by the Fire Marshal, were to get people into court and if they refused the ticket, they go to jail. Cool, I thought, I can do that.

My first experience went smoothly with the owner of a weedy, over- grown vacant lot in Chevy Chase Canyon. The man simply said to me, "I didn't think firemen could write tickets..." I showed him how it worked. The second experience required me to track down the miscreant before I could write him up. A local real estate agent and broker, the man owned a ton of property and hid behind post office boxes, several addresses he did not live at, and a solid door of a small real estate office. He did not like answering the door. He owned an abandoned duplex on property across from a hospital. He intended to develop the property into a medical building. In the meantime, the structure was left wide open and vagrants and kids entered it daily. The yard was covered in dry weeds. Trash and furniture littered the place and a small fire already occurred in the garage. With five warning notices written and sent to him, he responded to none. Finally I located him inside his office. I did a low crawl below a window and up to the door, announcing, with a loud knock, "Doctor Beauchamp? Got a delivery for the office manager..." The man I sought answered the door then denied who he was. I observed him at city council meetings and at the city hall over the years and the guy at the door was my target. He still denied it, pissing me off. "He's not here, I tell you. I'll get a number where you can call him." He stepped inside and walked to a desk and looked at a Rolodex. I walked in and stood near him. "Come on, Harold. Cut the crap," I said. "Get me your driver's license and let's get on with it."

He gave me a shocked look, became indignant and ordered me out. I refused. He shoved me. I shoved back. Once he touched me he was mine. The nudge was a prosecutable offense so I lifted my radio up to call for the police. He was going to accept this ticket or somebody was going to jail. I should have stepped out but my badge-heavy mode cranked up a notch. Testosterone was now the issue. If I were a "real" cop the confrontation would never have progressed, the man accepting his deserved licks for the violation. As I spoke into the microphone, Harold slapped at the radio and said, "What are you doing...you can't do that..," and he pushed me again and the radio tumbled to the floor. We grappled and the portable radio was kicked out the door onto the porch, and we managed to slam the door shut, too. I thought he intentionally kicked it shut and the act got my attention. Then he broke away and ran to the desk, pulled open a drawer and rummaged around. Afraid he sought a gun or knife, I reached across the plane and pulled his arm out, asking him to settle down. He pushed me back and dove in. Again I reached across and grabbed his arm, but I was off-balance and feared his actions, so I swung a half-strength punch and hit his jaw. I had never, in 28 years, hit anybody in the head with my fist. I had wrestled with crooks at Sears many times, but it was my job to subdue and handcuff, not pummel and punish.

My fist glanced off Harold's jaw and the act surprised me as much as it did him, but I needed to get his attention off the drawer's contents. I used that moment of hesitation to dive across the desk and get him into a chokehold (still an approved maneuver in 1979) and we fell to the floor struggling. I am not afraid to admit the man's actions scared me. I dragged him down and got the door open where my radio rested on the porch. He did not like the control I had with the hold, which I applied lightly, so he took advantage and sunk his teeth into my forearm. The force of his bite reminded me of the German Shepard attack, only Harold did not let go. I yelled at him with no effect. I loosened my grip and rose up and pummeled the back of his head, breaking a finger in the process. He did let go, however. I clenched him again and dragged both of us out the door, looking like tandem skydivers as we struggled. Reaching my radio, I ordered up some help. The assistance showed up in the form of the nearest engine company and several cops. Harold was arrested for assault on a peace officer. His version of the event: I punched him and he simply defended himself. I then noticed a ten-year-old kid walk out of the office. The boy was Harold's step-son, I learned later. Again firemen and cops teased me about an on-duty incident. Technically in the right, there was a better solution with my Harold encounter. When he claimed he was someone else, I should have backed out of the office and called the police. Failure to identify yourself or lying to a peace officer is a crime; without training/experience, I just did not know. Cooperation may have come immediately with one of those six-foot mirrored-sunglass types in a black and white. With a lack of experience and only my Sears background dealing with petty criminals, I went into a Dirty Harry mode and reacted poorly. Two days later a crimes-against-persons detective took the case to the District Attorney's Office for filing. The Deputy DA was told of my background persuing fire law violators and the detective said, "Orr's not really a peace officer, just a fireman, so this is more of a mutual combat situation..." No charge was filed but the DDA scheduled an office conference to hear both sides of the story before taking action. They treated the incident like a fist fight between two winos in a city park. Harold, the eccentric real estate agent, was well-known around town and made it plain a lawsuit imminent. Prior to the office conference the city assigned me a lawyer from their city attorney staff since the scoundrel intended to bring his own to the meeting. Before entering the DA's Office conference Julie, my city representative, said "We're not going to say anything. Just let the guy tell his story. He might sue so we don't want to give him any ammunition for later." I protested but she reassured me, "This is the way it's done." We sat down with the DDA, Harold, his lawyer, and the step-son. Harold said, "The fireman attacked me for no reason and punched me in the mouth when I wouldn't give him my driver's license." He admitted to a crime, not identifying himself, so I thought we were winning a few points. Then the step-son repeated the same story - verbatim. He sounded well-coached and coughed up the statement like a Chatty Cathy doll. I had not seen the boy but he was apparently in an attached office. Julie asked the boy no questions. Then the DA gave me my chance to speak. Julie piped up, "Since there is a civil action pending, we choose not to say anything at this time." The DDA looked quizzically at me and cocked her head slightly. I took my opening, "The city attorney chooses silence...I'm afraid I have to do what they say." Julie put a hand on my forearm, "We choose not to reveal our strategy because of the lawsuit." I sat back in disgust. I had no idea what my rights were so went along with my mouthpiece. I felt like a criminal trying to hide his offense, though I was guilty of nothing but inexperience. We adjourned. The DDA said a decision could be expected in a day or two. I did not hear from Julie for a week, despite several phone calls and messages left with her office. I ran into her going to a city council meeting and queried her about the conference results. "Oh, didn't you hear, John...?"

"No. You haven't returned my calls."

"Well, I thought someone from the fire department or the detective would tell you..." She glanced over her shoulder while making her statement and, still shuffling towards the meeting room, said, "Since we couldn't give our version of the story, they are taking Harold's word and considered filing charges on you...I'm sorry nobody told you."

"You're sorry? Nobody thought of calling me or my boss? Do I need to get a lawyer or notify the firefighter's union?"

"I have to get to a meeting, John. Just don't worry. The DA won't file on you. It's a dead issue." A dead issue? The citation quashed, his property remained unkempt for over another month, the charges dropped, and now a million-dollar lawsuit filed. Hardly a dead issue. I asked the Fire Marshal about the citation and he said the guy was "close to some city hall people" so the situation best left alone. I fumed and sweated through a civil deposition but finally gave my version of events. The lawsuit was later quietly dropped; nobody told me why so I snooped around city hall for answers. Apparently Harold was named in a police report, as a suspect, in an assault. The victim was a 65-year-old female neighbor walking her dog, according to my friendly source. The report never made it to the records bureau at the police department, only a referral to a city attorney file was noted. My friend said the incident emanated from a deposit of feces on Harold's lawn. It was unclear who dropped the excrement, the elderly woman or her pet. Shoving was alleged, perpetrated by the pacifist Harold. I never got the entire story but finally coaxed Julie into telling me the city settled my case for $500. In court, training and experience trumps mistakes, sometimes. To protect myself in the future I asked for permission to ride along with uniformed police officers to observe service protocol with citations. I needed some kind of training and no such class existed. Currently dating a Glendale police officer, Rachel "Mad Dog" Foster, I rode along with her on several occasions. I loved the woman. Definitely ferocious on the job, she had the ability to tone it down and be human off-duty. I felt comfortable enough to allow her along when I had Carrie and Lori on weekends. After Rachel and I participated in a pursuit, as a backup unit, with her driving, I decided my training was over. I would take my chances as a firefighter, where it was safe. Although involved in four pursuits years later, none were as wild and exciting as this one. All were white-knucklers, however. It is easy to understand the administration of "street justice" by police after a breakneck car or motorcycle pursuit. Almost afraid to write a citation now, I analyzed my options and settled on a new tactic. I used the tickets as tools. More like extortion, actually. When I encountered a reluctant violator, I threatened to cite, but granted a three-day grace period for willing property owners. Once I met them in person, I would collect valid ID so they were easier to track in the future, then gave them the three-day option, out- lining inflated fines I made up. I threatened and they gave me what I wanted: clearance of the offending property and a lessening of my work-load. Almost no recidivism was a bonus. Some were incredulous a fireman could write a ticket but the scheme proved successful. The exercise of tracking down the evaders was beneficial for my later career, too. Some slumlords were too evasive and I took their success in hiding as a personal affront. Their tactics improved mine. As Alexander Pope once said, "A little learning is a dangerous thing." Extreme hazards presented themselves frequently and getting a good fix on the owner proved strenuous. Out-of-towners made it difficult to serve a citation so I cut corners. These extreme fire hazards, on some occasions, already experienced fires or were such an attractive nuisance arson was inevitable. Serial arsonists hit our hillsides regularly, setting fires from roadside weed-choked lots, particularly in affluent Chevy Chase Canyon. A conflagration loomed. Lives were in jeopardy, many homes could burn and my fire prevention regimen required action. My solution? On at least three occasions I will admit to here, I picked up a phone and dialed a local commercial brush clearance company. In a business-like voice I requested a vacant lot be brought into compliance. I did not say I was the owner or refer to "my" lot, just stated, "Can you bill me, please..," and provided the real owner's address or P.O. Box number they hid behind. The post office routinely refused to provide actual home addresses from box applications because I was not a "real" cop. The larger brush clearance companies had no problem performing the work without up-front money or a deposit. If a property owner refused to pay, the brush crew manager simply placed a lien on the property. The tactic worked, the properties cleared, and serious hazards eliminated. Maybe on the edge of ethical behavior, prevention of fire was a priority. I briefly dated a letter carrier and she later helped me obtain addresses from P.O. boxes. She also introduced me to her supervisors and a postal inspector at a party. Letter carriers have great parties! From then on, post office cooperation was mine. The networking paid off for over twelve years; the relationship with Cher only six months.

Tracking down fire law violators and working fire prevention served as another training ground. The offenders I dealt with were minor bandits but their tactics of evasion were better than some career criminals. I found it challenging to conduct the "hunt," using all my tracking abilities to find them and make the kill - writing a citation and getting the hazard eliminated as the trophy rack.

Never a serious fan of sports, I preferred the company of women more than men. Law enforcement and firefighting fulfilled my competition needs. I never grasped the attraction of team sports and clashing with other men over a ball, goalpost, or punching each other out in a boxing ring. To me, team sports seemed a haven for schoolyard bullies using the contact sports as a safe harbor for their intimidating personalities. Built-in excuses to shove and kick, pull a face mask or ram a hockey stick into a competitor's side, hoping a referee does not notice. Being a relative non-participant furthered my eccentricity, but I did not care. When I observed blatant face mask violations in football, or the wink-wink banter between baseball broadcasters about how to conceal Vaseline behind a belt buckle or beneath the rim of a hat, I was discouraged. Illegal physical assaults? Advocating cheating? Using steroids to be better than your competitors? These characteristics are not my definition of sports. I enjoyed the company of my male friends, loved hanging out at the fire station or watching pitchers of margaritas evaporate over shop talk, but despised the ever-present testosterone exhibitions accompanying sports events. I have never once painted my face in L.A Rams or Raiders team colors. I much preferred the company of an intelligent woman and discussing similar interests of work, family or topics of substance. However, my treatment of women was antiquated. It took a close friend's guidance to bring me into the twentieth century. Paula Breaux joined the Sears security staff in 1979. It did not take her long to figure me out. Having morning coffee with her was a ritual and these encounters more like therapy for me. She did not giggle or blush like most girls. Probably because she was a woman; I just did not know the difference - yet. We worked the sales floor together as a plainclothes security team. A natural for the job, Paula made some great busts. I, of course, wanted to move in a bit closer to her. After successfully keeping my hands out of her knickers for a few weeks we settled into a wonderfully satisfying friendship. After covertly analyzing me for a while, Paula recommended I read The Women's Room, a best-selling novel by Marilyn French, and I did. The tome was an epiphany. I just did not know what an epiphany was at the time, but the novel got my attention. According to the protagonist, a young housewife with three children, the 1960's and 70's

female life revolved around two things: "...green beans and baby shit..."
My life with Jody fit this profile. I partied with co-workers at Sparkletts,
went racing and carousing while she had no choice but to wallow around
in "green beans and baby shit." My perceptions of life, women, career
and family forever changed, or at least altered, after Paula and I
discussed The Women's Room and my shortcomings. I did believe these
were personal failings, not just a ploy to get closer to the intriguing
Paula. She was a $100-per-hour therapist, but settled for my performing
plumbing and landscape chores at her nearby home. I experienced
periods of backsliding but Paula made a point to slap me into focus. As
provocative and challenging as firefighting was, I felt the need to be
proactive and not just sit around waiting for a victim to call for help.
People routinely died from smoke inhalation before fire crews ever got
the call and left the station. Prevention and deterrence seemed a logical
choice. I recall my first fire fatality; a 70-year-old alcoholic, living in a
rundown apartment building on Glendale Avenue. He apparently
dropped a cigarette in an upholstered chair and the resulting smolder
killed him as he dozed in a stupor. No burns appeared on his emaciated
body. An hour before, he lived and breathed. With no smoke detector in
his apartment, not required in the 1970s, he died. I felt helpless. A similar
fire occurred in an upscale neighborhood in my rookie year. Five people
died, including three children, when a visitor to the home dropped a
cigarette between sofa cushions. He quickly retrieved the Marlboro, but a
glowing ember remained. With no smoke detector, the sofa smoldered
into flaming combustion, several hours later, and killed the family and a
neighbor's kid on a sleepover. The only way to help our citizens, to me,
was to prevent the fire before it started or, at least, deter arsonists from
igniting the blazes by eliminating the roadside hazards and vacant
buildings. Fire prevention is the mission of all fire departments and I
needed to do something to save lives by not putting people in harm's way
to begin with. Fire law enforcement became a natural extension of my
decision. Even working an 8-5 schedule I put in time on weekends as a
firefighter. The second job also kept my firefighting knowledge and
skills current. I also enjoyed the camaraderie of the firehouse, cooking
for a dozen guys and blasting down Brand Boulevard in a quarter-
million-dollar cavalry steed – except for the ugly lime-green color
scheme. Otherwise, I was as much an adrenaline junkie as any firefighter. Attending many wildland fire calls over the years, I felt frustration at
our inability to apprehend the thugs setting fires. Conditions guided me
into a crude form of crime scene/suspect profiling many years before the
FBI programs became common knowledge. I take no credit for
originating profiling as applied to arson fires. My application of the
theories came from Arthur Conan Doyle's fine fictional detective novels:

Sherlock Holmes. The English detective had the ability to look at certain aspects of a crime scene or person and analyze the obvious. Not only was Holmes'/Doyle's ability valid, I adapted it with success readily. Most wildland fires are intentionally set; at least 80-85 percent. I responded to all city grass and brush fire calls when on-duty and frequently responded when called in while off-duty. When allowed, I searched for evidence of each fire's origin. Even if the scene was a day or two old, I parked near the area, observed, and asked myself questions about how the blaze was set and where it ignited. Was there heavy traffic along the road at the time it started? Were there nearby homes where the arsonist's activities observable by neighbors or passersby? Was it a remote site? I imagined myself in the fire-setter's car, since 95 percent of the fires were roadside starts, and thought about why the spot was chosen, what time of day the fire occurred and what direction a car traveled to enable the firebug to fling an incendiary device out the window. Where did the road lead? Did he have time to turn around to come back and watch? Incendiary devices were seldom found in Glendale in the 1970s. Scanning investigative archives, I located evidence photos of cigarette/matchbook and cigarette/match devices in the Fire Prevention Bureau files so I knew what I sought. A cigarette forced into a closed matchbook generally needed physical placement in the brush or grass since it did not have enough weight to be flung out from a moving car and sail into the fuel. Another type I saw in a photo was a cigarette with paper matches wrapped around the shaft by means of a rubber band and a metal wood screw added for weight. More thought was put into this setup. As an experiment, I sat back and theorized the type of area and terrain where this device was recovered. No scene photos were in file. The added weight indicated a basic, yet well thought out preparation. Not a rocket scientist, but this was not the guy's first attempt. This incendiary was picked up as evidence several years before I joined the department. I looked up the sketchy report and drove to the site on Chevy Chase Drive. Sure enough, this evidence had weight added (the screw) so its flight took it about twenty feet from the roadway; either from a car, motorcycle, or maybe a bicycle. This device, however, did not cause this years-old fire, even though this is what the report said. The cigarette, matches, rubber band and screw were intact and only about a ½-inch of the cigarette burned down before it went out. The matches never ignited. Apparently the well-flung device hit a rock, bush, or other object and, with the ash knocked off, the cigarette extinguished. The evidence showed it was found in an unburned area since there was no scorching on the setup except where the cigarette was lit on the tip. This told me several things. After the first attempt failed, the fire-setter came back with a second device and was successful. The report said an acre burned.

The investigators did not bother to seek out the device causing the blaze. They were happy to have this one. It is feasible to picture an arsonist using two different types of devices by modifying to suit his situation. It also said a vehicle drove by at least twice to accomplish this arson. If done in a short period of time, the car's description is likely remembered by witnesses. The report indicated no such interviews conducted. Both the fire investigator and detective assigned concurred that this intact device started the fire. I had to shake my head at this revelation, reflecting on the quality of investigations in the early 1970s. Ironically, I was convicted of setting a fire just 50 yards north of this site in a 1998 trial with literally no evidence.

Between 1972 and 1991, there were at least four arson fires ignited within this 100-yard stretch of Chevy Chase Drive. One of these fires took off in 1989 within seconds after my partner, Walt Beatty, made a traffic stop on an arson suspect. Before Walt and his surveillance partner had a chance to ask the suspect a question, the grass flamed and took off up the hill. This location attracted repeat arsons. At least three other areas in Glendale and a few in Burbank, Pasadena and Los Angeles experienced repetitive fires. While scanning this sparsely-populated area on Chevy Chase Drive, I realized something else. I recalled an instructor in one of my investigation classes vehemently relating how arsonists inevitably watch their creations. This creep, no doubt, observed his. Why set a fire without a motive to watch? However, there were only three sites in this narrow canyon where the hillside was observable, and two I quickly eliminated. Chevy Chase Drive is fairly busy from sunrise to around 9 p.m. During a fire, engines and the police routinely block traffic and access to the canyon. The street above the fire location also hosted fire crews and precluded anyone in the area but people walking. The remaining site I could not see from my Chevy Chase Drive location at the base of the hillside, but I knew it existed. Up a steep, inaccessible slope to the east was an area the arsonist could watch from unmolested. I drove down-canyon a half-mile and followed Glenoaks Boulevard as it serpentined through another residential ravine, ending up at a city park with baseball diamonds and tennis courts. The elevation allowed a spectacular 180° view of the San Fernando Valley, Los Angeles, Griffith Park and most of flatland Glendale. On a clear day, airplanes were visible taking off and landing 25 miles away at LAX. On a sweeping turn next to the ball fields, a low guardrail prevented cars from dropping off a 200-foot precipice. By sitting on a flat fencepost, I looked right into Chevy Chase Canyon. He most likely watched from this area, safe from prying eyes. After he tossed his second device (remember the first, intact, device was recovered), he had a ten-minute delay to make a U-turn, drive back down-canyon, and maybe buy a soda to establish an alibi before the fire started. Midday, when this fire erupted, he probably had the viewing area to himself. Did any investigator think to explore this possibility and drive up to the park? The report said nothing. The fire started at 3 p.m. Was the culprit a high school kid who lived in the canyon? The timing was right, but why set a fire that threatens your own home? Could the owner of the vacant lot have tossed the device into the brush to clear his lot before the city forced him to? Again, the report was inadequate. I checked tax records, even though this fire occurred years before and the statute of limitations long ago expired. The lot was still owned by the same couple and their home was directly above the fire area. Who would jeopardize their home and possessions to save $200 on a lot clearing bill? There were many leads on this old case but none pursued.

Arson investigation in Glendale in the early 1970s was abysmal. Also obvious was an incomplete file. The fire department investigator merely located the device, passed the evidence off to the police, who were expected to pursue leads. The detective's report was not a part of this fire department file. About one mile up Chevy Chase Canyon from this fire was a large paved turnout. With several nearby homes below street level and one 75 feet above, no windows looked directly onto the area. While on an orientation drive-around of the city with 9-1-1 operator Linda Blackwood, the patrol was called to a brushfire at this location in 1978. We responded from across town, arriving quickly at this slow-moving ½-acre blaze. Analyzing the scene, I noticed only large bushes and some were involved with fire at the base of a steep, rocky canyon. No remains of burned stalks of dry grass were evident at the point of origin. After ignition, the growing blaze set off more dry bushes as it marched up the slope. This location would have required the pyromaniac to physically get out of a vehicle, place an incendiary, or ignite the bushes with a match or cigarette lighter while cruising by or tossing the devices at random, hoping one snagged on the sumac. It was an improbable scenario, so with tumbling rocks and cascading water from fire crews, I checked for evidence before firemen destroyed the fragile area. A wary Battalion Chief saw what I was up to and had crews shut down their mop-up hose lines. I found no dud this time, but located an obvious point of origin at the roadside. With my training from investigation classes, I traced the path back to the remains of one chaparral bush. The bush had clear fire damage showing progression fanning out as if a small bomb detonated, pushing out from the area of origin. Since fire crews had no need to dampen this area upon arrival—the fire was almost out at the origin when they got there—they drove to the top of the hillside to protect homes. After ignition, the fire continued to burn unmolested and rendered the bush almost to ash. I had an untouched point of origin. With only vegetation ash, pencil-sized scorched branches and charred leafy material, the black and silvery-gray remains of a dull paper matchbook leaped out at me. Even the telltale grainy-appearing line of ash from a cigarette ignition source remained intact. No fire streams touched the device so it stayed, frozen like a mummy. Placement of this incendiary was by hand. The vegetation was too sparse at roadbed level and the flammable dry grass did not grow until almost eight feet up a steep slope. This was my first incendiary device discovery. I signaled the Battalion Chief and looked around to find a location the arsonist watched from. I did not see it immediately but found the site later, after driving around a bit. We had no clue to the crook, except he was familiar with Chevy Chase Canyon and its intricate web of hillside streets. Detective Rick Jauregui of the Glendale PD Detective Bureau showed up to retrieve the device. Rick and I were friendly despite his normal sarcastic demeanor. He was Rodney Dangerfield with a badge and a gun. We were quite close at one time; so close he felt comfortable hitting on my wife while he was on traffic control and I was nearby battling a three-alarm shoe store fire on Brand Boulevard. True to his profession, Rick was there to protect and to service. Jauregui worked arson cases follow-up off-and-on for several years until he promoted to sergeant. We had beers together a few times and he helped me out on a surveillance years later. We were not tight, but he accepted me. In 1997, while awaiting trial for murder, Rick wrote me a note telling me to "hang in there," and thanked me again for saving his daughter's life in the early 1980s. I was touched he remembered even though I did not actually save his child's life. I simply coordinated the rescue when Rick's Rottweiler police dog attacked the little girl and her mother. I happened to be in the dispatch center at the right moment, picking up a copy of a report. A complacent lead dispatcher gossiped with her husband, on a private comm. center line, while a rookie operator, Rose, tried to handle the horrendous situation of a mother screaming into the phone they were being mauled in their backyard while Rick was away. Police units were miles away from Rick's home so I had the nearest engine company dispatched. They arrived and controlled the dog and rendered first aid until paramedics showed up.

I continued analyzing my Chevy Chase Canyon fire scene but there were few clues to the mobile arsonist's identity. Locations of potential brush fire starts are identifiable, since many of the same vacant lots and hillsides erupted in flame almost annually, but investigators cannot pick the exact day and time of the hits. However, in April 1980, I bagged two serial arsonists in four days. One was mobile, the other territorial. The first fires were small, set around the grounds of convalescent facility on the south side of Glendale in Engine Two's district. All occurred just before dawn over a three-day period. I was unaware of the series. The on-duty captains passed information on the series to their own relief shifts, but did not call out an investigator or police. On the fourth day, I joined the on-call fire prevention inspector assigned for investigations that week. While trying to appear competent, I watched the inspector poke through a pile of burned debris on a porch when I noticed a 60-year-old woman loitering around a grassy area near a palm tree. When she saw me glance at her she walked onto the porch of a small cottage. My sixth sense caused a chill to race down my back. My scalp tingled and I smiled. The first fire sites were visible from her cottage. I took over examining the fire debris while the fire inspector interviewed the fire captain and a witness. I also photographed the scene. The inspector did not talk to the suspicious woman even though she loitered. She went inside and I figured the inspector knew what he was doing.

From April 19-21 there were four small fires in this half-block area. At 5:30 a.m. on April 21, the dispatch center called me at home and said the on-call fire inspector wanted me to handle an investigation at the convalescent hospital grounds. Another small fire erupted on a porch. This fire flared up right next door to the suspicious lady's home. Intuition told me she was responsible. Once I arrived, I examined the similar fire scene and saw the suspect peeking out between her curtains and decided we should chat. I was not supposed to interview; that was for the "real" cops. The detectives were follow-up investigators and I imagined would talk to the woman. They didn't, so I knocked on her door. I heard her talking to someone or herself before she opened the door a crack. I identified myself and she acted like all the juvenile culprits I apprehended at Sears—hunched shoulders and eyes cast to the ground. After throwing the phantom witness into the pot, my suspect simmered. Her responses were childlike when I told her she was seen placing the bag of trash on her neighbor's porch less than an hour ago. Did she happen to light a cigarette while she was standing on the porch? Could the match have fallen? She pondered the scene I painted, agreed, and went on to confess to the other fires as well, in a burst of conversation precluding a Miranda warning. Nevertheless, she was taken into custody and transported to Olive View psychiatric hospital. The four arson cases were filed by detectives. She was my first of over forty serial arsonists I apprehended in my 18-year career. Two days later on April 23, 1980 at 5:30 a.m., the comm. center woke me up and assigned another solo investigation. I guessed the on-call fire inspector enjoyed sleeping in while I practiced my new trade. This time a VW van burned, again in Engine Two's district. The three-man crew waited for me on a cul-de-sac in an industrial area off San Fernando Road. The air was cool and crisp just before sunrise, the street like a ghost town with the only noise a distant murmur of the I-5 freeway and occasional chatter from the captain's radio. The yellow and white van sustained minimal damage to the driver's seat and headliner. Early discovery of the fire was apparent since the interior windows were smoked up minimally and the door was left open, allowing the heat to dissipate instead of building up inside. At this hour, quick discovery of a fire was unusual. I documented the scene through photos, evidence of arson on the front seat (a rock possibly used to break a window), and an actual witness who strolled up carrying coffee and doughnuts for everybody. The woman arrived earlier to work in a nearby office and found the van smoking. I preferred interviewing witnesses after evaluating a scene to see if their account confirmed my own scene evaluations. This woman's did. The witness actually saw the arsonist walking away from the burning vehicle. This explained the minor damage. She called the fire department immediately. The VW's ignition was hot-wired, its window broken, and the witness provided a vivid description of the culprit. The young man had shaggy shoulder-length hair and two fingers of his left hand wrapped in a filthy, blood stained gauze or cloth. A police officer taking a report discovered the van was stolen the day before from the 1400 block of East Wilson Avenue, three miles away. Still supposed to do only a scene investigation and collect evidence, my recent experiences with arson follow-up by the police overrode policy. I assumed the detectives filed arson reports on the bottom of the things to-do pile. I still knew a few ER nurses so I checked three area emergency rooms for recent finger or hand injuries and found nothing matched. I drove around all day, looking at men's hands, searching for bandages, unsuccessfully.

When I got to work on the morning of April 24, I checked the department logs for incidents that occurred overnight. This was normal procedure for me now since I missed calls. A cold fire scene is typically hard to work, but a days-old crime excludes the possibility of locating viable witnesses. I spotted an apartment fire report and saw it happened in the same block as the VW van theft. Meaningless or coincidental, I did not know, but went to the police department and asked for a copy of the VW and apartment arson reports. The obviously complacent clerk said she could not find the VW document and the apartment arson report was not yet cleared from the sergeant's desk. I pressed a bit and she finally located the VW report in a pile of stolen vehicle summaries. The one-page CHP-180 form ensured this arson never got to the follow-up detective's In-box. Only the auto theft section reviewed CHP-180's. No system to cross-reference reports was in place. All that was required was an FYI copy sent to the arson detectives or sergeant but that took extra effort and nobody I knew did it. Nobody wanted them but me. I drove to the apartment and found Gil Rodríguez, a friendly Glendale Police lab technician, photographing the damage and dusting for latent fingerprints five hours after the incident. I pointed out the burn patterns to Gil and showed how the fire appeared to burn itself out. A pile of ashy paper, cardboard and charred bits of wood littered an area below a wall next to a floor furnace. The furnace was far enough away, so I determined that it was not a source of ignition. The gas to the unit was off. The debris looked more like a warming fire than a righteous attempt to burn the building. However, the negligence involved categorized this as arson. I felt that the scene, in keeping with the transient appearance of the disheveled VW suspect, might indicate he sought shelter here. Gil showed me a copy of his assignment sheet, accompanied by the police report for the fire. The sergeant's signature was affixed, indicating that the report was cleared hours ago. The document reported a transient-looking 20-25-year-old guy seen crawling in and out of an unsecured window. Further described as having long, shaggy hair, there was no mention of the bandages. The screen was still sitting on the landing below the window. The apartment sustained about $700 damage. Gil lifted a few good prints, finished, and left. I remained and looked around the barren apartment. As I readied to leave, a young scraggly-haired guy walked by, stood at the window like a zombie until he saw me, then continued strolling along. In his hands were an electrical wire, a brick, and a piece of cloth or rag. He had some difficulty holding the brick because two bloodied fingers wrapped in gauze on his left hand apparently made it awkward and painful. I discretely called my dispatcher and asked for police backup, advising I had an arson suspect at 1429 East Wilson. I trailed the man out to the street and he started lurching rapidly away. I confronted him while keeping my eye on his brick. His speech was slurred and unintelligible, but when I asked him to put the brick down he became quite lucid. "I might want to bash your fucking head," he stated. He continued to walk as I re-contacted my dispatcher for an ETA on the police unit. Talking in radio-code so the suspect remained dumb, she shocked me with her response. "PD advises they're getting a copy of the report to the arson detective and they'll probably respond shortly." I fumed as my suspect calmly changed hands, the brick now in his good hand, and keyed my mic again, turning slightly away so he would not hear. "Verdugo, advise the PD the suspect is being detained in front of 1429 East Wilson, has a brick in his hand, and is threatening to hit me in the head with it if I don't leave him alone. I don't plan on leaving him alone, but I'm not armed." I did have a 5-shot Smith & Wesson .38 in an ankle holster but did not reveal that fact on the air. I calmed the suspect down by asking if he wanted a fresh bandage for his fingers. After all, said I, "I'm a fireman. You know, a good guy. I can help you." While he pondered this, I heard what sounded like a chorus of coyotes yipping in the direction of the police building a half-mile west of me. The cavalry troop of black-and-whites, a couple of motor officers, and the detectives charged up about 30 seconds later and took the man into custody. His fingerprints were found on the inside window sill of the vacant apartment. The description from the VW fire witness and neighbors in the apartment building resulted in two counts of arson filed. Also charged was one count for the auto theft, burglary to the burned apartment, and one attempt auto theft—he had broken a window on a Chevy in the apartment's parking lot while Gil and I examined the fire scene. When he heard my radio in the distance, he decided to give up on hot-wiring the Impala, retreating to the apartment he forgot he made uninhabitable.

Two series fire-setter arrests in one week seemed to solidify my abilities and maybe secured my desired arson investigator ambitions. A position was on the horizon and a selection process neared. The next few weeks found me in court for the preliminary hearings on both the car thief arsonist and convalescent hospital firebug. I qualified as an expert witness for the first two times during a one-week period. I worked a half-dozen fire scenes on my own during the month. In June, a prominent local businessman managed to nearly blow his 22-year-old son up when fuel stored in 55-gallon drums in his residential garage exploded. His illegal storage and non-rated transfer pump almost leveled the garage, burned two Mercedes Benz sedans and a portion of the house. Walt Beatty, Tom Rickles and I all responded to the Saturday afternoon investigation and almost arrested the man for negligence arson. A speedy arrival of the Fire Marshal saved his ass. The investigators were ordered off the scene. His son suffered serious first and second-degree burns.

In July, Glendale lost its only Sizzler restaurant to an accidental fire and I was again granted sole investigative responsibility. Seven firefighters applied for the upcoming arson investigator opening: two were former Glendale cops who transferred to the fire department years before. Walter Beatty also applied. Interviews took place over a five-day period. Earlier in the year I started dating a cashier at Sears. Recently divorced, Sherry was cautious on our first few dates since I managed to develop a bad reputation at Sears as a serial dater. We had coffee breaks and a lunch before she decided I was reasonably sane and saw me after work. Walt's presence was also felt in the background since he went out with her briefly, and stopped abruptly. I never asked Walt about her and he was a true gentleman in the sense he did not talk about his relationships. Her relationship with me was awkward but after our lunch we both felt more comfortable with each other. She always dressed in attractive business attire and conducted herself in a confident manner while working in the customer service section and the armor-plated cashier's window. I loved the way she had it all together, but backed off a bit. She intimidated me. Sherry dropped by Sears one afternoon and paged me to meet her on the loading dock. While picking up her paycheck, she managed to lock her keys in the car. I retrieved them only to have her call later the same day. She ran out of gas while running errands around town and, again, I came to the rescue. We got her car started and, as we parted, she stood by my Blazer in her linen suit with a white blouse and asked me what I was doing on Sunday. I had my daughters, Carrie and Lori, for the weekend so Sherry invited us up to her family's cabin in the nearby Angeles National Forest. I could not picture this woman in the mountains; a chalet in Aspen, maybe. I told her we could get there by noon. On Sunday, Carrie, Lori and I idled carefully down a steep, dusty forest road, following Sherry's directions. At a blind hairpin turn, a cloud of dust preceded a beat-up old military Jeep coming up the path, so I pulled over to the side. The dust cleared like a curtain on a stage, revealing three beautiful giggling, dust-covered girls strapped beside and behind Sherry in the driver's seat. Clad in a t-shirt, shorts, and hiking boots, she said they drove up to meet us so we followed them back to the remote cabin site deep in a canyon beside a live stream of icy cold water. The five girls got along beautifully. Sherry's daughters, Betsy, Chrissie and Margie were jewels. Today, they still refer to me as Daddy. Sherry and the kids were the high point of the year for me, but nothing could cheer me up after July.

On a weekday morning, I arrived at my office to find a phone message from Engine Five's captain. I returned the call and the 20-year veteran firefighter told me of a problem he encountered getting a middle-aged couple to mow down a stand of dry grass that made their backyard look like a Kansas wheat field. The serious hazard was compounded by surrounding homes in the close-knit upper class neighborhood with highly-combustible shake-shingle roofs. The captain heard of my successes gaining compliance with the citation book, and felt these people deserved attention. His crew visited the violator's home five times without compliance. I agreed to swing by and check the problem out. As an afterthought, the captain added, "Be careful, John. The guy is a city official or on the planning commission." I had much better control of myself now and the citation program worked well, so I confidently drove up to the exclusive neighborhood. I gained access to view the trouble spot from a neighboring residence and peeked over a wall. The captain was right. I half expected to see Dorothy and Toto cavorting in the middle of the field of flammable waist-high dry grass. The front of the Spanish-style home was neatly trimmed, bountiful and well-kept, much like the 35-year-old woman answering the doorbell. She glanced at the fire uniform and my nametag as her jaw tightened. I explained why I was there and she responded, "I know who you are. We know Harold (my nemesis the real estate mogul) and what you did to him." I moved on without faltering and told the woman we needed compliance. I remained calm at her condescending attitude while explaining how the citation system works. I asked for her driver's license. I could have offered her another extension but two months and five prior visits was already too much preferential treatment. She told me the citation belonged to her husband and I countered with the fact her name also appeared on the tax assessor's rolls and I intended to give it to her. She turned around, saying over her shoulder as she slammed the door, "I'm calling my husband!" Recalling the real estate office fiasco, I walked to the street, asked the comm. center for a police unit and a supervisor to back me up, and explained what I had. A couple of buzzards circled overhead in the quiet canyon, silently riding the thermal columns above. Maybe they were just red-tail hawks, but there was no doubt who the carrion was—me. I decided the ticket would be issued, but I wanted a witness or two on-board the sinking ship with me. I seemed to attract politically hazardous fire law violators. Maybe these politicians felt they were above the law.

A black-and-white unit arrived. I told the officer what was up. She said, "What's the problem, John? Write her up. You have grounds. She refuses, she goes to jail." I liked my backup's attitude but decided to wait for the supervisor. The police sergeant drove up followed by the Fire Marshal; one supervisor more than I expected, or wanted. The woman inside called her husband, who called the mayor, who called the fire chief. He asked my boss to find out "What's John up to this time." I briefed the Fire Marshal and he simply said, "Go back to the office, John. I'll handle this. Let me have your cite book." I tried to give more background to strengthen the case since he knew little of what preceded my visit. He repeated, "Go back to the office. I'll handle it. Her husband says you scared the hell out of her." The female cop shook her head and walked away. So did I. I met with the Fire Marshal an hour later. When I entered his office I picked up my cite book from his desk and peeked inside. He had not written the citation. "John, he's on the planning commission. You gotta be more careful with these people."

"These people? They are all citizens to me, chief. Why is this couple exempt?"

"That's not the point. We can't just go out and blanket the city with citations." I sighed loudly, exaggerating my control.

"So, when some guy like this has an arson fire in his failing business, or at a vacant property, I can't investigate him as a suspect for fear of stepping on his politically-connected toes?"

"I'm not saying that. We just have to tread lightly." I queried the chief about the other businessman's garage fire violations.

"Is he getting filed on? His negligence almost killed his son."

"No, but we warned him."

"And you didn't write up this guy or his wife today because he's on the planning commission? The hazard's real. Is he going to get cited?"

"Well," the chief mumbled, quickly casting his eyes down, then looking back up at me with a tightened jaw, "we're considering it."

"So, Chief, you've gone around me again, and he's not going to court?"

"Probably not..."

"Are you comfortable that I didn't threaten or intimidate his wife?"

"No, no, she just said she was upset and embarrassed that her husband didn't cut the grass and she was having to answer for it. She took her discomfort out on you and your reputation was convenient."

"Are you reprimanding me for any of this?" I asked while staring him directly in his eyes. He inhaled deeply and his face was flush. I was on the verge of insubordination but did not want to leave this conference with my doubts.

"No," the chief said, and let out his breath in a foul rush I smelled from six feet away. "But you gotta treat some people delicately."

"I won't, chief. Is this how it's going to be if I'm appointed to do criminal investigations? You want me to give favorable treatment to the affluent and influential?" I stood up for emphasis, frustrated at the answers and non-answers I received. "I'd like the rest of the day off, and tomorrow, too, to think about this. I can use comp time, okay?" He agreed and I dropped the cite book back on his desk like a recalcitrant child throws a toy. I was so mad my eyes watered in frustration. I called Sherry to cancel our dinner date. I needed to get out of town and meditate. She said she could soothe me better than absence. I agreed, but I would be bad company so elected to depart for a few days. By noon I headed for the Kern River, 100 miles northeast of Glendale. Loaded down with a cooler full of beer, Cheetos and a frozen steak, I raced out of town. It took almost three hours to get to the icy cold, snow-fed river where I found a campsite thirty feet from the water. Setting up camp consisted of opening the back of the Blazer and placing a six-pack of Michelob in the water next to my folding chair. I went over the day's events and those of the past few months where the Fire Marshal countermanded me or made an end run around my field decisions. The brilliant late afternoon sun blasted down, reflecting off the silvery surface of the rushing river. A half six-pack and Chopin's Prelude on the tape deck sitting on a nearby rock accompanied my ponderings.

With minimal training, I was given the responsibility of enforcing fire laws. I made an honest effort at efficiency and effectiveness. My successes were measured by my supervisors in numbers. How many inspections performed per month meant something to them. The methods

I employed gaining compliance was my secret. Fewer cases referred to the City Attorney's Office were not even noticed by the lawyers. Their workload lessened through my efforts but I did not need recognition from them. I learned to write a monthly statistical sheet reflecting my workload and results. They received a copy. Report writing on unique situations revealed some of my tactics but my arson scene profiling theories remained hidden. My arrest scorecard shined, so I did something right. My cockiness surfaced, influenced by the Michelob, I am sure. Angered, I picked up a smooth, flat rock and flung it, trying to skip across the surface of a quiet pool near the river's edge. The stone careered off an unseen rock just below the surface and ricocheted off the side of the tape deck. I dove forward and caught it as it submerged. Water rushed into the speaker opening as the edge of the aluminum chair bit into my ribs. The freezing water splashed all over me but music continued to play as I fished out the player. I lay on my side, brought back to reality by my misdirected rock. The irony and insight were there but I failed to recognize the fact I tended to move forward with blinders on. Convinced I was right in my analyses of the past few months' events, despite the submerged tape deck epiphany, I made a decision. I calmed down, looked at the surrounding mountains, the billowy clouds blowing in on the late afternoon breeze, and enjoyed the sound of the rushing river. My aching ribs, with accompanying bruise, caused me to smile like an idiot. I missed Sherry and her girls. I wanted to be with them and run my ideas by Sherry. Known for my spontaneous and not always wise decisions, I needed her to evaluate the situation and advise me. I valued her opinions, probably because she was a lot like me, but with a bit more insight. By 5 p.m., I was back on the road accompanied by Donna Summer on the Blazer's tape player, and arrived at Sherry's place before my wet shorts dried.

I spent the night with my new family and took the following day off as planned. I did drop by work during the Fire Marshal's lunch hour and left a note for the chief. It seemed I made many decisions now via notes, avoiding confrontation with the subjects of my discomfort. A friend, years later, described this propensity to me: "Orr, you'd walk a block out of your way in a blizzard to keep from arguing with somebody." I did not perceive the description as negative. My memo to the chief was brief and read, "Please remove my name from consideration for the arson investigator position. I'm not interested." Going back to the firefighter 24-hour schedule was again attractive and I would have more time to spend with Sherry, and be a dad to her kids and mine. The pressure of the competition lessened and I welcomed the relief. A hollow feeling accompanied the decision to drop out, but I did not feel like a failure. I was known as an eccentric. This was me. Excelling in a strictly firefighting career enabled me to take my frustrations out at the end of a hose line or ripping apart box cars with the Jaws of Life. A fair trade-off. When I returned to work the following week, I busied myself around the silent office. The secretaries were pleasant but obviously aware of my discomfort around the Fire Marshal sitting in the nearby office. As I gathered my paperwork to leave for field work, my boss stepped out and caught me at the door, his only words, "You sure about this...?"

"Yeah," was all I said. The response spoke volumes. I still respected my boss and the position he was in as a buffer between "us" and "them." I smiled and said, "Gotta get to work. Nobody did my job since last week. Lots to do."

"I trust you'll handle it," he replied. He placed a fatherly hand on my shoulder. All was good. Walter Beatty, also in contention for the arson job, lined up as number two on the short list in my estimation. Little did I know about Walt's history with the Fire Marshal. Walt and I seldom got together since I started dating Sherry, but we periodically met for a pitcher of Margaritas at a new local cantina, Los Arcos. To present this latest revelation to him, in case the fire department's grapevine faltered, I asked to meet with him at an out-of-the-way German pub in nearby Silverlake, a favorite hangout of Walt's. The boisterous, smoke-filled pub atmosphere seemed tacky for the tone of the conversation I launched into, but Walt was generally stoic and sarcastic, so the dark beer flowed and so did I. He was pleased with the possibilities pending, but he told me he had reservations. He revealed that his first assignment after his rookie year was with the Fire Marshal when he was the captain on Engine Five. The relationship was oil and water. Walt, young and aggressive, was not known for holding back. He walked a block out of his way to initiate a good argument or one-sided debate. With a reputation as a loner and eccentric, I continued to hear about his negative actions even years after I went to prison and he retired. Some co-workers, and even citizens, found it difficult to relate to Walt's condescending attitude and inflexibility. Walt was just Walt, to me, and I worked around these idiosyncrasies. Others did not find it so easy to overlook. The Fire Marshal wrote the only negative, and accurate annual review Walt ever received until I wrote his performance report when I became his supervisor in 1988. It seems the interim supervisors took that long walk around the block to avoid the wrath of Walt. After all, those men only had to put up with Walt for a 24-hour shift at the fire station. Walter married briefly in his early twenties, divorced in two years, and never wed again. His longest relationships with women were less than a year. I sat on the sidelines of the brushfire season through August and September 1980. I helped extinguish the fires and acted as the eyes of the Battalion Chief when his command post location precluded an overall view of the battles. I did not participate in fire scene investigation anymore.

On September 5, 1980, I got off-duty several hours late from my eight-hour day shift. A 5-acre brushfire took crews quite a while to contain and extinguish, my duties ending when the Battalion Chief left the scene. I drove home and collapsed, exhausted from the vigorous fight. The final unit cleared the scene and arrived at their quarters just after sunset, around 8 p.m. As Engine Five's Ward LaFrance engine backed into the narrow apparatus bay of their 60-year-old station on Chevy Chase Drive, the mini-mall directly across the street exploded in a fireball. Talk about timing. The arson fire almost killed a man who was tied up, robbed, and left in a storeroom. I was not notified at home, but then neither was Walt. Police detectives and the Fire Marshal handled the case. I learned about the fire the next day at work. Physically ill at missing a good case, I kept my mouth shut. A series of car fires occurred on the south side of town and, again, Walt was not called to investigate, despite his training and experience. I heard about the fires by reading the newspaper. We both felt like designated drivers at a millennium celebration. It appeared the Fire Marshal made a silent statement.

During my self-imposed exile, I managed to make a down payment and buy the 750-square-foot box I lived in from 1977 to 1980 with help from a $1300 slot machine win in Las Vegas. I spent more time with Sherry and the kids at their own small home than I did at my new estate and found myself closer to this family than I realized. Still feeling the sting of guilt from my near-abandonment of my own girls, I perceived a second chance at fatherhood. My Ozzie-and-Harriet view of the world hung on, but I learned. My ex-wife, Jody, had a man in her life now and I saw Carrie and Lori more often, but I wanted to settle. I enjoyed having all five girls over to Sherry's for sleepovers and to trek in the mountains near the cabin. Just hanging out at home brought solace to me. The evaluation process for the arson position continued through August and September without announcement of a selection. There were still six or seven applicants vying for the job. In late September, the Fire Marshal paged me to meet with him in the fire chief's office. The two men sat me down and asked to reconsider my withdrawal. They related the selection process neared completion and the two finalists were Walt and me. They asked to have us go through the police pre-employment psychological evaluation process, since the new position required the man to carry a gun full time. Without querying them further, I said to put my name back on the list. There was a lot not said at the short meeting and I left it that way. I wanted the job and was qualified. The Fire Marshal ushered me back to his cubicle and shook my hand. "You made the right choice, John. You won't have any problems..." The conference made it sound like my selection was assumed. I did not elaborate on specifics of the meeting when I met with Walt, but felt he already knew. I could not relate other people's perceptions of Walt directly to him. The effort was fruitless so I remained mute. He no doubt saw himself circling the drain. Before we parted that evening, he told me a story. The year before, I captured a couple of residential burglars, after which there was a flurry of publicity about the apprehensions, and a publicized commendation from the city council. In the same week, Walt captured and held a burglar while off-duty, as he broke into a display case in the city hall lobby. The display contained a number of expensive, irreplaceable artifacts found in the Glendale hills. Walt spied the guy's pre-crime furtive actions and hid behind a planter nearby and let the guy make entry, then had a passing city employee call the police. Before the cops arrived, the crook started to leave with his treasures and Walt confronted the man. An altercation ensued but the guy was detained until the uniforms showed up. This was a noteworthy bust right next to the city manager's and mayor's offices. But there was no publicity for him, and no commendation from the city. The incident passed into history. Walt's revelation was significant to me. He never revealed feelings before and I could tell he was disappointed about the pending arson decision. We parted that night with him commenting, "I didn't really want the arson job anyway. Who wants to work 8-5?"

The psych interviews took about four hours and included my old pal the 500-question MMPI self-inventory, several word-association exercises, and a fairly in-depth interview with the psychologist. Within a week I was told the job was mine if I wanted it. I did. Walt, Tom Rickles and I were scheduled to take the final one-week-long Fire Investigation IV class starting the first week of November in Ione, California. The session gave Tom and me a chance to acquaint ourselves and work an arson fire scene and follow-up investigation during the 4½-day class. Based at the California Department of Forestry Academy in the Sierra Nevada Mountain foothills in the gold country, the class included documenting the pre-set/pre-burned fire scene, interviewing witnesses in a 30-mile radius around the academy, and arresting a "suspect." This was the final exam to become a recognized arson investigator. Both police detectives and fire department arson sleuths attended. On October 29, 1980, a memo came out of the chief's office to all fire personnel. On November 1, I would pair with police detective Tom Rickles, assigned to arson investigations exclusively; no fire prevention details at all. I had again appeared as number one on a Glendale Fire Department hiring list, despite the bumps along the road during August and September.

CHAPTER SIX
FIRESTORM

The following is an excerpt from the August 1982 issue of the American Fire Journal. Written by Glendale Fire Department Battalion Chief/Fire Marshal Elmer N. Spraker, this sidebar accompanied my first published magazine article. The sidebar, titled *Making the Decision and Seeing the Results*. "During the late 1970s and early 1980s, the City of Glendale was no exception to the growing arson problem. Incidents involving arson reached uncontrollable levels—as high as 52 percent during certain quarterly reporting periods. Fire scene investigation by fire prevention bureau personnel and hit-and-miss police follow-up investigations were not getting the job done. Perpetrators were not being identified and report writing and fire scene investigation for cause and origin were inconclusive. Consequently, filings with the D.A.'s Office were far short of the national average. Research and comparison studies by fire and police staff in late 1979, combined with a trip to New Orleans to the United States Fire Administration arson seminar in February of 1980 with the assistant city manager, set the stage for dramatic changes. The 1980 budget requested two additional personnel; one each for the fire and police departments to be identified as fire investigators and assigned to the fire department's Fire Prevention Bureau under the command of the Fire Marshal. Before budget approval, personnel were selected and limited training began after great anticipation, manipulation of some loose dollars here and there, and just a little coercion. The budget was conditionally approved by the city council. After satisfying their conditions and provisions, the fire investigation unit became a reality on November 16, 1980, and immediately went to work on a backlog of assignments, responded to new cases, and handled problems associated with the development of the new unit."

Working the fire patrol for over three years provided me with the basics of law enforcement. Tom Rickles acted as my field training officer and fine-tuned my expertise. Walking the razor-thin line between existence as a peace officer and firefighter made life arduous. When I worked overtime at a fire station on a weekend wearing the uniform, I was still under the guidance of the Glendale Police policy and procedures manual. Responding with an engine or truck company, I carried a gun, handcuffs and evidence collection materials in a small canvas bag. I told no one of the gun since my earlier experience put me on notice. Several law enforcement situations over the years showed me that risky can turn dangerous quickly. The pistol stayed close but was just an accessory, like a plumber's wrench in a toolbox, or the fireman's axe strapped to my hip. California Penal Code section 830 made my position about as clear as the U.S. Tax Code:

"Peace officers; persons included and excluded: Any person who comes within the provisions of this chapter and who otherwise meets all standards imposed by law on a peace officer, and notwithstanding any other provision of law, no person other than those designated in this chapter is a peace officer. 830.3 Particular officers: Officers of the Department of Justice. District Attorney investigators... (m) Arson investigators of a fire protection agency; members of an arson investigating unit, regularly employed and paid as such, of a fire protection agency of the state, of a county, city, or district, and members of a local agency regularly paid and employed as such, are peace officers.... (p) Statewide authority; the authority of any peace officer listed extends to any place in the state; any such peace officer shall be deemed a peace officer only for purposes of his primary duty, and shall not act as a peace officer in enforcing any other law except: When in pursuit of any offender or suspected offender; or to make arrests for crimes committed, or which there is probable cause to believe have been committed, in his presence while he is in the course of his employment."

Working overtime as a firefighter paid me from the fire suppression budget, not investigations. Where did that leave me when my overtime engine captain asked me to determine the cause of our fire and I found it arson, and the guy nearby did it? We could always call for the police, but simple situations had the habit of escalating. I did not dwell on philosophy or insight; I made better decisions acting on my instincts. The City of Glendale Fire and Police staffs planned the new investigation unit for over 14 months, but little thought went into the day-to-day logistics and operations. Tom and I were given a small 10'X10' office in the 60-year-old headquarters fire station in downtown Glendale. Fire Administration abandoned the grim edifice in August, fleeing to newer suites in the nearby city hall complex and leaving us the former Fire Marshal's office. Wood paneling and a bare linoleum floor were the cubicle's only features. Calling it austere was an overstatement. We had to scrounge desks, a typewriter and a filing cabinet. The office was, however, just ten steps from the station kitchen and its bottomless coffee pot. A pager was issued to each of us and, during our first few months together, emergency call-outs included both Tom and I. Doubling our overtime budget by both of us responding was not a problem and we needed to acquaint ourselves with individual strengths and weaknesses and formulate a scene investigation protocol, as well as follow-up operations. I also required training on Glendale Police Department policies, methods, monthly pistol/shotgun qualification training, and a multitude of standard operating procedures.

Even our car was a hand-me-down. The beast, a 1976 Ford Fairmount with 80,000 miles on the odometer, was equipped with a small V-8, red spotlight, no siren, police radio, and no air conditioning. The Ford looked exactly like what it was—a detective unit. The chrome/red spotlight and antennas gave it away immediately, especially when I drove through Sherry's neighborhood, home of the Frog Town Mexican gang. When I visited her, I roared down side streets, careered into her long driveway and covered the brute with a camping tarp.

Tom Rickles, a 10-year veteran police officer was over six feet tall and solidly built. With salt and pepper hair and moustache, he did not spend much time in a gym, but was a proficient bowler. Required to wear a suit or coat and tie to work, Tom's favorite attire was a blue/gray plaid sports coat, fashionable in the mid-1970s. Nobody told him we were in a different decade. Gruff and generally irritable, his overall abilities made him an excellent candidate for police sergeant. However, he had trouble expressing himself in front of the promotional oral boards. I respected and admired his knowledge and aptitudes but a standard-issue cop attitude made me a bit intimidated by Tom at first. He loved his kids and wife and respected his marriage and policy manuals; not necessarily in that order. Since full-time arson investigators in California are considered peace officers, I was ordered to abide by policy and procedures manuals of both the fire and police departments. There were some ambiguities. I could not carry a weapon on a fire truck, but police policy required all members to pack an on- or off-duty gun at all times. We learned to work around these variances.

Sitting in our office one weekday, Tom and I were paged to man the air utility unit and respond to a multi-alarm fire and explosion burning on the west side of town. Station One's personnel were in the field and already raced to the inferno when the request came in as we prepared to go, too. I jumped on board the ten-ton GMC, fired it up and pulled to the front ramp. Tom made me put my .357 magnum in the trunk of the car before we roared off. The Fire Investigation Unit soon found that bomb and explosives-related crimes fell into our province. The team's expertise in fire scene examination matched post-blast investigation as well. Relieving the detective bureau of bomb threat and explosives cases bought us some credibility, too. Everybody won and fire and police staff agreed to our proposal. The Unit was assigned on all explosions, explosives found, bomb threats, and suspicious package calls. This new responsibility also added a few dollars to our unit's training budget. Tom soon traveled to the Bureau of Alcohol, Tobacco & Firearms Training

Center in Glynco, Georgia for a two-week explosives/bomb scene investigation class. The training did not qualify him to deactivate live bombs; only to identify and evaluate suspicious packages and improvised explosive devices (IED's) before detonation and after. Much of the class time was devoted to fieldwork for post-blast scene evaluation and evidence identification/collection and documentation. My explosives/bomb training came slowly, primarily through local sessions taught by the Los Angeles and Orange County Bomb Squads, and explosion scene experience. We both joined the International Association of Bomb Technicians and Investigators. Contact and networking with FBI agents and the Glendale police intelligence section on a few early cases enabled us to get on a confidential quarterly mailing list of national explosives-related intelligence and incidents. The periodical included intimate descriptions of recent IED's and receiving such information required a law enforcement equivalent to a Top Secret security clearance in the military.

The marriage of a cop and a firefighter to combat the crime of arson worked. Tom taught me how to write a valid search warrant, get arrest warrants in the system, file criminal cases, and led me through the complex world of the D.A.'s office and court system. I taught him how to keep his head low when attacking a fire in a smoke-filled structure and how to make a meatloaf dinner to feed 14 guys for less than two dollars per person. The fire headquarters building became our second home. Tom had dinner with fire crews every Wednesday night before his bowling league met, during World Series games, and for Monday Night football.

Station One was quarters for a ladder truck, two engines, the salvage/air utility rig and the battalion chief. The department's mechanical shops and three wrench-turners were also part of the huge concrete mausoleum. The on-duty shift of firefighters consisted of 12 men. The dispatch center was on the top floor in a penthouse-like structure with at least two dispatchers on-duty at all times. If we tired of talking with the boys, there was usually a minimum of two female dispatchers working. My second home was the comm. center. Tom joined the station fund and paid dues that provided coffee, shoe polish and 26-inch TVs and VCRs. We frequently joined the crews for lunch, brunches on weekends and occasional dinners. Tom was married with three daughters and a son. I was living in my house but spent a lot of time with Sherry and her girls. We planned to marry in April 1981.

After successfully completing the week-long Fire Investigation 4 class in mid-November, Tom and I settled in to our new hovel. We spent the first quiet weeks developing forms for scene investigation and follow-up narratives as well as responding to as many fire calls as we could. There weren't many. An unusual series of three small brush fires in Chevy Chase Canyon was our only arson case for the month. The fires ignited between 11 p.m. and midnight, a real rarity. Neither investigator was called out and we had to find out about the fires the next morning. A suspect was seen holding a torch out the window of his car and lighting the brush. None of the fires progressed beyond a few square feet of burned grass. The dirty white '63 Ford station wagon was the only description we had and the vehicle apparently escaped over the hill into Pasadena after the fires were set. With a cold trail, we had nothing to go on. The incident exhibited a problem we would endure for years to come. We called it the warm bed syndrome. The later the hour when the fire call came in and the ambient temperature divided by the wind chill factor equaled the less likelihood an investigator called out. Fire captains and crews wanted to get the fire out and get back to the warm bed awaiting them in quarters. If they had to wait for a police officer to take an arson report or an arson investigator to be called from home, the beds grew cold. If a fire cause could be easily blamed on a smoldering cigarette or a lightning strike the crew returned to quarters. Many arson fires were overlooked due to this syndrome. Rats and matches was another favorite fire cause. The situation would continue if we didn't do something about it.

January 1981 was quiet but we continued to attend even small accidental fires, not just out of sheer boredom but to enhance our investigative expertise. Investigators normally are called to large loss blazes and the scenes are damaged by firefighters extinguishing the fire as well as by the fire itself. Such scenes are difficult to work with most everything rendered down to charcoal and ash. Seeing a number of fires with minor damage enabled us to observe proven causes before the blaze destroyed evidence of its origin. For example, we heard a dispatch for Engine Four to a "smoke-in-the-apartment" call nearby. A neighbor smelled smoke, dialed 9-1-1 and Four's responded, forced entry, and found smoke coming from a window-mounted air conditioner. The occupant took the excess of a six-foot-long electrical power cord, folded it over several times and shoved it into the side of the unit's housing to get it out of the way. The folds restricted the flow of electricity and caused resistance heating that eventually allowed the plastic insulation cord material to melt. Ultimately ignition could set the curtains, and room ablaze. Seeing this almost-fire gave us insight to the next fire we went to and found an air conditioner at the point of origin. If the remains of a folded power cord were found we could use our prior experience to gauge the probability this was the cause of the fire. This investigative strategy carried a great deal of weight when qualifying as an expert witness in court. I continued to work at Sears on weeknights and on Saturdays even though my new position paid about $330 more per month and came with a lot of overtime. I also worked as a firefighter in a station whenever I wanted to pick up another $250 per shift. Sherry didn't think the Sears job was necessary, and I agreed, but still enjoyed the work.

On February 12, 1981, Tom and I heard a radio call for another strange series of vegetation fires. A warm day, the three fires occurred again in Chevy Chase Canyon, at around 10 a.m. The fires were set along a ½ mile stretch of the street just north of Fire Station Three. We responded with the fire units and found two small grass fires and a roadside juniper bush burned. No incendiary devices were located. Two of the starts burned at locations we'd had fires at before—one at the same turnout where I found my first incendiary device in 1978. All three fires appeared lit with an open flame from the passenger side of a car. An indication of two people in the vehicle or the arsonist was ballsy enough to stop, lean out the passenger window and set the blaze. It was less than a quarter mile from our November midnight series with the Ford station wagon. We probably would not have been called out to these small fires had we not monitored the dispatch channel. Fire captains did not take the initiative to use us. Apparently warm beds grow cold even during the day. Tom and I decided to have a training session and actually burn some buildings and vehicles. We theorized that firefighters could better recognize the need for an arson investigator if they actually saw before, during and after scenes of fires. The fire department staff approved and we found a dozen vacant homes and apartments slated for demolition we could destroy at our leisure. Furniture was donated and we set up at least 12 fully-furnished rooms for destruction. The preparations for the event were time-consuming and the week of the festivities required us to work 12-hour days. The fire business is cyclic so we hoped for a continuing quiet month. The burning was planned for the weekend of March 28-29 with the fire crews coming through for two daily, 3-hour training blocks the weekdays following.

Friday, March 20, I went to Sears for my normal 5-9 p.m. shift. At around 6:30 I followed a suspicious teenager out to the parking lot, stepped on a piece of drain pipe and pancaked to the ground with a severely sprained ankle. I was sure I broke it by the rifle-shot sound of the snapped tendon. The guy took off, probably because I sounded like a gut shot grizzly. I called for help on my radio, went to the ER via ambulance and spent the weekend on my back. I was marginally off the crutches after four days and the planned burn went off on the scheduled weekend. The fire crews loved the fire training and the ability to actually sit and watch a developing fire rather than rushing to put it out. Seeing how a fire erupts, spreads to adjacent furnishings, climbs walls, races across ceilings and breaks windows is invaluable training. At the end of the day Sunday, we re-secured the structures so our fire scenes would be undisturbed for the expected 130 firefighter's participation in our fire scene investigation session. Both Tom and I got home around 7 p.m. exhausted, hungry and ready for a good night's sleep. Murphy's Law had other ideas. At 8 p.m. we were called to an attempted arson scene at a $225,000 home in Chevy Chase Canyon Estates. We arrived to find four gallons of naphtha-based camping fuel spread around the expensive home and several failed cigarette/matchbook incendiary devices soaking in the fuel. The liquid actually extinguished the cigarettes—there was insufficient heat to allow ignition and the glowing coal was snuffed out. We collected the evidence and carefully photographed the scene, praying the flash attachment would not set off the fume-filled home. Fire crews removed liquid-soaked furnishings, placing it all outside. The owner told us burglars must have gotten in through an unlocked sliding door. Burglars do not carry around four gallons of flammable liquid and incendiary devices. We cleared the scene by midnight, grateful for a workable case, but haunted by its timing. Tom and I shared instructor responsibilities Monday. My sore ankle did not allow me to remain on my feet long so I used my rest periods to pursue the attempt arson case since I was responsible for crime report follow-up for the week. I got no cooperation from the victim's insurance company when I tried to obtain information on his policy. I found discrepancies with the title to the home and, four years before, the owner experienced a previous arson fire at his nightclub in Glendale. New to the arson field, I had difficulty networking with someone to help me convince the insurance company their policyholder may have tried to burn his own home down.

On Wednesday we received permission to set one more fire during a break in the training tours. We obtained two gallons of camping fuel to simulate what would have happened if the fire we investigated Sunday night had actually gone off, and what the scene looked like afterwards. Three crews stood by while I spread the fuel in the furnished living room then brought in a lit incendiary device from the outside and placed it. Eight minutes later, it went off, pushing flames three feet out the openings. The naphtha-based fuel went off like gasoline. The fire crews let the blaze build for a few minutes but the smoky inferno threatened a neighboring structure and had to be knocked down. After we moved in we recovered parts of the still-identifiable device. Over 130 firefighters from Burbank and Glendale trekked through our training up to Wednesday afternoon, and we still had twelve more companies scheduled for Thursday. At just after 1 a.m. Thursday, a $225,000 home in Chevy Chase Estates exploded in flames. Tom and I were called out. The home where the attempt occurred Sunday night was gutted. Ironically, two of the same crews who extinguished our camping fuel fire on Wednesday responded to this blaze. Talk about déjà vu. We worked the scene until dawn, finding six one-gallon cans of camping fuel this time and, amazingly, several unexploded incendiary devices again. One or two had functioned this time. Cigarette/match devices had about a 50 percent failure rate. The owner claimed he came home late from work and the exact moment he opened the front door and stepped inside, the fuel went off. Our investigation showed at least one gallon of the fuel was poured on the floor of the foyer where the owner stepped in. He was unharmed, unburned and no scorched hair. Recalling the fireball put out by our test fire the day before, Tom and I nodded our heads sagely. We now had a compelling set of before and after photos of this fire scene—a very strange and rare occurrence. This happened one more time in my career and the oddball evidence helped convict me of four counts of murder. The prosecutor claimed such before and after photos were impossible to obtain unless the arsonist himself knew the target and was the photographer himself. My defense lawyer ignored this 1981 investigation and refused to use the scenario to refute the prosecutor's allegations. The jury was left with the impression that before and after photos of a fire scene was indeed evidence I was an arsonist. An unusual occurrence, yes. Proof, no, but without presentation to the jury by the defense, I was an arsonist.

Thursday went smoothly despite our fatigue. At the end of the day we re-secured the structures and released them to the developer with our thanks. He hoped we would burn them to the ground and save him demolition expenses. Over 170 firefighters and investigators participated in the exercise. Tom and I received a half-day off Friday to compensate us for the extra hours spent on the project. We picked up plenty of overtime for the two fire scene investigations Sunday night and Thursday morning. A carpet donated to our burn training managed to find its way into our office. The tacky '50s-style linoleum, now covered by an equally tacky brown/beige pile carpeting made the cubicle a bit homier. On Friday, before leaving for the day, Tom and I dropped by the police building to pick up reports. Parked in front was a dirty white '63 Ford station wagon—our Chevy Chase Canyon brush fire suspect's car. By April 1981 there weren't many '63 Ford wagons on the street. We contacted the driver when he came outside after inquiring about a traffic ticket. We ID-ed him and, within a minute, the street-wise guy said he wanted to talk to a lawyer before communicating further. Without any real probable cause, we kicked him loose but his description and ID were sent to every fire and police station in southern California as a probable brush fire setter.

Even after I developed my own investigative and follow-up abilities, Tom treated me like he was the training officer with a rookie-on-a-leash. He belittled me publicly once because I strapped on a gun when we were called out to a late-night fire scene. This was standard and according to policy. Procedure also required detectives called out after-hours to don a suit, or sports coat and tie. Tom and I never followed that requirement. At this fire scene, a newspaper reporter showed up at the command post and queried Tom about the unit's status. Tom responded, "John still has to work out his wannabe image. He's in there now, digging around a fire scene wearing a gun. What's he need a pistol for? It's a cold fire scene and we're the only ones around. I don't see any suspects." The quote appeared the next day in the Glendale News-Press. Tom was still a cop and I remained just a fireman to him. Apparently it did not matter to him I had cleared over 70 percent of the cases we solved in 1981, arrested two on-the-job burglars without his assistance, and bagged a car thief. This was beginning to appear as a marriage of convenience. Despite these minor differences, I liked Tom. As with most cop partners, we were close and covered for each other on occasion. At Christmas, we infrequently parted for lunch and spent an hour or two shopping in the middle of the day at the nearby Glendale Galleria. The trade-off balanced out in the city's favor. We never took an hour for lunch. Besides, we both loved this job too much to bring discredit to the unit. During 1979, I took the fire captain's promotional exam and ended up number seven out of 48 taking the test. By mid-1981, all six ahead of me on the list promoted to captain. The next retiring captain was scheduled to soon leave the department. The captain's civil service promotional list expired in August. I knew the old captain well. He was definitely ready to go fishing and relax. Out of nowhere, the captain pulled his retirement papers and decided to stay three more months. A friend of mine overheard a conversation between the shift battalion chief and the retiring captain. A reprimand for violating policy would be dropped and the captain would receive a preferred station assignment in exchange for delaying his retirement until the list expired. My boss, the Fire Marshal, didn't want me to promote out of the fledgling investigation unit after serving for only 16 months. The normal rotation was intended to be 3-5 years for the arson unit and the position wasn't slotted for a captaincy. I had been on the job for eight years. The almost-retired captain agreed to the terms. The raise in pay would have been at least $600 per month but I was enjoying my assignment despite the ups and downs with Tom and other cops but the overtime compensation was good. I may have even waived the promotion should it have been offered. I at least would have liked to have been given the opportunity to make the decision. As usual with me, the money was secondary. Pursuing the bad guys, the chase, the hunt and solving whodunit crimes was the ultimate high. I have to admit I also liked the positive publicity we brought to the city and its agencies, and to the unit. Much to the chagrin of our superiors, the unit ended up handling PR and frequently acted as public information officers for the fire department. Since we were already at fire scenes, generally available while others fought the blazes and were such a success, we talked to reporters constantly. As long as we were careful and did not discredit the department, we had free rein with the press. The local newspaper crime beat reporters made a special stop at our office after they made the police and fire report run each day. Tom and I networked with many agencies and, through the arson intelligence web, we learned of a series of fires set in brush and grass throughout the nearby L.A. area. A cigarette/match/rubber band device was found at some of the sites. Tom and I had seen similar devices in training manuals and found a few ourselves, verifying this particular set-up as fairly common. We sat down one day and evaluated this particular device and decided many different arsonists used this simple incendiary. The locations the devices were found in ran from small grass fires and brush blazes, to set-up delays to ignite Molotov cocktails and explosive trains. Even the Chevy Chase house-burner used the cigarette-match combo. The 10-12 minute delays gave perpetrators plenty of time to clear the soon-to-be crime scene and establish alibi, or to find a convenient place from which to watch. Nothing indicated to us that this simple device was put together by just one person. Feeling comfortable in our ramblings, we never openly theorized that only one person used this incendiary. We frequently revealed our discoveries of the cigarette/match combinations when sharing with other investigators. Others told us of their own recoveries. Nobody bought in the "only-one-guy" theory until I was arrested in 1991. Then, it was as if I was the most prolific serial arsonist in the country.

Little did I know what lay ahead. We attended occasional meetings of different organizations of arson investigators including the Fire Investigation Regional Strike Team (F.I.R.S.T.). The sessions were sparsely attended and I found them boring. Important information was gleaned from the round table discussions of area arson incidents but the core group was older fire and police detectives nearing retirement. Training was frequently discussed but nobody seemed to do anything but form committees. New to the group, I just listened. A surveillance van was donated to F.I.R.S.T. and three men were designated to find insurance for the vehicle. For six months I heard excuses by these three guys on why they didn't have time pick up a phone to find out insurance or none of the trio showed up for the meeting. It took seven months to finally insure the beast. In early April we were told neighboring Pasadena had two fires set inside retail stores while they were open for business. The blazes were set in displays of curtain or bedding materials—probably as a diversion for shoplifting. Two suspects were described. We picked up reports from the police station regarding a series of three fires set around a business in Glendale's industrial section. One of the fires was attempted arson and all three were related, probably due to a disgruntled former employee. The attempt was an incendiary device consisting of a cigarette with matches tied to it and a paper clip used to secure the device to a curtain pulled through an open mail slot. The device failed. In three months we had four series fires, totaling nine incidents and six cigarette/match incendiary devices.

In early April I gave notice and quit my job at Sears. The new investigator position took far more time than expected and the overtime money coming in made up for the loss of Sears pay. One week after the two incidents at the home in Chevy Chase Estates, the insurance company assigned a private investigator to examine the fire. Billy Dean McLaughlin was a former police officer from northern California and moved to L.A. to join an established Pasadena private investigative agency. If Bill was placed between Tom and me, you'd swear we were brothers. We resembled each other right down to the bushy moustaches. Tom met with us and after some initial sparring we decided we liked and trusted the guy. He provided copies of the entire insurance history of the burned structure and kicked in two new fires the owner experienced at the same nightclub in the San Fernando Valley in the early 70s. Where the company had completely stonewalled me on information requests before, we now had everything. In the 80s, insurance companies typically shared information as well as cops and firemen did. In Bill's file we found a number of significant things including the failed attempt to burn the house occurred on March 29. I tried to get information from the company on March 30 and April 1 with no luck from either of my sources. Unknown to us, the insurance policy was due to be cancelled, for non-payment of premiums, on April 3. Tom and I would have set up a surveillance on the doomed home had we been aware of that fact. The owner would have been caught in the act. Bill shook his head and so did we. Working the case together for the next eight months resulted in the service of three search warrants and the arrest of two men. The owner was taken into custody on December 17, 1981 and his alleged accomplice the next day. The abettor was fingered by the clerk who sold the man, a former employee of the owner, six gallons of camping fuel, all at one time. That, said the clerk, was an "unusual" sale. This extensive investigation and Bill McLaughlin's guidance allowed me to explore the complex world of property insurance and connect with insiders getting me access to files of the secretive business. I was pleased to have this "training" case early in my career. Bill gladly shared with us. Private investigators have difficulty getting police agencies to help out when there is a good insurance fraud case on a faked burglary, robbery or arson crime. Cops, normally suspicious, have a particular aversion to PIs. Tom and I ensured a solid case when we presented it to the major frauds section of the L.A. D.A.'s office for filing consideration. Or so we thought. Tom Rickles was in court when our appointment to meet with Major Frauds came up. I asked Bill McLaughlin to accompany me to meet with the head of the D.A.'s section. After a 30-minute wait, Bill and I entered a conference room where the assigned D.A., Al Botello, was seated. His supervisor hovered by an open door conversing with somebody. Botello was given our business cards; mine stating I was from the fire department and Bill's PI agency card. I already told Botello McLaughlin was coming along and he was a police veteran. As we sat down, Botello called over his shoulder to the supervisor and said, "We're ready, boss. No law enforcement present." Bill's face turned red and I took a moment to explain to Botello, unnecessarily, that the California Penal Code classified full-time arson investigators employed by fire departments as peace officers. He waved his hand around in the air as if his statement meant nothing but to provide information. I glared at him and our relationship over the next four months was defined by those first moments. Botello and his colleagues ultimately made a plea arrangement ensuring our suspect walked with minimal punishment. Like I said, this was a learning experience for me and, if nothing else, Bill McLaughlin was another mentor to help me along. There were times when Bill needed to locate someone for a criminal case he worked and I helped him in his endeavors. It was a violation of policy to obtain copies of protected computer documents or reports to private investigators but that was a local policy. I never provided hard copies of anything but I considered him a fellow law enforcement officer and his pursuit of criminals in the fraud field was the same as any other cop. I helped him. My arson-fraud suspect collected over $300,000 for his frauds, though he didn't collect on the burned house in my case. Officials provided him a new identity as part of the D.A. "deal;" a mere slap in the face. The man was a serial arsonist with a financial gain motive; an unusual combination.

In June, Tom and I witnessed a man dragging a woman down Central Avenue by her hair. Tom called for backup as I jumped out to rescue the woman. I blocked the man's forward progress and got within three feet of him when I heard Tom shout, "Knife, partner!" I didn't wait to confirm, backed up, dropped to a crouch and drew my gun from an ankle holster. The man had an 8" kitchen knife held in his free hand. In the time it took me to get my weapon I could have been slashed and stabbed repeatedly. I was not paying attention and Tom, as my training officer, verbally kicked my ass after the incident. I moved too quickly, probably trying to prove myself to my new cop partner by jumping into the fray blindly. I needed to think more like a street cop and not be so trusting that a suspect was going to lie down because I carried a badge. I'd been lucky over the years at Sears and most crooks tried to just flee; not aggressively fight back. Bound to run into a situation like this eventually, I am grateful the encounter turned out as it did. Silently, I enjoyed the fact we got another bad guy to add to our stats. This law enforcement safari never ended. We were constantly on the hunt. The knife-wielding suspect had done hard time for assaults in the past and was a veteran gang member.

Over the years, I was trapped in a fire, fell through a roof and a floor, stuck my finger in a live light socket and dragged a dead man from an inferno. Tom now told me I was in a "dangerous" new world and had to be careful. We worked two fatal fires—both suicides. A retired nurse doped herself up then poured alcohol over her body and bed and ignited it. Smoke and minor burns killed her. There was limited fire damage to the small, sealed bedroom. The other was a self-immolation by a troubled 22-year-old guy who used a can of lighter fluid to torch himself in his backyard. The follow-up investigations of the two deaths were handled by the robbery/homicide detail of the Glendale Police Department. During the early summer, I captured two more serial arsonists in-training. One was an 11-year-old who destroyed a beautifully restored 1968 Chevy, and later admitted setting various trash and grass fires around the middle-class neighborhood in Engine Four's district. The other was a 13-year-old who set off a trash dumpster, followed minutes later by two cars up the street from his home. This pair of incidents validated my early-arrival investigation formula. I monitored one call while on-duty and responded to the Chevy fire because it occurred near an elementary school just after students departed for the day. I heard the radio broadcast of the second series while driving home from work and quickly turned around and headed back in to Glendale. A call-out to the Chevy fire may never happened and been written off as accidentally-caused. The 13 year old's series may have resulted in a call-out, but too late to secure area witnesses who helped me locate the firebug. These were people fire crews generally neglected to pursue. Twenty minutes later, I had him in custody.

With the temperature hovering at 100° at just 10 a.m., Walt Beatty, my drinking buddy, and I headed to nearby flea market in Santa Clarita in the summer of 1981. Walt worked as a backup to Tom and me on surveillances and search warrant services, but I spent less time with him since Sherry and I were constantly together. I had my own warm bed syndrome. A spontaneous trip gave us a chance to hang out while Sherry went to the beach. The flea market was more of a beer bar than a place to shop. As we entered the event, I looked over Walt's shoulder and saw a guy sitting behind the wheel of his Blazer parked on Sierra Highway. It wasn't Walt of course. I brushed by Walt, walked quickly to the open passenger window and gawked at the disheveled man. Before I could say anything the guy remarked, "Tony said I could run down to..." as he reached down to the ignition with Walt's key ring dangling from it. I flamed. Another grand theft auto in front of me. Remembering Tom Rickles cautions, I hesitated a second, recalled I wasn't armed, and dove through the open window. I don't believe my body touched the window frame until my torso collided with the thief. Then my shins and tops of my feet took the punishment of my folly. I threw no punches, just concentrated on restraining him so he couldn't go for a weapon and hoped Walt would jump in and grab his or my pistol. Traffic whizzed by just over the felon's shoulder as I used every expletive I knew, letting him know I was crazier than he, and intended to inflict some real harm. The fool opened the driver's door and dragged me into the slow lane. Thankfully empty of the normal 55-mile-per-hour traffic, he hit the pavement first and we rolled, taking us into the fast lane. The asphalt was sizzling in the 100° heat and I knew I didn't want to end up on the bottom of this pile so got the idiot into a chokehold. Unfortunately, that put my arm onto the molten road surface. He kept trying to get to his waistband or pockets so I had to apply the hold aggressively. Walt called the cops and retrieved a pair of handcuffs from the truck. I would have preferred a .357 magnum but a CHP car whizzed by on the opposite side of the divided highway and squealed around in a U-turn. Screeching to a halt just a few feet from the pile on the roadway, the cop jumped out, gun drawn. As the cop approached I theorized it would not carry much weight to shout out, "I'm a fireman. Don't shoot." Knowing cop attitudes toward wannabes might lead him to the wrong conclusion, I used a ruse that became commonplace for me, "I'm a cop. This guy's a GTA suspect." My credentials established by use of cop jargon for a car thief, I did not need to flash a badge. We cuffed the crook, then accepted a cold soda from onlookers. I poured the contents of the can onto my stinging forearm. We then found out the thief tried to steal a car earlier and also flashed a pocketknife at a teenager and attempted a robbery all in the past 30 minutes. The folding knife was still in his pants pocket. I added one more serial criminal arrest to my stats. Walt bought me a 40 ounce Foster's lager as a reward, even though it was not quite 10 a.m. yet. Walt later asked me not to tell anybody about the incident. I guess he was embarrassed about leaving the keys in the truck. This is the first time I've related the story.

On September 25, 1981 I was called to a small fire at a 4-unit apartment complex. The blaze destroyed a furniture storage area and, at first examination, appeared to be caused by combustible materials placed too close to a water heater near the point of origin. Burn patterns substantiated my area of origin and I zeroed in on the heater when repeatedly interrupted by one of the tenants. I could not keep him away. He even stuck his head in through a breech in the room's wall from an adjacent garage. I told him to leave me alone but he came back three times, asking what was up. I finally escorted him out to the street. As I returned to the building the engine captain told me this same guy bothered him at the "other" fire two nights before. That small trash fire in a laundry room nearby happened late Friday and no investigator was called. This was Sunday and I had not been back to work to review reports so didn't know this was the second fire. I examined the water heater closer and found what appeared to be saw cuts and a hole on the underside of the exposed natural gas line to the regulator. The fire was arson and the lab later confirmed the saw marks made before the fire. The gawker got my interest and he enjoyed being the center of attention. He gave me several leads; all false. Two nights later, the garage on the other side of the storeroom burned. Again the bystander, Vincent, reported the fire and ushered residents out before the fire department arrived. He was quite a hero and showed me his scrapbook where clippings outlined his community involvement and an incident where he chased a purse-snatcher. This guy sounded like me. He even looked like me, right down to the moustache. I later included some of Vince's characteristics when I developed the antagonist serial arsonist in *Points of Origin*. Vince attacked the latest blaze with a garden hose and was overcome by smoke and transported to the hospital. That information surprised me because he was already back at the apartment when I arrived on scene. It seems an ambulance transported him to the hospital and, during treatment, two uniformed officers interviewed and accused him of setting the fire. Left alone, Vincent pulled the I.V. from his arm and fled the ER. His nurse and doctor provided the Glendale Police Station's address as his place of employment. Showing up back at the fire, he met with his good friend—me. I arrested him later after he admitted being near the hole in the garage wall using a flaming matchbook for light. He accidentally dropped the torch, he said. His statements and contradictions with the evidence gave me probable cause to arrest him. Four counts of arson were leveled against Vincent. Further investigation revealed he discovered at least two other fires in the area, admitted trying to burn an acquaintance's van a year before, and started a brush fire in nearby Eagle Rock four years ago. Some of the charges were not prosecutable because the statute of limitations had run. I became the first arson investigator in history to file bigamy charges in a fire case. Vincent's current estranged "wife" would be used to testify against him and we discovered he did not divorce his first spouse, thus, the bigamy charge. Despite my work, the case was lost in trial. Vincent was my first arrest of a pyromaniac. I'd nailed several series fire setters already but Vince was unique. His fires were set during times of personal depression and this fact helped classify him. Several years before I arrested him he was unemployed, having problems with his first wife and stormed out of their residence after an argument with her. He went for a walk and, as he returned, discovered a fire burning in the garage below his apartment building. He pounded on doors and evacuated the building, then attacked the blaze with a garden hose. He was the hero and gained positive attention for a time for his actions. This scenario repeated just before I arrested him. His latest fires, in 1981, were set because he was unemployed, depressed, soon-to-be evicted and his landlady screamed at him to get out and generally made his life miserable. At an all-time low, three fires brought temporary release from his depressing situation. In all the fire investigation classes I had taken, some portion of the training was devoted to pyromaniacs-psychology. Over the years, studies were based on a limited cross-section of identified firebugs. The pyromaniacs did have consistent profiles, however. They usually set fires within walking distance of their homes. Pyromaniacs discovered their fires. They frequently became the hero by helping with evacuations and putting out the fires. Pyros stuck around their fire scenes to help police and investigators. Vincent fit into all of these categories. Pyros are loners and losers and cannot hold onto jobs and have no friends to help them cope with their difficulties. They crave attention and their fires bring them attention, friends, admiration as heroes and self-worth; albeit, temporarily. Like a drug addict, one good score leads to the desire for another. More fire equals more attention. With all I learned about psychologically-motivated fire-setters, I felt I had enough probable cause to arrest Vince within ten minutes of meeting him. After my first contact I went to a deputy D.A. and ran the case by him. Since Vince fell into almost all the categories of a typical pyromaniac, did that give me probable cause to arrest? The D.A. said yes and no. Since an arson investigator cannot give psychological opinions in court, one could not use his opinions for probable cause either. A more experienced investigator could. More statements or a confession were needed to arrest Vincent. Arresting only a few series fire-setters this early in my career, the D.A. said, "After you pop a few more of this type of arsonist, a court may accept your opinion and expertise as probable cause for an arrest."

Pyros comprise less than 5 percent of all arsonists arrested. My chance of getting much experience bagging psychologically-motivated fire-setters was pretty slim. The Glendale Fire/Police Fire Investigation Unit blazed through 1981 spectacularly. In the article published in the August 1982 issue of the American Fire Journal, written by Battalion chief Elmer N. Spraker, the unit's first year success was outlined: "...during the first 13 months of continued training and operations, the following statistics were compiled: 153 incidents were investigated by the unit. 78 cases were cleared. 25 arrests were made. 23 cases were filed and 11 resulted in conviction, 2 were dismissed and 10 are presently pending court disposition. An additional 29 cases were referred to other agencies, such as the fire marshal or for other inter-agency counseling. 37 percent of the incidents investigated were cleared by the unit. This figure represents approximately 21 percent above the national average. Additionally, incidents involving arson dropped to 31 percent within the first year of operation. Management can only conclude that a certain deterrent factor had been established. When the news media carried stories of arrests, convictions and other court actions, it had an immediate effect on those who may have had arson in mind." Tom and I made more arrests for arson in 1981 than our predecessors had in Glendale in the past seven years. If the city doubled the number of detectives assigned to burglary or auto theft, a similar record would result. Unfortunately, most municipalities cannot afford to staff criminal investigative units with enough detectives to pursue the large number of cases reported. The quality of the investigative strategies and follow-up also had an impact on the final figures. Tom and I devoted our time to even the smallest case. Glendale made an excellent choice to attack the crime of arson during the early 1980s by putting the two-man arson investigative unit in place. Despite our questionable leadership in the Fire Marshal's office, early friction involving Tom, me, and Walt, and some conflict with veteran fire officers, the unit's spectacular success validated our place in the fire department's tradition-burdened existence. As law enforcers, we pursued criminal investigations, even when fire department personnel emerged as suspects. Placing Tom and I in a precarious position, the web of city politics and the shadowy, spider-ridden behind-the-scenes bargaining at city hall drew us in, giving us more than a little grief.

CHAPTER SEVEN
FIRECRACKERS

Another accidental fire death occurred in early 1982, enhancing our relationship with Robbery/Homicide detectives. Policy called for us to co-investigate fatal fire cases; we did the scene, the follow-up conducted by the assigned police agent. In addition, an epidemic of car fires materialized. The vehicle blazes, started with wads of newspaper shoved under the dashboards, puzzled us. About half of them self-extinguished when the arsonist closed the car door after setting the fire and a few caught early, leaving the telltale wadded up newspaper ash intact. Another whodunit to work on. Work took up much of my on- and off-duty time and Sherry and I experienced uncertainty in our marriage. We verbally battled about everything. I loved being with a family again but there was a power struggle with Sherry. Used to calling the shots at work, I brought my attitude with me and usurped her home authority. When Sherry and I met, the rendezvous was her second date with Walt. We shared similar schedules at Sears but she was unavailable to me. Walt lingered at that time. I was able to grab a few breaks with her and she soon related she and Walt were just friends.

"He hates kids, anyway," she told me one day. "I asked him if he wanted to join me and my girls at the Norton Simon art museum and he turned three shades of red and hasn't called me since." Sherry was the only woman I was acquainted with who actually knew Vermeer was not just the middle-aged guy who dressed mannequins in the ladies' wear department at Sears. Sherry asked me out the first time when she invited my family to her parents' cabin in the nearby Angeles National Forest. After that afternoon, the relationship launched as a brushfire fanned by Santa Ana winds. Trying to juggle my new career in investigations, and get a handle on my commitment to Sherry and family created conflicts. We ignored them as just growing pains. Lust had a way of dulling our common sense. After we married I tried to treat her as an equal but failed. She was better than me in many ways. I just didn't see it. At work, she was aggressive and thorough, handling customer complaints and troubleshooting minor problems in her department. With my own on-duty assertive persona coming home with me, Sherry and I clashed on some household issues. Apparently we didn't spend enough time on getting to know each others' day-to-day quirks before marrying. We treated each other like co-workers who were vying for the same promotion, but this was a marriage and there was no higher position to aspire to. We just didn't know it.

The Glendale Fire Department's 75th birthday celebration was scheduled for April 1982. Sherry and I volunteered to help put it on. The department was to host a 3-day firefighter's competition at out largest park and I elected to handle security, of course, and Sherry took on the sizable responsibility of producing a combination 75th anniversary historical tome and souvenir program She gathered old photos of fire department members, equipment, and memorable fires from various newspaper and private party collections and wrote the accompanying departmental history. Finished on time and ready for the printers, she asked me to drop off the proofs on my way to work. Instead, I took the paperwork and checked it out first. She had done a beautiful job. The program was attractive, informative, and was worthy of keeping as a great souvenir of our 75th anniversary. There were a few typos and some of the descriptions of equipment and fires described in "layman" terms instead of firefighter jargon. I corrected the text and added the appropriate terminology. Then I gave it to the printers. That evening Sherry met me at the door in a peach teddy and told me the kids were spending the night at their grandparents' house next door.

"Did you get to the printers?" She asked as we embraced.

"Yeah, there were only a few typos but I fixed 'em"

"Typos...fixed?"

I felt her stiffen in my arms.

"Yeah, a misspelling or two and, you know, a couple of terms needed changing into firespeak."

She stepped back and crossed her arms. "It didn't need any changes."

"Well..."

"None! It was perfect the way it was...and..."

"But some words were misspelled..."

"Bullshit!...well, maybe, but dammit, nothing else should have been touched. You didn't even ask me, you just changed it." Her eyes watered with anger and she stomped once, rattling dishes across the room in a china closet.

"I guess I could have called," I stammered.

"No shit, but you shouldn't have done anything. The program was my responsibility. It was perfect. Who do you think you are?" I stepped back this time. Sherry was not much for debating fairly. When our tirades reached this stage I could not reason with her, talk about the mistakes I may have made, or try to apologize for my own faults. She heard nothing after she challenged me with her key phrase, "Who do you think you are?" We'd been here before. The only way to deal with Sherry was to step back, let her vent, and not encourage any further debate. Let her cool down and hope the outburst drained her energy. It usually worked but this challenge to her floated around our relationship like the odor of three-week-old cheese fallen behind the stove.

I was wrong in this battle but no opportunity arose to apologize. Even if she conceded my editing was justified, the fact I didn't check with her first destroyed us. We never quite recovered from this epiphany. Subsequent arguments all had this faux pas hanging in the background. She had an edge in those debates, weakening me somewhat. Again, a power struggle instead of a relationship. Sherry and I seemed to get along only horizontally.

I couldn't always find witnesses available during the day when I needed to interview them so spent evenings doing necessary follow-up. Again, this loner cop spending all day and night pursuing the bad guys persona was effective. A high percentage of the employees punch a time clock twice a day and anything before or after is fun time. I was not among them. Success at work required more than 8-5 work days. Family was sacrificed, but that was me and my work ethic. Past jobs geared me up to get preliminaries done and prepare for the next rush period. Networking with Bill McLaughlin and his insurance contacts saved me countless hours researching areas I was not familiar with, so time spent bending elbows and ears at local watering holes was work time to me; usually on his expense account. Work was a refuge.

On a Monday morning in May, I discovered two suspicious car fires on the east side of town when I checked weekend reports. These didn't appear to be part of my wadded newspaper series. The fire captains did not notify the on-call investigator and wrote off the causes as accidental. The fires both started in the early morning hours, both in subterranean garages below occupied apartments, two miles apart on separate days. This seemingly unconnected series could—and does—happen in any city or in adjoining jurisdictions and their connection never made. Our efforts to overcome the warm bed syndrome were failing. Captains continued to overlook the obvious and refused to call out the arson troops. Tom's after hours response time was less than 30 minutes and mine less than 20. In the early 1980s the Glendale Fire Department was top-heavy with supervisors approaching retirement. The arson unit was progress and the fire service was burdened with tradition. We weren't around in the early careers of those men and we didn't quite fit, yet. They resisted us or were just brain dead after midnight. I examined both car fire reports and the cause and origin location in each was around the front passenger seat area. Both captains blamed electrical wiring shorts as the cause. No lightning that night, I guessed. Both cars were left in place and not impounded. Two things bothered me about the fires. One, the first fire occurred on Stanley Avenue, just a half-block from the home of a convicted serial fire-setter. Involved or implicated in many fires, "Red," as he was known on the street because of his flaming orange hair, had burned a garage and set several nuisance blazes over the years. The second peculiarity about the car fires was origins in the same part of the vehicle as my newspaper fires earlier in the year. I drove to both apartments and examined the cars. Both were obvious arsons. Both had open glove boxes, contents scattered on the floor and seats, and one vehicle's passenger door was left open during the fire. The responding fire crew didn't find this unusual, or else thought the discoverer of the blaze opened it. The undamaged door was opened before the fire ever started. Not only did I have to change the fire reports, I had to now write original arson crime police reports for both incidents. It appeared the thief rifled the glove box then set the fire for spite or revenge for not finding valuables. Maybe because he liked fires. Available combustibles were used to light the fires. No wadded newspapers brought in from the outside like my other series. A similar M.O., but I felt two different firebugs. This was the beginning of a seven month-long whodunit investigation. We had no clue who the arsonist was. When I went to Red's house on Stanley to talk to him I was met at the door by his 5 year-old step-brother and mother. As soon as I ID-ed myself, but before I explained why I was there, she ordered me off the property saying, "Tony (Red) didn't do anything. Leave him alone. He doesn't set fires anymore. If you come back again I'm calling the mayor and my lawyer." She slammed the door. It was an interesting statement. I had identified myself as "with Glendale Police Department" without saying fire or arson. How did she know what crime I was investigating? I left and later tracked down 19-year-old Red's other part-time residences and a few snitches who knew him. He was pretty well alibied on one case and in jail on one other. He was in the clear this time. On October 10, 1984, I was asked to return to 1455 Stanley Avenue to Red's part-time residence. A small fire occurred that evening in a closet, and the fire captain wanted me to investigate. I refused the call-out, remembering Red's mother's threatening me with legal action two years before and I was already at the scene of the still-burning Ole's hardware store fire. A closet fire is undeniably a juvenile-started fire. I wanted to avoid a confrontation with Red's mom, knowing her youngest son was now a fire-setter, and figured I could interview the boy at school the next day anyway. I refused the response, had a report taken so I could document the event and I'd follow up later. The captain confirmed the boy's presence along with a new step-father who had his belongings destroyed in the fire. The boy was making a statement. My refusal and reasons for it were not documented in a report. There was no reason to in 1984. In 1994, after murder charges were filed against me for the Ole's hardware store fire deaths, the refusal to respond to 1455 Stanley in 1984 as Ole's burned became evidence used to wrongly convict me of murder in 1998. My defense attorney in 1998, Peter Giannini said, "It's not important to the murder that you didn't go to Stanley that night in 1984. Forget about it. What does it prove?" My lawyer was wrong. The prosecutor used the refused call-out in closing arguments and the allegations went un-refuted or explained to the jury. The deputy D.A. said "Orr didn't go to the Stanley fire because he wanted to stay and watch 'his' fire—Ole's. Why else would an arson investigator refuse to go to a fire in his own city? Firebugs stay and watch their own fires." The jury never heard about Red or his mother's threats.

Four more glove box fires occurred during the summer months, all on Glendale's east side. I had a serial arsonist working and Red had alibi. The chase continued. In the early summer I had two more series fires at the same home, in the La Crescenta section of Glendale. The single man living in the two-bedroom home had no idea who was responsible. I profiled the now-cold scenes since no investigator was called out to either fire. The small fires appeared to be very juvenile in nature. Available combustibles were placed against the front door and a bush by the garage was ignited. Not very creative or aggressive starts. However, propping a rubber mat against the front door was a mild statement saying this act was directed at the occupant. The bush fire, I found out, was actually a trash bag physically moved from behind the garage and placed against the man's prized possession—his car. Someone near this guy targeted him personally, but the attempts were juvenile or set by a female. My theory was based on some training and a little experience with female fire-setters. An angry male adult breaks windows and kicks in doors to aggressively set fires. Females generally set less invasive or intrusive blazes, like the floor mat caper and attacking the guy's toy—his car—from the outside. A fire set by a man can be like a rape; a forcible entry accompanied by further aggression. It was a confusing profile but I was sure this man, Ray, was targeted—and not by a neighborhood juvenile. Three weeks of investigation showed the man a Lothario with a string of women and one close friend named Joanne he was stringing along. Ray was honest with Joanne about his other ladies and constant wanderings, but she still resented it. He received threatening letters ordering him to leave an unnamed woman alone. The letters sounded vague and contrived. Joanne was putting up with a lot from this guy, but actually being with him during one of the fires caused me to set her off to one side. Frustrated, I came down pretty hard on her during one spur-of-the-moment interview in hopes of at least deterring more fires. The next night someone poured a half-gallon of gasoline on <u>her</u> own front porch and ignited it. Her 15-year-old brother suffered minor burn injuries putting out the blaze. Now I was really lost. A month passed with no further incidents I was aware of. Three more glove box fires occurred, one of them spreading to six other cars, a carport, and scorched an apartment building. All the fires were on the east side of town. I checked the police "hot board" in hopes of finding a few police reports taken when a glove box was rifled without the fire. Maybe some fingerprints were lifted. Before I got to the reports, I came across a Be-On-The-Lookout flyer listing a number of known car burglars. A rash of car burglaries materialized all over the city during the first half of the year and an auto theft investigator compiled the list of thieves arrested for the crime before. The BOLO advised uniformed officers to watch for these guys prowling around at night. The detective who put the list together was my nemesis; Sharon's now-husband, Detective Dan. One of his listed suspects was caught red-handed a month before, burglarizing an unlocked Mazda in a subterranean garage. The victim, a weightlifter, heard noises in the carport under his apartment and investigated, finding a 19-year-old man inside his car. He held on to "Pogo" until police arrived. Pogo's home address was just one block from the weightlifter's apartment and right in the middle of the area where all my glove box fires occurred. Reluctantly, I approached Dan and inquired about Pogo's arrest. Dan told me Pogo was rifling the glove box of the Mazda when he was discovered. He added that most people will not report their car being entered if it was unlocked, unless the stereo or something of value was stolen. The most a guy could get out of a glove box was usually parking meter coins. Pogo was scheduled to serve a 45-day sentence for the car burglary. In the meantime, Ray and the lovely Joanne continued their unique relationship, but not without a few bumps. Joanne was kidnapped from work. A detective told me the following: as Joanne left work at a nearby hospital, two men forced her into their car and drove her around for two hours. They didn't touch her or even speak to her until they let her out of the car. One of the men told her to give a message to Ray: "Tell your boyfriend to leave my old lady alone. Stay away from her," and drove off. A few days later a pipe bomb went off in the window sill of Ray's bedroom. Joanne was at her own place that night. Ray, strangely enough, was alone. Again, he had no idea why he was targeted. The pipe bomb shattered the window, tore off the sill and blasted fragments all over the room and street. Over a week later on a Monday morning check of the police "hot board," I started to breeze quickly through because I was due in court. Skimming through drunk driving arrests and traffic accidents, I almost missed a crime report with the catch-all heading of "A.O. Misdemeanor." An "All Other Misdeameanor" could be anything from a theft from a patio to a stolen credit card. This morning, the A.O.

114

Misdemeanor report listed two juveniles as suspects. One of them was Joanne's brother. He was the one who discovered the blazing gasoline on their porch and been slightly burned as he put it out. This past weekend, according to the report, he rode on the back of a moped when a uniformed officer pulled the operator over for erratic driving. During a pat-down search, the moped driver was found with marijuana. All Joanne's brother had was a bomb in his jacket pocket. The bomb was not an "A.O. Misdemeanor." The explosive was described as a heavy glass bottle containing an "unknown granular substance resembling gunpowder or unknown compound with a fuse stuck in the opening of the bottle." At the time, policy didn't require an arson investigator to be notified upon discovery of a bomb so the officer made an arrest for the marijuana, took the bomb, released Joanne's brother, and booked the explosive into the property room; the basement directly below where I was standing. A bomb arrest is a good felony with the highest possible standard bail of any crime without enhancement—$60,000. I remembered the powerful homemade bomb that shattered Ray's house not long ago and rushed to the basement to examine this new explosive. It was a bomb and sat on a high shelf among stolen TVs, stereos and files. The filler didn't appeared to be gunpowder, but a homemade compound of chemicals that created a solid explosive. A blend such as this was sensitive to detonation by friction, static electricity, dropping, jarring or by the fuse. A gunpowder filler was stable compared to this stuff. Tom Rickles and I discreetly checked the yard at the home of the moped driver and saw scorch marks and shattered plastic shards strewn about. We got a search warrant that afternoon and stormed the house that evening. A small amount of explosive material was recovered along with bomb-making books, military manuals and a small marijuana farm in the kid's closet. Dad said he wasn't aware of anything blowing up in the side yard and nothing about the hydroponic farming in his son's closet. Both juveniles were arrested and readily admitted they were on their way to bomb Ray's house again when stopped by the cop. Joanne paid them to harass Ray in hopes he would think a jealous boyfriend and/or husband was troubling him. She wanted Ray to drop all his lady friends and concentrate on her. We asked about the fire on Joanne's porch. The brother said he set it at Joanne's instruction. She hoped the detectives would take the focus off of her as a suspect. He made the final decision on this decidedly male fire. She was in deep now. We arrested her, too, and closed the case with convictions on all three. It was gratifying to have profiled the fire scenes correctly. Except the gasoline blaze, the fires appeared set by a female as attention-getters. Even though Joanne didn't actually set the fires, she directed the boys on exactly what she wanted done right down to where the trash was kept behind the garage and where to place the bags next to Ray's prized car.

With Joanne and her gang out of the way we focused on the Pogo situation. We considered a surveillance, but figured Pogo would try to behave for a while before his jail stretch. Two nights later, the weightlifter's Mazda burned. We missed the chance to catch Pogo on the job. This was a revenge fire. While Pogo served his time, I caught a call-out to the scene of a burned Mercedes Benz convertible. The car was stolen after a residential burglary of the expensive home of an elderly couple. Guns, jewelry and household items were piled into the car and the crooks fled, unnoticed. The resident husband was the founder of the successful Hugh's market chain. Both well into their 80s, in poor health and sedated, the couple did not hear a thing as the house was ransacked. Less than an hour after the burglary, the Mercedes was set on fire, put in gear, and allowed to roll into the side of Toll Junior High School, just a ½ mile from the couple's home. I examined the fire scene for cause and origin and discovered the blaze set on both front seats at the same time. No flammable liquids were used. My report was taken to the auto theft detectives and they kissed the case off to burglary. I sent a copy of my report to burglary. A phone call to a caretaker was the only follow-up performed by the burglary detail. One of the burglary detectives was friendly so I asked him to assign the case to me. After a sergeant's approval and a smirk or two, the burglary/auto theft/arson report was mine. I had a lot on my plate but I felt the case was workable. The Mercedes was used to transport the stolen items somewhere and then dumped less than an hour after the crime. I verified the timing and felt the burglars lived close to the dump site. Since they stole the car to begin with, they didn't have their own transportation. When they dumped the flaming evidence, they again were without wheels so the abandonment took place close to the home of at least one of the crooks. This was a theory, but it was pretty obvious there were a multitude of clues overlooked by auto theft and burglary detectives. I was not an ace investigator yet, but was moving in close to a king's position. A chance interview divulged two possible suspects, Larry and Ron, and a probable neighborhood where Larry lived. No last names yet; just basic descriptions. The neighborhood was less than two blocks from the Mercedes dump site. Canvassing the locality gave me the possible house. I wore a public service department shirt to blend in with the area as I worked. Posing as the city water and power department, a phone call gave me a specific address. It was my first undercover operation. A ruse later got me to the front door where I learned Larry left town but personal items remained in his bedroom. With a typically scruffy appearance and longer-than-regulation hair, I fit in with Larry's associates. I successfully played the part of a friend of Larry's, looking to discuss "business." We obtained a photo of Larry and he was ID-ed as the suspect who was actually in the Hugh's home with Ron at a small party the night of the crimes. A search warrant was served that night when we recovered two guns and a few personal items belonging to the victims. Larry left town to visit relatives at an unknown location but we obtained an arrest warrant and put it in the national system. A month later, Tom and I flew to New Mexico to extradite Larry Garcia. Arrested by Santa Fe police and held on our warrant, Larry refused to talk to us on the flight back. We still had an outstanding suspect. Larry, the Hugh's burglar, had a preliminary hearing 10 days after we got back from New Mexico. In an unusual move, Larry took the witness stand and blamed everything on Ron, a guy Larry said he met the evening of the burglary. As the investigating officer in the case, I sat next to the deputy D.A. and Larry's Public Defender just to my left and the defendant to his lawyer's left. After testifying, Larry stepped down and sat next to his attorney. The D.A. talked with the judge as the hearing wound to a conclusion. I shuffled my reports and heard the Public Defender speak to his client. "Larry, that was good. You did good." Larry whispered something to the lawyer and he responded, "Well if they don't find Moreno, they ain't got a case!" Larry was held-to-answer despite his innocence pleas. They continued to chat while the D.A. droned on. I smiled like a 70-year-old geezer getting a lap dance. What do I do now? Was the conversation I overheard an attorney/client privileged discussion? If I put "Ron" and "Moreno" together and found Larry's partner, was this a breech of ethics? Tempted to ask the D.A., I remained mute. Tom and I discussed the situation since he was my training officer, and decided to see where the case went. Two Ron Morenos were located in the Glendale Police files and one was a good physical match to the description given by our witness. I ordered a copy of Ron's booking photo from another case and placed it in a photo spread with five other similar-looking guys. The witness positively identified Ron's photo. We located him just outside the Glendale city limits. His Uncle was an LAPD detective I went to high school with. He was in custody within hours of the ID with a confession that implicated both him and Larry. A trial wasn't necessary. A deal was cut and the case pleaded out with Larry doing state prison time and Ron getting probation. Three more incendiary devices were found in a brush area on the south side of Glendale on Marion Drive, the location of an annual brush fire or two. One was a cigarette device with matches attached and the others were plastic film canisters filled with diesel fuel and cigarettes jammed into a hole in the top. The canister devices failed.

My first published article came out in the August 1982 issue of the *American Fire Journal*. I wrote about our unique experiences with the live fire training burns in March 1981. The editor, John Ackerman, asked for more articles. While exploring the area around Pogo's home to set up surveillance procedures, Tom and I spotted two guys walking with stuffed pillowcases. There was no Laundromat around so we tailed them to a parked car two blocks away. The pillowcases had hard, sharp-edged bulges unlike any dirty clothes we'd ever seen. Affecting a traffic stop, we felt we both had enough experience with burglars to find out what these birds were up to. They had burglarized a home just two blocks from where we picked up their trail. In their possession was over $3,000 in jewelry, cameras and other personal items. Our unit was on its way to another successful year but we weren't through yet. A six night-long surveillance of Pogo was conducted the week he was released from jail. After 11 p.m., he prowled each night alone and on foot from his parent's home. We watched him enter several unlocked cars, rifle the glove boxes and prowl some more. At one point he peeped into the window where an 8 and a 10-year old girl slept. Pogo spent over an hour just staring at the girls, illuminated by a night light by their bed.

We could not get close enough to observe his actions but prepared to move in if he attempted entry. Half of the six shadowing cops wanted to administer street justice on him based on his peeping alone. He did not set any fires for the six nights we tailed him. Agreed beforehand, we would arrest only if he set a fire. The surveillance was terminated. On December 3, 1982, I was contacted at home and advised of a Volvo set on fire four blocks from Pogo's home. Only 10:30 p.m.—early for Pogo's M.O.—it pleased me to be called out to a fire instead of finding out about it days later. Just two blocks from the blaze, I spotted Pogo walking with another guy and two girls. Pogo was a loner. He was never with anybody else. Their travel was from the direction or the car fire. Our new unit vehicle was a dark blue 4-door Dodge Aspen and looked like a middle-manager's rental car. I was quick on my response to Engine Five's request for assistance so I drove onto a darkened side street and parked. The crew could wait an extra five minutes. Watching Pogo through binoculars, I saw one couple break off and walk north while Pogo and his girl headed east onto the 1500 block of Rockglen Avenue toward my position. Engine Five waited. Slipping away down a side street, I covered the three blocks in less than a minute, leaving Pogo and his lady friend to the tree-shrouded avenue. The Volvo was damaged minimally by a gasoline-soaked rag stuffed into the gas fill opening and ignited. Only the paint was scorched. There was no explosion as TV usually shows. The right fuel/air mixture does not exist at the fill pipe and will not allow a fire or explosion to develop. Water on the ground by the car indicated a neighbor extinguished the burning rag—maybe a good witness. I shined my flashlight down the fill pipe and it showed no fuel in the pipe itself. The rag was soaked with gasoline and brought to the car. Not Pogo's M.O., but then, he was with people now, not alone. Maybe he became more aggressive and demonstrative when he had an audience. A police unit arrived and as I told the uniform to take a report from the victim I heard three beeps on the fire radio. "Engine Five, are you available for a vehicle fire, 1500 block of Rockglen?"

Five's captain looked at me in question and I replied, "Yeah, take the call. I'll meet you there." Pogo was last seen in that block. I asked the cop to guard the scene while I went to find Pogo and roared off before Engine Five's crew mounted up. I sneaked onto the 1600 block of Rockglen from the east end after driving right by Pogo's house. I didn't see him. As I pulled onto Rockglen, I turned away from the blazing car and slowly U-turned, parking well up the street in the dark. The fire was about 100 yards west of me. Huge, overhanging trees lined both sides of the block and the fire appeared to be in a tunnel. I scanned the area with my Bushnell's, looking for Pogo. Engine Five's siren wailed in the distance as I spied movement next to a cypress tree about halfway to the blaze. Pogo had an interesting profile with an over-sized nose. It was he, silhouetted by a porch light, staying in the shadows of the tree next to an apartment building. I kept my binoculars on him with one hand and radioed Engine Five with the other. I told the captain to very delicately extinguish the fire to preserve any possible evidence and let him know I had a suspect nearby. Pogo stepped back into the shadows as two people emerged from the apartment and walked by him on the sidewalk. He returned to his position as the couple strode toward the blaze. In hiding and afraid before, Pogo now felt comfortable exposing himself to blend in with the bystanders. It fascinated me to watch him. His hands were deep in his pockets as he tentatively walked a few paces behind the gawkers. Standing in the edge of a group of the curious, Pogo trans-formed from the withdrawn, insecure and in-hiding arsonist to just another interested neighbor. He animatedly chatted with several of his new companions. His girlfriend was not visible. Engine Five rolled up and, in a minute, stretched a 1½ line and darkened the blaze. As soon as the flames disappeared Pogo was through. He lost interest and, like a post-coital Lothario, got up and left. His shoulders drooped and he cast his eyes to the ground while he strolled, hands in his jacket pocket. Between us was a small side street known as Zinnia Lane, leading to his house. As he approached the corner, I pulled out of my space and idled along with lights on as if I were looking for an address. He seemed a bit nervous at my approach and looked back at Engine Five several times. When he reached Zinnia I did a stupid thing; I gunned the car and aimed it towards him to see if he'd act like an innocent person and be startled or spook like a coyote caught leaving the chicken coop. He canined and loped down Zinnia Lane. In a four-wheel slide I turned onto the side street, hit the high beams and called in the cavalry. "Station, 51 Frank, I'm in foot pursuit southbound Zinnia from Rockglen!" I wasn't even out of the car yet but figured I'd end up chasing the freak. Pogo surprised me and stopped when I honked. I slid to a stop next to him. He was six feet tall, about 180 pounds and 19-years-old. Arsonists are weak and insecure but he was almost a cornered animal and I didn't want to push him any further. Police sirens yelped in the distance as I jumped out and Pogo meekly assumed the search position on a wooden fence. I didn't have to ask, he just knew that's where he was going to end up. I got back on the radio, "Station, 51 Frank. Got the suspect, pant, gasp, at gunpoint, Zinnia just north of Maple." I faked the breathing like I'd been running. A little melodrama never hurt. I was grandstanding but needed a bit of credibility on the cop side. It added to the re-telling of the story, too. I guess I was as insecure as Pogo, in some ways.

As the first police unit roared up I almost forgot to take my gun out to complete the scenario I'd just broadcast a minute earlier. With my back-up on-scene and Pogo on the fence I stepped up to frisk him. Instantly I smelled gasoline. In his jacket pocket was a plastic bag and in it was the source of the fumes. I had probable cause to detain but not to arrest. Running from a two-ton car bearing down on you is not illegal. The gasoline fumes did not connect him to the earlier fire yet. I needed something to solidify my detention so had the uniforms finish shaking him down and check his ID. I drove back to the fire around the corner. Engine Five's crew stood by, excited by two fires and the thought of being part of the pending arrest. They did a great job on the fire, using only a few gallons of water to extinguish the blazing MG convertible. Any more aggression and my probable cause to arrest might have been destroyed. At the curb across from where firefighters attacked the blaze were several fresh, clear sneaker shoe prints. Next to the prints was the plastic side window from the convertible top cut out before the fire and dropped on the ground. I called the cops and asked them to bring Pogo to me. He was wearing sneakers. The interior of the car was damaged, primarily in the area behind the passenger seat. The convertible top had burned, too, but the point of origin was clearly behind the seat, directly below where the plastic window was removed. I checked Pogo's shoe tread design. It was a match but I could not arrest him just yet. I had to officially declare the MG fire an arson. You cannot arrest a guy if the crime does not yet exist. Until I looked more thoroughly at the scene, this fire was assumed by the court to be an accidental fire. If and when I eliminated all accidental possibilities for this fire, I could declare it arson; not before. The Volvo attempt arson was prima facie: a gasoline-soaked rag stuffed into a fill pipe and ignited screamed intentional even to the layman. I was, however, detaining Pogo for the MG fire. After picking around the remains and snapping a few photos, I turned around to see Pogo's girlfriend. She was doing a slow dance, like a toddler who had to pee, just a few feet from me. She lifted her feet slightly, made a half turn then scraped her toes on the ground. I thought she might be psychotic until I realized she was dancing right in the middle of Pogo's footprints in the dirt. I arrested her, then I arrested him, and looked around for anyone else who might want to join them. I was pissed. Fortunately I took several pictures of the footprints before they were destroyed. The two suspects were transported to the police station in separate cars. I drove to the station to interview them. The girlfriend admitted to witnessing Pogo setting both fires. The gasoline-soaked rag came from her garage, just up the street from the Volvo fire. He also borrowed her pocketknife to cut out the MG's window. She claimed he could not be stopped when she saw he was going to light the rag and set fire to the MG. He was spontaneous. She fled down the street after he set fire to a map book behind the seat of the MG. My observations confirmed she was not with Pogo when I parked down the street. She also added Pogo had bragged about setting several other car fires and one night he "blew up six cars at the same time." The 6-car-fire was just one block from where the MG fire and his arrest occurred. Pogo, too, confessed to the two fires the night he was arrested. Implicating himself in two other car fires, I filed seven counts of arson against him. He later took a deal for two felony counts and was sentenced to three years in state prison. Talking to Robin, the girlfriend, I learned that Pogo shared many characteristics with Vince, the pyro I arrested in October. They were emotional twins. Pogo was very insecure and had problems with his friends and didn't feel comfortable with girls either. He was a heavy drinker, reportedly consuming two six-packs of beer on a typical night. The insightful Robin said he normally was a loner and only functioned around groups or other individuals after drinking. Pogo was a thief, stealing constantly, according to Robin who had only recently started hanging out with him. Pogo could not hold a job, had recently been fired for the third time that year, and his parents threatened to throw him out of the house if he did not straighten up. The parallels between Vince and Pogo were uncanny. Arresting one psychologically-motivated fire-setter was fortunate for a novice like me, but two in less than three months was unheard of. Their post-arrest interviews also revealed eerily similar evasion of the truth. It was as if series fire-setters attended classes to train for the pyromaniac trade before going to "work." Did they have a script to study? When asked a pointed question about setting a fire, and the query was close to the truth, both Pogo and Vince rubbed their brows and claimed the onset of an excruciating headache that caused them to conveniently forget. "I had too much to drink that night," was another common statement they used to avoid an incriminating response or to justify an action. A few seconds later when the topic ventured back onto safer ground the migraine disappeared and responses were again animated. Pogo had been caught on-the-job and the female witness got him to confess to the Volvo and MG fires readily. His boast to Robin about how he "blew up six cars at one time" brought on the migraine and drinking binge excuse of memory loss or, at least, foggy recollection. An invisible witness brought him up the driveway near the carport, and he confirmed this, but the curtain dropped when I got him into the car of origin. Placing him at the carport fire scene the night of the blaze gave him opportunity and he had the means to set the fire. He said he watched the carport and six cars burn from a distance. As an aside, I let Pogo know, truthfully, that there was a wallet with three one-hundred-dollar bills that survived the blaze, tucked under the driver's seat in the car of the fire's origin. His jaw dropped, then he smiled slightly and shook his head. He was also shocked to learn we had a six-night surveillance on him. He never saw any of us. Several of the experienced shadows from the Glendale Police Department Special Enforcement Detail were sure Pogo was onto them or, at least, suspicious of the tail or same car driving by too many times. When I asked him about the window peeping the migraine got so bad I had to terminate the interview. Technically, Robin was an accomplice but it was a weak case. A good defense attorney would have her say she did not know why he wanted a gasoline-soaked rag and by the time she figured he was burning the MG she could not stop him. Running away as she did was a good response on her part—divorcing herself from his criminal actions. The DA decided not to file against her.

On December 15, 1982, I made a pick-up run to the police department. One of the documents in my box was a crime report of a small fire in a 7-11 in the north part of Glendale known as Montrose. The fire erupted in a rack of potato chips and snack foods. The fire department sent an engine for a "fire-now-out" report and the captain didn't notify me to respond. I was on-call the night of December 14 when the fire occurred. With only $5 of damage listed, I assumed that both the police officer and fire captain felt it was too small an incident to request an investigator. Only 7 p.m. when it happened, it was too early for the warm-bed syndrome. A burned cigarette butt was located under the rack so the blaze was easily blamed on a careless smoker, but the captain felt strongly enough the fire was arson-caused to ask for a police report. The filter cigarette was booked as evidence by the police officer. Fourteen years later when I was arrested for arson and murder, the prosecutors and investigators theorized I set this potato chip fire in 1982 with what they called the "Orr device": a cigarette with paper matches attached by a rubber band. Several of these devices were recovered in retail fires in January 1982 and Tom Rickles and I found a few in brush fire starts. The prosecution and investigators overlooked the obvious in their theory; a 7-11 store is small, the clerk posted only eight feet from the entrance. The police report stated the store only had a few customers in and out prior to the fire's discovery. It was a slow period. If I had set an incendiary device in this 7-11's snack foods rack, I was forced to walk by or be seen by the clerk either on the way in or out. The potato chip rack was eight feet from, and almost in line with the check-out. Even if the clerk was busy upon the arsonist's entry or exit, this seems an unreasonable risk for the criminal to take. I was on-call and expected to respond for investigation within 30 minutes of this fire's discovery. It does not stand to reason I would set this fire then risk being recognized when I came back to investigate. Granted, I did not get called out to this fire but there was no way to predict that fact. This fire was caught very quickly because the clerk was close by and paying attention; however, he could provide no description of customers who were in minutes before the fire started. The prosecutors and investigators who theorized I set all the potato chip fires in the 80s were part of that high percentage of employees who just punch the time clock and haven't a clue or any insight of their jobs. Their collective shortsightedness came close to getting me the death penalty for things I did not do. It was an investigation by assumptions.

I have found that incendiary device construction varies with the arsonist, his or her target type and location, prior history of success or lack of it with the components, and probably a degree of individuality in some cases. (Keep in mind the cigarette/match combination devices have about a 50 percent failure rate.) Individual characteristics could show a device to be a "signature" of one arsonist. In the 1970s and 80s, the FALN terrorist groups on the east coast constructed a particular type of bomb they used repeatedly. The components were identical. The device was successful, and timing of detonations and distance between multiple incidents showed more than one individual using the "signature" device. A similar situation occurred on the west coast when animal rights activists set near-simultaneous fires in stores selling furs, using identical incendiary devices over a state-wide area. The "signature" devices were use of components copied by members passing the construction plans verbally or in writing to rebels in other states. Thus, a "signature" device may simply be a design used by someone who had been trained by a successful bomber or arsonist or has read about the construction. The so-called "Orr device" of a cigarette, paper matches and a rubber band was never and could never be a "signature" device as later theorized by prosecutors and investigators in the cases against me. Except in the eyes of those unsophisticated, uncommitted employees. None of these men had arrested 19 serial fire-setters or identified and apprehended an additional 20. They were too busy sawing to sharpen the tool. The addition of one component to individualize a device might, however, give the incendiary a "signature." The use of coins attached to a cigarette device in a case I investigated in 1985 created a signature pattern but, as an expert witness, I could never go as far as testifying even the coin-tosser devices were used by only one person. The cigarette/match/rubber band device has been displayed in crime scene manuals and arson investigation texts as far back as the 1960s. Military explosives/incendiaries manuals provide similar descriptions with drawings and photos of devices used for time delay ignition of fuses and to set diversionary fires. These tomes are readily available to the public through college bookstores and military surplus outlets as well as at gun shows. The basic cigarette/match device, as opposed to the matchbook delays, is the most commonly depicted in the college texts and military volumes with the occasional variation of the use of tape or string to secure the matches. An additional fact remains that should have been discovered by the half-million dollar background investigation of me from 1991-98. Several investigators, notably Bill Donelly, a Glendale Police Department detective, examined all cases I worked from 1978-1991, when I was arrested. A thorough examination of these files would have revealed the discovery of the rubber band device in Glendale alone, occurring on 10-12 occasions—maybe more—during this 13-year period. On over half of those evidence recoveries I was with my partners at the time the fire started; reports verify this fact. With only a 10-12-minute maximum delay on the device, it would have been impossible for me to have set those fires and been "the only one who used" the cigarette/match/rubber band device. The incendiary is common and was even used in a popular 1980s movie about a military academy. I asked a serial arsonist I arrested in 1985 how he learned to construct his device. He replied, "I saw it done on TV." This was at least three years before the military academy movie came out. The prosecutors and investigators also pounded the drum about how the rubber band device was found more often in Glendale than anywhere else so, "it must have been used by Orr frequently." Bill Franklin, an L.A. County Fire Department investigator stated in a 1992 interview, "Those Glendale investigators always found devices. In my 22 years as a fireman and investigator I only found one." I think that says it all, Bill. Discounting the instances I was with my partners when the responsible device discoveries occurred (as opposed to a device found that had failed and didn't start a fire), Glendale investigators found more devices because they were more efficient than any other investigative unit. From the inception of the Glendale unit, the assigned investigators persisted in responding to small fires; the "nothing" trash and grass fires most fire agencies ignore. A grass fire that burns 300-square feet in an L.A. county or L.A. city areas would not warrant an arson investigation because it happens a dozen times a day and those agencies maintain less than 3-4 investigators per shift for hundreds of square miles and hundreds of fires per week. On the other hand, an agency covering three square miles and only 5 or 6 small grass fires per year will provide a part-time sleuth whose primary function is checking fire extinguisher tags and arson investigation is only a sideline. It stands to reason that Glendale found more devices and cleared more cases than other departments. I did not meet many investigators who fell into that small percentage of all workers who truly enjoy, understand and appreciate their job. It takes training and a lot of experience to recognize a burned cigarette in a field of charred grass or other fire debris. The cigarette ash appearance is unique; the burned paper matches stand out against blackened grass stalks and the peculiar bubbled remains of a rubber band exposed to flame are like camouflage to the novice, but not someone who has seen the remains before. Establishing an area and point of origin can be difficult and, if the investigator cannot get close to where a device will be, most end up tromping up and down along a path that sometimes includes the remains they are looking for. I have stepped on fire causes myself. Glendale investigators found more incendiary devices not because there were more arsonists using them in Glendale or because I knew where the devices lay because I set them there, but because we were experienced, trained and treated even small blazes as crime scenes. Clearing 37 percent of an arson cases in 1981 didn't come to us because arsonists surrendered. We worked for the clearances and got them through evaluation of every fire scene we could get to and tied series cases together. By the end of 1982 we had fewer arson incidents in Glendale and still maintained a solve rate four times the national average. Unfortunately, deterring serial arsonists is like trying to find and stop a serial murderer. Their compulsions are so overwhelming they have to commit the crime.

CHAPTER EIGHT
FIREBALLS

From December 1982 to January 1983, a series of fires in retail stores began. The fires, set in snack food sections and other common combustibles on sales floors during business hours, seemed perpetrated as diversions for shoplifters. I was unsure if my 7-11 fire was related to neighboring Burbank's blazes and in Los Angeles, Monrovia, and in L.A. County jurisdictions. Again, the cigarette/match device surfaced in several of the fires. There was also a retail clerk strike going on at the time and we considered the possibilities of that scenario, too. Tom and I saw no uniqueness to this common incendiary device and did not relate them to any of our fires or theorize a relationship to the retail series.

Glendale Fire Department investigators frequently assisted the understaffed Burbank arson unit. Investigators P.K. Spooner and Jack Mitchell were allowed minimal duty time to pursue arson cases, fire prevention details taking priority. When two potato chip rack fires erupted within minutes of each other on the Glendale/Burbank border, Tom Rickles was on-call and took the assist request. One fire was ours and the other well into Burbank. Years later, Tom recalled that he and I were together at the time these fires occurred. I believe we were at an informal police officer retirement party at The Phone Company restaurant in Glendale when the call came in. I was too intoxicated to help Tom. The next day, Burbank received a tip on a possible suspect for the chip rack fires. The man, a 40-year-old truck driver employed by Hugh's Markets, lived in Glendale. Fired recently and known as a loner, he resided in a converted garage. His son was recently murdered in the San Fernando Valley and the crisis caused him to snap, according to our sources. This type of emotional trigger frequently initiates fire-setting sprees. Many of his characteristics fit the profile of a serial arsonist. Glendale volunteered to participate in a surveillance set up by the Burbank police and fire departments. L.A. City Fire Department representatives attended a pre-tail meeting but did not cooperate and join us. This was typical of the L.A.F.D. arson investigators. They did have an extreme workload and few detectives to handle their massive territory and huge number of suspicious fires. Interagency cooperation in the early 1980s was hit-or-miss. As it worked out, most of the fires were theirs, and the majority of our surveillance over the next week was in City of Los Angeles dominion. The suspect was followed for seven nights. On the first evening we tailed the man from his home directly to a Hugh's market in the nearby Cypress Park section of Los Angeles. The next five minutes were a frenzy to the shadowing team; pulses racing, stilted breathing and a heart rate like a golf ball fired into a closed ice chest.

Two of our shadows tailed him into the busy market. The first radio transmission from inside the store stunned us all: "All units, suspect just shoplifted a BIC lighter from an unmanned check-out. He's in the chip aisle." I don't think any of us on the outside breathed for the next minute. "Stand by...he's..." Again we waited, this time through four minutes of radio silence until, "he's out, heading for his truck," and the suspect started driving. The inside tails excitedly told us over the radio that the suspect entered a storeroom, tore a flap from a cardboard box into tiny pieces, piled them against filled cardboard boxes, then sat down, cross-legged, by his creation. One of the cops quietly clambered onto a mezzanine storage area for a better view. He watched the suspect feign using the lighter and pretend to light his cardboard "campfire." Then he acted as if the phantom fire was to keep warm and cupped his hands around the cardboard and rubbed his palms together. He did this for 2-3 minutes then got up and walked out of the store, unseen by any employees. One of the cops physically touched the faux fire to be sure. The man then drove through the San Fernando Valley for hours then went home. The next two nights he stayed home. On the third evening he drove back to the Valley and parked his truck at the Northridge Mall. Some of the recent fires had been set in retail stores. It looked like we might be in for another. The suspect stayed inside the mall wandering for 10 minutes then left, but not through the entrance he came in. He kept walking for two miles, as if in a daze. His truck remained in the parking lot. Instead of following him to Bakersfield, we decided to put a man on foot to befriend our lost soul and get him back to his vehicle. The ploy worked when our man, a Burbank PD sergeant dressed like a wino, struck up a conversation with the suspect at a bus bench. The sergeant got the guy to admit he was lost and gladly accepted an offer of a ride with a "friend" who was picking him up. After the suspect was returned to his truck, our sergeant got on the radio to tell us the guy was a "whack" as if we didn't know that already. But was he our whack? The whack drove to a country western bar on Ventura Boulevard where we all scattered around the dance floor and spent the next three hours drinking on the city expense money. After seven nights and only the first hour of the first night interesting, we terminated the surveillance. In the following week the suspect drew out $30,000 from his Hugh's credit union account and disappeared. No more chip or retail fires occurred for some time. Had our trucker gone "on the road?"

Fourteen years later, I was asked to provide alibi for myself during the late '82 and early '83 retail fire series. The fires were primarily nighttime blazes with some in the daytime hours as well. They were scattered all over Los Angeles County. The only alibi I could provide was the unverifiable fact I stayed home with my new family every night and during the day I was "married" to my partner, Tom Rickles. Finalizing and filing Pogo's case also kept me busy and I had to prepare for his preliminary hearing during the holiday season when some of these fires occurred. Fourteen years later, how can anyone prove where they were or what they were doing during certain time periods? I typically stayed home evenings helping the girls with homework, preparing brown bag lunches for the next day, and doing other Ozzie and Harriet-like family amusements. Our marriage was rocky but I worked at making it reasonably successful.

On January 23, 1983 I was headed for the north end of town on an interview when I spotted a column of gray/black smoke staining the clear sky about a mile away. Calling the report in to my dispatchers they advised 9-1-1 calls indicated a large home burning on Risa Drive. Before any rigs rolled up, I photographed the burning roof area of the 5,000-square foot home. The early pictures helped isolate the fire's origin and confirm an accidental cause after the blaze ripped off the attic and second floor. Fieldwork again placed me near a fire at its inception and ensured early determination of cause and origin. After fire units began arriving on Risa Drive, a second structure fire was reported just 2 miles away and less than a half mile from my original destination. No matter how you cut it, I would have been on the edge of an incipient fire on this day. The second fire was arson; gasoline poured on a service porch floor where the water heater pilot light ignited the blaze prematurely, engulfing the arsonist in a fireball. The injured man was tracked to a hospital burn ward 10 miles away where we arrested him and a companion later. The men, both veteran alcoholics, drank themselves enough courage to set the fire in an ex-girlfriend's home. Alcohol consumption was another commonality with arsonists. It was fascinating to interview the men separately and gain instant confessions from both. Showing a stunning lack of insight, these halfway intelligent losers had no difficulty admitting they were arsonists, but neither could cop to having a drinking problem no matter how I put it to them. They were social drinkers, consuming a quart of vodka each per day. Both were convicted of burglary, arson and conspiracy and did state prison time. In February 1983, Tom and I hosted a class, "Body Language Recognition for the Investigator." The first of over 16 programs Glendale put together for the F.I.R.S.T. organization, it was the only one to lose money. We brought a top-notch instructor, Tim May, from the National Fire Academy in

Maryland. Expenses ran high, but it was a great session. Twenty-eight students attended. Tom and I kicked in $100 each so the class actually broke even.

A small fire flared inside a Robinson's department store in Glendale in March. The blaze was arson. No device found and no suspect seen. It was a daytime fire. Tom and I were together when it started. Robinson's would burn again in 1990. In April we hosted a two-day "Vehicle Fire Investigation" seminar and actually burned eight donated cars for the students to investigate. Two of the fires were ignited by means of cigarette/match delays prepared by the outside instructors. Both devices functioned. This class was the first of a series of three we put together for the remainder of the year's training. The F.I.R.S.T. organization stagnated in 1983 and I felt we desperately needed specialized training to stimulate the membership. Designed for F.I.R.S.T. members, we offered the sessions to anyone interested. Forty-three fire, police and insurance investigators attended this class. A "Wildland Fire Investigation" class was presented in May as the second in the series. Tom, Walt Beatty and I set fifteen 50'x 50' plots of grass on fire using several different accidental and arson methods to ignite the training blazes. At least four cigarette/match devices were used by the three of us to ignite some of the fires. Students were broken down into 2-man teams to investigate the pre-burned plots. Incendiary devices, fireworks and even road flares are difficult to recognize after destruction in a grass fire. This live-fire training is the only way to become proficient at spotting the deteriorated remains of fire causes. The students were able to view 10-15 different scenes in a one-day class. Many of the students from smaller agencies would not see 10 fire scenes in two years, let alone one afternoon. Twenty-nine attended.

A fire in a three-story restaurant in mid-May nearly destroyed the business—or at least helped. It was called "Fins 'n Feathers." From the name, you'd think they served by-products. Apparently the public thought so, too. The fire only helped destroy the place; creditors already knew business was doomed—many hadn't been paid in months. The chicken and fish restaurant floundered. An extensive investigation revealed a former partner suffered fires to a rotting rental unit and a corroded Cadillac; both ended with sizable insurance recoveries. The man had only recently signed off on the failing business, giving it to two close friends. Sherry, had actually dated the former owner briefly. He had admitted to her the rental unit fire was "rewarding" and the insurance money paid for the necessary upgrading. He smiled broadly at the statement. After four search warrants and one arrest, the case, too, floundered. The D.A. wouldn't file and the rental and Cadillac fires were beyond the statute of limitations. Also in May, Tom was called out to a series of grass fires along the Foothill Freeway and nearby surface streets. He found a cigarette/match/rubber band device with a screw attached for weight. The distance from the roadway to the dry grass was substantial, thus, the screw was added to carry the device into the fuel. The basic device was identical to one seized over 10 years before in Chevy Chase Canyon in 1972. I don't recall where I was when these fires occurred so I didn't have an alibi. Case investigators, no doubt, theorized I set this series of fires, too.

After I was arrested in 1995 and charged with setting brush fires, my lawyer requested me to establish alibi for all these fires I was suspected of setting, even if I was not charged with them. How many people can establish where they were at 2:30 p.m. on May 23, 1983? I couldn't. For a brief period in the spring of 1983, I left Sherry and the girls. The marriage and concerns about the situation affecting my job caused me to flee for a while. There was never any question between Sherry and I that my career was a higher priority than the family. Sherry accepted that, but our emotional competition followed me to work and distracted me. After I moved out for a few days, Sherry visited me in my small cubicle at work while Tom was out. We had an air-clearing meeting where she pointed out to me I was again "running away" from problems like I did in my first two marriages. Instead of trying to stick with it like I did pursuing criminals, I walked around the block to avoid the real issues. She was, of course, correct. Taking refuge in work was more my style. She was immovable and had a debating style damnably convincing most of the time. Arguing with her in my tiny office with firemen walking by constantly was like trying to complete a sex act while waiting for a bus on Broadway. As the debate wound down we sipped some tea and she agreed to let me back into the house. She added, "If you ever empty your closet again, it's for good!" We toasted the arrangement, closed the mini-blinds and watched for the bus.

After the truce was struck with Sherry, I went to work on my relationship with my partner, Tom. We were like Nick Nolte and Eddie Murphy in *48 Hours*. After 2½ years together, I'd developed my own investigative styles and interview techniques. Tom had other responsibilities that took priority over work. I could not fault him for that but I resented his continuing condescension. He did not maintain my 24/7 motivated-employee work ethic. Tom was the training officer and I would forever be the "rookie." When he initially designed our business cards he used two badges as the logo in the upper corner. To conserve space, he overlapped the two images so the police badge partially covered the fire badge. He made a statement with that concept. Tom never quite got it—I did not want to be a cop, did not want to wear a uniform and even resented it when citizens and crooks spoke with me for a few minutes and said, "You're a cop aren't you?" I was a fireman. The good guy. All I wanted from Rickles was a little credit once in a while and same thing I craved from Sherry—equality. With Tom, I felt like the bitter middle-aged cynic who says at his father's funeral, "He never said he loved me." I just wanted acceptance. Like a typical couple married for a few years, we grew apart, but he later did change the badge concept—the fire badge on top. Tom became an administrator. With his new personal computer, he developed forms for interviews, forms for scene investigation and forms to keep track of forms. He spent many hours on a program to recover fire and police department costs from negligent hazardous material handlers, businesses with repeat false alarms that necessitated fire responses, and even from parents of kids who set fires and tied up our resources because of their negligence. The program was needed and brought credit to our unit and department. Tom became very active in the California Conference of Arson Investigators, joining the board of directors and moving into line for the various seats leading to presidency of the organization in 1987. However, he lost the edge for investigations. I inherited some of his cases when there were workable clues and he did not have time, or else refused to chase down leads. I gladly accepted good cases; my motive always to keep our clearance rate high. Open, unsolved cases lowered our 'case closed' statistics, reflecting poorly on both of us. For a while in 1983, I considered leaving the unit. Maybe working at a fire station as a firefighter was a way to give me more time with Sherry and the girls and I would not have to deal with Sherry reminding me, "Don't run away from your problems. Stand up and assert yourself. Work with it." The lady affected me. I decided to stay in the fire investigation unit. In July, a series of small fires occurred in a quiet residential area in the affluent Oakmont section of Glendale. We were not called out to one, a small grass fire by a mailbox on Thursday night. On Friday night Tom responded to another roadside grass fire 100 feet from the other. The third fire on Sunday night was apparently a false alarm. No investigator was notified. On Monday I took over on-call status and decided to check out the neighborhood. Just off the roadway I found a unique Molotov cocktail; a Coke bottle filled with gasoline and wooden matches stuck into the opening and secured with duct tape. The incendiary was placed at the side of the road; not thrown and broken to go off spectacularly. It was possibly the fire our crews could not find Sunday night and called it a false alarm. The matches burned out and the Molotov did not go off like the maker planned. I profiled the scene. One house and one house only had a view of all three fire sites. The arsonist would have to otherwise hide on a steep brush-covered hillside to watch the blazes after ignition. A Molotov was a masculine, aggressive gasoline-fueled device but it was not thrown; it was placed. Contradictory and baffling. The two grass fires were small and could not burn aggressively from their area of origin. There was no more dried grass, brush or fuel to allow propagation. These were simply "I want attention" fires. I theorized an 8-12-year-old male, afraid or too insecure to lob the bomb but ballsy enough to strike a match, set a grass fire and ran like hell. I left and had my dispatcher pal, Sue Saurer get the 9-1-1 callback location of the reporting parties on all three incidents. This was Tom's case initially but he had no desire to pursue it Monday morning. He was on-scene at his call-out fire for less than fifteen minutes. Sue came through for me, as usual. A police dispatcher for many years, she was extremely efficient. When Tom came over to the fire department, he recruited her to get away from the pettiness of the police station and join us. She gladly made the change and it was our gain. She went beyond my request. All three calls originated from the same house and she provided the name of the caller. Sue recognized the caller's name, too. Tina, who had worked at the police department in the past year, had called all three times. She was an explorer and performed menial filing and administrative functions in various parts of the police station while attending training to prepare for a career in law enforcement. Sue directed me to police officer Karen Krause, who knew Tina when she was an explorer before Tina was fired. Sue said she had heard police station gossip about Tina but didn't want me to pre-judge the girl based on rumors. She said, "Talk to Karen. Karen knows it all." Karen, a close friend of my former police officer girlfriend Rachel Foster, readily agreed to discuss Tina. Karen and I had lunch and coffee together a few times and I knew I could trust her to keep our conversations secret. Her own experiences with condescending cops were identical to mine and cops were supposed to protect each other anyway. My fire scene profile of the series fires being male-caused was slightly off-center. Karen brought me into focus. She described Tina as the daughter of a high-powered local attorney, with no mother around. Tina's desire for a police career did not sit well with Daddy. He wanted better things for her but she enrolled in the explorer program anyway. She had a rebellious and nonconformist streak, according to Karen. Tina did not fit in well with groups and was generally uncomfortable, trying to use her police-related work as an ego builder. These characteristics filled a few checkboxes in the serial arsonist column for me. Karen added that Tina was fired after being suspected of theft on two occasions. The last theft involved a stolen police badge from a locker room. Tina was the last one in the area where the badge was lifted. Petty theft history is another characteristic in the profile of a series fire-setter. My Molotov showed a more aggressive male-like tendency, but it was placed, not thrown, indicating insecurity or a female bent. Tina was an attractive 19-

year-old, had very short hair, and preferred wearing masculine attire; jeans or corduroy pants, men's shirts with long sleeves and buttons as opposed to feminine pullovers. I ventured a guess, "Karen, could Tina be a lesbian?" A masculine female would account for the semi-aggressive Molotov. Karen reluctantly replied, "I like to deal in facts. Something you can call evidence and present in court. I can't solidly say Tina is a lesbian but I think she looks and acts masculine. I can give you some names of her co-workers who can give you facts but I won't go there." That was enough for me. I went to Internal Affairs and talked with the assigned lieutenant, trying to get a clearer profile of Tina and the badge theft. He snickered at my profile and would not let me look at Tina's file. He confirmed the theft allegations and, in typical cop fashion, openly discussed the rumors about her sexual orientation. The lieutenant asked me who my source was since I apparently had good information already. The lieutenant wanted me to reveal my exact sources. I told him, "I won't give up a brother officer...Code of Silence, you know..." I hope Karen will forgive me the sexist reference. I already considered a search warrant for Tina's home to recover components of the arsons. I needed more information on the badge and other thefts to enable me to keep my eye out for them during a search but the IA guy refused.

That night another fire occurred but we did not know about it. No 9-1-1 call was received. The blaze erupted 100 feet west of Tina's swimming pool in an area accessible only through her side yard. A couple of bushes burned and Tina put out the fire with a garden hose and did not call it in. I drove up to survey the street and get a good description of the house for the search warrant. As I fooled around, Tina came out and approached me. I wasn't quite ready to interview her but opportunity knocked and she told me about the fire the night before. I called it in and had Engine Four come over to take a report. I'd need the documentation to prosecute. Tina stood about five feet six inches and carried a little extra weight. With a pretty pageboy haircut, she was neat, clean and talkative when we discussed the fires. Her movements were almost swaggering and definitely masculine, not fluid and graceful. I asked to see the new fire scene and she said she had to lock up her dog. The beast roared inside the house since my arrival. How could an arsonist get close to this house? The fire scene at the side of the house was at the end of the hillside cut. A steep drop-off to a home below cut off access to the burned bushes. Only a mountain goat could get to this area of the yard without walking by the house and I saw no hoof prints. The fire captain and his crew showed up, grumbled at having to take a report on a cold fire scene, and left. There were about fifty wooden matches scattered around the area of origin. Some burned, some partially consumed and some intact. The matches were identical to those on the

Molotov. The varied condition of the matches indicated they were bundled, then lit, possibly thrown, and when they hit the ground or the binder burned, some of them were scattered out of the fire area. The ground around the bushes was still damp from Tina's extinguishment efforts. She said she didn't see the matches the night before. Several outside lights lit the pool and side yard area and, even at night, the matches would have been visible. Tina, not expecting such questions, said that when her father was gone she left all the outside lights on for security. Father gone? Interesting. I believe she extinguished this fire when it began to spread aggressively towards a steep, brush-covered lot leading to several homes.

I pretended to look for an access point for an intruder to get through the yard and intentionally led her to a rear entry to the garage. The dog continued to bark just inside the bathroom window. I thought to myself, no way anyone got into this yard without Fido sounding off. Most of the house windows were open. Tina assured me the garage was secured the night before but the rear door left unlocked. She opened it and led me through the garage where the larger door was already open. Tina confirmed the garage door was closed during last night's fire, but not locked, and could be lifted easily. I scanned a workbench as I walked by – duct tape right on top. The trash area: three, one-quart Coke bottles sitting at the base of a water heater. They matched the Molotov found across the street.

I told her I was worried about her, "When is your dad coming home?"

"Tomorrow," she replied.

"Has he been gone long?"

"Since Wednesday night." The first fire was Thursday night. Lonely Tina? Needed some attention?

I was alone with her and concerned about our usual policy of having at least two investigators present when with a solitary female. Remembering how Vince and Pogo finally opened up to me when we were alone I decided to chance the interview. She must have read my mind and offered me something to drink. We went to the kitchen and she poured me Coke from a one-quart glass container. A large box of kitchen matches nestled on a shelf above the stove.

I did not intend to arrest her at the moment no matter what she confessed. Suspects are so much more cooperative when you tell them, "I'm not going to arrest you today. I have to report to the police sergeant and I'm just a fireman...The cops make all the legal decisions..." A non-custodial interview, when no arrest is imminent and the suspect is free to go, or throw you out, does not require a Miranda warning. Miranda slams doors; a non-custodial interview establishes rapport.

My opening statement about not arresting her that day got her attention. I guess she thought she could tell me everything and I might forget later. We verbally waltzed around the loneliness factor and I showed empathy whenever she became emotional. In minutes, I had a friend. She could not explain her reasons for the fires except she was "bored." I minimized the fact there was no damage done and she wisely extinguished the latest fire before it could spread, giving her a little hero-worship for her good sense. She liked that. I liked her. Tina had problems and Dad seemed to be at the root of them. I felt Dad's vacation without her may have been an emotional "trigger" that set off Tina's negative emotions and actions. Like Pogo and Vince's loss of jobs, pending evictions and general depression were their "triggers," Tina's feelings of neglect and abandonment by Father caused her fiery actions. Maybe it went deeper than that. I predicted there would be problems with Dad when he got home and found out his daughter was to be arrested. Then I recalled he was a lawyer. This could get interesting.

I made a stab at getting one last crime cleared up – the police badge theft. I'd love to have been able to hand the shield to the Internal Affairs lieutenant. I could easily get a search warrant and try to find it but it was a police matter. I remembered the lieutenant's smirk at my arsonist profile of Tina. Fuck them. They can get their own search warrant. Tina denied the theft and if she did it the badge was either buried in the backyard or would soon disappear now that I mentioned it. I wasn't about to ask for a consent search. My case was already cleared.

As promised, I didn't arrest her and terminated the interview; she was prosecutable for only two counts. The first fire damaged someone else's grass and was a violation. The Molotov construction and ignition was a solid felony even if it did not do any damage. The other two fires burned Daddy's grass and bushes. No doubt he would not be a victim for my case. Tina needed help, support and some guidance, not jail time.

The next day I filed the two counts and asked her to surrender herself. I would not handcuff and drag her in, the event difficult enough for her to be processed by jailers she had worked with at the Glendale Police Department.

I did not need to talk to her father, she was over 18, but knew he would call. He did. The contact was not good; he in his defense attorney mode. When I said my recommendation of an own-recognizance release and no jail time instead of bail and jail time, he cooled off. It put the case to rest and I never was called for a preliminary hearing. A deal was cut. I never saw or heard from Tina again. I did not expect to. She was not going to set any more fires. Her father was killed one year later when the private plane he was piloting crashed. I considered calling Tina to see how she was holding up, but didn't.

Like developing a character in a novel, I think my concern for Tina was defining for fire department investigators, in general, as well as for myself. Firefighters care for people and emotionally are attached to their communities and public. There are not many cops who would consider the feelings of someone they arrested. I never bought a beer for a guy I arrested but many times chatted with them amicably when we met on the streets; even the three I shared jail facilities with years later.

The Tina case was Tom Rickles caper but he chose to ignore the leads. I couldn't be too upset about it. Tina helped develop my expertise and validate scene profiling as an investigative tool. Three years down the road I would provide training that hinted at gender-specific fire scenes and using crime site location, time of day or components used to set a fire as keys to open the door to a suspect. In 1983 I was still a novice. It has been said, and I agree, that it takes about five solid years for an arson investigator to master his trade. I was still an unknown in the field but had the pleasure to work in a city that had the foresight to provide two full-time investigators to attack the crime of arson. One arson fire could cause more damage than lost through robberies or burglaries over a 2-3 year period in our city. We were trying to live up to the city father's expectations.

Fourteen years after the Tina case, in my trial on arson and murder charges, Karen Krause, my informant, would turn on me with a vengeance. She forgot to deal in facts and enhanced her memory of conversations held years before, to fit the prosecution's theories. I do not hold it against her. She suspected, wrongly, I had killed her sister-in-law.

Sherry and I split in September 1983. The martial difficulties were affecting my work and demeanor in general. I couldn't risk my career and what I had developed so I "ran away" again. The split was difficult with our girls directly involved. Sherry and I remained cordial and I still picked the kids up from school and participated in school and day care events as Daddy. I provided child support and we bought a car to replace Sherry's aging Pontiac. We still "dated" but the relationship stabilized as a good friendship. I many times considered reconciliation but Sherry would not discuss it. When I closed the door it was for good. I was grateful for the door opening just far enough to still be part of their family. I moved in with my private investigator friend, Bill McLaughlin and his wife Judy in a three-bedroom hilltop home in the infamous Chevy Chase Canyon. Bill charged me $250 a month rent.

In September 1983 F.I.R.S.T. hosted a one-day "Fire Death Investigation" class, the last of our series-of-three sessions for the year. Over 70 police and fire department investigators joined us to hear Jim Allen from the California State Fire Marshal's Office. Jim's presentation was fascinating, morbid and informative. Internationally known, Jim took his training on the road and taught in such far-flung places as Hawaii and Yellowknife in the Yukon. We were pleased he was a frequent visitor to the L.A. area from his home in the heart of wine country in Santa Barbara County, California. With 16 years law enforcement experience, as a deputy sheriff, he joined the State Fire Marshal's Office and became the premier fire investigator in the state. Jim became a standard in area investigation classes and a close friend. He was on my visitor's list at Lompoc Penitentiary.

My article, 'Problems of the Firefighter Turned Investigator,' came out in the November issue of the *American Fire Journal*. The piece outlined difficulties I experienced when transferred from being a smoke-eater into the world of fire law enforcement. I felt exposing these situations could help firefighters who found themselves in a similar predicament. Focusing on poor police-fire relationships, I continued to try and smooth the petty jealousies I found occurring between these agencies all over the state, not just in my jurisdiction. I was paid $106 for the piece and could now call myself a professional writer.

December 1983 was, thankfully, uneventful and I enjoyed the holiday season despite my estrangement from Sherry. With my girls, Carrie and Lori, Sherry and the rest of the family drove into the Angeles National Forest for our annual tree-in-the-wild decorating event. The girls helped string a popcorn garland, dress a small pine with bread and nut ornaments as well as collect tons of mistletoe from surrounding oaks, The local birds and squirrels had an early celebration.

CHAPTER NINE
FIRE & BRIMSTONE

As a firefighter-turned investigator, I enjoyed the best of working in both fields: the fire service and law enforcement. Having two sets of friends and co-workers caused me no grief. The law enforcement family keeps to themselves and the majority treats outsiders as just citizens—contributors to the tax base paying their salaries. I shied away from fraternization with police personnel off-duty, except when specifically invited by my current police partner. A few of the veteran police staff considered me a passerby, at best; an intruder at worst. No problem. I created the bed I reclined on and was comfortable with making my required daily visits to the police building after 5 p.m. when most cops were gone for the day. I had better access to the computers, friendlier records clerks, and amiable contact with detectives who stayed late and dedicated themselves to public service like I did.

In January 1984, I renewed an old friendship with a woman from my Sears days. She lived in Pasadena and frequented clubs in Glendale where I ran into her one evening on a surveillance at a jazz lounge. The nightspot suffered a series of phony bomb threats and the suspect's telephonic raids indicated familiarity with the inside of the place. One of the calls may have actually emanated from the payphone at the rear by an alley exit. Judy showed up one evening and we enjoyed a few drinks on the city, and continued our relationship for several months. The threats stopped after we posted the bomb threat penal code section next to the payphone at the club, and one in the fleabag hotel next door. One suspect resided there. The ploy worked. No more free drinking on the city tab, despite encouragement by a city councilman who frequented the club.

Sheila, my ex-wife, remarried and moved into Chevy Chase Canyon, near my new home. Her new husband was a Glendale city engineer. Sheila joined me for lunch a few times, near the Bank of America in South Pasadena where she was the loan officer, and drinks a time or two at the Nightwatch on the Eagle Rock/Pasadena border. She became an excellent source of training and information in finance.

My gracious new roommates, Bill and Judy, kept me occupied when I was not on a date or out for the evening on work-related forays. Our little adult family ate out often, usually on some insurance company's dime or Bill's expense account, and frequently discussed Bill's unique insurance fraud cases, or mine. He loaned me expensive eavesdropping equipment once when our firefighter's association/union haggled over a particularly hostile contract negotiation with the city's team. Bill and I ran into three of the fire department's mediators at a local cantina where the plot to bug the city hall negotiations room was hatched. We thought the pre- and post-daily meetings might reveal the city's true bottom line figures. Under the influence of several pitchers of margaritas, the plan sounded good. Not so much the next day. We did not follow through. I needed to test the equipment so put the bug in the secretary's break room instead to test the device. It worked just fine. I never found an occasion to use the bug in a case but it was reassuring to have it available.

Through networking at F.I.R.S.T. training sessions, I befriended a representative of Litton Industries. We were able to borrow expensive night vision equipment for surveillances free of charge on two occasions from this very helpful man. I couldn't justify a $3K-5K purchase for such toys in our small unit and he knew it, but Litton was known for their pro-law enforcement assistance and community support.

The longer I spent away from firefighting, the less familiar I was with my actual position of firefighter. Still carried on the books as a fireman, I got behind on knowledge of changes in tactics, strategies and equipment. The unit was on the fire department's mailing list for training bulletins but copies were seldom routed to us. It was the same for police communications. A take-home car, massive amounts of unlimited overtime, and no direct supervision made the arson unit positions the premier jobs in the city as far as we were concerned, but I truly missed working the firehouse. Another captain's test was coming up and I was not getting enough study time so I volunteered to work the fire station on Saturday or Sunday. During a 24-hour period at a fire station, I could access up-to-date training bulletins and manuals, get some actual drill as well as absorb knowledge from the line firefighters. I could also cook again. When living with Sherry, I prepared meals frequently but at home now, Bill was gourmet king. I could not get near the kitchen except to help clean up or sample his treats. Working a firehouse shift, I used my recipes again and I believe the firefighters appreciated the variety of meals I prepared. Working at a fire station on a weekend day and getting paid for it was like being a bouncer at a sports bar; hanging with the guys, watching football, and eating heartily. I got my fix of adrenaline from the emergency calls we answered. All this and $250-$300 overtime pay.

In early 1984, I worked at Station One, where my office was, as-signed to Truck Company One on a Saturday. We spent a quiet day until just after 1 a.m. Toned out to a structure fire on the Glendale/Los Angeles border, the address was definitely in Los Angeles Fire

Department territory. We had an agreement with them to cover this narrow industrial strip while their units responded from three miles south. The alert tone was new and mild compared to the old fire bells that used to assault us to consciousness. Before I realized it, I was riding next to a high-winding diesel motor the size of a Yugo and blasting through the streets of Glendale. I couldn't recall jumping out of bed, hopping into my boots and sliding a pole 30 feet to the apparatus floor. My first memory was of the siren blaring and the truck clearing the station. You don't get that kind of rush from being a meter reader or insurance salesman. Turning around in my jump seat, I peered out the front window of the ladder truck and saw a column of thick black smoke pushed into the sky by an explosive pulsing mass of flames. I didn't think it possible to increase my heart rate but was proven wrong. Two minutes later we crossed the railroad tracks and our 60-foot long truck serpentined through a small parking lot dodging parked trucks, dumpsters and police cars. L.A.F.D. wasn't on-scene yet; we were first-in. Donning my breathing apparatus, I stepped around the rig to finally see what confronted us. A small 20-foot long-house trailer, parked against a wooden warehouse, blazed away. The trailer fire leaped to the structure and it was well involved. Engine One caught a hydrant and, while their crew hooked up, two of us from the truck company stretched a 2½" hose line and advanced it to the fire. The captain led me into the blazing structure. The 2½" line was used to knock down the outer wall fire and prevent the spread beyond the house trailer. We walked through a destroyed wall, clambering over fire-damaged boxes enveloped in steam, smoke, and tremendous heat, snaking the 2½" line inside. When we set foot on the concrete storeroom floor it was like stepping on ice wearing glass slippers. I went down before we ever opened the nozzle. When I got up, the captain went down. Bracing ourselves against piles of unburned boxes and their contents, we finally cracked the nozzle and hit the flames. Gaining a foothold we advanced five feet, only to slide back ten when the nozzle reaction pushed against us on the slick floor surface. Visibility was near zero. I remember chuckling to myself as we chased the blaze while trying to figure out why the damn floor was so slippery. I felt like a Keystone fireman. In a few seconds we established a routine: brace against the boxes or a support post and open the nozzle; shut the nozzle off and advance a few feet, then brace and blast again. We couldn't spray water and walk at the same time. Finally the last flames were darkened and we relaxed. It seemed we had been in the warehouse for an hour but the audiotape I played later revealed we had knocked down the fire just thirteen minutes after we left the station threshold. When the smoke cleared we stepped into an unburned side room and slipped off our face pieces. The smell was overwhelming. I crinkled my

140

nose, looked down at the goo on the floor and shined my flashlight around. I started to slip again and reached out to grab something, feeling my gloved hand go through the side of a charred soggy box. My fingers were enveloped in warm gluey mass the consistency of lumpy gravy—or a badly burned body. My companion helped me up as we identified the cloying smell and confirmed it with the writing on some of the unburned boxes—Russell Stover. It was boxed chocolate candy. I love chocolate but the heavy scorched reek was like no Hershey bar I ever ate. The lumps were nut-filled candies and half-melted goo. We were ordered outside to allow L.A.F.D. to overhaul the mess and ensure the fire was out.

As we stood outside washing the stickiness from ourselves and equipment, I looked at the now-benign blackened skeleton of a structure. Shining my Streamlight around the rafters and roof support posts, I saw some of the six by eight and eight by eight termite-eaten wooden beams were almost completely burned through. Some split revealing clean, fresh wood splintered in shards through the charred covering. On the roof, in the center of the 30'x50' area we worked, was a huge air conditioning unit. The 800-pound cooler probably kept the candy at a constant below-room temperature. Another few minutes of exposure to fire and the metal monster would have crashed onto us, and the roof ending up sloping towards the entry area where we came through the wall. Acting like a trap door, it would have sealed us in and our hose lines severely restricted or cut off completely. The air conditioner sat on the roof like the Grim Reaper on top of a coffin. Each of us dealt with the possible outcome of that fire in our own way. Firefighters are survivors and very competitive. Fire is the enemy and you just do not give up when the dragon is still alive and breathing. By planning and conditioning yourself before you are ever faced with such a situation, you can explore the possible reactions and make better choices. With flames licking at your backside, running low on air and no windows found, what's the next logical step to salvation? Following the hose line takes you not only to your point of entry, but to the most logical place your comrades will force entry to save your butt.

When we got back to quarters after the warehouse fire, I didn't sleep the rest of the night. I don't know if it was the nauseating chocolate-smelling gunk lining my nostrils or adrenaline. At four a.m. I got up, made a fresh pot of coffee and took a full mug to my office. When I stepped in, I felt I didn't belong there. I was trespassing. On the clock as a firefighter, I realized I was not in my cop persona. I backed out and returned to the kitchen. I loved the headquarters station; the half-century old walls, institutional green paint and the tables that held the coffee cups and dinner plates of scores of firefighters for decades. For over an hour I sat there and reconsidered my arson position. I missed working with a team of firefighters and basking in the camaraderie of the kitchen and kicking a fire's ass. My captain joined me around 6 a.m., bringing the *L.A. Times* with him. We sipped coffee and read the paper in silence. I wondered if he thought about the air conditioner on the roof. He made the decision to have us go in. None of us saw the unit through the smoke and flames. How would he have felt if his decision cost a firefighter his life? I wanted to be a captain. I was ready for the test but was I up to making life and death decisions? Away from fire suppression for over three years would be a handicap in the oral interview. My studies prepared me sufficiently for the written test. I never had any problems taking exams, and had to concentrate on how I would convince an oral board I was capable of making intelligent fire ground choices.

On January 16, 1984 I sat in my personal truck on a surveillance at about 2 p.m. on North Columbus Street, near the downtown area. A small fire erupted the night before and I felt that a juvenile was involved and would come back. Typical of young firesetters he might skirt the site the morning after and return on his way home from school, letting a bit of time lapse before he checked it out. My intention was to watch for a reaction revealing the bad guy after the crime. After 10 minutes on the site, a guy about 20 years old and a little sleazy-looking, walked purposefully into view from California Street and headed south on Columbus. He was carrying a Sears bag containing a heavy box-shaped item. No problem; Sears was only a block away. He walked to a parked car, opened the trunk, took the item out and put it inside. Problem: the item was an automotive battery charger. Why was he parked two blocks away when there is a huge parking structure outside the store? Sixth sense sensibility. He folded the bag up, lighthoused over his shoulders and up and down the street then stuffed the bag in his waistband under his shirt. I was over two blocks north of him and no threat. He closed the trunk and headed back to Sears. I could see elementary school-aged kids in my rearview mirror. I knew the Sears guy would be back so waited for my arsonist. As usual, I was going to need a cop shortly and it was shift change. If I got my arsonist, I'd handle him personally but the thievery was a cop matter. The burglar showed up before my firebug, carrying another battery charger. In my mini-pickup with a camper, I didn't look very official and feared the crook might want to examine my badge—it said "Fire Department" and "Investigator;" not "Police." I called the cops.

Surprisingly, there was a unit nearby and we rolled up together on the bad guy. The trunk was still open. He had two battery chargers. I told the cop about my surveillance so he cuffed the crook, scooped up the contraband and headed for Sears. The cop was a happy camper. I gave him two hours of overtime to book the suspect and write an easy report. The man was booked for burglary. The second entry with the folded paper bag proved intent to enter the store to commit a crime; a requirement for a felony burglary charge.

On March 18, I was the on-call arson investigator for Pasadena Fire Department as well as Glendale. Their sleuths were out of town and I agreed to cover for them since I'd been spending more time in Pasadena with a couple of new girlfriends anyway.

The city of Pasadena, about half the size and population of Glendale, was re-building its downtown area. A combination of older established restaurants and newer fashionable bars and eateries provided a respite from Glendale's lack of nightlife. At about 9 p.m., my dispatcher called and advised me of several fires in Pasadena. Two more fires were reported in the same area I was headed for. A Pasadena engine was at a laundry room fire, holding the crime scene for an investigator and could not respond to the new fires until I arrived. I cleared them to leave, telling the dispatcher I was blocks away. I was not, but legal procedure sometimes gets in the way of efficiency. Still a half-mile away, the radio log showed the engine leaving as I arrived. I overheard Pasadena police on their radio and they had a juvenile in custody at the latest fire. With none of the fires officially called arson yet, they could not legally arrest. I slammed to a stop, spent about 2 seconds seeing the pile of clothes where the fire started with no accidental means to ignite the blaze and called it arson. I had my dispatchers relay the announcement to the Pasadena cops. I pictured the uniforms looking at each other and saying, "Who cares if the laundry room was an arson? We got this guy for two fires here." That may be, but the cops did not realize their fires were not arson yet and they could not arrest; only detain. A premature arrest tainted the whole case on down the line. I shot over two blocks to the tree and grass fires and declared both arson. The 13-year-old was found with a lighter in his pocket and verbal confirmation he walked from the direction of the apartment building where the laundry room fire occurred. The cops transported the kid while I checked the other three fires and determined they too, were arson. Six counts if we could make them stick. Normal Pasadena PD procedure required the kid to be questioned by a juvenile investigator but I wanted him now; not tomorrow. Another failing of law enforcement agencies is how they handle arson follow-up interviews. Many police departments want a fire investigator to simply declare a fire an arson and allow the "real" cops to question the crook. The peculiarities of arsonists and arson as a crime require creative interrogation and an experienced fire investigator present. A police detective is unaware that dropping a cigarette on a shag carpet will not set it on fire. A lit cigarette dropped into dry grass will not, 99 percent of the time, set the fuel on fire. Cops assume they know fires by what they see on television or in a movie. Mel Gibson tosses a cigarette into a pool of gasoline and it ignites. That's Hollywood. Interviewing a firesetter without an experienced arson investigator present is like allowing a dentist to give you an appendectomy.

Of course, what does a fireman know about interviewing? I conned the Pasadena sergeant by flashing my I.D. Tom's business card design, showing the police badge in front of the fire shield, lead to the assumption that I worked as a cop. He let me talk to the kid. The boy placed himself in the laundry room and at each site a fire occurred. It wasn't quite enough so I tossed in the phantom witness "seeing" him ignite the palm fronds as he used the lighter to illuminate his way on the fairly well-lit street. That scenario sounded good to the boy so he confirmed. I suggested the other fires were similarly ignited and he liked that even better. Means and opportunity equaled to six counts of arson.

I drove back to my Glendale office, typed up the scene investigation and interview report, made a copy for myself and returned to Pasadena and gave the documents to the police watch commander by midnight. I assumed the assigned juvenile investigator would appreciate a ready-to-file case on his or her desk. The fact that a quick beer with one of my Pasadena girlfriends was now possible had nothing to do with my efficiency.

Tom Rickles had me called in to assist when three fires erupted within minutes of each other in the downtown Glendale area. Two fires occurred around 1 a.m. One, a barber shop, erupted while Station One's crews were extinguishing those blazes. The other, a telephone company office across the street from the station was forcibly entered and ignited. Firefighters arrived and saved the phone company from destruction. We spied a good suspect in the crowd, talked with him and detained him. Tom smelled smoke on his clothes. The man had several unusual coins and currency in his pockets that came out of the barber shop. He was also pretty drunk and did state prison time for his impetuousness. Glendale appeared to have more than its share of serial firesetters.

Walter Beatty, Tom and I decided another live-fire training session was needed for our firefighters and to help us recognize unique signs of arson. We asked the California Conference of Arson Investigators if they would allow us to host the 5-day Fire Investigation 4 exam in conjunction with our burn training. They agreed. We weren't sure what we had taken on until we received a package of material from the State. Logistically, the session would be like the city of Glendale offering to take on the re-training of General Patton's army. We needed over 40 assistants, role players and coordinators. After a meeting, we decided it could be done. F.I.R.S.T. provided additional manpower and flyers generated over 60 interest responses. We accepted 58 students and worked 12-15 hour days while the 20 teams of investigators from as far away as Hawaii and Washington state pursued fictional arsonists during their five-day stay. It was a huge success and we cleared over $2,800 for F.I.R.S.T.'s training account. It was the first of five Fire Investigation 4 (later called 2B) final exams we hosted.

With work becoming my refuge, dating suffered. Between studying for the captain's exam, case and training responsibilities, I had little time to seek out quality companions and was tired of the bar scene. A friend set me up on a blind date. After a phone call, we arranged to meet on a Saturday afternoon for lunch at a Glendale Chinese restaurant. Before walking out the door to meet her, I heard a dispatch coming from the portable radio I monitored when I was on-call. Many calls indicated there was heavy smoke showing. I called my date's home but there was no answer. We weren't supposed to meet for at least an hour but I needed to have a few drinks before she arrived. Maybe it would be an easy, witnessed, accidental fire scene. It was a witnessed, accidental fire but my witness was dead. I radioed I was already enroute. It appeared the 40-year-old homeowner was cleaning wood paneling with a flammable liquid and a nearby kitchen stove or water heater pilot light set off the fumes. The bedroom furniture and kitchen contents were all on the back porch of the 800-square foot home and confirmed she was cleaning or maybe painting when the flames and fumes engulfed her. This scene required me to turn the body over to examine burn damage on her side where she fell face down fleeing the flames. The clothing on her back burned away but the light dress she wore was partially intact where her torso and stomach kept it protected as the fire burned over her prone body. The surface of the dress was scorched in a manner suggesting a fireball enveloped her. The lower portions of the garment were ignited by the low-hanging flammable liquid vapor cloud. Her forward movement drew the flames back, keeping fire from progressing to the front of the dress. I walked outside, took a deep breath, and let the curtain fall on what lie inside the house. I excused myself from the fire scene while we waited for the coroner and drove to the restaurant at the appointed time. Clad in my filthy, sweat-stained jumpsuit emblazoned with "Fire," "Police" and "Investigator" patches I scanned the parking lot for my date. She understood my predicament and we planned to meet later that night at her home in Monrovia.

One of my Pasadena girlfriends, Judy, a private investigator, started to get serious about our relationship and I backed off. She was a great lady, intense in her career and personal life, but I wasn't ready to settle in with her. She gave me a unique World War II French/American peace medal as a gift and introduced me to Gregorian chants, so it was hard to resist her, but I feared another Sherry-type power struggle. We still met for drinks occasionally and talked at F.I.R.S.T. meetings. When the fire business slowed I re-examined the Fins 'n Feathers case and connections with other players in the restaurant and property investment world. There was more to this case and it kept expanding. Sheila helped me whenever I worked an arson case involving fraud or financial gain motivation. I had a few cars burned and a residential and business fire, or two that could have been insurance scams and I could not decipher financial aspects of the owner's backgrounds. Unable to give me banking or credit information, Sheila steered me to a great source; the Chiefs/Special Agents Association. The group comprised of security and investigative officials of various businesses and corporations provided members with an annual handbook listing the associates names, addresses and phone numbers. With membership in the group, I got my foot in the door to the resources I needed to explore and understand credit histories, investments and especially the paper trail surrounding property and business ownership. Sheila had married a city engineer who owned many rental properties as investments and, between the two of them, I was able to gain insight of the tangled world of property management and transactions.

Glendale had a very low rate of insurance fraud fires. With the phenomenally successful Glendale Galleria mall and rejuvenated downtown, it seemed everything touched in town turned to gold. Our well-publicized prosecution of the arson-insurance fraud schemes of the nightclub owner in 1981-82 may have acted as a deterrent also. One of the reasons we cooperated with the news media was to keep our successes on the front page for its deterrent effects. Our PR plan was to have even small cases covered when we cleared them. Many in our city and elsewhere thought we grandstanded when we were in the limelight. We enjoyed the attention, but deterrence was paramount. We ran our unit like a corporation and our first priority was to run ourselves out of business.

In early-summer of 1984, I received notice I failed the written portion of the captain's promotional exam. Difficult to accept, I considered filing a grievance. I was sure I passed the latest test. I might not even accept a promotion requiring me to leave the unit, but I wanted the opportunity to turn it down. I rolled over and let it slide. I was having too much fun to consider moving on.

In June I worked overtime at Station Two. We responded to an afternoon brush fire on Marion Drive, location of several previous fires and incendiary device discoveries.

Marion Drive actually starts in Los Angeles and follows a serpentine route along the base of a large grass-covered hill, ultimately ending up as a narrow residential street in Glendale. One side of the street, at its origins, is taken up by upper-middle-class homes overlooking the vacant hillside across the road. Profiling that location as an arson site, it would not seem a very good possibility for an experienced arsonist. The homes across the street from the usual start sites are like sentinels guarding the frequently burned hillside; prying eyes to see an arsonist ignite the blaze by tossing a device out the window of a moving car. But the homes are set back, above the street level and the vacant hill has grass growing right down to the curb — no sidewalks. Someone watching from across the street would be above and looking at the top of the passing car; the passenger side effectively covered. It is a fairly busy road being both an entry and egress street to the densely populated Adams Hill area. Viewing this fire location for a roving arsonist who desired to watch his blaze would almost eliminate it as a possibility. He could be caught on the street above or below by fire trucks and police blockades setting up. However, the hill above is about 10 acres, steeply sloped, with a huge field of wheat-like dry grass that can be seen for miles from the hilly surroundings. The location probably advertises itself to mobile arsonists. Once lit, fire sweeping up the hill can be seen from the busy, nearby, Glendale Freeway and several distant hillsides. Devices found on Marion Drive showed the probability of at least four different arsonists igniting it. At least one may have been a hillside resident who could set the time delay, drive up the hill, pull a pop-top on a beer and sit on his patio or living room and watch his fire. Some of the devices we retrieved appeared to be experimental. There's the possibility of some vacant lot owners trying to save money by bringing the grass-covered lot into brush clearance compliance without spending more than few bucks on cigarettes and matches. One landowner was investigated by Tom Rickles and I but we came up short on evidence.

When Engine Two arrived at the fire, the blaze already swept up the hill and layed down along the ridge where we attacked it successfully with another six engine companies. My captain kicked me loose to investigate as soon as we rolled up our hose lines. Interviewing the first person to call the fire in confirmed an area of origin I already focused on. On my hands and knees for about ten minutes I located a burned cigarette/match/rubber band device in the scorched grass at the origin. On-duty at the fire station for hours, the incendiary had about a ten minute maximum delay before ignition; no way I could have set this fire using the "Orr device" as the prosecutor called it. Somebody else did.

In July, Tom and I were called to a small brush fire on the grounds of an ashram, nestled in the foothills of the San Gabriel Mountains on the northern edge of our jurisdiction. Before we left the office I looked up the word 'Ashram.' I didn't want any surprises.

Arriving at the three acre religious compound we examined the small burned area, along a footpath, in a remote corner of the retreat. Engine Eight had to drag about 400 feet of 1½" hose to effect extinguishment. We interviewed the informants, two holy men living on the ashram grounds, and got a good description of the nut-case who lived in the nearby foothills. The suspect was a dead ringer for Jesus – beard and all. The man was known to howl indiscriminately at the moon, as well as clouds and the occasional passing hiker. Meandering monks said they saw him frequently over the past month, as they strolled on the extensive game trail system leading into the San Gabriels. I found holey shoeprints surrounding the fire scene – holey as in breeched sneakers – not Nikes blessed by the monks. The next morning we hiked the trails, discovered another patch of recently-burned grass and bushes, and the same footprints nearby, but no Jesus impersonator. Fresh feces helped confirm the fact the new fire happened the night before and went unseen or reported in the protected arroyo.

I contacted the north-end area 15-car officers and one gave me a tentative ID on the suspect. He was known to dumpster-dive along nearby Foothill Boulevard. That night, a series of three fires erupted in the residential areas below the ashram. I found the holey shoeprints on footpaths beside two of the fires, adjacent to a flood control channel where grass, brush, fence and a large juniper flamed during a twenty minute period. Eight engines managed to quell all the blazes quickly, with only about $3,000 damage. Unable to find Jesus, I did manage to locate an old booking photo of the suspect on a spontaneous foray through the Records Bureau just after midnight. The photo showed a man looking like he was ready to sit down at The Last Supper.

Using two ATVs and five other cops, we surveilled the area the next night, hoping to ambush the bad guy on the mountain or on Foothill. We did locate him, followed for over two hours, then lost him when he slipped between a row of sumac bushes concealing a trail we did not know existed. With my observations, and the confirming footprints on the sumac trail, I was able to get a warrant for the man. A week later he was picked up inside a dumpster in Burbank. He pled out and was sent to Atascadero State Mental Hospital. This early autumn firesetting spree took a week to put together and we barely polished off the suspect's preliminary hearing when all hell broke loose.

CHAPTER TEN
FIRE TRAP

While writing this memoir at Lompoc Penitentiary, little documentation was available to me for research. With no Internet access and minimal case files stored in my 10'x6' room, I relied on enhanced memory for many recollections. I later obtained files containing enough information to make most of the anecdotes accurate. When I examined my unit's case highlights from our Monthly Activity Logs, my ability to confirm statistics and other information, produced accurate, factual entries. However, all I had to go on, in most circumstances, was the location of the incident, date, suspect name if there was an arrest, victim's name, and disposition of the case if it was an arrest incident. The main date I went by in the anecdotes was the event's inception date. Personal history dates, names and memory are, primarily, straight from whatever I could relate to the cases I worked. Critics of this memoir, particularly case investigators and prosecutors, will examine it for gross inaccuracies to show I'm the bad guy they portrayed in court papers.

In 1992 and 1994-98, my memory was a little better than now in 2000, but in 1995 I was provided with over 100,000 pages to review. I took two years to peruse some of the documents and make an index 200 pages long. Only allowed one box of documents (2500 pages) in my cell now that I am at Lompoc prison, I don't have access to the 100K pages I need to be totally accurate. The 100K are also on CD-ROM but I don't have computer access here either.

I make these claims now because the next phase of this book covers October 1984. Specifically October 10, 1984 when four people were trapped and killed in a fast-moving fire in the Ole's hardware store in South Pasadena, California. The million-dollar blaze at Ole's was determined to be accidental by a majority of the investigators on-scene the day after the fire. Some participants in the investigation, myself included, felt the scene examination was poorly handled by the police investigators. Five years after the fire, a wrongful death lawsuit settled in regards to the Ole's fire. The jury in the civil trial decided the cause was accidental; the thrust of the trial determining blame. Arson was not a consideration. An electrical contractor took the biggest hit for responsibility. The jury agreed that the fire was accidental.

In November 1994, arson/murder charges were filed against me for setting this fire. The jury in my criminal trial never heard about the particulars of the civil trial. The judge ruled the information was irrelevant and confusing, so it was inadmissible. The following is a timeline of events for that fatal day provided by prosecutors, using documents and audio tapes:

October 10, 1984-4:26 p.m. A radio transmission from Investigator 26 (John Orr) to Glendale FD comm center [Verdugo]):

"Verdugo, Investigator 26."

"Go ahead, I-26."

"Can you get the phone number of the Azusa Police Department and keep it handy, please?"

"10-4, I-26." I do not specifically recall this conversation or the exact incident provoking me to alert my dispatcher to stand by. In 1984 I dated dispatcher Lori Fitch and spent time at her condo in Glendora, east of Azusa. Dating for only weeks, I do recall spending the night with Lori on one occasion and she got up and left for work at around 5:30 a.m. Not due at work myself until about 7:30, I followed Lori at about 6a.m. to beat the horrendous westbound freeway traffic into Glendale from her home. In my haste, my handgun was left behind. I always carried a backpack or soft-sided satchel with my two guns (on- and off-duty weapons), checkbook, mini tape recorder, handcuffs, and a small amount of evidence collection supplies inside. It was my mobile office. The pistol either fell out or I set it on the floor next to the bag and missed it when I left in the dark. By 1984 I wasn't the badge-heavy, gun-totin' Wyatt Earp I was in my early career. Over that phase, the gun was a tool.

My only reason for being in the Azusa area at 4:26 p.m. on October 10, 1984 was to retrieve the weapon since I wasn't going to spend the night with Lori again. Since I was in my car when I asked for my dispatchers to stand by, I spotted something happening and thought I might need the local police quickly. Not wanting to dump an emergency request in their lap unannounced, it was my habit and personal policy to plan ahead when I could. I was now in the dispatch center's scheme of things; part of their current operations and allotted a percent of their attention. By 1984, Glendale was responsible for dispatching fire and paramedic units for Burbank and Pasadena, and there could be 3-4 calls working simultaneously. I showed them courtesy and respect for their very trying positions. Less than a minute later, the recording indicates I cancelled my request for them to stand by.

"Verdugo, Investigator 26, I'm 10-8. Thanks." That transmission indicated I wouldn't need their assistance. I was through with whatever I was doing. They could throw away the Post-it with the Azusa PD's number on it. Whatever I observed, a drunk driver or a suspicious person, was now resolved and I was on my way back to Glendale.

5pm (from defense documents):
Three documents in my case files are signed and hand-dated at 5 p.m. on October 10, 1984. My office is a 20-minute drive from Azusa. After the 4:26 p.m. radio contact, I returned to my office and completed these three handwritten, one-page, seven-item entry forms. They were known as P-5 forms. When a case was closed, a P-5 was needed to advise the police records people and my sergeant of the case status change. It was typical for me to do P-5s at the end of the duty day; thus, the 5 p.m. entry. At least two of these P-5s were for cases open for many weeks. I probably completed them on October 10 and hand-carried them to the police department. The sergeant did a monthly evaluation of each detective's open cases and within a week of the first of the month he'd send a nasty note saying, "Either close this case, inactivate it, or arrest somebody. It's taking up space on your assignment sheet and in the computer." The day before, I had inactivated ten cases between 3-5 p.m. and the varying closure times are handwritten during that three-hour period on individual case P-5s. They read like a log of my activity that afternoon. These ten cases required typing up interviews, scene investigation forms or follow-ups; thus, the wide range of closure times. The reports were all go-nowhere cases the sergeant just ordered me to close out the week before, no doubt. The October 10 P-5s reflected leftovers not requiring typed reports so they were carried over to the next day. With the World Series taking place that week, I would be rushing to finish my work to be able to get to a bar and find a good seat. Although not a huge sports fan, I did get excited with the baseball pool put together by one of the firefighters. Payoffs were substantial.

The October 9th P-5s were not important in 1984—just part of the job. During my trial for murder in June 1998, the lead prosecution witness, a wife of a South Pasadena police sergeant, testified she saw me inside the Ole's store on October 9, 1984, sometime between 3-5 p.m. The assumption was I was "casing" the place before setting it on fire. I didn't need an alibi in 1984. I had done nothing wrong. The October 9 P-5s were a good alibi but how would I know that before a fire occurred? If I needed an alibi, the P-5s on October 10 might have provided one had I placed the time of entry at 6:30 p.m. on October 10. Even 6:15 might have been an alibi. My lawyer in 1998 totally ignored the significance of the P-5 alibi evidence. I didn't fabricate anything or there would have been some evidence of it after the deaths occurred. My files and the records bureau documents were untouched. The original documents are still in the prosecutor's files for verification. In 1995, I investigated my October 10, 1984 activities evidence like I examined a criminal case. My life was on the line. Charges against me carried the death penalty. I developed a timeline in 1998 that positively exonerated me from starting the Ole's fire. After the 5 p.m. P-5 times were recorded, I have no knowledge of my activities. I assumed I hand-carried the P-5s to the police station since that was my normal procedure for items the sergeant wanted. Our outgoing paperwork was put in the sergeant's In-box. I typically made a run to the police station after 5 p.m. to avoid running into too many cops and I had easier access to the police computer terminal. I hated taking computer time during the day when the 8-5ers were using it. Someone always grumbled at my presence so I avoided the bureau until after 5 p.m. I assume that's what I did that evening but cannot document or verify it.

7:46 pm (Verdugo dispatch center audio tape):

An incoming phone call from Pasadena Fire Department Investigator Scott McClure, who had been at the scene of a 2nd alarm fire at an Albertson's market. The fire started in a rack of potato chips at about 6:36 p.m. McClure has been an arson investigator for less than one year and on-scene at this fire for less than thirty minutes. In the conversation with dispatcher Marilyn Blakely, McClure asks if "John or Tom" was available to call him at Albertson's. Blakely tells McClure that "John and Tom are aware of prior potato chip fires in the area" from the year before. McClure's call to Verdugo lasted less than one minute. Blakely called my home at Bill and Judy's but there was no answer. A tape recording verified this attempt. Bill and Judy probably were at a bar watching the World Series. My pager was activated at 7:47 p.m. and I called in almost immediately, indicating that I was very near a telephone. Blakely gave me the Albertson's phone number. There was no background noise discernable to indicate where I called from; it was quiet. I then called McClure but there is no recording of this call since neither of us was on a department line. McClure filled me in and indicated his fire was over an hour "cold" and that he was done with his investigation of the scene. If this was like our previous chip fires and part of a series, the arsonist would probably be gone by now. McClure had the scene in control and there was nothing for me to do to help him. It was basically an FYI call. I wanted to profile the scene so I told him I'd cruise the area. The call between me and McClure ended at approximately 7:49. Within ten minutes, McClure recalled I had a "face-to-face" with him. I do not recall the specific location I was at when I made the phone call to Scott. In 1994, when my lawyer sat down with me for the first time after murder charges were filed, one of his first questions was, "Where were you at when you made the 7:47 phone call after being paged? Can someone verify your alibi? This call location can exonerate you from setting the Ole's fire." I couldn't remember. Ten years had gone by and I didn't recall. I speculated, "Probably at some bar." My lawyer, Peter

Giannini, said, "John, you're charged with murder and you can't recall what you did the night of a major fire where four people were killed?"

"No, I can't. My memory begins later when I met with McClure." Giannini began to doubt me at that point. I could have easily said I was at a specific bar but how would I prove that ten years later? I may have been with one of my girlfriends or other friend, but I wanted to be truthful with my lawyer and not to guess only to be proven wrong. I told Giannini, "I can recall who I was with and where I was on my first wedding and my prom night. I cannot tell you where I was thirty minutes or an hour before either event was entered into my memory."

I recently read a fine non-fiction crime book by Jeanne Boylan, a forensic artist. Boylan developed an interview technique to assist querying witnesses in a way that does not cloud memories of their observations of suspects, events, and other relevant facts. Her broad base of experience and training enhanced her own efforts to analyze witness recall for her drawings. In her text, Boylan relates how humans clearly recall events like JFK's assassination or the 9/11 tragedy, right down to clothes the witness wore or the weather that memorable day. Ms. Boylan goes on to say, "...but asked to describe the day before, or the day after, the memory has long since released all non-pertinent detail." This occurred when I made the 7:47 p.m. call on October 10, 1984. My memory of that unforgettable night started with my conversation with Scott McClure. I was within a ten-minute drive of Scott's location at Albertson's because we remember meeting briefly in the parking lot at the store. I recall meeting and chatting for only a few seconds beside a small, boxy Pasadena fire rig, possibly Salvage Unit 33. After reviewing thousands of pages of documents, listening to the audio tapes, and tapping my memory, I am reasonably certain I was at one of my regular haunts during that period early in the evening: the Peppermill Restaurant and Bar in Pasadena when I made the call. I may have been on a date, or alone. The phones at the Peppermill were right next to the men's room and bar, as I remember. Answering my page within thirty seconds would fit with the Peppermill scenario. I was not traveling in my car when paged and was not at home. Many, many times in the 1980s, I was paged out while on a date. Typically, I'd have her bring her own car and meet me so she would have a ride home should I get called out.

At 8:04 p.m., the Ole's fire erupted over seven miles southwest of the Albertson's where McClure and I met in the parking lot area. The first call to the South Pasadena 9-1-1 line logged in electronically at 8:06 p.m. The prosecutors boldly insisted I was at Ole's to set that fire with a time-delay device around 7:50 p.m., and was inside Ole's at 8 p.m. The only payphone available for me to make the 7:48 p.m. phone call to Verdugo was the pay phone ten feet from the Customer Service counter, and 15 feet from five manned, operating check-outs. The defense had a sheriff's department video of this area, taken after the fire in this unburned portion of the store. The check-outs, customer service counter, and payphones are prominently shown. But I was not there, as the prosecutors theorized.

8:05-:20 p.m.

I left McClure and headed to the nearby Hastings Ranch shopping center. My car's scanning radio picked up radio traffic of a dispatch of South Pasadena police and fire units to a structure fire at Ole's on Fairoaks Avenue. Police units were dispatched to the fire a minute or so before fire crews. The dispatcher's voice was urgent and harried, as I remember. I caught the words "smoke showing" from one of the units over seven miles away. I jumped onto the Foothill Freeway at Rosemead and headed for Ole's. I normally drove freeways at 70 mph, but exceeded that and left the highway on the Fair Oaks/Marengo off ramp minutes later. At 8:07 p.m., I was again paged and quickly responded on my radio to Marilyn Blakely. A small closet fire had occurred in Glendale and I was requested to assist Engine Five on-scene. I advised Marilyn I'd respond, "...ETA 20-30 minutes." The address of the small fire was familiar but I cleared the radio frequency quickly so I could monitor the South Pasadena units. I planned on checking out Ole's first and then drive back to Glendale. My unit had no red light or siren and was considered an undercover car.

8:15-:20

I arrived at Ole's and saw only two fire units on-scene and heavy smoke coming from the interior of the large store. Parking about 300 feet from the store, I avoided a location where I might get hemmed in by fire trucks and broke out my 35mm camera and snapped my first photo. It was now my intention to stay at the Ole's fire but first had to notify Verdugo I wasn't going to the fire on Stanley Street in Glendale. I remembered that 1455 Stanley Street was the part-time home of Red, the serial arsonist, and his younger step-brother, Lee. It was easy to figure the step-brother was responsible for the blaze. I was thrown off the property before by their mother, and didn't want the grief of another confrontation with her. I had the legal right to investigate, but I figured I could always ambush the kid in school the next day. The decision not to investigate the Stanley Street fire came back to haunt me in 1998. Prosecutors said my turning down the Stanley Street response in Glendale validated their theory I opted to stay and watch "my" fire — Ole's.

8:21 p.m. (from audio tape):

My phone call to Verdugo is logged in and I ask dispatcher Blakely to have Engine Five's captain call me at the payphone at a gas station across from Ole's. I advised Blakely I was staying at the Ole's fire to provide mutual aid assistance and to have a police unit take a report at the Stanley Street location. Less than a minute later, I talked to Glendale Fire Captain Stu Jones. The fire at Stanley Street, in a closet, most likely was an intentional act of a child. Jones confirmed a nine-year-old's presence and I advised a police report be taken. I didn't elaborate on Red's family's history. Jones waited almost an hour to notify me and he was pissed for having to wait for a cop. If he called for me earlier, there would not have been a problem. He didn't follow procedure. Too bad, Stu. His attitude got worse when South Pasadena called for Glendale fire units to assist at Ole's and Engine Five was still tied up waiting for a police report. Engine Five was replaced by another engine. After advising I was staying at Ole's, I returned to the front of the store and started snapping pictures. My third and fourth photos are of Captain Bob Eisle on his radio asking for more help. His interviews and testimony years later confirm he first saw me by his engine taking pictures about 10-15 minutes after his arrival. His official arrival time was 8:10 p.m. He saw me immediately after I hung up from the 8:21-:25 phone calls. His memory was right on. The pictures also verify the encounter and times. Despite the size and magnitude of the fire, I didn't offer Eisle firefighting assistance. An off-duty firefighter typically does not step onto another agency's turf. It just isn't done unless there is a life at stake. At that point, I had no idea there were people missing. My mutual aid assistance was as an investigator. I took pictures from all angles of the rapidly-progressing fire and was around and near store employees and customers for about thirty minutes. The South Pasadena Fire Chief, Gene Murry, arrived at about 8:30. At 8:45, I heard radio traffic indicating S.P.F.D. investigator Bart Carroll didn't answer his page and was unavailable. There had been a second fire and units were requesting an investigator at that location, Von's Market on Fair Oaks. This fire was reported at 8:13 but never dispatched on the S.P.F.D. frequency since their only two units were already tied up at Ole's. An engine from neighboring Alhambra, en route to Ole's, spotted the second fire, a potato chip rack fire, and pulled in to extinguish it. I located Chief Gene Murry and volunteered to handle the Von's fire investigation since he had no investigator available. The engine still at Von's was needed at Ole's and my response would free them up. The mission of the F.I.R.S.T. organization was for such a situation---help out the overwhelmed smaller agency in their time of need. Murry accepted my offer and pointed south, telling me the Von's was about a half-mile away. At approximately 8:48 p.m., I was on the Verdugo radio frequency.

8:48 p.m. (audio tape):

"Verdugo, Investigator 26. Do you have the exact address of the second fire at Von's in South Pasadena? I'm enroute that location."

"Investigator 26, we weren't aware of any second fire..." I was not sure of my destination and was asking for the address for my report and to simply let Verdugo know my status at Ole's had changed. They didn't know about the Von's fire because we did not dispatch for South Pasadena at that time. We were all unaware of the Von's chip fire until 8:45 p.m. The prosecution in 1994 accused me of setting the Von's fire, too. If I had set that fire, would I have volunteered to go down and investigate where clerks, customers, or the manager might remember me? How could I have set the Von's fire and the Ole's fire and still have met with McClure at 8:05 p.m. seven miles away? I met with the night manager at Von's and got the basic information on the fire and released the Alhambra engine to respond to Ole's. I rushed the investigation, took a roll of photos, and examined the drenched fire scene. Three sprinkler heads went off and destroyed any hope of recovering evidence. Ole's continued to burn after an hour so I released the scene to Von's and returned to Ole's. Other members of F.I.R.S.T. had arrived by then. I volunteered to be on the interview team and located several Ole's employees bunched up across the street. If I set this fire, would I have volunteered to interview people who were in the store before the fire was discovered? I took down personal information of several employees, recording it in my "buddy book." The buddy book is a 3"x5" notepad used by cops for in-the-field interviews. This buddy book was later seized in a search of my office archives and ultimately disappeared. By 11 p.m., we knew we weren't going to conduct an investigation until morning; after the embers had cooled. A cursory body search took place overnight. I cleared the scene, returned to my office, and typed up the Von's report by midnight. Exhausted, I decided to return the report in the morning when F.I.R.S.T. started the official investigation—I thought.

From 1992-94, after my arrest for federal arson crimes, the L.A. District Attorney's Office conducted a re-investigation of the Ole's fire. They accused me of setting both potato chip fires and the Ole's fire, despite the fact that a half-dozen experienced fire investigators agreed the cause of the Ole's blaze was accidental. The civil case, of course, supported the accidental cause, too, but my jury never heard about it. I was convicted. The judge felt the civil case was "irrelevant." I returned to Ole's the morning of October 11, 1984 to find about 12 F.I.R.S.T. investigators on-scene. The four missing people had not been located in the debris overnight. Many L.A. Sheriff's units were in the Ole's lot, as well as media vans and fire trucks. The F.I.R.S.T. investigators got together as two of our leaders consulted with Chief Murry. We delegated who was going to handle diagramming, interviewing, photography, and digging. I asked for a "floating" position since I was on-call for Glendale that week and needed to be available for anything that came up. Before we could get started our leaders came back and said, "F.I.R.S.T.'s out of it. Sheriff's investigators are going to handle the whole show."

The bodies made the case a possible murder crime scene, but the small South Pasadena PD had no homicide detectives. When they had a murder in South Pasadena, they asked for help from Sheriff's Homicide. Sheriff's Homicide wouldn't work with F.I.R.S.T. "We want our arson guys to do the fire scene." Sheriff's arson guys were all cops; no firemen among them. When I saw what was going down, I called my friend Dennis Foote, an L.A. Fire Department arson investigator. Dennis was the primary detective in the potato chip and retail fires and I felt he needed to be involved in this investigation or, at least, provide information to L.A. Sheriff's investigators. Not being a leader in F.I.R.S.T., I felt the L.A.F.D. talent might be able to keep the cop arson guys moving in the right direction. Initially upset at this snub, F.I.R.S.T. members agreed the continuity if the scene was better handled by the Sheriff's people. To placate us, we were told we could help the Sheriff team dig when they found an area of origin. We had several L.A. Sheriff's arson guys as representatives in the F.I.R.S.T. organization but their attendance was spotty and they were, after all, cops; not firefighters. Rumors had it the cop fire investigators were making bad calls because of their lack of understanding of basic fire behavior, firefighting strategies, and experience.

I had one such experience at a fire scene assigned to me by my insurance investigator roommate, Bill. The Sheriff's investigator read some of the fire patterns in an inconsistent manner and was totally wrong on one count. Both of us ended up calling the fire arson, but his misreading could come back and bite him on the ass if an arrest were made and the crook contradicted the origin and cause. I kept my mouth shut at Ole's and leaned on a shovel for a while. I later decided better things to do than stand by… until some cop snapped his fingers. Word got back to the Sheriff's people that we weren't too happy, so they decided to have a meeting to establish priorities and stroke the perceived hurt feelings. It was a condescending and mildly threatening event. Gene Murry and his assistants heard about my photos so I agreed to return to Glendale and make copies and bring them to the scene. I had our one-hour-photo vendor make three copies of everything and returned at around 11 a.m. Apparently, after I left to get the photos, the Sheriff's brought body-locating dogs in and did some exploring. Failing to locate the bodies, the dogs left and the front wall was removed along with possibly critical evidence. The tractor scooped up piles of debris in what was determined to be the area of origin. I know that the bodies weren't going anywhere, and that the primary focus seemed to be to locate the cadavers. I later heard from F.I.R.S.T. members that witnesses said the fire probably originated in the attic spaces and dropped down into the store; a logical scenario. The first-arriving fire captain, Bill Eisle, concurred. My observations and photos depicted the possibility of an attic fire. Nevertheless, there were going to be lawsuits down the line and the Sheriff's investigators didn't give a rip about civil liabilities. They were criminal investigators and, if this wasn't going to be a crime scene, then, "Let's get the bodies and back out!" Their lack of sophistication of sound fire scene investigation practices raised the hackles on all of us. The condescending cop attitude toward fire department investigators was never more pronounced than at this scene.

I departed around noon. Tom stayed to assist. Later in the day, after handling my office details, I heard that my friend, Jim Allen from the State Fire Marshal's Office, arrived at Ole's and the bodies were located. I headed back to South Pasadena. I learned Jim Allen tried to intervene in the manner the fire was being pigeon-holed. He confronted some of the Sheriff's investigators who told him that, if he didn't back off, he would be arrested for interfering with the investigation. The L.A.F.D. investigators responded earlier, checked in, were ignored, and, in a 1992 report said about the Ole's fire scene, "...Didn't agree with the Sheriff's investigation and how it was being handled...After spending 10 minutes inside the burned store and being ordered out, we cleared the scene... It was a confusing investigation..." By 5 p.m. the day after the Ole's fire, the Sheriff's held a press conference and declared the fire accidental. We all had to live with their determination—so we thought.

On Friday, October 12, I picked up the report of the fire at 1455 Stanley Street. The school's system locater found my suspect, the infamous Red's brother, and I drove to interview him. After explaining my problem, the Marshall School principal gave me an office and had Lee brought in from class. The school was not required to notify a parent before an interview. The boy provided me with a brief history of his family and the new step-father before I led him into the fire scenario. He watched the World Series with the new step-dad then left the room to use the bathroom. A few minutes after he returned, the fire in the closet was discovered. I finally got Lee to admit being in the closet "looking for a toy." He eventually copped to setting the fire "accidentally." I thanked him and the principal, hoping a referral of Lee to some counseling sessions for evaluation might help. I ended up catching hell from Lee's mom and my friend, the principal. Lee's mom accused me of ambushing her son and coercing him to admit he set the fire in the closet. Ambushing, yes. Coercion, no; just creative interviewing. I guess I didn't fill the principal in with enough background on the family and I apologized. Turning down the scene investigation request nailed me after all. However, if I had confronted his mother right after the fire, she wouldn't have allowed me to talk to him, and I wouldn't have closed the case. My tactics ruffled some feathers but cleared the case. The mother never took her son to counseling sessions.

As of 1998, the last time I had outside resources to confirm such things, Lee did time in the California state prison system, possibly for arson. With his older half-brother's influence, his early arson experience, and a rumor of physical abuse in the family, it seemed expected Lee would continue to drain public resources. The Ole's debacle was not yet behind us. Tom and I, as well as several other investigators in the F.I.R.S.T. organization, felt uncomfortable about the drive-by cause and origin investigation perpetrated by the L.A. County Sheriff's Department. Our boss in Glendale, the Fire Marshal, told us to back off from further investigation. It seemed there was a mole in F.I.R.S.T. Our grumblings were passed on in other cities until they reached the area Fire Chief's Association level. South Pasadena's fire was none of our business. However, on Monday morning of October 15, Gene Murry, the South Pasadena fire chief, called my boss and asked for our discreet assistance. His arson investigator, Bart Carroll, suffered a heart attack the night of the Ole's fire and could not help with several tips called in to Murry's office, indicating someone responsible for burning Ole's. The Fire Marshal told us to help Murry, but to do it delicately. He did not want us to offend the sheriff's department's arson and explosives guys since they performed our bomb and explosives disposal duties. We could not afford to alienate such a resource. As we sat in South Pasadena Fire Chief Gene Murry's tiny office, I stared at the 50-year-old career firefighter and saw the stress he experienced: a major fire occurred, four citizens died, Fire Prevention laws were circumvented by his superiors during construction of Ole's, large lawsuits loomed, and the investigation of the blaze was removed from his responsibility. Gene looked like Lyndon Johnson while taking the Presidential oath-of-office on November 22, 1963. Chief Murry related how he interviewed a number of Ole's employees and customers after the fire and developed a timeline of events formulated from their statements. He was not totally unhappy with the fire origin called accidental, just the manner of indiscriminately tearing down of walls and scraping floors clean instead of the acceptable layer-by-layer examination. He went on to say less than twenty people shopped or were present in the Ole's store at 8 p.m., probably due to the World Series game televised, combined with threatening, violent storm in the area. At about 8:04 p.m., customers and employees heard the shrill sound of a smoke detector. One employee reportedly looked up and saw a column of grayish-black smoke coming from an area on the southeast side of the store's 8,000 square-foot annex attached to the larger 10,000 square-foot main building. Tom and I were fascinated by this information. We did minimal interviewing on the night of the fire before launching our cause and origin investigation with F.I.R.S.T. members. Most experienced investigators preferred examining their fire scene before conducting interviews with eyewitnesses, hoping to confirm their findings. The employee saw flames leaping up the extreme south wall, feeding on corn brooms, fiber, and rubber floor mats as well as plastic and rubber patio furniture. Another employee saw a similar spectacle from a different angle west of the growing and blaze; his testimony was nearly identical. Both men ran for fire extinguishers while the night manager in the adjacent main building tried twice to reset the smoke detector at the alarm panel in Customer Service. Still another employee saw the fire spreading rapidly with a frightening tide of smoke pushing across the ceiling, and got on a house phone to proclaim the fire over the PA system. There was at least a two minute delay between discovery and contact with the 9-1-1. The men returning with fire extinguishers saw the flames "racing across the aisles, climbing the south wall" and decided the fire was too big for their meager firefighting appliances. These three employees began warning customers to leave through the 15-foot wide opening between the two buildings. Several customers lingered, including an elderly woman carrying her three-year-old grandson. Employees heroically re-checked aisles, when a fusible link holding up a huge, roll-down fire door melted and allowed the aluminum blockage to drop, trapping five people. Intended to function after hours when no people are present, the safety appliance was designed for disaster when Ole's was open for business. Huge amounts of smoke raced through the opening before the fire door dropped, escaping out a loading dock, where neighbors called 9-1-1. The fire department never received a 9-1-1 call from Ole's. The first 9-1-1 call was logged at 8:06 p.m. The start time of 8:04 appeared accurate through comparison of the employees' and customers' statements. One trapped employee inched his way along to the south fire escape door. He crashed through the opening to the fresh air outside. The confined blaze blasted over the man's body, severely burning his head and shoulders. The remaining four—two employees, the grandmother, and the boy—perished. The bodies were found just 20 feet from the fire door.

South Pasadena's first arriving fire crew felt the conflagration started in the attic. Still, Chief Murry was concerned with the nearby potato chip arson fire at Von's and the cursory Ole's investigation done by the sheriff's detectives. All of them were police officers first, and fire investigation a sideline. Tom Rickles and I agreed.

When Gene received phone tips someone may have set the Ole's fire, he was in a quandary. The fire, deemed accidentally-caused, needed a closer look but the South Pasadena police chief, and Gene's boss, told him to back off and not confuse the "facts." But the tips had to be pursued and Gene wanted us to follow up the leads.

Tom and I spent that morning following up tips Gene Murry gave us. Interviewing several junior-high school kids led us to two high-schoolers. We got them to confess to setting two blazes, a grass fire and a garage, but were unable to get them into or around Ole's or Von's. Their alibis were solid. We were pleased to clear two South Pasadena cases so our time wasn't wasted. I think Gene Murry was happy but his boss, the police chief, soon put a muzzle on Gene — "No further Ole's follow-up. It was an accidental fire..."

I surreptitiously contacted the L.A. County Coroner's Office and talked to the pathologist who performed the Ole's autopsies. I explained the delicacy of the investigation and its problems and hoped he'd give me the name of the deputy sheriff's who attended the autopsies. He said no law enforcement representatives attended the dissections. It was standard for detectives to attend autopsies in suspicious fatal fires. I guess L.A. Sheriff's investigators were convinced their fire was accidental. I chatted with the pathologist and found out the bodies contained extremely high concentrations of carbon monoxide. This was expected in a fire that trapped them as it did. They may have perished before the fire trucks ever left the station. I considered quietly pursuing the case but my partner warned me off.

Later in the month we attended a F.I.R.S.T. meeting where Dennis Foote from the LAFD told us an interesting thing. The minutes of the meeting held on October 26, 1984, quote Foote discussing the 1982-83 chip and retail fires in the L.A. area, adding that 'six similar fires occurred since the 10/10/84 Ole's fire...' One blaze occurred at a hardware store, just three days after Ole's.

In November 1984, two more chip fires occurred. This time in Pasadena. No incendiary devices were found. McClure notes suspects, but no arrests are made. A revenge-arson arrest was our last for 1984.

CHAPTER ELEVEN
FIREWRIGHTS

You will not find the word "firewright" in any dictionary, but I felt the expression appropriate in this circumstance. "Wright" means a worker skilled in a particular field, such as a shipwright, or a wheelwright. A firewright may actually be a person stoking a boiler on a steam locomotive, but I apply the term to the multitude of serial arsonists I captured, many in the year of 1985. During 1985, arson hit an up-tick in its occurrence cycle in the Los Angeles County area. The incidence of serial arson in Glendale went up 55 percent from January to December. I apprehended twelve serial arsonists in 1985, arresting only three. The remaining nine confessed. Primarily juveniles, they received counseling referrals. Two of the nine without arrest included an elderly woman too senile for incarceration, and an attention-seeking male adult. I could not quite get an honest confession from him during a spontaneous interview. What he did reveal was just outside Miranda requirements and I could not, in good conscience, arrest the man. The vast majority of these apprehensions took place in localized firesetting sprees. An insecure arsonist seldom ventures far beyond his comfort zone—the neighborhood—enabling a good profile of his projected activities. A mobile firesetter is more difficult to identify and capture. One adult arsonist I arrested set a large series of fires in his home area in Los Angeles, then ventured into Glendale, where I arrested him in the act of setting his sixth fire. Although he ventured out of his comfort zone, the new series was localized on a college campus he was familiar with.

The series of potato chip rack and retail store fires continued throughout eastern L.A. County in January and February 1985. The times of the blazes varied, some occurring between 3-4 a.m. Many years later, I found that an Orange County fire investigation revealed a cigarette, match, and rubber band incendiary device. It appears now that there were several similar series going down in 1985. This incident was used against me in the 1998 trial. Specific fires were discussed at the monthly meetings of the L.A.F.D. and all agencies involved kept their case information restricted. I had not offered to assist beyond sharing Glendale-local knowledge and suspect research. When I learned of the additional 1985 fires, in 1995, while awaiting trial for arson and murder in Los Angeles, I profiled the old series. Since the prosecution in my case was telling the court in pre-trial motions I was personally responsible for all the potato chip fires, the inference was I also set all the retail fires. My lawyer, Peter Giannini, told me to study the documents and find some alibi for the mid-1980s fires. I told him the 4 a.m. fires were easy: I was home in bed. "Not good enough," he replied. The suspects in some of the fires were African-American men. "Still not good enough." My lawyer wanted a receipt for dinner with the mayor of Beverly Hills at the time of one of the fires. A time and date stamp on the receipt and a commemorative videotape of the event would also be helpful. By the time he was asking for these alibis in 1995-98, 10 to 12 years had passed. I had very little to work with when trying to document alibi. I had a few credit card receipts, no phone bills, and not even tax records that might have contained business-related bills attached, revealing a trip out of town or an engagement that coincided with one of these ancient fires. Even my employer, the Glendale Fire Department did not have records of my days off prior to 1985. Finally, I came across a gasoline receipt from Barstow, California that led me to an alibi for one fire. On April, 27, 1985 there was a fire at an Ole's hardware in the San Fernando Valley area of Los Angeles. The blaze erupted in foam rubber air conditioner filters. On April 25-28, 1985, I was on a four-day excursion with 25-30 firefighters and their families to the Calico Ghost Town near Barstow, 150 miles from the Ole's store; a verifiable alibi with a gasoline receipt and later, photos of the event. My lawyer never used it because I wasn't charged with this fire. I also found vacation or days-off sheets but there was no way to determine if, or where, I was out of town at the time of the fires 10-12 years before. While I wasn't able to pattern or profile these 1982-85 fire scenes by looking at the locations, the times of day, days of the week, and widespread locales indicated, some of the blazes appeared to be diversion fires to occupy store employees while arsonists stole merchandise or rifled cash registers. I think some set fires needed at least two people working together. None of the documents I reviewed included police reports where thefts discovered after the fire were recorded. One file I saw did have photos of Eveready batteries stacked in an aisle near the fire. Batteries are a very popular shoplift item. They appeared ready to be stuffed into bags, but apparently the fire grew too fast and the arsonist thieves ran from the store. The pile of merchandise was in disarray, different battery sizes stripped from the display and stacked together randomly. If the pile was made by an employee, why would the fire investigator have taken a picture of it? The theft of liquor, meats, or gourmet items during the fire would not necessarily be noticed by employees either. The Von's fire in South Pasadena was investigated by their own security people. They noted a "large amount of cigarettes" taken from an unmanned check-out and speculated that "the fire was set as a diversion. I've seen and heard about this type of crime before," said the head of security's report. The first documented potato chip fire I found was a reference to a 1979 blaze that destroyed a Ralph's market on Woodman Avenue in the Sherman Oaks area of Los Angeles. I was most likely on-duty at Sears or the Station the evening of that fire. My lawyer detailed a private investigator to verify the employee records on that date but never followed through to get this alibi.

In early February, Tom had a small fire in the mental health unit at a local hospital. We stopped at the hospital security office to pick up a copy of their report from Wanda, the secretary. The security director was a retired Glendale cop and we visited the office several times over the years. This time, I noticed Wanda. Really noticed her. Her efficiency reminded me of myself. The fire occurred early that morning and, by 9 a.m., she had the documents ready for us. I asked her out to lunch. She accepted. The lunch was so much fun I asked her out for drinks that night, too. She accepted. I was shocked. Fiercely independent, Wanda owned her home, drove a 12-year-old Datsun with only 28,000 miles on it, had no kids and no need for men in her life. But she opened the door a bit for me. Man-free for several years, she was content with her dog and two cats as companions—and now me.

After the fire investigation fiasco at Ole's, I worked with a few F.I.R.S.T. members to encourage more attendance from police department arson investigators at our monthly meetings. I felt South Pasadena's neglect in attending our sessions kept them in the dark about arson investigation. I put together an informational luncheon and invited police department representatives of F.I.R.S.T. and their police chiefs, Detective Bureau Commanders, and Public Information officers. There were over twenty member cities and agencies in F.I.R.S.T. in early 1985, and the dues paid by each city automatically included membership of their police department. I estimated only five of these jurisdictions had a good rapport or working relationship between fire department and police arson investigators. It was F.I.R.S.T.'s feeling that we could provide a press-kit-like package to attendees at our luncheon. Outlining the current fire department arson investigators' resumes and the organization's record of mutual aid responses and successes demonstrated the effectiveness of the team approach to fire scene investigation and follow-up. F.I.R.S.T. voted unanimously to fund the expected $500-$600 cost. Tom helped me put together an invitation letter to all area police chiefs and a separate invitation to police training officers to come to our free lunch and two-hour informational session. We also encouraged F.I.R.S.T. members to talk to their police counterparts to get the word out to all interested police detectives and even officers. In two weeks I received two confirmations and two phone queries. The phone contacts were courtesy calls. We cancelled the event. Not even a free lunch could breech the blue wall. Maybe we should have held it at a Winchell's donut outlet instead of a nice, centrally-located restaurant.

In retreat, Wanda and I fled town for a platonic three-day firefighter's clamming trip in Pismo Beach, California. We made it as far as Santa Barbara, where we were seduced by the beautiful coastal city, two bottles of Zaca Mesa Chardonnay, and each other. We never made it to Pismo Beach.

On April 10, Tom Rickles was called to a fire in a Thrifty Drug Store in downtown Glendale. A fire was set in a display of paper products at 8 p.m. as a shoplift diversion. A male African-American suspect was seen going behind a counter to steal electronic items during the fire. He leapt into a car driven by an accomplice and fled. No incendiary device was found in the charred mass of paper napkins and towels. The man was seen lingering near the electronics section for at least five minutes before the fire's discovery. It was assumed that he used a time-delay device. I describe the suspect as an African-American only because prosecutors later accused me of all retail store fires in the L.A area. Approximately 50 percent of Pasadena's population was African-American.

Wanda and I returned from Santa Barbara not quite in love yet, but we became exclusive. Cody, her handsome Irish Setter enthusiastically approved of me. Rock, the Siamese, allowed me in the house and settled on my lap when he was in a good mood, but Tinkerbell the haughty Persian did not recognize me as anything but an extension of a can opener.

Half Chinese, Wanda is a beautiful brunette with fascinating eyes and confident demeanor that frightens most men. Her circle of friends and co-workers, mostly ex-Glendale cops, surround her like a protective ring of Conestogas designed to keep out intruders. Apparently I passed. She let me move a few personal items into her house. Sherry and our girls were still a major part of my life. Carrie and Lori spent only about one weekend day a month with me; sometimes less. Jody had a new man in her life.

On April 5, a small trash fire erupted in a dumpster behind a laundromat in Engine Six's district. Just one block from Six's station, an old wooden garage erupted in flames while the engine was busy with the trash fire. Two fires had occurred in this alley only months before. The blaze spread from the garage to an adjacent garage and scorched a home before being contained by units from over two miles away. The first unit to arrive was Truck Six and they could do nothing without water on board. These two fires appeared to be set by the same person; one as a diversion to draw Engine Six to the far end of their district so the garage fire could spread. I later used this scenario in my book, *Points of Origin*.

There were no suspects in these fires. On April 17, a third fire erupted in this same alley. Glendale Fire Chief John Montenero's condo overlooked the fire. The 7:30 p.m. blaze started in a discarded mattress leaning against a wooden garage just five feet from a 2-story apartment building. Engine Six was in quarters this time and arrived quickly, saving the garage and apartment with Truck Six's assistance. I was not called to the scene, so I drove by to profile the scene the next morning. It was also my intention to canvass the neighborhood for witnesses but the area is a ghost town during the day—everybody works. I did spy a 60-year-old woman sweeping a spotless carport while I wandered around the alley. I wondered why she pushed around nothing with her broom. She said nothing when I approached her, but babbled while sweeping the imaginary dust. She complained about the trashy alleyway and was particularly vehement about the mattress that had burned the night before. The woman went on to admit cleansing the alley by destroying the discarded mattress and placed herself near the point of origin of a much larger fire across the street from her apartment earlier in the month. She hung her head and said, 'I'm sorry…that one got pretty big…' She promised to call me if there were any more irritations in her alley. I couldn't arrest her so called the L.A. County Psychological Evaluation Team to come out and chat with the lady. They did and she was moved to a mental health facility. I was not totally convinced that she was responsible for the larger fire. Well-publicized, the earlier carport blazes might have been copycat crimes, which were fairly common. I believed many of the retail and potato chip fires were copycat.

My unit handled bomb threat cases and, in April, I received a copy of an obscene bomb threat report. On the document, the sergeant stuck a Post-It note that read "Check with sex crimes investigators on this one." I found that my case was related to a series of obscene calls happening around Glendale over a few months. The bomb threat was a variation. The caller always used the victim's first name, or was familiar with the female victim's husband, or knew she had a husband. The initial calls were horribly innovative and insidious. Two prior obscene bomb threats were captured under sex crimes and annoying phone calls headings and not routed to me. Sex crimes investigators could find no commonalities or connections between victims or the M.O. I asked the investigator to assign the three bomb threat cases to me, removing that much of the case load from her shoulders. She was happy to do it. The M.O.'s on the bomb threats were identical conversations going like this:

"Hello?"

"Is this Jennifer?"

"Yes," she would respond.

"How are you doing? This is Mark…remember me?"

"I don't think so..."

"Jennifer, don't move. Stay where you are. I put a bomb next to your front door. Now listen to me. Don't move or I will set the bomb off. What are you wearing?" All three victims on my reports were scared and did exactly as the caller said. The conversation became vulgar and the women were forced to describe their clothing and undergarments. One actually was talked into disrobing for fear the caller would detonate the bomb on her porch. All finally hung up after several minutes of abuse. No bombs were found by responding police. The suspect used several different scams with the other victims but both the sex crimes investigator and I agreed it was the same guy. I re-interviewed the three victims at their homes and apartments. They were all in their early 20s, employed, stable, and the only connection was two of them shopped at the same Ralph's Market. All dated occasionally but no serious relationships or man problems existed. One victim, who I'll call "Wind Lady," had a wind phobia. A breezy day was enough for her to call in sick at work; a Santa Ana condition almost grounds for hospitalization. That night, she had a hang-up caller. I told her I would drive by for a security check of her duplex. Tom and I tried to tie the cases together somehow. There was a common denominator somewhere. The market was a good possibility, with the women writing checks for their groceries and the home phone number required. It would be difficult to pursue without getting close to the suspect if he worked at the store. One of the victims called me to provide a temporary number she could be reached at. "One of my girlfriends just got married and her apartment is still furnished so I'm going to stay there for a while. My place still freaks me out," she told me. I dropped by the Wind Lady's place on my way home from a cantina. We chatted while I looked at her porch and surrounding neighborhood. There was still a slight breeze so she stayed inside. When I came back inside, I reassured her she was probably safe. Obscene callers were insecure freaks and usually harmless. He probably didn't even have her address, just a phone number.

"And my first name," she reminded me. Her phone number was listed but no address, and only the first initial was listed. I got ready to leave and told the Wind Lady another victim decided to stay with friends for a few days and she might do the same.

"No, I can't," she said. "I'm selling some stuff in the *Recycler* and expect more calls. I really need the money." The *Recycler* was a weekly newspaper that listed items for sale from automobiles to zippers. I asked what she was selling.

"Just some furniture and tools I have in the garage. Oh, and a bridesmaid's dress. My friend got married recently and I'll never wear the thing again." A recently married friend... same as the other victim.

The Wind Lady already placed the ad to run for two weeks. It came out the week before. She showed me the ad. It said: FOR SALE - Gold voile bridesmaid's dress, short train. Call Zelda..." and the phone number. First name, phone number and, one could assume, most bridesmaid's were young. A perfect hunting ground. I called the other victim who was staying at her friend's apartment. She confirmed she had had a *Recycler* ad selling her bridesmaid's dress two weeks ago. Her first name and phone number appeared in the issue. I told the Wind Lady we had our connection and would work the case actively. I asked if she got a return call from the creep, try and keep him on the line and maybe entice him, possibly arranging to meet him. She was horrified at the thought and wouldn't consider it. I drove back to the office immediately and called the third victim. All three had advertised in the Women's Apparel section of the *Recycler*. Tom and I decided to lay a trap. I asked my boss if the city could fund the ad. His response was less than enthusiastic. "An obscene phone call case? You guys are arson investigators, not sex crime cops. Hell no! Get back to arson. Stop wasting your time on this shit!" We contacted the phone company and they agreed to do the phone trap but we would need a victim's signature. Two of the victims never wanted to go through another call with this guy. The Wind Lady was my last hope and she finally consented. The *Recycler* gave us the ad for free. They had received many complaints from advertisers about who they called "that guy." The bomb threats were a new scam but the obscene phone calls were common. Our ad read: 'FOR SALE — Sexy peach bridesmaid dress. Low-cut and revealing. Can be made into a cocktail dress. Call Maria..." and the phone number of the Wind Lady. We didn't think the ad was too over-the-top. I hoped the Wind Lady wouldn't screw up with her pseudonym. We had five days before the next issue came out. During the week, another obscene phone call had been reported to the wife of a Glendale Fire Battalion Chief. There was no *Recycler* connection. Maybe there were two of these jerks? Thursday night, the Wind Lady called the dispatch center and had me paged. She recorded the call but had hung up prematurely. I ran over and listened to the recording.

"Hello?"

"Is this Maria?"

"Uh, what...oh, yeah... this is Maria."

"You have a dress for sale, the one that shows the cleavage?"

"Uh, well," Wind Lady sighs, "I got it, yeah. It's blue, you know..." She was very nervous. It was peach, not blue..

"Did you wear it? Is it real comfy?"

"Yeah."

"Is it real silky and clinging?"

"Yeah."

"How do you get off, Maria?"

"Uh, get...what...get off? I'm not at work. I'm at home."

"I mean, how do you get off?"

"I'm not at work...what?...oh...you asshole!" She slammed down the phone. I thanked her and left, promising I'd let her know about the trace results. The trap was a bust. The one limitation the trap had was only a prefix was captured if the call was placed in the local dialing area and was not a toll call. We got '248' and nothing further. At least we knew he was local. I was in jail by the time a man was arrested for similar calls.

Two more carports and three cars in them were destroyed in April. I apprehended two juveniles in May and we experienced a few small brush fires. The grass blazes were flooded by fire crews before my arrival and any evidence of arson washed away.

On May 5th a one acre brush fire started in the 1100 block of North Verdugo Road. We've had several fires at this location. A cigarette/match/rubber band device is located at the fire's point of origin. A new twist is added — coins are attached to the shaft of the cigarette. We may have another serial arsonist to add to out carport/alley fire problem. The brush fire starts are similar locations, usually on busy streets and after 2:30 p.m.

On May 13th I arrest a 13-year-old for a series of three fires over a two-day period. All were within three blocks of his home. A description and first name is provided by a witness to the last blaze. Neighborhood canvassing produces nothing substantial but a school check of the first name and relating the kid's well-known erratic behavior provides me with a possible suspect's address. The guy set fire to a stolen motorcycle, a fence and later a field of dry grass. As I cruise the neighborhood after school I spot a possible suspect. As I approached, he "made" the car and ran. A short foot pursuit bags him and he is arrested and charged with three counts of arson. The witness confirms the ID.

Additional series fires erupt with still another suspect responsible. During the first week of the Glendale Community College summer session two fires start in dry grass on campus. Two devices are located in the small blazes. The incendiaries are a cigarette jammed into a large paper matchbook and the cover closed over it. The delay debris indicate only about a five minute ignition wait. Tom and I respond to the second fire since we weren't called out to the first one. Walking around the campus we locate a third device that apparently failed. The device nestles into a strip of dry grass between the other two fire locations We now have at least three serial arsonists working in Glendale and a similar series of carport and alley fires are occurring in neighboring communities of Pasadena, Burbank and Los Angeles.

On separate days, two more device fires erupt at the college; one a fire in a juniper bush next to the main building and a grove of junipers off the front of the school directly below two classroom trailers. About $3000 damage is done. We still have nothing to go on. Campus Security Chief Jim Sutherland bends over backwards to help but they can provide no suspects. Some minor thefts occurred on campus and a vandalism, too, but nothing out of the ordinary. I failed to check the vandalism report.

In the last week of the short summer session Tom Rickles left for Fresno and the semi-annual California Conference of Arson Investigators seminar. He departed Wednesday at noon. An hour later a tree fire is reported just 300' north of the college near the trailers. I arrive and see two palm trees and surrounding vegetation have burned. Engine Four completes overhaul and have blasted the area thoroughly, obliterating any possible evidence. I canvassed the neighborhood and actually find a good witness directly across the street from the fire. The man describes a college-aged boy who sat on a wall across the driveway from the palm trees. He was smoking and the witness paid no attention until about five minutes later when looked back and the trees were blazing. Five minutes; the burn time of the devices already found. The description provided matches at least 50 lads attending the school: 19-20-year-old, slim, light-colored hair, Levis, t-shirt.

I'm tied up in the morning hours the next day and can't surveille the campus. No fires occur anyway. With time running out on the summer session I decided to spend the next day at the college posing as a student. Thirty-six-years-old at the time, I didn't really look like a college kid but there were a number of adult attendees on campus. I wore a pair of cut-offs, t-shirt and carried a backpack. Unlike most college students, mine contained a Walther PPKS .380, handcuffs, Pentax mini-binoculars, and a portable radio. At 8:30 a.m., the only time of the daily campus schedule that hasn't experienced a fire, I set up on the north end of the campus at a small burger stand near the trailers. I let the police department know I was on a surveillance and give them my location so the black and whites will stay out of the area. I scope out the arriving students while I buy a cup of coffee and note a cop car cruise by on Verdugo Road. Asshole.

Seated in a patio by the burger joint I spot a good possible sauntering down the Verdugo Road. He's the right size and description and is looking up and down the street. My coffee isn't even drinking temperature yet. The suspect moved a few feet farther south and again peered around. I venture a peek in my binoculars and notice he's not carrying a cigarette. I'm across the street, about 100' away. Another teenager approached from the north and my suspect steps away as if he's shying from the approaching students. Nobody else is near. I peek into my binoculars again and as I watch my guy, I see the head of the other student veering off into the trailer area. A small cloud of smoke follows his head. Smoke? I focus on the new walking head. He stops and looks around like a shoplifter. I can only see his torso, his lower body covered by a large juniper bush. The first guy is just out of my sight and then I notice a car stop to pick up student number one. Back on the remaining suspect I see him take a puff off the cigarette, bend down, then pop back up. He walks into the campus.

The stand of junipers is right against the two trailers and hides me from his view as I jog for the street. It takes almost a minute to get across the busy thoroughfare. I don't want to leap out and pursue this kid since I didn't know for sure what I had and causing a couple of cars to screech to a halt might draw attention.

Finally climbing the far curb I stepped onto the campus and passed the location he stooped at moments before. I see him hovering around the corner of a building and he appears to be headed towards me but hesitates. I nonchalantly walk and glance down 10' away where he stood earlier. A matchbook device smoldered on the lower branches of the oily juniper. My heart rate doubled but I maintained my composure trying to decide risking a fire or a chase, or both if I didn't guess right. The suspect seemed comfortable with my approach and he starts back towards the device but as he passes me he reverses and heads into the campus rapidly. Other students have entered the driveway. Shit! I reach in and retrieve my Walther and radio as he turns and looks at me, then tenses as if to run.

"Police! Freeze! Don't move. Drop your backpack!" He freezes but looks around as if checking for an escape route. "Don't even think about it. Drop the backpack." He did. "Hands up...now drop on the ground...Now!" As he slowly drops to his knees I key the radio.

"Station, 51 Frank. I'm code six, north parking lot of the college. Suspect at gunpoint. Roll fire department on a brush fire, same location."

The students behind me freeze too and I see no fire yet, but can't get to the device either with the suspect on the ground at gunpoint. The suspect stayed nicely prone so I approached and handcuffed him without incident as I heard a pack of coyote-like sirens in the distance. The juniper bush still hasn't erupted so I got the creep up, grabbed our backpacks and hustled over to the trailers. The device had failed but sat intact on the branch.

"Station, 51 Frank. Suspect in custody. I'm code four. One unit for report and transportation...Notify campus security of my location."

The suspect started chattering about some "Mexican guy" paying him $5 to place the device. The spontaneous statement cost him dearly. I did not yet have him tied to the device other than close proximity, and no

171

fingerprints had been lifted from the devices before nor this one later. The spontaneous, outside-Miranda statement connected him to the device like a bloody fingerprint at a homicide.

Engine Four roared onto Verdugo Road with siren and air horn blaring, the crew fully expecting some smoke and flames. I was sorry to disappoint but felt a flush of pride when the captain cancelled the remaining units, most of whom had responded to some of the previous campus fires. "Verdugo, Engine Four on-scene, fire-now-out. Suspect now in custody. Officer Orr got him."

I transported David, my suspect, to jail, and booked him for seven counts of arson. Six fires occurred on campus and one, three weeks before, about a half-mile north. I was speculating but who knew what might come up in the post-arrest interview.

David looked at me, "Seven?"

"Yeah," I said smugly. "Six at the school or next door and the one about a half mile north of the campus by Fern Lane three weeks ago…"

"But, I didn't do that one…" Thank you David. As close to a confession as you'd want but I hadn't Mirandized him yet and couldn't use it. Most cops would discreetly slip the confession into the report conveniently after the Miranda admonishment. I didn't work that way. I didn't need it anyway.

After a booking inventory of his backpack contents revealed two identical matchbooks taken at earlier fire scenes, David told me the cigarettes came from his mother's car. He drove her car to school. She was giving up smoking and only puffed the cigarettes half way then put them out in the ashtray. This is why we only had five minute delays on the devices and only a small amount of ash in the remains of the fires. David said he would not buy his own cigarettes.

He was cooperative but maintained the "Mexican guy" paid him to place the devices around campus for unknown reasons. Campus Security Chief Sutherland brought me a report showing David listed as suspect in a vandalism the week before his arrest. David was failing one of his summer classes and did not get along with the instructor. After he was dropped from the class he argued, unsuccessfully, to be reinstated. That afternoon the instructor found all four of his tires slashed. During the post-arrest interview David admitted the tire vandalism, too. He also gave me written consent to search his mother's car to recover some of the cigarettes.

I left David in the jail and drove to the Cougar to find David leaning against a fender. David? He had a twin brother who also attended the college. I explained what happened, retrieved some of the ashtray contents and released the car to the sibling. In discussing his twin, the brother confirmed David's insecurities and having a hard time at home as well as at school. David fit the arsonist profile, right down to the vandalism. Many series firesetters act out by committing petty thefts or destroying property. His "trigger" may have been the failing grade at school or problems at home with his parents.

On a hunch I drove through David's neighborhood later that day. He lived in the Sunland area of Los Angeles, in a tract nestled against the San Gabriel Mountains. I felt David had been setting fires for a while. Those at the school were not his first. I found four recent blazes in a four block radius of his home. Two were juniper and cypress tree fires. Evidence of recent pruning of similar vegetation indicated a few more, too. The local engine company log revealed fourteen vegetation fires in the past three months. I mailed my arson and arrest reports to the LAFD arson investigation office advising them of my discoveries in Sunland. David's mother told me later that two LAFD arson dicks showed at their home one evening. Their interview strategy: "David, why did you set all these fires around the neighborhood?"

"I didn't," replied David.

"Thank you for your time." And LAFD left. No 5%ers were present that day. They never contacted me.

David accepted a plea bargain for two counts, resulting in over $2000 in restitution, counseling and 200 hour community service. I made a deal with the D.A. and David's lawyer to cancel the community service account if he would do an interview video for training purposes. The proposal was accepted. The video lasted 35 minutes but we later edited it down to 20 to eliminate some of the coaxing and coaching I had to go through to get David to share. The result was a fascinating tour through a criminal mind and all the evasions, lies and justifications used to avoid a responsibility. If I've left nothing else behind me, I think that 35 minutes of insight into a serial arsonist's mind-set is a satisfactory legacy.

After April 23 the carport and alley fires stopped. In their place, brush fires bloomed. Eliminating the college series, all of the new wildland blazes occurred after 2:30 p.m., including the one near the college I wanted to blame on David. Canvassing neighborhoods surrounding the incidents produced no leads. This tactic seldom worked for me in brush fire situations where a time-delay device was likely. A time-delay fire allowed the culprit to be down the block or two miles away when the fire erupted. The arsonist wouldn't return until there were sufficient passersby and fire activity so he could blend in. Watching crowds at fire scenes was supposed to be a standard tactic but fire crews never did it and I had a hard time focusing on anything other than the spread of the fire or protecting the area of origin at fire scenes. The arsonist was always there or watching from an adjacent hillside or cruising back and forth in a car.

A small wildfire erupts on May 6 at 5:10 p.m. There was no wind this late in the afternoon and Station Three was only a half-block away and kept this blaze to about an acre. The firebug was starting to slip. Charing Cross Road is a narrow winding throughway with homes built abutting the street itself. People getting home from work or children playing in the yards could see the crook and maybe remember him. Canvassing produced no witnesses, however. I wondered if the arsonist was venturing onto side streets to find new sites. The two mile stretch of Chevy Chase Drive that ran through the narrowest part of the canyon was the most frequently used start sites for brushfires in Glendale. The coin-tosser apparently used Charing Cross Road to move from Linda Vista Drive to Chevy Chase and had a device ready when he approached the major intersection. I theorized the firebug's car or truck might blend in with the affluent area. Linda Vista originated in Glendale and ran into Pasadena. My theory of the arsonist's car "blending in" was discarded after I canvassed the area and saw several older, dilapidated cars, construction workers' run-down trucks and middle class vehicles. Unlike serial killer crime scenes, there were literally no leads or evidence in most serial arson cases.

On August 7th, I was miraculously called to a vehicle fire in Engine Four's district at 2 a.m. I arrived about 15 minutes after the call and found a 1974 Chevy sedan with burn damage concentrated on the curb side of the car. The fire captain was correct: gasoline was dumped in the gutter and intentionally ignited. As Four's crew rolled up their hoses, I talked to the owner and he had no idea why anyone would burn the car. His mother died recently and he inherited the insured car. Could this well-to-do guy be liquidating his mother's assets? I considered it briefly but was ashamed of myself a few minutes later when I found that the gasoline trailed back to the car's gasoline fill pipe where the flow originated. The gas cap was missing and the owner said the tank was full: 18 gallons. It now held about $\frac{3}{4}$'s of that and about a gallon had burned along the curb. No siphon hose was found but if this was the mother-car, then the nursing vehicle was parked nearby during the transfer. It was a very warm early morning with no breeze. I walked about 50 feet from the burned Chevy and again smelled gasoline. Seventy-five feet away, I located a fresh stain of spilled fuel on the asphalt roadway. The missing car was parked at the curb, and a stain revealed a car with a gas fill in the middle of the rear bumper. The pattern flowed toward the lower side of the street exactly as happened with the victim's car. The recipient car pulled out and drove through the spill, leaving several nice tire tread patterns on the pavement. I retrieved an impression of the tread design, using a piece of blank paper. Where the driver's door would have been, about 6-7 feet forward and slightly offset from the gas spill, was a twisted piece of yellow paper. The tip was burned as if the device was used as a torch. After the fire was ignited by the torch, the suspect ran back to jump in the driver's side door and let the paper drop. This indicated two possibilities: The suspect intended to burn the car and walked forward to set it off or he was really stupid and used the torch for light and accidentally ignited the spilled gasoline around the victim's Chevy. It appeared intentional to me, or the suspect would have also ignited the gasoline around his own car. The twisted paper, when flattened out, was the bottom half of an automotive repair estimate with no garage name but the handwritten signature visible. Behind our fire station office was a Pep Boys automotive repair and supply store. It was the first place we checked and it was the right company, but the wrong store. The receipt was coded from the Burbank Pep Boys. I called Pep Boys security and arranged to search their auto repair receipt archives. Pep Boys provided two agents to help us. We were looking for a similar signature to give us the top half of the estimate with the printed name, address and vehicle information of the siphoning recipient. Two hours later we got a hit. The signature was identical. The address was just outside Glendale in the Cypress Park section of Los Angeles.

Returning to Glendale, I wrote up a search warrant for the guy's home and his car. I arranged to meet Tom a block from the suspect's house at 7 a.m. and got there 15 minutes early. The suspect drove off as I arrived. I notified the dispatchers but succeeded in pulling the guy over, despite the lack of a red light or siren. The 23-year-old driver was cooperative and said it was his Dodge. The tread pattern and gas fill location matched. There were two more Pep Boys receipts in the glove box. The signature was his, too. He said he never loaned his car to anyone. He was arrested, transported back to the Glendale jail and interviewed. He was not the right guy, but after we described the neighborhood where the fire occurred, he remembered he had loaned his car to his brother who had a band practice just a half block from the crime scene. I released the owner, located the brother and his accomplice, and arrested them. Arresting the wrong guy troubled me, but both the new arrestees confessed readily. They siphoned about five gallons of gasoline and spilled a couple in the gutter because the container they used had a very narrow opening. The fire was set on a whim as they left; pure malicious mischief. Both were sentenced to probation and restitution for the destroyed car.

Three more trash room fires occurred on Jackson Street, at a multi-unit apartment building near downtown. The task of investigating this annoying series is too time-consuming to pursue so we put up flyers in the lobby asking for information in hopes we may, at least, deter any more fires.

I had a theory. I wondered if the coin-tossing brushfire arsonist might also be responsible for the carport, alley, and garage fires. The brush blazes started after 2:30 p.m. and the carport fires stopped around 9 p.m. I wondered if the arsonist had an early morning job, or school, and got off at 2-3 p.m. He had to be home by 10 p.m. either because he was young, living with parents, or he wanted to get to bed early to be able to get up and go to work. It was only a theory. Tom and I set up two informal rolling surveillances. On-call, Tom used our unit and I borrowed an ugly lime-yellow reserve battalion chief's car. A blaze erupted a few nights later in a large bush next to a wood frame garage. The fire was discovered quickly. When the engine rolled up, the crew concentrated fire streams on the structure, leaving the smoldering bush alone. In the charred twigs, branches, and blackened leaf litter, I found a nickel and a couple of pennies fused together by a melted rubber band. The coin-tosser was setting both structure and brush fires. The coin connection was never mentioned in any news stories. I used this scenario in my book, *Points of Origin.*

During the first two weeks of September we had eleven more alley and carport blazes. Three coin-tosser devices were found, two had not functioned and were in unburned areas. We still had no clues and on the days Glendale didn't have any fires, neighboring cities did.

On September 17, another fireworks device with coins was located at a one acre grass fire in the 1100 block of North Verdugo Road (site of the 1990 fire I was convicted of setting). Finally we had a small lead. One of our more alert fire captains provided a description of a light blue, four-door Plymouth he saw drive by the fire three times. The captain fought the fire from the lowest point and was in view of Verdugo Road throughout the battle and gave a sketchy physical description of a guy about 25-years-old driving the car. By the time I got there, responding from a Burbank garage fire site, the Plymouth was gone. Driving the ugly yellow retired police car, I advertised my presence. Wanda hated it when I parked the monstrosity in her driveway but we were having so many evenings interrupted by fire calls I had to use it as my take-home car so I could get to scenes quickly. We couldn't even go to dinner and risk an interrupted meal, so we stayed home and she let me cook, or she would prepare one of her seaweed-tofu concoctions. Her home was just a mile outside the Glendale city limits and I used her place as my command post during the summer of 1985. On September 18th, I enjoyed a post-meal massage at Wanda's at about 7 p.m., when Engine Five and three other units were dispatched to a structure fire in a laundromat about two miles away. Not related to our carport fires, I didn't respond, but, minutes later, Engine Five reported a suspect still in the area. A small fire in a bathroom spread to the walls and customers saw a female suspect flee. I reluctantly left Wanda's and had the dispatch center get the suspect's description so I could watch for her on my way into the scene. She left some clothing inside according to Five's captain. When I pulled into the shopping center parking lot I spotted her on a bus bench nearby, watching the laundromat. I approached and engaged in a conversation with her as a witness and got a good "I didn't do it" story. As I wrote down her personal information, four units were dispatched to another structure fire three miles away. I could see a pulsing column of thick black smoke on the horizon west of me. The suspect should have been arrested but she was borderline mental, and a local resident, so I thought I could always get her later. I departed and investigated back-to-back fires at a dry cleaners and, minutes later, a carport. Both are arson and off alleyways.

September 20th found me cruising toward Chevy Chase Canyon at about 2:45 p.m., when I drove by Glendale High School. Students were being released for the day and I suddenly saw a jet of water streak out of a car window and douse a group of students at a bus stop. I laughed at the antics of the two guys inside the light blue, 4-door Plymouth. I whipped my Dodge around as they turned a corner. They were heading for the Glendale border. As I pulled up on them, I hit my red lights. When I tried to call out my location for the police department for backup, I found my portable radio battery was dead. The lime-yellow beast didn't have a police radio and, again, it was police shift change anyway. I stepped out and approached the Plymouth dressed in jeans and a flannel shirt, but with a badge and gun prominently displayed. The asshole took off into Los Angeles: my first legitimate pursuit and I had no police radio. I just followed quickly. Very quickly. When I caught up to the car I popped the siren but they continued evasion through the streets until they cut a corner too closely hit the curb and blew a tire. I called in my Los Angeles location to my dispatchers and advised of my predicament. The passenger jumped out and ran. The driver opened his door and yelled at me. He said, "You're a fireman. You can't chase me. You can't arrest me!" He reached down behind his seat and brought out a cut-down baseball bat. Before the bat cleared the door threshold, the driver stared down the barrel of my .357. The bat stayed in the car but he started to simply walk away saying loudly, "Fuck this..." I caught up with him and we tussled around until LAPD showed up. I booked the kid for interfering with an investigation. By driving off and impeding my investigation of the brush fire on the 17th, he actually interfered with progress of the case. I was so pissed when the chase was over I wanted to take the kid's baseball bat to him for scaring the hell out of me. The Dodge driver supplied me with alibi for the North Verdugo brush-fire —

he was legitimately at work. He did not, however, give up the name of the passenger riding in the car.

Six days and nights went by with no fires, but on September 26, Burbank experienced another carport fire. Exhausted from working 15-hour days for weeks, I stayed home with warm Wanda and simply monitored Burbank's fire on the radio. The fire was about a mile from the Glendale border. The next morning, I found a phone message from a new Burbank arson investigator: they had a suspect in custody on the carport fire. I called Kevin, who was thrust into fire investigation with almost no training but 10 years firefighting experience. He asked me to come over and help interview the 38-year-old suspect, found rummaging through the darkened garages and storage lockers placing household items and auto parts into trash bags. The man was arrested for burglary. He was booked in with a pocketful of loose coins. He also smoked the same brand of cigarettes we found in most of the devices. He also had paper matches. Searching the car revealed some loose rubber bands; something thousands of people carried around. He looked good, even better when I re-read the booking sheet information while waiting for the Burbank P.D. bureaucracy to approve my helping with the interview. A lieutenant who knew me finally gave the okay. The booking sheet revealed the suspect worked Monday-Friday, 6 a.m. to 2 p.m. at a hospital. Street-wise and cop-smart, he admitted the theft of hospital equipment found in his car, but said, "I been a thief all my life but I don't start fires." Not even the "phantom witness" who wrote down his license number in a Glendale alley could shake him. "I don't recall. I drive a lot looking for things in the trash I can clean up and sell at the flea market." The D.A. would not file on him. It was too far a stretch for an arson arrest. We told him to "get outta Dodge." Apparently he did. No more carport or alley fires occurred after we kicked him loose. We had no more coin-tosser brush fires either.

The fall of 1985 showed a large downturn in arson fires. After apprehension of ten serial firesetters and probable identity of the eleventh and most prolific, we relaxed a bit. I spent some quality time with Wanda and cancelled my deer hunting expedition with Bill, my roommate.

On October 17th, I was called to a small fire in an unoccupied one bedroom apartment in a twenty-unit building. There was no accidental means for the fire to start; it was arson. The living room looked like a jungle with all the ferns and potted petunias sitting around. Several spider plants sat in the kitchen sink and were watered recently. I asked the resident who discovered the fire where the manager was and she said that she lived on the third floor but was at work. Her 20-year-old son should be around, she added.

"But he's kinda slow, you know. His name is..."

I finished her sentence for her, "...Russell?"

"Right, you know him?" I did. Russell reported a trash fire earlier in the month. Tom suspected Russell. Confirming my suspicions, he had been the caretaker of the vacationing woman's apartment and he said he noticed nothing unusual in the unit when he watered the plants about 20 minutes before the fire. My investigation revealed the fire in the linen closet was ignited in fluffy towels and smoldered for about 10-15 minutes before heat built up sufficiently to breech the closet doors and flare into the hallway. Russell placed himself there during the ignition sequence. I had to arrest him. He confessed to setting the trash fire and the apartment blaze. He needed attention. He got it. With the potential to set fires in the future, we put him into the system to get court-ordered evaluation and treatment.

On November 1, 1985 the Glendale Fire Department Fire Investigation Unit celebrated its fifth anniversary of operation. We compiled our stats and Tom made up an impressive press kit using his computer. Pie charts, graphs and graphics revealed one thing to me: statistics can be a tool to stress the results you want and play down those annoying figures best left in footnotes. By recognizing more fires as arson-caused, our arson problem statistically increased even after our very successful years. Fire and police staff were worried about the perception of these figures and solved the dilemma in typical bureaucratic fashion: a sharp pencil and an eraser. All police reports taken were to be non-criminal headings initially. If the case proved to be arson then the heading would be altered when the case was filed or inactivated. I couldn't battle with fire and police staff, so I walked around the block when I encountered problems with the new rules. If I made sixteen arrests in 1984 and there were only eight convictions noted for the annual stats, the remaining eight picked up the next year. The results were skewed. We dropped the conviction category. Less than 4 percent of the unit's arrests resulted in a case not filed or a courtroom loss. Hardly worth noting. Our overall case clearance figures were always accurate and continued to be the highest in southern California through the mid-1980s. We added three more serial arsonist captures to round out 1985. The following year presented challenges of a different nature, altering the arson/explosives unit's operations drastically.

CHAPTER TWELVE
BUDDY

In this memoir, I have focused the text and anecdotes on serial arson and unusual cases because of the nature of the crimes surrounding my wrongful arrest/convictions in the early 1990's.

From 1980, when the unit began, to December 1991 when I was arrested, over 100 arrests were made by my two-man unit. My tenacity working the serial cases accounted for 85 percent of the firebug seizures. I was charged with and convicted of setting many grass and brush fires with literally no evidence. After I was very publicly arrested in 1991, the occurrence of arson brush fires in Glendale went down. Deterrence? Or was I the firebug? Arsonists love the gratuitous attention their fires get in the press. News articles after my arrest also revealed federal, state, and a task force of investigators examined area brush fires. Even the stupidest arsonist knew to avoid Glendale for a while. Investigators and prosecutors said the incidence of arson fires went down substantially because I was in jail and out of circulation. But within a few years, the number of Glendale area brush fires climbed back up again.

I don't have access to news sources and must depend on outside friends to keep me informed of what's going on in Glendale. One fire, set with a unique time-delay device was ignited the day after my first conviction when publicity was at its highest. News articles the next day carried the conviction story and indicated I was being investigated for "hundreds" of brush fires in the Glendale, La Canada/Flintridge and La Crescenta areas. A brush fire, set on August 1st, 1993, near Devil's Gate Dam in La Canada, was the real arsonists way of saying to the world, "It wasn't Orr. I'm still out here." It wasn't me. It never was me.

In 1987, Lance Heigner, my new partner, and I responded to that same location, even though it was in the Los Angeles County's jurisdiction, and we found a cigarette/match incendiary device. Lance and I were together so I could not have set that fire. It's a popular fire location. Another serial arsonist works along the Foothill Freeway in that vicinity and has set fires from 1993 to the present, year 2000, as I write. The means used to set these fires would also reveal, and confirm, much about the suspect, but I don't have access to the information. These fires will continue and one or more of these pyros is responsible for fires I was convicted of setting. They will continue until someone pays attention.

Despite the fact I am currently in jail, I am very proud of the direction my career took. I was fortunate to have an excellent training officer in Tom Rickles, and a broad array of fire scene and follow-up experiences in the early years. How many arson investigators can say they've arrested a bigamist or investigated an obscene bomb threat? The blazing year of 1985, like a final exam, tested the unit's abilities learned during the preceding half-decade. We passed the test and 1986 brought a new series of experiences and difficulties. Still living in the hillside house with Bill and Judy in January 1986, I spent 2-3 nights a week with Wanda. Sherry and I settled into our new, separate lives after the divorce was finalized but still got together for the girls' school events. Trips to the cabin weren't as frequent, nor were the mid-afternoon office visits I remember so well.

On January 19, 1986, a sixty-year-old, three-story Elk's Lodge building burned in Glendale. At first not considered part of a series, this large loss blaze fit a pattern developed some months later. It took two days to finally determine that the fire started with about a gallon of flammable liquid. The destroyed upper two floors collapsed onto the area of origin and it took two days to clear the debris away and expose the hallway where the fire originated. We pinpointed a flammable liquid pattern starting around a couch and trailed down the hallway to a short stairway leading to the main entrance. After removing tons of debris, I found the remains of a melted yellow one-gallon anti-freeze container in the pattern. Under the disfigured plastic, I could read the label and remnants of a beige plastic store bag also adhered to the mess. The plastic bag remained intact, covered by the partially melted container. It led us nowhere, unfortunately. Several motives took us on a long trek to eliminate suspects. A teenage dance held at the lodge the evening before broke up about four hours before the fire's discovery. Red was seen inside and outside the building by two Glendale cops who worked as chaperones at the dance. Most of January was devoted to follow-up of this $1 million fire. Again, over 100 "tips" were called in to "help" us with the case. Less than 5 percent were worthy of any action.

On March 3rd, another million-dollar fire flared, destroying an Internal Revenue Service auditing facility. The 4 a.m. fire extended into an adjacent bank, where a heroic attack by my old friend, Captain John Wray, and his crew halted the blaze. I arrived in time to witness and photograph the vigor of their attack. John's normal squeaky radio voice reached choirboy level during that battle. Since the building contained a federal agency, we assumed the Bureau of Alcohol, Tobacco, and Firearms and FBI would show up eventually. I had no problem with that but Tom warned me that the feds always moved in like a tidal wave and inundated local investigators, and gave nothing back in return.

While waiting for city equipment to arrive and help with moving debris, I went back to the office to get my pictures developed and clear the answering machine of the many media calls for information clogging the tape. In an hour I received calls from the fire chief, police chief and my boss, the Fire Marshal. All three wanted to know what the hell we were doing ordering the feds off their own property. Tom was adamant about nobody coming onto "his" fire scene until he was through with it. The responding B.A.T.F. agents were ordered out of the building by Tom. The feds called their boss who went up the line to some powerful bureaucrat who fell on the police and fire staff of Glendale. I referred my curious supervisors to Tom's pager number and went back to phone messages. No way was I going near that fire scene. Tom soon joined me in the office. The IRS fire belonged to the feds. People driving by the fire scene that morning shook their heads at the horrible destruction done by the fire, until they looked up and read the 'Internal Revenue Service' sign. Guffaws is a mild description of the reactions of passersby.

The only good thing to come of the IRS fire was an introduction to many federal law enforcement people. ATF brought in their National Response Team of 16 talented investigators from all over the country. In less than 24 hours, they confirmed that gasoline was used to set the fire. Their bags packed, they fled town. Periodic calls were made to me by "Bat" Masterson, the ATF case investigator; nobody wanted to speak with Tom. He was quite rude to the ATF guys who showed up the morning of the fire. Masterson asked for more than he shared, true to federal form. I helped him with local research as much as I could and tried to smooth the waters. He was a true gentleman. They had suspects but nothing panned out. I intimated the fire could be related to several other major-loss downtown fires and even mentioned Red as a possible suspect. They felt it was more "sophisticated" than a normal firebug's fun fire. I was left with the knowledge most local ATF agents had limited street smarts. With almost no fire investigative experience, the local ATF agents pursued only leads associated with IRS-related suspects. They let it be known I was to do no nosing around for Red as a suspect on the IRS fire despite strong similarities between at least three downtown Glendale fires in the past years. This advice from investigators who probably shaved just 2-3 times per week.

By noon the day of the IRS fire every cop and firefighter in the city, maybe the county, knew about the fire scene ejection. Tom became a minor celebrity. Everyone I walked by asked, "What did you guys do to those feds?" or "What did you say to piss the feds off so much?"

Tom kept an extra police badge in a leather case, in his unlocked office desk drawer. Our office was always open and unlocked, the door typically left ajar while we went to the bathroom, kitchen, battalion chief's office, or dispatch center. The badge disappeared and Tom had no idea when it went missing. The loss required him to write a police report. Over a year prior to this theft, I had made an informal query to the police department to have a police badge issued to me for specific case-related work when Tom wasn't around or out-of-town. The request was denied. "Work around Tom's absence" the staff said. When Tom wrote the stolen/missing badge report, he stated, "The badge was kept in a secure drawer with a locking mechanism. Only two keys exist and my partner John Orr has the only other one." No mention of the drawer and office always left unlocked and unattended for long periods while we wandered around the station. Tom was just short of accusing me. Fortunately, no Glendale police detective queried me about the loss. I silently fumed at this slur by Tom Rickles.

My first class of the year was a variation from the usual fire-investigation-related sessions. "Hazardous Materials in Public School Labs" drew over 100 cops, firefighters, and school officials for the March 27, 1986 event. I left Wanda's at 6:30 a.m. and, as I headed west, I saw a column of thick grayish-black smoke near downtown Glendale. Radio chatter divulged a three-story apartment building in flames on the third floor. I recognized the address at South Jackson Street. People were trapped on the top floor and firefighters had just made heroic rescues. A third alarm response was enroute and I had over 100 out-of-town students due to arrive shortly, so had Tom handle the scene investigation, even though it was my on-call week. Tom showed up at the class around 10 a.m. and briefed me on the fire at the Jackson Apartments. It was arson, started in the central, second-to-third floor stairwell, probably with a flammable liquid. The blaze ripped up the well and blew out into the third floor where occupants were trapped. There were no suspects.

After class, I went to the apartment and re-examined the scene. Only a handful of firefighters remained, but the Red Cross and Building Department officials swarmed through the halls. The second floor, where the fire originated, had smoke and water damage. The fire had only burned the door leading to the enclosed central stairwell to the third level. At the base of the damaged door, I found several fire-scorched rags stuck in the partially-opened door. Just inside the door it looked like an enormous firebomb had gone off. There were no stairs left. Minor scorching on the second floor just outside the door appeared to be where the rags were ignited as a fuse leading to the stairwell. I smelled the rag remains and detected cigarette lighter fluid or camping fuel. Foolishly assuming that Tom had secured other rag remnants for analysis, I left. I assumed too much. The next morning, I reviewed Tom's evidence from the Jackson Apartments. The photos showed the bottom of the door and the rag trail leading to the area of origin, but he didn't have a receipt for the rag evidence or a submittal form requesting analysis for flammable liquid presence. He told me he didn't take any rags and didn't smell any fluid. He assumed by the major damage that flammable liquid was used to start the fire. He said, "The pictures show the area of origin and the rags anyway. You've got a trailer created by the suspect so it doesn't matter if there's flammable liquid or not. It's an arson." He was half right.

Still troubled about the evidence, I returned to the fire building. With permission to re-enter from the manager, I ran to the second floor stairwell. The door had been covered with plywood, the carpet stripped and removed, the stairwell debris carted off with the rest of it. No rags, no solid evidence. Within a week, a witness came forward and named Red. The witness added that Red had stolen a one-quart can of cigarette lighter fluid from his apartment on his way out the door the morning of the fire. I had no evidence but my nose to confirm lighter fluid used to start the fire. Less than a week later, a print shop owner found a one-quart plastic jug hidden in the alley behind his business. Inside the container was lighter fluid. Across the alley was another three-story apartment building, identical to the Jackson Apartments. Was Red planning another fire? We set up on the container for two nights in hopes of seeing Red cruise through the alley on his bike. He never showed. A WeTip crime hot-line lead gave us the name of one of Red's friends and told us Red had dyed his hair dark brown the day after the fire. We desperately needed the witnesses but the many hours of searching produced no leads. Another lead brought me back to Glendale where his friend, a 17-year-old girl, was very nervous whenever Red's name was mentioned as I interviewed her in an apartment. She got up several times and paced, finally stepping into a nearby bedroom. She walked back in carrying a pistol. She held a stolen .32 for Red and feared arrest for having it. She provided no information on the fire. With enough probable cause for an arrest and search warrant, I located Red in a run-down pay-by-the-day apartment just three blocks from the Jackson Apartments. Booked for two counts of burglary and one of arson, I now had my first real interview with the infamous Red. He knew I suspected him of setting fires over the past five years—his network of friends kept him informed. He confirmed his presence in the Jackson Apartments a few times, where he had recently stolen a bicycle. Even a creative phantom witness couldn't get him at the apartment the morning of the fire. Very street-wise, he knew we had him.

The preliminary hearing a week later revealed the weakness of our primary witness. The man wasn't believable and had a history of mental problems the defense attorney brought out. One statement he made that could have carried the case to trial was the theft of the can of lighter fluid, but saying I smelled it at the fire scene wasn't enough. Not taking the rags and having them analyzed would create problems with a jury according to the judge. He was as sorry as we were when he said there wasn't enough evidence to bind Red over for trial except for the gun theft. Red was sentenced to a year in the L.A. County Jail.

I had reached the point where I could no longer work with Tom. The final incident was the Jackson Apartment evidence fiasco but I later came across a report regarding a fire I didn't know about. I answered the phone in my office one afternoon while Tom was out. The manager of a two-story apartment on Maple Street wanted to know how the investigation of his fire was going. It wasn't my case, so I got a copy of the police report out of Tom's file. It was buried, several weeks old, and there was no activity on it. I lied and told the guy it was progressing and that I'd have Tom call him. The flammable liquid fire at the man's apartment on Maple Street, was eerily similar to the Jackson Apartment blaze earlier in the year. I went to my supervisor and asked to have Rickles replaced. I did not want the move to be disciplinary, so I told the Fire Marshal about a few of the problems without giving ammunition the police staff could use against Tom. The Fire Marshal asked for more information and I took him into my confidence and told all, but reiterated I didn't want any hint of the move being disciplinary. Tom was advised that he would rotate back to the police department. An announcement went out for volunteers to replace him. I went on a week's vacation with Wanda and spent the last two days of it at her home.

The selection process for Tom's replacement brought out eight candidates from the police department. I was not allowed in the interview process but my views on the candidates and experience with them as uniformed officers was considered. I asked for more responsibility given to me in case management so we wouldn't have a repeat of the past problems. "You got it...what else do you need?" I was on a roll, so asked for a real undercover police car instead of an insurance salesman's wheels. "We'll slip in an order for a Chevy Caprice through the police department. anything else?" A new duty gun? "What kind do you want? We'll order it." The only thing I didn't ask for was more money.

Four weeks before the replacement selection was announced, the final three were revealed. At the same time, I was informed of my appointment as Senior Investigator, given an $800 per month raise and responsibility for all aspects of the Fire Investigation Unit's operation, case management, and assigned personnel. With the city Fire Marshal and the Robbery/Homicide Sergeant as my direct supervisors, we would still operate from the headquarter's fire station. Three weeks before the replacement announcement, I decided who I wanted: Lance Heiger, an eight-year GPD veteran who had written several arson reports as a uniformed officer and I heard reliable information from others about Lance's demeanor. About 10 years younger than I, Lance stood six feet tall and over 220 pounds. To get to know Lance better, I asked for a ride-along with him when he returned to duty after a shooting review where he killed a gang member. It was ruled a "good" shooting. He was a go-getter, handling any and all calls, and unafraid to work. His unique uniformed/undercover assignment made him stand out from the crowd and the watch commander obviously trusted Lance's judgment. During the 3-11 p.m. patrol, we met with many of the officers in his patrol group since Lance wasn't assigned to a specific area, but covered the whole city. Boisterous and deferent at the same time, he was well-liked by the troops and I detected no condescension toward me. I gave him my thumbs up to the Fire Marshal. Lance was selected and started July 1, 1986.

I gave Tom an acid-etched plaque commemorating "The First Five Years" of our very successful association. On it were the dates we served together and the overlapping police/fire badge logo he designed five years before. Our assignment together was filled with many good times but it stagnated. I was sorry to divorce him, but the continued success and reputation of the unit and its high clearance rate had to be maintained.

Lance Heiger was an avid bowler and country/western fan. Although a smoker, he puffed only outdoors. To him everyone was "buddy." His morning greeting was always, "Hey buddy, let's hit the trail…"

During Lance and my first month together we were like newlyweds. Never out of each other's sight, we responded to every fire call possible in Glendale, Burbank, and Pasadena when something interesting was going on. My roommate, Bill, and I planned deer hunts and Lance joined us frequently at local bars. Bill approved of Lance. Concerned about my dropping scores at the required bi-monthly qualification shoots at the police range, I finally gave in and had my eyes examined. I required glasses for distance viewing. In early September, I decided to grow a beard again. I wanted to appear a bit scruffy and be able to hang out at area bars. It was my feeling that a beard might let me get closer to a possible suspect in our brush fires. By 1986, I had a handle on reading suspects, and people in general, and felt I could focus on a potential firebug by observations. A loner hanging out in a bar might comfortably accept a friendly ear. Arsonists did this frequently and were much more open with people after they set fires. With Lance's arrival came new cases that again gave us a training ground. I tried to assign unique whodunits to him to test his skills in follow-up and deducing probabilities.

In October Lance was called out to a 10 p.m. fire in a cypress tree next to a real estate office. The blaze was unique, in that the office was on a busy thoroughfare, and the tree was seemingly set on fire with the intent to damage the building. I later incorporated this fire in my book, *Points of Origin*, and created a fictional diversionary fire as had occurred in this same area during the garage and alley spree fires in 1985. It was easy to write about fires I attended or observed during follow-up investigations. The beauty of writing fiction was my ability to add whatever I wanted to make the story interesting. After I was arrested and convicted, a Glendale firefighter, Jerry Jacobs, was interviewed. He recalled the cypress tree fire in the book, telling the investigators that they could use it against me. Like many witnesses who just wanted to be part of the investigation, this firefighter threw up "facts" to join in on the fun of my prosecution. Jacobs said he was at the cypress tree/real estate office fire on Engine Six. He added, "John was there investigating, he got there too quickly and there was a diversionary fire just like in the book. He set it!" In reality, this fire was not preceded by a trash fire as a diversion as in the novel. I was never at the scene of the real estate office fire until the following day when Engine Six wasn't there. Lance Heiger was the on-call investigator who responded from 20 miles away. Jacobs' interview was evidence of nothing and wasn't used in court, but the accumulation of similar interviews added fuel to the task force investigator's pursuit of the wrong man—me.

The Colorado deer hunts were successful, half of us bagging deer. We rented a thirty-foot motor home in Grand Junction and used it as a base of operations on the 10-day trip. Lance handled several cases in my absence for the deer hunt. The latter part of November Wanda and I were married in a private ceremony in our living room. We honeymooned at Jalama Beach in Santa Barbara County, California, just 10 miles south of where I pen this memoir at Lompoc Penitentiary.

On a weeknight at 1 a.m. I was called to the scene of a vehicle fire in a residential area downtown. Engine One found a Honda burning at the curb, most of the flames extinguished by a neighbor. The cause was obvious to the crew by the overwhelming smell of gasoline in the area. About one gallon of the flammable liquid was poured over the roof, windshield, and hood of the car and ignited.

A still smoldering knotted rag draped over the hood. Scorched paint, singed plastic trim and a heat bubbled tire were the only obvious damages to the three-year-old vehicle. Following intuition and experience I located a one-gallon plastic milk container about a half block away in the gutter under a parked car. The jug smelled like gasoline. The suspect parked a block away, on a side street, then walked into the area to set the fire. The scene spoke to me.

Gasoline use was a volatile and aggressive start — masculine. The car was targeted specifically; not a random act. The suspect parked a block away, most likely because his own car might be recognized even on this very dark street. He knew the victim and anyone angry enough to set a fire using gasoline has a strong motive known by the victim. The registered owner, a 21-year-old man, said he had no idea who would want to burn his car. Nobody was mad at him. The guy was lying. The rag, with three knots along its 12-inch length, piqued my interest, too, but I didn't give it much credence until later when it solidified what the scene already told me.

Something else bothered me. The car was not raped. Typically a man will break a window and enter a vehicle to burn it. In essence, a rape. This case appeared similar to the Joanne case where there was reluctance to be too aggressive — a feminine influence.

Whoever set this fire ran like hell, hopped into his own vehicle, and took off. He, or she, was very angry to set such an aggressive fire and desire to view the destruction irresistible. I hurried the fire crews along and asked the police officer to clear the scene and write the report elsewhere. I circled the block, parking 200 yards west of the victims' home, on the same street. A major thoroughfare, Pacific Avenue, was between me and the fire scene. Even at 2 a.m. traffic whizzed by steadily as I sat slouched down in my unit under the concealing branches of a large Chinese elm. A slight breeze dropped a mantle of leaves on my car. We now fit in. There were only two street lights for each long block, no moon, and trees lining both sides created a darkened tunnel-like atmosphere. With my best binoculars I still found it hard to make out anything around the victim's car. After 10 minutes a yellow Datsun pickup drove past twice on Pacific Avenue. I advised the police dispatch center I was code-5, on surveillance, and hoped a unit would still be close by if I needed one. Two-thirty a.m. was holing-up time for most cops — either to catch up on report writing or napping.

The Datsun drove by again, this time slower, and I was quick enough with my Bushnell's to see the two figures inside leaning forward to peer east towards the victim's car. I saw the brake lights flash briefly. Tempted to follow, I stayed parked, knowing instinctively they would return. They circled like vultures spying a carcass, spiraling in ever-descending passes.

Seconds later the Datsun reappeared, turned onto the street eastbound, away from me, and the idiot turned out his lights. This confirmed he knew the victim and didn't want his truck, or him recognized and could not risk an illuminated license plate in case a witness was around the burned car. Turning out his lights equaled a confession.

I cranked up the big Chevy and roared up to Pacific Avenue. The Datsun continued slowly eastbound and as I waited for cross-traffic to clear I saw the Datsun's brake lights flash on as he drove by the fire scene. Strike two in my mind. The truck sped up, turning right as I raced across the intersection. I left my lights off and screamed along the quiet residential street.

"Station, 51 Frank. Any units in the vicinity of Columbus and Milford for a traffic stop, arson suspect's vehicle in the area," I yelled into the mic while turning south on Columbus. The Datsun was two blocks in front of me already. I held back as he turned again, out of my view.

"12 Boy's at Colorado and Brand," a unit responded to my request before the dispatcher could confirm my query.

"51 Frank, 12 Boy's responding, Colorado/Brand, your 20?"

"Station, I'm gonna be westbound Broadway from Columbus, yellow Datsun pickup with two males on board." The 12 Boy car was the same officer who took the arson report earlier.

By the time I reached Broadway the pickup was a good two blocks away and accelerating. He couldn't have made me yet so I turned on my lights and rapidly moved up on them. I could see 12 Boy in my rearview mirror, screaming toward us. I'd never made a vehicle stop in the new car so placed the revolving red dash light, activated it and popped the siren once as the truck turned onto San Fernando Road in an industrial area. The 12 Boy car was close enough now to assist with one suspect if they decided to flee on foot. The driver pulled to the side immediately.

As my backup unit rolled up he called out our location and I added the plate number seconds later. We both shined our flashlights around the interior and took driver's licenses from the occupants. Standing a few yards back from the truck I filled the officer in on my probable cause for the stop. The uniform was still writing the arson report from earlier when I requested his assistance, so knew the basics of the case. He smiled and we agreed to interview the 20-year-olds separately and find out what they had been up to. The passenger fooled around under the seat as I chatted with the officer so he was asked to step out. The driver walked around to the curb, too. The interior reeked of gasoline. A dark stain on the filthy rubber floor mat was the source of the smell.

They gave conflicting statements about their activities. I asked the passenger why they were cruising around so late at night and inquired if they knew anybody in the area to justify their presence. He replied, "Yeah, my cousin lives on Milford Street. We were just swinging by to see if he was still up but his house was all dark so we drove on." The victim lived on Milford and was this guy's relative. Coincidence? I thought not and used a nearby pay phone to call the victim. The cousin confirmed the relationship and stated he had no problems with him and had no idea why he would be driving by to see him at 3 a.m.

We didn't discuss the fire as we probed so the suspects didn't seem to have a clue why they were stopped. The passenger thought I used the phone to run a records check on him. The driver gave me consent to search the truck. Under the passenger seat I found a length of identically knotted cloth as was located laying on the victim's hood.

I showed the cloth to the officer and advised the boys they were under arrest for arson and conspiracy. As another unit impounded the truck we transported the suspects separately to the jail. I took the driver and halfway to the police station he started confessing. I asked him to wait until I could read him his rights but he continued vomiting facts so I pulled over and hit him with Miranda. He waived his rights and wanted to tell his tale.

The driver said his passenger and the cousin had a recent homosexual encounter but the victim balked at any further contact or gay sex. The passenger wasn't handling the rejection well, pissed at being a one-night-stand. Driver and passenger met that evening at a party and became lovers, got drunker and decided revenge was in order for the cousin's offense. They obtained the plastic jug from a dumpster, filled it with gasoline and the driver followed passenger's directions to the Glendale neighborhood. Driver laid out the passenger, thinking he was in the clear by simply being the getaway guide. Unfortunately, he convicted himself of both conspiracy and arson. By discussing the fire-as-revenge plot he was okay, but as soon as they took the first step towards accomplishing the crime, finding a jug, they completed the conspiracy. As an afterthought I asked him about the knotted cloth left on the hood of the victim's car. He explained the gasoline-soaked rag was used to set the fire by igniting it with a cigarette lighter then throwing it into the gasoline covering the Honda. He added that a knotted cloth is also a common gay sex toy. He had to elaborate on its use to bring me up to speed but it was clear that the device was also a message to the victim as to who was responsible. The knotted cloth evidence was similar to the subconscious reasons a killer covers the eyes of a victim who knows him or a serial murderer poses a dead victim's body. The effort of leaving a message helped convict the two young men. This arrest was going to make an interesting preliminary hearing.

I interviewed the passenger after the booking procedure and he resisted confession for about 30 minutes despite the accuracy of the evidence I presented and the fact his co-conspirator rolled over on him. The man was a closet homosexual, like the victim, and resisted confirmation of the fact. The driver's confession had the ring of truth and the motive wasn't necessary for a case filing anyway. They both took plea bargains. Interestingly, the victim in this case was later arrested for the murder of his 78-year-old female neighbor. He was acquitted after a lengthy trial. My evaluation of this fire scene as having both feminine and masculine aspects was validated by the effeminate male homosexual suspect's confessions.

On December 2, 1986, I was called to a construction site fire in a large tract that experienced two other fires. The $50K blaze destroyed a 4,000 square foot home in the framing stages. The fire started under a staircase. One neighborhood witness recalled seeing a male black transient hanging around the remote hillside area and had been sleeping inside one of the partially completed homes.

Two nights later I responded to another cypress tree fire. The blaze flared at about 7 p.m. near downtown. The tree was flush against a 3-story apartment building and did about $3K damage, similar to the real estate office cypress fire. No suspects were seen. I canvassed the area, conducted an informal surveillance, came up empty-handed, and climbed into a warm bed at about 10 p.m. Less than 45 minutes later the dispatch center phoned and advised of a second alarm just called in for a construction site fire in Engine Four's district. A special request made, when I took the Senior Investigator job, was for automatic notification when a second alarm was called. The theory being, I was going to end up there eventually anyway, and in the confusion of a large fire investigator notification could well be late.

In less than five minutes I was in my jumpsuit and racing to the fire. The address revealed a horrible potential for a devastating fire. I knew the 3-story apartment construction was in the framing stages and wedged between two, 2-story, occupied buildings in a neighborhood with many shake-shingle roofs. The first radio chatter I picked up showed only Engine Four on-scene; the captain was also aware of the conflagration potential: he called for the second alarm before he got to the location.

It was a 6-8 minute drive from my home to the fire on moderately busy Canada Boulevard. I responded code-3 and just minutes into the drive I heard Engine Four declare the fire under control and ask for the investigator. He cancelled the second alarm assignment. I arrived two minutes later. As I rolled in I passed a bus stop two blocks south of the fire. A middle-aged woman sat on the bench alone, I noted. A potential witness.

Almost 50% complete, the building had plumbing installed and conduit already run. The fire started on the first floor. The base of the blaze was in a pile of wood scraps, paper and cardboard. A 3'x3' piece of plywood leaned against the framing and had fire damage in a 'V' shaped pattern, the narrowest part pointing like an arrow to the origin. It appeared a warming or cooking fire was built and the plywood used to shroud the flames from street side visibility. The unattended or neglected flames ran up the flat wood to the 2x4 framing members and the ceiling. With little fire-stopping material or drywall installed yet, the fire ran to the second floor. A new ordinance required fire sprinklers in this type of construction. They were in place and tested for leaks the day before. The test water remained in the system even though the pipes weren't connected to a water source. The fire, reaching the second floor, activated a fire sprinkler. Sufficient water and pressure from the third and second floor, gravity-flowed through the open head stopping the blaze on the second level, and leaked down the same path the fire followed ascending. Engine Four didn't have to pull a line. The blaze was extinguished by a disconnected sprinkler system.

The fire was man-set so I quickly checked the soft ground at the front of the site for footprints. Four's captain did a good job protecting the area. I had several good sneaker impressions around a portable toilet and at the unsecured chain link gate leading to the building. I glanced around the neighborhood to check for observation sites to view the fire and saw the woman at the bus stop now had a companion. It appeared to be a black male. As I retrieved my binoculars from the trunk a bus sped by and stopped at the bench. I got on the radio to have the police stop the bus and check out the man. Or not. The bus drove off and the man remained sitting at the curb. I directed the cop to detain the man while I checked the area for more footprints. Matching sneaker impressions were located in the wooden/floored hallway of the building. Inside the portable toilet were six burned paper matches and the same sneaker prints. About then I recalled the construction site fire from two nights before. A male black transient was seen inside the wood-framed sites before the fire.

After photographing the construction fire evidence I drove down to interview the suspect. The police officer informed me "Vern" was a few gallons short of a tank full. Being only a witness at the moment he was free to go, sort of, so I didn't read him his Miranda rights. I was pushing the intent of Miranda a bit but didn't think he'd truly understand the admonition anyway. What I had was, at best, a negligence arson, not an intentional felony fire. The evidence wouldn't hold up under a good defense attorney's attack. A negligence arson in California can be filed as a felony and is plea bargained down to a misdemeanor. This guy needed psychiatric help. His shoes matched the footprints at the scene and he had a paper matchbook in his pocket with many missing. I treated him like a 12-year-old and brought the phantom witness on board to get him to confirm he was at the construction site tonight. He bought it and added he was cold, thus the warming fire. Remorse hit him and he clammed up. The cop ran his criminal history and wants/warrants while I tried to get him to re-open the discussion. The dispatcher came back on the air and advised "Vern" was released from the Glendale jail at about 7 p.m. that evening. Brought in and held briefly for erratic behavior, Vern had to be cut loose earlier because he didn't seem to be a threat to himself or others and had committed no crime.

My earlier cypress tree/apartment fire occurred 15 minutes after his discharge from jail and just five blocks east of the police facility. To get to the construction site Vern would have walked right by the fire location. He clammed up so I arrested and booked the mentally unbalanced man. He was now a threat to the public. Nothing could get him to talk to me again that night. I have no doubts he set the cypress trees and construction site fires. Probably the real estate office and other construction site fires, too, but I'll never know. A check of his criminal and family history showed many arrests and his sister said he was uncontrollable and quite capable of setting fires. He had started small fires all his life. The state provided prison psychological assistance and we never heard from him again.

CHAPTER THIRTEEN
BUDDY, BYE

I asked my supervisor for permission to attend a training committee meeting at the January 1987 California Conference of Arson Investigators semi-annual session in Fresno. The attendance of Lance seemed more expedient since he was new and needed the training offered at the three-day conference. However, I wanted more exposure to the statewide group, particularly in developing curriculum. Lance required more scene management time. I delegated and he stayed home while I took the road trip.

I left Glendale on Tuesday, January 13, arriving in Fresno in the late afternoon. Checking into the Holiday Inn conference site, I enrolled later that evening. At check-in, the organization handed out a durable simulated leather notebook with the CCAI logo on the cover. In my room, I noticed the notebook was mis-stamped, the logo a slightly doubled image. I later turned it in and exchanged it for another. I am a bit hard to please, even if the item was free. I also handled several others and finally selected three more to take back to Glendale. One for Lance and two for door prizes at F.I.R.S.T. meetings. All of the notebooks contained pads of yellow-lined paper.

Classes started Wednesday morning. Unknown to me, a small fire erupted at a retail store in Fresno at 7:30 p.m. Tuesday night. About $30 damage was reported. I attended classes Wednesday and spent the evening drinking with a couple of private investigator friends in the hotel's bar. The weather in Fresno in January is icy, foggy and miserable. I never left the conference site during my stay except for one meal. Thursday, I attended several classes and spent one or two of the redundant sessions in the bar with friends on the training committee. Networking at these conferences was a major draw for me. After dinner and a few drinks I retired to my room and watched a pay-per-view movie and the late news. I recall seeing a story about a major fire at a Fresno fabric store. In five years I would be charged with setting that fire. I would also be found not guilty of that charge.

Friday was a half-day session so I got up early, packed my bags, took them to my car, and checked out of my room to avoid the post-conference rush after the last class let out at 11:30 a.m. I needed to stay for the last session, an arson-law legal update, to get hand-outs for Lance on these important topics. My unit had a rule: bring back hand-outs from each CCAI class to show the boss what we were learning as well as to provide the information to the partner who was unable to attend.

During the final morning of the conference, 40 miles south of Fresno at about 10 a.m., two fires occurred in retail stores in the small town of Tulare. In one store a sleeping bag burned. Two suspects were described: early to mid-20s, shaggy shoulder-length black hair, working together one as a lookout. Several employees described the same guys. One suspect was described as having not shaved in several days, a scruffy beard. I was 36-years-old at that time and had a full beard and neat, close-cropped brown hair. In the second fire the store manager walked right by the suspect who set the fire and described the man as being in his mid-20s, shoulder-length jet black hair and a 2-3 day growth of beard, an unshaven appearance. I knew nothing of these two fires or the other two that burned in Bakersfield, 100 miles south of Fresno, that same day. The fires were reported at 2-3 p.m. I left Fresno at about 11:30 a.m. and drove through Bakersfield around 12:30 - 1:00 p.m. I had no way to prove my location at the times of those fires. At the CraftMart fire at 2 p.m., a cigarette/wooden match/rubber band device was found. A filtered cigarette. A similar device with paper matches was found at one of the Tulare fires. Both devices were encased in a sheet of yellow-lined paper similar to the pads of paper inside the CCAI registration-gift notebooks. I knew none of this until after my arrest in 1991. None of the physical descriptions provided by witnesses included eyeglasses. My sight continued to deteriorate and I needed glasses to see anything clearly beyond 6-8 feet. I was okay for reading and maybe watching TV but couldn't drive safely or qualify on the shooting range without wearing glasses.

After arriving home on the afternoon of Friday, January 16, I took over the on-call status and gave Lance the weekend off. I swapped cars with him and he went home early. On Saturday, Wanda and I had a garage sale to sell off the duplicate items we accumulated after combining our two households. Wanda took a picture of me, with my beard, sitting on our front porch amidst the sale items. The picture later became vital to my defense but, of course, we didn't know it at the time. The department left me alone for most of the weekend, until 11 p.m. Sunday night.

I woke up to the sound of sirens in the distance and could tell units were rolling from both Glendale and Los Angeles. Five minutes later I was called out to the city's first fire fatality of the year. A 36-year-old Glendale High School teacher perished in a bedroom fire. He was trapped by burglar bars on the second floor. His home straddled the Glendale-L.A. border. The fire was accidental, from a combination of careless smoking, alcohol and prescription medication. The cushions on a sofa in the den showed three other smoldering fires started by the single man in the past. Tired of his smoke detector going off, he pulled out the batteries. A fatal mistake. While waiting for the coroner's arrival to remove the body, I chatted with a crew member from Truck One. He asked if Lance had shown me the picture of him at a party he attended while I was out of town. I replied I hadn't seen it. The truckee remarked it was "memorable" as he ran off to help his captain with a smoke blower. Later in the week I asked Lance about the photo and he reluctantly produced it. The Polaroid showed Lance engaged in a sex act, while fully clothed, with a stripper, at a policeman's stag party. The fact that Lance was married didn't concern me as much as his wearing the department-issue jacket with 'FIRE INVESTIGATOR' emblazoned on the back while he lay face down with a beer in one hand and a department portable radio in the other.

His face wasn't visible but, fortunately, he was recognizable. There were only two fire investigators in Glendale and I didn't want anybody thinking the picture was of me. He explained the party was in Canyon Country, about a 45 minute drive from town. I'm pretty broad-minded but the photo could create problems for the unit so I asked him to keep it among his friends only and avoid showing it to firefighters. I never heard from other firefighters about the picture. The incident caused some concern about Lance's judgment. Also, Canyon Country was a bit beyond the 30-minute required response time for after-hours call-outs.

The night after the fatal fire the department had its annual awards dinner. Wanda and I attended, along with about 70 firefighters, their families, and both fire and police staff. Over 150 were present. The next morning the Fire Marshal asked me to shave the beard. It was gone by January 20, 1987.

Later in the month, Lance informed me his fledgling security company had a contract to guard an Armenian wedding in Glendale. The police department approved officers working off-duty plainclothes security assignments and he asked me if I wanted to work the wedding with him. I agreed but was on-call that night and might have to leave unexpectedly. He said it was no problem and it wasn't. The easiest $100 I ever made for three hours of eating, dancing and hanging out with the very cool Armenian families.

In the latter part of January we had a series of nuisance fires in Engine Fives district. Two days later I apprehended two juveniles walking away from the second fire they set that day, just three blocks from the other series, but they wouldn't cop out to the four from the other day. Also in January, I cleaned out the narc car in my driveway, vacuuming the interior as the final part of the procedure. My mini car-vac clogged when I reached under the front passenger seat. As Wanda sat on the porch just ten feet from me, I pulled out the car-vac and found the reason for the clog: a pair of very brief, black fringed panties. They certainly weren't Lance's wife's size and I knew they weren't Wanda's either. Hers didn't have fringe. My wife's attention was focused on watering the yard so I stuffed them back under the seat and gave them to Lance the next morning. I wrote a 'PROPERTY FOUND' police report and packaged them in an evidence bag for him. I assumed he never turned in the report.

After a two-year absence from writing I had another article published in the *American Fire Journal*. Titled 'Effective/Affective Fire Scene Investigation,' the piece outlined the importance of reading a fire scene and confirming the investigator's discoveries by interviewing firefighters who actually extinguished the fire.

On February 6, I was called to the scene of a detonated explosive in a carport in the 1100 block of North Verdugo Road. Again, this area presented an interesting crime scene. The bomb was simply a one-pound can of black powder set off by means of a fuse forced into a hole in the top of the can. The detonation did no damage and created a nice boom and a lot of smoke. The fuse was set off with a delay device: a cigarette with several matches rubber banded to the shaft. Lance wasn't with me on this call. The device was placed in a subterranean garage where the suspect would have to drive, or walk, into the area and risk being seen by a resident or passerby. Not likely I could be responsible for setting off this blast with the exclusive "Orr time-delay device." I was driving the 4-door narc car that day.

In February, Lance and I assisted Pasadena arson investigators with two separate fatal fires---both accidental. Burbank also requested help on a vehicle fire. These agencies rotated their arson investigators every two years and it was routine for the rookie fire sleuths to depend on the Glendale unit for consultation and assistance. Also in February, I purchased a new soft-sided Cordura briefcase. My leather satchel was battered, damaged and waterlogged often when forced to take it into fire scenes and from bouncing around in the trunk of the car. The case contained my spare gun, ammo, handcuffs, a tape recorder, assorted evidence bags and containers, various types of blank paper and report forms. I also always carried a pack of Camel non-filter cigarettes and a lighter in it. I picked up the habit early in my career when Tom Rickles said the smokes were useful in post-arrest interviews. A criminal, always nervous just after being bagged, needed a cigarette to settle his nerves and over 70 percent of them seemed to smoke. Having a pack handy helped establish a rapport between the bad guy and the investigator. We had to be careful not to offer the suspect a smoke or a good defense attorney might intimate we were "softening up" the suspect---a forbidden tactic. If the crook asked for one, we could provide it without fearing a violation of post-arrest ethics. I made sure I always carried the strongest, worst smelling cigarettes---Camel non-filters. Being a non-smoker, if I was going to have to put up with the stink, then the suspect was going to suffer, too. Years later, I found out that most criminals prefer the potent non-filtered cigarettes.

My new black Cordura briefcase could be brought into a fire scene without fear of moisture soaking through the water-resistant sides or zippers. Fire debris and smoke smells were easily washed off the satchel.

My "black bag" was in my possession when arrested on December 4, 1991. The investigators and prosecutors called it my "arson kit" because it held cigarettes, matchbooks, and lighters.

In April, my article, 'Interviewing the Reluctant Witness,' was published. The phantom witness interviewing technique got its first publicity in the fire service. I encouraged the use of the procedure, even in accidental fires. A person who accidentally starts a fire can be as reluctant to talk as the hardened criminal.

In the third week of April I left for a 7-day vacation with Wanda. While out-of-town Lance had several early-season brush fires. With little rain the previous winter and spring, the hills were blanketed with dead, dry grass by late March. One of the fires occurred at the "annual" College Hills site in the 1100 block of North Verdugo Road. Lance's report stated a "transient-looking" man was seen walking by minutes before the fire ignited. Two other fires, both on Verdugo Road, blazed during the late afternoon hours in early May. Lance and I were together on both of them.

On May 16, at 7 p.m., I was on-call and played tennis with Wanda at Glendale High School. Another Verdugo Road brushfire erupted and I was forced to take my wife on a wild code-3 run with me. She wasn't impressed and said she would walk home next time I was called out and we were together.

Lance created a few more problems by being tardy on reaching fire scenes and showing up with alcohol on his breath. The alcohol "problem" came with the territory.

It happened to all the arson investigators at one time or another. We were allowed to drink when on-call but not get drunk. If we were forbidden to consume alcohol by the city, while on-call, then we were eligible for "on-call" or "standby" pay. The Fair Labor Standards Act made this declaration and the city did not want to compensate us to the tune of $110 per on-call week. The fire and police staff agreed the on-call arson investigator would be paid time-and-one-half with a two-hour minimum for each call-out but would not forbid us to drink alcohol. With my own fondness for good wine and Tom and Lance's weekly bowling leagues, it was inevitable we showed up at fire scenes smelling of alcohol.

The other minor problems with Lance were discussed between us as partners, not supervisor vs. subordinate. Cop partners covered for each other. An unspoken cop law was you would lie for your partner, and even get days off to protect him. My status as a "cop" partner was soon to be tested.

One morning, Lance showed up 30 minutes late for work and smelling like he just left a wine-tasting event. He wore the same clothes he had on when he left the office 14 hours before. His marriage was foundering and that wasn't my business but the perceptions of us by the Battalion Chief down the hall and fire crews that frequented our office were. Lance was on-call for the week so I ordered him to go home for the day but keep his pager on. I covered for him throughout the day but to have allowed him to stay on-duty in that condition was a crap shoot.

On June 3, another construction site fire occurred. This time, in Engine Nine's district, on the north side of town. The hillside development of 30 expensive homes, known as Oakmont View, was similar to the tract that suffered fires in 1986. There were hints of labor problems at the site. This location would later produce a non-fire disaster.

Jody, my first wife and mother of my two daughters, Carrie and Lori, remarried in the early 1980s. Her new husband, Lloyd, was a father, too, but his wife abandoned him and took their two sons when still toddlers. Lloyd hadn't heard from them since.

Jody called me at work one day and asked if I'd try and track them down. She didn't want Lloyd to know I took on this task, she planned a surprise for him.

In a lull at work, I went ahead and started my usual, and unusual, locate procedures. I got along with Lloyd but did not always agree with his parenting philosophies as applied to Carrie and Lori. Sitting the kids in a corner for 2-3 hours at a stretch for a trivial indiscretion seemed excessive and abusive to me. My daughters said he screamed at them instead of having reasonable conversations and made them do housework he was supposed to do because he was unemployed. I refused to get into the battle and trusted Jody to monitor their home life.

I got Bill McLaughlin to access a few computer databases he used frequently and picked up a couple of possible name matches with a Social Security number and partial birth date that seemed to be the ex-wife. A Department of Motor Vehicles history database gave me a few more name matches to work with. One driving record gave me a San Diego area address and a car license plate number a woman had received a ticket in while driving. Driver's licenses don't give Social Security numbers in California but I ran the car plate a different way and the car's lien holder jumped out at me. I had a friend at the bank where the loan originated. The car financing paperwork came back with a Social Security number match and an address where the payments were made from. Everything fell into place, down to a complete birth date and even where the woman worked.

I then called the area water and power department in San Diego and, ID'ing myself as "an investigator from Glendale," obtained a phone number for the home and workplace of the missing ex-wife. I assumed she was an ex-wife now since Jody had married Lloyd, but I didn't pursue it with her.

To solidify my discovery I pulled a phone scam I used regularly to obtain information. It was almost foolproof. Lloyd's boys were now teenagers and, I assumed, home from school at around 3:30-4:00 p.m. while mom worked. I set up two tape recorders on my desk at home; one with police and fire radio chatter I taped from a particularly busy period, and the other had a standard beep-tone. The Beep-tone is used by emergency services to let the callers know the conversation is being taped. Playing the two tapes together, my home sounded like a dispatch center.

I dialed my target's number.

"Hello," a teenaged male answered.

"This is San Diego Fire Department calling. Did you ask for paramedics at your address?"

"NOOOO...nobody's hurt here."

"Is this 2912 Santee Street?"

"No sir. We're at 3312 Overland Drive...Am I in trouble?"

"No, son. We must have our lines crossed down here. You're in Chula Vista, right."

"Yeah."

"But nobody needs paramedics there. Are you alone?" I pushed the envelope a bit.

"No. My brother Phillip is in the yard but he's not hurt or anything."

"Allright. Phillip is your brother and you are?"

"Darren."

Bingo, I had a solid hit.

"Okay, I'll check our lines here. Is your mom home?"

"No, she's at work, sir."

"She still works for the furniture company on Lacklund Street?" I held my breath hoping he wouldn't balk at this unusual query.

"Uh huh...she'll be home at 5 o'clock. Am I in trouble?"

"No, no. Everything's fine. You haven't done anything wrong, Darren. It was our fault."

"Okay."

"Bye, Darren."

With the boy's names matching Lloyd's missing family and the mom's particulars confirmed, too, I stopped for a moment and wondered why the boy's mom left Lloyd.

I trusted Jody would not let anyone near our kids who didn't measure up to our standards, but I ran a check on Lloyd's background anyway. Without anything derogatory on the surface, I was satisfied he would use the information to reacquaint himself with his children for legitimate reasons. I never heard whether Jody passed on the family's location and if there was a reunion.

In a few short years I would have reason to doubt my decision to help Lloyd.

On June 11, Lance and I heard calls on the fire radio for brush fires in the L.A. County area just northeast of our Chevy Chase Canyon district. We headed north when another brush fire came in around the hill from the first one, near the Devil's Gate Dam area and the well-known Jet Propulsion Lab. Arriving as the first County engines stretched their lines to protect a house, we picked out the area of origin quickly. Any evidence in the area was in jeopardy from the firefighter's efforts and a county arson investigator may not even be requested on the blaze. We ID'd ourselves to an L.A. County Sheriff Deputy and got his okay to search the scene. In minutes we located a burned matchbook with the remains of a cigarette jammed under the cover. Many of these devices were found in this vicinity and near our Chevy Chase Canyon. A fire captain protected the incendiary device remains with a helmet while their investigator responded from 20 miles away. Lance and I cleared this scene and patrolled nearby areas in case another fire broke out.

Sheriff's arson/explosive investigators developed a suspect on this fire. The occupants of the house above the blaze, a mother and her 20-year-old daughter, came home minutes before the fire started and saw a 50-year-old man in a white "construction-type" pickup parked at the dirt turnout where the fire originated.

They described him as a carpenter and his truck had a metal frame over the pickup's bed, used to carry lumber. In 1992, after I was arrested and investigated for "hundreds" of fires, these witnesses were shown a six-pack photo array containing my picture and those of five similarly appearing men. These eyewitnesses pointed out my image and said, "This is the guy we saw in the construction-type pickup just before the fire started." This was over five years after the event. I, of course, was miles away with Lance Heiger at the time the witnesses drove by this location and we did not go to their home. These two observers were like nine others who wrongly identified me as a suspect. Eyewitness identifications are horrendously unreliable. Coincidence is another matter.

At about 5 p.m., the same day we found the matchbook device near the dam, I was paged to the 1100 block of North Verdugo to the 150-yard long site later known as the College Hills fire start location. One fire already occurred there this year but at least an acre of dry, dead grass remained in the field to burn. I arrived fairly early and was joined a few minutes later by L.A. County Sheriff's Arson/Explosives investigator Rich Edwards. I knew Deputy Edwards for a few years. Assigned to the Sheriff's area north of Glendale and surrounding jurisdictions, Rich assisted many smaller agencies with arson and explosives cases. Monitoring Glendale's frequencies, he drove down when he heard the brushfire broadcast. It took us only a few minutes of searching to locate the point of origin and an incendiary device identical to the matchbook found earlier in the day. Two like devices located in adjoining communities on June 11, 1987 was not necessarily a coincidence. The coincidence was three years in the future.

On June 27, 1990, a five acre brushfire erupted just 100 yards from the Devils' Gate Dam area fire Lance and I secured the device from on June 11, 1987. The suspected accidental firesetter, from the June 27 fire, was apprehended. Also on June 27, 1990, another brush fire flared in the 1100 block of North Verdugo and became known as the College Hills fire. Two similar locations, two similar fires on the same day, three years apart. A combination of accidental and arson fires sharing similar locations and the same day. Coincidence? I was charged with setting the College Hills fire and later convicted of the crime.

As an investigator, I viewed coincidence skeptically. These two series of fires, three years apart, at identical locations, was coincidental and maybe two confirmed arsons, possibly ignited by the same person. Set by a mobile arsonist, there were, as usual, no solid leads to pursue my cases. Rich Edwards advised me of his suspect within days. The construction worker was sketchily described but Rich did not elaborate. I assumed the deputies were to conduct a surveillance of the guy since Edwards was so evasive with his information. Similar to federal agents, the Sheriff's arson/explosive investigators were known to share little information with the "locals." This situation improved as I got to know Rich better. He was one of the men who arrested me on the morning of December 4, 1991.

On July 18 I was awakened at 1 a.m. and asked to assist at the scene of a fire at a furniture manufacturing building near downtown Glendale. The blaze ignited in a front office then raced into the manufacturing and storage areas to almost destroy the 10,000 square foot structure. The owner's motor home, parked blocking view of the front office from the

202

street, was also damaged. I found the office window broken before the fire and about a gallon of gasoline poured inside and ignited. I experienced three similar fires and would have more. No suspects were seen. Several small grass and brush fires erupted on our freeways during the summer. No devices were located. Similar freeway fires happened every year in adjoining Los Angeles and in the Sheriff's area of La Canada/Flintridge in addition to Glendale's blazes. The freeway fires continue to this day, while I am incarcerated.

On September 1, another small fire took off at the Oakmont View construction site. Several thousand dollars damage was done to a half million dollar home still in the framing stages. Lance was on-call and responded to the 2 a.m. blaze. He met with Engine and Truck Nine. The property owner and site manager also showed up from their nearby homes. A disgruntled employee was identified as a strong suspect. I read the incident report from the computer that morning, just six hours after the fire. Lance was late getting in. At 8:30 he showed and we discussed the incident. In passing, Lance mentioned his security service now had the contract for guarding the Oakmont site.

He genuinely did not see the conflict of interest. I experienced a similar situation in the late 1970s and explained to Lance that, number one, you don't solicit work while on-duty, and number two, I didn't think he could take the contract since city regulations required uniformed security guards in stationary or roving positions. Lance's response was, "No problem. Who's gonna write citations to my guards? They're all off-duty cops!"

That afternoon a firefighter who worked the day before, and was at the Oakmont View fire, told me the owner of the tract mentioned to a fire captain that Lance's security guards were going to protect the site. At least two firefighters now knew of the conflict of interest potential. I informed Lance of the fireman's revelation and we could expect some feedback. Divorcing myself from the situation, I declined Lance's offer to work for him.

Four nights later I received a call at home from Sergeant Rick Jauregui. Working the construction site at Oakmont, his 2 a.m. relief did not show up. Rick had court the next day and couldn't stay the night. Lance advised him to call me if he encountered problems. I called Lance at home. His wife told me, "He's working security at Oakmont all night..." I paged him--no answer. As Lance's partner I couldn't leave the site unguarded but I was on-call and might end up getting paged out if I did relieve Rick. I had no choice and joined the conspiracy, relieving my old pal Rick. Later that morning, at about 4 a.m., the area Glendale Police patrol came by and we chatted.

I was hoping there would be no witnesses to my participation but I was stuck. I jumped all over Lance the next morning and told him I wasn't going to be put in that position again. Several days later the other shoe dropped. Called to the Internal Affairs office, Lance's solicitation of business while on-duty was discussed. It appeared word leaked back to the police staff. I met with Lance for drinks that evening and he was bummed. The situation was far worse than he expected. He told me he may have to give up the contract and take a few unpaid days off as discipline. The next day I was called into the Fire Marshal's office and asked what I knew about the Oakmont View security contract. Chris Gray was given the order of events and how I became aware of the contract. Fearing the staff was already onto my one-night-stand at Oakmont View, I copped to that, too. Chris Gray, the new Fire Marshal, was a very young, soft-spoken administrator who was good to the unit. Allowing us to make our own decisions, he simply needed a monthly report, an occasional update, and a weekly face-to-face with me and he was content. He saw no problem with my handling of the events and since I wasn't Lance's direct supervisor, only the Senior Investigator, the police staff would have to deal with his discipline. It was out of our hands. In parting, Chief Gray asked if I wanted a "loose cannon" in the unit. At that moment, I wasn't sure. Lance was now a more-than-competent investigator but still maintained the typical cop persona of a party animal.

I told Chris Gray that a few days off might get his attention but the conflict of interest damaged his credibility with some of the straight-laced firefighters who heard about it. The department was put in a bad light by an "outsider." Chris confirmed he already heard from a Battalion Chief, in confidence, and more firemen could have talked, too. Lance might be history.

On October 1, Lance was officially transferred back to the police uniformed services section where he came from. Chief Gray told me the decision was made by both fire and police staff. Lance was given days off without pay and, in a memorandum from the police Internal Affairs section I obtained later, they recommended to fire staff I be given days off for my using the department vehicle on an off-duty job. Chief Gray said he was evaluating the recommendation. He did not agree I had done anything wrong but I used poor judgment. I received no disciplinary action but was now without a partner.

Police staff quickly put out a memo stating Lance's return to their ranks was due to a manpower shortage. "The 7-year 'experiment' of a fire/police partnership was a success and the fire department could now staff the unit without police personnel," it read. At the same time, Chief

Gray put out a flyer requesting volunteers who wanted to work the unit to fill the vacant position.

On-call by myself from October 1 through December 31, 1987, it was a moderately busy period. I developed a suspect in several downtown fires and he looked good for a few of them. A roving security guard, the man worked in the Glendale area for over 10 years and was the same guy who fired a defective handgun in the concealed weapons course I took in 1978. I had run into the man during several late-night surveillances and he was at several fire scenes. I had no solid info-- but all of the fires were on his night route. My intuition and sixth sense said he was a good possible.

On October 7, at 4 a.m., I was jolted awake by the screams of sirens in the distance. The cacophony centered in the downtown area and my phone added to the din. As I picked up, the sounds of frenzied firefighter's voices littered the background as the dispatcher simply said, "Third alarm, 535 North Brand, First Interstate Bank." The 10-story bank was the only high-rise in town without fire sprinklers installed and a towering inferno waiting-to-happen. Less than four minutes later I raced towards the blaze.

Radio chatter indicated fire only on the first floor off the lobby entrance from the alley. Upon my arrival, at least eight engines and ladder trucks were operating. The entire building seemed charged with smoke but the fire was knocked down in less than ten minutes and confined to an electrical panel room. The third alarm was a good call even though the blaze was small. The flames, feeding on plastic, cardboard, and wooden storage in the 10'X10' cubicle caused only $100,000 fire damage but nearly a million in smoke and lost business to the many tenants in the structure.

I detailed two cops to try and scare up a witness or three from those working in the adjacent Burger King, the discoverer of the blaze, or whoever else was around.

The fire scene contained the electrical panels for the building's lighting, elevators and alarm system. The combustible storage shouldn't have been in there. Next to the room was a small mini-market and they used the handy storage next door for seasonal items and several plastic magazine display racks.

Concerned about my ability to eliminate an accidental electrical cause, I carefully isolated an area of origin, then slowly peeled back layers of plastic like an archeologist examines the strata of a multi-layered dig. Reaching the floor level I peeled back a piece of plywood and the sharp metallic smell of gasoline hit me. This was no accidental fire. I traced the gasoline smells and damage caused by the volatile fluid and re-created an actual pour pattern. The gasoline went against gravity

205

in several locations to prove an intentional pour as opposed to a storage container rupturing in one place.

Wishing for a partner or backup to handle some of the scene and interviewing requirements I briefly considered activating F.I.R.S.T.'s mutual aid phone tree. My assistance from the group's standby list that month had to drive from as far as 30, or more, miles and, being a weekday, morning traffic further complicated the request. I used available police personnel to conduct interviews for me while I re-checked and documented the fire scene.

The double, solid-core, wooden doors on the panel room were forced before the fire department's arrival; possibly by a large screwdriver or pry bar. The 9-1-1 caller was an attorney who arrived early, accessed the locked lobby entrance off the alley with his key, and was confronted with a wall of smoke pushing against the opening. He never entered and apparently neither did anyone else.

After igniting approximately two quarts of gasoline the arsonist had to lock the lobby doors on his way out. He wanted the fire's origin to appear accidental.

Most building employees had lobby keys according to a maintenance man. I pictured interviewing several hundred people over the next few weeks. Fortunately, one of the uniformed officers eliminated that need for me. One of the witnesses he scared up was my security guard suspect from the downtown fires: two blazes also ignited with gasoline: the IRS building, the furniture company and two others. The bank building was one of the guard's contracts. Required to only check the lobby doors for security twice nightly, he left a folded business card at entrances upon each visit. I found the cards in the lobby. Neither card had a smoke smell or stain on it. He could have only been there once and left two cards. Was he supposed to shove them inside the door? Did he have keys for the lobby anyway?

The guard told the officer he had shaken the rear doors at about 4 a.m., noted nothing unusual and as he walked back to the front of the bank he passed "one of the lawyers who always comes in early." This had to be the 9-1-1 caller he described. The timing was way off. The security guard viewed the lobby seconds before the lawyer and the area would have been filled with smoke yet he said he "saw nothing unusual..." There was no way he could peer into the tunnel-like entry leading to the lobby and not see smoke produced by the gasoline-fed blaze just 20 feet away. Re-interviewing the collection of witnesses, I spoke with the lawyer. He didn't recall walking by anyone on his way in and he was running for a phone when coming back out of the alley. You would imagine the lawyer remembering passing a security guard in the dimly lit alley or street area at 4 a.m. He "wasn't sure." This meant the door shaker lied and feared he was seen by the lawyer as he sneaked off into the night after setting the fire. He concocted the story to explain his presence.

When I returned to the office my answering machine was filled with the usual offer of "tips" on suspects for the fire. This was before the cause was even announced publicly as an arson. Over the next 10 days I categorized and processed nearly 70 "tips." Only 3-4 were of any substance.

The Deputy D.A. in charge of filing cases would not approve a search warrant for the security guard's home, office and car, based on the out-of-sync timing and statements of two witnesses. My hopes were to find a key to the lobby entrance for the bank or maybe the IRS building. If I could catch him in a major lie it might tip the scales in my favor since he was adamant he did not have keys to the building. His story reeked but the D.A. said I didn't have enough probable cause for a search warrant---yet.

I later discovered the bank building's alarm system shut down approximately 30 minutes before the fire. Whether it was intentionally shut off or went into a "trouble" mode we'll never know. The central station alarm monitor received a tamper signal on the system but a maintenance man said he'd simply "check it out" when he went to work. There was no fire department contact---an ordinance requirement. Had the fire system been functioning a heat and smoke alarm would have been sent to the central station and fire units dispatched. Somebody physically turned off the system or disabled it. Most likely the culprit shut it down and stayed nearby to see if the fire department arrived in response to the inactivated system. When units didn't come, he went back inside, set the fire and watched it grow without fear of an alarm going off. If the attorney hadn't discovered it, the blaze would have breeched the electrical panels, entered the walls, gone through the ceiling, spread to the adjacent mini-mart and into the building. The alarm system deactivation added a new motivation to the fire. Could owners or a tenant in the building had a motive to destroy the structure or maybe records in one of the offices? Was this a re-model fire to use insurance money for needed, electrical or decor upgrades? A multitude of possibilities existed but I pursued none. Without a partner I had to get several full-time detectives or burden another agency within F.I.R.S.T. to detail me an investigator to assist. I contacted the Bureau of Alcohol, Tobacco & Firearms and they were somewhat interested but the dollar loss was not large enough to fulfill their requirements to open a file. The ATF wanted over a million dollars fire damage and I had only about $125K for fire and the rest smoke damages. If I came up with a motive that involved interstate commerce they might be able to help. Three insurance companies involved in the loss hired private investigators to look into the fire, too.

For sake of efficiency, I delegated some follow-up tasks to the two private investigators I knew. Both former F.I.R.S.T. members, I trusted them enough to feed information back to me and I would do the same for them. I still zeroed in on my security guard. His statements were too far out of line with reality.

More interviews with building officials led me to dead ends. The PIs developed no new motivation or confirmation of building owners or tenants involved. It wasn't unusual for me to work readily with the privates. Since most were ex-fire or police investigators, we were all on the same side. Typically, a PI aligned with arson and fire investigation conducted little follow-up. Cause and origin confirmation is all most insurance companies wanted and if their insured didn't appear involved, the PI did nothing further. In the First Interstate Bank case both of my "assistants" were allowed some flexibility. There were subrogation possibilities against the alarm company and the building owners.

During the following month I conducted informal surveillances of the security guard when I was called out to other fires between 10 p.m. and 6 a.m. I knew most of his schedule and route from my one brief interview with him after the bank blaze. In that query he suddenly veered off the fire topic and told me a tale of "spies" and "underworld" figures who tried to kill him several years before. I couldn't bring him back to the fire, but he knew I was fishing. The side trip was evasion but it also showed his instability. The surveillance did turn up an interesting fact: the security guard had two cars. One he drove to and from home 20 miles away and the actual vehicle he used on his nightly route and parked in an industrial section of Glendale. Another man relieved him periodically, for one night, each week.

The selection process for my new partner drew seven applicants from the ranks of Glendale Fire Department. Two were former Glendale police officers and one applicant was a fire captain who was willing to lose rank and money to join the unit. Unfortunately, he lived over an hour outside of town and I couldn't accommodate him. Most candidates had no fire scene or law enforcement background. The only person ready to slip right into the spot was my estranged, and strange, friend, Walter Beatty.

Reluctantly, I approached him in a pre-interview discussion over a couple of pitchers of margaritas. The meetings brought back pleasant memories of our younger days when we worked at Sears and partied regularly. After a few drinks he knew where I was leading and I simply asked him if he had any problems with completing reports and having our secretary type them up and getting them in on time. I didn't question his ability to examine a fire scene. In ways, he was better than me. Electrical and mechanically-caused fires were his specialty and my weakness. We would complement each other. Use to my being his follower, Walt was told I was not his supervisor but had complete control in unit manning, operations and would participate in writing his annual review. In typical Walt fashion, the crux of the conversation was evaded when he skillfully replied, "We'll make a good team..." I recalled the last Christmas card I received from him and the message inside clear: 'You can ride my back-trail anytime, pardner...' I was in a bind and needed help. He was the only possible choice. In my normal cut-to-the-chase way, I talked with Chief Gray and gave my support to Walt. He was selected and scheduled to start January 1, 1988.

On the evening of December 12, the Santa Ana winds howled down the canyons north of Glendale, gusting up to 70 miles per hour. Trees were felled, signs and roofs sent flying, and many electrical lines damaged and dropped. At about 2 a.m. on the 13th, I was called to a car fire in the downtown area. After clearing the scene at about 2:45, I drove around looking for the security guard. His route car was missing so he was at work somewhere, I just couldn't locate him on the west side where I figured he'd be returning home by 3:30 a.m. I hit the pillow but couldn't sleep with the high winds and the fire radio alive with wind-related calls. With an earphone, I monitored calls so I wouldn't disturb Wanda. She, too, slept fitfully but spooned me for warmth. Cody, our 85-pound Irish Setter, paced and ultimately crawled up with us to snuggle. He didn't care much for the wind and its strange accompanying sounds. I generally monitored the fire radio when on-call and off-duty but it was unusual for me to listen in while in bed. To me, I felt my standby status required vigilance the same level as an engine company crew at a firehouse. High winds were critical periods and a brush fire or similar conflagration imminent. Although I didn't fight fire often, my presence at a major fire enhanced the Battalion Chief's ability to know what was happening on all fronts when I acted as his eyes in areas he couldn't get to.

I dozed off eventually and slept with one ear open only to be awakened at 4:30 by a dispatch to a structure fire on Fairmount Street. Station Six's two units arrived minutes later and gave a corrected address, asking for a second alarm to a "well-involved 2-story office building." The blaze was on the security guard's route. I dug out from my nest and called the dispatch center on the phone to let them know I was on my way. I didn't want to come up on the radio and let the security guard know I was around in case he had a scanner.

Before I drove a half mile I saw the smoke and Engine Six asked for a third alarm. The fire took hold of the second floor in the 10,000 square foot building and threatened an identical structure less than fifty feet away. Expensive furnishings and computer equipment on the first floor also had to be protected from leaking water.

The building was next to a freeway off-ramp and the 60-mile-per-hour Santa Anas blew the smoke across the lanes like a heavy fog hugging the ground. As I drove by, the heat was intense. Fire crews surrounded the building, attacking from the outside, one overhead ladder-pipe operating, and two-2 1/2" lines snaking up interior stairwells to confront the flames inside. I circled the building, snapping photos. The early pictures later helped in reconstructing the progression of the flames. Strolling across to the Command Post I used a tree to steady my camera and opened the lens a bit and slowed down the shutter speed. As I focused on the flames and framed the Command Post in the foreground I saw an extra body, in civilian clothes, standing next to the Chief---it was my security guard. He hadn't seen me in the shadows, walked down the sidewalk and into my range. I took two great photos of him with the blaze in the background. A jury would eat this up, if I ever got him to court. He finally noticed me and started to walk away. This guy was legally armed so I called for a police unit. The guard continued strolling up the street and I tailed him while staying in the shadows. My backup arrived and we approached him at his regular car, not the route car earlier missing from its parking space. I chatted with the man as a witness, appealing for his help. He confirmed the building was part of his door-shaking route and he had already left two cards on doors of the structure to prove his earlier visits. He said he was at his nearby answering service office when Station Six's rigs flew by and he followed them in to the fire. He noted nothing unusual at the building when he was by at about 3 a.m. When queried about the route car he said he had finished early and was going to head home. Willingly, he gave me consent to search both cars and they were clean, no gasoline smell inside either. Nothing solid was learned and the fire was knocked down after a 45-minute battle. Almost 80 percent of the second floor was destroyed but the lower level received only water and very minor fire damage.

After I was able to get into the building the area of origin was easily located. A small office waiting area and lobby had the heaviest damage and appeared to have suffered a broken window before the blaze was set. An arson fire. The involvement of flammable liquid was possible but I could not confirm it. Some of the first items to ignite were a polyure-thane-stuffed sofa and chairs which leave burn patterns similar to flammable liquid damage. A highly flammable six-foot Christmas tree also ignited early in the blaze but burn patterns confirmed the fire starting in the adjacent area with pieces of unsooted window glass on the floor level. Like several other of my fires that year, a window was breeched, no entry made, flammable liquid simply poured on the floor and set off. Few other leads were developed but I found the building's electricity turned off thirty minutes before the fire. Clocks in offices confirmed it. A similar scenario to the bank building fire two months before. Turning off the electricity shut down smoke and heat detectors again, as well as terminating the system's capability to send any kind of alarm. With high winds knocking out service all over L.A. County there was no police or fire response to the interrupted system. Whoever turned off the service wanted to be sure there was no fire or police response before setting the fire. I did use several F.I.R.S.T. members to assist me on this fire and BATF showed an interest since the loss was over a million dollars. I put them on hold, convinced my security guard was the suspect.

The D.A. still wouldn't provide me with a search warrant so I decided to just drop in at the guy's home and chat with him. Maybe he'd give me a consent search. I obtained templates of the lobby keys to the bank and office building and hoped to match them to those in the guard's possession. He claimed to have no access to either building but I learned he did have access keys and rights to both structures early in his contract in the late 1970s.

Maybe he had the keys.

I arrived at his home in West Covina at 4 p.m. and he was extremely cooperative. We chatted again. I shared my concerns about his statements of the bank building fire and he had no doubt I was accusing him without my saying it. He provided his key rings, allowed me to search his office, garage and car. I found nothing unusual. No newspaper clippings about the fires. No calendar notations. Nothing to implicate him. He ultimately got back on the "underworld" figures attempt to kill him and added, "These guys want my contract to all the Glendale sites I work. Maybe they're trying to set me up..." He mentioned another local security service who were also troubled by these bad guys. Strangely enough, one of the partners in that firm was murdered. If he was trying to deflect me, it worked---somewhat. I thanked the 65-year-old guy and told him I'd check it all out. If nothing else, I let him know I had tailed him on several occasions and he'd never know when I was out there with him.

I let BATF know I didn't have the manpower to pursue the leads generated on the security guard suspect or the interesting theories of another company trying to get their foot in the door. I sent them all my reports of the related fires in the downtown area.

The BATF agent said he'd get back to me. I never heard from them, but in 1997, during my pre-trial preparation, I found a copy of the BATF report on their investigation of my security guard suspect. They had several interviews with him. The guard mimicked previous interviews and tried to lay off the fires on the other, unnamed, guard service. He also refused to take a polygraph, which proved nothing. Of course, the BATF never told me any of this. They closed their case after two months. December 1987 wasn't a total loss. On Saturday the 19th, I relaxed at home with a glass of cabernet, Wanda, and Cody the dog. While Wanda dozed and Cody watched a boring video, I organized the security guard reports scattered around the den as I monitored the radio at about 9 p.m. My wife's snoring was the indicator of the boring video, not Cody's evaluation. It was a typical weekend for us. Still almost newlyweds we enjoyed staying home and shared similar TV and movie interests. She didn't mind my having the fire radio constantly chaperoning and, occasionally, interrupting our solitude. The portable radio was like a slot machine, it sometimes paid off--in overtime money.

Just after nine, Burbank's Engine 13 was sent on a trash fire near the Burbank Airport Terminal 8 miles from my home. Ten minutes later another dumpster fire occurred in 13's district, this time just one block from the station. Engine 13 was by then available and responded. A third trash fire, and a fourth shortly thereafter, along the railroad tracks, got me to put down my pen and look at the radio like it was a TV screen. Still, no request was made for a Burbank investigator. Trash fires are just that —trashy. Nothing calls. I perked up each time a fresh call came in because the direction of the fires approached Glendale. The fifth blaze was on the Burbank/Glendale border, along the tracks again. Our Engine Seven was sent and I didn't have to be paged to start rolling.

I whispered to Wanda as I planted a kiss on her forehead, "Payday, see you in a couple of hours."

My dispatchers had only to hear me call "10-8" on the radio to know where I was headed. Sevens found a pile of pallets and trash burning. It was only a matter of time before this idiot found debris piled against a building and got a real fire going. A second Glendale fire was reported a half-mile south of Seven's blaze minutes after their arrival. I was racing along the Ventura Freeway at about 90 miles-per-hour and decided to ambush the pyro instead of heading to the latest fire. The D.A. wouldn't file on a serial firesetter unless he was actually observed setting a fire, I got a confession or other strong evidence. I was ready to park and go out on foot to follow this creep.

I pulled into an industrial area known as the 'S' turn and parked next to a police impound lot to watch the tracks. With my binoculars I looked a mile up the rails to see Engine Seven at the latest fire. Smoke and steam drifted across the railroad tracks like a fog.

A lone figure walked southbound in the shadows, just a hundred yards from my position. He was on a stretch with no possibilities for fires since the trash dumpsters were all on the sides away from the tracks until he was just fifty yards away. I couldn't move or he'd eyeball the unit so I stayed put with lights out and engine off as he stopped at the overflowing trash bin. He reached in, then looked over his shoulders, up and down the tracks. I called for a police unit to back me up. The suspect walked away from the trash without igniting it. When the cop was less than a half-mile away, I pulled out and parked at a railroad crossing. The unit was too obvious parked at the impound lot and I was sure he'd already made me as he walked so decided to confront him. He would not set a fire after seeing the narc car.

I had to bullshit my way through this one.

The disheveled man was about 40-years-old, with several layers of baggy clothing. Fairly clean, I didn't think he was a transient. He ID'd himself as "Tony" and displayed an L.A. County Hospital Health card. He had no driver's license. I told him he stumbled into a burglary surveillance, to get him to relax and asked if I could search his backpack. I patted him down for weapons first as the black and white roared up. Discreetly, I clued the uniform in on what I had with the trail of six fires starting at the Burbank Airport over the past hour. The man stood shivering and the cop watched as I checked the backpack. Inside was a stack of letterhead stationary, dirty and damp around the edges, and a dozen pieces of still-connected computer paper from a printer. I asked the guy where he'd been since sundown and he said, "That paper came out of a dumpster up the tracks. I didn't burglarize anybody's place."

"Right, man," I said. "We haven't had a burglary. We're just watching the area. Where you been?"

"I was at the Burbank Airport looking for a job."

"When did you leave the airport?"

"About an hour ago..."

"Which way did you walk to get here?"

"Took Hollywood Way to the tracks then followed them to here."

"No shit," said I.

The cop and I looked at each other and smiled. While the uniform ran the guy for wants and warrants I raced up to the last fire location. Arson had not yet been determined. He was only being detained. Engine Seven was still there. Inside the dumpster were several reams of the same letterhead stationary and computer paper. From the amount and layers of damaged and unburned materials in the bin, I estimated the burn time. The suspect's walking time was figured in and estimated to place him at the dumpster when it caught fire. I was guessing, but had set enough training fires by this time to know at what speed fire travels in certain fuels. The ballpark figuring and the matching paper should be enough for a filing. Maybe a mercy filing after all my security guard requests were shot down. I photographed the dumpster and its contents and returned to the cop and suspect. She already had him hooked up---he had several outstanding warrants. During the booking search I found two cigarette lighters. He clammed up and would not talk to me without a lawyer. The D.A. filed six counts and the guy plead out to two misdemeanors. Even with his extensive petty criminal history he only did 30 days. The man, a long-time, on-and-off Glendale resident may have been responsible for many fires in my town. I saw him around and spoke with him a few times after his release just to let him know I was present. He was not a complete whacko, actually held an occasional job, and had family nearby in Highland Park. In 1990, I was contacted by a Glendale Police Department homicide detective. He queried me about my trashcan pyro arrest and asked if I knew any of Tony's associates.

"Nope," I answered. "Talked to him about three times since 1987, the last time over a year ago. Haven't seen him since. You want me to keep my eyes open for him?"

"No need," the detective replied. "We know where he is---the morgue. Somebody bashed Tony's skull in last night down on the south side of town. He's dead."

Tony, no doubt, set many fires over the years. If I hadn't been monitoring fire calls that night I may never have reached the 'S' turn area in time to intercept him. His destination the night I arrested him was on surface streets just a short way from the 'S' turn. He would not have set any more fires, most likely, and I could have lost him. More fires may have resulted from the missed opportunity. But again, Glendale paid attention to small incidents and the practice produced dividends in the future---maybe even a saved life somewhere along the line. I didn't notice a drop in fires around town after his death, but I think we already deterred him anyway. There were plenty of other pyros. His murder, to my knowledge, was never solved. I have no doubt some boneheaded detective looked at me as a suspect after I was arrested.

The Orr family home in Los Angeles (1962).

Rescue of "Lady" by John Orr, during a fire in a two-story house in 1989. Orr was a half-mile away at a bar, with partner Walt Beatty, when the alarm rang in. Lady survived heavy fire and smoke but nearly succumbed to drowning while locked in a downstairs washroom. A river, created by firefighting upstairs, cascaded to the first floor, into the tiny bathroom. The small dog treaded water for several minutes before rescue. Photo by Gene Blevins.

Prosecutors theorized John Orr "…arrived early at many fires…indicating he set the blazes and stayed near to watch." Orr's evaluation of 60+ "early-arrival" fires between 1980-1991, showed over 80% were legitimate responses with partners along, arson fires with apprehension/arrest, or accidentally-caused fires. Orr's lawyers did nothing, in trial, to refute the allegations and supply the documented alibi. Above photo was one of these fires. Note empty hoses on ground and firefighters preparing to attack. Orr and his partner Tom Rickles were near this accidentally-caused fire when the call came in and arrived with first-in units (1982, 700 blk. W. Milford Avenue).

Another "early-arrival" fire (1982, 712 E. Windsor Road). Again, Rickles and Orr were together in-the-field when the accidentally-caused fire came in (NOTE: Firefighter prepares to battle fire as first-in engine company. Couch placed over top of floor furnace can be seen just inside front door.).

216

Orr on a solo investigation in-the-field when this alarm on Kennington Drive rang in. He arrived with first-in companies (1985). Three suspects later arrested, by Orr, for this revenge-motivated arson. Photo by John Orr.

Orr saw smoke from this accidentally-caused fire in Engine 4's district on Risa Drive and called it in, arriving before first-in units (1984).

Orr and partner, Lance Heiger, in-the-field and nearby when this accidental fire occurred at a restaurant under construction in 1988.

Photo of South Pasadena Fire Captain Bob Eisele (now fire chief) at the October 10, 1984 fatal Ole's fire, approximately 20 minutes after the first alarm. Photo taken by John Orr.

Photo of Kennington Drive home, taken in 1990, showing extremely poor brush clearance practices. Videotaped and photographed as part of a presentation put on by Captain Orr, in March 1990, this location and seven other hillside neighborhoods were examples of poor clearance. Locations used were areas with histories of arson-caused brush fires. This particular stretch in Chevy Chase Canyon, experienced five known arsons. Eighteen months after the photography, in October 1991, a brush fire ignited below the structure, destroying it. The 1991 fire resulted in Orr's conviction with literally no evidence, except this "before" photo.

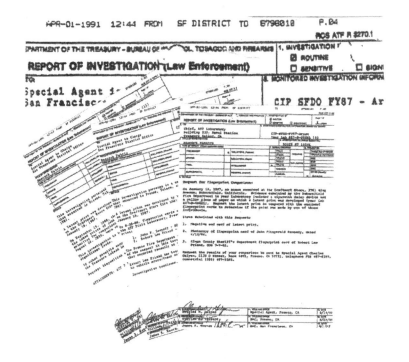

In the federal case against Orr, many documents were found withheld by prosecutors and not provided to the defense team. A fifteen-page BATF report, regarding the Fresno-area fires in 1987, was provided prior to the Fresno trial, but three pages (shown above), in sequence, were missing. Orr's lawyer requested them and they were deemed "irrelevant" by prosecutors. Orr's lawyer did not pursue their exposure. In 1996, after federal conviction, Orr found the missing three pages. The material revealed the reason for their concealment—viable suspects in the Fresno-area fires Orr was convicted of were revealed. None of the suspects were cleared, yet the information was still deemed "irrelevant" and hidden. One suspect was implicated in a fire at CCAI conference site at the Fresno Holiday Inn. When Orr attempted to obtain the missing pages he was told by prosecutors/BATF investigators that, "...we don't know anything about them...," and "...we never had those pages and don't know who you're talking about...." The newly-discovered three pages countered BATF denials: The fax tag line (enlarged above, top) reveals the documents sent to the San Francisco BATF District Office, then re-transmitted to the phone number listed to the L.A. BATF Arson Task Force Office, on April 1, 1991, well before Orr's first trial. At one point, Orr personally talked to a Fresno Fire Department investigator involved in developing two of the suspects. He told Orr, "Talk to the feds. We gave them everything we had on those guys and they (BATF) told us not to talk to you or your lawyer. I'm sorry, John..."

CHAPTER FOURTEEN
LESSER OF TWO EVILS

The latter three months of 1987 provided Wanda and I with several thousand dollars of overtime money, so Christmas was especially agreeable, despite the long hours I put in working by myself.

At a swap meet in Pasadena, Wanda spied a beautiful antique lapis lazuli ring and tried it on. Blue her favorite color, the ring fit perfectly. She loved shopping but had a frugal streak. With about $700 cash between us to play with, she passed, calling such a spontaneous purchase frivolous. My dad kept Wanda occupied at another booth while I excused myself to buy a beer, as a ruse. I slinked back to the jewelry vendor, haggled the lapis down $25, and bought it. I slipped the boxed ring into her bag of clothing purchases and she seemed pleased at the discovery of the gem among her other treasures.

By late 1987, I felt confident our unit functioned smoothly without a police officer assigned. Maybe better, and with less anxiety. I worked law enforcement since my Sears days in the late 1970's. Enhanced by the excellent basic training by Tom Rickles, I filed dozens of criminal cases, wrote and served over 15 search warrants, chased down fleeing felons, and testified as an expert witness at least twenty times.

Walter Beatty started work as my partner on January 1, 1988. After Lance's premature departure, word filtered back to me, from police officer friendlies, a little resentment simmered at the cop shop. Rumor had it I initiated Lance's transfer so I could slip my close friend, Walt, into the unit. Apparently, the unthinkable happened — a secret remained covert at the police department. The real reason for his return, the conflict-of-interest scenario, never circulated. Without any other information to go on, the cops assumed the rumor correct. I was not bothered too much until I heard Lance voiced support of the gossip to several people at a cop event. At least the prick could have been discrete. I covered his ass when he was my partner and I did not appreciate his using me as scapegoat for his own failings. Tempted to plant the seed of reality about the scam, I remained mute. It would take little to alienate the police fraternity and I needed their support. Lance also retained the Oakmont security guard contract. It seemed they looked out for their own despite the three days off the situation cost Lance. The liability of retaining Lance was reinforced when a police employee, working out of the police chief's office, bought me a drink and intimated the alteration to my unit was best for all. He did not elaborate.

I still respected my police counterparts. Using the police lab and technicians, jail, interview rooms, property storage facility, uniformed officers and detectives as backup, I also had to ensure they would accept Walt's unusual personality. Naturally insecure in the new, unfamiliar position, he exuded overconfidence to the point of insolence. Going through a Wyatt Earp stage, his aggressiveness came out inappropriately a few times. A reluctant witness on a bomb threat case was shocked when Walt snapped at her when she didn't answer questions quickly enough. He spoke condescendingly to superiors, including at least one Battalion Chief, at fire scenes. Whenever we went to the police station I made sure I was available to go with him. The Unit didn't need any more grief and Walt's overcompensation wouldn't set well with police officers or detectives. He was Don Rickles, without the humor.

Russ Pierce became the Robbery/Homicide sergeant and our liaison with the police department on January 1, 1988. Hopefully, we'd all grow together. My associates in the police department jail, lab, and records bureau were allies and I nurtured them. Lunches, a box of doughnuts or an occasional bouquet or card of appreciation went a long way in keeping the fire investigators high on police support staff's Christmas card list. I could live with a few uniforms pissed off at me but could not afford to offend the support services. I would not allow Walt to threaten the relationship either. He was a loose cannon, but a talented and knowledgeable guy. Like a troubled marriage we had to work to make the pairing successful. Unfortunately, it was a one-sided effort.

Right out of the gate I wanted Walt to ride along with uniformed officers in a black and white. Recalling my own difficulties with writing citations and controlling my temper early in my law enforcement experience I forced him, creatively, to do the ridealongs. He endured two stints and that was it. He procrastinated until we got too busy and he had built-in excuses.

We started January off with a police report of a small fire at an elementary school. A fiberglass picnic table burned on a Sunday morning. Descriptions of the two suspects enabled us to go to the school and track them down. Isaac and Manny, both 10-years old, were left alone every Sunday morning while their parents wandered off for the day. Left on their own they amused themselves burning the table and getting into who knows what kind of mischief. We counseled the boys at school, touched base with the parents and had all scheduled for follow-up counseling sessions. Neither parent attended more than one meeting and we couldn't enforce attendance without an arrest. Six months later we heard from the boys again — in a big way.

In February, I returned from a run to Van Nuys in the San Fernando Valley, on a Saturday, when I spied a column of thick, black smoke reaching into the sky of Burbank. In Wanda's turbo T-Bird I raced through the surface streets and arrived as several first alarm units rolled up at the National RV Center. Parking over a block away and without radio or camera, I ran back to watch as a dozen motor homes and the building went up. Within seconds of my arrival I saw Glendale dispatch supervisor Rich Kaufmann drive by. He waved at me and I watched him videotape as the spectacular explosion-punctuated fire roared through the RV lot. Watching his videotape at work the next day I decided I had to have a video camera. I spent over a thousand dollars for a Pentax 8mm videocam and extra equipment. The set-up could be used for post-fire scene investigation documentation as well as capturing the very important early fire stages when I was able to get to the fire quickly. The beauty of the videocam was one-hand operation. I could document as soon as I arrived, or before, without worrying about shutter speeds or lens openings. Everything was automatic.

Also in February my article, 'Dangers of Hazardous Investigative Evidence Storage' was published in the *American Fire Journal*. The 2000-word piece outlined an incident I experienced at the Glendale Police hazardous evidence storage facility and how it was mitigated. Hazardous storage included flammable liquid, car batteries, fireworks, and anything deemed unsafe for the indoor property room. I walked into the 6' x 10' concrete facility one day and found a 12-volt car battery with exposed terminals on a shelf just below 2 gallons of gasoline and five gallons of acetone. I called in a haz mat response to the police building. It cost over $3000 for the police department to remove some of the unidentifiable miasma. Upgrades and correctional procedures were recommended. The rules were not followed and I had little power to mitigate the continuing problems. Politically, even my boss, the Fire Marshal, couldn't enforce the needed expensive maintenance and changes. In May, 2000, a Glendale Police Community Services Officer was overcome by fumes from an unmarked 55-gallon drum of booked evidence from a drug lab. A full haz mat response was called, the jail and police building evacuated, and two personnel transported to the hospital. I guess they didn't read my article back in 1988.

Less than a week after I bought my videocam I relaxed at home, on-call, and heard a radio broadcast of a structure fire in Engine Seven's district. Only a minute later Engine Seven called in "...heavy smoke showing, requesting a second alarm." I raced to the D&L Bindery fire, five miles from home, and arrived with the last part of the first alarm units. Ugly black and gray smoke billowed from the 8,000-square-foot single-story structure next to the railroad tracks. With a stiff 15-20 mile-per-hour wind out of the west, the flame travel was quickly traced back as I videotaped the area of origin on the outside of the property fence just 30 feet from the tracks. I continued to tape as two other structures burned while third and fourth alarm units arrived to help.

I considered calling out Walt to assist but the area of origin was confirmed and there were only three people to interview. A fire of this magnitude, with several million dollars damage and three businesses involved might cause most agencies to call out an army of investigators. I had that option but didn't need the massive response. With a confirmed start in a pile of trash and pallets on the outside of the building's loading dock, the motivation was most likely a nuisance fire that got out of hand or possibly accidental. If arson, the motive was not for insurance fraud. A fraud fire would start on the inside, late at night, to ensure a late detection and total destruction. Three people were inside this building when the fire started. My intuition told me this wasn't a revenge fire either. If someone was pissed off at the business or owner, the attack would also be on the inside, not from 30 feet away and a hope the blaze would spread.

By the time I returned to the area of origin it was obliterated by firefighting activities. But I had it all on videotape and later confirmed by the tow truck driver who called it in. He traveled on a nearby overpass, saw the two pallets burning and the 9-1-1 recording verified his observations. The blaze was just spreading through the perimeter fence onto the littered loading dock as the driver reported it. No leads were developed on this early Sunday afternoon fire. The National RV blaze struck at almost the exact minute on the previous Sunday afternoon. No connection between the two fires was established.

Over the years I found much of my time wasted on leads going nowhere. Big-screen detectives or fictional investigators in mystery novels often wander off into herds of clues, running every one to the ground. In reality, unless you form a task force of detectives, following up on every lead is impossible or a waste of time. Using what a fire scene told me helped narrow down motivation, suspect age group and even gender. A trash fire in an alley behind a 7-11 store at 3p.m. is going to cause me to look for a school-aged kid, not a 50-year-old man. A gasoline-initiated blaze in a failing restaurant screams of owner involvement, not a burglar who happens to carry around cans of flammables. With seven distinct motivations for arson it was necessary to identify one or two possibilities before wasting hundreds of man-hours on bad "tips" or leads. I know spending more time on some of my follow-up investigations may have revealed a suspect eventually, but I think the Unit's tactics were verified by our high clearance rate.

With Walt Beatty on board and functioning as a partner in just two months, I started a new program. Simply a twist on the mission of the fire department, fire prevention, I attempted to expand on the concept. We experienced so many construction site and vacant building fires in the 1985-87 period, I targeted these locations for special attention. Typically littered with cardboard, old furniture, wood piles and accumulation of trash, these unsecured and seldom patrolled areas were frequent arson targets. I intended to focus on these potential disasters and prevent the arson.

The idea came to me when Engine Six's captain called me to be present at a fire prevention inspection problem at a small business in the industrial area on the west side of town. The company housed a large storage area containing thousands of gallons of flammable paints, thinners, chemicals and vats of caustics. Six's captain warned the owners twice to clean up the site and added he would shut the place down if compliance wasn't met. He didn't expect any headway and asked me and Walt to join them to add a hammer to their nail. The fire department has the power to shut down a business if the hazards are sufficiently dangerous but the ordinance is seldom used. This place qualified.

The cheapest way for these owners to correct all the violations was to burn the place down and start over. Nothing was done since the last visit. The captain wrote the order to cease business and I directed Walt to write a citation for the continuing violations. Walt and I had taken off our coats to display guns, handcuffs, and the ability to enforce the law. Additionally, we took IDs from the owners and two employees present and asked for license numbers of their cars, home addresses and phone numbers. By the time we left they knew the department was watching the dump. As we departed I told the men a special request would be made for additional police patrol also. As an afterthought, I asked for the owner's insurance policy and he readily produced it. The fire-trap did not burn but they did finally get the problems corrected and re-opened.

Arson prevention seemed to work well. We spread the word to all fire companies to contact the arson investigators when they encountered resistant owners of hazardous locations. We assisted fire companies on many "final" inspections. Before we started the program, a third visit resulted in the problem being referred to the city attorney's office for prosecution. The lawyers simply started an additional 90-120 day warning notice procedure forcing fire crews to return again and again to re-inspect. If Walt or I wrote a citation the city attorney was required to prepare and prosecute the case within ten days. We effectively eliminated the middleman and just the threat of a citation now resulted in an average of 3-5 day compliance, saving us from writing the citations. With a few months track record of success I made a request to formalize the referral-to-arson program. The Fire Marshal and fire department staff accepted the proposal and we were in the fire and arson prevention business.

We made surprise visits to filthy construction sites and forced compliance of fire laws including re-securing perimeter fences, removing large amounts of combustible materials and, in some cases of large tracts or sites, forcing the owners to provide overnight security. Owners of vacant structures were ordered to do the same or the city would contact board-up services to do the work at substantially higher prices than doing the work themselves.

Walter hated the program. The idea of writing a citation was cool, but the constant fire prevention inspections and follow-up calls, meetings and drive-bys with slumlords and building managers seemed beneath his new law enforcement position. It was just busywork. To me it was survival of the Unit. We were so successful in catching arsonists the past few years, our number of fires dropped. If the stats tumbled too far, we would be out of jobs. It happened in nearby Pasadena. They had a two-man unit of a cop and a fireman, then just a fireman/investigator, then no full-time investigator. Their problem wasn't a lack of cases but political issues and the possibility was real to me. My idea was to keep the Arson/Explosives Unit working, producing and visible. Even if arson stats dropped we'd have a record of keeping busy and even bringing in money for re-inspection fees and cost recoveries. Despite Walt's grumblings, I added vacant lot and grassy hillsides to our fire/arson prevention duties. Over 80% of our brushfires originated on street side vacant land so by eliminating these targets the roving firebug would be forced to move into another jurisdiction to play. In theory, at least.

In September and October 1987 we had trash fires behind a neighborhood grocery store in the Montrose section of town. Phil's Market had an alley behind it and the dumpster was torched twice in the late evening hours. On February 23, 1988 the container took off again at about 10 p.m. Like a fuse, the fire extended from the dumpster, entered a leaf-clogged rain gutter and ignited tarred roofing material, then flames crawled through a breech in the wall to set off the attic space and a storeroom. A second alarm was called and a heroic stop made before the fire destroyed the building. I misread fire travel initially and when Walt arrived to assist he put me back on the right track and we traced the origin back to the dumpster.

Examining the earlier trash fire reports, I noticed a description of a pick-up truck written down by a fire captain. A little canvassing revealed information on the former employee who owned such a truck. A background check showed him now employed for several months as a security guard at the First Interstate Bank building in downtown Los Angeles. The 30-story high-rise suffered a $20 million fire several months before. One man was killed. Los Angeles Fire Department arson investigators took over a week to announce the fire was "probably" accidental.

Still, such a coincidence was intriguing. I elected to contact LAFD and gave them the Phil's Market report and suspect's connection to their fire. LAFD asked me to hold off on contacting the man until they could check him out. Turning an accidental fire into an arson with a suspect would be controversial and almost unfilable. (this was, however, done to me several years later.) LAFD never called back so I talked to the kid on the Phil's fire as a witness and he gave me nothing usable. So much time had passed by the time I got to interview him, he had trouble recalling his activities on a particular night.

With my devotion to work and Wanda, contacts with my family were random. Calling Carrie and Lori periodically I was only able to connect with one at a time, if that. Both teenagers, their high school years were filled with social events, dating, and the rigors of getting an education. They also worked together at the local Del Taco. Lloyd, their mother's husband, didn't work and was at home whenever the girls were there. They tolerated him but the relationship with step-dad was fragile.

Wanda and I took my mother to dinner once a month or had her over for drinks in the evenings. She lived close by and kept active with her senior group's activities and occasional bus trips to Laughlin, Nevada.

My dad worked at his retirement "job." On weekends he went to the garage sales and swap meets buying used tools, machinery, and collectibles. During the week he cleaned up his purchases, sanded and oiled the tool and machine surfaces and made everything serviceable again. Then he'd hold his own garage sale or rent a stall at the Rose Bowl or other swap meet venues and sell his finds at two or three times, and more, of their purchase price. Honest guy that he was, he dutifully kept meticulous records of buying and selling and paid taxes on his profits.

Dad's garage was almost wide enough for two compact cars but there was never an oil stain on the floor. Since I was five years old I only saw a car in our garage once and it was a VW Dad just purchased. Within a week the newness wore off and the multiplying swap meet detritus took over again. There were several narrow paths running through the cubicle, just enough room to open a drawer or remove boxes from a shelf. It was like jamming the contents of a 7-11 store into a bathroom.

At least once a month I'd cruise by Dad's and have a beer or a can of sardines with him. We'd sit around on the two stools in front of the workbench and chat, reminisce, and joke around. He always told me he was in the process of cleaning out the garage and "soon" there'd be enough room to park his truck inside. It hasn't happened since 1966 but I religiously came by to check on his progress. He didn't date much but kept his social life active my visiting his nearby siblings and the widows of a couple of childhood friends, He helped them all out with household chores and remains spry today at 87-years-old. He even had my mom over occasionally when he hosted holiday events. With a barbeque in full swing Dad and I still found reasons to gravitate to his garage so I could check on his consolidation progress.

I actually saw some headway gained once. Only because there was a leak in the garage roof and two large boxes of old magazines and clothing go soaked. He threw it all away and left enough room for the four boxes of junk collected the following weekend.

On my 39th birthday, April 26, 1988, Wanda and I went to bed early after a terrific dinner and a bottle or two of excellent Riesling. The dispatch center woke me up just before midnight with a gift of three hours overtime. I rolled to a failed attempt to lob a one-gallon Molotov cocktail at a house. Some idiot filled the Gallo Hearty Burgundy jug with gasoline, stuffed in a wick, lit it, then tried to toss the nine-pound device from the street to the man's house. It fell short, shattering on a driveway and did limited damage. The victim immediately fingered two neighborhood punks who hassled him. He ran them off earlier in the evening. The area cop taking the crime report knew the pair. After collecting the bottle evidence and photoing the scene, we drove two blocks to the home of one of the crooks. The engine on his truck was still warm at 12:30 a.m.

We had his mother wake the 20-year-old and got a good story on his activities that night and he also gave consent to search his truck. The interior smelled like a refinery. On the littered passenger side floor, among McNuggets boxes and greasy napkins, I found a black metal wine jug twist-on lid. Great wine, that Gallo. I seized it and we left.

Still feeling the effects of my own wine consumption, I drove home. The next morning I figured the nearest place for the purchase of a jug of Gallo was at the 7-11 store in the area. When Walt and I arrived at about 9a.m. we noticed the store had a video camera. The silent observer was out of service the night before. The night clerk did provide us with a sketchy description of one of our suspects.

I transported the broken glass bottle neck and metal cap to the Los Angeles County Sheriff's Lab that morning. Attached to the bottle neck was a black metal band used to crimp the cap in place to seal the jug after it was filled with liquid at the winery. I felt maybe the lab's comparative analysis technicians might like a challenge and could try to match the band from the Molotov to the cap from the truck. The Glendale Police Lab, as capable as they were, didn't have a comparative analysis section.

Skeptical, the Sheriff's lab technician accepted the request and evidence, saying he'd get back to me. Used to matching pry marks on locks to screwdrivers and crow bars or bullets to the gun barrels, this must have been a first-time challenge for the very busy techies. I expected at least a week's turnaround on this relatively non-violent "nothing" case.

I got a call back from the Sheriff's lab the next morning. We had an exact match. There were tear marks fitting the jagged edges on both pieces. Like ripping a piece of dense cloth, the frayed, torn ends microscopically matched.

Warrants were issued that day for both suspects. I got the warrant information in time to be included on the "Hot Board" read to the 3-11 p.m. cop shift. Only two cars worked the extreme north end of town where these clowns lived but I had great success with the uniforms working the north side.

At 5:30 p.m., as I headed for the local cantina to meet my old roommate Bill, the police department paged me—a very unusual occurrence. The cops normally had the fire dispatchers locate me. I called and the sergeant advised me an L.A. County Sheriff's patrol had one of my suspect's under surveillance near the fire scene. I don't know how the deputies got the Be-On-The-Lookout info on my suspects but was pleased something occasionally worked out between me and the cops.

As I raced to the area, a Glendale cop came up on the radio, joined the deputy, and stopped the 20-year-old when he got antsy. It wasn't the driver I had talked to, but the passenger I had not met yet. Just before I arrived, the idiot started resisting with two burly deputies and a gutsy female Glendale cop present. I joined in the fray as the fool was spread-eagled across the hood of one of the units. It took all of us to subdue and handcuff the slippery kid. I thanked them all for their help and had the GPD transport him for booking. I also found out the north-side Glendale cops met and shared the BOLO information on the two well-known suspects. I was only two blocks from the other suspect's home so cruised over to see if we could score a double.

I drove into the L.A. County Sheriff's jurisdiction, just off the Glendale border and as I approached the house I saw suspect number two, Larry, leaning into the open driver's window of an occupied car in the street. He didn't "make" the narc car but checked to see if there was room for me to pass. I slowed and considered parking for a few minutes but maybe the car's occupants saw the arrest of the partner and were informing him. The suspect looked nervous and checked me out a second time. Instinctively, I moved up behind the car parked in the street and activated my red and yellow lights. I expected the group to perceive I was approaching them because the car was illegally parked. At the same time I called the police dispatcher.

"Station, 51 Frank, I'm code-6 on an arson suspect, 3200 block Evelyn, roll a back…"

The suspect looked up as I got out and he started to walk away. "Is this your car…can you move it to the side…"I said, hoping to keep him on the street and off guard. He looked over his shoulder and slowed, but I was now moving up on him. "Larry! I need to talk to you…" He bolted.

"You're under arrest, Larry," I shouted and took off after him. He was headed for his house. I didn't want him to get inside and complicate matters. Advised he was under arrest, he was a fleeing felon.

"51 Frank…foot pursuit," I screamed into my radio.

Larry rounded the end of a four-foot high hedge along a sidewalk leading to his front porch. I couldn't follow in his tracks and catch him in time so I leaped a three-foot high split-rail fence, touched down twice in the rock garden, dodging cacti, then launched myself towards the sprinting figure.

I screamed at him as I flew. With a portable radio in one hand, my trajectory was aimed two feet in front of the running 220-pound youngster. We collided and my radio went flying. To keep from losing him or impaling myself on needle-sharp hedge or cactus branches, or both, I grabbed his shoulder-length hair and held on as our momentum carried us forward, away from the hedge. I recovered before Larry and slipped my left arm around his neck in the reliable, and now forbidden, chokehold. I dragged the struggling firebomber to my radio and again called for help. I wasn't sure if my first request went through or they responded to it while I took a solo flight moments before.

"Station 51 Frank, foot pursuit…now…3200 block Evelyn Drive…"

The return response was good news/bad news. The good news—the two assigned units were authorized code-3; the bad news—they were three miles away and I was already tired. Adrenaline seems to overpower me quickly, draining my strength instead of enhancing it.

More bad news popped out of the radio, "51 Frank; you're in Sheriff's area on Evelyn…?" I hoped the borderline location would bring twice as much help, not a jurisdictional hesitation or question. I didn't have time to ponder. Larry was busy trying to squirm out of my grasp. We struggled almost upright but I wanted us on the ground where he couldn't use his weight and youth advantage against me. As he twisted, I simply relaxed and let my 195 pounds drag us back to the ground while tightening the modified "half-Nelson" I tried to get on him. We fell and the wrenching broke open a retainer on my shoulder holster. The Smith & Wesson 9mm, still in its clamshell, hanging by its left strap, swung around and smacked Larry in the chest. He reached for it but I tightened my forearm and distracted him while rolling over to get the gun out of his reach.

We'd been on the ground less than a minute when I heard sirens screaming in the distance. One of them was the distinctive keening wail of a County Engine 63's mechanical growler warning device. Actually, I didn't care if a fire truck or a tow truck showed up to help me out. All I knew was I was breathing hard and didn't want to die by my own gun. He could kick my ass to death but I wouldn't give up the Smith. I later found out Engine 63 just happened to respond on an unrelated emergency at the time.

Larry didn't really seem to want the gun, just wanted to get away. He didn't talk as we struggled but he, too, was tired. With his right wrist in my grasp, I tried to twist his arm so he couldn't reach up again. We rolled around and I finally got him into the street in a sitting position. I squatted behind him using my greatest strength, my legs to lift when I needed to control the bruiser. The 9mm continued to swing precariously under my left armpit and occasionally around to the front of us. A few neighbors showed up and offered to help. One asked if I wanted a rag to stop the 'bleeding." I had no idea who was bleeding but was pleased these people had no love for Larry, either.

Thankfully, a Glendale black and white roared onto Evelyn Drive and went into a four-wheel slide, narrowly missing my narc car. Officer Yang, an old friend, barked into the radio as he jumped out, "14-Boy, 97 on Evelyn…they're fighting…3219 Evelyn."

"My gun's loose, Yang…"

He hesitated a moment, eyed the shotgun mounted in the front seat, then decided the best course of action was his baton. He charged us like Bruce Lee with the stick cocked at head height. When Yang was four feet from us, Larry saw the coming attractions and didn't want any part of it, violently turning to the left. The club crashed onto my right elbow. I guess Yang liked that maneuver because he cocked and fired the baton again. This time striking my bicep. I almost lost feeling and my grasp on Larry when the third blow smacked my forearm.

"Cuffs, cuffs, my gun's hanging loose over here…" I shouted.

We managed to get one handcuff on his right wrist as a Sheriff's unit screamed towards us. I whispered into Larry's ear, "Larry, I'm tired. If you don't put your left arm behind your back I'm going to choke you out. I'm too old for this shit. You're fucking busted." He listened to reason and we successfully cuffed him as I collapsed on my back to catch my breath.

I heard the Sheriff's deputy radio for a paramedic unit. I didn't think we thumped Larry that badly. He appeared okay to me. Then I realized

231

the medics were for me so I sat up and had him cancel the ambulance. If I could have seen myself the paramedics would have continued in. Three large welts decorated my right arm, a cut on my nose dabbled my shirt front with blood, and one ear was rubbed raw by road rash. The torn shirt and abraded pants added to my ensemble, but I felt okay. We had both idiots in custody and euphoria overcame any pain. An extremely satisfactory conclusion to a "nothing" case.

Both suspects appeared at the preliminary hearing ten days later in front of J.D. Smith. After I testified to the matching of the bottle cap and crimping seal, the suspects went on to take a plea bargain. The assault-on-a-peace officer charge was dropped. I still wasn't considered a cop in the eyes of the D.A.'s Office, I guess. Both firebombers served a year in the county jail for the offense.

On May 13 a fire flared in a Ralph's Market storeroom while open for business. Rubbing alcohol stolen from a shelf was used to try and ignite a pallet of bundled firewood. No suspects were seen. Probably a diversionary fire to enable shoplifting of meat, liquor or cigarettes while employees were busy with the fire.

Two more fires went down in the trash room at 433 North Jackson Street. No damage was done. Like most series fire cases, the more incidents occur the likelier of turning evidence. I went back through the files from the past three years and obtained the latest tenants list for the 40-unit building. Several names appeared showing residents still living there since the first fires and two were home during the daytime hours when all fires occurred. I talked to the first and struck out after almost accusing the tenant of setting the blaze. I was wrong and felt badly about how I handled the situation. Especially after I chatted with the other suspect. He escaped scrutiny during the previous investigation because he had a job that took him away from the building all day, we thought. Actually, he freelanced and was in-the-field frequently and could have been at the building for the other series. The small blazes started by ignited material being dropped down a trash chute next to his third floor apartment.

A 42-year-old single man, he was insecure, almost effeminate, and enjoyed being the center of attention during the interview until I got to the accusatory stage. The phantom witness got him close to opening up but the remote hallway precluded visibility of the exact area so the invisible spy couldn't be an eyewitness for the interview purposes. We reached an impasse. He knew that I knew he was the guy. With no evidence to get a filing I left him by asking for his "help."

"Please keep your eyes open when you're home during the day. You never know what you might see. I don't think we're going to have any more fires, are we?"

He hung his head as he replied, "I'm sure there won't be any more problems..." And there weren't. I don't use this case as a serial-arsonist-captured statistic on my resume. He was identified but not arrested or apprehended. The fires stopped. That's all that counted. Low stats.

On Sunday, May 12, at about 10 a.m., I was on-call and stopped at a nursery in Glendale to pick up fertilizer for Wanda's garden. While inside I heard a siren approach and several in the distance. Walking out to my unit, I watched the Battalion Chief roar by and saw a huge column of oily black smoke on the near-horizon, less than a mile away. From the size of the blaze I knew I'd end up getting called to it. Again I found myself near a fire at its inception, and I had nothing to do with its origin like prosecutors and investigators theorized years later.

A second alarm was called by Engine Seven as I started to roll. Arriving less than four minutes later I saw Seven's already had a 2½" handline stretched to protect a 2-story apartment building from the well-involved Studio Auto Body fire. The small converted gas station building blazed, along with 6-8 cars and trucks inside a lot to the rear. I videotaped the firefighting efforts as a total of 10 vehicles inside and outside were destroyed. After the smoke cleared, fire travel was traced back to the area of a Ford van where I determined the blaze started. Splattered on the ground was a bizarre rainbow of a dozen open cans of flammable enamel auto paint. I noted the door of the van was open before the fire.

An undamaged paint booth building at the rear of the property was examined. Inside the garage-sized structure someone discharged a dry chemical fire extinguisher in a fashion that was not directed at the fire area. The empty extinguisher was thrown to the floor just inside the door. Inside, a thin layer of flour-like chemical covered the concrete floor and captured two sets of child-sized sneaker prints. The white tracks led out the door and disappeared into pools of water from the firefighting. I located a section of perimeter fence where the chain-link had pulled away from the ground and disturbed dirt beneath the breech specked with white powder. The suspects were somewhere in the crowd of 30-40 kids loitering on the apartment property.

Entering the driveway I kept my eyes glued to the ground, looking for white powder. In less than three minutes of tracking I located two pairs of sneakers decorated with the evidence. Glancing up I saw the powder in the hair of a pair of 10-year-olds and open-mouthed gapes on their faces. We recognized each other.

"Isaac, Manny, we need to talk..." They obediently followed me to the manager's apartment where I separated the pair and we talked. Isaac and Manny were responsible for burning the picnic table at a nearby school in January. They reluctantly shared their tale, Isaac apparently the leader, Manny the follower. Again on a Sunday, the parents left the two boys alone while they wandered off to who knows where. Bored, the boys played in the body shop lot where Isaac fired off the extinguisher, entered the van, ransacked it, then began tossing the full paint cans. The paint hit the parking lot with a pleasing plop and colorful display so Manny joined him. Over ten gallons were thrown about before Isaac produced a matchbook, lit if off and dropped it in the flammable liquid. Fortunately, the flash point of paint wasn't anywhere near gasoline and they fled as the flames spread.

I recalled the National RV and D&L Bindery fires in February. Both were Sunday fires when the boys were traditionally left alone. I talked to Manny, the weaker of the two, and asked if he and Isaac watched the big fire by the railroad tracks. They did, returning from a visit with a cousin they used the tracks as a shortcut home. Manny clammed up when he saw where I was going with the story and I could only get the pair to agree they watched the fire. I couldn't place them near the pallets or gain a confession for the bindery fire but they were nearby.

Tempted to arrest them, an aunt showed up and took custody of the pair. Glendale PD didn't like arresting 10-year-olds. The boys' parents later attended counseling sessions and were further referred to a psychologist. The total loss for Studio Auto Body was over $500,000. Isaac and Manny repeated their firesetting because their parents neglected them. The acting out was predictable, particularly when they didn't attend the first counseling sessions we ordered in January. After this incident, Manny, Isaac, and their families disappeared from Glendale. I believe the threat of civil suits for the fire damages caused their flight.

On June 22, I had a series of three nuisance fires and a Molotov cocktail in the Engine Five's district. The blazes and firebomb detonation occurred around a 2-story apartment building under construction in the framing stages. A quick canvass of the neighborhood produced a possible suspect, a 14-year-old. "Ramon" saw me nosing around the Molotov site and hung around a while. I remembered Michael doing the same thing around his fires. "Ramon" matched the suspect's description. I let him follow me across the street from the Molotov's splashdown while I located the exact point where the bomb was launched. A single wooden match on the ground was a clue number one, spilled gasoline, number two; and fire damage in the hedge the third. When the incendiary was tossed, the near-full bottle spun and flaming gasoline splashed on the bush, setting a small fire. All this took place at the edge of his apartment building, just twenty feet from his garage. A bottle matching the Molotov container was located in Ramon's garage and similar wooden matches found in his kitchen. Case closed with a referral to counseling, four fires cleared and how many prevented?

The summer of 1987 kept us busy, particularly in the late night and early morning hours. We were making good overtime money but the responses to so many small arson fires and accidental blazes where we weren't needed were taking a toll. Walt suggested a program similar to Pasadena Fire Department's shift investigator procedures. Pasadena had several qualified arson investigators on each shift 24 hours a day and they were used from 5:00 p.m. to 7 a.m. instead of calling out the day arson detective. Handling only cause and origin investigation, a day detective was requested only when a suspect was developed and immediate follow-up necessary.

Walt jotted down notes on the pros and cons of such a program and I researched overtime cost savings if the proposal was accepted. Walt and I were averaging $5-6,000 annually for after-hours overtime. I figured the city could save $5-8,000 per year if we could get the program implemented. The summer kept us active with several more series fires so we tabled the "shift investigator" research for a while.

On August 9, Walt and I sat in our new office at the Municipal Services Building, near city hall, at about 4:30 p.m. when we heard Engine Four dispatched to a mattress fire beside a street in the affluent Greenbriar area of town. Minutes later Four's captain called "at scene of a small fire, now out, we have an incendiary device and need an investigator..." Walt was on-call and since it was near quitting time I stayed in the office while he took the call. He found three cigarette/match/rubber band devises in the area of the discarded mattress and a description of a blue sedan provided as a possible suspect vehicle seen cruising the area. The car was similar to one belonging to a South Pasadena arson suspect. A flyer was distributed earlier in the summer depicting the car and an actual photo of the suspect. We passed on the info to the South Pasadena Fire Department. The case went nowhere but again the "Orr-device" had been found and at the time of the incident I was with my partner when the fire went down. I obviously wasn't involved, yet years later it was theorized I was the only person setting fires with this device.

On August 15, Walt and I responded on a one acre brush fire in Engine Six's district. The dangerous afternoon blaze started at roadside and raced up a steep hill to threaten five homes. Quick action by Station Six and three other units put the fire down. An "Orr-device" was found at the bottom of the hill, partially destroyed by flames. All parts were recognizable. I photographed the burned components as Walt held it. Again we were together, this time for hours before the fire.

On September 14, a five acre blaze broke out along the western border of Glendale in Los Angeles' Griffith Park. Walt and I raced to the Command Post and watched as a huge response of LAFD personnel, equipment and helicopters made quick work of the fast-moving fire. Again allowed by an outside agency to search their area of origin, we got on hands and knees and looked for a device in the charred stalks of grass. Minutes into the search a one-acre blaze erupted in nearby Burbank. We rushed to our own fire but found no device. First arriving companies obliterated the area of origin. Four years later, a near-identical circumstance occurred with two Griffith Park-area and Burbank fires preceding a final fire in Glendale. The Glendale blaze destroyed a $500,000 home and I was later convicted of setting that fire on literally no evidence. I believe the suspect on the 1988 and 1991 fires lives in the Chevy Chase Canyon or La Canada/Flintridge vicinity. Similar fires continue to plague the area. One was set the day after I was convicted in 1992 while I was in Fresno, California.

On October 17 I bagged a 14-year-old boy for another Molotov cocktail incident. The firebomb went off at curbside in an affluent area of Engine Six's district. It was a whodunit upon arrival but examining the spatter marks of the liquid gave me direction of travel. The splash patterns led me to a nearby house. A few questions brought me to a teenager I previously apprehended in the late 1970s when, as a 7-year-old, he set three brushfires in his backyard. Released to his parents, this repeat firesetter later attended counseling and paid a $250 fee for the investigation, my overtime and the fire engine response. Our unit enlarged on Tom Rickles original cost retrieval plan and collected an average of $8-10,000 per year for violations such as this. We avoided clogging up the court system with an arrest, got the parents attention and enforced the counseling requirements through straight-up extortion. If the culprit didn't pay-he went to jail. The program worked nicely and we had total flexibility to hold off on billings if they created a hardship on the family. The fees were sometimes just a tool.

December produced a unique series crime wave. The first two crimes were captured as burglary reports so I never saw them. On the third, a burglary detective finally contacted me with questions. The suspect's m.o. was taping powerful "quarter sticks" fireworks to windows of drug stores. The resulting blasts breeched the windows, set off the alarm system and brought police, owners and alarm company patrols to the scene. After the damage was covered with plywood, or sometimes not, the burglar came back, knowing the alarm system was now compromised. He entered, broke into the drug supplies and stole other merchandise with a good chance any alarm transmitted would be perceived as a "false" alarm. He was right. Pretty good scam. The detective asked me to evaluate the evidence, write a report on the device properties, and submit the remains for analysis to tie the cases together or help identify a suspect.

In two of the cases no evidence of the explosive was recovered yet was described in the original report, In the first of the series the officer mentioned "tubular cardboard pieces" in the area but didn't recognize them as an expended quarter stick. No arson/explosive investigator was requested, of course. In the second incident the officer taking the report saw scattered remains, correctly ID'd them and even mentioned the "end plugs, colored paper wrapping and fuse remnants." He didn't gather or book any evidence, The officer was Tom Rickles.

I drove to the drug store and found the window still broken two days after the detonation. Below the window, on a side street, I found the expended explosive pieces littering a hedge and collected it. Tom's oversight broke the chain of custody connecting the crimes.

A display board was prepared exhibiting the similarities of evidence as well as m.o. The burglar was captured days later when he hit the only accessible drug store left in town and an alert uniformed officer lay in wait for the man's return.

A search of his apartment and car revealed matching tape used to secure the explosives to the windows and another dozen quarter sticks. The arson/explosives unit had little to do with this case but the display board and my report helped get the D.A. to issue a search warrant and a case filing. Testifying in the preliminary hearing bolstered the case and allowed me to qualify as an expert witness in an explosives case, a rarity. The career criminal took a "deal" and did state prison time.

CHAPTER FIFTEEN
BURNING BRIDGES

In late January 1989, a low-grade explosion, followed by fire, brought five companies of firefighters to a large supermarket in the west-central part of town. Crews arrived at about 3 a.m. and found several small, separate fires burning inside and a thick oily smoke filling the cavernous building. Crews extinguished the fires quickly. Inside, firemen tripped over 5-gallon blue plastic containers and slipped on pools of unburned gasoline. Gasoline, brought into the structure in the benign-appearing blue water containers, was spread throughout the store. Some of the trails or poured "fuses" were incomplete and did not ignite, the mixture too rich and the initial fire consumed all the oxygen before the other pools took off. The scene spoke of two possibilities: serious revenge, or insurance fraud. Without signs of forcible entry, keys used, the fire screamed "owner involved fraud fire." I was contacted by former L.A. County Sheriff Arson/Explosives investigator Bruce Kamann. Now retired, Bruce hired out to insurance companies. I had worked with him on several fires in Glendale and even been to his home a time or two. He was a member of F.I.R.S.T. and the only police office fire investigator who I felt truly understood fire behavior. Bruce explained he had a near-identical fire in a market two years before in nearby Temple City. The gasoline used to burn the place was transported in blue 5-gallon jugs. His theory, as was ours, was that using the blue water containers did not draw attention. The price tags on some of his undamaged containers matched some of ours purchased at a Hollywood Pep Boys store just four blocks from the suspect we developed. The suspect had recently sold his interest in the Glendale market but had financial ties, nonetheless. He was a full partner at the Temple City store and the business was failing. We were able to get a search warrant for the suspect's Hollywood home, but little was learned. Another motive was discovered after a lengthy investigation: the owners of the market and an investor had requested a zoning variance recently. The request was to demolish the market and build a very lucrative 3-story medical building. The project was on the edge of several residential areas and the Zoning Commission turned them down. If the market burned down, demolition would automatically follow and possibly be the foot-in-the-door leading to a variance. I had heard of it happening before. A case filing required an inside witness. Insurance money enabled the market to re-build and get back into operation. At one point, we felt there might be another attempt to burn the market, so we conducted a week-long surveillance using a pool of on-duty firefighters we were grooming for the shift investigator program. Nothing happened during the week, but the training was excellent and I had the opportunity to evaluate each man on his strengths and weaknesses.

In January, my article "Profiles in Arson — The Serial Firesetter" was published in the *American Fire Journal*. Also in January, the three-part captain's exam took place and after scoring well on the written, I advanced to the oral interview and practical evaluation. I felt good about all three phases. Although some of my reviewers seemed to look down on a firefighter who hadn't fought fires for the past eight years, I tried to turn that perception around. A fire captain's job required life or death decisions, good report writing and oral presentation skills, top-notch time management abilities, and people perception. I explained to the oral board members that, not only had I developed and honed these traits as a fire investigator, my Senior Investigator position had me practicing supervisory skills for over two years. The oral board asked what I felt was my greatest accomplishment in my career. I replied it was the strides I'd made training hundreds of police officers and detectives, as well as firefighters through the F.I.R.S.T. classes and the impact of furthering better relations between fire and law enforcement agencies, particularly in Glendale. I added that I was prepared to give up fire investigation for a career as a fire captain. I later heard that a L.A. Fire Dept Battalion Chief on the oral board said my oral presentation was the best he had ever witnessed. I recall being very comfortable during the interview, but never imagined doing that well.

In February, my shift investigator program got into full swing. We selected nine firefighters, three for each of the firefighting shifts to handle after-hours fire scene investigation. Training was scheduled and we were on our way. On March 3, 1989, I left Glendale for a week-long business and pleasure trip up the central coast of California. The California State Fire Marshal's Office sponsored Symposium IV, an arson conference and workshop. I left two days early to do some exploring and maybe some hunting with Bill McLaughlin, my old roommate.

I arrived in San Luis Obispo and checked into a Motel 6. Prowling around the beautiful college town nestled in green hills below a larger mountain range, it was too late in the day to head out to explore so I retired early and watched TV. I spent Saturday and part of Sunday in area mountains and checking out public land around a nearby army base. Late Sunday afternoon, I checked in at the Symposium IV held at the Asilomar Conference Center on the beach in Pacific Grove. The arson workshops lasted through Wednesday. Over 200 fire and police investigators and other fire service professionals attended, more than 110 from Southern California. While at the conference, I ran into my old friend Jim Allen from the California State Fire Marshal's Office. I planned on meeting Wanda in San Luis Obispo on Friday afternoon and made arrangements to meet Jim and his wife for dinner that night. I drove the scenic Route 1 through the spectacular Big Sur area. Pausing several times to videotape the rugged coastline and shop at the gift stores along the way, I arrived back in San Luis Obispo at about 3 p.m. to stay at the same Motel 6. Wanda wasn't due in on the train until Friday afternoon, so I spent Thursday, March 9, in an area known as the Cuyama Valley, 40 miles southeast of San Luis Obispo. I prowled around the Twitchell Reservoir area and cruised surrounding foothills, finding most of it private ranchland and no access to the public. Most gates were locked so I couldn't even go to a ranch house to ask permission to hunt. "No Hunting" signs decorated most of the gates, adding insult to injury. I chatted briefly with a ranch hand in a small flatbed Chevy truck and a government worker during the day, and returned to the motel by 3 p.m. Unknown to me, a pair of fires damaged two stores in Atascadero, 20 miles north of San Luis Obispo earlier that day. Atascadero was 40-60 miles north of the area I traversed in the daylight hours of March 9. At least five other similar fires had occurred in retail stores up and down the Central Coast over that past week. I was aware of none of them. A cigarette/matches/rubber band incendiary device, wrapped in yellow, lined paper was found in an Atascadero store the next day. There was no fire.

On Thursday evening, San Luis Obispo closed off about eight blocks of its downtown area and held a farmer's market and street fair. The weekly event drew thousands of residents and students from the Cal Poly campus just north of SLO. I napped from 4-7 p.m. and woke up famished. I drove to the edge of downtown and had trouble finding convenient parking. Walking three blocks to the street fair site, I scanned the area for a good restaurant. Everything was packed with people. The streets were far too crowded for me, so I retreated to the extreme south end of the main street and found a BBQ set up in the parking lot of a liquor store and feasted. At almost eight o'clock, I heard a slew of sirens heading to the north of me. I looked up the crowded street and saw a haze about five blocks off, but it appeared to be another BBQ at first. I walked toward the growing cloud when it rapidly increased. Within one block, I saw the smoke was from a burning building, but the wall of people prevented me from getting closer. Police weren't moving the crowd back and no fire engines were on the front side yet. I moved back a block before cops finally started controlling the crowd and fire equipment showed. I retreated to my motel and watched the fire on the news later on. The blaze consumed the three-story building called the Party Exchange. It was the only fire I saw or heard about during that week until I was arrested and charged with setting three of them in December 1991. Ironically, I was not charged with setting the only fire I saw, the Party Exchange. Apparently investigators did not even know I was at the fire scene a block away. I was charged with setting the three Atascadero fires, even though witnesses saw a man wearing a straw cowboy hat at two of the locations. The straw cowboy hat was again described at another fire the week before in Morro Bay. I didn't match his description of "thin" and I didn't own a straw cowboy hat.

Wanda arrived the next day. We hung around town and shopped, then drove to Pismo Beach and dined with Jim Allen and his wife. Jim was called to the Party Exchange fire. I vaguely recall his mentioning something about a fire in Atascadero, but he could not recall the conversation specifically years later, either.

Wanda and I returned home the next day. The telephone jarred me awake at about 1:30 one Saturday morning. Picking it up on the first ring, I heard what every parent dreads: "This is the Anaheim Police Department calling. You have a daughter Carrie and she owns a 1972 Datsun?"

"Yes," I whispered, readying myself for the worst. My free hand grasped Wanda's leg hard enough to wake her.

"We've had a disturbance call," the dispatcher quickly responded. "A vandalism, actually, and your daughter's the victim. We ran the car plate and her license and both came back to the Glendale Police Department. They gave us your number." California law enforcement officers can fill out a Department of Motor Vehicles form protecting them and their family's addresses. I had both Carrie and Lori protected. I breathed easier and got the particulars from the dispatcher. I knew Carrie experienced an on-going problem with Lloyd, her mother's husband. As she grew into an independent teenager, she rebelled at what she perceived as Lloyd's lack of parenting skills. He continued treating my girls as children and Carrie not only stood up for her sister, she challenged him, balking at his persistence. Almost always jobless, Lloyd garnered little respect from my daughters when he ordered them to do housework and other chores that were his responsibility. Both Carrie and Lori went to school full time, got good grades, and worked after school and on weekends. This night's problem originated with Carrie's early evening falling out with Lloyd, so she decided to move out and into a girlfriend's home nearby. Lloyd tracked Carrie down and created a disturbance at the girlfriend's home when he tried to force her to her own house. The parents stood up for Carrie and ordered Lloyd off their property. He returned later and was seen under the hood of Carrie's Datsun. Again he was chased off. Sparkplug wires were ripped out, a windshield wiper and other small parts damaged. The police were called and, while taking the report, they discovered Carrie's law enforcement connection. The dispatcher gave me the phone number where Carrie was and I immediately called. The girlfriend's father assured me Carrie was okay but the police were talking about taking Carrie into custody as a runaway. I asked to speak with the police officer.

"Sergeant Monty. Captain Orr?"

"Will it help if I come down? I don't want Carrie taken in. I'm her dad. Can you release her to me?"

"Sure, no problem, Captain. I'm off-duty at 2, but I'll stick around. This could be fun. Maybe we could go arrest this prick who messed with your daughter's car?"

"Hold off on that, please. My other girl's living with him. I'll be down in 30 minutes. Is that okay?"

"No sweat. Come on down." I made the 35-mile drive in about 20 minutes in my narc car and embraced my daughter when I arrived and told her we'd take care of the problem. She could live with me if she wanted. Her eighteenth birthday was only months away. The police sergeant went out of his way to be helpful. Assuming initially I was a police captain by the license confidentiality reference to the Glendale Police Department, I straightened him out quickly and told him I was a fireman. My business card firmed up the fact I was a peace officer. I also dropped the names of two Anaheim police detectives who had attended my classes and we got down to business. Carrie stuck close to me and filled me in on her run-in with Lloyd and the shouting match she feared might, at one point, get physical. I trusted her judgment but didn't want to take sides. Running away at her age wasn't legal, but maybe logical. I just didn't want her going back to her mom's place. Long absent as an omniscient father figure, I still felt comfortable making the legal decision to take custody of her and approve her remaining with her girlfriend's parents. The guardians were responsible people and gladly accepted. The sergeant still wanted to go over and arrest Lloyd but I used the situation to keep us all happy. I called Jody and told her that I had talked the police out of an arrest, and that I was taking custody of Carrie and made the decision to support her moving out even though she was underage. Jody reluctantly agreed. I met with Jody the next morning and we chatted in her tidy living room while Lloyd eavesdropped from the nearby bedroom. He occasionally threw in a comment or two but the mediation ended when Lloyd said, "You haven't been a real father for years. You just paid your child support and don't care about being a father until now. You bought their love." Not trusting myself to stay any longer, I left Jody with a hug and reassurance that she could call me and we'd continue our chat when Lloyd wasn't around. She agreed. My girls turned into intelligent, resourceful, trustworthy adults and I have to give some credit to Lloyd. He was present during the girls' early years when I chose remoteness, and must have had some positive effect on their development. I thank him for helping keep them safe and secure during those years.

In late March, I walked into Fire Station One and entered the kitchen to find a "Tentative Captain's List" written on a chalk board. The Personnel Department mailed the standings out two days before and fire department tradition was for each recipient to call in his score and placement as he opened his mail. The top ten spots were listed. When I walked in, six of the ten were filled in. I sipped a cup of coffee as the ten firefighters present chattered about the possibilities of who would be the first two men promoted. They assumed that I wouldn't have scored high enough because I had been away from the fire suppression section for so long, or that I wouldn't take the promotion anyway and elect to stay in the arson unit.

My mail delivery at home was around 11 a.m. and it was already past noon. Setting my coffee down discreetly, I slipped down the stairs, ran to my car, and raced the two miles to home. Cody's guttural bark behind the front door greeted me. I retrieved the detritus from the mailbox and sat on the steps leading to the porch. Nested between a Montgomery Ward catalogue and a telephone bill was the business-sized envelope with a return address headed by "City of Glendale — Personnel Department." Cody bounced onto the porch and licked my face as I tore open the envelope to find the pink copy of the three-part testing form. Pink designated passing. My raw score was very high. I was number one on the captain's list. Without Wanda there to hug, I placed a wet one on Cody and embraced his hairy body. Once inside, I picked up the phone and dialed Station One.

"Station One kitchen, Keplar speaking."

"Hi, Al, John Orr here. Got my results..."

"I thought you were still here. Your coffee's still steaming on the counter!"

"Right, Al. Pencil me in for number one." The next month was a whirlwind of planning and decision-making. I delegated much of the shift investigator training and scheduling to Walt Beatty while I expanded on our fire prevention program and watched two captain's appointments go by. The positions were at fire houses and my supervisor's counseled me to hold on, they were trying to get the authority to open a slot in arson. I had to sign a waiver twice to allow the process to bypass me. Civil Service rules allowed me to waive only twice. I recalled the department's maneuvering in 1983, when I lost the promotion and would not allow it to happen again. I told my boss I would take the next opening, even if it was a captain's slot counting nuts and bolts in the department shops. Fortunately, they came through. The unit was slotted for a captain and a firefighter. On May 1, 1989, I was appointed fire captain and realized about a $600 per month raise. My daughter Carrie was to turn 18 in June and child support would end. In two months my income increased almost $1,000. Not generally motivated by money, this was still a nice reward. I went out and bought a new Chevy Blazer and was approved to use the truck as my unit's second vehicle. The city paid a car and gas allowance also. The snow white Blazer was soon equipped with undercover red and yellow lights from surplus kept around the department shops, and some I scrounged from the police garage.

Two more of my "Profiles in Arson" articles came out in the *American Fire Journal*. The first "Profile" piece, in January, outlined my Pogo serial arsonist case from 1983. The format I used to write was complimented by my editor and a number of my peers, and the tale was apparently entertaining as well as informative. The next two "Profiles" followed a revenge arson case I worked in 1984. I did not perceive myself as especially literary, but I did like telling the stories. I flirted with ideas for a fictional novel, scratching out a basic outline.

Walt's annual review was due before my appointment to captain so Chief Gray was the author, with input from me. I praised Walt's abilities and investigative intuition but marked him down for lack of people skills. I specifically stressed a need to work on his condescending attitude and he must be more patient and tactful. He argued with me and Chief Gray over the 'Areas of Improvement' section, proving the very things I was citing. Before I asked Chief Gray to stress these remarks on the review, I asked for access to Walt's personnel file to see how he had been rated by previous supervisors. I was shocked to find only one performance rating where Walt was dinged for his well-known and recognized misbehavior. Ironically, the negative comments were nearly identical to my observations and were pointed out in an 18-year-old review done by none other than the Fire Marshal who didn't want Walt appointed to the arson position in 1980. The early 70s evaluation stated Walt needed to use more discretion and have patience when dealing with citizens and his peers. No other subsequent supervisor mentioned the shortcomings despite common knowledge the problems persisted over his 18 year career. I hoped my critique would help bring him into line. Walt reluctantly signed the form but gave me the silent treatment for several days. His next evaluation would be produced solely by me.

On June 23 we had an early afternoon fire in an expensive hillside home, situated at the end of a cul-de-sac. The 900 square-foot palace was in poor condition. The land itself was expensive. The owner and his wife left approximately 40 minutes before a neighbor across the canyon, an off-duty Glendale detective, spotted smoke pushing out of the home and called 9-1-1. Two separate pools of gasoline inside the house were ignited with wooden matches. The mixture was too rich and the fires did not spread, but died down after the oxygen in the small structure was consumed. We found a number of items, including a computer and all the wife's shoes, removed before the fire. It looked like an insurance fraud fire. Again, we found a zoning variance requested by the owners to enable them to enlarge the home and add a second story. We couldn't quite put the case together for a criminal filing or get enough information for a search warrant to try and find the woman's shoes, the computer, or anything else of value they removed before the planned fire. The insurance company did, however, refuse to pay the claim. A civil case would have to resolve the issues.

In July, we had enough brushfires occurring to pattern one of the arsonist's activities. I felt there was more than one. I contacted Captain Gary Seidel of the Los Angeles Fire Department arson detail, and suggested we use the pattern and schedule an afternoon surveillance in the Glendale area. He agreed and provided three units and five men to assist, including himself. Walt and I were the fourth and fifth units. It was a mobile surveillance, no fixed locations, and designed to gather intelligence, write down license numbers, and maybe act as a deterrent. The Glendale brushfires were occurring on Thursday and Fridays after 3 p.m., but in several different eastside locations. At 2:30 p.m., we met at Glendale Station Four to discuss strategy. L.A.'s units were 4-door sedans with red spotlights. I provided F.I.R.S.T. portable radios with a common frequency and we plotted areas of responsibility. We no sooner finished assigning zones when the tones went off for a brushfire a mile-and-a-half away. All the surveillance units caravanned to the small brushfire blazing behind a medical building at the mouth of Chevy Chase Canyon. The surveillance teams cruised the area while two engines made quick work of the fire. Not wanting to give the surveillance away on the radio, I flagged down a black-and-white to get a report taken. It was Lance Heiger. He agreed to do the cause and origin investigation of the fire while we headed out. Our intent was to look for someone suspicious. We didn't have a suspect or vehicle description. Our plan was simply to write down license numbers on cars occupied by single males—our most likely pyros—and pull over anybody acting weird or who looked out-of-place. In Southern California, such drivers were the norm. After cruising for about 10 minutes, we split up and headed for our patrol areas. The fire units cleared the scene on Chevy Chase and for ten minutes the radio was eerily silent. Walt Beatty broke the hush a few moments later. In his two-man unit, he stated they were following a teenager on a moped who had been circling the fire scene. The bike was now headed into Chevy

Chase Canyon. Three miles away, near Station Six, I lost radio transmissions from Walt when he entered the narrow gorge and reception deteriorated. One L.A.F.D. unit was in the next canyon over and our own Verdugo dispatch center was monitoring so if Walt needed backup they were handy to assist. The radios were again silent for several minutes as I prowled the Greenbrier area. Static and garbled shouts leaped in fragments from the radio. Verdugo dispatch efficiently re-broadcast Walt's transmission on our frequency so all surveillance units could hear what was going on. Walt reported a brush fire in densely populated Chevy Chase Canyon. As the surveillance net tightened around the area, five engine companies were dispatched to the fire. I arrived five minutes later and asked two surveillance units to pass the fire and shake down any suspects up-canyon before fire engines blocked and shut off Chevy Chase Drive. I rolled into Walt's location and had one L.A.F.D. unit remain down-canyon. Walt initiated a traffic stop on the moped and, as he and his partner exited their unit, a fire broke out exactly opposite of their location, only 75 feet away. The moped operator seemed as shocked as they were. Walt called in the fire then shook down the kid while the rest of us roared in. The fire was contained quickly, despite the steep terrain. Walt searched the area of origin, locating the remains of a golf ball. About 15 feet from the street, the area of origin was unquestioned with three eyewitnesses. The only thing suspicious in it was the golf ball with most of its vinyl cover burned off to expose the rubber band-like inside. If it was some kind of incendiary device, other components of it weren't discernable. Since the moped kid had been under surveillance for at least 10-15 minutes prior to the fire, he was released after a consent search of him and the bike. They chose to stop the kid because his slow progress up the canyon caused him to pull over to let traffic pass, and they took the opportunity to stop him there.

We experienced at least two prior fires along this part of Chevy Chase Drive, one just 100 feet south was the location of an early 70s fire, where a cigarette/match/rubber band device was found before I joined the department. This start was popular with pyros because traffic typically moved quickly through, and the chance of prying eyes witnessing the act minimal. For the 60-70 minutes prior to this fire, I was at Station Four responding to and cruising the earlier fire down-canyon and three miles away in Six's district. No way I could have started this fire.

Two years later, on October 2, 1991, another brush blaze erupted within 10 feet of the July 28, 1989 fire. In 1998, I was convicted of setting the '91 blaze with literally no evidence but the fact the jury heard I was convicted of setting fires already. My lawyer chose to not even mention the prior fires at this location.

Walt packaged the golf ball evidence and we all cleared to return to our areas of surveillance responsibility. Traffic increased as residents returned home from work. Some of our fires occurred this late, so we opted to stay in operation until at least 5 p.m. At about 4:40, Verdugo came up on the radio again. "Investigator 20 and surveillance units, we're getting reports of a brush fire, Sinclair Drive." Again we abandoned our patrols and flooded the area with investigators. The blaze was less than 200 yards from the first fire and a quarter mile from Station Five. They arrived and reported a small fire on a steep hillside next to the freeway with one home exposed and a fence burning. Five knocked the bulk of the fire down in minutes. I arrived with Walt and we located the remains of a golf ball on the charred hillside. We turned no suspects on these three fires. L.A.F.D. units were released by 5:30. In the weeks that followed, three more golf ball devices were found by a shift investigator at the sites of two freeway-side grass fires. No suspects. Just another roving arsonist or one of our "regulars" altering his M.O.

On a Sunday afternoon, I relaxed in my backyard hot tub with Wanda under beautiful clear skies. I wasn't on-call. A perfect weekend, a perfect woman, and our 14-year-old Irish Setter lounging nearby. Rapidly deteriorating, Cody's body was giving out on him. To give Wanda a deserved break, I left my pager and radio in the house, confident Walt would handle whatever the city offered. In late afternoon, after a pitcher of sangria, Wanda wandered into the house for a moment while I dozed contentedly in the spa. The warm water lulled me and the next thing I remember was Cody's bark announcing Wanda as she stormed out of the house and handed me the portable phone. "Mister Beatty seems to be lost," she said. The dispatch center had paged Walt three times over thirty minutes and received no response. He had called "10-8" at 10 a.m. and they hadn't heard from him since. There was no answer on his home phone. Engine Four had a large fire in a half-million dollar house in the Greenbriar area and a body was found inside. Detectives were waiting at home to be called out if the death was suspicious. Family members were present outside the home and firefighter's wanted to finish overhauling the fire scene, but were hesitant to move anything that might be evidence. Without an investigator on-scene, nothing could happen. I gave the dispatcher a ten minute ETA for me, asked them to keep trying Beatty, request an on-call Glendale police lab technician and have a police unit interview neighbors and family. Some of this may have already been done but I wanted activity taking place on the scene and on the radio. It might divert some of the tension of the delay in getting an investigator to the fire. The fire was accidental. A seriously disabled middle-aged man tried to light a cigar, ignited the sofa he reclined on, and hadn't enough mobility to escape. He perished in the sitting position. A box of wooden matches and the full ashy remains of the cigar were found. The firefighters were so careful with extinguishment, the scene was virgin. According to the distraught wife, her husband would have had extreme difficulty lighting a cigar with his frozen limbs. There was no way he had the strength to roll over if he dropped the match on the sofa or blankets surrounding him. I wanted to be able to tell the family the man didn't suffer but couldn't, and skirted the issue. He, no doubt, watched in horror as the sofa or blankets burned like a fuse to ultimately engulf him. Smoke may have anesthetized him somewhat. I had the lab tech photograph the scene as the coroner's investigator and I examined the body. The dead man's trachea and nasal passages were clogged with inhaled soot. He was alive when the fire started and he took in a great deal of smoke before passing out and eventually expiring. I returned home and left instructions with Verdugo to place me on-call until Walt revealed himself. He called me an hour later and explained he was in Topanga Canyon, an area out of pager range usually, and the battery on his beeper was dead anyway. His excuses fell on deaf ears. I put strike one on his score card.

My continuing problems with Walt were sufficient for me to let Chief Gray in on the status of our working relationship. As part of a state-of-the-unit paper I presented to him, I alluded to the difficulties of being a close friend and supervisor to Walt. The Chief already received word on the fatal fire tardiness. I hadn't informed the Chief about the specifics. He had conducted his own research and learned that Walt had screwed up. A few complaints about his demeanor in the field filtered through the Chief's office as well, but the worst problem never surfaced beyond me. Walt was involved in an off-duty physical altercation with a juvenile. The LAPD listed Walt as a suspect. Charges were not filed but Walt got a lawyer and neither of us reported this to our superiors. The less I knew about the situation, the better. This was, however, strike two for Walt. I was guilty of covering for my partner again.

The year 1989 ended with very low arson stats and fewer fires overall, too. Still maintaining a 15 percent-18 percent clearance rate and conducting more training for F.I.R.S.T. than ever before, we stayed visible. My "Profiles" articles brought further credit to us as a unit.

CHAPTER SIXTEEN
VIRGIN VETERAN

The beginning of 1990 brought the unit's tenth year of successful operation. After the disastrous 1985 arson spree, I went through three partners. Still, our clearance rates remained higher than the national average, despite the relative inexperience of two of these associates for the first six months of assignment. Post-1985, the number of arson incidents dropped back to normal levels. Our well-publicized success rate had no deterrent effect on the jilted lover who throws a Molotov cocktail at his ex-girlfriend's apartment while she watches TV with her new beau. An owner of a failing restaurant may reconsider ending his financial woes by fire because of the unit's reputation, but with a 70 percent revenge-motivated arson history, we were not likely to enforce our way out of business.

Early in 1990, I voluntarily toured our canyons and brush areas to evaluate the potential of our coming wildfire season. I did not like what I saw. A major wildfire had not ravaged Glendale since 1961, with the exception of a 1975 blaze burning on the northern edge of town. The Santa-Ana-fanned flames swept across national forest land, destroying only a few acres of Glendale brush, but six homes burned. What I saw in Chevy Chase Canyon alone revealed a potential conflagration. Complacent homeowners allowed natural vegetation to climb right up to their properties, sometimes surrounding the expensive homes. Since 30 percent of our city existed inside brushland zones, the number of structures in jeopardy was in the thousands. Our department could not possibly enforce brush clearance laws effectively on all of them. It was up to individual owners to police themselves. Our agency, like most, was reactive. If a citizen called in a dry grass or overgrown brush complaint, an engine company drove by and issued a warning to the landowner to clean the problem up. Otherwise, nothing was done by our department except the occasional public information booth at the January Rose Festival in the dead of winter, attended by only a few hundred citizens. The scenario was a design for disaster. With 85 percent of our wildland fires arson-caused, I decided to extend our prevention duties. We could not predict exact arson fire-start locations, but knew the events were inevitable, and many occurrences destined for overgrown vacant lots. I recalled seeing aerial photography of fire-ravaged areas in Malibu, Bel Air, and Topanga Canyon in southern California. Blocks of devastated homes, burned to the ground, were speckled with islands of structures able to survive the firestorm. Homes with tile or non-combustible roofs and adequate brush clearance endured the conflagration. By surveying the Chevy Chase Canyon and other sections of town, I saw many homes capable of surviving. Common to most brushfire zone homes was their insurance situation. Almost all of them were forced to pay exorbitant rates for living in such a hazardous location, and the majority couldn't get insurance at all. State Farm, Allstate, and Century insurance companies simply wouldn't write a policy in a brushfire zone. Forced to buy insurance in the state-sponsored California Fair Plan, kind of an assigned-risk policy, homeowners never challenged the traditions of rate structures.

I proposed to inspect the properties capable of surviving a brushfire, photograph the location, write a report certifying survivability, and ask the homeowner to submit the report to an insurance company of their choice. My goal was to have the homeowner ask for a reduced rate or, my preference, getting a major company that didn't write policies in brush areas to sign some up based on our survey. I contacted a local State Farm agent and she agreed to consider locations I surveyed and found survivable in a major brush fire. My criteria was for a home to have the potential to survive with no firefighters or engines present as the fire sweeps through. In less than six weeks, I had four properties realize an average of a 40 percent savings on their premiums. Two were with State Farm. Chris Gray accepted my proposal and asked that I prepare a presentation for a city manager's staff meeting in March. If we showed homeowners they could save substantially on insurance premiums when they replaced wood roofs and maintained adequate brush clearance, many might be inclined to follow. A full-blown ad campaign would follow if the city management team bought our ideas.

In mid-March, I again drove around the canyons and hillside neighborhoods to survey selected areas for my video presentation. I taped a half-dozen areas with graphic potential for disaster. One of the locations was the neighborhood in the 2700 block of east Chevy Chase Drive. We had many fires along this stretch, the last when Walter Beatty made the traffic stop of the moped. With a string of homes directly above the hazardous hillside, I taped the brushy lower slope and panned to the half-million dollar homes hanging precariously above the fire potential. Eighteen months later, one of these 30 homes I videotaped burned in a brushfire I was later convicted of setting. Since I had a "before" video of the home and the hillside as it burned, and had filmed it after the fire as well, the prosecutor turned the "before/after" tape into evidence that I was an arsonist. My presentation to the city manager's staff meeting went well, but many questions were asked, and further study and research requested before resources could be committed. We needed at least 10-15 successes before we could consider going forward. I was a bit perturbed at the setback and how the bureaucracy functioned—or didn't.

Now a supervisor, I had to work within the system as much as possible. Walt wanted nothing to do with the brush surveys. It wasn't law enforcement stuff. I had to agree that it wasn't as sexy as chasing down arsonists, but the roving brushfire pyros were killing us. We could not catch them so had to protect these properties by building defensible perimeters and eliminating roadside start locations in the canyons.

The shift investigator program cut down on our late-night call-outs but created its own problems in management difficulties. The Battalion Chiefs on each shift didn't want to release their men as often as we needed them for training purposes because the shortage of their shifts. Most of the investigators wanted to be given time off, have the department pay for all training, and they all wanted to carry guns. I tried to delegate as much of the liaison needs to Walt. "Make me the bad guy if you have to. The city will never allow them to carry guns, but I'll go to battle to get the training," I told Walt. My priorities were in the arson prevention program, brush surveys, day-to-day operations requirements, and maintaining my own caseload of criminal investigations. Walt had trouble understanding behind-the-scenes workload.

On May 12, Walt was requested at the scene of a small brush fire on Verdugo Road. A shift investigator handled the initial scene investigation, but needed Walt's assistance. An incendiary device was located but it was unlike any we'd ever seen. Consisting of an empty .45 caliber brass casing, several matches were stuffed snugly inside, struck, then thrown out the window of a passing car. No time delay. We had a new arsonist on the block. Similar non-time-delay devices appeared later, too, all on the north side of town. During early to mid-June, we had our traditional freeway vegetation fires as the dry grass along the thoroughfares turned to wheat-like straw. Similar freeway fires happened all over L.A. County, and especially in the Pomona and Diamond Bar areas. Walt made a few arrests. One case related to a domestic violence situation resulting in a revenge fire. Policy called for us to co-investigate with police detectives when injuries were involved in a fire case, or there was potential for worse to happen. Walt did not like being subordinate to cops, and the investigation didn't go well.

A three-day California Conference of Arson Investigators seminar was funded for both Walt and me, but my needs at home took priority. An enthusiastic shift investigator, Bruce Stuber, filled in for me to share a room with Walt. They departed on Tuesday, June 26; the third day with temperatures in the Los Angeles Basin exceeding 100°. The day they left, a number of brush and grass fires erupted around southern California.

The Santa Ana wind conditions and hot weather brought out the crazies. A full moon had a similar effect on people. Arsonists seemed to compete with each other. I'd seen as many as three columns of smoke from brushfires mushroom over the San Fernando Valley area at the same time. Fortunately, the competitors missed Glendale that day. With a full load of vacant lot and hillside inspections to follow-up, I also actively worked several open arson cases. Chris Gray had given me a "special" to work, too. A straight fire prevention engine company detail, the fire hazard report was in an exclusive hillside area near his home and required special attention. He took the report over the phone himself and called me into his office to give it to me directly, bypassing normal procedure. This "special" helped convict me of 18 felonies in 1998— wrongly, I might add.

June 27, 1990 started off crystal clear and my Blazer's outside thermometer read 86° at 7 a.m. when I drove to work. Gusty winds were predicted. I spent a few hours in the office preparing for the day and answering phone messages before heading out at 9:30 a.m. Within 30 minutes, a brushfire was reported on the south side of town in Engine Two's district. Just a small grass fire, Two had it out before my arrival and we cleared the scene a few minutes later. I checked my notebook clipboard itinerary and saw I had one out-of-town detail to attend to. I wanted to be in the city during the hottest part of the day, so decided to run over to the Burbank Airport area and take care of business. I notified the dispatch center I'd be out of the city but available on the air and pager. As soon as I neared the airport, the alert tones sounded and a combined Glendale and Pasadena response sent on a brushfire near Devil's Gate Dam. The fire threatened the police heliport. A second alarm was called within minutes. Pasadena's investigator was also at the Fresno conference, so I included myself on the second alarm response, abandoning my Burbank detail. When I hit the freeway, I heard the Battalion Chief ordering an engine to protect the aviation fuel tank at the police heliport and one to the hangar. It was 108° at 11 a.m. My response took me about ten minutes and I arrived as ten engine companies managed to get a handle on the eight-acre blaze with help from the L.A. County Fire Department and helicopters. On the border of Pasadena and the county area, it appeared the fire originated in a small canyon right on the border. The bowl-like 5-acre draw seethed like a volcano's crater. Smoldering tree trunks and debris smoked, mingling with waves of heat generated by flame-scarred boulders and the hard-packed, scorched earth. Unfortunately, my video camera was in for repairs so I couldn't document the blaze. I stood on a freeway frontage road and scanned the bowl for an area of origin. My binoculars were almost useless with the heat distorting the view, but I spied what appeared to be a small campsite near the edge of a clearing under a copse of sycamores. A splotch of color caught my eye. I hoped it wasn't a child's body. Moving down the road gave me a clearer view. The colors were from several backpacks and a blanket. Peering closer, I saw a canteen and nearby, ropes leading up a tree. Mountaineering equipment still hung from the ropes. I identified myself to a sheriff's deputy and an L.A. County Fire Battalion Chief. Jurisdictions aside, they were happy to let me explore the fire area and collect evidence. Trees smoldered and unburned deadfall threatened to catch fire and destroy the camp and the evidence. Donning my Nomex jumpsuit, I grabbed a county firefighter and we descended into the cauldron. The temperature must have been at least 120° in the bowl. The scene said the fire erupted and chased the campers away so fast they could not take time to gather their belongings. There was still a possibility a body would turn up. In minutes, my companion and I were drained from the intense heat, even though little fire remained. I located a probable area of origin near the camp and we bailed out. Returning to my truck drenched in sweat, I turned the evidence over to the sheriff's deputy, along with a diagram of the probable area of origin so the county and Pasadena could resolve the jurisdiction issue. I waited a while to see if things would cool down a bit, but the chief wanted to burn out a small area in the bowl so it wouldn't re-ignite later and bring them back. Tempted to follow up on the evidence, particularly a brown bag with a name on it, I decided my return to Glendale was advisable. Chief Gray had cautioned me to limit out-of-city activities. Seeing how harried I'd been with new prevention program research and needs, Gray indicated I should slow down a bit on my activities with F.I.R.S.T. and focus on Glendale's requirements. This mutual aid assist to Pasadena didn't quite fall into those parameters but I was drained, drenched and smelled of smoke.

Thirsty and hungry, I drove home to shower, change my clothes, wash my jumpsuit, and rehydrate. Completing my rejuvenation at home, I headed back to Glendale. The thermometer on the Blazer read 112°. A slight breeze blew. I still had several details to attend to, and checked my itinerary at a stop light. My "special" hazard inspection in the La Crescenta area was a priority so I hit a freeway on-ramp and headed north. Picking up a fast food lunch, I wheeled onto Whiting Woods Road to eat and check the hazard. At the end of a cul-de-sac, I found the minor problem then parked in the shade of overhanging oak trees. At least 15° cooler in the shade, I opened up both truck doors and the rear window to take advantage of the cooling down-canyon breezes. In seconds, I dozed off with one ear open to the radio. The portable was alive with wind-related fire and medical calls. The police frequency was mysteriously silent. People stayed indoors to avoid the heat, even criminals, apparently.

At about 3:20, a female police juvenile investigator announced on the radio, "53 John, we've got a brush fire, Verdugo and Sweetbriar ... Fire's burning up the hill towards some homes ... 53 John, we're getting calls, 1100 block North Verdugo Road ... 53 John, that's affirmative." Radio reception in the cul-de-sac was poor because the Verdugo Mountains loomed above blocking some of the broadcast, and I knew I couldn't call out on my portable radio at all. Like bells at a fire station, 53 John's broadcast jangled me awake and, before I knew it, was roaring off Whiting Woods Road and toward the fire. My siren was inoperative but I had red and yellow lights to help me along. Thirty seconds after pulling out, Verdugo dispatched fire units and my pager went off as I was automatically added to the brush response. Two to three minutes after I heard Glendale detective Kim Lardie report the fire, I acknowledged I was responding to Verdugo dispatch center. These three minutes were later critical to my defense of charges that I set what would become known as the College Hills fire. At the moment I made the radio acknowledgment, a retired U.S. Air Force pilot drove by the fire's origin and saw a man standing on a landing at an apartment building.

Two years later, after I was arrested and my face shown on TV and in newspapers, the pilot came forward and swore I was the man at the apartment. His statement contradicted my own fire after-action report. I said I was still three miles away at that early stage of the fire. The investigators, prosecutor, and jury didn't believe me. I later heard about the actual man who was standing at the apartment and, no doubt, seen by the pilot. The man was a city employee, and an African American. My lawyer was reluctant to pay the man's expenses to subpoena him from San Diego and put him up in a hotel while he testified. The jury never heard about the man.

It took me about 5-6 minutes to get to the fire on Verdugo Road, but by then it wasn't even there anymore. The blaze swept up the hill like a tide of fire crashing against a dry shoreline and engulfed four homes immediately. The fiery tide didn't ebb, but continued up the large, heavily-populated hill. I drove to the ridge above the fire on Sweetbriar Road and made a quick survey of the extent of the fire. Set up on Verdugo Road, the Battalion Chief's Command Post could not see the fire's progress, and he would soon need this information on fire spread. With no fire patrol unit around, I circled the upper reaches of fire extension until I was enveloped by a shroud of smoke, the miasma so thick my Blazer's engine died for lack of oxygen. I walked to the back of the truck and retrieved my freshly-laundered Nomex jumpsuit and slipped it on. The street was like a ghost town. Surrounded by homes in the range of $750,000, there were no cars or people around. Walking to the passenger side to get my black Cordura bag, I opened the door, forgetting the driver's side was already cracked. Wind blasted over my front seat like through a tunnel, sucking up lunch leavings, a hat, and my clipboard/notebook. All went sailing by me. An explosion of paperwork erupted when the notebook struck the ground. Flying away on the wind was my alibi for the 18 felony counts later charged against me. One of the fluttering items disappearing with the gust was a small 4"x6" F-10 Fire Hazard Complaint Form. Chris Gray had taken the Whiting Woods fire hazard over the phone and handed it directly to me, bypassing the usual procedure of logging it in a master file first. At the time, it meant nothing. The missing form became vital five years later when it would help prove I wasn't lying and actually sat on Whiting Woods Drive at the time the College Hills fire erupted. At the time my alibi blew away, I had more important things to consider with at least six homes in my view burning and no engine companies on the street. For over 45 minutes, I put out fires on two wood roofs, tried to help Engine Five's crew for a while, then decided to report to the Command Post and see what assistance I could provide. I isolated what I felt was the area of origin and had a police officer string yellow "Crime Scene" tape along the road to protect it until I could return for an investigation. The flames, pushed by 30 mph gusts, jumped the 200 yard wide Glendale Freeway and started what was, in essence, a second fire. At least fifteen homes burned in the first hour and the hottest front of fire made a determined run for the heavily populated Chevy Chase Canyon. I finally drove to the fire's origins to conduct a cause and origin investigation, 15-20 feet off the sidewalk and about 40 feet from a 2-story apartment building. An incendiary device tossed from a passing car could reach the area with some difficulty, if weighted. A relatively flat stretch ran from the sidewalk to the edge of the steep hillside. It appeared an engine made a stand here to protect the apartment building. Some water and mud run-off covered areas of interest. With the misleading debris, I found it difficult to isolate an exact point of origin. The charred stalks of grass indicated heavy growth and included the curly tendrils of burned crabgrass. Smoldering cigarettes seldom started vegetation fires, despite Smokey Bear's warnings; matches to light the butts cause most wildland blazes. However, with several days of 110°+ weather and constant breezes, a carelessly discarded cigarette could smolder to ignition. The origin area was within cigarette-tossing distance of the sidewalk, but not a car. I discounted this cause, but it was a possibility. Three vehicles were parked next to the apartment building when the fire ignited, but were moved before I showed up. Evidence of tire tracks were obliterated by the fire streams used earlier. Only nine years later did I see a news photo of Engine Five pouring water on the area of origin from a top-mounted water cannon. In the foreground were the three vehicles. A car maneuvering into a parking spot here placed its exhaust pipe at the very level of the area of origin. On that day, I wasn't aware of this and did not consider the scenario. I did find the remains of three different plastic cigarette lighters in the area of origin. No incendiary device components were found and I located no striker aberrations. Several TV film crews hovered by the "Crime Scene" tape, so I was careful not to allow their long lenses focus on the remains I collected. Some pieces of shattered plastic were melted and others survived intact despite exposure to the fire. The grass was shorter in the area where I found the components. If the plastic parts were in the crabgrass area nearby, the evidence would have been destroyed. Because of the history of arson blazes on North Verdugo Road, I leaned toward calling the fire arson. Without any solid evidence, I could not eliminate all accidental causes. I was hesitant about calling it arson. A constant, stiff breeze, blowing on a cigarette coal in thick crabgrass with a 112° temperature could set off the blaze. I fought my way through the TV crews and walked to where the generals did battle with the fire inside the command post, a converted bus and dealt with logistics. I did not want to disrupt the 5-6 fire and police staff members, so I waved at Chief Gray to come over to where I stood on the bottom step of the bus entry door and leaned into the air-conditioned atmosphere.

"A cigarette lighter can be locked open and thrown from a car," I briefed Chris. "It's a possibility. There's nothing else there. No devices. I'm gonna call it arson for now." At that point, I detected a presence over my left shoulder and looked back to be face-to-face with the end of a boom mike extending to a cameraman and sound guy. Another mike was about five feet back and withdrew as I turned. "Move the fucking mike and get back," I said quietly as I excused myself. Profanity generally rendered footage unusable. The rumor of the cigarette lighter moved through the crowd of reporters like a wave. I had passed on disinformation to the media before and thought it might be advantageous to let this float around for a while. If I changed my mind later and called the fire accidental, there was no foul; but I couldn't say accidental, then change to arson when I caught the suspect. A defense attorney could ruin my career.

I didn't totally believe a modified cigarette lighter could be tossed 20 feet or more from a moving car and stay lit. The following day proved me right: using three different lighters, I locked the butane flow open, but when thrown or even dropped, the flame went out upon striking the ground or in flight. When I finally broke loose from the Command Post, I answered the media questions about the fire's origin by simply saying, "We believe it's arson. We have some leads to follow."

The conflagration was brought under control when the winds died at about 6:30 p.m. after destroying only 300 acres of wildland, but doing over $15 million damage to structures and vehicles. During the firefight, I had notified uniformed police that I needed a basic police report taken so I could impound an abandoned car and charge overtime to the report number later. They were occupied with other matters, and the police radio was tied up with fire-related traffic. On two occasions I called the watch sergeant's phone and found the line busy. I assumed the detail would be worked out somewhere along the line. A cop flagged me down while I chatted with Moe Gomez from the California State Fire Marshal's Office near the apartment building. Moe drove to Glendale when he saw the fire on TV and knew my partner was in Fresno at the conference. The cop said he had a female witness who saw something suspicious and he briefed me on her tale. Her information related to an abandoned car over 100 yards north of the fire origins and sounded bogus to me. As a courtesy to the cop, I had him lead the three of us to her apartment. The 40-year-old woman pointed out her bathroom window at the abandoned car far up the street, and said she saw a man walk away from the car into the edge of the grass, then back onto the sidewalk. Minutes later the fire started right next to her apartment; not 100 yards away where she saw the man. I didn't write down her name or take notes; I could always come back later if needed. We departed and, as we walked to the street, I again mentioned the police report I needed and explained to the cop that I had leads and asked if he'd canvass some of the neighborhood for witnesses. I assumed my request would be fulfilled. Over the years we had problems many times with police officers who did not want to take arson crime reports when an investigator was on scene. They felt the investigator was familiar with what to put in a police report, so we should do it.

The College Hills fire was the worst blaze to strike Glendale in 30 years but the follow-up investigation was going to be like most brush fire cases. If a roving serial arsonist started it, then my chances of catching him were minimal. Basically, all I had was a 10'x10' area of origin and limited witness possibilities on a very busy street. I considered calling Walt in Fresno and having him return, but felt I did not need to call in extra help yet. I turned down requests from the Los Angeles Fire Department Arson Unit and the Governor's Arson Task Force, because all the extra resources would only duplicate what I had already accomplished and—I thought—the police were canvassing the neighborhood. There were only 10-12 houses to door-knock for witnesses, so I didn't need 8-10 out-of-town investigators. I could handle that with Walt's assistance when he came home. This decision would come back to bite me on the ass years later.

With Moe Gomez assisting late into the evening, we cleared a number of leads and spent some time at the police department conducting computer research. Walt and Bruce Stuber saw the College Hills fire on the 5 p.m. news in Fresno and elected to drive back to Glendale early in the morning. They caught up with me at the Command Post around 8 a.m. I was surprised to see them and relieved at the same time. My title of Administrative Captain allowed me to delegate investigative details, assist, or do them all myself and let Walt take care of day-to-day operations at the office.

Gray wanted the exact cause and origin of the fires that destroyed or damaged each of the properties effected by the College Hills fire. Chris Gray wanted them all evaluated, photographed, and a report written on each scenario. I delegated follow-up interviews to Walt and Bruce while I started the Chief's project. It was then that we found out that the neighborhood canvass had not taken place. The officer never initiated it. Also, a police report had not been written. I decided not to impound the abandoned car, so didn't attempt to get a report number the night of the fire, and was just now learning that the official police report was not written. I understood why it did not get done. If I decided to call the fire accidental, I didn't need one. If I arrested somebody for the blaze, the report could be written later. This was standard procedure until years later.

Walt and Bruce conducted follow-up while I researched the damaged or destroyed properties. The Glendale Police helicopter enabled me to snap a roll of aerial shots of the entire fire area, and discover damages unseen from the street. Even with the overhead assistance, the task was formidable. I asked for help from shift investigator/pro photographer Mike Richardson, a firefighter assigned to an engine company who used my notes to photo all the targeted homes. This saved me at least a half day and his photo skills were much better than mine. After categorizing anonymous tips, over 80 in all, I found about six worthy of attention. I insisted to Walt that we didn't require any further investigative help, other than locally through the department. A few witnesses pointed us to a blue Honda, but we had no license number. The neighbors who had been home at the time of the fire gave us nothing workable. There simply were no witnesses to interview, no suspects to surveil and, after a couple of days, no leads to chase down. I could understand Walter's frustration. This was the largest dollar-loss fire in the city's history and we could not solve the case if it was arson. I continued having my doubts. If I took a police report with an arson heading, a criminal statistic, the city would show a huge spike in arson losses, and such a call could affect insurance rates and the cities "safe" standing on various annual lists used in Chamber of Commerce and business-seeking brochures. I decided to wait.

Walt wanted to go out and chase down leads and I told him to go ahead. They were simple face-to-face interviews of the mediocre "leads" or research details. I had enough on my plate finalizing the tasks related to the cause and origin surveys, and keeping up with the paper flow for the day-to-day office operations. Additionally, any large fire resulted in an influx of fire hazard complaints called into the department. Neighbors get antsy about overgrown weeds and shrubs on adjacent properties that they have ignored for years. I told Walt I'd handle the office and prevention duties while he conducted follow-up. He wanted me to go with him. I substituted shift investigators but, after several days of this, Walt complained about me not helping him investigate. I told him Gray was delegating and so was I. That's the way it worked. Walt stormed out and walked to the Fire Marshal's Office confronting the bewildered man with his complaint. Gray ordered him out. He returned to our office more frustrated than before. To placate him, I joined in the pursuit of tracking down a report of a gas company truck parked by the fire scene at the time the fire originated. It was a legitimate lead that could produce a new witness, but got us nowhere. A week later, we continued receiving occasional tips on the College Hills fire but settled back into a routine. One of the leads included reports a local teenager had bragged he had set the fire. Walt took the call and I let him handle the interviews. The witness said the guy was generally an idiot but he was just stupid enough to have set the fire. He owned a white Datsun pickup. We surveilled the guy occasionally and agreed that an interview with him might not produce anything other than a denial. We kept our eyes open for him at other fire scenes and, if spotted, we'd swoop down on him.

On July 6, Walt and I got back to the office after lunch together and a brush fire was reported about ½ mile west of the College Hills start location. Shift investigator, Ted Verdone, had found an incendiary device. It consisted of a firework tied together with an incense stick as a time delay. I had an arson report taken so we could book the evidence. We had seen similar, but not identical, devices before. I indicated on my report the fire would be "co-investigated with the College Hills fire" only because of proximity. I still felt we had 2-3 active serial arsonists working the Glendale and surrounding areas. Later in July, neighboring Pasadena had a series of alley fires including carports and garages. The firesetting spree culminated with a brush fire near the Glendale/Pasadena border. Many years later, I found documents from Pasadena investigators indicating a Pasadena firefighter as a suspect in these blazes.

Walt continued complaining about unit operations and refused to accept me as a supervisor. We were just antagonistic friends to him. This wasn't Starsky and Hutch. Unfortunately, our problems made me consider a move. After 10 years in the unit, I was considering seeking a job with another agency in a more rural location and leaving the Glendale unit. I suggested to Chief Chris Gray that we transfer Walt back to a firehouse. Gray agreed. When I informed Walt of the transfer he went ballistic. Chris was apparently intimidated by Walt's outburst. After just ten minutes, I received a call from Gray. "Walt's on his way back. Let's keep him until December. Then he'll have three years in and we can call it a 'normal' rotation." I would have to endure for another five months.

In the first week of September, Sergeant Russ Pierce, my supervisor at the Glendale Police Robbery-Homicide detail, asked me to meet him in his office. Unfortunately, the topic was Walter Beatty. The latest co-investigation involving Walt and one of the detectives did not go well. Walt had irritated the lead detective on the minor case. In a weekly detective bureau meeting, Walt was discussed and similar experiences were related by several of the veteran cops. Most of the detectives agreed they would no longer work a case with Walt. I'd already tried to alter Walt's behavior with two annual reviews citing his problem areas with no success. Detectives refusing to work with Beatty meant one thing: I had to handle all cases involving co-investigations, a burden I could not accept. I was furious. Walt's bullheadedness now forced me into demoting him. Tempted to initiate a disciplinary action, I thought it over and decided to be rid of him without anything hanging. I had enough experience to feel comfortable with that decision. I informed Chris Gray of the detective's situation and the requirement for me to work all co-investigations. I would not allow him to force me to take on an even heavier workload. He had to go. Walt was informed that "departmental needs" required his premature return to a firehouse. A selection process started for a replacement. Beatty maintained ties to the unit by becoming one of the three 'B' shift investigators. At his request, he went to work at Station Three, a 3-man station in the middle of Chevy Chase Canyon.

Years later, while preparing for a state arson/murder trial, I listened to a number of audiotapes seized from my office during execution of a search warrant. One of the tapes was from our office answering machine. I had preserved it for one of the messages related to a case. The taped messages were a reflection of Walt's participation in the arson/explosives unit. Twenty-two of the messages from the tape, covering a two-day period, were for my cases, an upcoming Investigation 2B class, consultations, and office-related operations. Only two of the 24 messages were for Walt and one of those was confirmation of a date from a lady friend.

In October 1990, Joe Lopez, a firefighter with the Glendale Fire Department, was promoted to fill the position as my assistant in the arson/explosives unit. He joined me with limited law enforcement experience, a minimal amount of fire scene investigative background, and the pliability and devotion of a puppy. From October to December 1990 we were tethered almost 14 hours a day during the week, usually more, with unpaid surveillances and after-hour meetings with private investigators and insurance company sleuths. Built like a distance runner, Joe lived up to that appearance and worked out at the YMCA several times each week and played tennis with Chief Gray. His wife, Jan, was the fire chief's secretary. I was ultimately pleased with the Chief's selection. Joe's first requirement was to qualify with the city-issued Smith & Wesson 9mm and his off-duty gun, a 5-shot .38 Caliber pistol. Earlier in 1990 he attended a basic weapons-handling course and, after two attempts on the police pistol range, he was allowed to officially carry a concealed weapon. During our first three months together we doubled up on after-hours emergency call-outs. Joe needed exposure to as many fire and explosion incidents as possible. His move from working the 24 on-24 off shift schedule to 10-hour workdays was not an easy transition. On the 24-24 schedule, a smoke-eater labors only ten days a month. When Joe accepted the position he slipped into Walt's schedule and had Friday through Sunday off. My own 10-hour day, 4-day workweek gave me Saturday through Monday off. This schedule didn't work out. We only had three days a week together so I gave up the 4-10 plan and went back to a normal 5-day workweek.

In November, 1 was called to the exclusive Oakmont View area to a Molotov cocktail on a front porch. I arrived and found a one-gallon milk jug filled with gasoline just inches from the front door of a $600,000 home. The device had not gone off. The owner of the house, an Asian restaurateur, had been threatened by gangs at his business in nearby Los Angeles. The gasoline-soaked wick had a cigarette/match/rubber band delay ignition device attached to it. The cigarette was lit, but liquid gasoline saturated the cloth and extinguished the igniter before the matches torched. LAPD's Asian Gang Task Force was contacted and the investigator assigned to the extortion gladly took over the attempt arson, too. He would be able to maneuver in the Asian community much easier than I. He also commented on the delay ignition device, "Yeah, we've seen those before." So had I. The "Orr-device" was almost as universally used by arsonists as Molotov's.

In the late summer I decided to put on another Fire Investigation (now 2B) final exam class for the state. Joe Lopez jumped in to help with the massive preparation. During the latter part of October and early November neither of us got home before 8 p.m. Our 2B session was worth every minute. Class critiques from the students at the end of the week and word-of-mouth accolades showed we put on a quality show. I remember being called into a Glendale Police Captain's office several weeks after one of our 2B classes in the mid-1980s. The captain received a letter from the police chief of a northern California town. One of his detectives had attended our 2B session and wrote a glowing account of the trip and encouraged the department to send all their detectives to the annual event, not just the arson detectives. Unfortunately, this pat on the back came with an inadvertent barb. The text of the letter referred to me as "Detective Orr of the Glendale Police Department." The Glendale cop captain was not pleased I presented myself as a police department employee. My business cards were handed out to each participant in the session and the cards clearly stated I was a fire department investigator. I had absorbed the vocabulary and demeanor of a cop and this student, or his chief, misunderstood. What was meant to be a compliment turned sour and I turned my back on the captain and walked out. It seemed I would never live down the wannabe-a-cop image. A copy of the letter was forwarded to my chief, with a handwritten comment that I should be "counseled" about the situation attached to it.

I have said I never impersonated a police officer and that's not exactly correct. Like Bill Clinton's definition of what is and isn't sex, I interpreted the definition of impersonating one way and the captain and others figured it differently. My intent, when I took on this disguise of being a cop was for efficiency. Periodically, it was necessary for me to say I was "an investigator with Glendale P.D." when talking to suspects, witnesses. or officials of other agencies. Many times I found myself spending an extra 10 minutes discussion to convince a records clerk why a fireman wanted a copy of a burglary, robbery, or similar crime report. When interviewing suspects or witnesses it was sometimes detrimental to ID ourselves as arson investigators. This immediately gave away the crime we were investigating and could destroy a good investigative technique. It was a tactic I had to develop to proceed successfully as a firefighter doing peace officer work. When I was charged with murder in 1994, "impersonating" became a key part of the prosecution's case. I later special-ordered a Glendale police-type badge that had fire department wording on the banners but had a replaceable banner with the word "Police" on it. It was used on those few occasions I truly needed it. The last thing I ever wanted to be was a "real" cop. My loyalties were with the fire service.

My wife, Wanda, and I had two children: a cross-eyed Siamese cat named Rock and our 14-year-old Irish Setter, Cody. In December 1990 Cody was dying. His hips deteriorated rapidly and he was barely able to get up by himself without pain. He had a minor stroke one evening as we watched TV. After the stroke, we left him in the kitchen of our home while we both went to work. One of us would come home at lunch to let him outside to do his business. On the bad days he was not able to help himself and defecated and urinated on the tiled kitchen floor. He looked forward to our new mid-day visit schedule and so did we. Wanda and I knew he would not be with us much longer. December 10, 1990, was my day to visit Cody. I left my office while Joe lunched with his wife and as I approached my home in Eagle Rock I saw a column of smoke. The header was about 3-4 miles southeast of Eagle Rock, around Highland Park. I briefly considered sneaking over to check it out even though it wasn't my jurisdiction, but Cody's needs were more important. I continued on home and spent some time taking care of him, then drove back to the corner. A right turn would take me back to Glendale. I looked left and the header was a towering column of thick grayish/black smoke and reached a few thousand feet into the clear blue sky. This was a major structure fire. I had a 10-minute response time requirement to Glendale emergencies during the duty day and my calculations, and typical high-speed driving propensities equaled a quick trip into L.A. I took off. Light traffic enabled me to get into the area in about eight minutes without going code-3; I didn't use red lights and siren in outside jurisdictions. I used my red spotlight at an LAPD-controlled intersection on Figueroa Street and glanced up the street to see an ancient, one-story department store blazing. Hose lines littered the street like wet serpents in an Indiana Jones movie, so I shot down a side alley and found a parking space next to a funeral home. I started taping as soon as I got out of my unit. The first few frames of my 8mm tape show L.A.F.D. unit Air Utility 4 parked in front of the blazing department store. Many other L.A.F.D. units were also operating. Less than a year later, December 4, 1991, I would be charged with setting this fire. Prosecutors and investigator's reports stated, "Orr was at the department store fire in it's early stages." One employee was shown a photo spread containing my picture on August 8, 1991. Ana Ramirez, working in the general area of the fire when it started, pointed to my photo and said, "I've seen this man in the store, not on the day of the fire but about two weeks before." These statements were made eight months after the blaze. She added, "He was wearing a uniform-like tan shirt and pants and was carrying a piece of yellow paper, like a utility bill when I last saw him." This identification and my videotape were the investigator's probable cause to arrest and charge me with this felony. Ana Ramirez was wrong.

At the time I was arrested I thought back to the videotaping of the People's fire and told my lawyer, "No problem, they can't get a conviction of this fire." The video's first frames show Air Utility 4 with open side compartment doors and equipment laid out beside it on the ground. AU4's crew is observed changing air cylinders for firefighters having already exhausted their 20-30 minute self-contained apparatus.

AU4's air supply quarters were on the edge of downtown Los Angeles 6-7 miles away. AU4 would not be dispatched on the first report of this fire but maybe 4-5 minutes later when the first assigned units arrived and saw the need for extra air cylinders. AU4 did not arrive until after the fire had been burning for 20 minutes minimum; maybe more. This was hardly in the fire's incipiency as stated in the investigator's probable cause. I still ended up indicted for this fire.

Four days after the People's fire, on December 14, 1990, I separated from Joe to pick up a friend's daughter, Alix, from a daycare center in La Cañada, just north of Glendale. I picked up Alix at about 4:30-4:40 and headed to Burbank to drop her off at her home 10 miles away. Arriving at her apartment, I walked Alix in and let her mom know she was home, then left to go to a nearby liquor store for a bottle of wine. As I got back into my unit, the radio was alive with fire activity on two channels. I soon picked up both Burbank fire and police units and the location of the blaze: Mort's Surplus store on Victory Boulevard, just a mile away. I could see brownish smoke drifting over the area, and headed for the fire. I shopped regularly at Mort's Surplus, a sporting goods and used junk outlet; unlike People's Department store where I had never shopped or been inside. At least one Burbank engine arrived before me and reported the one-story building was fully charged with smoke. I parked across the street and down about a half-block away. I didn't get too close because incoming fire equipment would be laying hose lines and block my route from the area if I got a call to Glendale. Most Burbank cops didn't know me and I planned on moving up close to videotape, so I put my badge on a belt clip. I then considered the possibility of this fire being related to People's and I didn't want to be IDed as a cop if there might be a suspect in the crowd—another reason I videoed fire scenes. Arsonists always stayed in the area to watch. I took the badge off. After a few more units arrived, I crossed the street but saw superheated smoke pushing out the front of Mort's, and high voltage wires ran right through the smoke. It was probable that the wires would drop from the heat so I moved back to the opposite side of the broad boulevard. Joe showed up a few minutes later after hearing the same radio chatter I did. He was taking this joined-at-the-hip habit seriously. He knew I was headed for Burbank and would be at this three-alarm blaze. We videotaped for at least 40-45 minutes. I called and made sure Alix's mom was home and cleared the scene, leaving Joe behind. I was not charged with setting this fire, but mention of it was allowed in pre-trial motions.

On December 26, three fires erupted on Ventura Boulevard in the Sherman Oaks area of Los Angeles, about 12 miles from downtown Glendale. The fires occurred within twenty minutes of each other, spread over a half-mile stretch on the busy boulevard. One was minor, but the other two started almost simultaneously and destroyed a pair of retail outlets, Stroud's Linens and Pier I Imports. When these fires erupted at around noon, I was in Montrose, a northern suburb of Glendale. Joe was on his day off and had volunteered to work overtime as a firefighter at Glendale Station Nine. After picking up lunch from a nearby deli, I drove to Nine and backed into the front driveway in front of the reserve ladder and went inside at about 12:30, 15 miles from the now-blazing stores in Sherman Oaks. Nothing marked my arrival time. Just a normal duty day. After lunch with Joe, we lounged around the station and I started to depart for nearby Tujunga on a follow-up investigation. As I checked a map while sitting in my unit, the station's tone-alert sounded, followed by three short beeps on my radio and through the station's speakers. "Engine 8, engine 9, County engine 63, truck 9, Battalion 2, roof fire." I cranked up my Ford and headed west toward the reported fire. About a half-block later, I pulled over to the side of the street and grabbed my video camera from the floor of the back seat. As I got it out and ready, Station Nine's equipment was already rolling. I taped the approaching rigs by focusing on my outside rearview mirror. As they roared by, I followed closely behind. The tapes date-line clearly showed 12/26/90. The fire alarm came in at 1:36 p.m. This was as close to establishing an alibi as I could ever come to on the day of the Sherman Oaks fires. Of course, on 12/26/90, I had no reason to establish an alibi. I wasn't aware the three retail stores burned 15 miles away until I saw it on the TV news that night. A suspect was arrested the next day and held until 1994. He was seen and identified as being inside the Pier I and Stroud's store just minutes before the fires started. The fires were reported within four minutes of each other. Prosecutors and investigators later wanted to charge me with the Ventura Boulevard fires even though a suspect was arrested, charged, and indicted on the felonies. The District Attorney's Office pursued me in the same crimes. Mention of these fires was allowed in building a case against me. Investigator Tom Campuzano said he never thought the man convicted was a good suspect for the Ventura Boulevard fires, and had fought with the Deputy D.A. to not pursue the man. This statement was in a pre-trial hearing to include these uncharged acts as evidence against me in the 1998 murder trial. No evidence of his attempts to stop the prosecution of this man was presented. The L.A.D.A.'s Office desperately needed as many uncharged acts as they could to present at the murder trial. There wasn't enough evidence to convict without similar acts crimes they could try and blame on me as "the only one" who set retail fires in southern California.

In the early 1990s there was no formal network for arson investigators to pass along information on series fires. Law enforcement had a teletype system and could transmit such intelligence on a particular crime or crimes but it went to the agencies specified and the teletype printers were in police stations. Messages marked "Attn: Arson Investigators" didn't always make it to fire departments.

In January 1991, I spoke with Captain Steve Patterson of the Burbank Fire Department and he told me the Ventura Boulevard suspect had ties to his city and had been possibly IDed as being near Mort's Surplus. He hinted that the guy had been acting suspicious and a Burbank police officer stopped him and wrote out a field interview card on the man. When the defense requested this information during pre-trial discovery in the murder case, we were told such a card did not exist. Maybe Steve Patterson was in error when he told me this in 1991.

In September of 1990 The Bureau of Alcohol, Tobacco & Firearms sent out a teletype detailing series fires in retail stores set by a suspected serial arsonist in Texas, Oklahoma, and the latest group occurring in Phoenix, Arizona in the late summer. The arsonists traveling in a westerly direction would have put him in the L.A. area in December 1990. Serial arsonists, much like serial murderers, do not respect borders and know their chances of capture diminish as they move around. The B.A.T.F.'s flyer outlined the fires set in polyfoam-stuffed toys, dolls, and animals in chain stores like K-Mart and Toys-R-Us stores. I felt these incidents might be related. Several could also have been copycat fires—a common occurrence in televised fires. The L.A.F.D. arson unit had 18 men assigned to it and a liaison with the B.A.T.F. was detailed full-time to work with both arson investigative agencies. I assumed they were on the job. When I received my copy of the B.A.T.F. bulletin in September 1990, I filed it in my pending file in case we experienced anything similar in Glendale. It disappeared after investigators searched my office the day I was arrested.

CHAPTER SEVENTEEN
FIRE BUGGED

By January 1990, I still had several "Profiles" articles owed to the *American Fire Journal*. During the previous year I was too busy with my caseload, the College Hills fire, Walt's dismissal, and Joe's training period to take the time to write and submit any more. Coworkers and my peers occasionally reminded me of the series of articles I promised in the first installments. A few friends suggested that I consider writing a novel. I had no idea how to go about it and knew nothing of the publishing world. I took a night school novel-writing class in February 1990. I enjoyed the two-hour, once-a-week sessions and the instructor, Les Roberts. Les was a well-known producer and mystery novelist. He complimented me on the three chapters I submitted for criticism as part of the class. I decided to use my experience investigating and apprehending serial arsonists as the basic plot line for a firefighter-gone-bad thriller. I based the protagonist in *Points of Origin* on myself, and I used Glendale as the primary location of my manuscript. Finding time to write was easier than I expected. The arsonist in the manuscript, Aaron, a Los Angeles fireman, set fires primarily in alleys and dark locations at night, and grass and brush fires during the day. My original concept was to have him escalate his firesetting from the nuisance type blazes and graduate to larger wildland fires, as typically happens with the growing needs of firebugs. I felt readers would be interested in what makes these guys tick. My plans included having Aaron set a fire in a 7-11 as revenge; an out-of-character act providing clues to keep the story going. Character development wasn't an easy task. Considering the scenario of Aaron setting structure fires, I originally didn't feel his characteristics would be secure in a crowd, so shelved the idea until the story developed. The original three chapters I submitted to Les Roberts included mention of a fire that killed five people, including a child. Concepts for various characters and scenes were taken from real life. It was easy to sit in front of my computer and pound out descriptions of fires I actually fought or witnessed as a fireman, and create characters drawn on the quirks of real people or those I'd seen on the streets. The class instructor stressed making my protagonist the kind of person a reader cared enough about to hang out with to the end. Early chapters in all books are devoted to creating the personalities and characteristics of the main players. Mr. Roberts said, "Develop your protagonist to be a decent, likeable person.

Give him a few peculiarities to endear him to your readers. Your antagonist, on the other hand, must be a despicable person who does detestable things. Make your readers hate the bad guy." I felt I was a likeable person, and successful in my career, so I based the protagonist in *Points* on me. Aaron was given characteristics of serial arsonists I had arrested: Pogo, Michael, Tony, Vern, and others. The first chapter is devoted to establishing who Aaron is as a criminal, but not revealing his occupation as a firefighter. Chapter two introduces Phil, the arson investigator and his characteristics, then chapter three meshes together both of their lives. I typically started writing on weekend mornings in April of 1990. Later, I became so involved in the project I occasionally took my lunch hours, and more, at home pounding out the tale. I'd pen 10-12 pages a day, then print them out and edit. Aaron set about thirty fires in the early drafts and only three involved structures. Only after I saw the People's Department store and Mort's Surplus store fires in December 1990 did I seriously consider having Aaron graduate to retail blazes.

I recalled the 1987 retail fires in Fresno during the seminar, but knew little of the fire's origins. A Fresno Fire Department investigator took me into his confidence in mid-1987 and asked me if I had heard of any similar fires in the L.A. area, but kept specifics to himself except that the stores were ignited by "cigarette delay devices." I later talked to two private investigators who worked the fires for insurance companies and gained some knowledge from them as well. I did not relate the two December 1990 L.A. area fires I saw to the 1987 Fresno blazes. I hadn't sufficient knowledge to tie them together. Fires set in open retail stores are unusual, but not the rarity prosecutors and investigators later said during my trials. Glendale experienced less than ten in my 18 years with the department. We found evidence of over 115 in Southern California from 1979-1995 prior to my 1998 trial. They were about as rare as a Mercedes Benz car fire; they happen, but not every day. I considered having Aaron set store fires and actually wandered through a few outlets and tried to imagine how an arsonist would go about this task. With my years of shoplift surveillance experience from Sears in the 1970s, I knew how thieves operated and theorized that an arsonist would handle himself in a similar manner. I developed Aaron's methods from those of the insecure personalities of arsonists I apprehended. It was hard to imagine anyone ballsy enough to set a fire inside a store occupied by 30-60 people. Arsonists generally avoid people, at least until after the fire takes off and he can blend in with bystanders and mingle. The retail firesetter personality had to be a bit more aggressive and, in essence, sociopathic. There were contradictions in my Aaron, but I was writing fiction, not a documentary. The beauty of fiction writing is the ability to improvise, so

I did. Aaron's character is sexually motivated. Out of the three dozen serial firesetters I apprehended, I felt only two were sexually motivated pyros. They existed, but were in the minority and it seemed that nobody knew how they acted or were motivated.

In 1992, after I was arrested and a psychologist examined my manuscript he said Aaron was inaccurate. I portrayed him as masturbating as he set up his fires. The psychologist stated that a human cannot process two major emotions, such as sexual excitement and fear, at the same time. If Aaron was in a retail store ready to set his device, he experienced a tremendous fear of discovery. Overwhelming fear would override sexual excitement and he could not maintain an erection at the same time. After he left the store, yes; but not while gripped with fear. The effect is similar to a rapist unable to complete the act because fear of discovery is overpowering. The psychologist related a rapist committing an assault in a public area or inside an apartment where others are nearby would have trouble completing the act. So, Aaron was an enigma. No problem: I wrote fiction. In statements and investigative documents, prosecutors and investigators said I was Aaron in the manuscript and based the story on my real firesetting experiences and masturbatory fantasies. The inaccuracies in *Points of Origin*'s Aaron, and the reality of psychological abilities should have helped convince a jury that it was simply made up. My lawyers refused to even address the small issues and didn't want to spend the money on a fiction-writing expert or two to testify to the facts.

During 1990, I edited various chapters, scenes, and characters. I let the plot carry itself forward as a typical serial arsonist case developed. With only nuisance fires and brush fires initially, I concentrated on the psychology of the investigation as opposed to explosive movie-like action. The title, *Points of Origin* was to apply to the two main characters as well as arson vocabulary. Phil and Aaron's pasts were to be explored to show how close these men actually were in general makeup and background but expound on "triggers" in Aaron's life that made him go in a different direction than Phil. The moments their lives split was to be their point of origin. It didn't work out that way, however. I got into Phil's pursuit of Aaron and didn't look back. Phil's tenacity mimicked my own investigative style and I didn't see a need to delve into backgrounds.

When Desert Storm kicked off in January 1991, Joe and I continued to work together all day, four days a week. We picked up a 50 percent increase in "suspicious package and possible bomb" calls as well as many more bomb threats. Citizens, fearing terrorist activity related to American invasion of Iraq, called in daily and reported abandoned cardboard boxes, briefcases and other ordinary items as suspected explosives. I had 10 years experience with explosive cases, but was not qualified to disarm or defuse actual devices. If we could not make safe entry to examine a package, we contacted the Sheriff's Bomb Squad. Joe quickly learned how to handle—or not handle—suspicious packages. Even with an explosives background, I nearly blew up my partners and myself on two occasions, despite exercising care. While burning off a pound of confiscated homemade fireworks flash powder at our fire department training center, the blend detonated. Flash powder usually burns with a brilliant, smoky flash. The mixture, nestled inside a plastic container, was set inside our heavily reinforced concrete burn building and surrounded by combustibles and old fireworks. Joe and I stood outside about 25 feet away as the small fire inched its way to the powder. The unexpected blast was heard 2 miles away at our fire headquarters station. Heavy steel shutters on the windows crashed open and about 30 pounds of concrete dropped from the roof of the room where the blast went off. We quickly shoveled the evidence into a cardboard box, swept the floor, deposited the detritus into a dumpster, and fled. Fortunately, we were the only people at the training center that morning, other than the 50 employees at the adjacent city yards who walked away shaking their heads after we reassured them all was well and the explosion expected and planned. It was the second time in 10 years that I had nearly blown up a partner at the training center while burning off supposedly safe items. Even before these incidents I decided I didn't have the proper mindset to get bomb technician training. The L.A. Sheriff's Department Bomb Squad was a phone call away.

In January 1991, along with all our bomb calls, we worked 23 arson cases. One resulted in the near arrest of a Glendale Fire Department member. Joe was on his day off when I received the call from shift investigator Mike Richardson. The night before, he had responded with Engine 27 to an attempted arson of a small wood-framed garage on the west side of Glendale. Wooden matches were found stuffed between wooden siding slats but the heat was insufficient to get the fire going and an alert neighbor saw the smoldering and called 9-1-1. A teenaged boy hung around the scene, according to Mike, showing an unusual amount of interest in the activities. Richardson told me he thought the boy may have been a Glendale Fire Department Explorer, yet the boy never mentioned it to any of the firefighters. Fire Explorers were 16-20-year-olds who went through extensive training with our agency to obtain the coveted firefighter certification required to obtain many positions in southern California fire departments. When the certified explorer reached 18 they were allowed to work at Glendale fire stations, responding to emergencies, but limited to relatively non-hazardous labors. He lived two houses north of the fire scene. When Mike gave me the address it clicked with me instantly: a similar unsuccessful attempt happened at the same location two years before. I drove to the fire scene, located in a quiet, well-kept residential area on our west side, and approached the garage. A narrow fenced-off walkway behind a large apartment complex allowed ready access and the teenager could not see me from his yard. The ground was still wet and the garage still damp from the previous night's light rainfall; one of the reasons the fire didn't progress. The gates at both ends of the walkway were locked. Firefighter boot prints surrounded the rear side of the small structure and led to a short chain-link fence the smoke-eaters used to access the area. I found a single wooden kitchen match nearby, covered by some leaves. Only the head had burned and even a very thin band of the red phosphorus head remained. It was as if the head may have been damp and wouldn't continue to burn or it was used for a brief illumination. While stooped down I saw faint foot impressions coming to and leading back from the garage. Not shoe prints, but what appeared to be slipper or socked feet impressions. Thirty feet away I found a four-foot-high chain link fence. Several pointed links above the top frame rail were crushed down recently. The weathered, slightly rusted wire was bent and the underlying shiny metal was exposed. On the other side of the fence was a barren backyard with no grass and a large patch of muddy ground leading up to the back porch. I saw two sets of muddy shoeprints coming from the back porch. Two more sets led back to the concrete steps. Studying the disturbed ground by the chain link I figured out the probable scenario. The suspect, apparently aware of the muddy footprints he would leave behind, stepped out of his shoes and leaped over the fence, landing on the dampened ground of the walkway in his socked feet. The return trip required him to drop off the fence directly onto the shoes. The deeper impressions and sideways sliding confirmed his leap. He appeared to have put the shoes back on and returned to the porch. The second, fresher, set of prints appeared to be impressed since the rain the night before. The oversized work boots sat at the base of the stairs. Dog paw prints also littered the muddy ground, along with two piles of dog feces. Having an eighty pound Irish Setter for years made me a near-expert on dog feces; its consistency, the age and size of the dog, and maybe even his diet. I observed that this pile was from a large dog and he had gone once before the rain and once this morning not long before my examination. Corresponding paw prints matched the two mounds and the two distinctively different ages of the dog tracks were the same as the boots left behind. I had a pretty good idea of what took place, but not enough evidence to be called probable cause to arrest unless I was on an Apache reservation. Unafraid of discovery now, I fired off a couple of flash photos of the poop piles and footprints, hoping to draw out the suspect. It didn't, so I walked around and knocked. The dog responded and confirmed his size by the deep bass of the animal's bark. A door slammed and I assumed—and hoped—the dog was locked in a far away room. When the young man opened the door I recognized him instantly. I had seen him at the training center and riding on the department's engines. I didn't mention it and neither did he. I played dumb and let him tell me his story as we walked into his kitchen. While he told me how he was awakened by the sirens and what he did after he woke up, I scanned the kitchen for clues. On a small shelf near the stove was a shot glass holding 15-20 wooden kitchen matches. The shade of red on the tip matched the one in my pocket. I steered the conversation around to his dog and whether he had seen or heard anything suspicious when he took the animal out to do his business the night before. He told me he didn't go outside last night or this morning. He said he let the dog out the door and stood on the stoop until he was done and then cleaned off the dog's muddy paws when he returned to the house. I took down his name and left—the boy's, not the dog's.

Thorough oral and written tests precede an explorer's placement in the program. An extensive background investigation is conducted as well. My unit was never asked to do the background checks until after this incident. Neither his class, nor he had his past examined. I did a routine scan of the Glendale Police Department contacts file and his name leaped out at me. Four years before, he had been arrested for arson. When I cross-checked, the report revealed that my partner in 1986, Tom Rickles, had captured and arrested the explorer for setting a couch on fire in an alley. The furniture was next to a garage. This kid was now staying overnight in our fire stations and riding our fire engines. This pissed me off enough to go out and arrest him immediately. I analyzed the follow-up reports and found that he had attended counseling after going to court and he had no further police contacts, now that he was 18 years old. I had enough probable cause to arrest with the sketchy lies, footprints, and the dog feces evidence, as well as the matches. Not real solid stuff, but enough to grab him if I saw him on the street. I picked up my crime scene pictures from a one-hour-photo place and arranged to meet with my boss, Battalion Chief Chris Gray. He fit me in even though his schedule was tight. I avoided the administrative offices as much as possible, particularly since I was dressed down in jeans and a flannel shirt with a down vest. Chief Gray listened intently as I explained how an arrest would allow the media to see how we dropped the ball on the kid's background investigation. It was part of the report which would become public record. I suggested letting me make the final arrest decision after one more interview. Chief Gray left it up to me. I found it hard to arrest the kid. He was intelligent and probably had a promising future. He

272

needed psychological intervention, not jail. I confronted him with the evidence and an embellishment of a shadowy, and totally fictitious, witness. He confessed immediately, but marginally. I left him and called his mother at work, offering an ultimatum: Get him to cop to the fire completely and accurately and he would not be arrested if he sought counseling, and quit the explorer program. It was blatant extortion, but legal. She called me back a half-hour later. He still resisted complete disclosure, almost willing to roll the dice with a jury to preserve his fire department position. He did not want to quit. I drove back out to his home and he finally collapsed and gave in. I desperately wanted confirmation of my evaluation of the scenario, but desired it to be spontaneous, not coached. He obliged me but played down the incident, saying he used the matches to light his way, yet would not explain why he was at the garage at 11 p.m. There were 14 matches stuffed into the garage and between the wooden slats. His intent was to burn it. I didn't arrest him and the follow-up investigation file was buried in the police department records bureau where it belonged. He had his family's support and enough potential to overcome this setback and lead a successful life. I didn't want to be responsible for a felony arrest or two that would affect his future. As it was, the loss of an almost-guaranteed firefighter job was a heavy price to pay. I feel it was the right decision. This apprehension was the forty-first serial arsonist, or series fire setter, I had identified and captured.

During March 1991, at least 11 fires occurred in retail stores in the Los Angeles County area. Six were in the Los Angeles Fire Department's jurisdiction, one in L.A. County area, two in Redondo Beach, and two in Inglewood. All four agencies had their own arson investigative units. Damage estimates ran from a $16 box of pillows to a total loss of one store valued at over $9 million. Minor injuries were reported at several locations. One suspect was seen at two of the fires, only miles apart and minutes before each fire erupted in the San Pedro area of L.A. He was either a former employee or related to one of the employees and had some sort of problem with each store. Another suspect developed was an employee of a Hollywood Pier I imports store and had been an employee of another Pier I that burned to the ground on December 26, 1990. Three female suspects were intimately described and seen at both Inglewood fire sites before the blazes started. I knew none of this until I read investigative reports in 1995 and 1996.

My first knowledge of the current series was from a monthly session of the Fire Investigation Regional Strike Team (F.I.R.S.T.) on March 29, 1991. I gave a presentation at a F.I.R.S.T meeting: a slide show on the serial arson case I successfully cleared in January 1991. The suspect was the Glendale Fire Department Explorer. It was a unique and amusing incident and the feces factor made it all the more perfect for presentation at a meeting of this diverse group. In the latter part of the session, just prior to my presentation, Investigator Tom Campuzano of the L.A. Fire Department Arson Unit outlined the December 1990 and March 1991 series fires in retail stores. It was rather startling information since most of us knew little or nothing about the March series, but had discussed a few of the December blazes at January and February meetings. Apparently the best suspect information came from a series of three fires just two days prior to this meeting of F.I.R.S.T. The March 27, 1991 fires were in the Lawndale and Redondo Beach areas of L.A. County. A composite picture of the suspect, drawn by a police sketch artist, was given to all members present. The picture was created from the description of one or two eyewitnesses. The composite picture brought about a few chuckles. The sketch looked just like two members of F.I.R.S.T.: Moses Gomez of the local California State Fire Marshal's Office in West Covina, and my partner, Joe Lopez. It was funny at the time, but not after I was arrested eight months later. Joe and Moses weren't present to share our jocularity. Campy passed out another sheet of paper, this one listing all of the December and March fires, locations, type of material first ignited, and damage estimates. A physical description of the suspect and his vehicle were also discussed. The man walked right by two staffed cash registers, within 10 feet of the two witnesses, minutes before the incendiary device was discovered. They watched the suspicious man walk to a silver Nissan in the parking lot. The crook was described as a male, early 40s, possibly Filipino, slim, 6'- 6'3", clean shaven, and had a full head of hair combed straight back.

In March 1991 I was 42 years old, 5'9", 195 lbs and portly, had a bushy moustache, and a receding hairline with two distinct bare spots on the sides of my upper forehead. I didn't look Filipino. I was later charged with the three fires in this series. I also wore glasses 90 percent of the time—I can't see clearly beyond 6 feet away. These two witnesses were later shown photo line-ups with me included. Both witnesses were adamant the bad guy they saw was not in the photo spread. One of them did, however, later pick my partner Joe Lopez out and say, "I'm pretty sure this is the guy." While Campy gave his brief on the case he added more information about who to contact if we had anything to help. I wrote some of the information in the margin of the sheet he gave me. I had no usable tips for him even though I was aware of 6 similar 1987 series of fires in Fresno. I saw no connection to the 1991 fires in L.A. I never learned the specifics of how the fires in the Fresno area were set, where in the stores they were set, or anything else. There was no possible connection, in my opinion, except the connection I was considering for my book, *Points of Origin*. I did not hear Campy mention anything about how the 1990-91 fires were ignited or about an incendiary device. It would not have been appropriate for me to pick his brain for more information so I could use it in my novel-in-progress. I gleaned what I needed and moved on. As treasurer for F.I.R.S.T., I busied myself with the monthly drawing for a small prize, logging incoming and outgoing checks and preparation for my presentation. My manuscript, *Points of Origin*, was nearly finished at the time of this F.I.R.S.T. meeting, but I was continuing to edit, delete and plan for more chapters. After this informative session, I decided to alter my antagonist's methods. So far, I had focused on nuisance fires set in alleys and other out-of-the-way places the typical insecure firebug would use, a few brush fires and the out-of-character store fire mentioned in early drafts of the manuscript. My antagonist, Aaron, had become infuriated with his own ineptness in several chapters and graduated to setting fires inside businesses to get back at his perceived enemies. After hearing Campy's information, Aaron was developed into a more serious fire-setter. A total of 6-8 retail fires are described in *Points*. Over 35 other types of fires are presented. I used the personalities of several serial arsonists I had arrested as models for my new and improved Aaron. Originally planned as a typical, insecure firebug, Aaron now became more aggressive. From the beginning, he was developed as a firefighter, but smoke-eaters are not normally insecure and weak. To be more realistic, I had to make some changes. To obtain a fireman's job, Aaron had to jump through the hoops of a rigorous oral exam as well as psychological testing and interviews.

Unfortunately, I didn't have enough knowledge of how important character development is to a manuscript. I sat down to write the novel and immediately got into the story like I do any investigation. The tale flowed out of me and I pursued it like I would a real serial arsonist or other criminal. The facts and evidence were put on paper and my instincts led me to forego the background character development. The story became more important and the original version of *Points* read like a police report rather than a psychological thriller. I liked it that way.

Later, Campuzano wrote a report reflecting that I showed a consciousness of guilt by not coming forward at the F.I.R.S.T. meeting and telling him what I knew about the 1987 Fresno fires' similarities and his latest series of retail store blazes. He indicated I should also have told him I had a manuscript I intended to sell and that it paralleled the real case. After the meeting, an investigator from the California State Fire Marshal's Office, Scotty Baker, did come forward and talk to Campuzano about the Fresno and San Joaquin Valley area fires as well as a similar group of fires in 1989 in the Central Coast area of California. Baker was a primary investigator in those fires and had complete knowledge of details in those fires. I did not come forward because I only knew of some retail store fires in the Fresno and San Joaquin Valley area from what Fresno Fire Department investigator Tom Kuczynski told me in 1987. It would be a long jump from 1987 to 1991, and a 250 mile distance, to mesh these two series of fires. I had nothing to offer Campuzano.

After the meeting I did chat briefly with Campuezano. He did not put this in his report, or else he simply didn't remember. My statement to him was an advisement to add the Mort's Surplus store fire in Burbank on December 14, 1990, to his list. He did not have it marked down. I also mentioned a Be-On-The-Lookout flyer issued by the Bureau of Alcohol, Tobacco & Firearms (B.A.T.F.) in September 1990. The BOLO flyer outlined a series of retail fires similar to his latest spree. This was similar to Campy's fires and I mentioned it in passing. That series moved in a westerly direction and put the arsonists on the west coast in December 1990. The L.A. Fire Department maintained a full-time investigator paired up with a B.A.T.F. man to work arson fires in the L.A. area, and it was my assumption they had already made the connection, but I mentioned it anyway. Campuzano did not remember my statements. They weren't important to him, or me, at the time; I wasn't a suspect. L.A.F.D. investigators had a reputation in the local fire service as prima donnas, so his blowing me off was expected.

I walked away and got on with my presentation. I had nothing to offer him. As for not telling him about my novel-in-progress, it would have been self-aggrandizing and out-of-context in a meeting as serious as this. Had I told him, he would have asked that I not use anything learned in the meeting, so I just ignored it. After I was arrested on December 4, 1991 for the March 27, 1991 fires, the federal case began to fall apart, according to reports I got back from various friends in the fire service and law enforcement. The credibility of the two witnesses who provided the best physical descriptions seemed to be unimpeachable and I wasn't such a good suspect for those fires; one where the distinctive incendiary device was found intact. I did not have enough hair, had a moustache, wore glasses, and was too short. At that point, Joe Lopez began to look awfully good to them and the investigators even theorized that Joe and I were working together to set fires 25 miles from Glendale in the middle of the duty day. Fortunately for Joe, he was on a day-long ski trip with eight other firemen and had a great alibi. The B.A.T.F. still investigated his phone records and interviewed him accusingly on at least three occasions. He was angry and scared. I wasn't quite as lucky. The following information was gleaned from B.A.T.F. reports and other documents provided to my defense team as part of discovery, as well as through my own discrete sources: The B.A.T.F. and L.A. Fire Department arson investigative units formed a task force to investigate the L.A.-

area 1990 to early 1991 fires shortly after the March 29, 1991 F.I.R.S.T. meeting. I still was not IDed as a suspect; this did not occur until two weeks later on April 17, 1991.

B.A.T.F. representatives April Carroll and Mike Matassa became lead investigators. While one part of the team pursued information about the 1987 series fires in the San Joaquin Valley, others re-opened the case involving the 1989 central coast of California arsons. The 1989 fires occurred around San Luis Obispo, Atascadero, Morro Bay, and Salinas, California. This spree happened before and after the Symposium IV arson conference in Monterrey. Again, I was not aware of this series of fires until my arrest on December 4, 1991. The statute of limitations on the 1987 series, to expire in January 1992, was running out. After the expiration, federal officials could not prosecute. The state limitations expired after three years. On April 3, 1991, as Joe and I relaxed after lunch in our temporary office in a double-wide trailer in the city hall parking lot, a B.A.T.F. investigator dropped in. Special Agent Howard Sanders, part of the task force of detectives circulating through the L.A. County area fire departments, asked us about the retail series fires mentioned at the F.I.R.S.T. meeting the week before. He presented another flyer with more suspect information, and asked if we had experienced similar fires. I mentioned the occasional small retail fires Glendale had over the years including the Robinson's Department store blaze involving a rack of sweat suits the previous November. Howard wasn't interested. Recalling the prolific coin-tosser suspect who used various cigarette/match delay devices, I theorized he had the right make-up to graduate to retail fires as a diversion for shoplifting. The coin-tosser bore a vague resemblance to the B.A.T.F. composite drawing. Sanders, a chubby, bespectacled 30-year-old, seemed more like a computer programmer than a cop, and again had little interest in my Mayberry experiences. Treating us like we were only a step above Barney Fife, Sanders condescended while querying me further. He obviously had no concept and limited experience with series fire-setters of any kind. While chatting, I pulled an informational flyer from the coin-tosser file and asked Joe to run over to the city hall and make a copy of it. Interested in how the B.A.T.F. chose their arson "specialists," I evaluated Sanders while Joe was out. From the agent's description, arson investigation was an interim job on the way to some other specialty. With almost no arson experience other than minimal classroom instruction, the B.A.T.F. patted their agents on the butt, pointed them toward burned federal property and said, "Go forth. You are now an arson expert." Through Sanders' statements and my own experience with the B.A.T.F. locally, none of these special agents had any firefighting knowledge, and extremely limited scene experience. Fortunately, they did have the foresight to add an experienced L.A.F.D. arson investigator to their ranks to assist with the task force—Glen Lucero.

Joe returned and I gave the coin-tosser flyer to Sanders. He put it in his notebook, thanked us, and left Mayberry. I don't know what Sanders did with the flyer, but in his 1992 and 1998 testimony, he stated we gave him nothing verbally or in writing during his visit to our office. I imagine Sanders used all his vast arson experience to evaluate the coin-tosser, and immediately eliminated him as a suspect. What I can't understand is why he chose to say, under oath, that we gave him nothing. He needs to review the ethics and professionalism chapters of the B.A.T.F. agent's manual. Joe Lopez testified he recalled making a copy and Sanders taking it with him. Why would Sanders choose to "forget?" The coin-tosser may not have been a good suspect on the surface, but use of a similar device and a fire setting history was certainly worth a computer work-up to see where he currently lived and worked.

Joe progressed well and in April I felt comfortable taking a break from the past six months of being on-call 24/7. The week following Sanders' visit, Wanda, her best girlfriend, and I took a seven-day cruise to Mexico. It was a refreshing week of no phone messages to answer, no pagers, and no middle-of-the-night call-outs to fire scenes. Upon our return, we decided to get a Dalmatian puppy. Domino became our only child. We left him secured in our service porch during the weekdays and I made lunch hour visits to let him out to play and do his business. Quickly housebroken, he made a padded basket-bed in the kitchen his territory. Wanda wasn't able to come home for lunch as often as she did with Cody since she started working in the Television Publicity Department at Warner Brothers Studios in nearby Burbank. Domino bonded with both of us and even had his own observation area above our hot tub where he kept his eyes on us as we soaked.

Also in April, while conducting follow-up on an obvious vehicle insurance fraud case Joe worked on, we pulled into the parking lot of a large shopping center on Foothill Boulevard in La Crescenta. Half of La Crescenta was L.A. County Sheriff's Department jurisdiction and the western part was Glendale's. Our fraud took place in our area and the Builder's Emporium-anchored shopping center belonged to the Sheriff. Well within our policy's 10-minute emergency response time for Glendale calls, we were not required to let the Sheriff's Department know we were in their district. If we served a search warrant, made an arrest, conducted a surveillance, or other potentially emergent situations, then a courtesy call to the locals was necessary. A simple witness interview was generally benign. A beautiful spring day, the brilliant blue skies swept clean by a day-before Santa Ana breeze, we dressed down in jeans and polo shirts. We were in our "cool" mode and looked like a couple of swimming pool contractors checking out prices—except for the 4-door Ford Crown Vic narc car. I was on-call that week so we performed fieldwork in my unit. I stopped using my Blazer on-duty when it was determined the truck did not qualify as an actual emergency vehicle. I then inherited an ancient Ford Crown Victoria with 110,000 miles on it. Waiting for a Honda to pull out of a space near the store in the unusually busy parking lot, I noticed a man being shadowed closely by an employee in a drug store uniform. Coming our way, the customer stepped up his pace while the store worker spoke loudly to him. I raised my nose up slightly and cocked my head like Domino did when I ripped open anything wrapped in cellophane. I pulled the Ford into the vacant space as the guy climbed into a battered Toyota four-door two spaces away from us. It instantly clicked that the Toyota guy might be a shoplifter. I told Joe to sit tight since he hadn't yet caught on and was ready to get out. Backing out, I wanted to try and get behind the Toyota to prevent his leaving. He pulled backward too quickly for me and I could only watch as the employee held up his hands and yelled, "Stop!" at the bad guy, then stepped to the side of the parking lane out of the Toyota's way. The man aimed the car directly at his pursuer and accelerated. The employee, forced to jump sideways, narrowly missed being struck. Had the culprit done this to me or a cop, firing at him would have been a justified shooting—assault with a deadly weapon: the car. Once again, I found myself at the right place at the right time. Just a year before, Battalion Chief Gray and the Fire Chief amended the arson unit's code-3 response policy in a memo. First on the list of the hated changes was this statement: "The arson investigators will not engage in police-type pursuits of arson suspects. If an investigator needs to chase a suspect, contact with police dispatchers will be made on the radio and responding uniformed police will affect the stop." This was our first test of the new policy. However, this guy wasn't an "arson" suspect. Cool, a loophole. The Toyota careened through the crowded parking lot and I knew he had not noticed us as cops or witnesses so I decided to simply shadow him. Still not positive what went down prior to the assault-with-a-deadly-weapon, I got on the radio to the Glendale police since we were in the Los Angeles County Sheriff's area and didn't have their frequency. "Station, 51 Frank, we're shadowing an ADW suspect, eastbound Foothill from La Crescenta Avenue, Sheriff's area. ADW occurred at the shopping center, possible shoplift involved." A nearby Glendale unit advised she'd back us up as I caught up to the now-speeding Toyota. I straddled the middle and left turn lanes of the wide boulevard to keep out of the crook's rearview mirror vision while he used the far and gutter lanes to pass the moderate traffic. He still hadn't made us. "Station, 51 Frank we're still eastbound Foothill, passing Oceanview. Approximately

279

50 miles-per-hour." He was actually hitting 70 at times, but I kept that to myself. If the guy did make us as a cop car and he split, I didn't want to be in the position of deciding to make it an official pursuit or having to make a police radio broadcast that everybody would hear: "We aren't allowed to pursue felons so are discontinuing." A truly embarrassing situation. The police department was not aware of our "no-pursuit" policy. Fortunately, the crook stayed in the gutter lane and I saw two Sheriff's black and whites going in the opposite direction. They blew past us, wondering why we were flashing a red spotlight and waving at them. They never saw the fleeing Toyota, but focused instead on their "hot" call to the Builder's Emporium. The relay communications between Glendale and the Sheriff's was about 30 seconds behind us. This was going down pretty fast. Just after the deputies sailed by and I was busy on the radio, I heard the Glendale unit advising she was a half mile behind us so we had back-up nearby even though I couldn't yet see her. Murphy's Law reared its ugly head and the crook made a quick right-hand turn onto a side street while I played with the radio. Joe hadn't yet been qualified for the police radio so I drove one-handed and almost missed the Toyota's slide onto Descanso Drive. I blew across three lanes of traffic in four-wheel slide that would have made Steve McQueen proud. There were now no cars between us and only one lane in our direction as we paced him just 50 yards behind. A ½ mile ahead was a blind, busy, signaled intersection and the light just turned red for us. The Toyota driver checked his rearview mirror, made us, and accelerated on the downhill side street. It didn't look like he was going to respect the red signal ahead so I hit my red lights and siren to try and clear the intersection before he got there. Still not officially declaring a pursuit, I called out our location and the dispatchers and cops monitoring our progress all knew the blind cross street we approached and heard my siren on the air. The Toyota screeched to a halt just short of the red light. He was blocked by two cars in front of him and another turning onto our street in the opposite direction. The thief was hemmed in. I pulled up to the Toyota's bumper so he couldn't back up and drive around the obstructions, and hoped the car in front of him did not drive forward. Throwing open our doors, Joe and I both drew down on the suspect with twin Smith & Wesson 9 mm's. This was my first real application of all my Officer Safety and Field Tactics felony traffic stop training. I ordered the guy out and onto the ground as the Glendale black and white roared up. Joe covered me while I cuffed the guy and brought him to the curb to wait for the deputies' arrival. From start to finish, I doubt the incident lasted more than four minutes and covered three miles. Deputies arrived while I moved the Toyota out of the street and spied about $50 worth of Panasonic AAA batteries on the passenger side floorboard. When we

returned to Glendale, I ran the guy's rap sheet. The criminal history for the 28-year-old man ran 21 pages: about 32 arrests for theft, burglary, assault, and many drug-related crimes. This was our first felony arrest for the year and I was pleased with how Joe held up while we went through the experience. Thankful for the Officer Safety courses we both attended, I wrote a report of the incident to Chief Gray and asked the sessions get continued funding for us and the shift investigators. Ironically, I was scheduled for my fourth trip to the class in San Luis Obispo at the end of April.

During April 1991, I spent a great deal of time on an arson/fraud fire from January. The scam was not a typical arson-for-profit fire; the business, a spa sales showroom, had no insurance on it. The owner did, however, owe many customers for returned defective merchandise and had a large tax bill outstanding. The motive appeared to be defrauding the federal and state governments as well as numerous customers. When a customer turned in the under-warranty, defective spa, his payment was delayed, and the receipt stated, "Not responsible for damages caused by fire, theft...," while in the spa owner's care. The fire wiped out the business owner's responsibility. One of his statements to me was the fact he now had a sizable casualty loss to write off on his taxes. The owner disappeared on me in February. This happened very shortly after the flammable-liquid-enhanced blaze destroyed, very specifically, the defective customer-owned hot tubs, and little else. I asked the B.A.T.F. for assistance in gaining IRS information on the suspect, but they were not willing to help out. They were very closed about offering aid. Agent Mike Matassa was my contact. On April 23, 1991, B.A.T.F. agent Matassa called me in my office. Mike typically had a strained, heavily-accented Massachusetts tone to his voice. That day he sounded like a constipated Pekinese's bark. I remember the call clearly. Six days before, the fingerprint from the Bakersfield CraftMart fire was identified as mine. This was law enforcement's first contact with me as a suspect. Mike mentioned the serial fire investigation but remained vague. I assumed it was the standard federal agent's reluctance to reveal anything about a case. Then he asked me about a training session Glendale was hosting the following week and if a few of his people could attend. I readily agreed. The seminar was the third of a series of one-week long classes to certify an arson investigator with the state of California. The fourth session, the final exam, would be held in November. Matassa and his people only wanted to attend on the day we burned six vacant apartments. I already scheduled LAPD's forensics unit to attend and test new black light techniques to see if flammable liquids were fluorescent after the blazes were extinguished. Their lead technician, Doreen Music, was a comparative analysis expert on, among other things, shoe tread patterns and footprints; one of my favorite topics. Last time she taught a class for me, she was partnered with Ron George, the very same man who operated the AFIS computer to declare me a suspect on April 17, just days before this phone call. He left the LAPD in 1990 and joined the L.A. County Sheriff's Dept. I told Matassa that Joe Lopez would be in charge in my absence. I was headed for San Luis Obispo for a week-long Officer Safety and Field Tactics class. I don't recall much of the remaining conversation, but Matassa's later report indicated he queried me about my departure date and what route I'd take. After hanging up, he wrote an affidavit for a surveillance bug to be attached to my car during the trip. My supervisors were not yet told I was a suspect, so I assume Matassa knew I would take my Ford Crown Victoria car on the drive. He may have asked but I don't recall. No reports indicate the bug was attached to my car before I left L.A. As I recall, I left home on Sunday, April 27, and traveled to San Luis Obispo that afternoon. Matassa, his crew, and an airplane shadowed me all the way, according to reports I later viewed. They must have been pretty good because I never saw them. But then I was not looking for a tail either. San Luis Obispo is about 180 miles north of Los Angeles. With a population of about 40,000, it is the largest city between Santa Barbara and San Jose. Nestled at the base of several low foothill ranges, SLO is the home of Cal Poly college and is bisected by California route 1 and 101. It is a beautiful, anti-growth community, just a few miles from the ocean, surrounded by national forest and agricultural land. I stayed at the Embassy Suites hotel on the south side of town. A welcoming party held in the hotel bar allowed me to renew some old acquaintances and nurture new ones. A firefighter trying to do police work must use every avenue available to gain acceptance by law enforcement counterparts. Whenever possible, I encouraged firefighters to pass out business cards and network with others, both cops and firefighter investigators. After I arrived, the party looked like a realtor's convention: business cards flew around like snowflakes in a blizzard. If I leave nothing else behind when I die, I will be happy to have at least fostered a better cooperation between cops and firefighters.

The training was held at the California Specialized Training Institute (CSTI). The class curriculum, a hybrid of a course designed for police officers, included vehicle stop techniques, felony suspect vehicle stops, building searches for suspects, weaponless defense and baton techniques, as well as day and night shoots at a nearby firing range. The interactive training included some classroom instruction but primarily real-life physical activities. For searching, vehicle stops, and self-defense, each student had the opportunity to play both the cop and the crook. It was cowboys and Indians for adults with real guns and blanks.

In one scenario, the officer may be a bad guy hiding in a warehouse while a police team searches. Everyone was armed with handguns and/or shotguns with blanks. The next session could find us acting as a cop wrestling with a "crook" trying to take away our gun. All of the scenarios were adapted from the police course, but designed for fire department arson investigators. In the police course, a scenario might be a call to a drunken male at a taco stand. For us, it was a drunken male with a Molotov cocktail at a taco stand. This very special training is one-of-a-kind. Most fire department arson investigators never had any training in these areas. They had to work with half their brain tied behind their backs. After the first day's primarily classroom sessions, we adjourned at 5 pm and headed back to SLO. It was very cool in the evening and I had not come prepared for the breezy night-shoot scheduled for Wednesday. Having been to the class twice before, I still forgot how miserably cold the firing range could be. I needed a pair of heavy wool socks, ammo for my .45 Colt Commander, and rounds for the AK-47 fully automatic demo. It was necessary for us to provide our own shells for the AK-47 show. First, I needed Tic-Tacs and a few snacks for my room. A shopping center near the hotel provided all the stores I wanted to hit. I went to a Thrifty or Sav-On drug store first and checked for heavy socks. They didn't have what I wanted, but I bought 2-3 packs of Tic-Tack breath mints; enough to get me through the week. As I left the store and walked to my car in the parking lot, I slipped the mints into my shirt pocket. I don't remember my exact movements, but I was monitored by my shadows all the time. Their report said I went to the trunk of my car and put the just-purchased items into a bag, then drove to the Embassy Suites. They followed me back to my room. At least one of the followers drove back to the drug store and contacted the manager and clerk who checked me out. The report estimated they searched the check-out trash receptacle about 15 minutes after I departed. When the feds interviewed the clerk about my transaction, he thought I purchased cigarettes. I imagine the interview went like this:

Agent: "Did he buy cigarettes?" The check-out's trash was searched by the clerk after he told the agents he thought I had left the receipt behind and he threw it into the trash. After a minute, the clerk came up with a receipt for two packs of Marlboro Light cigarettes—all of the recovered devices in the '90 and '91 fires were comprised of Camel, non-filter cigarettes. Marlboros are filtered. The date was the same. The clerk was "pretty sure" that I bought cigarettes. The surveillance team was also sure; "sure" I was getting ready to set fires. Agent Noriega's report neglected to mention a few things, like the fact that I also went to another store immediately after I left the drug store. The Big 5 store about 150 yards from the other, sold me .45 caliber ammo and wool socks. I spent a minimum of 15 minutes at the Big 5. There is no mention of this additional time spent shopping. Once I read the report in 1992 just before trial, it took me a while to decide why they would eliminate this additional foray into a store. I didn't like to think a brother law enforcement officer would be such a creative writer. I had the Pollyanna syndrome: I always tried to think the best of fellow officers. It isn't reality. The federal officers simply wanted there to be as little time as possible between when I left the drug store and when they arrived to search the trash and "discover" the incriminating evidence: the receipt for cigarettes. A jury might not believe the clerk's statement, memory, or the receipt actually being mine if a long period of time lapsed between the two events. After I left the drug store, it took at least five minutes to get into the Big 5, plus 15 minutes to shop, and five to get checked out, another 10-12 minutes to get back to my car and up to my room where they put me to bed. At least 30-40 minutes passed, not 15 as the ATF report reflects—one of many omissions on their part. Fortunately, I save receipts for deductible items such as ammunition. I don't save receipts for Tic-Tacs. During pre-trial preparation I was unable to find the Big 5 receipt in my 1991 tax papers. They were seized in the search of my home the day I was arrested. They were never found and turned over to me. They are still missing. So are the surveillance videos and logs the feds say they didn't have, yet the footage showed up on several TV programs years later. No doubt there were logs for each day of the tail. It is required. I have been on hundreds of hours of surveillances and there are always surveillance logs. The feds denied there were any, and withheld them from our view.

On Wednesday, a classroom session outlined current surveillance tracking device technology. I was amazed at the sophisticated bugs available for law enforcement. Another session was taught by an SLO sheriff's deputy who was also a bomb technician. The topic was explosive device recognition. He also related anecdotes about bomb tech pranks, including the caper pulled on a student of the same type of class we were in. It involved a fake bomb. He thought it was funny and some of the class did, too. I didn't. Bombs, real or hoax devices, scare the hell out of me. That afternoon in our own cars, we drove four miles to the firing range. Each student fired a minimum of 50 handgun and 20 shotgun rounds as well as the AK-47 if they brought their own ammo. The session ran well, as usual, and ended at about 10:30 that evening. Part of the course was a 100-yard run, with four stop-and-shoot targets. The final stage at the end of the course found the student out of breath and with difficulty in keeping rounds on the small metallic targets. A very realistic scenario simulating a foot pursuit ending with a shoot-out. It was windy, wet, cold, fantastically exhilarating and realistic. Again, no

ATF report reflected activities of the rest of the week. There certainly weren't any fires.

Thursday was spent in a small village on the training grounds where the students again were broken into good cop-bad guy teams. We used real police vehicles and responded to various "calls" in the "town" and applied all of our newly acquired skills. From vehicle stops and handcuffing techniques to managing a shootout with numerous suspects, we chased fleeing crooks while civilian observers and other suspects got in the line of fire—just like in the real world. This session alone was worth the trip. Watching the confusion at the end of police pursuits has always baffled me. Ten cops pointing guns at suspects, other law enforcement officers, media, medics, and civilians all in the area. No control at all. Everybody wants to be the one to kill the bad guy; nobody wants to shoot a civilian. I managed my six-man team and did not get anybody killed, but we did not get to shoot any "suspects" either. Most of the scenarios ended up in a shootout. I was pleased to learn these tactics in a class and not in real life. Out-of-control adrenaline junkies have no place in law enforcement. CSTI classes should be mandatory in-service training for all cops. The day was exhausting and the Thursday night end-of-course half-price drinks party didn't help much. I retired to my room early, no doubt with my shadows nearby. Some may have been drinking with us. Two more class sessions remained for Friday morning before we would be released at 11 a.m. Wanda was taking the train up to meet me in San Luis Obispo, arriving at about 1 p.m. I headed for class at about 7 a.m. My car was parked in the rear lot of the shopping center next door to the hotel, just below my fifth floor room. I put my black Cordura satchel in the trunk and looked for a towel to wipe down the dewy windshield. It wasn't there so I went to the rear driver's side door, where I peeked in and saw it on the floor of the rear seat. I knew it was locked since I secured it the night before but pulled up the handle as I walked by anyway. It was unlocked and opened. This startled me since I had a pair of binoculars under the front seat, about $1,000 worth of radio equipment under the dashboard, as well as my collection of George Winston tapes in the glove box. When I looked at the floor of the backseat, several items were in disarray. Nothing too obvious, just a black foam pad and a pillow askew on the floorboards and a mechanic's rag exposed when it should have been pushed under the seat. Stooping down, I checked for my Bushnell binoculars under the driver's seat. They were there, but exposed, and so was everything else. I had not moved anything around and these items could not have been in the positions I found them by rough driving. They had to be physically relocated. No windows were broken and I could detect no Slim Jim marks along the window tracks but the dew had accumulated and pooled in that area, obliterating any telltale signs. Shaking my head, I drove to school. Promptly at 11 a.m., class ended and I drove back to town. The Ford was filthy and dusty from driving the firing range roads so I searched for a car wash. I didn't want the car to be dirty for Wanda's arrival. While I wandered around the downtown area, a Porsche I recognized passed going in the other direction. It was Tony Perillo from the School staff. I whipped around and followed, catching him as he pulled into an auto repair garage. I parked on the street and met up with Tony in one of the repair stalls. I thanked him for the great class and he gave me directions to a car wash, but when I approached my car, there was a wire hanging down about eight inches below the rear bumper. Thinking it was a piece of detritus from the range road I grabbed the thin, frayed strand and pulled. It had exposed wire strands sticking out between the insulation material and didn't give much when I yanked it. Getting on my knees, and hoping the wire wasn't connected to the taillight, I pulled again; it gave a little. I had to look up underneath the rear bumper and saw it was attached to a small, black box. It was heavily anchored by a strong magnet. I immediately thought back to the bomb tech's story about a prank pulled on a student, using a hoax bomb. The wire appeared to be an antenna, but was so frayed and used I could not imagine the item being anything functional. The thought of someone pulling a joke like this angered me. The possibility of the device being a surveillance bug crossed my mind, but I've never seen a real one except what was shown in class. Those were compact and sophisticated. This device had some mileage on it. I walked back to Tony, prepared to ream him out if knew anything about it. My query was evasive enough to get him upset so he came out to the car and looked at the device. He proclaimed ignorance. I wasn't convinced so I laid it on him:

"Tony, If you don't know anything about this, I'm going to the SLO cops. I'm pissed. This isn't funny."

"John, I don't know where it came from and if I were you I'd tell the cops, too." He now sounded sincere. "I don't want to get anybody at the school in trouble so let's end it here." He continued to deny knowledge and actually gave me directions to the SLO police department, adding that anyone at the institute had probably left for the day so calling them would do no good. There was no other class going on and it didn't seem likely to either one of us anyway. It was the start of a weekend. We were both now baffled. I left my card with him and asked that he call me if he found anything out when he went back to the school on Monday. I drove the half-mile to the SLO P.D. and had a sergeant come out and take a look. I explained my explosives background and said it did not appear to be a bomb or hoax device, but it would not be a good idea to screw around with it either. Like most cops, he was as inquisitive as a three-year-old in a kitchen with open cabinets. He wanted to touch it, pick it up, and see what it was. I told him no and he called his bomb technician who happened to be at the police range just north of town. After the call, I agreed to go out there. It had not gone off yet so it wasn't a motion-detonated device. Besides, it was too small to do much damage. The surveillance team, of course, was busy circling the block to try and see what was going on. The police parking area was off the street and somewhat hidden. I noticed nothing unusual, oblivious to what was happening. Later, I saw reports indicating the ATF officials saw me discover the bug and talking to Tony at the garage. After I drove off, they contacted Tony and he was brought on board. The SLO P.D. sergeant was contacted an he told them of my destination. I was leaving a wake of witnesses littering my course as I tried to find out what was happening. Later ATF reports indicated my "consciousness of guilt" by the way I acted upon discovery of the bug. It was theorized I wasn't acting "normally." When I met with SLO PD Sergeant Jerry Lenthall at the police range we removed the device and I photographed it. While I fiddled around, Lenthall walked off to answer his phone inside the facility. A serial number and frequency number appeared on a tag on one piece so I wrote that information down on a sticky note. The call taken by Lenthall was the ATF shadows, anxious to find out what was happening. When he returned to me he said he would take charge of the device and check with CSTI after the weekend and get back with me. I was very tempted to hold on to the box and wait for the rightful owner to come and get it but I reiterated to Lenthall I didn't want to get any brother officers in trouble. I left my business card and the bug with Lenthall with instructions for him to call me and let me know what was up. I was also tempted to attach it to a northbound semi, but didn't. Before I drove off I wrote 'Eagle Electronics' on the sticky note. Eagle was a Glendale-area center for electronics buffs, ham operators and CBers. I intended to try and find out who in the area used that frequency, if I could. As I drove off I recalled the apparent entry of my car that morning. The two things together were beyond coincidence. I pulled off the side of the road and retrieved my fingerprint kit from the trunk. Tony didn't touch the bumper when he bent down to look at the device. The local cops didn't either, only playing with the device itself. There were two disturbances on the dusty chrome bumper and they corresponded with the area where the device was located. I got 3-4 good lifts from the bumper and placed them on white 3X5 index cards. I had already touched my rear door handle but saw another disturbance in dust on the lower edge of the door itself. It appeared at the right location for someone stooping down to look at the items on the rear floor of my car, using the door as a support. Only two partials were lifted from there, but they still appeared to be good enough for a match. I knew they weren't mine. I thought about my binoculars but they had a rough textured surface and weren't suitable to accept fingerprints. However, they had been moved around to the center of the underside of the driver's seat from their usual place nestled next to a mechanic's rag against the driveshaft hump.. One lens had a beautiful print. It looked like whoever rifled my car had reached under the seat and connected with the glass before he knew what it was. Making the lift was difficult. The recessed lens was small, but I got it. I had used the binoculars the day before to watch a hawk on the school grounds. They were spotless at that time. I checked them closely. Somebody entered my car. Somebody left prints. I know now it was the BATF agents on the surveillance. Their entry was without a warrant, but I really don't care about that. There was nothing for them to find anyway. What really irritates me is the fact that after they seized everything from my office in December 1991, the prints were part of what they took. The 3X5 cards were clearly marked 'SLO PD range-night before?' and the date. Even after my lawyer made a specific request for the cards, they said they couldn't find anything like them. I arranged for a day to search my office files for the express purpose of retrieving them and matching them to the surveillance agents. I couldn't find them. They were gone. Investigation by omission. I picked up Wanda later and we kept the Embassy Suites room for another day or two. I didn't tell her about the bug or car entry. At that time I had been involved in a brief affair and considered the possibility Wanda knew about it. Maybe she hired a private investigator? I remained mute and found Wanda to be in her usual playful mood — very playful and content. We kept the Embassy Suites room, abusing room service and watching every in-room movie they offered. We visited wineries and explored nearby Paso Robles where I considered putting in an application for a brand new fire department the city was staffing. It was a pleasant week and weekend despite the odd happenings. I didn't burden Wanda with my discoveries. It wasn't until October 1991 that I would get any solid information about the bug. Lenthall did call me and reassured me it was all a joke and nobody got in any serious trouble over it. He advised me to forget it. This was less than a week or two after I got home. In late October I received a call in my office from George Williams from the CSTI staff. George, a friend for several years, came to the L.A. area and taught weaponless defense classes for F.I.R.S.T and his own business. George was planning a class for November in the Glendale Holiday Inn. He asked if I would pass a few of his advertising fliers around at some of my arson meetings. I readily agreed. I also pointedly asked him about the tracking device. His response: "It was no joke, John." He was reluctant to tell me more, saying he was sworn to

288

secrecy. He added he would tell me more when he came down for his class; ironically it was to be held during week-long class I was teaching. His parting comment: "Those San Luis cops were serious." ...and he hung up. San Luis Obispo cops? I had no idea. Apparently George wasn't told everything but he never called me when he came to Glendale in November either. Involved in my own logistically massive training session, it slipped my mind that he was in town. We never got together. I never checked the frequency number either. I figured if somebody wanted to talk to me they could come forward. I later learned, after I was arrested, that the bug frequency was issued to the BATF and was on loan to them from an out-of-state ATF office. The frequency was listed in California radio texts as belonging to BATF.

The prosecution never provided surveillance logs of the San Luis Obispo tail but I would have loved to have read their comments about the moment Wanda and I walked into a fabric store to shop. It didn't occur to me until 1992 when I went over some receipts and recalled the event. It was just two hours after I had found the bug. Then there was the fifteen minutes Wanda and I spent getting frisky in the hotel parking lot after a late dinner. I hope they didn't have night vision equipment.

CHAPTER EIGHTEEN
BURNING QUESTIONS

My new partner, Joe Lopez, still needed law enforcement training, even after six months with me, so I had him ride along with uniformed police officers to get a feel for traffic stops, handling irate citizens and arrest procedures. Also important was Joe's exposure to as many police department members as possible. Joe's mere presence healed any damage done to the unit's image by Walter Beatty, or me. Women loved him, men wanted to be him. One of the most sincere, honest, and straight-up people I ever met, he had a laid-back Harrison Ford-like demeanor and a desire to learn. In early 1990, Joe attended the week-long Officer Safety and Field Tactics course to give him realistic, hands-on sessions with police officer instructors. He now needed some fine-tuning. On a slow weekday, we drove through residential areas on the west side of town where I captured five or six burglars over the years. I wanted Joe to grasp the concept of the sixth sense for knowing a situation or person is suspicious. We cruised for an hour, finally finding a strange character wandering around an upper-middle-class neighborhood. We watched through binoculars from two blocks away as the clown circled the same block near an elementary school. He stopped occasionally, leaned against a fence or telephone pole, and continued circling like a vulture. I pointed out this was a common tactic used by residential burglars. I learned it through experience and from veteran burglary detectives. The crook walks around until a resident hops into a car and drives off. The burglar then knocks on the door and if nobody answers he can be assured 20-30 minutes to commit the deed uninterrupted. Teaching Joe police-type procedures were meant to expose him to an on-the-job criminal like when I worked at Sears. In this controlled situation, with me as back-up, I could observe, his experience would broaden, and later apply to arson or bomb suspects. The guy we followed just circled the school but we both agreed he didn't belong and was up to something. I decided to give Joe a chance to demonstrate his ability to shake down and question a suspect. We tailed the guy for over 30 minutes and I told Joe we'd jack him up as if we just came across him and give him a chance to lie about his activities first. I drove up to the 20-year-old as he leaned against a chain-link fence on the perimeter of the schoolyard with his hands in his pockets. Joe was supposed to shake the guy but the flake had something in his hand and I feared a weapon. The crook looked up as we got out of the car and his expression showed shock as well as a glance up and down the street for a clear escape path. I took over, IDed us as cops, and watched his eyes for signs he was going to rabbit on us. At least he removed his empty hand from his baggy right pants pocket. I ordered him up against the fence, now in my hard-ass cop mode, showing Joe how it was done. The guy didn't want to take the position so I helped him by shoving him solidly into the fencing and coaxed him into grabbing high. Fearing that weapon, I placed my left leg between his legs to control his movements and reached into the pants pocket. There was no pocket, only a semi-erect penis. He wore no underwear and had removed the pocket to enable him to masturbate while he watched the kiddies in the schoolyard. I had Joe finish the "interview" while I retrieved water and a bottle of Phisoderm disinfectant soap from our trunk and lathered my tainted hands. We told the kid to get outta Dodge and advised police dispatch to roll a car to check the idiot out. I just wanted to get away from there. Joe was a true gentleman and didn't tell anybody about the incident, as far as I know. Common office details kept us busy and Joe also took a week off to attend an LAPD homicide investigation class at their academy. I had a reciprocal training agreement with the academy staff to allow one of my people into their class and I reserved two positions for LAPD detectives in the annual Fire Death Investigation session we hosted in Glendale. Upon my return from San Luis Obispo, on May 10, Joe and I conducted a quick bomb investigation resulting in one felony arrest. Assisting in the investigation was a female L.A. County Sheriff's Deputy--the 30-year-old suspect's sister. Her brother was out-of-town at the time we got onto him and conducted consent searches of an apartment and a garage. She offered to surrender him when he returned to town instead of us having to track him down. We agreed. Components from the 9"x2 1/2" pipe bomb were from a San Bernardino location and included a volatile military gunpowder I'd never seen before. Carol, the deputy, was very protective of her errant brother and we found he had no criminal history so were cooperative despite the severity of the crime. Nine months later, after I was arrested and charged with 13 counts of arson, I read an L.A. County Sheriff' Department report on the March 27, 1991 D&M Yardage fire I was charged with setting. The report was written by uniformed deputy Carol, our bomb suspect's sister. After hearing of the series of retail fires around the L.A. County area over the past four months, I made major alterations to my manuscript of *Points of Origin*. Aaron now graduated to setting multiple fires in stores and I used intelligence from the BATF flyers to salt my fictional fire scenes in the potential novel. Not really serious about being able to have my book published, I nevertheless sent out a few queries to literary agents and publishers to test the waters. Having no prior experience with fiction publication, I used the wrong formats and approaches to the literary people. In several of the query letters I said my manuscript was "fact-based fiction" and paralleled a "real" case. I took literary license in one letter and even said the real case being investigated had a "firefighter" as a suspect I based this on the tidbits of information I knew from the Fresno investigation when fires occurred during the arson seminar periods. I juiced up the appeal of my solicitation letters by implying even the L.A. 1990-91 cases were included in this "fact-based" scenario of a firefighter suspect. I figured an agent or publisher would be interested in such a parallel to a fictional manuscript since it had been successful in many cop-gone-bad novels in the past. The letters were later used against me; the tie-ins to the real case too provocative to be simple literary license On June 13, 1991, I took off work a few hours early to drive to Orange County to attend my daughter Lori's high school graduation. As Wanda and I cruised southbound, a series of three brush and grass fires erupted along freeways on the Los Angeles/Glendale border and in Glendale itself. Two of these fires were in areas I was later convicted of setting grass fires. Twenty-five miles away at the time of these similar fires provides good alibi but my lawyer never approached bringing up alibi cases of a less than lunch-with-the-Pope variety. Another seminar approached, this one at the end of July, and I elected to allow Joe to have the city on-call responsibility for the four days I would be out-of-town. From 1989 to 1991 I let my partners attend whatever training was offered since I had been in the unit for 10 years and took advantage of every seminar available during the early to mid-1980's. CSTI in San Luis Obispo was my first in a long time. The July session was the semi-annual California Conference of Arson Investigators meeting, held in Fresno, California at the Holiday Inn. It was the setting for a large part of *Points of Origin* and I wanted to visit to update my descriptions and settings in the manuscript. Somewhere along the line ATF Agent Matassa learned I was attending. As a member of CCAI's Education/Training Committee I planned to give a short presentation to the board covering the outstanding CSTI course: Officer Safety and Field Tactics for Arson Investigators. I had videotaped both classroom and field exercises and felt the thrill of the actual class would make more of an impact through the tape rather than my own dry lecture. I intended to gain CCAI's support in spreading the word about the class and provide more students for this spectacular training. The number of fire represent-atives in the course dwindled to the point CSTI might drop the offering. Part of the problem was advertising. Word-of-mouth, so far, hadn't cut it. Few fire department investigators knew about the semi-annual sessions. I felt a strong enough presentation might get CCAI's support and have the course advertised in the organization's quarterly magazine, *The*

Investigator. Maybe gratis. An article, with photos could also help and I was prepared to volunteer to write it. I left home on Tuesday, July 30, 1991, again driving my big Ford. It was a dog when it came to acceleration but once it got rolling it cornered fairly well and was a great road car. After the car was issued to me, I added an AM-FM cassette player and four speakers at my own expense. I loved road trips with the Ford. It reminded me of a Douglas DC-3 or a VW bug---it lumbered along, but was dependable. I didn't have an off-duty car since the Ford was mine 24 hours a day, all year long. Of course, the ATF shadows were with me, according to reports I read much later. Two new names were added to their team: Glen Lucero, LAFD Arson and Larry Cornelison, Special Agent In Charge of the L.A.-area ATF office. A couple of the agents actually enrolled in the seminar, apparently so they could discreetly follow me and fit right in. Again, the session started with a pre-registration get-together the night before classes actually started. As part of the registration, I was pulled out of line and had a Polaroid picture taken of me. The ruse was, the photo would be in the next issue of *The Investigator* magazine because I was on the Education Committee. In reality, the picture, with me half smiling, ended up in a law enforcement 6-pack, a photo-spread with five other similarly described individuals to be shown to witnesses. Six witnesses, out of over 70 shown the 6-pack, picked me out. My usual m.o. at the seminars was to hang out with private investigators and insurance people. They were generally retired fire investigators, had a tremendous amount of experience and access to information I periodically needed, and much bigger expense accounts than their civil servant counterparts. The networking worked both ways. Seldom did I buy a drink at CCAI conferences. ATF head Larry Cornelison surprised us by sitting with me and several private investigators. Very uncharacteristic of a fed, but I didn't know Larry well so it was meaningless to me, until later. I thought he was being cordial. The Holiday Inn we stayed in was the location of three chapters of *Points*. As I sat and sipped a Jim Beam, I remembered the chapters I wrote just six months before. In those sections, my protagonist, Phil Langtry, was tailed by a team of law enforcement and fire department investigators, in the same hotel, at the same bar. Six months before. It was now happening to me, in reality, but I wasn't aware of it. *Points of Origin* was written, primarily, without an outline. I just plugged in a few ideas and let the story take shape. The investigation aspects of *Points* were based on my own experience with arresting over 20 serial arsonists in Glendale and adjoining cities. Serial crimes are investigated differently than heat-of-passion crimes. I also had worked several cases involving suspects who were firefighters or related to the fire service and law enforcement community. Aaron, and, the investigation of him, was a composite of my past and professional experiences. I had dinner with several old friends that night and returned to my room to watch a movie. Probably bored my shadows senseless. The next day, Thursday, August 1, they would get what they wanted—a fire, with me nearby, and the suspicious circumstances they longed for. After lunch Thursday, I went to my room, lounged around, then headed back to the classroom. Over 200 people were at this session. The Education Committee was getting together at 2:30, in a small meeting room off the atrium area near the hotel's restaurant. I talked to one of the board of directors earlier and he assured me I had an allotment of time for my presentation. At about 2:15 I left the classroom and walked about 100 feet down a wide hallway then jogged left by the restrooms and stepped into meeting room 'A.' It had a glass door and windows overlooking the atrium next to a waterfall, but thick curtains were drawn as I entered. Several people were already seated at a conference table, sipping coffee and chatting. I saw my TV and VCR were in place.

THE FOLLOWING IS AN EXCERPT OF AN OFFICIAL BATF "REPORT OF SURVEILLANCE" FOR AUGUST 1, 1991, WRITTEN BY GLEN LUCERO, LOS ANGELES FIRE DEPT:" I followed Orr out of the classroom at approximately 2:10 p.m. He walked down a long hallway then stepped out of my view. I was followed by two other agents, one of who alerted others on the surveillance team. As I reached the end of the hallway I couldn't find Orr. We checked elevators and hallways, bathrooms, the restaurant and bar. He wasn't anywhere. Outside surveillance personnel were alerted. We determined Orr was not in his room. Outside surveillance began driving around surface streets surrounding the hotel. At 2:35 p.m. agent Albert reported a fire approximately 1/2 block from the hotel in an alcove on the outside of the Fresno Convention Center. A combination trash can/ashtray was burning. We alerted the fire department and the fire was extinguished. I personally examined the burned container and found it to be made of plastic, metal and foam material. There were no accidental means for this fire to have ignited. I determined it to have been intentionally set near where John Orr was seen only minutes earlier. There is a side entrance to the hotel where seminar participants take smoke breaks. John Orr had been seen in this area several times during the conference. John Orr was not seen the rest of the day." When I went "missing" from the surveillance crew, I had simply stepped inside meeting room 'A' for my presentation. After sitting in on 10 minutes of this session I realized I wasn't going to make my pitch here. This branch of the Education Committee was concerned with arranging speakers for the next seminar and other unrelated areas. It would have been fruitless to make my appeal to these guys. I explained this to one of the committee and excused myself at about 2:45; minutes after the inferno down the block was extinguished. I returned to my room, watched some more movies, ordered a room-service dinner and continued editing my manuscript. The BATF's investigators actually presented their surveillance fire at my trial in July, 1992; the inference, of course, I set the fire after "eluding" their dragnet, ran down the street and set the trash can ablaze. They never queried me after I was arrested and try and find out where I went. My lawyer didn't think they would ever present something so ludicrous as evidence, but they did and we weren't prepared. Their inferences went unchallenged and without explanation. To refute their claim we had to find one of the Education Committee to verify I was at the meeting. My lawyer refused to let me testify. On Friday morning I checked out early to beat the crowds. One of the last two sessions was repetitious and the other was a legal update. I went to the classroom, found the instructor and picked up his handouts dealing with recent arson-related case law. Before I got into my car I got down on my knee and checked for a bug. Nothing there. An ATF shadow snapped several pictures of me doing the pre-launch search. After topping off my gas tank I headed back to Glendale where I had an early afternoon appointment in regards to an arson/insurance fraud fire I was working. The ATF surveillance report on the trash fire ended with: "We followed Orr back to L.A. without further incident." But they weren't through yet. August 1991 was a busy month for Joe and I. The arson/insurance fraud from July heated up and we served two search warrants almost nailing the guy after a lengthy surveillance. I also appeared as investigating officer in the Glendale Municipal Court for a bomb arrest I made on July 15. In July I was asked to make a presentation at the quarterly meeting of the California Arson Prevention Committee in San Francisco in August. My boss agreed to give me the time off and I could take my trusty Ford plus, the city would reimburse me for gas. The CAPC picked up the room tab. I zoomed off on Wednesday, August 7th, arriving in San Francisco in the late afternoon. No ATF reports reflect a constant tail on this trip. One document did relate a conversation between an ATF agent and a Los Banos(CA) Fire Department investigator. He was asked if Los Banos had any fires in their jurisdiction on the afternoon of August 7, 1991. They had no responses at all that day. I had detoured off the freeway, through Los Banos due to a closed freeway on-ramp. I didn't know the ramp to get back on was closed and the only other way northbound was to go through Los Banos. I got gas, found the ramp shut down and drove 12 miles through onion fields to get back on again. Somewhere along that stretch was the hamlet of Los Banos. I have no idea how they knew that fact if they didn't tail me, but no other reports reflect a constant surveillance. They may have been following too far back and didn't know I got off the freeway and couldn't get back on. I don't know since they never provided surveillance logs. My presentation, ironically, was about a serial arsonist I arrested in 1985. He set a series of brush fires on, and around the campus of Glendale Community College during the summer session that year. I videotaped a post-arrest interview with him. The original 30-minute tape was edited down for me by a friend in the Burbank Fire Department. He added an introduction, title credits and a soundtrack by Queen. It was a bit dramatic but the price was right: free. The suspect fit the classic profile of a serial arsonist and that may have been one of the reasons his arrest appeared simple. The CAPC heard about the tape after I showed it at several meetings and classes in southern California and asked me to make a presentation of it and give an overview of the June 1990 College Hills brush fire in Glendale. My presentation lasted about 20 minutes. I left San Francisco within the hour and drove five hours to King City for a two-day deer and wild pig hunt with my close friend, Bill McLaughlin, a private investigator. We bagged a nice three-point coastal buck and I got over 100 pounds of excellent pork from my 150 pound boar. While I enjoyed my combination business/pleasure trip, BATF agent Mike Matassa and LAFD investigator Glen Lucero showed their week-old photo spread to Ana Ramirez. Ms. Ramirez worked at the People's Department store in Los Angeles on December 10, 1990 when a fire gutted the building. After the fire had been burning for about 20-30 minutes I arrived and videotaped the activities. Ramirez said nothing about suspicious activities or suspects on the day she was first interviewed the day after the fire. When shown the 6-pack photo spread on August 8, 1991, 8 full months later, she pointed at my picture (mounted top row, center) and said she thought I was in the store on a few occasions, but not on the day of the fire. Many other photo spreads were presented, including a number of different composite drawings circulated among witnesses. Only the one 6-pack with me and one composite drawing from the D & M Yardage store were ever provided to the defense after I was arrested. We don't know if any other suspects were developed. The summer of 1991 was a busy time for the Task Force investigators. On October 1st, I was off-duty and played around the house with Domino as a series of brush fires occurred in South Pasadena. No suspects were developed and no devices found. Temperatures in the 90's kept fire departments all over southern California jumping. The City of Pasadena also experienced a three acre brush fire that damaged two homes. The next day, October 2, I worked alone; Joe was off-duty. Puttering around the administrative offices, I saw smoke from a brush fire in the Griffith Park area just west of Glendale. The fire actually occurred in the Hollywood Hills area but I didn't find this out until years later. Recalling two prior occasions when

Griffith Park fires erupted, followed by a Burbank and Glendale fire, I left the office to an informal patrol towards Burbank. As I headed west a fire erupted in the Griffith Park area only 200 yards from the Glendale Burbank border. I got into the area, scoped it out briefly and decided I'd better head back into Glendale in case the same arsonist who did the west-to-east series before now hit Glendale. Chevy Chase Canyon was my destination. Two miles into town, headed toward Chevy Chase Estates, I saw a column of smoke go up simultaneous to a dispatch for a brushfire in the Chevy Chase Drive/Kennington area. Both Engine Five and Three were ahead of me when I hit Chevy Chase Drive. First reports indicated a house involved. The beginnings of black clouds of smoke were added to the grayish-brown brushfire emissions. This 2-acre fire destroyed a half-million dollar hillside home. Units at the base of the fire used a top-mounted deck gun to affect the extinguishment along Chevy Chase drive--the area of origin of the blaze. Too much water brought down the hill. The mudslide obliterated any chance of recovering an incendiary device or evidence of an accidental fire cause. I spent a moment or two looking around for anything to help me write a cause and origin report. About that time a bystander told me of a possible witness, a construction worker employed at a nearby project. I recalled the Sheriff's Department developing a suspect in a series of fires in La Canada and he worked in construction. Cautiously approaching the man I listened to his tale of hearing what sounded like a backfire or fireworks explosion and a car accelerating away. Then he saw smoke. Surrounded by 8-10 co-workers when the fire went down, I considered his story valid but he had no vehicle description. His information could prove a problem if I called this fire arson and he provided two alternative accidental fire causes: A car backfire and fireworks. The backfire theory was a consideration because burned dry grass was close enough to the street to be ignited by a jet of flame or red hot metallic meteor emanating from a car's exhaust pipe. If I wrote this information down it would become part of the report and possibly cloud issues. I noted the man's license number and the address of the worksite in case I needed to re-contact him. I may have captured more info, too, in my pocket-sized police field notebook but don't recall and these documents went missing after I was arrested. I didn't want to make an arson or accidental fire cause call on this incident until I checked with the Sheriff's investigator. I cleared the scene and later returned when L.A. Sheriff arson/explosives investigator Rich Edwards showed up. Rich's construction worker information was over two years old and he said he'd check and get back to me. My construction worker was just a witness at this point unless he matched Rich's information. On October 9, Joe and I responded to a brush fire near the north Glendale border with Los Angeles. By the time we arrived only

Engine Eight remained on scene. The fire began about 25 feet off a freeway on-ramp. A nearby CalTrans work crew reported it quickly and Engine Eight's early arrival kept the fire from extending beyond a flat field into heavy brush that hadn't burned in 35 years. With an interview with a police officer witness in a pipe bomb case pending, Joe and I did a cursory overview of the field and followed burn patterns to the area of origin. The melted, bubbled remains of a rubber band and several burned paper matches attached to a rock were located. The device was identical to at least three other similar found over the previous month in La Crescenta. There was no time-delay. The match bundle apparently was struck and as the lit match head ignited the others, the device was tossed out a car window into the grass. A crude but effective fire starter. Two of the devices were found in residential areas and this one by an on-ramp. Two of these "instant" fires occurred when Joe and I were together. It was my feeling the non-time-delay incendiaries were responsible for many of our freeway fires as well. Very delicate after burning, the components frequently disappeared under assault by fire streams. In court documents, investigators and prosecutors theorized I set all these fires. In 1996 and again in 1999, after I was incarcerated, similar, but larger fires erupted along the freeway within 100 yards of the October 9, 1991 fire location. On October 20, 1991, another affidavit was written and signed by a judge to enable the attachment of a more sophisticated bug to my city car (By now, my supervisors were advised I was a suspect). This affidavit was written by Rich Edwards, an L.A. County Sheriff's Department arson/explosives investigator. On October 26, 1991, the Glendale Fire Department's head mechanic asked me to turn in my car for "routine maintenance." I left it for several days, picking it up on October 29th. The Teletrac tracking device printed log shows my car stationary for over 24 hours after the bug was activated. At 8:30 a.m. the car starts to move. Joe Lopez dropped me off and I started on a 54-day, 24-hour-a-day tail. The Teletrac's signal beamed to a series of antennas scattered around the L.A. area and the system triangulated the bug's location at 5, 10, and 15 minute intervals. Whatever the computer was programmed to track that day. The printed log showed the day, date, time, direction of travel, approximate speed and location of the car down to two or three intersecting streets at the moment of the "hit." After I was arrested and charged with arson and murder in 1994 (the state arrest wasn't until this time, the federal arrest was in 1991), I was able to evaluate the Teletrac log. It was not considered a part of the federal case since the L.A. County Sheriff's were doing the monitoring. Along with the log was several hundred pages of related documents. These items were primarily fire response reports that showed fires occurring near my travels during the Teletrac period. The rest of October and into

November, Teletrac shadowed me and revealed a number of fires occurring in my vicinity, but these were ignored by Task Force investigators. These events would later become important. The prosecution contended accusingly, "Orr was always near fires when they started....," the inference being, "He must have started them." The Teletrac proved their theory, in part, since I was in the area of fires during the tracking period, but these fires were not started by me since the Teletrac accurately shows me nowhere near the location before they ignited so it was impossible for me to have been involved. Some were accidental fires, too. Anyone can pass near an area where a fire occurs and never know it if the blaze starts several blocks off their street of travel or ignites after they left the vicinity. It is a natural occurrence. Two of these fires happened within a half mile of a classroom where I was teaching the week of November 18-21. Both were suspicious, but I was in class with 31 witnesses. Teletrac coverage also was found to fluctuate by as much as mile, but a quarter-mile error was more common. Basically, Teletrac proved to be beneficial to the defense, but a lackadaisical lawyer chose to ignore its potential good. An ignorance that nearly found me convicted of a lunch with-the-Pope alibi fire. The Task Force's case was ready to heat up. Class adjourned Friday at about 11:30 a.m. I gave Joe the rest of the day off since I was taking the next week off myself and the remaining details of closing out the class could be accomplished by one man. Popping the final exams in the mail by 2 p.m., I headed home to perform the final detail for the class—returning borrowed equipment to Tri-Ess Services, a business in Burbank owned by a chemist and old friend, Ira Katz. Teletrac documents show me just blocks from the I-5 freeway in Burbank as I headed for Tri-Ess. Recording locations every 15 Minutes on that day, Teletrac hit at 3:08 p.m., three miles east from a fire erupting next to the Walton's cabin TV show outdoor set at the Warner Brother's Studios. The next Teletrac hit shows me at a school less than a mile from the blossoming fire. I saw the smoke, heard the fire call go out on the radio and dutifully stayed at the school for a parent-teacher conference I was attending for a friend's daughter. At least until I found I was fifteen minutes early. With a few minutes to spare I headed for the studio area but could find no adequate videotaping sites due to traffic and inaccessibility so returned to the school. I didn't set this fire. Teletrac exonerated me. The next Teletrac hits place me back at the school. This was a better-than-lunch-with-the-Pope-and-a-receipt alibi. Four years later I was still charged with setting the studio fire at the Walton's cabin. John-Boy the arsonist. Seven years later, in 1998, most of a jury voted to convict me of setting the studio blaze despite the solid Teletrac alibi. After the conference at the school I stayed for dinner at my friend's apartment and went over her daughter's evaluation from the parent-teacher conference. Before eating, I was paged. Burbank arson investigator Steve Patterson, still at the studio fire scene, wanted a second opinion on the fire cause he determined. Steve had been a fire department investigator for about 18 months. Continuing Burbank's tradition, he called on Glendale's assistance several times each year and, ironically, was in my class all week long. He was assigned to one of two teams evaluating mock fire scenes at my own home on Monday, four days before. Steve, still a novice in terms of a working knowledge of fire scene investigation, did well on his class fire scene but my experience with him showed more book learning than actual live-fire experience in fire investigation. Like many newer investigators, he used outdated textbooks as guides and substitutes for practical training. I was the same way early in my career. Books were bibles. Investigating at least eight scenes with Steve over his 18-month assignment I tried to get him interested in setting his own training fires to observe fire setting in it's incipiency, as it gains headway in the fuel, during extinguishment, and finally the aftermath. It was the only way to explode several of the fire scene investigation "standards" still being published. For example, the condition of common window glass exposed to various fire scenarios is supposed to be a standard indicator of whether a fire was arson-caused or accidental. My live-fire training sessions over the years exploded that myth. Post-fire window glass condition may be an indicator, or a clue, but not the textbook miscues perpetrated in texts and articles I read even today. Steve swore by the bibles. After being paged, I hooked up with Steve on the phone and he asked me to come to the studio. I told him I was only minutes away and he started to give me directions to the fire scene. I knew approximately where the fire was from my earlier excursion but was unfamiliar with the gate number or street names Steve used to guide me in. I stopped him mid-description and suggested I meet him at the Hollywood Way studio gate. My friend's apartment was just off Hollywood Way and the thoroughfare dead-ended at the studio entrance. We agreed and signed off. I decided to skip the incoming pizza delivery and drove quickly to the studio. I was early, Steve not there yet, so I left word with the gate guard to advise Steve I'd driven on in to the fire area. I figured I'd probably catch him before he headed for the nearby gate anyway. I got turned around in the maze-like studio but finally spotted a fire department car and Steve's assistant investigator. The brightly-lit fire scene was just beyond the car. After suiting up and meeting with a few other fire personnel, Steve joined us. He showed me around the scene that was basically a vegetation fire that spread to the Walton's cabin facade, a few outbuildings, and fencing. The area of origin was difficult to trace after thousands of gallons of water and many firefighters had flooded it or trekked across the surface. Steve led me to the remains of what he described as a chicken coop. He pulled away a few boards and proudly pointed to partially fire-damaged flooring. The burning structure above collapsed onto the floor, covering some unburned wood and preserving it. The damaged portion had charred wavy edges like dark clouds painted on the flooring. Steve immediately said the wavy patterns indicated burning flammable liquid damage: gasoline in the chicken coop. Black, rounded damage is another of the textbook standards sworn to as evidence of arson and flammable liquid on the surface. Unfortunately, the patterns can also be caused by several other factors including fire burning across a ceiling and radiant heat etching the exposed floor as it travels. Steve wouldn't listen to an alternative. He proclaimed the evidence caused by gasoline on the floor and added he wanted authority to call out F.I.R.S.T.'s arson dog, Blanche. The canine trained to alert on over 20 different kinds of flammables, was owned by a former L.A. Fire Department investigator who now worked as a firefighter and off-duty for insurance companies. I was tired, hungry, and saw this fire scene needed to be searched on hands and knees to trace fire travel. I could tell by the foot and boot prints it hadn't been done thoroughly. The other glaring sign was the supposed use of gasoline to start this fire: it would have been overkill. Judging by the amount of burned grass and fallen leaves, a dropped match would have been far more efficient in getting the fire going. The scene could be an arson site but I didn't see a strong enough motive for an aggressive act such as use of gasoline. Flammable liquid would also draw immediate attention to the fire and although in a remote forest-like setting, a 3-story office building looked down on the set from just a few yards away. I placated Steve, instead of arguing with him, and we placed an order for Blanche. The arson canine wouldn't show up until morning. As I left I advised Steve to trace the area of origin again. I don't know what he did after I left but later learned Blanche alerted on nothing; no flammable liquid presence. Taking on-call status until Sunday at noon when I'd officially be on days off, I got up Saturday morning and took my mother to the Burbank Airport in my narc car. Teletrac shows it. Returning home about 11 a.m., I readied my camping equipment and guns for my solo trip to the desert. Wanda's idea of camping was a 30-foot motor home with shower and wet bar. She wouldn't let me take Domino either. Her .22 Beretta and the dog made her much more secure in my absence. Working part-time as a private investigator for my old roomie, Bill McLaughlin, I had a payroll timesheet to deliver to his home since I wouldn't be in town at the end of the pay period the following week. Borrowing Wanda's car for this personal errand to Tujunga, eight miles away, I grabbed a couple of rolls of film from the city car and headed out to complete my tasks. One of my shift investigators at Station Nine

301

needed film for his investigation kit and I planned to swing by and drop it off. He had left a message on the office answering machine on Friday. Wanda and I had an agreement. She was our groundskeeper and I took care of her car's maintenance, washing, waxing, and filling her gas tank since she periodically let the fuel level drop to fumes-only operation. This brief trip was also a freeway shakedown for me to check on the car's condition. With the city car at my full-time disposal I seldom drove Wanda's beast except when we went out to dinner or out-of-town. I flew up to Bill's place, dropped off my paperwork on his porch since he wasn't home, and headed for Station Nine. Getting off the Foothill Freeway at Oceanview Boulevard I spotted a red and white L.A. Fire Department car just ahead of me. Pulling up to the fresh stop light I glanced to my left at the car's occupants and saw and old friend, Captain Gary Siedel and his son. He didn't see me so I idled forward a bit and popped my horn twice to get his attention. We waved in recognition and greeting, then made our opposite turns and drove away. I cruised to nearby Station Nine and pulled into the rear parking lot. My shift investigator's car wasn't in the lot, he was off-duty, so I walked into the kitchen and left the film in his food locker in the kitchen and left. Then I returned home on the freeway and topped off Wanda's gas tank at the gas station/car wash next door. I puttered around the kitchen grab-assing with Wanda for about 10-15 minutes. At about 2:12 p.m., I monitored my portable radio for a "smoke investigation" call assigned to Engine Three in Chevy Chase Canyon. Three's cleared the station quickly and the dispatcher came back on the air, "Engine Three, we're upgrading your call to a brushfire, 3300 block Saint Elizabeth Drive." I threw my stuff together and ran to my city car parked across the street. My pager went off as I was included automatically with the assignment of three more Glendale engines and one from nearby Pasadena. As I rolled code-3 to the fire I glanced up to the ridgeline as Engine Three reported they were at the scene and saw nothing, but I saw a wisp of smoke against the hillside at the top of Chevy Chase Canyon. Pasadena's Engine Eight came up on the radio to report a small fire on Figueroa Street just below Three's location. At that moment my scanning radio picked up traffic on another brushfire about three miles northwest of us. I rolled up to Eight's location on Figueroa and saw a very small bush burned and a fireman poking at it with a shovel. Chatting briefly with Eight's Captain, we decided I should divert to the larger fire over the hill. He said he'd call me if he found anything suspicious at his scene. Flying over the pass into La Canada, I caught up with Glendale Engine Nine on their way to the Hilldale Avenue fire. Hilldale is approximately ½ mile east of the freeway off-ramp where I waved at Captain Seidel about 45 minutes earlier. I didn't recognize the name Hilldale so followed Engine Nine and

302

then the column of smoke to get to the fire that was actually in L.A. county's jurisdiction just off the Foothill Freeway in a residential area. The street was strewn with engines and hose lines so I stopped short and directed traffic until relieved by a Glendale motorcycle cop. Knowing the small blaze was in county area, I did a quick walk around of the base of the fire and noted the fire appeared to have ignited inside the freeway fence near the sidewalk. An old fallen tree formed a natural "fort"-like structure and I immediately thought kids may be responsible. Fire hoses and firefighters covered the obvious area of origin, destroying any possibility for a good search. It also didn't seem possible to throw an incendiary device from a moving car at this location and have it successfully clear the fence. Near simultaneous roadside fires were suspicious but I couldn't solidly connect the two and was reluctant to do so. An arsonist who likes to watch his fires would miss one of these since they went down within minutes of each other so what would be the point? Wanda and I were having an early dinner out and attending the City Employees Association-sponsored Las Vegas Nite that evening. Anxious to get home and finish my vacation preparations and get cleaned up for dinner, I drove off. Since Engine Eight's Captain didn't contact me I assumed he found nothing but I was not aware of his investigative experience I decided to have Joe Lopez go by the location and check it out later. When I got home I called and left a message on the office answering machine for him to check out the scene when he came in on Monday morning, and also submit my overtime slips for the call-outs. That way my overtime slips would be put in before the end of the pay period since I wouldn't be back to work until December 2nd. I left the next morning at about 11 a.m., my narc car with Teletrac still functioning in the city hall multi-deck parking structure. I would return to work for one day, Tuesday, December 3, then start two weeks of jury duty. On Monday morning, November 25, 1991, deputy Rich Edwards scanned the Teletrac read-outs and discovered I was near the Burbank studio fire on Friday afternoon. Captain Seidel of the LAFD was also privy to the on-going investigation of me and he notified the task force of my presence near the Hilldale fire "just minutes" before it ignited, according to his statement. I knew none of this, of course, and enjoyed relaxing for the next eight days puttering around the desert and back at home with Wanda. Apparently the task force members examined the Teletrac read-outs for November 22 and 23 and decided I set all the fires. Teletrac exonerated me from the studio fire. No Orr-as-the-studio-fire-setter scenario worked. It just didn't fit in any way with the time-stamps and location showing me in Glendale all day until just minutes before the fire is reported, then my car is three miles away. It couldn't happen but the task force used my "close proximity" to the studio and the two small brush fires on Saturday to obtain search and arrest warrants on me. Their probable cause and press releases said the task force members felt "Orr was out-of-control and had to be stopped..."

CHAPTER NINETEEN
ASHES TO ASHES

On December 3, 1991, a Tuesday, I returned to work and Joe filled me in on what I missed while I wandered around the deserts of southern California. I spent the day shuffling paperwork and caught up on finalizing some of my older cases. With investigation narratives and summaries necessary on several large matters, I decided to use my upcoming jury duty time effectively by penciling the reports while in the juror's waiting room. As a law enforcement officer for over twelve years, I felt there was no chance a lawyer would allow me on any jury. I dated the jury coordinator in the 1980's, and she managed to assign me to jury duty in the courthouse directly across the street from my office, instead of downtown Los Angeles or Van Nuys. Networking over the past decade paid off in many ways. If not seated on a jury early in the day, release was possible and my office just five minutes away so I could catch up on paperwork. I looked forward to the pre-Christmas lull.

At this stage of my career, I was comfortable with stepping back and considered many options for my future. The Paso Robles Fire Department in central California transitioned from a volunteer agency to fully paid, and a captaincy or battalion chief position in that beautiful area beckoned. Wanda found this agreeable but neither of us really wanted to leave L.A. An administrative battalion chief position also opened in nearby Burbank. This, too, was a consideration since the appointee oversaw investigations. I pondered.

On December 4, 1991, at 7:10 a.m., I walked out of my house to find a cool, clear day, and a man crouched behind a neighbor's juniper bush. An odd sight, even in L.A. Even weirder was the fact he held a gun. The rising sun shined through my driveway in front of my Ford while the man with the gun peeked around the far side of the juniper, looking up the street, away from me. He stooped in the early-morning shadows created by my neighbor's house. My first thought was to reach for my off-duty gun, a Walther PPK/S .380, strapped securely to my left ankle. In that same split second I realized I also held a Ruger .41 magnum pistol in my hands, inside a zippered case, ready to be placed inside my trunk. Within the same instant, while still scoping out the man-in-the-bush, I thought of Wanda hovering above me on the porch. She puttered in a planter of flowers with Domino. With my back turned, I pictured her in a helicopter-like holding pattern. She always did this prior to swooping down on me and enforcing her own "never say good-bye without a kiss" policy. I am not a morning person and always felt her last minute clinging was her way of forcing me to think about her as I single-mindedly zeroed in on my work day. My job was my life, my mistress, and Wanda knew it. I appreciated her tenderness. The latter half of that split second's thought was spent determining I had my car for cover, I could draw quickly, and the .380 was deadly accurate at 30 feet; the distance to the juniper. Wanda would be out of the line of fire if I dove for the hood and as I formed this decision I saw the object of the gunman's attention: an LAPD black and white drove halfway into my driveway.

My thought process downshifted when I realized the cops would handle the offender next door. I looked back at the bush and saw the man looking at me---and I recognized him. He was an LAFD arson investigator and friend. Rolling my eyes back to the cops I found them pointing guns at me.

My left leg froze in an 'L' position as my right thumb found the combination Velcro/snap holding the fully loaded Walther in the ankle holster. Had I continued, shots would have rained down on me.

"John...John! Don't move. Stay where you are!" The shouts came from behind a camper parked in front of my house. I turned and recognized Larry Cornelison as the source of the racket. Larry, head of the L.A.-area Alcohol, Tobacco & Firearms office was holding a gun as he jogged towards me. He repeated, "Don't move, you're under arrest."

By then I'd dropped my left leg but remembered my law enforcement training automatically: "An officer never gives up his gun." I had no idea why Larry wanted to arrest me. I didn't particularly want to shoot him either. At least not at that moment.

"Wanda, step inside," I heard myself say as Cornelison ordered me to put my hands on top of the car. He was 15-20 feet away now. Putting my trust in Larry, my body tensed to resist this travesty, but the .380 stayed in its holster.

"Left leg, small auto on the ankle," I said as Larry patted me down, he obviously as nervous as I.

"John, you're under arrest," he repeated.

"For what?"

"Arson, John."

Arson? I couldn't believe it. I tried to pursue the question but was quickly handcuffed and led to a plain Ford parked in the street. I counted at least five undercover cars and saw a multitude of L.A. area arson investigation talent: all people I had worked alongside for the past twelve years. Rich Edwards and several other L.A. County Arson/Explosives Unit; Tom Campuezano and Glen Lucero, LAFD Arson and Mike

306

Matassa, also an ATF Agent. There appeared to be over ten investigators in front of my house. Glancing over my shoulder I took a last look. Wanda was being shown paperwork at the front door where Domino joyously barked at all the attention he received. A piece of paperwork now in Wanda's hands was a search warrant, I was sure. I wasn't worried, however, I'd done nothing wrong. We didn't even cheat on our taxes and I had no illegal fully-automatic weapons in my home, so why were the feds here?

Larry Cornelison rode in the back seat of the Ford with me as I was driven by Mike Matassa to the LAPD Northeast Division. There I was taken to an interview room where I was paraded by several uniformed LAPD officers.

"How's it goin', John?"

I looked up to see Officer Will, the beat cop working day watch in my neighborhood. I'd talked to him many times at a car wash next door. I shook my head as I passed him, not knowing what to say. His query was neither contemptuous nor probing, just a greeting. I don't think he knew I was handcuffed. My shoulders slumped and it felt like my hands were dragging on the floor. I was outraged, confused and prepared to strike out at anyone handy, particularly the ATF idiots, but controlled myself.

The interrogation was brief and inept. I was shown an affidavit supporting the search warrant but given only a moment to glance at it between questions by Matassa. Somewhere I may have been read my Miranda rights. I don't recall. Matassa took the lead, obviously the case investigator. Cornelison didn't allow it for long though. Matassa faltered somewhat, expecting an immediate confession from the queries and statements he posed to me. A lack of response baffled Matassa and Larry attempted to gain some headway by making a half-assed compliment about my reputation since 1980.

He added, "When we developed you as a suspect, none of us believed it. We didn't believe it, but you did it all."

His blatant declaration, not just an accusation, pissed me off enough to have decked him had I been uncuffed. I hung my head and bit my lip...and strategized. I also couldn't understand what he meant by "all."

The affidavit, as I glanced at it, mentioned three different retail stores in the greater Los Angeles area. Two in December 1990 and one in 1991. I was aware of only one of the three fires. It occurred at the People's Department store in nearby Highland Park. I looked at Cornelison and slowly turned to Matassa and simply said, "You're fucking crazy. This is fantasy." I dropped my head again and thought about a lawsuit against these pricks but shook my head and snickered audibly. They must have thought I was as whacko as they portrayed me to be.

"What was that, John?"

"Nothing, man. This has got to be a joke." I replied sarcastically. Overwhelmed by the situation and afraid to say anything, I limited my responses and let Cornelison rattle on. An old interrogator's trick is to maintain silence and the other person will generally fill the void automatically. I let Larry vomit his trash talk. But I had to speak one more time.

"Larry, I haven't done a fucking thing. This is all bullshit and I just want it to go away." This statement was followed by an ATF good cop/bad cop routine straight out of Police Academy III. Cornelison, veteran that he was, saw me ready to clam up and ask for a lawyer and quickly reverted to another textbook maneuver.

"All right, John," he said. "This is as hard on us as it is on you, let's talk off-the-record for a minute."

"Yeah, John. You're the last person we wanted to arrest. We just need you to help us understand why?" Matassa chimed in, "Let's talk off-the-record a minute. Man-to-man." I saw Larry grimace at Matassa's intrusion into his question effectively diluting the original off-the-record offer. While watching Matassa finish his statement, I missed Cornelison's eye or head jerk, indicating Matassa should leave the room, but I expected it anyway. Matassa mumbled something to his superior and stepped out. Cornelison looked back at me, "Off-the-record, John. Why?" Tempted to jump heavily into his face with my comeback, I felt pity for this middle-aged man who, by his lack of interview skills alone confirmed my years-old theory of the ATF as Keystone Kops. I felt some allegiance to a fellow law enforcement officer but this interview was far too bizarre; I had nothing to volunteer. I was disappointed as well as angry. I walked around the block to avoid a confrontation with this man. They told me the interview wasn't being recorded. It was. Like most federal recordings, this one, too, ended up with built-in gaps at strategic moments. I said, "I don't want to talk to you anymore. I didn't do anything so let's just get the procedure moving." Cornelison stepped outside and disappeared. While he was gone I scanned the affidavit and support information attached. The two additional counts suggested I had burned two retail stores. I never visited either store and wasn't even sure where the city of Lawndale was as the paperwork articulated.

Continuing to check the sheets, I found several pages and maps listing two or three series of fires that occurred in Central California. Some went back five years. I then realized the scope of the ATF's investigation. I was aware of the 1987 Fresno series fires but never heard about the discovery of a fingerprint associated to one of the fires. The series of Fresno-area fires were in a list attached to the affidavit. I could see that the ATF considered me an arsonist roving California and burning stores. The documents related to the fingerprint indicated it was mine. I'd never been in Bakersfield in my life. Through it, yes, but never in it. The accusation seemed indefensible. A series of retail fires in Central California was mentioned but I wasn't aware of them until that moment. Cornelison and Matassa transported me to the Federal Court Building in Los Angeles where I was strip-searched, fingerprinted and confined until 2 p.m. when I met with Federal Defender Drew Edwards. We briefly went over the affidavit and I explained, in the short time we had, that I was not guilty of any of the charges. He too, noted that the evidence was extremely weak, except the fingerprint.

At least two witnesses had viewed a common photo spread line-up of six photographs (mine included) of people of similar physical characteristics. The people who were present at the fires "positively" identified me as being in the stores. These IDs were made seven and nine months after the incidents. Drew and I also found my recently-completed manuscript, *Points of Origin* was being used as evidence Drew told me no bail was recommended. This meant I would remain in custody until a bail review hearing could be arranged. Still, Drew attempted to get bail at my arraignment and it was denied. A bail review set for December 18 coincided with a scheduled preliminary hearing.

As a law enforcement officer I had to be isolated from the general jail population. For this, at least, I was grateful, and the isolation allowed me to sort out my thoughts. At 5 p.m., the evening of my arrest, I was taken to the Metropolitan Detention Center in downtown Los Angeles. Processing in required a strip-search, fingerprinting, and some commingling with other prisoners. They were not aware of my "keep away--law enforcement" status. I initially shied away but being caged made everyone's senses very acute. Too many sideways, suspicious glances directed my way indicated I needed to fit in a bit better. Carefully, I entered conversations by shaking my head affirmatively and agreeing with their complaints of it taking so long to process us when the inevitable question cropped up: "What're ya in for...?" The question came from a 45-year-old, heavily tattooed biker-type with long hair and a beard. Somewhat prepared and not wanting to reveal that I was accused of being a pyro, I blurted out, "Possession of automatic weapons."

"Whoa, alright, my man. We'll talk later..," the biker replied as some of the others nodded in agreement. The biker, J.C., later helped me adjust to this new experience. It appeared I had to play a guessing game if I was to survive. I kept telling myself I'd be out soon, but I should at least try and learn something from this experience. Ironically, this was the only instance during my 15 days of initial incarceration that anybody asked what I was in for. I never heard anyone ask another con the question. We appeared to all be brothers, involved in a common situation and simply sharing the experience. A bit like survivors on a lifeboat drifting into an uncertain future. Taken to the isolation cells, or the "hole" as it was called, the door slammed behind me with a decisive metallic clank.

The hole was an 8-foot by 8-foot cubicle with stainless steel toilet and sink, a small metal table and a round, swing-out seat. It also came equipped with three well-worn novels I devoured in the next 48 hours. The only appetite I had was for reading. The food was palatable but I just didn't have any desire to eat. Milk sustained me. I was able to call Wanda a few times from court and discovered the crew did search every inch of our home, garage and even my mother-in-law's studio behind our garage. They acted like gentlemen, she said, even playing with Domino. They took several boxes of documents with them. Wanda was a basket case. A few of her friends and my relatives dropped by and called, offering help. Normally quite social, Wanda crawled into a shell and rejected offers of assistance. Our conversations were filled with long silences, both of us obviously in shock. I asked her to contact a Glendale attorney.

Hagop "Jack" Dirakjian handled primarily civil cases but represented a man I intended to arrest for an arson/insurance fraud scam. I used a ruse to get Jack to bring his client in for a discussion about the case and possible reasonable conclusions. I didn't have enough to arrest but Jack and the client didn't know this. I was going to either spend an additional one-hundred-plus hours working up the questionable case or be forced to drop it and move on. The major case developed from the failed attempt to burn an insured home but my investigation revealed at least three other probable insurance frauds of staged burglaries and two auto thefts. I couldn't quite bring the cases together and probably wouldn't, even through there was an anonymous informant sending me intelligence information. I sat with Jack and the client going over the case for about 10 minutes when Jack and I both realized the man hadn't told him everything. It gave me an advantage. I left the interview room and told Jack the man could roll the dice on me getting the final pieces to the puzzle or he could drop his nearly $100,000 in pending claims. One had already paid off. When I returned 10 minutes later Jack had convinced the man to withdraw the claims.

Jack's efforts on his client's behalf saved me many hours of, no-doubt, fruitless searching for clues or a witness willing to talk and testify. When I was arrested, Jack was the only defense attorney I was acquainted with. He agreed to meet with me at the jail.

On Friday, December 6, Jack visited me, bringing along an associate, Douglas McCann. I hated McCann instantly and it was obvious Jack wanted Doug to represent me. Tired of years working criminal defense, Jack wanted to handle civil cases only. I listened to the staccato presentation of McCann outlining defense strategy. Only 32-years-old, he cut off his superior, and me, choosing to take total control of our brief interview. He was arrogant, opinionated, sly, and a complete asshole...I retained him on the spot. I wanted a cutthroat to go after the feds who exposed Wanda and I to this travesty. He required a $10,000 retainer. Wanda made the arrangements and early the next week Doug announced he moved up the bail review hearing to December 10. This pleased me immensely and renewed my faith in the man despite both Wanda and I initially wondering if he was the right choice. He was young enough to be our son. Later I'd wish he was devoured at birth.

Despite the initial snubbing of her friends and our relatives Wanda accepted them back quickly and mapped out what resources were available to us in this expected expensive nightmare. An excellent planner and expert at follow-through, she overcame her depression and helped build me back up during my 15 day incarceration. The hardest part was putting our home up as collateral for my $50,000 bail. She owned the home before we married and I told her she would never lose it. The residence would only be forfeited if I ran and that wasn't going to happen. I told Wanda early on, "I'll serve ten years for something I didn't do before I'd see you lose the house." Processing my release took until December 18. Forced to submit to home detention with a tracking device attached to my ankle, ATF supervisor Larry Cornelison and Agent April Carroll picked me up at the detention center and drove me home where the anklet was attached and then left. Alone with Wanda for the first time in over two weeks, we collapsed and tried to make sense of what was happening. Sipping my first cup of fresh-brewed coffee in weeks Wanda added a shot of Kahlua.

After a couple of cups each we mellowed out but remained depressed. Everything about the future was speculative. Even though I was innocent, the fingerprint identification hung over us as the sole "evidence" that could convict me of dozens of charges being considered. There was no other evidence. The manuscript of *Points of Origin* didn't seem to mean anything to us, but prosecutors, and now the media, made the novel into a journal of my "crimes." A few very close friends offered substantial loans to get us through the quick demands for money McCann made.

We were able to keep up on our own initially but later required the assistance--and more. My father also provided help despite his fixed income and nearing age 80. My mom made frequent appearances at the house and ran errands for me when Wanda had to go back to work. She even went out and did my Christmas shopping for Wanda. The holiday season meant little that year and, unfortunately, for the following years as well.

After years of making my own business and work decisions, supervising a 10-man unit and literally making life and death choices on occasion, I found myself helpless. Strapped with the court's orders and unable to bring home an income we depended solely on Wanda's salary and our savings. Unable to emotionally handle work even if I could go back, I was denied the ability to even use sick time as a resource. Every time I attempted to accomplish something a wall was put up to halt my progress. My network of friends, co-workers and associates, for the most part, dried up as available help. With very few exceptions. When the mounting frustration threatened Wanda and I, we set down the rules we were to live by to survive this trauma. I would handle all the case requirements, deal with McCann and our investigators, and insulate her from anything related to my battle. She was to handle the household, our finances and trying to keep her life as normal as possible. Wanda resented any intrusion by media and even shied away from discussing the case with her own friends and co-workers. In essence, we divorced this prosecution as part of our life. It became an 800-pound mistress-from-hell and was my sole responsibility except when it came to overlaps like pending deadlines of payments by McCann. Wanda paid the bills.

I settled into an investigative mode and acted as McCann's lead investigator. I couldn't gain information for us over the phone, even from my old sources. Once a person is arrested, the aura of suspicion remains. Nobody would help. On occasion I resorted to ruses to obtain documents or information. Pretending I was "Mr. McCann's investigator," some cooperation was gained. I even managed to extract statements from people who knew or had met me, but would have stonewalled a true statement if they knew who the "investigator" actually was. I handled the case against me as if I was the prosecutor gathering evidence for court.

In mid-December we received a piece of devastating news and copies of a report. The federal prosecutors provided us with limited copies of documents they intended to use in trial and this one report hit us like another fingerprint ID. After my December 4th arrest and vast media coverage, an L.A. County Sheriff's deputy came forward and talked with the task force investigators. He handled traffic and crowd control at the D & M Yardage store fire on March 27, 1991, in Lawndale, 25 miles from Glendale. While keeping people away from the blazing structure he found a man approaching and asked him to get back. The bystander flashed a badge, stating he was an arson investigator and was "helping out" the fire crews. The deputy kept his eye on the guy for a while then lost track of him. After my arrest, photos and videotape of me flashed across the deputy's TV screen and, nine months later, he positively identified me as the investigator he encountered in front of D & M Yardage. It wasn't true. Who would a jury believe? An arrested and accused fireman or a trained observer deputy sheriff? There were discrepancies in the report of interview of the deputy. He described the badge "I" flashed as having a bear on top. The badges I carried as an investigator all had no bear and were oval-shaped like a standard police badge. The prosecutors launched a search for a bear badge. They found a F.I.R.S.T. badge, with a bear on it, had been issued to the Glendale Fire Department several years before. I signed for it. It couldn't be located. It wasn't found during the searches of my office and home. I knew where it was and attempted to recover it so we could ambush the prosecutor in court. The badge had not been in my possession for years. Walt Beatty was the last person to have the F.I.R.S.T. badge. He was forced to turn in his Glendale Fire/Arson badge when he left the unit and took the bear badge for his own personal ID. He didn't think I knew he had it. I didn't mind so let it go with him. Barely on speaking terms since my arrest, I called and asked him to turn the badge over to me or, at least, retain it in a safe place so he could bring it to court. He said he didn't know what I was talking about---he didn't have it. I delicately explained the devastation the missing badge could cause to my case and he said he'd "look around" for it. In the meantime, I launched a search for the person the deputy actually saw. I knew it wasn't me. I was in Glendale, 25 miles away when the store burned. The description the deputy provided could have been any one of a hundred firefighters in southern California. My take on the encounter was the man could have been a firefighter or arson cop just saying he was an investigator to get in close or could even be the actual arsonist. I bet on it being an investigator. After a few phone calls to former associates, I hit the wall. Nobody would help. I wrote a pleading letter to F.I.R.S.T asking for assistance. The memo read: "If anyone knew a firefighter who was at the D&M Yardage fire and met with a deputy, please call my "investigator"(me) or lawyer. The letter was published in the next F.I.R.S.T. Minutes of the Meeting sent out to several hundred southern California agencies and individuals. In the first week of February I reclined on my bed with Domino at 8:30 a.m. before walking to my "office," actually our dining room table, to work. The phone rang and I answered.

"Hi...is this...John's...is this you, John...?"

"Yeah, John Orr, who's this?"

"John, this is Barry Pape, Hermosa Beach Fire Department. I think you're looking for me."

"Oh shit, you were at the Lawndale fire?"

"Yeah, and I ran into a deputy..."

"Hang on a sec, Barry...," I said, sitting up in bed and taking a deep breath. I'd known Barry for over five years and he looked nothing like me. Only about 5'7", Barry had a full head of salt and pepper colored hair and a distinct bushy moustache that matched his hair. With a fireplug appearance we may have weighed the same, but I was three inches taller and had a severely receding hairline, my most distinctive feature. "Okay, Barry, tell me about the deputy." Barry told me he had been at a nearby shopping mall and when he came out he saw the heavy black smoke and heard sirens. Driving to the scene, actually in an L.A. County Fire Department jurisdiction, he parked a block away and walked in to see if he could help. As he approached the well-involved building a deputy shouted at him to get back. Barry flashed his badge, one with an bear on top, and told the guy he was an investigator and was allowed to hang around. "What's the big deal, John?" Barry asked.

"Did you see me anywhere around the fire?" I queried.

"No, of course not."

"The deputy has positively identified me as being the guy that flashed the badge at him."

"Bullshit, the guy's wrong, John. I'll testify for you, and I'll bring the videotape."

"Video?" I asked.

"Yeah, you haven't seen the tape of the fire."

"No, I didn't know it existed."

"Oh, yeah, I thought maybe you were at the (South Bay) Arson Control Team meeting when we showed it, a Redondo Beach fireman shot the footage. He even caught me flashing the badge at the deputy."

"What," I exploded.

"No shit, the video shows the deputy shouting at me, then me flashing the badge and him walking over to talk to me. It's right on the tape." Lunch-with-the-Pope-and-a-receipt, and now a videotape, too. Ecstatic I asked for the firefighter/videographer's name and number. Barry gladly passed it on. When I asked him to keep the information quiet he said he had to tell his supervisor. It seems all firefighters and investigators in Southern California were circling the wagons and were told to report any contacts with me. I understood and thanked Barry. He said he couldn't provide me with a copy of the videotape unless his boss okayed it. With my profuse thanks I started to hang up but Barry added a peculiar statement.

"I'd like to keep it quiet, John, but lots of us are scared."

"What do you mean scared?"

"Well, me and some other guys were at fires you're accused of setting and we're all afraid the feds'll start looking at us, too."

"I can understand that, Barry. They are out of control...," I said, baiting him shamelessly.

"I was at that fabric store fire in Fresno. You know, the one in '87 they're charging you with..." I smiled, hoping he wouldn't clam up.

"Did you see me there? I may need you to testify."

"Like I said, I don't want them to start picking on me, John. Those fuckers are scary, and I sure didn't see you in Fresno." We parted cordially and I immediately called McCann with the good news. Then I tracked down Beatty and asked him about the F.I.R.S.T. badge.

"Yeah, I...uh...found it. It was under a bunch of stuff in my console in the truck. I didn't even remember I had it." He turned it over to the ATF investigators several days before. After all our years together, Walt seemed to be working for the feds. He didn't even have the courtesy to call me and let me know the badge was located. It was the last conversation I ever had with him.

It took a week for the task force to get a copy of the D&M Yardage videotape to us. Nobody would provide it without getting the feds permission first and even then it was denied. Our hopes were to refute the deputy's "trained observer" ID of me with Barry Pape's testimony and the videotaped encounter. Nevertheless, with several other similar "positive IDs" of me by civilians, we hoped to show how poor eyewitness accuracy really is.

The videotape of the March 27, 1991, D&M Yardage fire was spectacular. Both the fire itself and the revelation of the deputy/Pape encounter. Barry is clearly not me. We hoped this would result in the D&M charge being dropped. The charge wasn't dropped, and the judge later ruled he would not let us use the deputy/Pape encounter. "The deputy was wrong, end of story. It's (the encounter) no longer relevant. Get over it." The encounter could only be used if we had an expert witness on mis-identifications testify.

315

CHAPTER TWENTY
COURTING DISASTERS

After my arrest on December 4, 1991, each day presented a rollercoaster of emotions. The euphoria of locating the D & M Yardage videotape, and obtaining Barry Pape's testimony, was replaced by the shock of Judge Rafeedie's disallowing the presentation of the gross error made by the sheriff's deputy. With at least two other witnesses making "positive" ID's of me at the crime scene before the fire, we hoped to show how unreliable eyewitnesses were by using Pape's statements and videotape; graphic evidence juries love. One witness said she saw me inside the store "sometime after the fire," too. With no specific timeframe, I could not establish an alibi, so attacking the witness memory credibility was a valid defense. Asking for a dismissal of the D & M Yardage charge, based on our discovery, Judge Rafeedie decided the witness was already proven wrong so there was no relevance to the issue now. This was the judge's prerogative, but made no reasonable sense to me. The prosecution countered also, stating the D&M charge was not seriously weakened by the loss of the deputy's wrong ID. They had two more witness IDs to back them up.

Rafeedie's decrees against the defense side were critical but another major decision was on the horizon and the decision favored us. I retained Douglas McCann with $10,000 in December 1991. In January he wanted another payment. At $10K per month our ability to pay him would expire quickly. The financial aspects of this nightmare were an extra burden that almost sent Wanda and I over the edge.

With no established "Attorney Payment Schedule for Felonies" in existence I had to deal with McCann like a vendor at a weekend swap meet. Maybe I should have had my father do the honors. By January we assumed McCann would handle the two separate trials I faced. Eight counts of arson were filed in the Central District (Los Angeles) case and in January 1992 a Fresno Grand Jury indicted me on an additional five counts, just days before the statute of limitations ran out on the federal charges. McCann wanted $40K for the Fresno trial and preparation and we would negotiate if a second trial was needed. The prosecutors in the L.A. case agreed to allow the Fresno trial to take place first since, they said, it was the stronger case. I would pay for all private investigator's services, any trip expenses to and from Fresno, and any expert witnesses we needed over and above McCann's $40K. Any income McCann derived from interviews, book deals he negotiated for me or case related sources would be deducted from the $40K I owed. We didn't expect any such income.

Fortunately, Wanda and I had clear credit, owing no one but the mortgage company. But we didn't have the entire $40K. A few friends fronted us money for short terms but we could not borrow from my credit union even though a $10K loan would have been easy. As of January 1 I was on unpaid leave and with about four months worth of sick leave accumulated I hoped that could be our buffer. Vacation and comp time on the books carried us into January, ensuring a paycheck until, at least, the middle of the month but when that money ran out I applied for sick leave.

The city stonewalled me. They said I wasn't sick so couldn't get sick time. I told the city fathers I was too emotionally ill to work and they replied, "You're on unpaid leave so whether you are fit to work or not is irrelevant. We can't evaluate your fitness to work since you aren't here so you can't qualify to access your sick leave." Employee/city contracts did not allow sick leave to be cashed out until retirement so I was in a Catch-22 situation with no recourse. I ultimately lost over $20,000 in accumulated sick leave.

The Glendale Firefighter's Association had a fund to help its member's families when in financial difficulties. After paying dues faithfully for over 18 years I hoped for assistance. They did provide some short-term relief but they, too, found a loophole to escape their obligations. I had neither the time or energy to take the city or Firefighter's Association to court. These incidents set the tone for the ebbing of friends, co-workers and associates who wanted nothing to do with a man accused of arson. My partner, Joe Lopez, was my union representative and he helped immensely dealing with the GFFA.

Several other old friends stood by us as well. Jim Fitzpatrick and Paul Phillips, and their wives, and a few others, called to offer emotional support and sometimes money. Shortly after my arrest, my dad and brother Pat came by the house to talk with Wanda. Distraught and confused she simply wanted this horror to go away. She told me later she felt by closing the doors, drawing the curtains, not answering the phone, and staying away from the TV she would be protected. Dad and Pat brought it all inside our home. Frustrated, she shunned their offers of help and asked them to leave, alienating my brother, but not Dad. We would never hear from Pat again despite my efforts through phone calls, cards and letters.

Wanda, a strong, independent woman in many ways, stood up to surly waiters, aggressive suitors, phone solicitors, and even egotistical TV stars she dealt with where she worked at Warner Brothers studios, but my arrest was foreign ground to her. You can't vent anger at prosecutors or a judge in a courtroom. The justice system doe not have a network of checks and balances like the business world. A bad meal at a restaurant or shoddy business practices at an electronics store have recourse: you can complain or otherwise get satisfaction at management levels or through consumer groups such as the Better Business Bureau. Not even God has power over the courts or a judge. They are Gods; at least hiding in their courthouse caves and courtrooms they are. Wanda retreated, handling our household and wishing every day the nightmare would end. She even requested I make sure McCann was out of my workspace and ordered the dining table office cleared of casework by the time she got home from the studio. To her, McCann was a necessary evil, like a mechanic, or the guy who picked up our trash each week, albeit, paid much better. After release from the initial two weeks of custody, it took me only days to realize I had no control, leverage, or say so in any aspect of my life. Tethered by a home detention anklet the size of a Volkswagen, I couldn't leave to go shopping or even to work. Home detention meant jail without bars, but was infinitely better than the alternative. The anklet, a sending unit hooked up to our telephone to broadcast violations, was simply a front. When I took my first dip in the backyard spa after leaving jail, Wanda and I soaked for about 45 minutes when our cell phone beeped. I answered.

"John, this is Mr. Barron, manager of the home detention monitoring company. Are you still home?"

"Of course, I'm in the backyard..."

"Well, the alarm went off about 45 minutes ago and shows you out-of-range of the sending unit. My associates at the center called me just now..." We verified the anklet broke contact as soon as I lowered my feet into the spa. The pool heater metallic housing blocked the beams and showed me beyond 100 feet from the telephone. As soon as I propped my foot up on the ledge above the heater, the beam showed back-in-range. I didn't discuss the 45 minute notification period with Mr. Barron and neither did he. In 45 minutes I could have been on a plane for Houston. But I had no intention of fleeing. The innocent stand and fight.

With the limits on my movement I was only able to make phone calls and coordinate private investigator activities, but that, too, was limited by how much money I could afford to pay them.

Typically outgoing and quick to step forward with confidence to thwart any threat to me or my family, I found myself helpless. My certitude evaporated and I wouldn't recover it for years. I lost weight, became paranoid and woke up sweating in the early-morning hours and could not get back to sleep. Some days I got up and went to work on the case, other times it was all I could do to crawl out of bed to urinate.

Wanda and I clung together like children lost in a snowy forest one moment, and five minutes later couldn't stand to touch each other as we slept. Domino, our Dalmatian, was confused but seemed to be the only constant. His attention was like an adhesive. We couldn't stay away from him and were drawn together by his needs for love. Our neighbors stood by us more than lifelong friends and co-workers. Support was shown by them daily. I was afraid, or paranoid, and didn't show my face in front of the house, except to pick up the mail. Neither did Wanda, for fear a camera crew was nearby, Neighbors watered the lawn and plants, weeded Wanda's flowerbeds and picked up trash blown around by breezes. Their silent support was appreciated, but every minute of every day, we hurt.

McCann muzzled me initially and forbade me to talk to the press, but I found I did have some control. The local crime reporter I'd worked with for several years, Tori Richards, pressed me for an interview and I felt a screaming need to shout my innocence so consented. The article was positive so I did more, chatting with reporters from the L.A. Times, Glendale News-Press and even the Daily Breeze from the beach area. Later, McCann actually held a news conference at the Burbank Holiday Inn in an attempt to provide positive press for our side. The crowd of reporters dispersed when they found I wouldn't be present to answer questions. Tabloid TV shows haunted our phones, neighborhood and front porch. One crew caught me sitting on the back porch holding Domino and quietly weeping on a particularly bad day. I contemplated firing a few rounds over their heads but even that misguided plan was blocked – the court ordered all my guns confiscated. I couldn't even protect my family from the media or other criminals.

The emotional and physical hurt was constant. Although I was innocent, I told Wanda one day, killing myself might be easier on us both. Suicide would end the hurt: the pain gone instantly for me, and her grief would heal quickly knowing the looming trials, financial woes, and under-the-microscope scrutiny would evaporate. The lesser of two evils. In a rare moment of lucidity she took my hand and said, "If you go, I will, too. Without you around I'd have to go back to cleaning the house, cooking and picking up dog poop. You're doing it all now, househusband." She broke the tension and we laughed for the first time in months. The next day Wanda brought home a copy of a best-selling non-fiction book, The Final Exit. The text, a how-to guide on committing successful suicide lay unopened on a coffee table for months; like a loaded gun.

With the L.A.-area federal case on hold we focused on the Fresno charges. The five counts included a fire in a fabric store that destroyed the building, an attempted arson at a small department store in Tulare, 30 miles south of Fresno, and fires in two stores in Bakersfield, California,

110 miles from Fresno. These four blazes occurred during a 3-day period in 1987, five years before, while a California Conference of Arson Investigators (CCAI) seminar was going on or just ending. One additional felony filed surrounded the discovery of an expended cigarette/match incendiary device in another fabric store in Fresno but it wasn't found until two weeks after the conference ended and I could prove I was in Los Angeles. Employee activity in the area of the discovery of the device seemed to indicate it could not have been in place for more than a few days. Small victories for us. The strength of the Fresno prosecutor's case was a fingerprint on a piece of paper attached to a cigarette/match device located in the CraftMart crafts store attempted arson. The print was impressed on a piece of partially burned yellow-lined legal notebook paper. I was aware of several of these fires in 1987 when Tom Kuczynski of the Fresno Fire Department called me in my Glendale office. Tom related the series to me saying only a "cigarette/match device" was used, without elaboration of specific components and hinted the fire's timing during the conference.

I asked him, "You think it's a CCAI attendee?"

His response, "We don't want to speculate. We're keeping it all quiet. Let me know if you hear of anything similar in the L.A. area." I later talked to two private investigators, one of them a former L.A. Sheriff's Department arson investigator, Bruce Kamann, and CCAI director Tom Fee, and two other fire cops. All were either attached to the insurance company investigations or had also been contacted by Kuczynski. The information was far from "confidential." After a second series of fires occurred in the Central Coast area of California in March-April 1989, the investigation broadened. Another fire-related conference went off in Monterey, California during this period. I wasn't aware of this series until the day I was arrested in 1991. Investigators compared attendance lists from the 1987 and 1989 seminars to see who was at both sites; a sound investigative strategy. At least 12 people were identified, including me. The fingerprint from the 1987 CraftMart fire was sent to the California Department of Justice, along with fingerprint cards from all the "suspects." Knowing the prints were from police officers, investigators, firefighters or private investigators, two DOJ experts compared the impressions. Both the worker-bee examiner and his supervisor signed off as "no match" between the evidence and any of the suspects. No match from what they labeled "a clear, identifiable latent impression." There were reportedly 7-8 identifiable points on the evidence; only 6 were needed to take a match to court. It wasn't my fingerprint in 1989. The comparison to the evidence used my own fingerprint card.

However, in 1991, after similar incendiary devices appeared at L.A.-area fire scenes in still another series of retail store fires, the CraftMart print again was compared. By then, all law enforcement personnel in California were on a computer for matching. The print, actually a photograph of the print from the paper, had, by 1991, faded enough to be unidentifiable so the picture was utilized. The print was enlarged, a few lines connected and added, then the now-completed drawing entered into the Automated Fingerprint Identification System computer database on April 17, 1991. In minutes, the AFIS machine spit out a list of ten names as possible matches - mine was number one.

This very strong evidence was the cornerstone and foundation of the prosecution's case against me. It was also the only evidence against me. Fingerprints were also discovered on the filter of the CraftMart cigarette in 1987 but we couldn't use the AFIS technology to enhance the less-than-perfect images: The Bakersfield Fire Department investigator who recovered the CraftMart device, Marvin Casey, threw the evidence away just months after the crime. Photos of the cigarette butt were available but the prints unclear. Casey said, in his own defense, "The device wasn't useful for anything further so I tossed it...I had pictures of it anyway." He discarded the evidence about "two weeks" after the original trip to the DoJ in mid-1987.

Casey did not consider the possibility of ever arresting a suspect. I think that reflects on the quality of his investigative abilities. To him, this $10-loss fire in 1987 was a "nothing" case despite the fact a $50,000 fire followed the CraftMart attempt by just minutes. He didn't photograph the CraftMart fire scene either. The device had an identifiable filter, tobacco to be matched to later evidence, remains of several wooden matches and, of course, a fingerprint that just by its size could be used as circumstantial evidence against any suspect developed. The device he threw away as "unusable" was a veritable bonanza of potential evidence. Tobacco could have been vacuumed from a potential suspect's car or home and the matches might be microscopically examined and confirmed to those in a suspect's possession. Circumstantial evidence, to be sure, but enough to add to a case for a filing.

But Casey never considered these issues in his "nothing" case. The statute of limitation in California arson cases in 1987 was three years. Retention of the evidence is required. In trial, Bureau of Alcohol, Tobacco, and Firearms (BATF) expert Jerry Taylor was asked about the destruction of the CraftMart evidence. He replied, "If I destroyed evidence that soon I'd get at least 30 days off without pay, if not actually fired..."

Good news, bad news. Good news, bad news. This case was like being diagnosed with cancer. Every trip to court was dreaded as a visit to the oncologist; you expected the worst and usually got that news. Motion hearings were like sitting down with the doctor after chemotherapy - maybe the announcement would be good for you, or maybe the information meant death. Small victories weren't enough to pull me out of the abyss of depression.

No positive IDs of me were made by witnesses in the Fresno-area cases. On the contrary, the best witness walked right by the arsonist at the Family Bargain Center in Tulare just minutes before the fire started. The suspect, described as in his mid-20s, scruffy-appearing, and with shoulder-length black hair was clearly not me. I was 38-years-old at the time, had short brown hair, a moustache, and wore glasses. We were later to discover I also had a full beard. Two other witnesses describe the same suspect with a similar-appearing man acting as a lookout at a small fire in a surplus store, also in Tulare. The team obviously created diversions so they could shoplift. Three employees actually observed and described the team of thieves. I was not charged with the surplus store fire, for easy-to-discern reasons, but the Family Bargain Center fire occurred minutes later and I was to be prosecuted for it. Still another witness, in an auto parts store next to the Family Bargain Center, described the "scruffy-appearing, mid-20s guy."

Both sides wanted to believe some witness suspect descriptions were good observations, but the defense wanted to, at the same time, show eyewitnesses were notoriously inaccurate. A lot depends on the quality of the observation. The Family Bargain Center witness walked right by the suspect and got a good look at him because he had reason to note the young man. The guy carried a piece of yellow paper and appeared to be comparison shopping so the witness/store manager had reason to allow his memory banks to start. This "trigger" was because the man was more than just a regular customer. The paper caused the focus. The surplus store witness's attention was drawn and memory started because the actions of the two men were suspicious. They looked like a shoplifting team. These were all good observations and should be considered credible. As an investigator I would have no problem relying on these witnesses for use in a case filing.

The good news/bad news of the fingerprint on the yellow-lined paper was daunting. How could I explain the impression found at a fire scene in a city I'd never visited? A close look at the evidence by experts in 1989 showed it was not mine. Then it is John Orr's in 1991. If the print was mine, I assumed the yellow-lined paper came from the CCAI seminar registration gift: a notebook with the CCAI logo embossed in gold on the front and a pad of yellow-lined paper, of the same dimensions as the CraftMart device component, inside. I handled several notebooks and pads, other than my own, as I searched for the better quality items I purchased for door prizes at my monthly F.I.R.S.T. meetings. Back in Glendale I handled legal pads daily.

But then we had to explain how the paper got to Bakersfield from the Fresno Holiday Inn. Did the real arsonist have access to the conference room, seminar storage areas, hotel rooms or did the paper come from my office or a seminar I hosted in the L.A. area? This bridge existed but was kept hidden from the defense by prosecutors for obvious reasons, and none were related to fairness or justice. Juries tend to simplify evidence and believe the most logical assumption. As an investigator I would also lean towards the obvious. Without another suspect(s) we had to live with the print or substantiate our suspicions the print was doctored. The "identifiable latent impression" from the 1989 comparison showing no match to me, was enlarged and additional features added and enhanced before being entered into the AFIS computer in 1991. But why would I be the focus of the BATF investigators before the print ID, instead of someone else? *Points of Origin...* BATF sleuths swore, under oath, they never saw my manuscript of *Points of Origin* until July or August 1991, after the fingerprint match, and had no idea I wrote a fictionalized version of their real case. Yet I found an investigator's report where BATF Agent Ken Croke was in Atascadero, California "...showing six-pack photo line-ups containing the photo of John Orr..." on April 5, 1991. This was two weeks before the print match. The agents were lying to us. Only the *Points of Origin* manuscript could make me a suspect. Could the agents also have taken the ultimate step of doctoring the photographic fingerprint, after reading the manuscript, to fit their case? A photo is easier to phony up than a real fingerprint image. We would not expose the April 5 Croke report until trial to help bolster our theory of outright fabrication of evidence. A lying ATF agent could cast much reasonable doubt on the prosecution's case in trial. *Points of Origin* was fact-based fiction. Nothing in the 417-page manuscript was usable as evidence "only the real arsonist would know." The book was provocative, and might mislead a jury, but certainly wasn't "evidence." Its presentation in trial would cause confusion and take a great deal of extra time since jurors had to actually read the entire manuscript before they could properly analyze it. McCann, in a motion to exclude *Points of Origin* as evidence, said as much when pleading with Judge Rafeedie in the L.A. case.(Even though the Fresno trial would take place first, we had to make pre-trial motions in the L.A. case, too.) Rafeedie agreed with McCann, scoring one of the few extra points we'd get from the prosecution-oriented court system. Without the manuscript the L.A. case was almost un-prosecutable. With literally no evidence against me except several iffy witness IDs, there was no case. On the verge of dismissing the L.A. case, the prosecutor appealed Rafeedie's decision to exclude *Points of Origin*. The appeal to the Ninth Circuit Court might take 6-10 months to decide.

With the L.A. case effectively on hold and thousands of dollars spent on private investigators, McCann started pressuring for more money. I told him I refused to sell the house Wanda owned before I ever came into her life, so there was no income there. I had a retirement account and advised it would remain intact - for now. I assured him his $40K would be paid before trial - and it was. He needed more now but Wanda and I had to keep the house running and the private investigators were pay-as-you-go, for the most part. There was also the expected expenses of our accommodations during trial in Fresno, maybe expert witnesses, and defense witness accommodations and meal reimbursements as well as transportation.

McCann told me, "I'm not trying to pressure you for money. You are my client and you don't need any more pressure. But, I have to set your work aside to find paying clients and their cases take time from your casework." In other words, I responded, "we're getting close to trial and you are telling me I have to buy your time to prepare for my case?" "No, no, John. It's not like that...it's just...giving me some more money allows me to set my other client's casework aside..." At the time of this conversation, in May 1991, McCann had been paid over $30,000.

McCann ended up getting a payment anyway. He worked out a deal with a TV tabloid show: provide a client interview and pick up $5000 -- so he did. We discussed this type of payment early in our association. It would be deducted from what I owed. He neglected to tell me he was paid for the tabloid interview. I only found out much later when a middleman who intended to write a book about the case let it slip in conversation. He brokered the deal and received $1000 for his help. When I confronted McCann about the payment he said he intended to tell me about it.

I should have fired him over the scam but we were approaching trial and he had performed reasonably well. Getting *Points of Origin* thrown out as evidence in the L.A. case was a major coup, but the Fresno judge ruled the other way. Still, there were other incidents that warned me of his propensities.

McCann was uncomfortable in the courtroom. With his long, unruly hair and rumpled suits he gave an unprepared look. On at least three occasions he tripped over his briefcase. The pratfalls seemed almost a part of an image he wanted to project to get the prosecution off-guard or he was just a buffoon. He was, however, canny and ambushed several witnesses and the prosecutor on occasion. He could think on his feet - when he could stay upright.

From January - June 1992 McCann and I ran back and forth to Fresno at least once a month. He even let me drive his new Lexus each time. I told him he'd better, it was my car. His purchase price - $40,000. Another motion hearing battle was the issue of precluding "uncharged acts" evidence. Normally, the playing field in a trial must be level with no outrageous advantage given to either--just that facts. Typically in a trial, a defendants "prior bad acts", bad behavior, kicking a dog, an arrest for being drunk, or crimes not proven to be committed by the defendant, cannot be used in trial, unless he/she testifies. The theory being a jury might tend to convict based on behavior having nothing to do with the current case. This was a factor in the O.J. Simpson trial - the prior domestic abuse allegations where he wasn't arrested or convicted. A trial should be only about the "instant" case, as it is called. In the Fresno case the prosecutor wanted some of the Central Coast 1989 fires and 1990-91 L.A. fires allowed as evidence of "uncharged acts" even though I wasn't charged with but a few and convicted of none of them. Besides, all those crimes occurred years after the allegations in the instant case. They wanted to bring up 15-20 fires, as if I set them all, even if there was no evidence to tie me to the cases. The prosecution needed to bolster their obviously weak theories because the fingerprint alone was questionable. As if we didn't have enough problems dealing with the Fresno charges, now we had to defend 15-20 far-flung fires, adding hundreds of hours of preparation time and expensive PI work.

The uncharged acts presentation would infer I was guilty of all mentioned fires even though many were without evidence other than I lived in the metropolitan L.A. area or went to a conference near some of the blazes. The "signature" incendiary device of cigarette, matches and rubber band was found in several of the cases. The prosecutor's assumed I was the only suspect in the state to use the "unique" device. I wasn't their suspect and the device far from unique. Prosecutors wanted to sway the jury by this overwhelming evidence.

With the limited number of reports provided to us on the uncharged acts, I still was able to develop my own theories. I deduced at least two, and maybe three to five suspects were involved in the widely separated series fires. I based this on the subtle variations of device components, types of targets, timing and spacing of individual series as well as the huge variances in time and distance.

I was still not convinced the Fresno fires were directly related to the conference. It was probable, but the significance of the device discovery two weeks after the seminar indicated a local arsonist. Maybe a firefighter, maybe not. The Central Coast series in 1989 seemed more likely a copycat series and probably a firefighter, investigator, cop or fire service groupie type, but probably a male. With several of the Fresno-

325

area fire witnesses noting the second, "lookout" suspect, I was convinced this series was a team of arsonist/thieves learning their trade.

By 1992 I'd arrested many serial arsonists and investigated over a hundred series fires involving well over three hundred incidents. McCann laughed at me when I intimated I wanted to testify as my own expert witness on serial arsonists. He said, "No way." The first fire in Fresno was a small blaze set in a retail store, possibly as an experiment since it was a failure. I was not charged with this fire. No stolen merchandise or cash was mentioned in reports we received from this incident. No purses of employees or customers rifled in the confusion, but we didn't get a follow-up report or accompanying police report, only a short fire incident form. The second fire was set two nights later in a fabric store and the ill-placed ignition site resulted in total destruction of the building. From witness reports, the fire developed so quickly employees and customers barely got out alive. Again the novice fire starters failed if these were shoplift-diversion fires. No time to steal--they had to flee, along with customers and employees. Some small fires in nearby locations may have been extinguished by employees or customers and gone unreported. Was any canvassing done in this primarily business district? No indication of it in reports we received. Following the complete destruction of the Hancock Fabrics store on Wednesday night, the two "scruffy" appearing suspects are seen in Tulare where two small blazes are set. Again, no police reports were provided to me and McCann even though we asked for them. The Friday morning Tulare series included the surplus store and Family Bargain Center, but the same description is provided at an auto parts store next door to the Family Bargain Center. A man was seen "casing" the outlet and the only employee inside was drawn to the odd activities of the suspect. No fire was set, or maybe the device failed and a customer/employee discarded the discovery later. The arsonists seemed to learn how to set small blazes in isolated areas so the fire would become the focus of employees but not build enough to keep the crooks from foraging in the confusion. The CraftMart fire occurred about 90 minutes after the Tulare sets. Again, a small target for the incendiary is selected - a rack of dried flowers. An employee reports a suspicious male loitering in the store and the small blaze gets the attention of several employees. Put out quickly enough to salvage the device and paper, the fire scene yields the partial fingerprints on the cigarette and legal-pad paper.

This 1987 series of fires, even though it occurred while the CCAI seminar was held, appeared to be motivated as shoplift diversions by relatively new arsonists, not perpetrated by an "experienced/knowledgeable" fire setter as ATF experts and investigators theorized later. By then they had me as a suspect to whittle down and force into their investigation. The CCAI series fires in 1987 may have been triggered by experienced criminals who heard about the well-publicized semi-annual event and fit it into their shoplifting plans. Strangely enough, a culprit later identified was suspected of setting fires in the CCAI Holiday Inn conference center...

I was reminded of Tom Rickle's 1985 fire in a Sav-On store. A small, slow-developing, time-delay fire was set on a shelf holding paper products, well away from the front of the outlet. Once discovered, the fire got the attention of customers and employees, many of whom gravitated to the area and allowed a shoplifter to jump a counter in the front of the store and steal valuable merchandise. This is a fairly rare occurrence and we seldom heard about such events at area arson meetings particularly if the fire never got large enough to entail fire department response. But they did happen. A similar series went down in Garden Grove, 30 miles south of L.A., in 1988. Fires were set in several stores in rubber and polyfoam products. The shoplifter was observed but escaped. One store burned down, minimal damage in the other. Years later, in 1993, Christian Tallini was arrested for the Garden Grove blaze, as outlined in an *Orange County Register* article. Tallini claimed responsibility for the blaze, saying he "frequently shoplifted by setting small fires" to mask his misdeeds. During preparation for my trials, our investigator queried Willie Dumas of the Garden Grove Fire Department about his retail store series fires. He related there were devices discovered but he had been ordered by federal ATF agents to not talk with me or my PIs. Dumas added, "We even tried to get Orr's photo to show to witnesses..." before Tallini was identified and arrested. I have dated videotape alibi for one of the fires. BATF agent-ordered concealment of evidence showing many device-retail-fires were set by several far-flung arsonists would have helped our case. The playing field was far from level.

My theories come from experience apprehending many series fire setters and investigating hundreds of series fires scenes. The combination of profiling fire scenes and later obtaining confirmation on fire origin by actually talking to the suspect, verifies my ability and experience in the field. But McCann balked at allowing me to take the stand and testify as an expert witness. Nobody else had the record I did, so we were stuck. We also needed an expert witness to testify to the commonality of the cigarette/match/rubber band device. Few investigators were adept enough or fortunate enough to recover the incendiary as we were in Glendale. The few who might have this experience refused to testify for the defense. I again told McCann, "I have to testify..."

McCann stated, "We'll see...I don't let clients testify usually, but allowing you to take the stand as an expert witness may be too provocative to the jury..." Maybe he was right. How would a jury look at an accused arsonist testifying about his vast knowledge in fire setting? The experience was from career-related arson investigations, not as a criminal. It was scary to McCann, and me. McCann couldn't even use my expertise in his motions to suppress the uncharged acts evidence. The prosecution relied on an ATF arson/bomb expert, Jerry Taylor, who wrote a report for the prosecution, after he viewed only six fire reports where a device was discovered. The following are actual excerpts from his 1-page evaluation:

"Although different in exact details all of these fires have unique similarities indicating the same individual(s) assembled and placed the incendiary devices. The m.o. involves the construction of a cigarette/match delay device encased in paper which is then positioned into common combustibles favoring wooden bins and pillows...the construction and placement of the device is critical if the individual is to attain a high rate of fire propagation thus implying extensive fire starting experience, an above average knowledge of fire setting, or both. The use of yellow-lined paper, three matches, and a rubber band is a definite signature of the perpetrator(s). The use of tan filtered cigarettes in 1987 and use of unfiltered cigarettes in '90 and '91 is also a unique signature. In conclusion, it is the opinion of the assigned that the same individual(s) assembled and placed these incendiary devices." Taylor, of course, didn't generate this slanted, short report until after a fire investigator (me) with 18 years experience was the listed suspect. Would the report have been written in this same manner if completed before a suspect's occupation was known? Profiling all the scenes should have been done.

Taylor's experience was 15 years as an ATF agent, bomb/explosives expert and he provided "technical assistance" on arson investigations, according to his resume. He had never arrested a serial arsonist nor been the lead investigator on a serial arson investigation. Series fires, however, are similar to serial bombings, so I gave him some credibility. In the 1970's and 80's, series bombings perpetrated by the Puerto Rican FALN terrorist groups in the Eastern United States revealed near-identical "signature" bombs put together by different people at widespread locations. Using verbal or written instructions of the original device-maker, many followers constructed the "signature" devices.

Similarly, a West Coast animal rights group claimed responsibility for fires set in furriers' shops in the 1980s and, again, the incendiaries used were of "signature" components but constructed by different people. McCann never listened to me when I provided these jewels of advice. "Too complicated" was his response. Finding an expert to testify for us was impossible, McCann said.

"Use Taylor as our own expert then. Ask him about these well-known 'signature' facts," I pleaded.

"He will refuse to talk with us before trial and I don't ask witnesses questions I don't already know the answer to in trial..." He was right but I already knew the answers and Taylor would have to tell the truth. Wouldn't he?

Taylor knew of these signature device incidents when he wrote his report. Yet, on one hand, says "only one person" set all the Fresno, Central Coast and L.A.-area fires he evaluated and then contradicts himself by pluralizing the "suspect(s)", individual(s)", and perpetrator(s) revealed in his study. He left himself an out yet Judge Wanger in Fresno believed Taylor's assertions and allowed uncharged acts as "evidence" against me. The $7,000 I spent on private investigators produced very little usable defense information in the Fresno case. I could provide little alibi in the 5-year-ago arsons since I was at the seminar site when all the fires occurred. No fires corresponded to times I made phone calls from my room. None of the conference attendees we interviewed could remember what they did in January 1987, let alone whether I was with them at the time. Many, of course, refused to talk with us. Several advised that ATF investigators ordered them not to speak with the defense side. In particular, two of my PIs tried to interview Fresno Fire Department arson investigator Tom Kuczynski. Tom and his associates refused to cooperate. A request for further documentation from them elicited a referral to the U.S. Attorney's Office where they provided minimal documentation.

This procedure of obtaining documents and information from the prosecution before trial is called "discovery." Required to turn over to the defense all relevant material, specifically necessary was exculpatory information; data tending to exonerate a defendant. U.S. Attorney's Pat Hanley and Carl Faller were masters at deceit and deception, providing partial reports and "forgetting" to include reams of multi-page documents. Blaming their copying machine or subordinate assistants was also common. The U.S. Attorneys had valid reasons to ask investigators and ATF agents to stonewall our efforts. They intentionally withheld several reports outlining suspects examined by the Fresno Fire Department and other northern California jurisdictions. One suspect had a prior history of setting fires in retail stores as diversions so he could shoplift. He had been arrested before, using the same m.o. The arsonist was apprehended again in Central California.

He was picked up just four blocks from a $100,000 Woolworth's fire in Salinas, California. The Salinas fire was one of the uncharged acts used against me in trial and in pre-trial motions in Fresno. The Woolworth's, and other fires in that series were relevant to the Fresno case.

The defense was provided with an abbreviated fire report of the Woolworth's fire but nothing about the four other nearby blazes and zero about the suspect himself and his subsequent arrest. All were withheld by prosecutors Hanley and Faller, and L.A. prosecutors. These intentionally corrupt actions of concealment almost ensured I would be convicted. Hiding and cowardice was their strategy. The statute of limitations on their violations of obstructing justice ran out in 2003. There's still time. An ethics committee, I'm sure, also could pursue these verifiable charges but who will listen to a convicted felon? Concealing information about one arson suspect was bad enough, but they weren't through yet. A 2-man team was investigated for responsibility in fires set in the CCAI seminar site at the Fresno Holiday Inn. Could one of these men have taken a pad of yellow-lined paper with my fingerprint? Did he have access to Holiday Inn conference rooms, seminar storage areas or even my hotel room? Apparently that far-fetched possibility was too threatening to U.S. Attorneys Hanley and Faller. The investigation of these suspects in 1987 and 1988 didn't surface until I found out in 1997. Even then, only a reference to the men was found in a redacted 14-page ATF case summary. The reference also indicated the two men were examined closely by the Fresno Fire Department investigators. With the Fresno detectives avoiding us we had no clue. Five years after my Fresno conviction I obtained the mug photos of these two suspects from arrests that took place about the time of the 1987 fires. Both men were in their mid-20s, lived in the Fresno and Bakersfield areas, one had shoulder-length black hair and in both mug shots the suspects hadn't shaved in a few days and had a scruffy appearance.

Had we known of these suspects, my $7K private investigator fund would have been spent on exploring these men. Their exposure at my trial could have helped explode Taylor's "one person" theory since reality revealed at least two, separate retail store arson series, in widely distanced areas, possibly perpetrated by 2-3 individuals. No wonder Taylor chose to pluralize his suspicions that only one "suspect(s)" or "perpetrator(s)" committed the fires he evaluated. The information I found many years later may have been enough to create reasonable doubt in motion hearings and at trial in Fresno.

Nearing trial in 1992, we also discovered I had a full beard in January 1987 and, of course, I wore glasses. No witness noted a suspect with glasses. My memory of the 5-year-before Fresno seminar was refreshed when I sought pictures of how I appeared during that period so we could show them in trial or to witnesses. During my search, we examined a photo album Wanda put together to commemorate our relationship. On a fall 1986 deer hunt I started to grow a beard. Subsequent photos in the album show me at a retirement dinner in October with a longer beard, our wedding photos in November confirmed longer facial hair, and 1986 Christmas snapshots substantiate the beard's continuing existence. The last, most vital, confirmation of my beard was in a photo taken on the front porch of our home. The caption read "January 17 - Garage sale." With household goods scattered around the background, on our front lawn, Wanda snapped the picture to document our post-wedding sale to sell off items duplicated when we wed. The sale was held less than 24 hours after the Tulare and Bakersfield fires and I had a full beard. Not lunch-with-the-pope alibi, but damn close. McCann took my discovery under advisement and said, "See, you don't have to testify. Don't lower yourself to defending your integrity. Make the bastards prove their case. Besides, Wanda can testify..." Despite the beard revelation and supportive evidence, we still could not substantially counter the fingerprint or prove its fabrication. With any alibi only marginal, our task was formidable. Trial was only weeks away. Reciprocal discovery was also required. Any alibi we expected to present in trial must be revealed to the prosecutors in advance. McCann said he'd sandbag the beard issue until the last minute since the prosecutors were slow in giving us discovery material we requested and seldom gave us all we asked for.

The U.S. Attorneys seemed to think we should ask for specific items and they'd get the documents to us, but without knowing what existed, how were we to be specific? I suppose if McCann had asked for "any and all materials related to suspects investigated, other than the defendant," we might have forced them to provide what they ultimately withheld. He didn't and I felt the prosecution was supposed to be fair. How naive of me.

CHAPTER TWENTY-ONE
FIREBOMB

Working in my dining room/office 8-10 hours per day, lawyer McCann dropped by at least twice a week, sometimes more. At times I acted as his secretary, taking calls from clients, the courts, and trying to track him down. He should have paid me. Apparently he gave out my home phone number as his "Glendale satellite office." I tried to keep weekends clear for Wanda and I to enjoy some normalcy. Unable to go out to eat, shop or visit, we frequently had guests who brought food and, sometimes, wine and beer. Carrie and Lori brought their boyfriends by several times and we spoke on the telephone weekly, for updates. I seldom had good news for them, but they were additional support we desperately needed. Mom and Dad, too, cruised by and called all the time.

Immobility crushed me daily. I hated idleness and was pleased to have case work to keep me busy. Each time McCann brought a box of discovery materials I had mixed feelings. We hoped for nuggets, as we mined the documents, but feared the rattlesnake that might hide in the ROIs (reports of interviews), lab analyses and occasional photos. Again and again there were ups and downs.

One PI was forced to quit when McCann mistakenly revealed, in a news conference, the guy was working for a defense attorney. The PI wanted the information kept confidential. His replacement team of PIs tried to rip me off by bumping hours worked and conducting unnecessary interviews. I fired them after receiving a bill for $3000 that should have been less that $1500. I never heard from them again.

My old friend, Bill McLaughlin, stopped by weekly, depositing a bottle of quality wine with us. Like a drug dealer, he hooked me and Wanda on the premium California vintages and now we could barely afford Gallo-by-the-gallon. Bill was interviewed several times by the ATF and local investigators and feared discovery of some of his creative sources of information. All information he obtained was for insurance fraud criminal investigations but, as a PI, he generally had to rely on public law enforcement agencies for material. Many times I made calls to detectives and verified Bill as a good, solid, dependable PI and asked for their courtesy in dealing with him.

The attention given Bill by the people investigating me caused him to become secretive and uncooperative. At one point the feds intimated they felt Bill and I were in collusion to burn retail stores for some obscure profit motive. An interesting concept, but totally bogus. I earned $800-$1000 per month working for Bill. I'd also frequently do phone scams to locate someone like I did for Jody's husband Lloyd in the 1980s. Surveillances, witness interviewing and public record searches were also on my job list.

We approached trial hopefully, knowing the only evidence against me was the fingerprint from the CraftMart fire. The fact the print did not match mine in the 1989 comparison almost nullified its use but the 1991 ID was positive. The introduction of uncharged acts evidence weighed in favor of the prosecution, but we had no identifications of me from witnesses, except a weak attestment from a Bakersfield store. She was shown a photo line-up with me and five other individuals in it and she pointed to my photo and said, "He looks familiar..." We also enjoyed the fact I had a full beard at the times of the 1987 crimes and wore glasses to see anything beyond 6 feet in front of me.

We could not verify why agents lied and said I wasn't a suspect before the April 17, 1991 fingerprint confirmation yet showed my photo around the Central Coast of California almost two weeks before. Our theory of the *Points of Origin* manuscript being their stepping stone toward doctoring or fabricating the print was validated by the April 9 photo show-ups. It seemed they obtained a copy of my base manuscript and decided I was a suspect on this fictional tale. Parts of the manuscript kept in my office and sent to literary agents, and others, in early 1991, might have found their way into ATF agent's hands but no one was telling. Did agents illegally enter my office without a warrant to get the manuscript, like they did my car in San Luis Obispo, or did they have my supervisor obtain the document at their request? Both activities would be illegal. Nevertheless, we told the prosecution this was part of our defense.

Early in our trial preparation I contacted a psychologist who worked with law enforcement and firefighters. Dr. Fishkin also wrote a monthly column for the *American Fire Journal*. Despite my depression, I didn't feel the need for psychological intervention but McCann felt a profile might be beneficial somewhere down the line. I agreed. Fishkin dropped by weekly to interview me and the psychological report he produced came out exceptionally well, stating I had "none of the characteristics of a serial arsonist."

In February 1992, I wrote a letter to Michael Cabral, the L.A. Deputy District Attorney in charge of a task force of investigators examining me for state arson charges. With copies to the Glendale Police and Fire Departments as well as the U.S. Attorney's Offices I outlined my offer to freely give an open interview and undergo a complete psychological exam. The defense never makes such offers, but I did. The local press quoted investigators as saying they were examining all arson cases I worked over the prior ten years to see if I was involved in setting any of the fires I actually examined. They also intimated strong evidence I did set fires, in collusion with one or more of my partners. These irresponsible accusations attacked the integrity of my unit and co-workers. I offered to talk with investigators to answer any of these insidious charges. There was no response to my offers of an interview or psych exam. Dr. Fishkin's report, done several months after this offer, proved why the prosecution did not want to take me up on the offers. I, in no way, fit the profile of a serial arsonist.

In April 1992, one of McCann's visits corresponded with an appointment with Dr. Fishkin. We gathered in my office, sipping tea, when McCann asked me if I'd take a polygraph - a lie detector test. I told him, "Nope."

McCann and Fishkin bantered and agreed a denial to take a polygraph would come out as an indication of guilt. They talked about me in the third person, then came back with McCann offering "We really think you should take one. We'll hire a guy to do it, in confidence, and if it turns out okay we'll ask the court to appoint another examiner for court presentation." A court would order a polygraph and the results allowed in trial only if both sides agreed beforehand. I vacillated, recalling the polygraphs I took as pre-employment exams.

On both, I reacted as deceptive or outright lying when queried about drug use. Strongly anti-drug, I never saw a marijuana joint until 1974 and then only from a distance, yet the polygraph said otherwise. The machines were bogus. My feelings were later confirmed again when I used a polygraph in two of my investigations. Again, the machines were off-base and created more problems than answered questions. Technology and the passage of time did not increase their reliability. The FBI-spy Aldrich Ames fiasco further confirms this fact, but we weren't aware of Ames in 1992. McCann and Fishkin were worried about the negative publicity should the U.S. Attorney ask, in open court, whether I would submit to the testing and I said, "No."

I gave in to their reasoning and said, "Okay, let's do it." McCann and Fishkin shook hands, smiling and sighing with relief as if their performance was pre-planned. Then McCann added, "We can teach you how to pass the poly..."

"Yeah, John," Fishkin piped in, "it's actually pretty easy to do..."

"What are you saying?" I cautiously queried, trying to lay an ambush for what I knew now was coming, "I can actually beat the test?"

"Yeah," McCann offered, "...digging your fingernails into your palms, putting a thumb tack in your shoe or curling your toes during the test raises stress responses so you don't register much higher when you lie..." I stared at both of them, controlling months of frustration, anger, and hurt I wanted to vent. "You bastards," I whispered, "you're coaching me on how to lie, or expecting me to lie, or both."

"No, no," they said in unison.

"Bullshit," I shouted. "I will not fucking lie anywhere at any time...both of you please leave...now."

My mind raced, gauging how I'd replace McCann and whether I could get any of the thousands of dollars already spent back into my pocket. Weak and depressed I found I couldn't even follow through with kicking them out of my home.

Both men backpedaled, trying to justify their charade as just part of their tactics to defend the case. I don't think I had the physical strength to punch them out or throw them out the door so simply deflated and deflected my anger into another area.

I still should have fired McCann but with the money already fronted, and trial looming, caused me to make another bad decision. It was not the first and wouldn't be the last. I already knew: McCann would justify his expenses and not return a dime. I continued to pursue my investigation of the prosecution's case as if it were a crime, and it was, and I the detective. I played devil's advocate for both sides, gathered evidence to weaken their felonious suspicions I was an arsonist and tried to put a credible defense together. It was like an innocent man being accused falsely of child molestation with no physical evidence. Without solid alibi, how do you defend yourself?

Almost every document we needed had to come through the court. Witness interviews were another story. If we re-interviewed a prosecution witness or found a new one, whatever we learned could be kept confidential, unless the results were written down. Reciprocal discovery required us to give the prosecution all "relevant" written material. I assumed they were forthcoming with us and naively insisted McCann follow the letter of the reciprocal discovery requirements. He ignored me but that was his choice. Springing a "newly discovered" document or witness in trial could result in the judge disallowing it altogether. Lists of potential trial witnesses were required to be exchanged between prosecutors and the defense a week before the trial start date. My Pollyanna perceptions of justice were again shattered. McCann warned the prosecutor's witness list would be loaded with unfamiliar names and people they never intended to call into court. This tactic forced the defense to spend many extra hours tracking down these phantoms to find out what they might say on the witness stand. Over 120 names appeared on the prosecution roster. We didn't have time or money to track down and interview all the potentials.

Just before trial McCann made a suggestion. Since all five Fresno charges were similar, including the 2-week-later discovery of a device, he wanted to tell the jury we agreed all the fires were set by the same person. Not the uncharged acts, just the Fresno-Tulare Bakersfield blazes. He theorized the jury might agree and find the solid alibi of being in L.A. the week the device was found as indicative someone local was the arsonist despite the fingerprint. This proffer could also backfire. The jury might believe all the fires were set by the same guy and even though I had solid alibi on at least one count, they could convict on all anyway. It was a gamble, but I was a gambling man. I agreed with McCann's strategy.

The prosecution also offered a plea bargain: Plead guilty to three counts and they would recommend a 10-year sentence. The judge agrees with prosecutorial recommendations in 98 percent of all plea bargains. I would serve only 1/3 time with good behavior and be out in about four years. I said, "No deal. Let's go to trial." And we did.

On June 18, 1992, jury selection started. Before noon we had a jury and two alternates. Trial time was expected to be three weeks. Wanda remained in L.A., McCann and I camped out together in the infamous Holiday Inn.

The courtroom was fairly small but the 14-foot ceiling and Great Seal of the United States behind the judge were ominous. With the millions spent by the United States on this prosecution and courtroom, what chance did my innocence and a $40K defense have? The courtroom was almost full each day; many people I'd never seen. The court clerk, Candy, was a dynamo and managed Judge Wanger's realm as if it were hers. She helped the defense as well as the prosecutors. Candy pointed out court-watchers, media and local politicians in the audience. Michael Cabral, the L.A. District Attorney's Office prosecutor attended a large part of the trial. His presence hinted of local, state of California, charges on the horizon.

During opening statements I had to contain myself. The prosecutors took turns pointing at me, calling me an arsonist and telling the jury I betrayed the fire service and public's trust. Pounding the fingerprint hammer repeatedly I was tempted to give the orators the finger during their presentations. Instead, I sat stoic, following McCann's orders to show no emotion. The papers reported it correctly : "The defendant showed no emotion..."

McCann's opening titillated the jury by intimating fabricated evidence, doctored/altered reports and outright ATF agent's lies. He did fairly well, until he tripped over his briefcase again. I was surprised the court reporter didn't include it in the transcript. A witness and videotape of the January 14, 1987 Hancock Fabrics fire opened the prosecution's

336

case. No witness ID of me; I didn't appear in the video footage nor was there anything to tie me to the fire. If I was tried on this charge alone, the jury could not convict.

Additional witnesses provided insight into the Tulare Family Bargain Center and Bakersfield arsons. The Family Bargain Center manager, James Peret, set off the first explosion of the trial. He changed his suspect description.

Peret's interview, just minutes after the small fire, in 1987, revealed the suspect "...in his mid-20's, scruffy appearance, and had shoulder-length black hair." When Mr. McCann interviewed Peret several weeks before trial he also showed the manager the 6-pack photo line-up he'd already been shown by ATF agents. McCann displayed the 6-pack, with my photo in it, and Peret told him, "Nah, none of these guys is the one I saw. They're all too old." Cool, we thought. In trial Peret confirmed his original post-fire description of the suspect, given to a Tulare police officer less than 30 minutes after the incident. The prosecutor side-stepped the "no pick" photo show-up and talked Peret into the following:
PROSC: "Mr. Peret, when you described the man you saw before the fire, you said he was in his mid-20's, correct?"
PERET: "Yeah, mid-20s, maybe a little more..."
PROSC: "Maybe a little older... you only got a quick glimpse according to the report..."
PERET: "Yeah, only a second or two..."
PROSC: "So maybe a little older than you originally reported?"
McCann did not object at this point and should have. Peret turned his head towards me.
PERET: "Oh, yeah...maybe older..." It is a well-known fact trial lawyers do not ask questions they don't already have an answer for...
PROSC: "How much older, if you recall...?"
PERET: "Oh, you know, he could have been 30 or more."
PROSC: "Thirty years or more could mean 34 or so...?"
McCANN: "Objection! Leading the witness..."
JUDGE : "Sustained."
The jury already heard it, of course, as the prosecutor planned.
PROSC: "Mr. Peret, what would you estimate the upper limits of your age estimate would be of the suspect you saw on January 16, 1987?"
PERET: "Oh, 34 or so..."

McCann, of course, was allowed to cross-examine Peret and despite the original minutes-old, mid-20s statement, and his "these guys are too old" account about the photo line-up, Peret stuck to his guns. I was 38-years-old in 1987. The witness was obviously prepped or coached by U.S. Attorneys before his testimony. The female Bakersfield witness also upgraded her original description from the photo line-up of me as "looking familiar" to, in trial, "I'm 70 percent sure, maybe more, that the man sitting over there," pointing at me, "is the one I saw in the store just before the fire." She, too, was unshakable...now. Her original description was fairly close to me but the man was dressed "in cowboy clothes," with a western-style shirt with pearl buttons, clean shaven, large rodeo-type silver belt buckle and a straw cowboy hat. I owned no such clothing-- ever. The man did not act suspiciously. Ironically, the western attire and straw cowboy hat were consistent with Central Coast series fires descriptions by three separate witnesses.

A younger, mid-20s guy did come into the Bakersfield witness's store just before the fire and he asked about the store's security and fire safety devices. The man's actions and questions were "unusual" according to her. Again, a mid-20's guy. McCann showed obvious discomfort with the courtroom. His questions of witnesses were sometimes overly long and complicated causing him to have to repeat himself.

He did not have the confidence I expected. It was standard for him to think 2-3 sentences, or a paragraph, ahead of himself and lose his train of thought. His trips back and forth from the podium to the defense table put several extra miles on his unpolished shoes as he came back to refer to his notes. There was a lot of information to decipher and he often made factual errors on dates, names, and situations. I went through stacks of Post-it notes providing him with the correct information or pleading with him to ask specific questions. Some of the questions were for investigators involved in the case. Since they would not talk to us outside the courtroom I wanted to conduct the relevant interview in the trial while the witness was on the stand and get the answers for the pending L.A. case. McCann blew off the tactic even though the statements I sought gave us an advantage before the next trial. Lawyers seldom listen to defendants, even those able to pay their way.

The fingerprint information came out early and McCann valiantly fought to counter it by cross-examining the print examiner who proclaimed "no match" in the 1989 comparison. Despite all the print man's errors and discrepancies in his support documentation, the testimony came down to his only defense: "I simply made a mistake in 1989..." He could not be shaken. During McCann's cross-examination of several ATF witnesses the groundwork was lain for the revelation of Agent Croke's lies in his reports.

Prosecutors Faller and Hanley were visibly shaken when the hints of Croke's, and possibly Agent Mike Matassa's lies came up. Huddling at the prosecution's table I'm sure they discussed the value of putting Croke on the stand only to have him proven a liar. Croke's expected testimony was put off several times. Matassa was queried several times about his status as lead investigator and the fact Croke worked under him and that Matassa gave specific instructions to him and tasks to perform. Faller and Hanley cornered Matassa immediately after he left the stand for the first time. ATF expert Jerry Taylor's testimony that "only one person(s)" set the six fires he examined in his survey was attacked by McCann. In a field he wasn't entirely familiar with, McCann didn't come on very forcefully. He didn't assault the witness over his lack of expertise in actual arson investigation and the fact he never arrested a serial arson suspect. He was only a consultant. I wanted the groundwork down so my own expertise in serial arson investigations and apprehensions would give me some credibility when I took the stand.

McCann explained, "It's a bad tactic to attack or belittle law enforcement people. Juries want to believe them and when a defense lawyer attacks a credible witness they hold it against the defendant."

"But he's wrong," I countered. "I don't care if you appear to be a prick for attacking obvious shortcomings in a witness-- I hired you to be a prick."

"I have more experience in court than you, John. This is the way I work."

I shook my head as I tried to get in the last word, "I guess my TV docu-drama perception of aggressive defense attorneys was in error. Do you think Hanley and Faller will treat me as well when I testify? I'm in law enforcement, too..."

"I just let a client testify in San Diego last month. The guy might have gotten off but he insisted on getting on the stand. We lost. He came off guilty to the jury."

"Was he?" I queried.

"What?"

"Was he guilty?"

"Well, yeah...but...I just don't see the need for you to take the stand. What would you say about the fingerprint?" We argued each evening when we adjourned to the Holiday Inn bar or a restaurant. It was eerie sipping a beer at the bar and hearing a news broadcast about my case on the 6 o'clock news. I kept my head down most of the time.

On Wednesday, Agent Croke took the stand. Croke, a short, 30-year-old agent, had a scraggly beard and black shoulder-length hair. A prosecution witness, Faller took Croke through his involvement in the uncharged act fires on the Central Coast to let the jury know I was registered in a motel just 21 miles from three fires in Atascadero on March 9, 1989. The Woolworth's fire in Salinas was also mentioned. Croke discussed showing photo line-ups in Atascadero and opened the door for McCann's queries. If the 6-packs weren't mentioned we would have had to bring Croke back later as a defense Witness. Obviously the prosecution knew nothing of our trap.

When McCann cross-examined a wary Croke he smoothly breezed by the dates he investigated in the Central Coast area then moved on to other fields. Then he struck.

McCANN: "Agent Croke, were you present when the CraftMart print was run through the AFIS computer?"

CROKE: "No."

McCANN: "Do you know the date of the AFIS print run that indicated John Orr as a suspect?" The prosecutors fidgeted, Faller started to stand to object to something but there were no grounds so he sat back down.

CROKE: "Yeah, it was April 17, 1991."

McCANN: "April 17, 1991...This was the first time John Orr was considered a suspect?"

CROKE: "Yes, he became a suspect after the AFIS computer IDed him."

McCANN: "Not before, right?"

CROKE: "Nope."

McCANN: "Have you read the manuscript, *Points of Origin?*"

CROKE: "Parts of it, not every word."

McCANN: "When did you first read 'parts of it' ?"

CROKE: "I'm not sure but it was summer 1991, I think."

McCANN: "Not earlier, say May or June 1991?"

CROKE: "No, no. No way that early."

McCANN: "Agent Croke, you testified John Orr wasn't a suspect until April 17, 1991 and you didn't read the manuscript until months later, correct?"

CROKE: "Correct."

McCann approached the witness and handed Croke a copy of his Central Coast activities report dated April 9, 1991, and asked Croke to review it. He did.

McCANN: "You wrote this report?"

CROKE: "Yes."

McCANN: "When is this report dated?"

CROKE: "April 9, 1991."

McCANN: "Please read paragraph five..."

CROKE: (looking at the prosecution table for help)"...Paragraph five...uh..." Croke read the entry stating he showed a 6-pack "containing the photo of John Orr in position #5." It still didn't hit Croke but the prosecutors saw the problem and shuffled papers trying to find something...anything to get them out of this jam. The jury noticed the activity, alternating glances at Croke and the prosecution table like spectators at a tennis match.

McCANN: "Agent Croke, you testified John Orr wasn't a suspect until April 17, 1991, and you didn't read the manuscript until the summer of 1991...Please explain what made John Orr a suspect on April 9th when you were showing 6-packs with his picture on display as noted in your report?"

CROKE: (scans the report, looks at McCann, me, then the prosecutors) "Uh, it... I don't see...this isn't the right report."

McCANN: "Please answer my question Agent Croke... Why was John Orr a suspect on April 9th if you hadn't read the manuscript yet?"

CROKE: "He wasn't...wasn't until...this report's wrong."

McCANN: "You've testified that this report, prepared, dated and signed by you, is false?"

By then Croke is squirming so McCann moved on, but re-visited the falsified report before returning the witness to the prosecution. Hanley gets Croke to admit an error but promises to study his notes which he conveniently left in L.A. McCann leaped up and shouted "Objection!" All interview notes must be copied and turned over to the defense as part of discovery. We never received Croke's notes. The jury is dismissed while the issue is argued out of their presence. The prosecutors dispatch Croke to L.A. to retrieve the notes and, maybe, his credibility. After the jury returned Agent Mike Matassa took the stand again. Matassa arrested me and his testimony covered the actual arrest and post-arrest interview. Before they get too far another prosecutorial faux pas jumped up.

Matassa drones on, "...I later reviewed the transcript of the interview..."

"Objection," shouts McCann, "we were never given a written transcript of the interview. The audio tapes the prosecution provided us were unintelligible..."

The prosecution, again caught withholding evidence, asked for the jury to be excused. The judge sent them to lunch and demanded a copy of the transcript be copied and given to our side. After Wanger leaves the courtroom and only a few media reps and spectators loiter, Carl Faller shouted across the courtroom to McCann.

"Don't you ever do that again..."

"What?" McCann replied quietly.

"Don't you ever accuse the prosecution of withholding evidence in front of a jury like that...that's unethical and unconscionable."

"But you've withheld evidence at least twice now."

Faller started across the room towards McCann, his jaws clenched and a growling sound emanating from his throat. He scared me. "Don't you ever pull that shit again." Faller stopped several feet away. McCann

341

turned to face Faller and said, "Mr. Faller, first you tell us the interview wasn't recorded, then you gave us tapes that were unintelligible, now you inform us the tape was clear enough to make a transcript. What's going on here?"

Faller moved on McCann and I'm seething too, so stepped between the two and Faller stopped within an inch of me. I whisper, "Back off asshole, this is my lawyer you're fucking with." Faller peered over his shoulder toward a bailiff whom I'd become friendly with and said, "Bailiff..." The court cop slowly pushed off a desk he was leaning on, amused by Faller's posturing and headed our way. I glared at Faller and stepped back, diffusing the situation. Had I known the depth of the prosecutions evidence withholding I would have goaded him and not backed off, bailiff or no...

The transcript of the post-arrest interview revealed a few nuggets. Large gaps in the recordings were explained away as background noise interfering or, at one point, "damage done to the tape while rewinding..." Yeah, right. For months prosecutors and investigators claimed the interview was not recorded. There was nothing in the tape to indicate I said anything about guilt so the prosecution tried to hide the tape. Apparently concerned it might later surface they transcribed portions of it and gave the defense only an unintelligible taped version and no copy of the abbreviated transcript. Then the prosecution had the audacity to state, "Orr never denied (in the taped interview) he set any of the fires...an indication of guilt." Of course, my vehement denials and "you assholes are fucking crazy if you believe I set fires" were well hidden in the background noise, or maybe the repudiations were concealed in the 'gaps'.

When Matassa took the stand again, McCann made one more strong point about investigator shortcomings.

McCann asked, "Agent Matassa, for many months you claimed to me and Mr. Orr the post-arrest interview was not recorded, correct?"

"Well, yeah."

"Please read this highlighted portion of the transcript just provided to the defense of this 'unrecorded' interview."

Matassa fidgeted, then Faller jumped up, "Objection. Counsel is intimidating the witness."

The judge responded, "Overruled, he's just inquiring."

"Please read, Mr. Matassa," McCann reiterated.

"From the recording, I said, 'Larry (Cornelison, his interview partner), I'm going out to the car and get some more batteries for the tape recorder, these are almost dead..."

"You told us the interview was not recorded, you lied, correct?"

Matassa admitted his falsehood to the jury. I, too, had lied during post-arrest interviews with people I detained, but never to defense lawyers or in reports to avoid providing exculpatory information.

We made a few gains here and there but the prosecution recovered some loss of face the next day. Croke returned to the stand with copies of his pencil-written notes from the Central Coast investigation itinerary. Croke said he made several trips to the Central Coast from April to July. The photo spread showings took place in July, not April. When he wrote the report later, he couldn't recall exactly when he penned it, but somehow he erred and dated even the July activities April 9, 1991. This explanation, though questionable, could not be disproved one way or the other, particularly when he produced copies of trip reimbursement vouchers with the July dates. McCann did force Croke to identify the three reports with erroneous dates and admit they were false. Ups and downs, ups and downs. After only four days of testimony the prosecution announced they were almost through. We had to scramble to get our witnesses lined up since they weren't expected until next week.

The prosecution finished off with a blitzkrieg of witnesses testifying to circumstantial evidence such as my Holiday Inn hotel bill for Fresno, Motel 6 bill for near the Atascadero fires and rosters showing my attendance at both the 1987 and 1989 seminars.

The Fresno hotel bill showed a check-out time at 6:40 a.m. on January 16, 1987. This, the prosecution theorized, was my actual departure time from the seminar and gave me several hours to travel to Tulare to set fires by 10 a.m. Actually, I checked out at 6:40 a.m., put my bags in my trunk, and returned to have breakfast and attend the morning sessions. My check-out so early was to beat the crowd of over 200 attendees who didn't have the foresight to avoid the rush when the seminar ended at about noon. It took about two minutes at 6:40 am.

There was no way to verify my stay until noon. I paid cash for breakfast, made no calls and apparently didn't even buy gas or I paid in cash. Any handouts from the morning sessions were long ago thrown out. Tom Rickles, my old partner and CCAI seminar director, testified he took my conference completion certificate home to me from "one of the two 1987 seminars, I think it was January's, because John didn't pick it up or he wasn't there that morning." Always one to avoid crowds, I elected to allow Tom to bring it home with him instead of waiting around for a hundred or more guys to pick their certificates up.

The defense case was slated to begin and end within two days. McCann had me coordinate getting the witnesses into town and arranging transportation and accommodations. We found out the court would pick up the tab.

Our defense was subdued, simply designed to counter the allegations, yet we felt confident. McCann refused to put me on the stand. I'll admit I didn't project the confident nature I had before I was arrested. The trial was a battle but without the ability to at least get up on the stand and say, "I didn't do these things," I felt unarmed, stripped bare and helpless. McCann would not let me on the stand. If I were convicted I could not testify in any future trial without the conviction being exploited. I was the only one to provide alibi in three of the Central Coast fires and McCann knew it. Still, he didn't tell me of the future ramifications if I were convicted. Had he been forthcoming, I may have been more adamant.

McCann took an out another lawyer would use 8 months later. These guys must take classes on "Keeping Your Client Off The Stand."

He said, "I don't know what I'd ask you...what should I ask you?" Then added, "Make them prove their case...we've done pretty well, we only need one juror to believe us." Wanda came up to spend this week with me because she also had to testify about my beard. The judge examined the photo album and the series of pictures that showed the development of my facial hair from stubble in October 1986 to a well-trimmed beard in January 1987. The battle to get the entire series of photos in front of the jury was important. Like the uncharged acts evidence required by the prosecution to accuse me, our series of pictures would help bolster the beard issue, and our defense.

We also felt the viewing of the photo album demonstrated I was a normal husband, father and friend who attended retirement dinners, a birthday gathering, Christmas with the family, and hosted a garage sale. Not voicing this character-development-without-having-to-testify tactic, the prosecution was aware of it anyway. They fought, and won. The judge allowed only the garage sale photo and excluded the album itself and the others.

After Wanda verified the authenticity of the beard photograph, the prosecution rebutted with a witness. Giselle Niva, and insurance company claims adjustor from Burbank attended the 1987 CCAI seminar and met me, and many other people, for the first time. She testified I did not have a beard in January 1987. McCann, not his usual self, didn't know what to ask her. I met her only once and knew several other CCAI attendees who had beards and may have worn one at the time. We needed to query her further about her other meetings but McCann let her off the stand without any questions at all. "I don't want to ask questions I don't know the answers to..." Despite the last minute decisions and difficulties, we were confident of success. McCann's closing argument was weakened by his meandering, digressing and thinking ahead of himself but covered most of the bases. At least he didn't trip over his briefcase - I kept it hidden under the defense table. Prosecutors Faller and Hanley each got their turn to scream their accusations during closing,

344

repeatedly pointing at me while I showed "no emotion." The jury finally adjourned Wednesday afternoon.

Wanda and I stayed with McCann at the courthouse until five p.m. waiting for an early verdict. Thursday, too, we spent loitering around the trial venue. Candy, our court clerk, let us know a long deliberation was usually good for the defense - "It shows there is some reasonable doubt." She added, "There was screaming and yelling from the jury room this morning. You have some hold-outs..." The revelation sounded promising.

Everyone returned to the courtroom twice to allow part of the transcript read back to the jurors. I don't recall what portions they were interested in, I was in a daze and could barely function. On Friday, just after noon, we all gathered once again in the courtroom. Today I can't picture even one of those people who held my life in their hands. The spokesperson told the judge they were hopelessly deadlocked - no possibility they could come to a verdict on any of the counts. I dreaded going through another trial but breathed a sigh of relief we had some advocates. I turned to Wanda in the audience. She sat in the last row and showed no emotion, unsure of what was happening. Judge Wanger admonished the jury and told them to return to deliberations and try to break the deadlock. He reminded them if they were not able to reach a conclusion today, Friday, return on Monday and Tuesday was required. The courtroom handled only routine matters on Mondays so even if the jury had a verdict on Monday, they might have to come back on Tuesday as well. At least two jurors commuted long distances each day, one from Bakersfield, over 100 miles away. The jury returned to their lair.

Three hours later, Wanda and I huddled in an office on the same floor as the courtroom. We held hands, she wept occasionally, and we both shook and shuddered constantly as the clock ticked.

I thought back to Monday morning when we left our home for what could be my last time. I walked onto the back porch and Domino stuck his head between my legs from behind as I surveyed Wanda's gardens, our refurbished garage, the spa we spent so many hours soaking in, and the beautiful Chinese elm sheltering the gazebo. I bent down shaking my head in bewilderment at how this nightmare could happen and nuzzled Domino. I'd had no control of my life for the past eight months and I flamed, angered at....I didn't know. The wrath could not be vented on any particular individual.

I released Domino and took one last lingering look at the yard, but it blurred, so I walked back inside only to run into Wanda. We wound our arms around each other and cried.

Friday afternoon at about 4 p.m. I perused a magazine and held Wanda's hand while she stared at a wall. A nearby secretary's phone buzzed, she answered it, looked at me, hung it up, then leaped up and disappeared down a hallway. Seconds later McCann stuck his head in and said, "Jury's in, let's go." I was glued to the bench but wanted desperately to get the news. Wanda stood and I remained seated trying to catch my breath. She bent down and whispered to me, "Let's go." We trudged down the hallway and entered the nearly packed courtroom.

As we entered, Wanda hugged me briefly and peeled off to take her seat in the back row as I followed McCann to the defense table.

The judge came in, followed by the jury and no time was wasted handing the verdict sheets to the bailiff. He carried them to Judge Wanger. He read each page then handed them to the bailiff who then took them to Candy to read out loud. Candy scanned the top sheet and I saw a half-smile as she intoned, "...as to count one, arson to Hancock Fabrics on January 14, 1987, we find the defendant not guilty." She flipped the page to count two, the device found two weeks after the seminar. Still a half-smile. "...the attempted arson to House of Fabrics, we find the defendant, not guilty." Candy's smile broadened a bit. I thought our tactic of agreeing all the fires were set by the same person might ensure exoneration.

After flipping to the third charge, Candy's smile disappeared but she didn't skip a beat, "...at the Family Bargain Center in Tulare, we find the defendant guilty as charged." Twice more I heard "guilty": the CraftMart and other Bakersfield fabric store incident on January 16, 1987. I had to put my hands on the table to steady myself as McCann pleaded to allow me to remain on bond. He rambled and faltered, repeated himself and looked around at the floor as if trying to locate his briefcase. I finally put my hand on his arm to stop him. The judge ordered me taken into custody immediately. My Monday morning observation came true--I had looked at our backyard, home, and Domino for the last time. I didn't think I could feel any worse as I turned to see Wanda in tears, waving to me and scurrying out the door ahead of the media slugs. Could it get any worse? It could and it did.

CHAPTER TWENTY-TWO
FIRE AWAY

Many writers have penned vivid descriptions of the actualities of incarceration. I will spend little time in this text trying to illuminate what the common person imagines behind-the-bars life is really like. Everyman reads about prison life, sees documentaries or movies outlining this existence, and creates the horrific images in their mind. In reality, the facts are unimaginable. A holding facility is not like the refuge created by your mother's loving hug. There is no femininity in a sally port. A cell is not a building block of life, but a place to tear you down and destroy you. Not even a freshly-calved block of ice from an arctic glacier is colder than the steel bench, sink, and toilet inside a block-walled holding cell with concrete walls and floor. The only warmth in such a cave emanates from a fetid breeze escaping the caked, slimy drain opening in the middle of the floor. Thankfully, a constant cold wind of fresh air floods out of a ceiling vent, like Niagara Falls in January, and keeps the stink at ground level. But you want the heat and inevitably cover the vent with wet toilet paper so, at least, your feet stay warm. Use too much toilet paper and you have none when you truly need it for its intended purpose.

Wanda left the courtroom in Fresno and drove the 200 miles back to L.A. after my conviction was announced and arrived before I even got out of the courthouse lockup. Slammed into the hole, or Administrative Segregation as it is called, I found a phone mounted at the head of my steel cot. Ad Seg is required for former peace officers and I welcomed the conveniently placed phone and avoidance of the general population of the Fresno County Jail federal holding area. I talked to my wife but I do not recall what was said other than attempts at building some hope for the future. A general numbness did not sink in as far as my stomach where a deep pain burned for days. A sentencing date loomed in about 45 days. Carrie's wedding was scheduled for October 31, 1992. My dad would stand up for me - there was no possibility of release. A court-ordered pre-sentence psych evaluation was written after a 90-minute chat with the good doctor. His findings were similar to Dr. Fishkin's. The court psychologist could not slant his findings. Fishkin's analysis said I did not have the characteristics of a serial arsonist, so the court-appointed shrink's conclusion revealed his allegiance to who wrote his paycheck. He penned, "Defendant vehemently maintains his innocence and the findings show no ideation of a serial arsonist. If defendant is, in fact, guilty of the heinous crimes he was convicted of, then he is a threat to society and should be incarcerated for a lengthy period." End of report. McCann told me if I threw myself on the mercy of the court I would probably get 10 years for each count, to run concurrently, and only have to do the same 1/3 time the plea bargain offered earlier. I would be out, with good behavior, in 3.5 - 4 years. He added that copping out at this point might affect the next trial or state charges. I reminded McCann of my innocence and intended to take the pre-sentence opportunity to write the judge and speak out on the day of sentencing. McCann replied, "Then you'll get 10 years for each count, to run consecutively...a total of thirty years."

At sentencing Faller and Hanly were allowed to re-visit the substantial "evidence" of my guilt and recommended the highest end of the jail time guidelines - 30 years. During their dissertation Hanly stated, "In the city of Glendale and surrounding communities, the incidence of arson fires has gone down over 70 percent since the defendant's arrest..," implying that I burned a swath across southern California while I was loose. I didn't have enough time in my busy schedule for office needs, let alone playing General Sherman.

This statement caught McCann and I off guard and we certainly weren't prepared for it. The prosecution, of course, was not required to provide documentation of this "fact" in a sentencing hearing. With the few minutes to prepare to plead for me, McCann had no time to hear an explanation of the real reason such statistics occurred. Their inference was outrageous but I knew exactly what happened, just did not have time to relate it to McCann. Besides, the judge had already made up his mind.

My unit ensured over 70 percent of all fires in Glendale had an experienced investigator on-scene to assist the assigned fire captain with cause and origin determination. We responded to even small grass and trash fires as well as larger loss vehicle, structure, and brush blazes. The two individuals who replaced Joe and I when I was arrested had limited fire investigation experience and background. One was a former fire department shift investigator with, at least, some training and scene experience. The other was a full-time police officer with specialties in narcotics and undercover operations working for the Special Enforcement Detail, but no fire investigation training or scene time. I doubt they spent any time looking into nuisance trash and grass fires that were traditionally arson-caused but too small to consider worthy of an investigator's time. Without an experienced fire cause expert in attendance at fire scenes, fire captains were left to their own limited training and experience. The warm-bed syndrome reared its ugly head again after I left. If a fire captain called a blaze arson-caused he was required, by fire department policy, to write an investigation report and, generally, wait for a uniformed cop to take a police crime report. Early a.m. trash, vehicle and small structure arson fires suddenly became caused by "carelessly discarded cigarette," "electrical shorting," or "ignited by faulty car exhaust causing sparks to ignite dry grass..." The incidence of fires remained stable, but arson fires were now, after I was arrested, neglected and not investigated and mis-called as accidentally-caused: The arson stats then "dropped."

Even the replacement investigators, I'm sure, opted to call suspicious fires accidental rather than risking an upsurge of arson on their watch. One more solid reason intentionally-set fires went unreported as to their true origins.

Prosecutors also did not consider the fact 1992 was an unusually wet year in Southern California and the excess rain ensured the fire season did not start until June or July - cutting brush and grass fires by about 25 percent. Something else prosecutors and investigators did not ponder when they made the unsupported statement "arson stats went down" after my arrest - the very high arson case clearance rates posted during my 10-year tenure in the Investigation Unit. Our clearance rate was the highest in Southern California, maybe the entire state, because we were efficient, thorough, and reliable. Why would I set an arson fire in Glendale where an unsolved case damaged my clearance rate? It was a ludicrous assumption.

I had no answer for the "surrounding jurisdictions" Hanly spoke of. With only a 1986 Ford Crown Victoria 4-door at my disposal, it defies the imagination I would cruise around neighboring cities setting fires in my plainly marked narc car with a red spotlight and four antennas. McCann and I could not respond to Hanly's vomiting stats we could not refute, but I did read a five minute statement declaring my innocence, even citing a recent series of fires occurring along Blackstone Avenue in Fresno. The exact same stretch where the January 1987 fires erupted.

McCann, for once, was right - I got a sentence of 30 years. I could parole in 10.

Just before I was moved from Fresno County Jail to the Metropolitan Detention Center (MDC) in Los Angeles in preparation for the next trial, McCann was invited to orally argue the U.S. Attorney's appeal to get *Points of Origin* back in as evidence. The 9th Circuit Court of Appeals allows oral arguments in very few appeals and the appellant, the U.S. Attorney/prosecutor Stephen Stein, only gets relief less than 5 percent of the time in such actions. We went in smelling good. McCann could have cruised through the hearing by simply stating, "I stand by our response to the prosecution's argument. *Points of Origin* isn't evidence, it's a time-consuming, provocative manuscript of no evidentiary value."

Judge Rafeedie had already agreed. McCann called Wanda the evening of his oral argument in September, saying he was nervous being in front of the 9th Circuit but was confident we would prevail. He added, "Even if we lose, there are a few things, exculpatory chapters, in the manuscript we might find beneficial." He was trying to prepare Wanda for the potential loss and at the same time make her feel better.

The next morning I called Wanda and she read me a short article from the *L.A. Daily News.* Quoting McCann's oral argument, the piece was thankfully brief. It summarized McCann's closing statement to the justices, in open court, before the people who were already leaning towards agreeing with the defense to exclude the manuscript from trial. McCann said to them, "I might actually end up using parts of the manuscript, some of it is exculpatory." Horrified to hear this, I told Wanda my lawyer just told the justices they didn't even need to hear the motion and the oral arguments were a waste of time; he might use the manuscript anyway.

Within weeks Judge Rafeedie's decision was overturned - *Points of Origin* came into my next trial as evidence.

A combination of McCann's nervousness and lack of experience weighted the upcoming trial in favor of the prosecution. I told Wanda, "Start shopping for a new lawyer and cash in my retirement account. We need help." The Public Employees' Retirement System put a rush on processing my withdrawal and I was surprised my contributions over my 18 year career came to just under $100,000. We could now pay off those who had loaned us money to pay McCann for the first trial and have enough, hopefully, to cover the cost of a new advocate. A rule of thumb among lawyers was most felonies warrant about $10K each to defend. The L.A. federal case consisted of eight felonies. We were to have only about $65K after we paid off our debts and the taxes taken out.

I arrived at L.A. MDC federal holding facility in time for Thanksgiving, days after Carrie was wed. The pain of missing the milestone of my daughter's wedding was compounded by news Lori, too, was engaged to marry. McCann did little in preparation for trial in the L.A. case but we paid him for his efforts anyway, knowing he was on his way out. We interviewed two potential replacements and ultimately were referred to Peter Giannini of Century City.

Giannini walked with confidence and had a deep modulated voice that commanded attention. He did not ever raise his voice. While his 5'7" size didn't match his authoritarian manner, he did dress like a Fortune 500 CEO and had a look of experience: thick salt and pepper hair and he alluded to a list of courtroom victories. The image made him a poster boy for defense attorneys. He had recently succeeded in getting series arson charges against a police sergeant dismissed before a preliminary hearing could be held. The sergeant was arrested and accused of setting a series of fires in abandoned buildings in a small L.A. county jurisdiction. A TeleTrac locator system was attached to his police unit and he was near locations of some of the fires. There was no other evidence so Giannini made a motion to dismiss and it was granted.

With some recent arson experience and an interview by Wanda and I, we accepted Giannini and took him onboard. Shortly after Christmas 1992, Giannini called McCann and informed him he was no longer my lawyer. After the manuscript appeal failed I could barely stand to talk to McCann, let alone have the fortitude to enjoy firing him, so opted out to Giannini. McCann came to MDC for a final visit desperately trying to regain his place. I refused and he approached Giannini asking him to take second seat in my defense and share the $60K I agreed to pay for the next trial. McCann was gone by January 1993 and the PERS finally disbursed my retirement proceeds. Giannini made an attempt to have me sign over the PERS disbursement directly to him before the processing was complete. Something told me defer.

Giannini had Wanda and I sign a "standard" client contract. The form said there would be no refund if the charges were dismissed or a plea agreement worked out. I didn't intend to take a "deal" and if Giannini got the charges dismissed, it would be worth $60K. Troubling, to me, was a clause stating the fee did not cover expert witnesses or private investigator costs. I balked when I read this since Giannini knew I had no more money left after the retirement check was cashed. Giannini said, "We'll work something out..." I reminded him our home could not be re-financed since Wanda was unable to make house payments as it was, let alone a second mortgage fee. My father was subsidizing her mortgage until we could get back on our feet.

Giannini responded, "It'll be okay. These cases take priority over everything in your life...we'll be alright." Naively I believed him. He said much of the private investigator work he could perform to cut costs. Giannini came with the recommendation of one other lawyer and his name was recognized by jailhouse lawyers I had contact with so assumed we would be alright. At his point, anybody was better than McCann.

Without my home office and access to documents, I did little pre-trial preparation as I had for the Fresno trial. My room at MDC was small and I shared it with another guy so had almost no space to store materials. MDC was Club Fed. No steel benches, sinks or bed frames. Wood, porcelain and carpets outfitted the cubes we lived in. There was even carpet in the TV rooms. A garden spot compared to the Fresno County Jail.

Giannini requested documents through the discovery process and provided me copies of some, but not all. He was not used to giving case files and reports to defendants and soon overcame that reluctance. The tradition of withholding materials was based on defendants in the past discovering witness and victim's addresses and following up with threats. Giannini showed no fear of this.

Several federal affidavits and reports referred to the TeleTrac locator and its daily logs of my movements between October - December 1991. This period didn't cover times of any of the cases I was charged with so was not really alibi. Peter ignored the TeleTrac. However, the fact I was electronically surveilled and didn't set any fires spoke volumes. Hearing Michael Cabral, the L.A. District Attorney's Office head of the "John Orr Task Force Investigation," attended much of the Fresno trial, Giannini feared state charges down the road. He requested the Teletrac log from the Asst. U.S. Attorney, Stephen Stein. Stein responded, "The TeleTrac is not part of the our case since that period is well after the last fire we charged you with in March 1991. We don't really intend to use TeleTrac logs but if you request a copy of it you may not like what you get..."

Stein left it hanging and Giannini thought there was evidence to convict me of something during the tracking period to be used later in state court. He came to MDC and queried me, "They've got you on something on that TeleTrac. If you set a fire and even if it's not a federal charge, our requesting the log might result in that uncharged act being used against you in federal court. Did you set any fires from October - December 1991?"

"No. None. Ever. Understand?" I replied. "We can use TeleTrac for a variety of reasons having to do with the federal charges. There's nothing on it to hurt us." Giannini apparently didn't believe me and dropped the TeleTrac log request.

Assistant U.S. Attorney Stein started making noises about uncharged acts immediately and said he would also try and get my Fresno conviction in, too. The uncharged acts now were the Fresno-Tulare-Bakersfield fires but he may only be successful getting them in, and the fingerprint, but not the fact I was convicted of the blazes. Stein wanted more uncharged acts, as well. He proposed inclusion of over 15 additional, above the eight he charged. The current charges were: March 9, 1989-Pacific Home Improvement-Atascadero-$10 loss; March 9, 1989-Cornet Store-Atascadero-;$20,000; loss March 9, 1989-Coast-to-Coast store-Atascadero-$16 loss; Dec. 10, 1990-People's Dept. Store-L.A.-$1.2 million loss; Dec. 14, 1991-Builder's Emporium-L.A.-$30 loss; Mar. 27, 1991-D&M Yardage-Lawndale-$1 million loss; Mar. 27, .1991-Stat's Floral-Redondo Beach-$0 loss; Mar. 27, 1991-Thrifty Drugs-Redondo Beach-$75,000 loss.

Circumstantial evidence in these eight cases was limited to witness IDs in three, and proximity in a few others. In the three 1989 Atascadero cases I had attended an arson seminar in Monterey, California, 120 miles north of Atascadero and stayed in a Motel 6 in San Luis Obispo, 21 miles south of the fires the night before. I responded to the People's store fire from my home and videotaped the blaze. All three March 27, 1991 fires occurred 25 miles from Glendale while I was on-duty on a weekday. Two more fires on March 27 went down in Inglewood, five miles from Redondo Beach and suspects seen and listed in reports at both locations. The description matched - a team of three females. I was not charged with these fires.

Each of the charged fires could not be prosecuted on its own merits. A typical rule of thumb for case filings, in my unit, was you only take a Deputy D.A. a case if it could stand alone, without inferences or past history. None of the cases charged against me in the L.A. federal court could; not even with an employee pointing a finger to the 6-pack photo and identifying me. Eyewitness IDs were inherently weak. In the March 27, 1991 D&M Yardage fire, an employee, Evelyn Gutierrez, was interviewed minutes after the blaze by an L.A. County Sheriff's Deputy (ironically, a woman I knew), and described only females inside the store and nothing strange going on before the flames were discovered. Two days after the fire, she was interviewed again, by ATF agents and again describes no men and confirms nothing suspicious. Sixty days later, an L.A. County Sheriff's Arson investigator re-contacts Gutierrez, for a final chat before inactivating his case due to lack of leads. Again she says nothing about a male inside the store and nothing unusual happened before the fire. In October 1991, almost seven months after the fire, Gutierrez is again approached by ATF agents and shown the infamous "John-Orr-in-position-#5" 6-pack (2 rows of three pictures, mine top-row-dead-center). The employee not only now describes a man in the store, "acting suspiciously," she somehow manages to point to my photo and adds, "This guy was in the store just before the fire started. He asked me a question, then headed toward the door and veered off into the area where the fire started 15-20 minutes later."

Less than 40 minutes after the D&M store burns, an attempted arson occurs a mile away at Stat's Floral Supply. Only one man enters and leaves this outlet and as he exits he strolls between two check-outs, walking within 5 feet of Ana Bonilla and Ruth Ervin. Less than five minutes later a customer walks up to Ervin holding a folded piece of smoldering yellow-lined paper. (this paper is smaller than the CraftMart paper, measuring only about 8"X5", made for a half-sized notebook). Inside the paper is a cigarette/match device with a rubber band. There are

6-8 matches. The incendiary was found smoking in a bin of Styrofoam flower stands - a not-very-flammable material.

The police and fire departments are called and Ervin and Bonilla interviewed, separately, providing very similar descriptions of the man they saw walk right by them. The suspect was 6' - 6'3", clean shaven, hair combed straight back, possibly half-Filipino, 40-45 years old, and thin. (I was, in March 1991, 42, bushy moustache, 5'9", 200 lbs., wore glasses and my receding hairline pronounced.)

An additional fire takes off 30 minutes after the Stat's attempted arson, at a nearby Thrifty Drug outlet. The Thrifty fire does over $75K damages but fire sprinklers help control the smoky blaze set in patio furniture. No suspect was seen.

The next day, Ervin and Bonilla meet with a police sketch artist and produce two composite drawings. The pictures are nearly identical. Both show the suspect with a full head of hair styled mid-length, close-cropped on the sides, clean shaven, no moustache and a long, narrow nose. I hadn't possessed that much hair on my head since high school.

One drawing depicts a slightly pudgier face but both have the Filipino/Hispanic features. Ervin and Bonilla are both later shown the Orr 6-pack and neither ID's me. My partner is very close in appearance to the composite drawings and a 6-pack with him in it (but not me) is displayed. Ruth Ervin picked out Joe Lopez as the suspect. Fortunately, Joe was skiing, 100 miles away with 15 witnesses at the time of the fire. Still, federal agents obtain and serve a search warrant on Joe. He is exonerated, of course. But they never tell him that fact.

I provide Giannini with requests for documents and ask him to interview several witnesses to provide alibi for me in the March 27, 1991 fires. I repeatedly scan the Barry Pape videotape of the D&M Yardage fire looking for anybody recognizable, or a vehicle. The Stat's employees watched their suspect get into a silver car with Nissan written across the back and I drove a white Ford Crown Victoria. I know I wasn't there but wonder if a similar car appears in the video footage and the prosecutors may use the image in trial. Neither type of vehicle is noted.

It took Giannini many weeks to get me some of the documents I needed. I tell him I can re-build my work days from fire department dispatch center (Verdugo) records, reports, and recordings. Unfortunately, the 24-hour reel-to-reel tape of all fire department phone and radio conversations for March 27, 1991 has been recycled and erased. ATF investigators could have preserved it, or did and didn't give it to us, since I was a suspect just three weeks after the March 27 fires.

I asked Giannini to interview Glendale Fire Department dispatchers Sue Saurer, Lori Fitch, and Susan Marchmann. These three have been fire/police dispatchers almost as long as I've been a firefighter, all know my on/off-duty habits of keeping them advised of my activities and can testify intelligently for us. I was meticulous, almost anal, about keeping the dispatch center updated, particularly when I was on-call. Even when Joe Lopez was on-call and handled emergencies, I was the supervisor of an 11-man unit and called or radioed Verdugo if I was going to be out of the area or had a delayed response. The department implemented a 10-minute response requirement to emergencies for the arson/explosives unit and I made sure we adhered to it or, at least, documented variations affecting the requirement.

On March 27, 1991, Joe was out of town. I was not only on-call/on-duty that day, I was the only available on-call investigator in Glendale when the three South Coast fires occurred between 11 a.m. and noon. I was not able to use shift investigators as daytime stand-bys after late 1990. One of the day arson guys had to be around. I normally wouldn't leave town except to hop over the city-limit line to visit neighboring cities on investigations, to visit Dad or Mom, or sleuth.

If I did have to travel beyond the 10-minute response requirement zone I'd come up on the radio and tell Verdugo, "Investigator 20, out-of-city, delayed response." The reel-to-reel would preserve my status. Upon return or when I reached the 10-minute response zone, I'd say, "Investigator 20, back in the city, available." It was a simple courtesy to keep Verdugo advised. Like the Walt Beatty fiasco of 1989 when a fatal fire occurred while he was the on-call investigator and didn't answer his pager. Both fire and police departments repeatedly tried to find him and couldn't. I didn't want that to ever happen to me or Joe.

I could imagine the Fire Chief calling Verdugo and asking, "Where's Orr...?" and a dispatcher responding, "We don't know. He called in-service at 7 a.m. when he left home and he could be anyplace and we wouldn't know it." That never happened and I think the comm. center people appreciated the fact they always had the answers concerning ability to find an investigator when one was needed.

During my single years in the early-mid 1980s, I simultaneously dated a Glendale and a Pasadena lady friend. My love life was no secret. I couldn't leave my pager on all night without a charger if I slept somewhere other than my home base. I had to let Verdugo know my overnight phone number. If I called after 10 p.m., the dispatcher, no matter who answered, would say, "Hi, John. Who is it tonight? Miss 242 or Miss 795 (the Glendale or Pasadena telephone prefixes)?"

One night I thought I was slick when I ran into an old flame in a Burbank bar. Before leaving the Bombay Bicycle Club to go to her apartment, I found myself without a quarter for the payphone and had no telephone charge card. I dialed 9-1-1, knowing the call funneled into Verdugo without the 25 cents. I needed to let them know I'd be on my pager all night because my battery was freshly charged and I could risk it. I planned to leave Burbank in the early a.m.

The police transferred me to Verdugo. "Fire department, what is your emergency?"

"I'm out of quarters, Lori,"

"Hi, John. What's up? Miss 242 or 795 tonight?"

"I may be..."

"Oh, Sue," she shouted to her partner, "John's back with Miss 848...he's in Burbank!" Another voiced chimed in from the monitoring police dispatch center, a common practice, "Yeah, Lori, he's at the Bombay Bicycle Club. I think her name's Kathleen..."

The 9-1-1 lines provide emergency centers with caller location and the name of the business where the phone call originates. Only blocks from Kathleen's apartment, the girls from Verdugo deduced I reconciled with my old flame. Some of the comm. queens should have been detectives.

I told Giannini at least Sue Saurer was still a friend, if not an advocate, and she would make a credible witness testifying about my habits. My communications habits, anyway. Any comm. center witness could testify I would never leave Glendale and drive 26 miles to Redondo Beach without letting them know I was out-of-town and had a delayed response. Being the only available on-call investigator that day meant I had no back-up and simply did not wander off to the beach. It would be like a fire captain deciding to drive his engine and crew 10 miles out of Glendale to an auto parts store in Van Nuys, hoping they wouldn't catch an emergency call while on the personal errand in another jurisdiction. We had to give the jury something. The prosecutorial assumptions could not lay unchallenged in front of the panel. I cited one more example to Giannini, an anecdote I hoped convinced him that dispatchers are good witnesses. Many times, while on-duty, I'd slip into Sears Glendale and descend into the basement hardware section for a tool or similar purchase. The pager was out-of-range in the depths of the store, beeper activation impossible through tons of concrete and re-bar. The same scenario was true for some parts of the Glendale Galleria Mall and a few dead spots in the city's canyon lands. Along the same lines, if I were at a noisy construction site, bar or riding a motorcycle, I occasionally forgot to swap the pager from audible beep to vibrate alert. In the loud environments I might miss a page and not hear an audible beep. My pager was like a purse to a woman. I constantly touched it, fiddled with the modes and checked its status: audible, vibrate, on, off. My lifeline sat on my hip, next to my other tools: gun, handcuffs and badge.

When emerging from Sears or the other questionable environments and found I was on audible and may have missed a page (as depicted in the *Points of Origin* manuscript, Chapter 2), my habit was to pick up the radio and call Verdugo, "Investigator 20, still on pager..." If I had missed an alert or the dispatcher was looking for me, they now knew I was available. A simple courtesy to the comm. center, but new dispatchers always asked, "How come Orr comes out of the clear blue like that telling us he's available? He's been on the pager all day..." The dispatchers always knew where I was - on the air, available for them, or updated constantly to any change in status.

Giannini, skeptical as always, side-stepped comment. He wanted solid alibi I was in the city limits on March 27, 1991. A toll call to show me in my office or a lunch receipt with my signature on it and a date/time stamp. We had nothing so to present the scenario to the jury we must depend and dispatchers to relate my habits. I told Peter if I had advised Verdugo I was "out of town, delayed response," on March 27, there would be a notation on my Daily Radio Log. I was not shown "out-of-city, delayed response" for that day. A pretty good indication I spent the day on duty. But how do you prove a negative?

After my lengthy explanations to Giannini, he went directly to the comm. center and interviewed the supervisor, Rich Kaufmann, not the dispatchers. Rich kept a good handle on his 3-city comm. center but wasn't as close to me as the day-to-day operators. Giannini ran my potential alibi by Kaufmann who said, "Basically, Orr could be anywhere on his pager. It works in Ventura and Orange County, 40 miles away. He could tell us he's in Sears and be in Santa Monica and we'd never know the difference."

That short interview, playing devil's advocate, convinced Giannini my alibi was useless. Sue, Lori, and Susan never spoke to my lawyer. Years later, all three women were interviewed by my private investigator on another case. All three confirmed the alibi solidly.

In early March 1993 Giannini visited me at MDC, dejected he wasn't "getting any viable alibi." For the 1989 Atascadero fires, my alibi was only verifiable through me or two men I met in a remote corner of the Cuyama Valley east of Santa Maria, California. In this potential hunting area 45 miles southeast of Atascadero, I scouted for wild boar sign and talked to a ranch hand and a federal employee at the time three fires blazed in Atascadero. Four years later, Giannini felt it impossible to find these two men let alone hope they'd recall the encounter. I had to agree and, again, I was limited by funds. A private investigator's search might cost $3-$5,000 and he may never find the men. Giannini wouldn't spend the money and I didn't have it.

One man was a 30-35-year-old, weathered ranch worker driving a light blue or green 70's model Chevy pickup truck with a flat bed instead of a box: There was a large utility box mounted behind the cab. I drove a

357

dark grey Ford Ranger with camper. The other guy was a 40ish, thin-faced man in a light-colored Dodge pickup with government plates. He may have been working for the EPA or other federal regulatory agency since we were near oil drilling facilities. I also poked around an old homestead site and its dump, finding a unique, tiny glass medicine bottle in the debris pile. When I got home I catalogued my artifact and displayed it with my Indian arrowheads, pottery shards, and weathered rifle cartridges from prior trips. The entry I wrote wasn't exact, as to the date, "Cuyama Valley - March 1989", but it should have been enough. Only I could testify to the find, the witnesses or date. Wanda could verify the artifact log entry but Giannini said juries don't tend to believe the wife of a convicted felon.

Wanda testified I had a beard in January 1987 during my 1992 Fresno trial. Apparently the jury chose to believe a casual acquaintance who met me only once rather than one who slept with me. Maybe I should have slept with the prosecution's witness.

After the Fresno trial, news articles and media talking heads no longer described me as "the alleged firebug" or related "fires he allegedly set..." Now it was "the arsonist fire captain" or "the blazes he ignited." As of July 1992, I was a convicted felonious fire setter, not just the accused. Anything said by my wife was now suspect even though we were both innocent.

I was baffled by the Central Coast 1989 series of fires. The man described as the suspect wore a straw cowboy hat. He sounded like a local and a Atascadero citizen was actually stopped and identified by police a few days after the fires. He had no connection to law enforce-ment or the fire service and was somewhat evasive about being in any of the victim locations. He was a handyman and matched four witness descriptions down to the hat. His alibi was a handwritten date book showing he was repairing stairs at a ranch house 10 miles out of town at the time of the fires. We found no reports the alibi was confirmed by a witness at the ranch. I spent over $2000 in 1992 sending a private investigator into the Central Coast area to try and verify the alibi as well as conduct other research. The handyman agreed to meet my PI and allowed photographs to be taken. We, too, could not confirm alibi.

From my evaluation of the Fresno and Central Coast series fires I could not connect the two positively. The similarity of devices, targets, and timing seemed significant. Fires just before the conference in Monterey in 1989, 120 miles north of Atascadero, followed by fires after indicated a conference attendee traveling north, then returning south. A good indication of a firefighter, cop, or insurance representative who was at the symposium IV conference in Monterey. The similar physical descriptions of the cowboy suspect were provided at a fire before the conference, and a day after. Focusing on the Atascadero fires I scanned one important statement by a credible witness at a Coast- to-Coast Hardware store fire who said, "Only 'locals' had been inside the store before the fire. No strangers..." Could it be a local firefighter or cop who was aware of the 1987 Fresno series? A copycat? The Fresno fires were not a huge secret. I had been consulted, Tom Fee of the Pomona Fire Department had, too, as well as at least two insurance private investigators. Without adequate documentation and interviewing this avenue could not be pursued.

Unknown to Giannini and I, the March 9, 1989 Salinas fire, which was included in this series, was probably perpetrated by still another suspect. We never learned of this man, his prior convictions and same m.o., or his arrest in 1989 in a motel just four blocks from the Salinas Woolworth's store fire. Years later I also found a copy of a short news article from a San Luis Obispo newspaper describing two similar fires in retail outlets near the beach at Morro Bay, near Atascadero. The fires occurred in March 1989 but no reports, interviews or other information ever reached the defense. The article was found in piles of the federal prosecutor's documents.

Regardless of my speculation and analyses of the Central Coast fires, Giannini was adamant I couldn't be an expert witness in my own defense.

I repeatedly shouted my innocence to lawyer McCann and Giannini and both ignored the proclamation. It wasn't until years later I figured out their philosophy. Jailhouse lawyers explained to me: A lawyer cannot suborn perjury and allow a client to take the stand and knowingly lie. If the client tells his mouthpiece, "I killed the dude," the defendant cannot then take the stand and, under oath, say, "I didn't kill the dude." The attorney is bound by the Code of Ethics to not let the lie be heard in court. How do attorneys handle this potential conflict? If it may be advantageous to have the client testify then the question of guilt or innocence never comes up, thus leaving the option of testifying open. McCann and Giannini never asked me if I was innocent, I volunteered it. Neither of these men ever expected to let me testify, either. The legal profession seems to be an elaborate game designed to optimize per-hour profit.

With much of the fight taken out of me by arrest and later the wrongful conviction, I hoped getting back in to the battle would strengthen me in 1993. During February and March Giannini didn't visit me often, provided little documentation and performed almost no interviews I was aware of and those he did were of the wrong people.

He occasionally talked to Wanda when he felt guilty about not taking my calls when I knew he was in the office. He placated her, outlining his strategies and case shortcomings, deftly preparing her for his plan. He never intended to go to trial.

I had sources of information in several fire and police agencies who acted as a clearinghouse on the John Orr investigations. This network passed on information about who of my friends and co-workers were being interviewed. Giannini indicated to me he spent time talking to individuals he never spoke with and didn't generate requests for documents needed to conduct my case research. He was a master at placating. He took no time to present pre-trial motions or respond to those pending, or if he did, I never received copies of them. Many years later I reviewed the court docket for 1993 and found no notations of his attempts to block uncharged acts evidence. His standard reply to me was, "The judge will rule against us anyhow." I silently seethed until the anger was replaced with fear and indecision. Do I fire Giannini? His contract said no refunds. Could he do that?

On March 20, 1993 Giannini came to MDC and had me brought to an interview room. As I entered, his somber, downcast look reminded me of the Fresno jury when they entered the courtroom with their verdict. I physically recoiled like he was a shadow that moved in a dark alley. Still, I sat down.

"John, I'm having no luck on any alibi. I've got nothing to work with."

Luck had nothing to do with it. Research, intuition, creative interviewing and aggression gets results. He'd shown none of these traits and its easy for me to flame with anger now, but in 1993 I was beaten down. The thought of another trial and the accompanying publicity was frightening.

"The U.S. Attorney is offering a deal. A very good deal."

"I don't even want to hear it. I'm not guilty. I won't cop to something I didn't do," I replied with all the force I could gather.

Going over my alibis for each case I confirmed Peter had neither interviewed the right witnesses nor examined pieces of physical evidence, not even Wanda. Without testimony I had no alibi for the Atascadero charges.

"John, we need to win all eight counts, not just five. You could get another thirty years if you roll the dice."

Weak as some of the alibi was, testimony of the right witnesses could bolster the proffer and give the jury something to consider. I wouldn't leave Glendale on a duty-day and drive 25 miles to set a string of five fires. No witnesses describe or ID me in the three Atascadero fires. On the contrary, at least five people describe the thin, six-foot guy wearing western-style clothes and a straw cowboy hat in the stores before the fires. No such clothing or hat were found in the searches of my home, office and car. The People's Department Store fire I videotaped showed I started filming at least 30 minutes after the fire ignited, not "in its incipient stages" as the prosecution contended. A half-dozen fire department witnesses, or less, could easily verify this. The People's employee who said I was "in the store a few weeks before the fire and another time" was simply wrong. Sixty years old and not wearing her prescription glasses when she saw the similar-appearing man 30 feet away, the witness wasn't credible, let alone, wrong. The woman did not ID the 6-pack photo of me until eight months after the incident, then only to say, "He's been in the store a few times wearing khaki pants and shirt like a uniform." She did not see the man on the day of the fire so without a definite date/time she did see him I could not seek alibi. Still, People's was a loser case for the prosecution. Giannini didn't see it that way.

Peter countered, "I don't have the money to investigate these leads. I need more money..." He was hired in mid-January and this was mid-March. At this rate he made $30K per month. I called him on it.

"Well, trial would have to be delayed to investigate and I need to take care of my family; your payment gave me flexibility to delay and the trial is expected to last 5-6 weeks..." Smoke and mirrors.

"I have no more money. Wanda cannot make the payments now let alone if she got a second mortgage. My dad is having to subsidize her now as it is..."

"Your dad?"

"No! He's 80-years-old, on a fixed income and can't help any further."

"You could sell instead of re-financing."

I stared directly at him. "We discussed this when I hired you. Wanda owned the house before I came into her life. She was barely able to qualify for the loan but the owner carried back some. She will not lose her house. I'll do ten years for something I didn't do before she'd lose her home." I thought I detected a slight curl around the corners of Gianini's mouth.

"John, the deal's good until Friday afternoon."

My shoulders drooped a bit more as the pressure mounted and Peter continued without my prompting. "Plead to three counts, they recommend no additional jail time, no restitution ($221,000 had already been leveled in the Fresno sentence), and any time you receive runs concurrently with your Fresno sentence."

I still wasn't interested in the deal but asked, "What about the Fresno appeal? What happens if it's reversed? What about the state case? One of the fire's their looking at had fatalities."

"John, I looked at the Fresno transcript and had another lawyer examine it, too. She and I see no reversible errors. Less than 3 percent of all convictions are reversed."

"What about the state charges?"

"From what you told me the Ole's fire was termed accidental. How can they change that finding nine years later, call it an arson and indict you? Tell me?"

"I don't know Peter. You're the lawyer."

"This is the deal of the century. No further jail time, no lengthy trial."

I sighed, took a deep breath and used my last bit of strength to tell him, "No deal. I won't admit to something I didn't do. We'd lose the support of those on our side now. My friends, relatives and co-workers...they'll all disappear."

"I'll come back tomorrow. Think about it." He left and went directly at my weakest link - Wanda. By the time I called her that evening she had caved in. Threatened with the loss of her home and me at risk for another 20-30 years if I went to trial and lost, she urged me to take the deal. We could see the end of ten years before I was eligible for parole, but twenty or thirty? Neither of us could imagine surviving the trauma of another trial. Wanda said it was my decision and we both knew my daughters and family would understand why we took the "deal." Nobody else would, however. The deal required me to stand up in court and, under oath, admit I set three fires. If I revealed I was taking the deal for financial reasons the judge might be offended enough to go beyond the prosecution's recommendations and add time. As it stood, Peter said the judge goes with the recommendations 95 percent of the time.

There were so many ramifications I couldn't even think about the pending state charges. I assumed Peter Giannini knew what he was doing. He'd been a lawyer for years. But the deal was like signing a confession for things I did not do. State prosecutors and investigators drooled in the wings. (I found a copy of the plea bargain in the state files years later. The fax tag line showed it sent from then U.S. Attorney's Office to the state prosecutor and one to the L.A. Fire Department Investigations fax.) Giannini came by the next day like he said, just 24 hours before the deal would be withdrawn. I had no leverage and no strength. My anchor, Wanda and my family, supported the decision. I would lose everyone else in my life. All would believe I took the deal because I was guilty. The real reasons remained a close-kept family secret or the judge could retaliate. With no funds to fight or change lawyers I told Peter we were forced to take the deal. We agreed to plead to the three Atascadero counts. Two had the least amount of damages and he wanted to keep the admissions away from the L.A. area. He was concerned about the possible state case. Peter left a happy man after making the "deal-of-the-century." It was no bargain for me. Three hours later he returned with the seven-page plea agreement and an additional requirement. The U.S. Attorney, no doubt in conjunction with the L.A. County Assistant District Attorney Cabral and lead investigators of the John Orr Task Force Investigation, demanded I plead to one count in the metropolitan Los Angeles area. Peter said it wasn't a major stumbling block. "Take the Builder's Emporium fire in North Hollywood. There was only $40 damage so you have no civil liabilities. One of the Atascadero charges involves $25K damage and they might sue you and Wanda." Unknown to me, and maybe Peter, the same North Hollywood hardware store suffered a small fire on October 13, 1984 - just three days after the Ole's fire. This added the linchpin connecting me to the fatal fire in the prosecutor's eyes. If Giannini received a copy of the 1984 Builder's Emporium fire report during the discovery process he ignored its significance. He did not pass a copy on to me. I would have noted it during my pre-trial investigation. If I had actually been the arsonist they portrayed and set a fire three days after the Ole's fatal at the Builder's Emporium, how stupid would it be for me to now plead guilty to the connecting incident?

I blindly signed the plea arrangement and on May 12, 1993, committed three felonies. Standing in front of Judge Rafeedie, I was sworn in and he read the charges.

The jurist asked me, "Did you set this fire?"

Three times I glanced up at him and said, "Yes." Each time I answered I committed perjury. The courtroom, a friend and ally over the previous 15 years, was now the site of my becoming a felon by admitting, under oath, something I didn't do. A conundrum. A classic Catch-22.

A member of the audience that day, an old friend, said my body language spoke volumes. Each time I said "yes" my head slowly shook side-to-side saying "no." I didn't even realize it. Involuntary body language had always been an investigative tool I used sparingly. Now I swore by it. Judge Rafeedie, a former carnival barker before turning to the law, abided by the U.S. Attorney's recommendations and sentenced me to 98 months on each of the three felonies to run concurrently with the Fresno sentence. With good behavior, I would serve only 6 years and 8 months. I finished that sentence in time to celebrate the new millennium; January 2000. I continue to battle with Judge Rafeedie in 2001, trying to break that plea bargain based on the new evidence of important withheld documents and because the advice of lawyer Peter Giannini nearly killed me in 1998. Many years later I found out the prosecutor did not initiate the plea deal – Giannini went to them. He lied to me again.

CHAPTER TWENTY-THREE
SMOKING GUN

After a short stay at the United States Penitentiary at Lompoc, California in June 1993, I traveled to Terminal Island Correctional Institution to begin my federal sentence and start the appeals process. At seaside in the harbor at San Pedro, Terminal Island prison was designed, in the 1930s, as a military disciplinary barracks for 600 prisoners. With few modifications since World War II, TI housed over 1200 in 1993.

Living in a hallway containing 30 bunk beds, I quickly adjusted to prison life. This was the only option I had. In jail you either fit in and get with the program or die – by your own hand or another's. An ex-cop becomes a fly-on-the-wall and must blend in with the prison population, or constantly fight to prove himself and end up losing the battle anyway, by going to the hole. Like the old west, there is always a young gunslinger wanting to take a shot at the older cowboy. My case notoriety stressed I was a firefighter---I left it at that and was ignored. A former L.A. County Sheriff's Sergeant, imprisoned for stealing drug money, befriended me and acted as a guide. I found a niche, taught evening creative writing classes, and worked in the institution's business offices.

A federal defender from Fresno, John Balazs, was assigned the task of filing my first appeal. He drove down from Fresno and spent three hours with me at Terminal Island. He cited several gross errors in the trial, contrary to Giannini and his associate's evaluation. With renewed hope Wanda and I welcomed John's involvement as he moved forward.

When sentenced by Judge Rafeedie, one order stated "Defendant must undergo psychological intervention to discover and treat motives that precipitated his crimes." After several months without any contact from the shrinks, I provided them with a copy of Rafeedie's order. Dr. Ihle responded back that TI did not have sufficient staff to provide individual evaluation or counseling so she'd gladly enroll me an a drug rehab group session, AA, or anger management seminar and even offered me drugs to control my "compulsions." I thanked her and went back to work teaching my therapeutic creative writing classes and inventorying incoming produce and canned goods for the business office.

Several weeks later Dr. Ihle told me they acquired a new psych intern who needed one-on-one session experience and, under the department head's oversight, administration of a complete psych evaluation. Did I want to be a guinea pig? I agreed, and spent weekly 45-

minute sessions with the intern looking at ink blots, telling stories about pictures I was shown and proclaiming my innocence. It was a cool experience, lasted about six months and the evaluation findings were identical to Dr. Fishkin's analysis and two others I suffered through over the years. I was pretty normal, according to the report, and showed no characteristics of a serial arsonist and was not a threat to society. I guess that satisfied the court's order but I missed my weekly sessions after they ended. It was the only chance I had to talk to normal people.

My depression showed in the psych evaluation findings but that was to be expected in a jail atmosphere. Having a regular schedule, and two jobs, kept me busy and passed the time. I learned more teaching creative writing than the students did. Producing a half-dozen articles and short stories, I started submitting some to magazines and contests. I was pleasantly surprised when two of my tales won awards in the 1993 PEN American Center's Prisoner Writing Contest. A memoir about my two Terminal Island cat buddies won first place and $50 in the contest. "Running Springs," a semi-fictional account of an off-duty cop chasing down two murder suspects in the desert near Death Valley won an honorable mention. I had my $50 prize sent to the Glendale Chapter of the American Red Cross earmarked for earthquake relief after the 1994 Northridge temblor. The Red Cross helped me relocate fire victims many times during my years with the Glendale Fire Department and I thought maybe I could return a little something to the city.

Wanda, my mom and dad, Carrie and Lori, and a few Glendale firefighter friends visited me while I was at TI. The TI Visiting Room was like a seaside restaurant. Large plate glass windows overlooked the harbor with the ocean only 10 feet from the openings, albeit through two 8-foot-tall, razor-topped fences.

Joe Lopez and I talked periodically. He said co-workers at the Glendale Fire Department were constantly interviewed by the L.A.D.A.'s Task Force conducting an on-going investigation of me, my old cases and even chatting with suspects I'd arrested for arson. Information about what cases were examined was sketchy but Wanda and I feared the worst, hoped for the best.

The Fresno appeal moved rather quickly. John Balazs was a jewel. He always took my calls, talked to Wanda periodically, and answered every letter I wrote. In May 1994 John submitted his final brief after the Fresno prosecutor, Patrick Hanly, forwarded his reply. Hanly, in typical prosecutorial fashion, violated appeal rules. An appeal is supposed to deal solely with what is "on the record"; information directly from the trial transcript—nothing outside the record. In a short footnote Hanly slipped in the fact I accepted a plea bargain in the cases from Atascadero, the "uncharged acts." The violation had already been sent to the Ninth

Circuit Court of Appeals and Balazs could not stop it from being seen. Our strongest argument to reverse my case was the inclusion of uncharged acts at the Fresno trial. Now the prosecution seriously weakened our efforts by a clear-cut violation we could do nothing about.

Within weeks of John's final brief submission, the appeals court invited him to orally argue the case on July 11, 1994. Only a small percentage of cases are heard orally. Our hopes soared.

In a letter to me dated July 12, 1994, John excitedly described how the oral arguments went. Allowing only 20 minutes for each side, John was helped along when one justice interrupted his "destruction of the cigarette butt" claim and said, "Isn't your Atascadero claim really your best claim?"

Taking the hint, Balazs brought it home. In his letter he wrote, "The judges indicated that they agreed with our argument that it was wrong for the government to use evidence of the Atascadero fire to prove the five charged arsons, while at the same time using evidence of the charged fires to meet its burden of showing you committed the Atascadero arson." The letter continued, "Other good news is that the panel did not seem to believe the error could be considered harmless... my impression was that they acknowledged that the case was close and that a significant trial error would not be harmless."

Balazs then wrote about the bad news: "Judge Rymer pointed out that after the Fresno convictions you pleaded guilty in L.A.---one was an Atascadero fire. Rymer indicated whether it might be fruitless to reverse the conviction for a new trial when on re-trial the government could use the guilty plea to establish you, in fact, committed the uncharged act fire." Balazs responded that the Atascadero guilty plea was not on the record and should not be considered. He wrote, "I also brought up the fact that you pleaded guilty with the government's recommendation that you would get only concurrent time. I could only argue that you pleaded guilty because of the no-time deal, even though you are innocent. But I, at least, gave that impression to the judges.

"Rymer acknowledged my arguments. She seemed to agree that technically I was right. But in practice it was a wasteful exercise. It would give you two chances with the very same evidence. She seemed unsure.

"Pat Hanly did a typical Hanly argument. Rather than address the one issue that the court was obviously concerned with, he argued other issues in making a quasi-personal attack on me. He attempted to insinuate that I argued outside the record, ignoring the fact he went much further in his. He conceded the prosecution presented insufficient evidence to show you committed the Atascadero fire." Both Balazs and I realized the plea bargain seriously wounded my chances for a reversal of the Fresno case. Giannini's "evaluation" and consultant did not consider the ramifications of the "deal."

Six weeks later the appeals court ruled and affirmed the conviction, not citing the plea bargain as the reason to not give me a new trial, but allowing the uncharged acts was "harmless error." Wanda and I were devastated again. Picking up the pieces, we busied ourselves and tried to get back to the routines we had earlier in 1994. Lori married and Carrie moved to Tennessee with her new husband. I missed another milestone, but Wanda became my presence at family functions and on holidays.

On November 30, 1994, I listened to my radio through headphones to block the din of inmates returning from work at 3:30 p.m. An advertising teaser for the 5 o'clock channel 7 news came on the air, "Fire Captain charged with murder." I physically held my breath hoping for more information like, "Fire captain kills wife in Beverly Hills love triangle," but no information was available on the radio. Nearing 4 p.m. lockdown I couldn't get near a telephone and couldn't call Wanda anyway; she was still at work. After count time I avoided the TV rooms but word soon spread. The fire captain was me. With murder charges filed by the state, and me at a medium security prison, I was quickly taken to the hole. My security and custody level shot up demanding a transfer to a high level penitentiary—back to Lompoc.

I had no lawyer, no money to retain one, and the L.A.D.A. didn't even have the courtesy to serve me with papers regarding the pending charges. In limbo, I couldn't even contact Wanda to prepare her or draw on her help---the phone availability in the hole was a first-come, first served basis and I just arrived. For hours I agonized over how Wanda would find out about the new charges and how she'd react. I pictured The Final Exit, still sitting on the coffee table. Shortly before 9 p.m. a corrections officer dropped by my cell to advise I had an attorney visit at 8 a.m. Attorney? I didn't have an attorney. Maybe the state appointed one already. I expected the L.A. County Sheriff to come down TI to arrest and interrogate me. I had no idea how these things worked and imagined Wanda laying in bed with the covers over her head. The officer asked if I wanted to use the phone before lights out and I finally dialed home. Wanda answered quickly, blurting out Peter Giannini had met with her after work and broke the news. He stayed with her for over an hour and explained what would happen next. His presence saved her from learning about the murder charges from the news or having a friend call. Strangely, I was grateful for Giannini's concern. Bitter about the whole plea bargain fiasco I didn't think I'd ever speak to the man again and now Wanda said he arranged to come to TI and explain everything to me. Desperate for information I actually looked forward to his visit. I neglected to ask Wanda if Giannini stepped off the square footage of her home or asked to see the foundation. Giannini and I were allowed an hour to go over the brief information provided to him by Michael Cabral, the L.A.D.A prosecutor. He gave Gianini a courtesy call before the media was advised even though he wasn't yet my lawyer. Peter understood I couldn't pay him and he said appointment by the state was a strong possibility. I gave our past history no thought, glad to have someone on board who was already familiar with the case. The list was actually good news/bad news. There were an assortment of brush fires but the murder/arson counts were in regards to the Ole's hardware store fire. I could see no way the Ole's fire could be changed from accidentally caused in 1984 to arson, 10 years later. Plus, I was seven miles away from the blaze, meeting with Pasadena Fire Investigator Scott McClure moments before or as the fire erupted.

McClure's name was even in the paperwork, referred to as the "Prosecutor's Summary." The notation read, "Orr had just left a meeting with PFD investigator McClure." How, could they now turn this case into a murder? I told Peter we were in good shape. First, I'm innocent, and two, McClure's pretty credible. I was baffled by the studio fire charge, too. We knew TeleTrac was on my car at the time of that fire and exoneration clear. I was 4 miles away when the fire started. The two small fires on November 23 occurred after I drove within 1/2 mile of the area of one blaze and nowhere near the other until I was dispatched to it. I had no alibi for the 10/2/91, Kennington Street fire. I videotaped the burning home but the Summary also noted I had before footage of the structure, too, indicating I "knew" it was going to burn. Almost true...I videotaped the entire Kennington neighborhood over 18 months before the fire, along with 4-5 other areas as target hazards for a brush clearance enforcement program I was putting together for a city manager's meeting. The College Hills fire charges infuriated me as much as the rest. I was over four miles away for an hour and a half before it ignited yet the Summary said I "lied" about where I was and a witness put me at the point of origin within minutes after the 300 acre blaze started. Ludicrous. I wasn't in the area until at least an hour after it started because I was fighting fire. I felt better after Peter left, knowing we had a fighting chance this time if I could only convince him to take on the battle. I knew I would not take a deal this time—no way.

Below is the actual document (verbatim):

PROSECUTION SUMMARY

On December 4, 1991, Glendale Fire Captain John Leonard Orr was arrested by federal agents from the Department of Treasury, Bureau of Alcohol, Tobacco and Firearms, and charged with multiple violations of 18 U.S.C. § 844(1) (arson of a structure or property used or affecting interstate commerce) based on fires set throughout the State of California. The indictments charging John Orr involved the following facts:

1.) The January 15, 1987, arson fire at Hancock Fabrics, 5179 North Blackstone, Fresno, California. This fire originated in the Styrofoam and foam rubber displays at the location and was set by the use of a time delay incendiary device. The fire was set while the location was open for business. The loss was estimated to be in excess of $500,000.

2.) The January 30, 1987, attempted arson at the House of Fabrics, 5265 North Blackstone, Fresno, California. Although it was unknown when the device was placed at the location, a time delay incendiary device was recovered from the foam rubber display at the location.

3.) The January 16, 1987, arson fire at Family Bargain Center, 1167 North Cherry, Tulare, California. This fire originated in a display of pillows at the location. The subsequent cause, and origin investigation resulted in the recovery of an incendiary time delay device. This fire was set while the location was open for business and resulted in only nominal damage to the pillow display.

4.) The January 16, 1987, arson fire at Craft Mart, 3761 Ming Avenue, Bakersfield, California. This fire originated in a dried floral display at the location and was set by the use of an incendiary time delay device which was recovered from the location. The fire was set while the location was open for business and resulted in a nominal loss at the location. A latent fingerprint was recovered from one of the components of the device, a piece of yellow lined paper. This latent print was later matched to the prints of John Orr.

5.) The January 16; 1987, arson fire at Hancock Fabrics, 26015 "H" Street, Bakersfield, California. The fire originated in the foam rubber display at the location, and was set by an incendiary time delay device. The fire occurred while the business was open for business and resulted in a loss in excess of $200,000.

6.) The March 9, 1989, attempted arson at Pacific Home Improvement, 9370 El Camino Real, Atascadero, California. This attempted arson occurred in the rolled foam padding display at the location and the remains of the device were recovered. The attempt occurred while the location was open for business and resulted in no loss to the location.

7.) The March 9, 1989, arson fire at Cornet Department Store, 7101 El Camino Real, Atascadero, California. The fire originated in the foam padding display at the location and was started by the use of an incendiary time delay device. This fire originated while the location was open for business and resulted in a loss in excess of $25,000.

8.) The March 9, 1989, arson fire at Coast to Coast Hardware, 5805 El Camino Real, Atascadero, California. This fire originated in the rolled plastic sheets and toilet seat displays at the location and was caused by an open flame being applied to available combustible materials. The fire originated while the location was open for business and resulted in a nominal loss to the location.

9.) The December 10, 1991, arson fire at People's Department Store, 5817 North Figueroa Street, Los Angeles, California. The fire originated in a curtain display at the location and resulted in a loss in excess of $1,000,000. This fire originated while the location was open for business and was set by the application of an open flame to the available combustible materials.

10.) The December 14, 1991, arson fire at Builder's Emporium, 6601 North Laurel Canyon Boulevard, Los Angeles, California. The fire originated in a display of throw pillows at the location and was started by the use of an incendiary time delay device which was recovered at the location. This fire originated while the location was open for business and resulted in a only a minimal loss to the location.

11.) The March 27, 1991, arson fire at D & M Yardage, 16510 Hawthorne Boulevard, Lawndale, California. This fire originated in a display of hanging drapes and was caused by the application of an open flame to the available combustible materials. The fire originated while the location was open for business and resulted in a $1,000,000 loss to the location.

12.) The March 27, 1991, attempted arson at Stats Floral, 2021 Artesia Boulevard, Redondo Beach, California. An incendiary time delay device was discovered while it was still smoldering. The device had been placed in a display of Styrofoam at the location and was recovered by an employee of the location. This attempted arson occurred while the location was open for business and resulted in no loss to the location.

13.) The March 27, 1991, arson fire at Thrifty Drug Store, 1720 Aviation Boulevard, Redondo Beach, California. This fire originated in a display of patio furniture cushions and was caused by the application of an open flame to the available combustible materials. The fire originated while the location was open for business and resulted in a loss of $100,000.

Subsequent to his arrest and indictment, John Orr was convicted by a jury in 3 out of 5 counts charged in the San Joaquin area. Seven months after conviction in the Eastern District of California federal court John Orr pleaded guilty to three counts of arson in the Central District of California federal court. These fires were related to the retail store arsons occurring on March 9, 1989 in Atascadero, California and an attempted arson on December 14, 1990 at a Builder's Emporium in North Hollywood, California.

After John Orr was sentenced in the Central District case the L.A. D.A.'s Office formed a Task Force of investigators from the L.A.

Sheriff's Office, BATF, L.A. Fire Department, and Burbank Police and Fire Departments. Thousands of man-hours were spent evaluating the personal and professional life of John Orr to determine his relationship to fires in his own city of Glendale, neighboring Burbank and Pasadena, as well as throughout Los Angeles County. Hundreds of interviews and examination of over 85,000 pages of documents resulted in the Task Force's determination of proof John Orr was involved in setting hundreds of fires. Twenty-five felony counts have been charged against the defendant, including four counts of capital murder.

NARRATIVE OF OFFENSES

COUNTS 1. 2, 3, 4, PENAL CODE SECTION 187(a)/190.2(a)(3)
OLE'S HOME CENTER 452 FAIR OAKS AVENUE SOUTH PASADENA
OCTOBER 10, 1984

On October 10, 1984, at approximately 8:04 p.m., a major structure fire occurred at the Ole's Home Center located at 452 South Fair Oaks Avenue in the City of South Pasadena, At the time of the fire the store was open for business and had numerous customers on the premises. The fire resulted in the death of two employees of the location Carolyn Kraus, age 26, and Jimmy Celina, age 17. In addition, the fire caused the death of two customers who were in the location at the time of the fire, Ada Deal, age 50, and Matthew Troidl, age 2. The fire also result in losses in excess of $1,000,000 to the structure and contents of the location.

Fire companies from the City of South Pasadena were initially called to respond to the fire and the initial fire captain requested additional assistance from the fire personnel of Pasadena, Alhambra, Sierra Madre, Glendale, San Marino, Monterey Park, Arcadia, Monrovia, San Gabriel and the City and County of Los Angeles. These fire companies were also assisted by the personnel of Pasadena and South Pasadena Police Departments.

The building involved in the fire was initially designed and built to accommodate two separate occupancies. The east side of the structure was initially occupied by the Von's Grocery Company, and was equipped with an internal fire sprinkler system. The west side of the location was previously occupied by a Thrifty Drug store and was not equipped with a fire sprinkler system. When the premises were remodeled to provide for the new occupancy, two door openings were cut into the existing common wall between the two locations in order to create one large Ole's Home Center within the area that was formerly the two occupancies. Instead of installing sprinklers in the west portion of the occupancy the Ole's Home Center, with the City of South Pasadena's approval, installed a automatic steel roll down fire door across each of the new openings cut into the concrete wall between the two occupancies. The fire doors were designed with fusible links which would melt when the temperature in the location reached 160 degrees. When the fusible link melted the fire doors would come down and prevent the spread of any fire from one portion of the premises to the other.

When the fire occurred on October 10, 1984, the fire doors worked as they were designed to work, and rolled down upon the melting of the fusible link. Unfortunately, the closure of the fire doors and the speed of the fire travel resulted in the four victims being trapped in the location and unable to find their way to one of the other emergency exits prior to being overcome by the toxic smoke within the location. Based on the magnitude of the fire, and the four fatalities, the City of South Pasadena requested the assistance of the Los Angeles County Sheriff's Department in conducting the initial scene investigation. Sergeant Jack Palmer of the LASD arson explosives unit was assigned primary scene investigation and was responsible for determining the cause and origin of this fire. Sergeant Palmer arrived on scene on October 11, 1984, at approximately 6:00 a.m. At approximately 11:00 a.m. on October 11, 1984, Sgt. Palmer formed the conclusion that he was unable to determine the cause and origin of the fire. Sgt. Palmer based his conclusion on his inability to eliminate all accidental causes. Based on the information available to him, on the morning after the fire, Sgt. Palmer concluded that he could not eliminate a possible electrical malfunction in the attic area of the location. Once Sgt. Palmer reached this conclusion the investigation at the location was terminated and the possible criminal investigation was closed.

The Task Force review of the investigation conducted by Sgt. Palmer on October 11, 1984, revealed that during the course of his investigation he had conducted interviews with only two witnesses who were at the location at the time of the fire. In addition, it was determined that he had given no consideration to the fact that there was a arson fire a short distance away from this location, both before and after the fire at the Ole's. Finally, it was determined that Sgt. Palmer was unaware that John Orr was at the scene of this fire at, or shortly after, the time of arrival of the first arriving fire company, Based on the absence of consideration of these factors the District Attorney's Arson Task Force attempted to interview all available witnesses from the Ole's Home Center fire.

The interviews of the employees present at the scene on the night of the fire revealed that the fire was first seen by two employees of the location, James Obdam and Marc Lewis. Both of these individuals informed the Task Force that they saw the fire within seconds of first hearing the fire alarm sound; that the fire was only a couple of feet tall when they first observed it; and, that the fire was on the floor or bottom shelf of a rack located near the polyfoam stacks in the house wares section of the store. The various employees who were located in the west end of the structure informed the Task Force that within minutes after the alarm sounded the fire had traveled up the south wall, jumped across the aisle, and began spreading rapidly down the south wall and across the top of the merchandise racks in a northwesterly direction. Employee James Cuellar informed the Task Force that he was lucky to get out of the location without injury even though he was only 30 feet from the southwestern fire door and the starting point of the fire was the entire length of the store away from his location. In addition, employee James Obdam informed the Task Force that he suffered serious burn injuries as he attempted to exit out of the northwest fire door only minutes after the fire alarm sounded. All the employees at the location stated that it was only a couple of minutes between the first sound of the fire alarm and the closure of the fire doors between the two portions of the business. Furthermore, the Task Force examined the building plans and blueprints to determine the building construction impact on the fire. The building blueprints reflected that the building's attic space contained fire safety devices called draft stops. Draft stops are placed in the large attic space of any structure to avoid the extension of a fire across the entire ceiling/roof line prior to detection. The draft stops work to contain any outbreak of fire to a smaller area of the attic and thus allow a fire to be discovered prior to consuming the entire roof area which would then collapse on the occupancy below. The existence of the draft stops in the portion of the Ole's Home Center destroyed by the fire would have acted to prevent the type of fire that Sgt. Palmer felt he could not eliminate during his cause and origin determination. In addition, the building plans revealed that the roof of the western portion of the Ole's Home Center was equipped with roof vents. The existence of roof vents within each of the areas covered by a draft stop would have allowed the smoke from any fire to escape through the vent. Yet, even with the vents, there was not a single witness who observed smoke showing from the roof of the location prior to the fires discovery by the smoke detectors located on the ceiling of the premises.

Once the Task Force had completed its review of the blueprints and the witness statements this information was presented, independently, to two fire protection experts of the Los Angeles Fire Department. Each of these individuals independently reached the conclusion that the fire was inconsistent with an electrical fire and could not have been the result of a slow smoldering electrical fire in the attic that then erupted into the occupancy below.

The Task Force also interviewed Frank Holmes who was the electrical contractor on the remodeling of the west portion of the structure.

Mr. Holmes informed the Task Force that during the remodeling work no electrical wiring was installed in the attic area of the location and that all the electrical work done at the location was done in the southwest corner of the location. Mr. Holmes stated that while the plans called for the running of electrical wiring to the exit sign above the southeastern fire door that such work was not done because he installed special radioactive exit signs that did not require electrical power to operate.

Finally, the Task Force examined John Orr's role at the location and the fire's similarities to the fires that John Orr was convicted. This fire bears striking similarities to the fires John Orr was convicted of, as well as numerous other fires throughout Los Angeles County.

1) The location was a home improvement/hardware/house wares store that was open for business at the time of the fire;

2) The Ole's chain of stores was in the process of being sold to the owners of the Builder's Emporium;

3) John Orr was not on duty at the time of the fire yet he is seen at the location within ten minutes of the first alarm. Captain Eisele of the South Pasadena Fire Department observes Orr taking pictures of the fire as he attempts to locate his support units from the San Marino Fire Department. When Captain Eisele asks Orr what he is doing at the location Orr tells him that he just happened to be in the area and asked if it was o.k. for him to take some pictures;

4) John Orr had just left the location of an arson fire in the City of Pasadena that was attributable to a Potato Chip Pyro that had been striking throughout Los Angeles County;

5) Moments after the Ole's fire was discovered a fire was discovered at the Von's Grocery store one mile away;

6) The Von's grocery store fire was investigated by John Orr and attributed to the Potato Chip Pyro;

7) On October 11, 1984 John Orr called Investigator Dennis Foote of the Los Angeles Fire Department and requested that he come to Ole's and bring his entire file on the potato chip fires;

8) The investigative file that Investigator Foote gave to John Orr has not been seen since John Orr took possession of it;

9) John Orr was the only investigator who was adamant that the Ole's fire was an arson and that it started in the poly-foam;

10) John Orr has told several individuals since the Ole's fire that "we" know who set the Ole's fire but we just can't prove it.

11) John Orr has never shared the information as to who set the Ole's fire and why he reached that determination with any other known investigator;

12) John Orr failed to go back to Glendale to investigate an arson fire within the city because he wanted to remain at the Ole's fire;

13) Even though John Orr was required to inform his Battalion Chief that he would remain in South Pasadena to examine their fire he never obtained such approval;

14) The Glendale Battalion Chief was never made aware of the fact that John Orr was on scene at the Ole's fire;

15) Subsequent to the fire, John Orr wrote a novel, which he himself described as fact based. In this novel Orr describes in great detail a fire strikingly similar to the Ole's Home Center Fire. The similarities cover all aspects of the fire including the number of deaths and the fact that the fire is determined to be accidental. The fire in the novel is set using a device that is identical to the device John Orr used in the fires of which he was convicted in the federal proceedings. Finally, the arsonists in the novel, much like Orr in the Ole's case, becomes infuriated when the investigators determine the fire to be accidental

16) In the novel Orr writes about how the arsonist sets another fire in the same type of store approximately six weeks later in order to make it clear to the Ole's investigator that the first fire was not an accident.

17) On or about, January 31, 1985, the John Orr signature device was found partially burned in a stack of poly-foam in the Ole's Home Center located at 3425 Colorado Boulevard in Pasadena. Just as the arsonist in the Orr novel said was necessary to prove the first fire was an arson.

COUNT 5 PENAL CODE SECTION 451(b)
Kennington Fire
2740 Kennington Drive Glendale, California October 2, 1991

On October 2, 1991 a fire destroyed the house located at 2740 Kennington Drive in the City of Glendale. The fire started at the bottom of the hill and burned up to the house that it ultimately destroyed. At the time of the fire John Orr was assigned to conduct the investigation into the fire. During his time at the scene John Orr was informed that a witness was available who had seen a white full-size car in the vicinity of the location just prior to the fire. When John Orr was informed of this he refused to interview the witness at that time and never conducted an interview with the witness. This very general description matched the car being driven by John Orr. The witness ultimately left the scene before being interviewed by any investigator. Subsequently, John Orr conducted a momentary and cursory examination of the potential area of origin and conclude his investigation.

The Task Force investigation has revealed that John Orr prepared a photo spread of the location which contained pictures of the location both before and after the fire. That while the victims of the fire made several attempts to contact Orr for information on the fire that he failed to contact them concerning the fire. Finally, when the Bureau of Alcohol,

Tobacco and Firearms served search warrants on Orr's residence and office they seized a videotape, prepared by John Orr. This videotape, of the location, was taken from across the canyon while the fire was in its incipient stage. In addition, the video further shows John Orr sitting in his car and videotaping the arrival of the first in fire companies to the fire scene. During this videotape John Orr makes no effort to advise the Verdugo Dispatch of the fire location and condition but merely shows him observing the fire and the arrival of the fire companies.

COUNT 6 PENAL CODE SECTION 451(c)

WARNER BROS. STUDIOS FIRE 4000 Warner Boulevard
Burbank, California
November 22, 1991

On November 22, 1991 a major emergency structure fire destroyed the "Walton" set located on Warner Bros. Studio in Burbank. The investigator on the case was Captain Steve Patterson of the Burbank Fire Department. During the course of his investigation Captain Patterson requested the assistance of John Orr. During his initial conversation with Orr, Captain Patterson was informed that John Orr would come to the scene if he was given directions. After giving Orr directions Captain Patterson was requested to wait in the street outside the studio so that he could direct John Orr to the appropriate location within the studio's back lot. Captain Patterson waited at the appointed location for approximately 15 minutes without the arrival of John Orr, and then returned to the fire location. Upon Captain Patterson's return to the fire location he discovered that Orr was already at the location even though he had said he would not be able to find the location without Captain Patterson's guidance. Captain Patterson ultimately determined this fire to be an arson. Subsequent investigation has revealed that John Orr was identified entering the studio in the area of the Walton set on the day of the fire, that John Orr admitted going to the area of the fire after observing the smoke (to take pictures of the fire), but claimed that he did not observe the fire due to the height of the berm surrounding the studio lot. A review of the Teletrac tracking device that was attached to John Orr's car during this period of time revealed that John Orr's car was parked in the parking lot next to the Walton Set on the day before the fire.

COUNTS 7, 8, 9 PENAL CODE SECTION 451(c)

Hilldale Fire
2000 Hilldale Drive
La Canada, California November 23, 1991
San Augustine Fire
3860 San Augustine Drive Glendale, California
November 23, 1991
Oceanview Fire

210 Freeway and Oceanview Drive Glendale, California
November 23, 1991

On November 23, 1991 three brush fires struck the northeast corner of Glendale within minutes of each other. Within twenty minutes of the first alarm for the fire at 2000 Hilldale, John Orr is observed at the intersection of the 210 Freeway and Oceanview Drive. This location is approximately 5 minutes from each of the locations where the fires occurred.

The Task Force investigation revealed that as the Verdugo Dispatch is dispatching the first fire companies, John Orr self dispatches from his residence at 5222 Sumner in Eagle Rock. John Orr is then seen driving southbound on Figueroa Street to the fire sight behind 3860 San Augustine. Without stopping to conduct any investigation he turns around and heads northbound on Figueroa Street where he eventually meets engine company 29 which he then follows code three to the vicinity of the fire at 2000 Hilldale. When he arrives at the vicinity of the Hilldale fire he begins directing traffic at the intersection of Hilldale Drive and Florencita Avenue and at no time does he conduct an investigation into these fires or contact the investigator responsible for the fire investigation.

COUNTS 10-26 PENAL CODE SECTION 451(b)
COLLEGE HILLS FIRE
1000 Verdugo Road Glendale, California June 27, 1990

On June 27, 1990, an arson fire struck the hillside located at 1000 North Verdugo Road. The fire burned up to the top of the hill and eventually resulted in damage to 66 homes in the area of Glendale known as College Hills. The fire originated at a location on North Verdugo Road where fires had occurred almost on a yearly basis for several years prior to the fire. As the senior investigator in the City of Glendale it was John Orr's responsibility to conduct the investigation into this fire.

When the Task Force began the investigation into this fire it was determined that John Orr had not requested that a D.R. number be issued from the police department. Without such a D.R. number no investigative reports could be issued and tracked concerning the fire. As the Task Force investigation into this fire continued it was determined that no investigative reports were ever written concerning the largest fire in the City of Glendale history.

Although there were no Glendale investigative reports located, the task Force did locate several documents relative to the fire. These documents included an Interdepartmental Communication written by John Orr, an overall review of the fire and police departments response to the fire, and a report written by the investigator from the State Fire Marshall's Office. In addition, the members of the Task Force conducted interviews with the majority of the City of Glendale personnel who participated in the fire suppression activities. Based on the review of all known data and the witness interviews the following facts were ascertained:

1) According to John Orr he was in the vicinity of Whiting Woods Road when the initial dispatch for the fire occurred. That he immediately drove to the 1200 block of Sweetbriar to assist Glendale Engine Company 29 in fire suppression activities, rather than conducting any investigative work. That he continued to assist the fire department with various activities until approximately 6:30 p.m. when he then conducted an approximately one-half hour cause and origin investigation;

2) Although John Orr told the press, Battalion Chief Chris Grey, and Investigator Moses Gomez of the State Fire Marshall's Office, that he located a device involving a lighter, held open with a pen, at the area of origin, he later recanted that statement and has never shown anyone a device that was used to ignite this fire;

3) Investigator Moses Gomez stated that he arrived at the fire scene at approximately 6:00 p.m. on June 27, 1990 and that when he met John Orr he was just undressing after conducting his cause and origin investigation;

4) Investigator Gomez stated that John Orr told him that the fire started approximately 10 to 15 feet up the hillside off North Verdugo Road in an area that would create a chimney effect. That while John Orr told him he found a cigarette lighter in the open position he never showed him the device. That after his arrival at the scene he and John Orr conducted two interviews of potential witnesses, examined one vehicle in the area of origin (that was later eliminated), conducted a surveillance on a house waiting for an unknown car to arrive (the vehicle never arrived) and ran some information on the police computer attempting to locate some vehicles;

5) Investigator Gomez stated that several offers of assistance to John Orr, from the State Fire Marshall's Office, are declined and the defendant ultimately tells him that he is no longer certain of the cause of the fire.

6) In addition, an examination of the records of the Glendale Fire Department further reveals that there is no record of any previous code violations on Whiting Wood Road which would have warranted the defendant being at the location and conducting a re-inspection a code violation. Furthermore, based on an examination of the times of dispatches, and distance of travel, it is impossible for the defendant to have been in the vicinity of Whiting Woods Road and still arrive at the fire scene at the same time as the first arriving fire companies.

7) Subsequent to the arrest of the defendant, Retired Major Richard Jiminick of the United States Air Force informs federal agents that on June 27, 1990, he observed the defendant standing in the vicinity of the area of origin before the first arriving fire companies were on scene. During the course of his statement, Retired Major Jiminick also describes the clothing that the defendant was wearing and such description generally matches the clothing that the defendant is wearing on the day of the College Hills fire.

8) Finally, a review of the course and scope of the investigation conducted by the defendant reveals substantial irregularities. On June 28, 1991, Glendale Fire Investigator Walt Beatty returns from a training seminar in Fresno to assist in the City's investigative efforts. Upon his arrival in Glendale he speaks with the defendant and discusses various investigative techniques that should be employed. During this discussion the defendant informs Investigator Beatty that a thorough canvassing of the residents of the area of origin has been done by members of the police department. Later, Investigator Beatty learns the there was no request for a canvass of the neighborhood and that therefore no canvassing was done. Subsequently, Investigator Beatty complains to the defendant about the defendant's failure to support the investigative follow-up, and that the defendant is in fact impeding the investigation. The defendant tells Investigator Beatty that Battalion Chief Chris Grey has him doing too many other activities to assist in the investigation, and that if Investigator Beatty has a complaint he should direct it to the Battalion Chief. However, when Investigator Beatty complains to the Chief about him preventing the defendant from assisting in the College Hills investigation he is removed from the arson unit and a subsequent interview with the Chief reveals that Investigator Beatty removal from the arson unit is based on the defendant's previous reports to the Chief that Investigator Beatty complains constantly and needs to be replaced. Therefore, when Investigator Beatty begins to complain to the Chief, the Chief determines that the defendant's complaints are valid and Investigator Beatty's removal occurs. The Chief feels that the defendant's reports concerning Investigator Beatty's chronic complaining is accurate since the defendants only responsibility at this time is the investigation of the College Hills fire. After Investigator Beatty's removal from the arson unit, the investigation into the College Hills fire terminates and the majority of the information Investigator Beatty generates is thrown away.

While the novel written by John Orr does not deal directly with the College Hills fire it does deal with a large number of fires that actually occurred. In examining these fires the Task Force discovered that some involved the Fresno and Bakersfield fires charged in the indictment in the Eastern District. In addition, the novel involved a series of fires in the

Glendale and Burbank areas during 1985. During the course of examining the items seized from the residence of John Orr the Task Force examined a scrapbook belonging to John Orr that contained numerous newspaper clippings from 1985. An examination of these clippings revealed that John Orr had informed the reporters that the same person who was responsible for these fires was also responsible for the yearly fires that occurred in the vicinity of 1000 North Verdugo Road in the City of Glendale. Yet, in interviewing the various personnel of the Glendale Fire Department the Task Force was unable to locate anyone who John Orr had informed of these serial fires and their connection to the consistent burning of the College Hills area of Glendale.

OTHER UNCHARGED CRIMES: On February 4, 1984 at approximately 4:05 p.m., an arson fire occurs at the Howie's Ranch Market in San Gabriel, California. While no witnesses observe a suspect in the location, a device is recovered from the potato chip rack at the location. An examination of the device reveals that it is a cigarette with 3 matches attached to it by a rubber band. On January 31, 1985, an employee at the Ole's Home Center in Pasadena, California recovers an incendiary device. The employee finds the device in a stack of foam padding at the location. The device is found to contain a cigarette with at least two matches attached to it by a rubber band. While the employee found the device on January 31, 1987 it is unknown when the arsonist left the device at the location.

On February 8, 1988, an attempted arson fire occurs at a real estate office on West Olive in Burbank, California. The device is found after someone places an incendiary time delay device inside the mail slot of the location. The device found consists of a sheet of yellow lined paper with cigarette, rubber band and three matches contained Inside the paper. A fire strikingly similar to this one occurs in the novel by the defendant. Although this location, unlike the one in the novel, is not completely destroyed by the fire.

On October 9, 1991, at approximately 1:30 p.m., an arson fire occurs in the brush at the intersection of Lowell and the 210 freeway in Glendale, California. While several firefighters and police officers spend several minutes trying to locate the cause of the fire they are unable to locate any device. However, immediately upon the defendants arrival he points to an area in the middle of the field, walks to the area, moves a stick and picks up a rock with at three matches attached to it by a rubber band. This type of device is one of the types of devices used by the arsonist in the defendants novel. In addition, on the day of his arrest federal agents seize and search the defendant's briefcase and find rocks, rubber bands, matches and cigarettes and other components used In the preparation of incendiary time-delay devices. On October 30, 1991, at approximately 4:06 p.m., an arson brush fire occurs in the vicinity of the intersection of York Boulevard and the 2 freeway. Although investigators do not recover a device, the defendant's vehicle is in the vicinity of the area of origin within minutes of the time the fire occurs. During this period of time the defendant's vehicle is equipped with a Teletrac monitoring device and his movements are monitored by investigators. On this day the defendant only left his office on one occasion and his vehicle goes to the vicinity of the #2 freeway and York Boulevard only minutes before the fire occurs.

On December 13, 1990, at approximately 3:41 p.m., an arson fire occurs at Mort's Surplus Store In Burbank, California. The fire originates in a stack of cardboard boxes at the location. Although no device is found at the location, employees of the location observe the defendant at the location before the first fire companies arrive on scene. In addition, the defendant videotapes the arrival of the first arriving fire companies and the suppression activities but fails to inform the fire investigator, assist, or offer assistance during the early stages of the investigative activities. Since the charges in this case are based on circumstantial evidence relating to the defendant's activities surrounding the fires charged in this indictment, the federal indictment, and uncharged crimes, the People believe that the corpus delicti in each of the counts charged can only be established by examining the facts surrounding the other crimes evidence. While there are large numbers of additional fires that also would provide substantial evidence of the defendant's guilt in this matter the People believe that the above reference fires provide a clear and concise picture of the defendant's activities and the nature of the charges in this instant action.

CHAPTER TWENTY-FOUR
FLAME OUT

Removed to Lompoc Penitentiary from TI, I stayed in the hole upon arrival. Primarily due to my law enforcement background, but also because of the recent notoriety of the case. Lompoc received all the L.A.-area TV news stations. Thankfully, I remained in the hole until January 3, 1995, when an L.A. county jail bus picked me up at about 5:30 p.m. The weekly shuttle from San Francisco to L.A. broke down earlier in the day and ran late. The motor coach was fully loaded with prisoners taken from county jails up and down the coast of California. The sewage system of the vehicle overflowed, adding to the already-tense situation. Segregated, again, this time in a small cage near the driver, only one other prisoner needed isolation. A nineteen-year-old African-American girl from L.A. was picked up in San Jose for an L.A. prostitution warrant she skipped out on in Santa Monica. About ten feet in front of the other prisoners, we chatted amiably. It was a pleasant surprise to find such an articulate youngster along. She wanted to talk about family and children. I obliged and we had a pleasant conversation until we both fell asleep; her with her head against my seat back, only a thick steel mesh separating us.

Arriving at Sybil Brand, the L.A. County jail for women, "Tara" got up to leave when her name was called. She stuck her fingers through the mesh to grasp mine and said, "Good luck, Pops. You'll be okay." I smiled. "But don't tell your wife you slept with a black woman. She may not understand." We both laughed as she started her trip into the unknown.

Her humor helped relieve the tension a bit, but I didn't know what to expect when we arrived at the infamous L.A. County Jail, just northeast of downtown L.A. I was due in court at 9 a. m. the next day and it was 11 p.m. before we stepped off the bus. Standing in a line outside the receiving area I was surrounded by 30-40 huge LACJ buses. We had to wait while an idling behemoth next to us spewed diesel fumes and a line of court-returnees emerged from the sally port. I'd booked prisoners into LACJ many times over the years and sent at least 100 through the jail since 1977, but I didn't expect to see anyone I knew. In the ultimate irony, the second from the last in the "chain" of prisoners headed for Wayside Honor Rancho jail after a day in court, was none other than "Red." I arrested "Red" in 1986 and he was suspected of setting dozens of fires over the years. He was about 20 feet away and I could have let him go by and he wouldn't have seen me, but I said, "Hey, Red. What's up?" I forgot he needed glasses. He wasn't wearing any and had no idea who I was. Still, he looked up, squinted in my direction, raised his head pointing chin at me as he said, "Hey homie. What's up?" No telling what he might have said had he known. During my LACJ stay I ran into 3 other men I arrested or apprehended during my career. Only one recognized me. Processing in took about three hours. I was kept isolated in a stinking holding cell. Fortunately the special handling allowed me to avoid the mandatory de-licing and cold shower. Somewhat acclimated to prison by now I still wasn't prepared for the horror L.A. County Jail presented. I walked by dorms holding hundreds of bunk beds. Early in the morning the lights were dimmed but pockets of youthful offenders chatted and screamed across the rooms while others tried to sleep. The scene reminded me of the movie Blade Runner where streets in futuristic L.A. are overcrowded with huge masses of moving and stationary bodies.

My assigned pod consisted of 15 single cells and was quiet. Just 25 feet from a companion row, O.J. Simpson would soon be the only occupant in that area. I fell asleep in seconds only to be awakened to cold eggs and bread thrust through the cell's food slot at 5 a.m. Processing out to court required lengthy stays in holding cells again, then a short ride to the downtown courthouse known as the Criminal Courts Building. More holding cubicle transfers finally found me on the ninth floor. I hadn't shaved or showered in two days, had no comb or deodorant, so appeared for arraignment looking like a disheveled homeless man fresh off the street. Cameras flashed and video lighting illuminated me as I stood next to Peter while my plea of not guilty was taken. As Peter departed he said he'd be down to visit me in a few days. A copy of the *L.A. Times* was passed to me the day after arraignment and a photo of me appeared on page 3 of the Metro section. The accompanying story read, in part, 'The former Glendale fire captain looked the part of the criminals he used to pursue, unshaven and disheveled during his brief court appearance...'

Again, I won't spend much time describing conditions inside the L.A. County Jail. Suffice it to say a county jail is everyone's nightmare magnified 10 times--but it is survivable. Maintaining strength and fortitude is easy when the alternative is not existing at all. Peter told me this case might take a year or two be resolved. If I had known then that it would be almost four years of this hell, I would have found an out and the result not pleasant. At least eight suicides took place at LACJ while I was there. One man was stabbed outside a shower stall just 30 feet from me. He bled to death before medical help could be alerted and got to our remote module. I witnessed countless fights, most head-butting and kick fights because we were handcuffed each time we left our cell. I had a small verbal altercation with a 30-year-old veteran gang member one morning as we readied for court. The escort deputy cuffed us up while we were still in our cubicle and less than 30 seconds later our gates were racked open and my opponent had already slipped out of his handcuffs. He expected me to be the aggressor and when he saw I was still shackled we both laughed and he managed to get himself back together before we reached the deputy. I never quite mastered using a paperclip to unlock my handcuffs.

Survival in LACJ meant I had to have finesse, aggression in the appropriate doses at the proper times, discretion and show total, almost exaggerated, respect at all times. Dealing with hardened criminals was easy compared to the often inexplicable behavior of some deputies charged with our welfare. The Stockholm Syndrome at LACJ was never a consideration. Brutality common, intimidation the norm, I was very careful not to do anything to draw attention to myself. Unprofessional deputies routinely baited and belittled me and I had to take it---for now. Deputies stole everybody's mail regularly, usually magazines. Even discreet complaints went nowhere. so I learned quickly to roll over and play dead. I documented many instances of the tolerated outrageous behavior of LACJ deputies but before I can pen another book most of the culprits will have escaped into the general population of L.A. County--as full-fledged deputies, not jailhouse overseers. Most of the corrections deputies were professional and just put in their time, but those few out-of-control amateurs seemed to be a larger group than they actually were. Their lack of supervision is the root of the problem. If I write about LACJ in the future I may just title it *Hell Revisited*. In the weeks following arraignment Giannini came to visit occasionally for short periods, each time bringing a few documents and reports the prosecutor used in putting the case together. Peter shocked me when he said there were over 30 file boxes of documents related to the case. He later spent almost $4,000 copying the mass. Total pages —85,000. An index 120 pages long gave us generalized knowledge of the contents of each box but each page had to be analyzed. I knew from past experience most of the examination would fall to me.

During 1995 Peter was only able to bring me a third of a box, about 1,000 pages, at a time. The documents, copies of my old case files from 1980-91, reports involving uncharged acts and local fires, interviews, phone records, lab reports, transcripts from civil and criminal trials, were in disarray and many times duplicated. Additional boxes contained Wanda's financial files, cancelled checks, credit card statements for us, and thousand of pages of innocuous material. After the defense went to work, we secured more material through discovery until the total was about 100,000 pages. Eventually I was able to arrange to have Chris, a long-time friend and legal assistant pick up one box (about 3,000 pages) per week from Peter's Century City office and bring it down to me for review. Unable to keep any more than one box in my tiny cockroach and rodent-infested cell, I had to rotate them out weekly. I soon found there were a multitude of retail L.A. fires we never heard about during the Fresno and L.A. plea bargain/trial preparations. Some may have been valuable to our defense in those cases. Water under the bridge for the moment. I noted them and moved on. Unsure of how many, and which, uncharged acts cases Cabral would try to bring in for trial I asked Peter to get a ballpark figure if he could. Trying to defend 6-8 cases instead of 100 would cut the amount of time being wasted. I was spinning my wheels keeping track of a multitude of dates and times trying to cross-reference them with possible alibi. For example, if a retail store fire occurred at 11 a.m. on April 4, 1988 in Santa Monica, I needed to find any bit of information I could placing me somewhere else at that moment, even if the fire was not a charge against me. Since uncharged acts had to be defended, too, this effort was necessary. A strong showing against uncharged acts could be a decisive edge for us in motion hearings and trial.

I checked phone records (for toll calls only, local calls are not generally noted on regular phone systems), credit card receipts for meals eaten at the time of a fire or purchases at stores, and even checks written that might coincide with the day of the target fire. I went as far as examining my investigative case files for witness interviews or scene investigations where I might note a time that provided alibi. But with over 100 possible uncharged acts the task was formidable. I didn't have a computer to log the target dates/times on for easy reference. and cross-checking---I had a pencil and pad of paper. Cutting down on the number of cases to check would help tremendously. Giannini told me an evidentiary hearing was required to get Cabral to cough up the uncharged acts.

He added that we should be able to whittle the mass down to about 10-12 extra cases. Relaxing a bit, Peter destroyed my comfort zone by saying, "But any retail fire case where you had alibi could be beneficial..." I was back to square one even before the evidentiary hearing. The earliest retail fires I found were in 1979. Several small potato chip rack fires at a Ralph's market in the San Fernando Valley ultimately led to a $4 million fire that leveled the store. The place was re-built and another fire went down. A strong indication, to me, a localized, non-mobile arsonist was at work. Although the oldest retail fire, I felt I had a better chance of finding alibi in this series of blazes, especially the burned-to-the-ground incident.

Cabral, in numerous motions and in front of the judge, said I was the potato chip fire setter and was responsible for "all the major retail fires in the L.A. area."

The total-loss 1979 Ralph's fire occurred at about 7:10 p.m. In 1979 I either worked the 24-hour shift at a firehouse or was on-duty for my regular weeknight Sears shift. Fire department records and journals could easily reveal if I was on-duty and were just a phone call away. Giannini's PI, Larry DeLosh, contacted Sears personnel and was informed time cards and payroll records were available for that period but they needed a subpoena. For weeks I asked DeLosh and Giannini to get the verification for, at least, the night of June 15, 1979 to confirm an alibi.

To this day I have no idea why they didn't follow through on this request. If they had and it was a dead end I would have been informed. They simply didn't find out. A fire station journal or daily operations log sitting in the archives of the Glendale Fire Department now probably has information disproving Cabral's statements "John Orr did it all." I simply may have been on-duty at a fire station that night. The dusty, faded green-bound station histories, at this moment, are located at Glendale Fire Station 22. The Sears time card is probably long-since been destroyed. I don't have the $500-$800 for a private investigator to seek these items out now.

I soon found out Giannini had more than one client. Reportedly making $125,000 as my state-appointed counsel, he still solicited other paying customers and accepted a minimum of 8-10 other appointments by the state, some for murder, including death penalty cases. My requests for further discovery, subpoenas and interviews fell on deaf ears. DeLosh said he was only to pursue leads if Giannini approved them. Informed early in the case a minor witness needed to be located, I told Peter and DeLosh a simple way to find this guy, and several others we would eventually need, was to join a national arson investigator organization for just $50. The membership automatically provided a member roster with addresses and current phone numbers. I was ignored and DeLosh ran up at least $600 in charges to find the witness. He failed. A PI brought on board later found the man in minutes, or at least the substantial lead that got us to him. The source? The same organization I told them to join three years before. I constantly worked with one hand tied behind my back. Peter went through a series of short-term legal assistants but several took time to put my analyses and research on a computer and provided me with hard copies. It was a start. Mining the 30+ boxes of documents allowed me an inside view on how the case was investigated by the 'John Orr Task Force.'

Like an archeological dig, my examination of the prosecutor's paperwork divulged layers of responsibilities. I would dive into a box of credit card statements and phone records then hit a strata of interviews and old fire reports. The interviews were conducted and signed by a particular task force member and this box then became "Edwards' box" or "Sheurell's box." Apparently Cabral delegated aspects of the case to the individual detectives and all the reports and research done by that man were in sequence for me to evaluate--both the man and the task.

For example, Sgt. Walt Sheurell, of the L.A. County Sheriff's Arson/Explosives Unit, a friend and associate for years, was given the sizable job of evaluating and transcribing a 24-hour long audiotape. The tape, with at least 10 different tracks, was from the Glendale comm. center for the day of the Ole's fire, October 10, 1984. Both radio and phone lines were recorded and Sgt. Sheurell listened to hundreds of hours of conversations and transcribed those pertinent to the case. Most were radio or phone transmissions involving me.

Walt also was tasked with investigating various fires in the South Pasadena area where Ole's was located. Trying to blame some on me, I suppose. I gave Walt an 8 out of 10 for investigative abilities, thorough analysis and fairness. He didn't slant anything or try to twist a tidbit into a fact and connect it to me. A true professional.

Investigator Bill Donnelly, a Glendale Police Department detective assigned to the task force, was the total opposite. If John Orr was a square peg and didn't fit into the round hole of his responsibilities, he'd whittle the evidence down to suit himself. Given the sizable job of analyzing all the cases I worked in Glendale from 1980-91, Donnelly went as far as interviewing at least two serial arsonists I arrested, and who confessed, to see if I framed the individuals for fires he thought I set. This ludicrous avenue of pursuit is verifiable by reviewing interviews of Pogo the serial car fire setter and David, who set fires at the Glendale Community College.

I examined Donnelly's box of reports and found a handwritten notation by him. In *Points of Origin*, I referred to Aaron the arsonist driving a Chevy V-8 that had a "throaty roar" to its engine. Donnelly found an arson investigation report from 1982 where a witness had described to me a car leaving the fire area and it had a throaty roar sound to it. Donnelly circled the entry and noted 'THIS IS JUST LIKE IN *POINTS OF ORIGIN*!' Wow, Dave, good work. On October 1, 1991, Joe Lopez and I responded to a small brush fire at the 210 Freeway and Lowell Avenue. We were together, having just finished lunch and had a 1:30 appointment with a police officer on a pipe bomb case where another cop was the suspect. We took the brushfire call when the first engine reported "smoke showing." We made the code-3 run and slowed down when the fire reported as small. Joe and I arrived, and with the appointment looming, did a cursory scan of the scene. Joe was on-call so I let him work but wanted to hurry along, too. I visually followed what I felt was the fire's path and trudged through the light brush and grass coming back to a point that looked good. Joe took another route but he, too, came back to the right spot. It was like watching a good bird dog track a pheasant. My 12 years of brushfire investigation experience allowed me to spot it a bit quicker so I stepped to the street by our unit as GPD sergeant Rick Young drove up, joining the assigned report officer.

Joe retrieved a camera from our trunk and I confirmed that he spotted the remains of an incendiary device. Rick Young strolled up and I asked him to join me in examining the device so we could complete our scene and hit the road. I walked directly to the device location and explained to Rick we'd seen the same kind before in the La Crescenta area. It was a quick-start incendiary consisting of matches bundled together with a rock added as weight. The fire setter drove by the grassy roadside start, lit the device from a cigarette lighter or striking on a matchbook, and tossed it into the weeds. The fire would start immediately but the car already put a few hundred feet behind it and hit the nearby freeway on-ramp. He probably drove a mile or two and came back by. All 3-4 prior fires were at similar well-traveled locations with grass growing down to the roadside. In Donnelly's box I found a copy of his Prosecutor's Summary and accompanying reports where he attempted to charge me with the 210/Lowell fire.

His evidence? An incendiary device fire, my presence, and one interview. Donnelly interviewed Sgt. Young after I was arrested, who stated, correctly, "I responded to the report of a brush fire...When I arrived Joe Lopez and John Orr were already at the scene standing by the trunk of their car...John Orr approached me and asked if I wanted to see what started the fire. He entered the large fire area and walked directly to where it started..." Then Sergeant Young got flaky, "...as if he knew exactly where it started. He pointed out the device. I thought it highly unusual that John Orr could just arrive and walk directly into a large burned area and know exactly where to find the cause of the fire."

Detective Donnelly didn't have enough sense to realize the quick-start device coupled with the fact Joe and I were at the scene in one car, together, eliminated me as the firebug. Unless it was Joe and I working as a fire starting team. An interview with Joe or a thorough discussion with the fire captain would have illuminated his "case" and divulged we already walked into the fire zone and checked it out before the cop's arrival. Since I was arrested, at least three similar fires have occurred at this location and along the 210 freeway just 50 yards from the October 1, 1991 site. I have no knowledge of how these fires ignited other than they were deemed arson. I have a lead on a suspect, even as sit here in the Lompoc Penitentiary, but can do nothing about it. Donnelly submitted this horribly inept investigation to Cabral and requested a felony filing added to the growing list of "my" crimes.

Also in Donnelly's files I found what appeared to be a draft of the "Prosecutor's Summary of Evidence." The 14-page document was issued by Cabral's office, apparently as a press release, and also later showed up in a pre-trial motion. It appears Donnelly wrote the original but I can't be sure. Based on his writing style, syntax, conjecture, and outright lies contained in it and other reports he generated, I'd bet he was the author. He, at least, had a hand in it.

By mining the boxes I found several other copies of the Summary---one in each task force members' files---and theorized it was a guidebook as well. Usually near they front of the box, most had copies of identical reports following the Summary in the same order. I assumed a task force meeting was held and piles of the interviews, Summary, and other key case documents were stacked on a table and, upon entry to the conference room, each investigator picked up the copies as he sauntered to his seat. Analyzing the tactics used by Cabral gave me insight to the individual investigators' strategies, tactics, and how reliable Cabral thought the man was by how much work, and what type, was delegated. It was never my intention to attack the men personally in court, they were just doing their jobs, but if they failed to explore exculpatory evidence I was not an arsonist, these facts would come out in trial.

Investigator Tom Campuezano had one of the thickest files. His order of documents, notes, and follow-through indicated he took his job seriously. An L.A. Fire Department investigator for many years, Tom had experience and it showed in his well-kept files. One of his tasks was to investigate a small grass fire that occurred on October 30, 1991, just days after the TeleTrac was installed on my city car. I was near the fire's location, about mile as the crow flies, 30 minutes before ignition. The fire started next to the southbound lanes of the #2 Glendale Freeway just one-half mile north of the York Blvd. off-ramp. This was just outside the Glendale city limits. The TeleTrac hit just one-half mile from the freeway site showing my car traveling in a southeasterly direction at 14 mph at about 3:30 p.m. Campuezano speculated I traveled on, entered the northbound freeway at York, drove one mile to the next off/on ramps at Colorado, went through two signaled intersections, headed back southbound one mile to the fire site, dumped an incendiary device, exited the freeway at York again, and traveled almost four miles along surface streets (at least 9 signaled intersections) to the next TeleTrac hit location at Orange/Harvard streets. The "hits" were every 15 minutes. The theory was impossible unless I hit 100 mph on the freeway and drove code-3 on the surface streets to Orange/Harvard which happened to be the Glendale Fire Headquarters at that time. Campuezano went as far as to board a fire department helicopter and flew the route taking photos over the freeway and area surrounding the fire, but not the surface thoroughfares. Like the 210/Lowell cases, this effort did not result in additional charges. At least Campuezano produced something for Cabral. He made mention of this fire in the trial to bolster the theory that "Orr was always near fires when they started because he set them..." Of course, this fire scenario, in no way, worked. I could not have set it.

(When the prosecution's files were originally scanned, the mass was stored on 7 CD-Rom disks and given to the defense along with a brief index of the contents of each box. We downloaded the disks and made up our own boxes we stored at Giannini's office. The ROM disk contents were paginated starting at 00001 - 85465. The ROM index was 120 pages long originally and expanded to over 200 later as I sub-indexed the contents.)

Determined to gather alibi on all uncharged acts, I referred to my notes and the ROM Index to refute Campuezano's allegations I set the #2 Freeway fire on October 30, 1991. Cabral had, early on, indicated there may be "alterations" to the original 25 charges so I attacked everything in case he decided to file more later.

In reality, I found the following circumstances surrounding the #2 Freeway fire: Before the fire, TeleTrac dutifully tracks me leaving my civic center office early, at about 3:15 p.m. and headed southeast towards my dad's home; no doubt for my occasional check on the condition of his garage contents and a freebie beer. At about 3:15 a car fire was reported at Fremont Park in north central Glendale, in Engine 6's district. The dispatch caught my attention. I don't specifically recall it but I later obtained a copy of the report, since Capuezano didn't. I wasn't officially called out to the small blaze but I must have heard something on the radio that alerted me---the sixth sense. I reversed my southeasterly direction and headed toward the park. The next TeleTrac hit shows me stationary at the headquarters station, probably at the gas pumps. The next hit shows me at Fremont Park. At about that time, around 4 p.m., the grass fire at freeway-side takes off. It's in Los Angeles so we, Glendale, don't get dispatched and I never knew it burned five miles away. What would be my motive to set that fire?

My attempt to further refute this possible felony charge halted at 4 p.m. on the TeleTrac. Coverage mysteriously stops and doesn't start again until after midnight. Why did it stop? Or was it simply the redacted version of the TeleTrac was given to the defense because I ultimately drove to my dad's house? This was one of the few questions I had about the integrity of Mr. Cabral's cooperation with the defense. Another key uncharged act case centered around TeleTrac, too, and, again, coverage was missing for that brief time period. "Orr was always near fires when they started so he must have set them..." I also requested a copy of the headquarters station's gas/diesel log for October 30 to bolster my alibi. It wasn't available, destroyed after three years.

The car fire report from Fremont Park showed no request for an investigator and no entry from me indicating I took no action once I did arrive at the scene. According to times, Engine 6 cleared before my arrival. The car was a VW bug and the park was a thoroughfare from the local high/middle/elementary school complex a short walk away. A tunnel under the freeway by the park led to a large multi-unit residential area. At 3:00 p.m. school just let out and I assumed the interior fire to the VW noted on the report was possibly arson and that's why I headed in that direction initially. I worked this alibi up as far as I could and moved on.

After my research into the TeleTrac/freeway fire, I decided to pro-file the charges against me in the same manner and find support documents for alibi or witnesses to refute specific allegations from the Summary. It took less than 20 minutes to write out the synopsis above surrounding the freeway blaze. It took me almost 18 months to gather all the documents and finalize the research. Requesting documents through discovery was a tedious process but I had to put these cases together because any investigation conducted by the task force could later appear as uncharged acts in court. The TeleTrac/freeway fire appeared on the Summary, but was not yet charged.

I soon found out the prosecution intended to use these uncharged act fires as circumstantial evidence to bolster their weak charged fires. If the defense did not refute the prosecution's assertions then the jury would accept them as fact. All Cabral need do was have Campuezano testify to the TeleTrac hit placing me 1/2 mile away 20-30 minutes before the fire and then move on to the fire itself, its determination as arson, and theorize it could have been set with a cigarette/match device. The jury would take the next step and picture me setting the fire. I had to provide Giannini with information to refute with facts; documents, and witnesses, when possible. It took me less than a year to realize Giannini was not accepting my research and ignored my take on the case. I'd brief him on the phone one day, outlining a significant discovery, and send my written analysis only to discuss it a week or two later and he'd have no idea what I was talking about. His own progress in researching the 35 boxes was abysmal. At this rate it would take 3-4 years to get to trial. And it did. I gladly gave four years to my country, but never signed up for four to my county, too.

While examining each box I used Post-it notes to mark significant reports and to block off the huge sections containing irrelevant piles of cancelled checks, credit card statements or miscellaneous reports. I hoped by cutting Giannini's time researching we could cut to the chase and save time. My exam and culling of one box containing 3,000 pages might result in only 100 pages for Peter to examine. Still, we made little progress.

The research kept me busy. Some days the cell block was so cold I had to wrap a blanket around me and wear socks on my hands to keep warm. When inmates were restless and trouble brewed, a deputy tactic was to make it so cold we only desired to stay in bed under the covers, unable to emerge because gales of icy wind blew out of the vents. Good tactic, but I had to work so channeled the vent's breezes with cardboard file folders, tape and sheets of plastic from trash bags. Unfortunately, when I did this, freezing gusts sank to the tier below where the atmosphere became arctic. Other days the cell temperature topped at 90° and to keep cool we'd have to take bird baths periodically. Showers came only every other day. By early 1996 Cabral confirmed he sought the death penalty. Giannini didn't tell me or call Wanda. I read about it in the *L.A. Times* the day after the announcement and Wanda had to hear about it from a friend who called.

The constant barrage of ups and downs wore Wanda down. Not part of my battle researching and refuting, she kept the household going and tried to lead a normal life. Leaving Warner Brothers Studios in 1996 she returned to work locally at the home office of an HMO. Her increase in salary allowed her to wean herself off my dad's assistance and once again survive comfortably. My old friend Joe Lopez helped Wanda around the house, played with Domino, and they periodically dined out. Joe and Wanda, not he and the dog. He kept her spirits up and encouraged her to get out more often, and she did. I didn't ask Wanda to visit me at LACJ. I left it up to her. Visiting in the filthy facility was a conversation on a telephone through smeared, almost opaque, bulletproof glass. No touching, hugging or kissing. The wild uncontrolled children and mass of clustered bodies made a visit like hanging out inside a homeless camp on Skid Row. I didn't ask her to visit me---I let her decide when she'd come down. I saw my grandson, Gabriel, Lori's first boy, through the bulletproof glass. I haven't seen him since.

In mid-1996 Wanda asked for a divorce. I had no choice but to agree. The arrest, trial, incarceration, exposure of an extra-marital affair and related financial difficulties had worn her out, but she stood by me. After five years of this hell she needed relief. It was time for us to move on. Self-sufficient again, as she was before I met her in 1985, she had a new kitten and Domino to keep her company. She continued to accept my calls after the divorce was filed and we chatted as friends. From her and another source I soon found out she had a man in her life.

Our calls were less frequent after that discovery but she remains a friend and supporter.

I was fortunate to have Chris still present as a legal runner, adviser, friend and colleague. A bit of a tyrant at times, she never allowed me to get too deep into depression and hyped our collective discoveries frequently. After I finished a box-o'-documents she, too, analyzed and catalogued the contents, frequently coming up with jewels I missed. She would have made a great detective. Using her computer, she transferred my handwritten evaluations to hard copies and did further research on her own.

After two years in custody at LACJ and no trial in sight, I confronted Giannini about the lack of progress in getting to an evidentiary hearing and other routine matters before the court. His claim of being busy fell on deaf ears-- he wasn't busy on my case. He handled at least 3 other inmates living in my cellblock and they were all convinced to take a deal by Giannini. How many others were there? He gave away his tactic in one conversation: "It's always better for the defense the longer it takes to get to trial. Witnesses disappear, die, or forget things..." By mid-1996 Peter hired 6'7" attorney Ed Rucker to assist us. Ed, a 45-year-old easygoing intellectual, had a sound reputation and thoroughness Peter lacked. Spending several hours with me just after our introduction, he outlined his case responsibilities. Handling only the Ole's/murder charges, he would use his own PI and pursue that investigation solely. The Ole's fire had initially been determined to be an accidental fire in 1984 and confirmed in a subsequent civil trial in 1989. Over $3 million was awarded to survivors and heirs for wrongful death and injury based on faulty electrical wiring causing the blaze originating in the attic. Ed went to work.

In 1996, I saw Giannini six times for a total of less than six hours. From October 23, 1996 to April 1997 I didn't see him at all. Ed sat with me for 45 minutes on November 14, 1996 then I didn't see him again for 18 months. On April 11, 1997 I saw Giannini for one hour then not again for one year : April 22, 1998. I saw more of the PIs than I did my lawyers. I might have been a pain-in-the-ass, but I was making progress. Ed was, too. Despite his absence Ed always took my calls and these bi-weekly contacts proved to me he was competent. Absorbing fire cause and origin vocabulary and investigative techniques, Ed took it a step further and became a cause and origin expert. When I talked with him I spoke to a colleague.

I began to wish he was lead counsel, and so did he.

The "Prosecutor's Summary of Evidence" soon revealed itself to be Cabral's outline. In a motion before the court the 14-page Summary was used to support requests for uncharged acts. The arrangement of the investigation files, including a box of Cabral's handwritten meeting notes, divulged the Summary's importance. I wrote to Peter and explained what I discovered and the need to attack the uncharged acts at the upcoming evidentiary hearing based on what I found in the files. He ignored the facts and said unless I could provide airtight alibi on some of the fires the judge would rule in the prosecutor's favor. I gave alibi in a half-dozen of the retail fires but needed a few interviews and research conducted to solidify.

An alibi fire occurred about six months after the fatal Ole's blaze, at another Ole's in Van Nuys, on April 25, 1985. The fire started in foam rubber products as a possible shoplift diversion and I was on a weekend trip with 30 firefighters and their families, and Wanda. No doubt some of these people had photos of me and Wanda sipping margaritas in Calico Ghost Town 125 miles from the Van Nuys incident. A confirming gasoline receipt for my uncle's motor home helped support the scenario; the receipt from Barstow, California.

The photos and gas receipt would make a great display in court. Judges and juries love show-and-tell. Peter never pursued the Calico alibi and I had to have a friend make contact for verifications. This alibi fire was ignored. A March 3, 1991 series of retail fires included two Thrifty stores, again in the South Bay area, and a department store blaze, over a two-hour period. All three were set in foam rubber products and one destroyed the store. The final fire was described in a short L.A. Fire Department investigation report where a group of teenagers were seen stealing merchandise while the fire progressed and employee's attention diverted. Again, the shoplift-diversion fire surfaced. I found a receipt, through my cross-referencing, dated April 3, 1991, a meal with my wife and a friend, but not lunch-with-the-pope as Peter wanted. The receipt was for lunch and had to be during the period of the three fires that day 10-20 miles away. Giannini ignored the alibi fire. When the evidentiary hearing was held, scheduled over three days, Giannini was totally unprepared. L.A. Fire Department investigators Dennis Foote and Tom Campuezano testified to their continuing investigation of retail and brush fires dating from 1981 - 1990. Potato chip series fires were lumped together with brush blazes only because of a cigarette/match device found a few times. Some of our alibi fires were listed and some excluded. Peter didn't want to "add any more fires to the prosecutor's list for the judge to see" and didn't present any alibi fires. The judge even said, in the hearing, "I'd like to see some alibi..." Instead, Peter countered, to me, with, "I also don't want to give away any defense secrets before trial..." Secrets they were, and secrets they stayed ---Giannini never used any of the alibi fires. Had an effort been made at the evidentiary hearing we may have had a chance on a favorable ruling. In typical Giannini fashion he chose to avoid any effort at countering the uncharged acts.

The two LAFD investigators stated the "John Orr device" was found at some of their listed fires but some of the components were different. A couple of the incendiaries were bound together with cellophane tape and located at brush fires. Some found at retail stores were held together with rubber bands, yet these "experts" blatantly stated, "Only one person set all 30 fires" in their 10-year-list. No similar retail fires occurring since my 1991 arrest were presented even though we found several, but received no investigation reports for post-arrest periods where devices were located. All post-arrest fire cases we received reports for did not include investigation supplementals, only incident forms with computer numeric coding instead of written narrative. Gentle evasion.

Four cases on their list of 30 showed strong revenge motives and mentioned an employee suspect at the same store in the San Fernando Valley. One serious potato chip fire in a market occurred in the middle of South Central L.A.---Watts. Not likely I could maneuver unnoticed in a store in this area. Giannini did little cross-examination and almost no confrontation over discrepancies on the list. Had he been prepared, introduction of alibi on several of the blazes or exposure of the commonality of cigarette/match devices, would have seriously undermined the "experts" credibility. There were 3-4 witnesses to counter the "commonality" issues; none were called.

In their effort to get uncharged acts into trial the prosecutor forced Foote and Campuezano to either stretch expert opinions to the limit or simply lie. Their expertise on device commonality could only be measured by the number of times they actually found cigarette/match incendiaries or read/studied about in training texts. All training texts and instructors I personally have read or heard, consistently confirm the cigarette/match combinations are the most common device around. Variations with tape, twine, string, gauze, band-aids or even wax to secure the matches in place indicates the variations available to the arsonist. One firebug could use the same device but his construction influenced by available material. No competent arson investigator can say with certainty only one pyro uses a particular device unless there is a signature attached to it. Addition of a piece of colored string or paper might establish a signature but the generic cigarette/match combo is universal. Undercutting the two "experts" was an easy and necessary task but the opportunity evaporated.

Both Foote and Campuezano left the LAFD within a year after the trial. One, before retiring, cleared his "cold case" files of garage, brush and similar fires in the Hollywood and Wilshire areas of Los Angeles by blaming me. I viewed a number of these report histories where he said, "This fire and similar in the area are suspected to have been set by convicted arsonist John Orr. Case closed by exception."

Peter ended the evidentiary hearing after only one day's testimony—the prosecution's side. No defense, other than a summation, was presented on the key to my defense: eliminating uncharged acts as evidence.

We lost the uncharged acts battle. Judge Perry said in his decision, "I will allow the 14 uncharged acts requested by the prosecution and entertain more if desired..." We were now almost three years into trial preparation and Judge Perry demanded a firm start date.

During the final days of 1997 I renewed my attack on the files and came across a vein of pure gold. Material I evaluated earlier referenced documents I had not read or made connections to the importance of until I got these nuggets. Handwritten notes I'd found could not be matched to any investigator's scratching I recognized. One of the last boxes seemed to be a monotonous clearinghouse of miscellaneous detritus.

This day I discovered the missing fax pages and "other suspect" references. An 11-sheet, paginated fax from the San Francisco Regional BATF Office sent to the L.A. U.S. Attorney's Office turned out to be actually 14 pages long. In discovery in 1992, I noted the fax pagination said "Page 1 of 14" and "Page 13 of 14" and told McCann to order up the missing pages. The document was a case investigation log from the BATF, opened in January 1987, chronicling the feds involvement in the retail fires in Fresno up to 1988. McCann never followed through to get the missing pages. Now I had them. It was here the two suspects from the Holiday Inn fire(s) were listed and investigated for the retail fires in 1987. Both suspects were named, their fingerprints compared to the CraftMart device and physical descriptions provided. Several other suspects and print comparisons were mentioned, too. No results were given. The fact the men were investigated/suspected was significant and required the prosecution to provide the information to the defense. If the suspects were alibied then the information was harmless and could have been passed on to us. Obviously they had no alibi.

Now I also knew why the Fresno Fire Department investigators stonewalled us when we requested documents, interviews and information from them. They said, "Talk to the U.S. Attorney's—we've been asked to provide nothing and refer you..." This U.S. Attorney tactic was unethical and possibly illegal; at the very least, actionable.

With close working relationships between the L.A. USA's Office and their Fresno counterparts, Faller and Hanly, this information was undoubtedly shared. The investigative chronicle was housed in the San

Francisco BATF Office, sent there from the Fresno BATF Office, and faxed to the L.A. USA's Office three months before my 1992 trial.

A second discovery solidified the intentional hiding of exculpatory material. A 5-page California State Fire Marshal's investigative supplemental written after an assist to the Salinas Fire Department for a March 3, 1989 retail fire, outlined ignition in foam-stuffed pillows. In the report, Investigator Greg Smith states the blaze at a Woolworth's store was the first of several within a 15-mile radius that same day and after. An additional fire at an OSH hardware outlet a few days later was investigated and led to a suspect. The man had prior arrests for setting small fires in retail stores as shoplift diversions. On parole for such crimes, they tracked him down and arrested him at a motel he'd been staying in just four blocks from the Salinas Woolworth's.

An affidavit for the search/arrest warrants served on me December 4, 1991 mentioned the Salinas Woolworth's fire at least three times, makes no mention of the other four area fires nor the suspect who was arrested. BATF Agent Mike Matassa obviously infers I set the Woolworth's fire since he states I drove through the vicinity on my way to Monterey. So did 68 other Southern California attendees. Matassa goes on to say his affidavit used reports he reviewed "from Salinas police and fire departments and the California State Fire Marshal's Office" to help him determine John Orr set these fires. The jury in my Fresno trial heard about the Salinas fire at least four times, yet the defense never received the information about the suspect with prior retail fire setting history. The prosecution is required to not only present such exculpatory information to the defense but also divulge it in the grand jury hearing room where I was originally indicted. Another prosecutorial violation.

What did the three-years-old reports have to do with my 1998 trial? Uncharged acts defense. All the Fresno, Central Coast and other fires were potential uncharged acts evidence. If the original Fresno conviction was reversed, 20 percent of Cabral's case went out the window and he may have lost the evidentiary hearing as well. I also could have withdrawn from my plea bargain case based on the same evidence and taken that, too, away from Cabral.

Mr. Giannini wasn't too happy about my discoveries. I asked him to get a federal public defender appointed to start an appeal to reverse the federal cases, based on the egregiously withheld exculpatory evidence. He refused. I asked him to start the appeals and he'd not only win his trial delay but might just get the charges dismissed. Cabral could not proceed without uncharged acts evidence. Gianni refused, citing he didn't have time to pursue the federal cases. Understandably, to a point, it was a tough enough fight doing the murder trial, let alone taking on federal procedures, too. I wrote the Federal Defender's Office myself, seeking help. No response. Trial loomed. Depression and frustration hit me hard but I was fighting mad so hit the document piles again. Unknown to me, an Anti-Terrorist Act bill passed in 1997, putting a one-year filing period for federal appeals. Four years later I was repeatedly turned down by the courts for missing appeal filing limitations. Giannini burned me again and I'm still fighting in 2001.

With so little time before trial I changed tactics and devoted all my time to using the Prosecutor's Summary as a tool. I took each sentence, each accusation and every statement of the guide and tried to counter the assumption or presumption. I found it surprisingly easy to do, probably because most of the documentation was available, and I was innocent.

The summary was an outline of the method Cabral used in his evidentiary hearing and I knew he'd follow this successful ritual in trial. The insidious assumptions and speculations, such as "Orr arrived in the fire's incipiency" had to be refuted. If just the videotape played in trial (as it was), Cabral's closing statement would add, "Orr arrived in the early stages of the fire and did not report in on his radio because he did not want anyone to know he was there---he started the fire and simply watched it destroy Mr. Kim's home." Cabral didn't need a witness to testify to the statement---just play the video. I saw it coming and warned Giannini. It happened exactly as I predicted. Giannini ignored preparation, the tape played, and in closing arguments Cabral repeated his Summary's assumptions. Giannini made a last-minute attempt to counter them but acted as though the first time he heard of the issues was on the last day of trial. If the defense doesn't offer a defense, what does a jury do? Assume the prosecution is telling the truth.

I prepared the countermeasure sheets and provided Peter with a multitude of options to use in mitigation of the expected tactic. With the allegation statements referenced by page number, Peter could look at it, then go to the mitigation page numbers and examine the countering interview report or other document. The CD-ROM allowed quick access to almost everything. Simple, but still not enough. Some of the sheets were put on the computer and the Ole's fatal fire mitigations sent to Ed Rucker---I hoped.

Innocent, I found defending myself fairly easy despite airtight alibi missing in the 14-year-old Ole's case, but finally found it, too. Once I had my massive ROM index completed and sub-indexing established, the mitigation sheet brought me home. Only one aspect of the Ole's case blocked me. Where was I when paged to call the comm. center and phoned them at 7:47 p.m. the night of the Ole's fire? We were fortunate to have the multi-track audio tape recording of the dispatch center's activities and incoming phone lines. As outlined in Chapter 10, most of my locations and movements were solidified by the tape and accompanying documents I later found.

The Summary, and other prosecution documents, repeatedly blared I was at Ole's for that 7:47 pager/phone contact—the assumption I was actually inside the store 10 feet from the Customer Service counter and check-outs. Cabral screamed, "Orr was inside the store and close enough to hear the soon-to-be victim and her husband discuss buying ice cream. We know it's true---he put it in his novel." Fine. I knew he was wrong. Now, how do I put it in my mitigation sheets? I drew a map. I drew blank clock faces. I paid my cellmate next door two Snickers bars to draw more clock faces for me to speed my research. I wrote down the times the Summary placed me somewhere: "Orr met face-to-face with McClure at 8:05 in Pasadena," or "Orr talked to Verdugo on his radio," and so on. I just couldn't recall, 14 years later, where I talked on the phone to Verdugo at 7:47. From the audio tape we knew there was no discernible background noise, no elevator music, no bar glasses tinkling, no traffic, and no voices, so we knew I wasn't inside Ole's. I assumed I was on a pay phone at a restaurant/bar in Pasadena. I answered the 7:47 p.m. page and was on the line to Verdugo in 21 seconds after the pager alerted me so I was very near a phone. I finally figured I'd never recall clearly and I refused to make up a location to please Peter Giannini or fit our scenario. With multiple lady friends in Pasadena in 1984 and my usual hangouts also in the area, I narrowed it down to two possibles and both fit the bill. One was the Peppermill Restaurant and the other next door. Both had pay phones outside the bathrooms or in nearby hallways and the floors were muted by carpeting. No background noise. I was within a 5-8 minute drive to McClure's 90-minute-cold fire scene because I met face-to-face with him at not much beyond 8:05. My review stopped cold at this point. My clock face studies were filled with scribbles and unreadable etchings but one thing was excluded by both Cabral and me. One half mile south of Ole's, another fire erupted, in a Von's Market in a potato chip rack, just 4-6 minutes after the Ole's fire was reported. All of my maps, clock face studies and time-lines were geared to Cabral's assertions and neglected this second fire. Drive time estimates were for my McClure-to-Ole's meeting. Cabral's time-line(not a graphic, just a conglomeration of miscellaneous reports, references and the Summary) proved nearly impossible. Neither of us included the Von's fire—him probably intentionally.

In the Summary and in motions to the court, Cabral said, "Orr set the Von's fire, too." With both time-lines reaching the same conclusion - almost impossible to accomplish - the inclusion of the Von's fire made everybody's time-line impossible...except the study of my actual movements. I could not have been at Ole's at 7:47 for the phone call, set the Ole's device, returned to my car, drove to Von's, found a place to park, enter the store and place another device, return to my car in the parking lot, and drive 7.5 miles to meet McClure in Pasadena. I tried it Von's-to-Ole's-to-McClure and it still did not work. Totally, utterly impossible. Vindication and airtight alibi. I didn't even have to testify to it. Cabral's Summary lays it out and all the defense needed was a PI to drive the course. Not even that really. The time-line of Cabral defeated itself.

I pictured a nice poster-size graphic time-line, on a display board, supported by documents of the Prosecutor stating where they thought I was, then Peter and Ed showing a map projected up on the courtroom wall, and dramatizing a bit with audiotapes and some photos to prove the alibi. Maybe even parallel time-lines like I did originally, showing Cabral's and our theories. But mine wasn't theory, it was fact. Who cared now whether Ole's was an arson or accidental---John Orr wasn't responsible for the fire. Nobody listened except Chris. I bullet-proofed the time-line, played devil's advocate, and found no way to breech its invincibility. I was not guilty. Peter and Ed looked at my studies of the time-line skeptically.

Chris and Joe Lopez drove the time-line; proof positive. Ed, at least, dispatched his PI to drive it but, unknown to me, he only traveled the McClure-to-Ole's leg, not the Von's trip. I didn't know this until trial. Ed placated me and it was one of his few failings. Apparently he felt anything other than Ole's, like McClure's fire and the Von's chip fire, were Peter's responsibility. I also tightened up one more alibi to counter the Prosecutor's Summary statements of "Orr's consciousness of guilt." Cabral stated that at approximately 8:10 p.m., on the night of the Ole's fire, I was paged by Verdugo Dispatch Center and advised, on the radio, an on-call investigator was needed at 1455 Stanley Street at a closet fire. Cabral said, "Orr was the on-call investigator for that evening and should have responded to his own city. Instead, he opts to stay and watch 'his own' fire the now-burning Ole's." The jury would assume Cabral was correct if Giannini did not offer the truth of the matter. The Prosecutor's Summary predicted this tactic, if Giannini had chosen to use it as an guide, and about the only way to counter the allegation was for me to testify. I was ready but Peter said, "No way. What would I asked you once you were up on the stand?"

Tom Rickles memory of such long-ago events was weak. This became apparent in an early 1996 interview with Giannini and our private investigator. Tom was aware I got thrown off the 1455 Stanley property by Red's mother in 1982, but would he remember it? No way to tell. Giannini never asked him and the ejection wasn't part of any reports since the actual suspect in the long-ago case was arrested by me: the serial fire setter, Pogo. Red was in the clear so no reference was made in writing. I did locate support documents where Red was a witness to an arson fire and told the police officer interviewing him that his home address was 1455 Stanley Avenue. I also possessed the case file for the 1984 Stanley fire and the follow-up to it, written by me, clearly states the closet was set on fire by Red's brother Lee, and he admitted it The difficulty I experienced from Red's mom at ambush-interviewing her child in school is captured in the report. It may have jogged Rickles' memory if he was shown the report but we'll never know because it wasn't. Not responding to the Stanley request the night of the Ole's fire had no bearing on the case's outcome. Turning down a request for an investigator at a fire scene was optional, the decision left up to the detective assigned - a long-time policy of my unit. We followed this procedure in an effort to cut down on overtime expenditures and to condition fire captains not to depend on us so heavily. If Tom or I responded the fire captain did not have to write a report of the incident if it was arson. Otherwise it was on them so many chose the option of calling us out for everything despite the department's call-out guidelines saying otherwise. We wanted to wean the captains off our tit and encourage them to make their own cause and origin decisions. A fire captain's job description clearly states they are responsible for cause and origin determination at every fire they attend. Most took that definition a bit too far and used us as the tool to make their cause and origin decision. I did, on October 10, 1984, order a police officer to take a report on Stanley to fully document the victim's names, addresses of witnesses, and the potential suspect. I opted to not respond to this small case because of the prior problems I had with the mother, and fear she would not allow me to talk to the boy at the home right after the fire. If she closed the door that night, she probably would have ordered me to leave her kid alone and I could not approach him at school. My ploy worked and I did ambush the boy the next day, gained school officials permission to interview him and gained a confession. This a jury could find easy to believe. Tom could testify to the case report from our files where I interviewed the kid as well as the report where Red listed his home address on Stanley and maybe some of this would jog Rickles' memory. Again, however, Ed Rucker read my mitigation plan and ignored it as not his Ole's responsibility. Since the Stanley fire was in Glendale, it was unrelated to Ole's - Ed's only responsibility was to deal with the Ole's fire and nothing else. He directed me back to Peter. Giannini later told me the Stanley fire was Ed's caper and if Rucker ignored it, obviously it was not important to my defense. After finding myself not guilty of murder, Chris and I were pretty excited so moved on to the College Hills fire mitigations. Cross checking a sub-index I found a note referencing a

Glendale Water Department after-action report written about a month post-fire.

The only witness against me in the College Hills fire was a retired air force pilot, a major, who says he saw me moments after the fire started, standing in front of the apartment next to the fire's origin. The pilot said the guy he saw was me and I was dressed in clothing that appeared to be a "city uniform or work clothes." I didn't wear a uniform on or off-duty and I was miles away when the major/pilot drove by the apartment. Like my search for the investigator at the D&M Yardage fire who the deputy said was me, I knew I had to find the guy Major Eyewitness said he saw. My own after-action report of the College Hills fire said I was 4 miles away at that time. With the Major countering this scenario the jury would assume I lied.

I always maintained the pilot saw a city employee. At 3:15 - 3:30, city workers from Parks & Recreation, Streets, and the Water Department are returning to their home bases or the city yards, nearing the end of their 7 - 4 work day. When I saw the sub-index for the Water Department after-action report there was a note stating, 'water dept emp's helped evac apt.' I froze. We never saw this report, Cabral never got it either since it wasn't in the ROM. We had to request it through discovery. It took Peter 14 weeks to finally get it but it was worth it. In the early part of the overview, it stated, "While returning to the city yards Don Morring and Bill Reen saw the fire start and stayed on scene until the fire department arrived. While Don directed traffic Bill Reen assisted tenants evacuating from the apartment nearest the fire." The men could have been located three years before but Giannini refused to dispatch a PI to Glendale to research the College Hills witnesses I theorized we'd need. Giannini didn't even bother to call anyone at the Water Department to get a description of Reen or Morring to see if they looked like me. The men were in the wind.

I had no idea why Peter Giannini didn't move forward on my case. He was secretive and always distracted when he came to visit. I heard he was in the Attorney's Room at LACJ frequently but it was to see other clients. In early March 1998 I had not heard from him, and he didn't take my calls for over two weeks. He was always "out of the office" even though one of his other clients, residing close to me, talked to him minutes before. On March 23, 1998 I was awakened for court at 5 a.m. Not scheduled for any hearings I was surprised and enjoyed the opportunity to get out for a while and ride the jail van through downtown for a few minutes. But it wasn't a dry run. I walked into the courtroom to see Giannini talking to Cabral on the far side of the room. He turned, saw me, and his jaw dropped for a second but he quickly regained his composure and walked to me. He explained he had a motion requesting more time before the judge and it wasn't really necessary for me to be in court and I could request to be returned if I wanted. I didn't want. We had been waiting to start trial for, literally, years and I was pissed. Three years and 2 months, to be exact, and Judge Perry had been adamant about an April trial start date.

Moments later the judge came in and we all listened to my lawyer begging for more time. "I'm not prepared, your honor. We need more funds for investigators and I need until at least September or October to be really ready." Judge Perry's jaw tightened as Giannini spoke but his response was clear, concise, and direct, "Trial starts in three weeks. See the residing judge for additional funding." Thirty-nine months apparently wasn't near enough time for my lawyer to prepare. I called him on Monday morning and spoke to one of his legal-assistants-of-the-moment. He informed me, "Peter left for a vacation. He'll be back in two weeks. Can I help you with anything?" I needed help, but no one could provide it. Giannini says in open court he isn't prepared, needs another six months, is ordered to trial in three weeks, and he takes a vacation? I hope his suitcase was the size of a CEO's desk so he could carry all the paperwork I'm sure he took with him on vacation to help him prepare.

Less than a month before trial, Peter said his PI tracked the water guy down. When I finally asked about it the first week of trial he said, "Yeah, we found him about a month ago," Peter sighed, "but he's African-American and he doesn't want to testify so that's it." I felt the fact the man was black alone was great news---we proved the major was wrong. Peter looked at it differently and replied, "The jury won't believe the pilot was that wrong. They'll just figure you were there, too." The PI had limited information and documents and failed to ask Morring if I, a fellow city employee, wearing a gun and badge on his belt, was known by sight or if he saw me or any other men at the apartment. Did he see the first engine pull up and where was he when this happened? The major said he saw me, continued on and seconds later an engine rolled by. A confirmation from Reen and/or Morring would solidify they were there at the same moment the major said he was there. Even a face-to-face interview with Morring by the PI, would have been sufficient. What the man said might be disallowed as heresay but the point we needed made was a simple physical description—the man was black and this the PI could testify to. My efforts to obtain documentation/confirmation of this interview fell on deaf ears, and the PI later died, taking this contact to his grave.

The lead was abandoned by Giannini. The man could have been compelled to testify by use of an out-of-county subpoena. Again my lawyer dropped the ball. I told Giannini, "Expect me to testify if these witnesses aren't brought in and the small allegations from the Summary refuted."

"We'll see," my lawyer replied. We saw. They weren't brought in. He wouldn't allow me to testify.

I also viewed over 200 photos provided by the prosecution. At least two were used to place me at the Ole's fire during the periods I was not there. Cabral fit me into his scenario using photos of Tom Rickles – not me. I never wore a watch until 1986; the photos show Rickles with his digital watch on his left wrist. Giannini ignored this scenario. I knew this was a small brick in the defense wall but could be used to discredit witnesses later. Left unrefuted the jury assumes everything the prosecution says is the truth.

The final challenge to my lawyers involved DNA. Away from resources for many years I did not know how DNA-matching worked. My little knowledge came from occasional *L.A. Times* articles I read from the OJ Simpson trial. Those stories related how a blood drop could provide enough of a sample for one typing/comparison. As far as I found in my case only one piece of evidence remained where my DNA could be compared-the cigarette/match device from the Stat's Floral fire on March 27, 1991. I asked Giannini if the remains were adequately preserved for a DNA comparison. His knowledge seemed less than mine. Ed Rucker chimed in and said, "I'd never allow my client to voluntarily submit to DNA comparison-especially in a death penalty case!" Both lawyers asked me if I was sure my DNA wouldn't appear on that device and I vehemently said, "Yes! Let's Do it!"

Further conversations on the DNA issues elicited no concrete answers except Giannini stating "…it's so expensive." To me it could mean exoneration or an unchanged act that could challenge the prosecutions cornerstone. With a minimal sample available from the cigarette alone they speculated there wasn't enough and maybe that's why Cabral didn't ask for the comparison. To me, he sounded scared. I insisted the matches, rubber band, tobacco and the burned paper might retain additional saliva for comparison. Again, the issue died without resolve.

CHAPTER TWENTY-FIVE
RITUAL

Jury selection took about four hours. Peter provided surprises before, but his panel-picking paralyzed me. Granted, he had more courtroom experience than I, but I never heard of law enforcement and lawyers seated as jurors in criminal trials. Peter and Ed agreed to allow a retired L.A. county sheriff's deputy, a welfare fraud investigator, and a *criminal prosecutor* to sit on my jury. Not only was the L.A. City Attorney's Office prosecutor kept on the jury, she managed to get elected foreperson, a near fatal mistake.

By the trial start date, I knew everything I said to Peter went nowhere. Ed, at least, humored me and listened. The prosecutor stayed on the panel. Peter and Ed double-teamed me and said she would lead the jury fairly through the intricacies of evidence and help decipher the letter of the law to her fellow jurors. The rest of the jury was racially balanced and about equal in males to females. There were four alternates selected and ultimately we used almost all.

Since the uncharged acts evidence was coming in, the judge disingenuously allowed the transcript of the 1993 plea bargain hearing to be read to the jury. Opening statements by Cabral exposed the upcoming revelations, "John Orr admitted setting fires before...fires in retail stores...using a signature device...you will hear where he was asked if he set fires in stores like Ole's and he said, 'Yes'." That got the trial rolling. The Builder's Emporium linchpin from the plea bargain allowed this opening statement. Gianni had me "admit" I started this fire in his "deal-of-the-century" plea bargain.

Peter followed with the defense opening, "Yes, the defendant admitted to doing terrible things...but he has pleaded not guilty to the crimes presented in this trial."

We could have adjourned the jury at the end of opening statements and allowed a vote and I'm sure I'd have been found guilty. No evidence presented and no witnesses heard and I'll bet most would have convicted me. Sitting through the next few weeks was agony. Spoken about in the third person, I might as well have stayed in my cell at LACJ. When the jury was out of the courtroom and I attempted to be heard, the judge shut me down, "You have lawyers to speak for you," he wisely imparted. If I wanted to fire Peter I could not do it because the judge wouldn't allow me to speak. If I had pleaded with the judge to let me testify he would have referred me back to the lawyers. Another Catch 22

The day-to-day, up at 5 a.m., go to trial, back at 9 p.m. schedule wore me down further. I listened to the parade of witnesses give their little piece of the puzzle with the Ole's witnesses first. One of the first obstacles of the prosecution was to have the Ole's fire changed from accidentally caused to intentionally set. The lead Ole's investigator, Jack Palmer, L.A. Sheriff's arson/explosives, told the jury he determined, in 1984, the fire was accidentally started by an electrical problem in the attic. Cabral got him to say he did not have enough information in 1984 and "could have been wrong" about his call of an accidental fire.

Another early prosecution witness, Judith Miller, stated she saw my face on TV in 1994 after the Ole's murder charges were announced. Her reaction at my image on TV? She immediately said to herself, "I've seen him before. In fact I saw him in the store while I shopped with my husband." Her husband was a South Pasadena Police Sergeant. Her 10-year-old "memory" of seeing John Orr in the Ole's store the night before the fire left the jury with the impression I was casing the store before setting the fire. Ed did an admirable job of cross-examination and cast some doubts on her credibility. We, of course, had documents saying I was in Glendale doing paperwork in my office at the exact time she said the encounter took place. We couldn't present the documents to a prosecution witness and had to wait to refute her when Tom Rickles testified for our side. Miller's small piece of the circumstantial case started the puzzle-solving process for Cabral. The Miller piece remained glued to the table. The defense would not attempt to soften the adhesive by presenting either a witness or the alibi documents. The jury never heard my alibi. Rucker later said, "Rickles is too dangerous a witness. His memory is faulty after so many years..."

"Did anyone show him the documents from October 9, 1984?" I asked.

"Well, no...but he might just say the dates and times could have easily been placed on the P-5 forms at any time before or after October 9."

"Maybe, but doesn't it make sense that if I was going to fake and create an alibi it would have been for the night of the fire, not the day before?" I offered. "At least give the jury something to consider. Don't let Miller's off-the-wall identification stand by itself. The damn jury might just believe her if we don't offer something." Ed replied, "It's early in the trial. They'll forget her testimony by the end anyway---"

"Except when Cabral brings it up in his closing arguments..." I had little trial experience but I sure as hell knew how Cabral intended to present his case. It could be won or lost in closing.

406

"She's toast, John," Peter added. "We don't need to overcome every little thing...It's not good defense tactics to attack prosecution witnesses." The jury never heard alibi to counter Miller.

As I predicted, Michael Cabral and his associate, Sandra Flannery, proceeded using the Summary as a guidebook. If they stood at the courtroom door and sold the 13-page Prosecution Summary like a program at a ballgame, they'd have made a fortune. The parade of over 84 witnesses produced little we weren't already aware of. At least little I wasn't aware of. Cabral consistently brought up statements and referred to documents Peter knew nothing about. He'd turn to me periodically and ask, "What's he talking about?" I'd reach into my files and produce the interview or report Cabral's witness was discussing. I could only carry a small amount of paperwork with me to court so I had to tell Peter where the other items he needed could be located, usually by ROM page number. I had my handy 200-page index; he didn't. On one occasion he handed me his cell phone and asked me to call his office and have an associate dig out what we needed. He drove to his office on the lunch hour to pick up the copies after I provided the ROM page numbers. Cabral confidently marched forward, consistently bringing up the "nothing" issues Peter said did not need to be addressed. The "Orr police badge" was a favorite Cabral liked to jam down our throats. Every chance he got he'd ask a witness if "John Orr ever flashed his fake police badge" or "Did you ever see John Orr's fake police badge." It was a non-issue —until closing arguments when Cabral used the badge as a mallet to hammer home the idea John Orr was sneaky, a wannabe cop who thought he was better than everybody else, and he thought he was putting something over on the cops.

The badge was genuine, just the modification not approved by my supervisors. The simplest explanation was: I arrested people. I wrote and served arrest and search warrants and testified as the Investigating Officer in over 60 cases. I was a cop, even if the fire department paid my salary. In trial I gave Peter a copy of California Penal Code section 830. It defined law enforcement and peace officers in the State of California (It cost me 2 Snickers bars to buy the sheet from one of the jailhouse lawyers with access to the law library.) The definition included "all full-time fire department arson investigators" as cops...police... law enforcement. I told Peter to simply ask one of the law enforcement types Cabral used as witnesses and asked about the badge issue, to elaborate on my status as a peace officer. Querying just one prosecution witness could clear up the matter and deflate Cabral's issue that was a non-issue. It was a charade but Cabral was going to jam it in our ears in closing if we did nothing about it. Peter ignored my plea.

Another piece of the prosecution's puzzle stayed on the table unrefuted. It, too, haunted us in closing.

After the Ole's presentation Cabral moved on to the College Hills witnesses and another "badge issue" circumstantial piece fell into place. I was charged with 18 felony counts emanating from the College Hills blaze. I was the lead investigator of the "largest loss criminally-caused fire in Glendale's history, yet John Orr didn't make a crime report, a police report of the incident." These accusations alone could have been capitalized on to counter the badge issue but Peter dropped the ball. Cabral implied I was pretending to be a cop on one hand, and the next moment he's saying I was derelict because I didn't write a <u>police</u> report as the lead investigator on a criminal fire. He got his cake and ate it, too. I had asked two uniformed police officers and a detective to ensure a report was taken while I conducted my scene investigation and fought fire. Several years before I had written a form letter entitled, "Why Arson Investigators Don't Write Original Police Reports" and sent them to officers after they balked at writing an arson police report. We had trouble like this for years. Thirty percent of my arson cases were solved while on the fire scene. Focusing on the scene itself and preserving the evidence before it was destroyed by the firefighters was paramount. Uniformed cops took the report and interviewed witnesses while the arson detective worked. The officers I spoke with at the College Hills fire were all extremely busy and forgot the request and didn't pass on the need. Very understandable with the huge amount of requests for fire and police service in the early stages of the 300-acre blaze. They forgot. I didn't find out until the next day. By then I'd announced, prematurely, the fire was arson-caused, but overnight had second thoughts.

Many arson fires started along the 100-yard-long stretch of North Verdugo Road where the College Hills fire originated, but none next to the apartment building. This was unique. With my own propensity to discount cigarettes as fire causes I was unsure whether conditions were just right for a carelessly discarded smoke to start the blaze. I knew the fuel, dry grass and weeds, must have less than 25 percent moisture content to ignite and the necessary fire triangle was completed, except the heat source. I found no cigarette butts in the area of origin, only the remains of several plastic lighters. A non-filter cigarette could burn down to nothing and water from Engine 5's deck gun might have completed the destruction. It was easier to leave the cause as arson and change it to accidental later, if necessary. If I wrote a crime report the city instantly suffered a $14 million crime spike and I wasn't prepared to be responsible for that---not yet. Busy with many post-fire and daily tasks, I didn't generate the report. Gianni was informed of these facts. I could have easily taken a non-criminal "Fire, Other" report heading but there was no requirement. Investigator's discretion. Insurance people were only interested in fire department incident reports to adjust losses so I ignored the police department's faux pas. The case, if arson, was technically still open and we investigated leads right up to the time I was arrested. If I did arrest someone for the College Hills fire I could file the case with the D.A.'s Office with only a fire report---no requirement for a formal police report. I'd done it before. The College Hills police report was another non-issue unless it was unchallenged.

The no-police-report issue was brought up subtly with at least six prosecution witnesses. Cabral intended to magnify it in closing. And he did. He said, "John Orr didn't take a police report, a crime report, because then there would be nobody tracking the case to make sure he followed up on it. John Orr didn't want anybody looking too closely at 'his' fire because he set it..."

Another facet of the College Hills scenario for the Prosecution was in the Summary. The assertion, "When John Orr's partner, Walter Beatty, continued to actively investigate the fire, John Orr took notice. Beatty was getting close to discovering the truth so what did he do? He had Walt Beatty removed from the arson unit, the College Hills investigation taken out of his hands, and sent back to work in a firehouse." Another provocative assertion for the jury to consider, and established through two witnesses. Beatty himself, and Assistant Fire Chief Gray. Peter knew why Beatty was removed. All he had to do was subpoena Beatty's 1989-90 annual personnel reviews I wrote. Cabral balked at supplying the "privileged" records and Giannini did not pursue it. I wrote the reviews and they were my work product so could be provided. Giannini dropped it.

Beatty was soundly criticized in the reviews, by me, for his poor people skills and alienating the public as well as co-workers. Two years running these propensities were laid down on paper. When police detectives in the Glendale Police Department had enough of Beatty's attitude problems in July 1990, they voted to refuse to work with him and the added duties fell on my shoulders. I couldn't allow that and had him replaced. Cabral didn't know this. Beatty didn't even know this because I just wanted him out, and never told him.

At least four detectives and our sergeant, Russ Pierce, could testify to the Beatty problem. Chief Gray could testify to the transfer, and did. Giannini let it slide when Gray only remembered Beatty's transfer was a "normal rotation." Gray didn't recall, and was not asked, about the detective issues. Giannini never prepped Gray before testimony. The jury was left with the insidious motives of John Orr having Beatty removed not-so-coincidentally following the College Hills fire. Cabral's plan worked beautifully. I had to admire him. It seemed like Giannini was cooperating voluntarily.

The prosecution presented no surprises. The Summary was their index, their guide, their bible. If a mediocre NFL team had a copy of their next opponent's playbook their chances of victory soared. Giannini and Ed Rucker had a copy of Cabral's playbook and ignored the dog-eared Summary.

Cabral and his first-time-in-the-courtroom assistant, Ms. Flannery, took just over three weeks to put on the prosecution's case. With an average of only five hours of testimony per day, we spent a total of about 66 hours listening to prosecution witnesses and housekeeping issues. Out of 84 prosecution witnesses, 24 testified to uncharged acts evidence. Almost 30 percent of their case dealt with fires and issues to support allegations in the instant case. Without the uncharged acts evidence the 25 counts were un-prosecutable. It was like putting a serial burglar, with prior convictions, on trial for every burglary in a city during a time he was within 30 miles. He'd be convicted with little or no evidence.

While the prosecution presented witnesses to convince the jury the Ole's fire origin was mis-called in 1984 by at least eight competent investigators, the issue still wasn't resolved by any measure. The jury heard there was a civil trial in 1989, but Judge Perry, in his infinite prosecutorial-like wisdom, ruled the panel would not hear a settlement was made to injured employees and heirs based on the accidental cause. The criminal jury would not hear a civil panel before them agreed the fire was accidental. They could hear I had a prior history, but not the prior history of the alleged murder case they were judging. Apparently Judge Perry didn't want to confuse the jury with facts.

The defense opened with the Ole's case and Ed Rucker shined. He prepped his witnesses by showing them documents and advising of the questions he'd be asking before they took the stand. The testimony went smoothly and expertly. Law enforcement and fire witnesses seemed comfortable with Ed because he spoke their language.

Mr. Rucker paraded several former Ole's employee witnesses in front of the jury. They testified to frequent electrical problems in the store, including dead outlets, long extension cords stretched to enable appliance and light use near the dead outlets, and flickering lights. These same witnesses provided this information in the Ole's civil trial, but my jury did not hear this. Even the prosecution witness, Judith Miller, stated that the store lights flickered on the night before the fire when she says she saw me in the annex area of Ole's. One witness said there were several soaked ceiling panels removed from the area above the fire's origins after a recent rain leaked through the roof, into the attic, and onto the panels just above the store display area. She added, "I also saw electrical wires in the attic running through the places where the panels were removed..." An electrician stated he had repeated call-backs to the store to repair electrical problems, many of them in the attic. We couldn't see how my jury could take this testimony lightly. They still could not hear that the civil jury agreed the Ole's fire was caused by an electrical malfunction in the attic. Judge Perry said those findings were irrelevant to my case. At the beginning of the trial, and before deliberations, Judge Perry admonished the jury that "...if facts presented during trial to support a conclusion (such as the accidental vs. arson at Ole's) are equal, the juror should favor the defendant." There was no way to determine how the jury perceived this close battle. My lawyers chose not to interview jurors after the trial was over. After all, Ed Rucker and Peter Giannini, just weeks before the trial, told me they were working the trial period for free - the money allotted by the state to defend me was gone. Interviewing jurors, post trial, would have taken time and they weren't being paid. It was over. Peter met some of his witnesses for the first time, in the hallway, minutes before they hit the stand to testify.

My legal assistant friend, Chris Blancett, watched Giannini do his pre-trial preparation with just seconds to spare before they took the oath. Although the trial transcript doesn't show them, gaps of silence filled Giannini's questioning of witnesses. He'd scan documents in front of him at the podium, then return to the defense table to retrieve forgotten items he didn't set up for his witness. When he presented a document for a witness to peruse and read a sentence, the witness, sometimes never having seen the material, spent 2-3 minutes scanning to refresh their memory. All this lack of preparation took time and bogged down the trial. It appeared very unprofessional and disorganized, except when Ed took over.

Giannini seemed uncomfortable and his questioning, which can be discerned from the transcript, validated his lack of preparation and unfamiliarity with the information. Like McCann, he made errors in references to names, dates, times, and places. With so many cases he handled over the previous 3.5 years and during trial, he just did not absorb enough to put this trial on successfully. At least he didn't trip over his briefcase.

There was also one bump in Ed Rucker's witness prep road. I heard we had a great fire behavior expert lined up to testify to confirm Ole's was an accidentally-caused fire and erupted in the attic, then dropped down into the floor area. He had a fantastic, credible, extensive curriculum vitae in the field of fire behavior. Ed talked to him many times and he wasn't a cheap expert but Mr. Rucker never met him in person. The expert's name was called and the bailiff escorted the man into the courtroom. He looked like he just stepped off his Harley-

Davidson chopped hog motorcycle. About 50-years-old, he had long, scraggly thin, gray-brown hair below his shoulders and a full, untrimmed moustache and beard down to mid-torso. He was a ZZ Top lookalike. But he had an exceptionally nice, well-cut suit and tie. Speaking well, he waltzed through his credentials and had no problem qualifying as an expert witness. His knowledge of polyfoam burning characteristics actually caught Ed off guard. He volunteered more than expected and some should have been researched further, but Ed moved on. His conclusions were the same as the first investigators in 1984 had come to: accidental and started in the attic, dropping down to ignite the interior. We established what we needed. His knowledge and background were far beyond the two prosecution expert witnesses, but they had an edge because they were both experienced firefighters. We hoped the jury found him believable despite his down-home appearance. Chris, even though she was a witness, was allowed to stay in the courtroom throughout the trial. As a trade-off, the prosecution let two witnesses remain, too. They were the mother and father of the three-year-old boy who lost his life in the 1984 fire. The father stared evilly at me initially, whenever I turned around to scan the audience or look at Chris. After a few weeks I didn't feel as threatened and his demeanor softened. The mother never looked at me. Chris was the fly-on-the-wall and listened to audience members and press talk and kept us apprised of perceptions of witnesses by the public.

I was able to wear a suit and tie during trial. Chris brought down fresh clothes once a week and I changed out of my jail blues every morning. The comfortable clothes, freshly laundered and pressed, sometimes by Chris herself, helped me feel somewhat normal, at least for a few hours a day. No cameras were allowed in the courtroom but local news reporters attended every day.

I talked to Chris very seldom during the proceedings since I usually got back to my cell in LACJ late and others had phone time ahead of me. Exhausted after leaving the trial and forced to wait in a series of stinking, filthy holding cells for sometimes as much as four hours, I collapsed into bed by 10 p.m. Sleep never came easy. Going over the day's testimony in my mind I was frustrated at Giannini's ignoring a viable defense. I frequently got up and dug through my files to prepare for the next day. A fruitless exercise, it seemed, I still attempted to participate. The defense was over in a minute. Comparatively speaking, anyway. After 66 hours, three weeks for the prosecution, I expected Peter and Ed's defense would go on for at least a week. In the second day I overheard Peter say to Ed he was working on his closing arguments because he expected to be done with the defense the next day.

412

My requests and pleadings for the Water Department witness, Tom Rickles, a dispatcher, badge-issue testifiers, Walt Beatty, or anyone, went unanswered. The bullet-proof Ole's time-line testimony took less than five minutes. Our PI simply set up the driving time he ran from my McClure-to-Ole's run at about 14 minutes. No maps or documents were admitted as evidence, no graphic time-line for the jury to review during deliberations, just the 14 minute drive time offered. Peter said, "They have all your time-line components in evidence. They're not stupid people. We don't want to insult their intelligence." Ed placated me by saying he'd elaborate during closing arguments. I wasn't placated. Anything Ed or Peter showed or did during closing arguments wasn't considered evidence and would not go into the jury room for review. All the panel had was the 14-minute-drive-time and little mention of the importance of the Von's fire. Total defense witness testimony time clocked in at 14 hours to the prosecution's 66. *Closing arguments* by the prosecution exceeded the defense's total testimony time: 15 hours. As expected, the prosecution touched briefly on all the Summary's allegations during their closing: "Orr failed to go to a specific request for his assistance at the Stanley fire while Ole's burned and he watched...The defendant never approached the on-duty Glendale Battalion Chief at the Ole's fire and asked him for permission to stay and assist...Orr never offered to assist South Pasadena firefighters even though people were still trapped in the burning store - he took pictures instead...Orr made no attempt to investigate the Kennington fire, looking at the area of origin for seconds, then walking away and never even wrote down a witness's name and address...The defendant never took a police report for the largest loss fire in the city of Glendale's history...The defendant had Walter Beatty removed from the fire investigation unit when he tenaciously continued investigating the College Hills fire...Orr lied when he said he was on Whiting Woods Road at the time the College Hills fire started - the former Air Force pilot saw him at the apartment building just seconds after the blaze ignited - Orr lied." The tirade continued for hours, in closing arguments, with Cabral using his Summary as a map. Giannini scribbled notes on a legal pad as the prosecutor steamrolled along, jotting down Cabral's assertions as if this was the this was the first time he heard them. Cabral re-hashed the "Orr-police-badge" non-issue and stopped just short of saying I broke the law by impersonating a police officer and I "tried" to be a real policeman. Later on he again says I failed to write a police report on the College Hills fire. He discreetly waited for a while so as to keep this badge-issue and the police report I did not write topics separate. Giannini still did not see the strategy and ignored it. For 15 hours the two prosecutors went unchallenged. In Giannini's closing he spent less than 15 minutes feebly trying to counter the Summary's assertions hoping the jury would believe him, with almost nothing concrete to retaliate with. I had given it all to him but without witnesses testifying, there was no "evidence" before the jury to use in closing. He never once said, "Orr was a cop, the badge issue is a non-issue, witnesses have told you he arrested people, wrote and served search warrants," or "Walter Beatty was removed from the investigations unit because of his long history of poor people skills, the Glendale Police Department Detective Bureau's unanimous vote of no confidence, and their refusal to work with him." Giannini only attempted countering about 30 percent of the Summary's allegations in closing.

The prosecutions closing lasted 15 hours, the defense less than three hours. Ed started our closing with the accidental vs. arson argument and continued doing a superb job, until he reached my time-line alibi. He still spoke with confidence, still had facts memorized but didn't quite tie up the loose ends. He didn't re-cap the references to Cabral's time-line of where they theorized I was. No dramatic effect at all.

I truly wanted something like this to be presented to the jury: "The prosecution said John Orr was inside Ole's at 7:47 - 8:00 p.m. because that's when they want you to believe he overheard the ice cream conversation between Mr. and Mrs. Deal. Mr. Deal testified he only remembers talking about the ice cream in the car as they pulled into the parking lot but Mr. Cabral wants you to believe the defendant was inside Ole's, at that moment, setting up an incendiary device. (Play audiotape of the 7:47- 7:49 call of me talking to Verdugo with no background noise like you'd expect at a large hardware store). Fire Captain Scott McClure testified he met face-to-face with John Orr at a little after 8 p.m. Captain McClure recalls this specifically. Scott McClure is not lying. He met with John Orr, 7.5 miles away at a few minutes past 8 p.m. We know John Orr was at Ole's at 8:21 because he was paged and he talks to Verdugo again (Play tape). He was at the gas station about 100 yards from Ole's. John Orr could not be at Ole's ending a two-minute phone call, telephoning McClure to talk at around 7:49, drive 7.5 miles to meet McClure in Pasadena at a bit after 8 o'clock and drive back to Ole's in time to make the 8:21 recorded phone call. There isn't enough time for the prosecution's scenario. No time to even have a conversation with McClure before turning around and drive like a bat-out-of-hell to get back at Ole's at 8:21. Now, ladies and gentlemen of the jury, there's one other thing. The prosecution wants you to believe John Orr also set the Von's potato chip fire one-half mile south of Ole's. With an 8-10 minute delay device and about 10 minutes driving time from Ole's-to-Von's and back, WHERE IS THERE NOW TIME FOR THIS EVENT, TOO, TO TAKE PLACE? There isn't sufficient time to get from Ole's to McClure and back in the 30-minute time span, let alone to also include the Von's trip. It is simply impossible. The prosecution wants you to believe John Orr set Scott McClure's Pasadena fire, drove down and set the Ole's fire, set the Von's fire and maybe the Great Chicago fire, also."

"Objection," says Cabral, "Assumes facts not in evidence!"

"Sustained," I imagined the judge saying.

Ed Rucker would continue, "What the prosecution alleges didn't happen, couldn't happen. The Ole's fire was an accident. John Orr met with McClure at a little after 8 p.m., heard the South Pasadena fire and police radio traffic about the Ole's fire as witnesses have stated, drove to South Pasadena, arriving there 14 minutes later in time to spend two minutes to find a place to park his car, find a pay phone and call in answer to his page. Take 8:05, plus 14 minutes to drive, that's 8:19, plus two minutes to park and walk to the gas station, equals 8:21 p.m. That, ladies and gentlemen, is a time-line that fits. The defendant, John Orr, is not guilty. The Ole's fire started accidentally, in the attic. Thank you." But Ed didn't close this way. Neither did Peter despite the fact they were given the time-line alibi months before trial. I cannot explain why they didn't. I never got any answers from them. Now, three years later, in 2001, I'm still incarcerated, trying to find someone to listen. Someone to look at the time-line and supporting documents and come to the same conclusion --I'm innocent. It is that simple.

After closing arguments, Judge Perry issued jury instructions. One of the directives was to ignore uncharged acts or consider them only peripherally. Right, forget the defendant said he set fires. One of Peter Giannini's reasons for keeping me off the stand was, "They heard you admitted setting fires. They won't believe anything you say." Nice tactic counselor.

Deliberations started and after several days without a verdict I was allowed to stay at LACJ instead of in courthouse holding.

I went back over the trial in my mind, gratified for a few defense victories. Peter managed to cast reasonable doubt on the cause and origin of the studio fire by embarrassing Burbank Fire Investigator Steve Patterson. Steve stated he eliminated electricity as a cause of the fire because he was told no power was on in the area. Our PI found the first firefighter on-scene from the Studio Fire Department and he also was the first to put water on the blaze. He said, "I directed my hose line on the fire and as the water hit the set's junction box, there was an explosion of sparks..." Patterson never interviewed the first-in firefighters, something I preached in my classes Patterson attended. I figured we proved the fire could not be called arson now because an electrical cause could not be eliminated, a requirement before a fire can be deemed criminally started. The TeleTrac supported my innocence, clearly displaying me and my car over five miles away when the fire erupted. Hopefully, disproving the prosecution's theories in the studio fire would weaken the remaining cases.

The jury returned in six days. Solemnly they filed in and sat down. I breathed shallowly as the judge spoke about the jury hung on one count---the studio fire. How could any of the jury vote for conviction on a case with the airtight TeleTrac alibi and the doubt about the fire's origin? Then it hit me, as the clerk read the verdicts: The jury was convinced of my total guilt because of the uncharged acts and guilty plea in the federal case. I was right the first day of trial. I could have been convicted after opening statements. Testimony and facts had little effect on this criminal-prosecutor-foreperson-led jury.

Twenty-four times the clerk droned on, "Guilty," after reading the charge. I was lead away quickly. We had a few days off before the death penalty phase began. In the death penalty phase of a murder trial the prosecution is allowed to bring up anything and everything about the defendant the prosecution wasn't allowed to use in trial. It was the prosecutor's job to kill me. Since Judge Perry let just about everything in anyway, I expected a short hearing. A brief opening statement by each side got the hearing going, followed by a parade of repeat, and new, witnesses by both sides.

An old girlfriend, Rachel "Mad Dog" Foster, a former Glendale cop, testified that John Orr, "didn't like uniformed cops. He thought he was better than them." She added, "and he probably was...."

Lori, my short-term dispatcher girlfriend, said I told her how to burn her car for insurance money. This 14-year-old conversation was in jest and I only shared my knowledge of insurance fraud with a friend and lover. The car never burned. Giannini let her off without questioning her. Several witnesses from additional uncharged acts cases not used in trial were allowed to speak. One, the wife of a Burbank Police Officer, said she saw me at the scene of a November 1991 fire in the alley behind her store.

As the small fire blazed she saw a man jump a six-foot-tall fence and attempt to evacuate people from a home. After I was arrested in 1991 she saw my picture on TV. Months later Investigator Patterson showed her the Orr 6-pack montage and she picked me out. She added that the man she saw IDed himself as a deputy sheriff. The prosecution attached me to another fire through an ID witness. The TeleTrac shows me home, on my day off, with no transportation available to me, at the time of this fire. I had no off-duty car. Giannini didn't bother to bring any of this up. I guess he figured it was only the death penalty phase. A line of witnesses continued to try and attach me to other fires. The defense remained mute.

When our turn came, Peter put on my daughters, Carrie and Lori, Mom and Dad, and a few co-workers. My family, of course, tearfully pleaded for my life. I hated putting them through this ritual. I cared about living but despised the fact my family had to be put through this additional trauma. I had the option of testifying in the death penalty phase but it was my choice to say no this time. The jury had convicted me. How could I now get up and say they screwed up and I'm really innocent. The prosecution could have kept me on the stand for days asking about anything they wanted. It would have been my opportunity to counter all the allegations but even if a juror or two wavered, the conviction was in. It was over. I opted out. The jury hung again. We later heard eight voted for death. The prosecution could have re-tried the penalty phase but decided to accept the jury's decision. Sentencing was scheduled for September.

After returning to LACJ from the death penalty phase, I was actually relieved. I knew I'd be returning to a prison soon - a resort compared to my 3 year 8 month stay at the hell-hole. I didn't have to make the court run but one more time. Knowing I'd get life without parole, plus additional years, my biggest concern was how I'd keep myself from punching Mr. Giannini in the mouth. The man nearly killed me. I did not hate Mr. Cabral or Ms. Flannery. They did their job but were misguided and ill-advised by overzealous investigators. I didn't agree with their lack of thoroughness and I believe the prosecutor was aware of the solidity of my time-line.

On the morning our PI, Ted Woolsey, was to testify to the time-line findings as Ole's alibi, Cabral asked Rucker specifically what the testimony entailed. When Ted's name was called, the mother and father of the Ole's three-year-old victim, got up and left the courtroom, not to return until the short testimony was heard. Their departure at this particular time indicated Cabral was concerned about the time-line and its importance. Apparently the parents did not want to hear the reality of the alibi. I believe Cabral and Flannery knew the time-line testimony would weaken their theories, if not their whole case, substantially. The next logical step is they knew I could not have set the Ole's fire, or the Von's fire. Could they have figured out the reality of the time-line mid-trial, or earlier, and still continued gambling with my life? There are aspects of conversations I heard and notes I read in the ROM files that almost confirmed this. I'm still working on recovering this information. Interviewing the witnesses will have to come later. Someone will ask them someday. Why did the Troidl couple choose that moment to leave the courtroom? Their hallway conversation must have been intriguing.

If I hold anything against the prosecution, my wrath lies mainly in the fact they entered the lives of the Ole's victims. After the trauma of the initial loss in 1984 and years of grieving, the civil trial brought it all back to the surface. I quietly wept when Mr. Deal testified about the last time he saw his wife and grandson just moments before the fire erupted and drove him from Ole's. He, no doubt, was forced to relive it in the civil trial, too. Years after the civil hearing, Cabral or one of his misguided subordinates had to bring the tragedy into the survivor's homes again.

There was no evidence I set the Ole's fire. There was no way my activities on October 10, 1984, based on tapes, reports or witnesses could be construed as evidence I was involved in the Ole's fire other than as an assisting representative from a neighboring agency. Many competent investigators examined the fire cause and agreed it was an accidental fire in 1984 and subsequently.

At the time I did not agree totally with the methods investigators used to evaluate the scene and voiced that opinion. I spent less than 15-20 minutes inside the building so had no time to do a competent analysis. With my years of scene profiling experience now, I can say that the Ole's fire was, most likely an accident. I evaluated all the reports, interviews, civil trial testimony and multiple scene analyses. The Von's fire was a righteous arson. Whether it was a shoplift diversion, fun fire for juveniles or a firebug igniting it for a thrill, the ignition of Ole's counters any motivation for the arsonist. Why light off Ole's? As a diversion to shoplift? Only one place could be pilfered at a time. Von's and Ole's were separated by a half mile and three signaled intersections. It makes no sense. A juvenile motivation for fun negates the "fun" because they can't watch both at the same time and there was near-simultaneous ignition of both stores. A thrill-seeking pyro wouldn't, in my opinion, touch off two fires at the same time for the same reasons juveniles wouldn't. A time separation was necessary for a pyro to enjoy both of "his" fires. The logical conclusion is Ole's was a coincidence, and truly accidental.

The Ole's fire has now claimed another victim - me.

CHAPTER TWENTY-SIX
ENTREATIES

The night before my sentencing hearing, I managed to secure an appointment for a haircut. At L.A. County Jail, inmate haircuts are provided based on the availability of experienced barbers in custody for petty crimes. I drew a Russian-Armenian whose command of English equaled my ability to write Cyrillic. My hands shackled to my waist, I could not point to what I wanted trimmed. With only a handful of hair strands remaining on my crown, I desired those few locks left untouched, in kind of a comb-back.

"Nothing off the top, Ivan. Okay?" I said.

"Da...da," 'he replied. "Nuttin' on de top...da, da." Before I could correct him the clippers zipped from forehead to crown, leaving stubble from ear-to-ear. I appeared at sentencing looking like John the Monk. At the hearing I was given the expected four life-without-parole sentences and assorted additional years to run consecutively to the LWOPs. In essence, a death penalty - I would die in prison but on a non-specific date. The feds would keep me until their mandatory release date in 2012.

Within weeks I found myself in a small L.A. County jail van headed to Lompoc Federal Penitentiary 125 miles northwest of Los Angeles. The two deputies transporting me stopped at a Burger King in Ventura for lunch. After almost four years of LACJ slop I hoped for, at least, an order of French fries. I assumed, like most of my prior inter-jail transport crews had, an allotment to buy food for their charges. One deputy stayed with me in the smelly van while the other retrieved two lunches - not even a soft drink for me. Neither cop said a word for the entire 3 1/2 hour trip.

By now my family knew the routine. The state trial was just another bump in the long road. At least that's how we all handled it outwardly. Nothing changed except the locations of my battlegrounds. Prison is no picnic but compared to a county jail the penitentiary is like a resort. I made the choice to treat the latest convictions lightly when talking to my family and closest friends. I still felt my strength would help them weather this nightmare. My repressed anger was always near the surface and for years I feared losing it totally when the opportunity to vent these feelings presented itself. Always an idiot youngster or similarly angered inmate handy, my release would have been on the wrong person for the wrong reasons. Like the irate husband, angry at his wife, I had plenty of dogs available to kick around, but chose not to. I was too concerned about having my in-custody record blemished by an outburst of violence. I probably should have feared my potential opponents but I maintained a strong, experienced con stance and knew what to say, how to say it, and how I would be perceived by how I acted. This prevented minor altercations from escalating but what went through my mind when I did get in minor skirmishes truly frightened me. Weaponless defense training from my law enforcement years was geared to taking an opponent out quickly because you had to always protect your gun. I was not armed now, of course, but I only knew how to strike at the three N's to quickly devastate an attacker: hit the neck, 'nees, or nuts. A sternum strike was another alternative but all these techniques could potentially do permanent damage. Well chosen words to avoid a physical confrontation and allow both of us to back off without losing face seemed to work well. But I was pissed all the time and seethed silently. Arriving back at Lompoc Penitentiary just after 2 p.m., I was taken directly to ad seg (the hole) because of the "former law enforcement" flag in the prison file. Told I'd be released to general population as soon as a lieutenant approved the move, I welcomed being back in a "normal" world.

After three days bunked with a heavy smoker, I was transferred to general population only to find out the prison was under a lockdown order from a 40-man melee on the football field. Apparently a bad call by an inmate ref led to the brawl.

Celled in a 6'X 10' cubicle with a man convicted of killing two prostitutes on a military base, nobody seemed to recognize me from the news broadcasts. Despite his criminal history, Eddie, a former staff sergeant, was a congenial, clean, intelligent, and fairly normal companion. His propensity to end his "dates" with a claw hammer didn't phase me a bit. I didn't plan on dating him. Hitting the recreation yard immediately upon release from our 14-day lockdown was a breath of fresh air - literally. It was the first time I'd been outdoors, other than to and from buses, in over four years.

Getting back into prison routine, I retrieved my property, left behind when transferred to LACJ in January 1995, and found a receipt for my telephone account with a few bucks still on it. The only number still good after four years was Wanda's, my ex-wife. Toiletries in my property still appeared usable but a stick deodorant caused a horrendous reaction and an infection blazed away for about six weeks. I was able to get antibiotics to finally chase it off. Welcome to the wonderful world of prison. Hired into the Education Department/Law Library complex, I began teaching creative writing again. Long absent from Lompoc's night class schedule, there were over 45 applicants for my 12-week course.

The job evolved as I took on more responsibilities and established some trust with staff members. Eventually I acted as a liaison between inmate GED tutors, evening class instructors and staff, handling all the details of logistics for copying, class material ordering, registration and attendance. The position was similar, in many ways, to my work with F.I.R.S.T. in the 1980s and 1990s. I created advertising flyers, handled incoming requests for attendance, sent confirmations, set up classrooms, arranged for reproduction of hand-outs and took roll in each class. I found I had no patience for GED tutoring so eased myself out of that arena until I did no student training in the GED program, only taught my evening creative writing sessions and my daytime liaison chores. The writing students volunteered to attend my class and wanted to learn; most GED students were forced to go to school and their resentment showed. Disrespect in the classroom was frequent with spontaneous conversations breaking out periodically and loud radio playing common. A middle-aged white guy trying to maintain order of Latino and black youngsters and adults without staff presence was a touchy situation. I was prepared to maintain the proper stance but, again, opted to step aside rather than risk exposure to potential violence.

In late 1998 I received a notice from the California State Court of Appeals telling me the notice of appeal for the murder/arson convictions was filed but no proof-of-indigence and request-for-appointment-of-counsel was received. The stern warning gave me 30 days to respond with the requested items or I'd lose my appeal rights. Was this Giannini's back-door way of responding to my snub of him at the sentencing hearing? How was I supposed to know of these requirements? It was his responsibility to ensure the proper paperwork was filed, or I had the information, and this was the first I'd heard of these needs. More was to come. I connected with a few jailhouse lawyers in my writing class and found I may have already lost my rights to conduct further appeals of my federal cases.

In 1996, the Anti-Terrorism and Effective Death Penalty Act (ATEDP) passed and included severe restrictions on filing post-conviction appeals. Being totally out of news contact and with no law library access at LACJ I never heard about the ramifications of my not filing federal appeals while in state custody. Besides, I thought, I should be covered since my federal public defender, John Balazs, told me specifically I should not file any federal habeas actions until my state case was adjudicated. Giannini mimicked this recommendation, not wanting to "give away any defense secrets" prior to the murder trial, and refused to do anything about the federal cases. This defendant-out-of-the-loop lack-of-latest-legal-knowledge was not a legitimate excuse according to case law. A possibly fatal catch-22. Giannini told me he had four clients on death row in California, made frequent trips to death row prisons and was very active in the California defense attorney organizations. He was very involved in post-conviction relief issues. The ATEDP statute of limitations on prisoner filings was, no doubt, well known to him yet he never applied these restrictions to my cases, or my needs, and never informed me of them. On February 27, 1999 I received two letters. One from the California State Appeals Court advising me of appointment of counsel to handle the state appeal and one from Ivy Kessel introducing herself as my new representative. She stated she had been "an appeal lawyer for 14 years, seven as a prosecutor with the AG's Office and seven years handling complex criminal defense appeals in state and federal courts." She went on to say, "I am telling you this to assure you your case is being handled by a very experienced criminal appeals practitioner."

Her intro included a questionnaire that read like an MMPI psych evaluation. The subtle queries seemed to be her way of gaining insight to her new client's knowledge, intelligence level, education, mental stability, and degree of potential hassle she might encounter. It was a good tactic. Ivy readily accepted my phone calls and answered all my letters - a major improvement from my past experiences with lawyers. She waded into the 9,000-page transcript from the murder trial and ensured Giannini released all his trial files to her. On April 19, 1999, Giannini sent me a letter confirming his delivery of 34 boxes of documents from the state trial to my friend and assistant, Chris Blancett. I was now totally free of him.

Giannini was a paradox. He seemed to initially welcome my efforts perusing the 100,000 pages of documents, thus saving him time cutting through the chaff, but seldom took note of pertinent nuggets of information I found. Face-to-face, at his infrequent interviews with me at LACJ, were perfunctory wastes of time. Letters I sent and studies I conducted to counter prosecution claims went unanswered despite their later importance in trial. Defense lawyers seldom pay any attention to their clients other than in initial interviews about accusations. Peter Giannini's strategies seemed incredibly naive and I was unable to do anything about it. His failure to inform me of ATEDP limitations and how they affected my cases haunts me to this day. Ivy Kessel filed her 91-page opening brief in my murder case appeal to the state court in the late summer of 1999. Her primary thrust cited insufficient evidence to convict on any of the 25 charges. Additionally, she accused the trial court of erring by admitting the 14 uncharged acts, guilty pleas in federal court, refusing to sever the murder counts from the arsons, allowing the *Points of Origin* manuscript as evidence, and imposing consecutive sentences on the 16 College Hills counts. The final cite contended the multiple College Hills convictions, involving homes burned after the brush fire spread, should run concurrently, not consecutive. The government was advised to respond to this opening brief by December 1999. Ms. Kessel refused to make any comments about a DNA comparison.

In the interim, I researched appealing my federal cases based on the newly discovered evidence. The withheld material was scanned by me while at LACJ then passed back to Giannini for his continuing research. I could not keep the detritus in my cell and had no copying capabilities anyway. The accumulation of withheld documents I found were important to me but without viewing them in their entirety or having sound legal knowledge they remained just that -interesting. I had no idea how, or if, the material could be utilized until I started examining the bits and pieces Chris extracted from the boxes and sent to me. Then I was able to put together the pattern of deceit by the U.S. Attorneys involved in the Fresno and Los Angeles federal cases. The document's eventual importance was only noted after I allowed a jailhouse lawyer, T.J., to review them in the summer of 1999. T.J. told me withholding such material was enough to reverse my Fresno conviction and enable me to withdraw the Giannnini "deal-of-the-century" guilty plea. The pseudo lawyer added that because the L.A. D.A.'s Office used so much of the federal case material in their prosecution (almost 30 percent) the state conviction would almost reverse automatically.

My primary source of information and legal mentor, T.J., was a 42-year-old convicted bank robber serving a couple of hundred years. With my many post-conviction relief motions in the system, I valued his experience and perception. The fact he was a co-worker enabled us to get together frequently and kick around strategy. Paying T.J. with Snickers bars and Pepsi, we worked together researching case law, writing writs, and typing. The law library had only ancient IBM Wheelwriter typewriters available - no computers. Between class preparation, teaching, and other chores at work, I located a workspace and helped T.J. as much as I could. We decided to go after the federal plea bargain case first.

After a convicted felon's direct appeal is decided, the court does not appoint a lawyer in subsequent filings. If you don't have the money for a lawyer, you represent yourself. The ATEDP Act included a rider limiting prisoners to only one legal action after a direct appeal. My direct appeal was never filed in this case since I took a "deal." I now had to file what were known as 2255 motions in my federal cases. The 2255 is actually a "Motion to vacate, set aside or correct a sentence by a person in federal custody." The intent of my 2255 was to prove a need for the court to appoint counsel, at government's expense, to assist in researching my allegations of withheld material that would have affected the outcome of pre-trial motions and/or my decision to accept the terms of the plea agreement. A request for an evidentiary hearing was included in the request to present the issues and witnesses to prove the accusations, many of which could have swayed the jury sufficiently to vote for acquittal. The Fresno trial was well-known as a close decision. With much shouting and indecision in the jury room, as well as an initial hung decision, the judge had to order the jurors to return to their deliberations. That jury caved in on a Friday afternoon, before a three-day weekend and convicted me wrongly. The Fresno 2255 would follow the L.A. motion.

My 20-page opening brief on trying to withdraw my guilty plea in Los Angeles cited the discovery of withheld documents, also known as Brady material. Brady was case law where the prosecution was caught withholding exculpatory items tending to prove the defendant innocent and these items would have helped a jury decide to acquit. My brief, written in the 3rd person, explained, "In order for petitioner(me) to adequately expand the record pursuant to the rules governing 2255 motions and to include all Brady material not disclosed prior to defendants signing the plea agreement, Orr respectfully requests that the court appoint counsel on his behalf to inspect the previously undisclosed materials in search of additional Brady matter." T.J. told me the court didn't want to hear about, or see any facts (i.e., copies of the withheld documents), just violations of the law that resulted in my not "intelligently" accepting the terms of the plea arrangement. He suggested not even including the samples of Brady material. In his experience, T.J. said, the judge ignores such evidence in 2255 motions. I countered with it ludicrous to make the allegations without giving examples of the solidity of the evidence. I won out and we included almost all the exemplars I had found. T.J. also discovered a very simple short-cut that should have ended the plea agreement instantly. The plea bargain was actually a civil contract, despite it being related to a criminal matter. Any civil contract can be voided if one of the principals is found dishonest in any way. Our Brady material confirmed dishonesty on the prosecution's part and, in the motion, I asked to withdraw from the agreement. It sounded good on the surface. The judge ultimately disregarded the tactic. So did the prosecutor. The topic was shoved aside like a loud, recalcitrant child in a restaurant is ignored by thoughtless parents. The motion further stated, "A defendant should be allowed to challenge a guilty plea when the prosecution withholds significant exculpatory material evidence. The newly discovered and undisclosed significant evidence reveals other substantial suspects under investigation with prior convictions for the same offenses that defendant was depicted as the only possible suspect."

Evidence used against me in the Fresno trial was going to be used in the Los Angeles federal case, including many uncharged acts and the prior conviction, so if we gained value in the "withholding" in the Fresno case, the outcome would have ultimately affected the Los Angeles jury, I contended. After all, I was never aware of the other suspects and how their mere existence would have helped us shoot down pre-trial motions and the prosecution's expert witness's theory of "only one guy" set these fires. Had I known, and Giannini been aware of these guys, we might not have gone to trial after all. I also insisted T.J. request a DNA comparison to the Stat's floral incendiary device in regards to weakening the unchanged acts evidence. My DNA profile was now in the California data base – requested post-trial by Prosecutor Cabral.

Providing proof of indigence, I made only $40 per month, we filed the 2255 motion with Judge Edward Rafeedie's court on August 19, 1999.

Wasting no time, T.J. and I filed a near-identical 2255 motion in the Fresno court of Judge Wanger. The withholding of the three suspects investigated and the "Salinas" factor were much more important in the Fresno conviction. The suspect arrested for the Salinas Woolworth's store fire in 1989 had direct impact on the Fresno case. Salinas was an uncharged act in the affidavits for arrest and search warrants, in the federal cases, and Salinas was repeatedly mentioned to the Fresno jury, including on maps sent into the jury room during deliberations. The Fresno jury was fed the Salinas fire implying I had set it even though prosecutors were aware another man was arrested for the crime.

The mug photos of the other two suspects were powerful evidence the jury should have seen, especially when placed side-by-side with eyewitness physical descriptions. This would solidly explain why these suspects were withheld/concealed from the defense. I also cited the DNA issues in my plea to Judge Wanger. Cigarette butt saliva residue could be compared to my DNA sample if the court would only heed my requests for counsel and an evidentiary hearing.

On October 26, 1999, the government responded to my Central District of Los Angeles federal 2255 motion. In his 5-page reply, Assistant U.S. Attorney (AUSA) David Vaughn wrote, "Plaintiff, United States of America, hereby moves to dismiss defendant John L. Orr's 2255 motion for failure to file his motion within the 1-year limitations period established in the ATEDP decision of 1996." The USA was actually the defendant, not the plaintiff. Without addressing any of the facts cited, exactly as T.J. told me would happen, Vaughn added, "Defendant pleaded guilty to three counts on March 24, 1993. Defendant did not take a direct appeal, and, by operation of law, 30 days later defendant's convictions became final."

Again without addressing the Brady issues, Vaughn further argued, "In 1996 (while I was still in LACJ) Congress passed the ATEDP Act which imposed strict limitations for the filing of 2255 motions. These time limits apply to all 2255 motions filed after April 24, 1996. Except in unusual circumstances the time limit of such a motion is one year from '[t]he date on which the judgment of conviction becomes final.' Since defendant did not file direct appeals his conviction became final on June 20, 1993. Since this preceded the effective date of the ATEDP, the defendant had until April 23, 1997 to file his 2255 motion. Consequently, defendant's motion should be dismissed as untimely." All this rhetoric was about the time I was in custody in 24-hour lockdown at the L.A. County Jail.

"Oh, shit," I said to myself, and probably out loud as well. Taking the avoidance of the actual issues as a good sign, I assumed Vaughn was afraid of their impact. T.J. reminded me the court didn't care about facts, just the law. My "civil contract' argument was ignored, too. We fired back a response in opposition to Vaughn's request to dismiss. Citing the rules of 2255 motions we wrote, "A 1-year period of limitation shall apply from the latest date on which the facts supporting the claims presented would have been discovered through exercise of due diligence."

My review of the 34 boxes of documents, while preparing for state trial did not constitute my first understanding of their importance to the federal case. It wasn't until after April 1999 when Chris began sending the documents and I was able to analyze them and understand the rules of 2255s that the 1-year statute of limitations began. "Newly discovered" evidence is one of the few detours around any statute of limitations. T.J. also said there was no way "lack of due diligence" applied because I was not only in state custody (this stays the limitations run also), but I was also without newspapers, TV, or law library access while in L.A County Jail. On top of that, two of my lawyers told me not to pursue a 2255 until after the state charges were decided. Confident of success, we fired off our reply.

Less than three weeks later, on November 5, 1999, Judge Edward Rafeedie denied my 2255, citing, "...motion is untimely, absent equitable tolling...9th Circuit Court of Appeals permits equitable tolling if 'extraordinary circumstances' beyond the prisoner's control make it impossible to file a petition on time. Petitioner, however, does not claim any such circumstances..."

Apparently being in jail and against lawyers advice does not qualify as an "extraordinary circumstance" despite these facts articulated(with exhibits) in my motion. Again, facts were ignored. Frightened at how the court ignored my pleas of the prosecution's misconduct, I agonized over how to go back to Rafeedie. T.J. told me a letter would be ignored. It seemed, to me, courts totally disregarded motions presented by inmates. We still had an appeal possibility with Rafeedie by asking for reconsideration and apply for a certificate of appealability from him to advance to the 9th Circuit Court of Appeals.

On November 29, 1999, the prosecuting attorney from the L.A. D.A.'s Office, Michael Cabral, responded to my direct appeal in the state murder case. The 115-page response reiterated the sufficiency of the evidence in trial to convict and credibility of his witnesses. Ivy Kessel said she was prepared for this rebuttal and we had one more opportunity to respond. She told me to "Hang in there..." I filed a request with Judge Rafeedie for a Certificate of Appealability(COA) to go over his head to continue my 2255 motion to the 9th Circuit. I explained my lack of knowledge of the ATEDP Act limitations, lack of notification by Giannini, and provided a copy of the letter from John Balazs telling me not to pursue a 2255 until after the state case was decided. Balazs' letter stated clearly, "I strongly (underline is his) recommend against filing a federal habeas petition until your trial in L.A. has concluded..." Inclusion of a copy of Balazs' letter was at my insistence since T.J. said it was meaningless to a court that rules on law, at this point, not facts. We mailed the request for a COA to Rafeedie.

On December 10, 1999, Ivy Kessel sent a 50-page reply brief to the State of California Appeals Court. In response to Mr. Cabral's vehemence his witnesses were credible and there was sufficient evidence to convict me in the Ole's fire case, Ivy wrote, "Respondent(Cabral) cites the testimony of Deputy Rich Edwards as evidence the Ole's fire was arson. The problem with Deputy Edwards testimony is that he was NEVER AT THE OLE'S FIRE SCENE(Caps were Ivy's); he was merely one of many people asked MANY YEARS LATER(again, Ivy's) to review the various reports and give an opinion based on those conflicting reports. Moreover, Deputy Edwards never actually testified the fire was definitely arson. The most he could say was that the fire appeared to have started in the southwest corner of the store." Kessel added that two other prosecution fire experts, both after-the-fact reviewers who never were at the actual post-fire scene investigation, were not clearly cause experts. One was never assigned to an fire investigation unit and did not even view any photos of the fire scene. He admitted, in testimony, he was only an expert on fire codes, and not an expert in fire cause and origin. He had never testified as an expert witness in court.

Kessel continued, "Such expert testimony was woefully deficient in establishing the fire's(Ole's) was arson and does not meet the substantial evidence test on appeal." Continuing her argument in regards to the Ole's accidental arson conflicts, she stated, "A mere possibility of such causation is not enough; and when the matter remains one of pure speculation or conjecture, or the probabilities are, at best, evenly balanced, it becomes the duty of the court to determine the issue in favor of the defense as a matter of law." In regards to the court admitting the facts of my federal plea bargain to the state jury, Kessel wrote, "Once the jury learned appellant pled guilty in federal court of the crimes of arson, the inference that he 'probably committed the Ole's fire, too' was compelling and could never have been overcome despite the lack of evidence, connecting appellant to the Ole's fire, and despite insufficient evidence that the Ole's fire was an arson fire.

"The prejudice to appellant was especially pronounced with regards to appellant's plea to the Coast-to-Coast(Atascadero, CA) fire where no incendiary device was found. Since no device was located at Ole's, admission of this plea allowed prosecutors to improperly urge the appellant's guilt to the Ole's fire despite insufficient evidence as the jury now knew appellant pled guilty to an arson where no incendiary device was found. The prejudicial effect of the trial court's ruling was fatal."

On December 17, 1999, a new AUSA in Los Angeles filed opposition to my request for a COA to carry my 2255 motion to the 9th Circuit Court of Appeals. Without addressing the 1995 letter from Federal Public Defender Balazs to me, advising not to file a 2255, Ranee Katzenstein wrote to Judge Rafeedie, "Defendant here has simply presented no evidence whatsoever that his failure to file timely his 2255 motion was not due to his own negligence."

I was appalled at Katzenstein's vehemence in light of the fact Balazs' letter said it all quite articulately. It wasn't my lack of due diligence, it was advice of counsel. T.J. told me, "Well, we can file a new 2255 saying there was ineffective assistance of counsel by Balazs start all over again..." I was becoming a litigious son-of-a-bitch but shuddered at the thought of going back to Rafeedie again.

My frustration mounted as I observed similar situations with many other inmates filing their own writs. Probably 70 percent of all motions filed by these jailhouse lawyers are frivolous pipedreams or misguided revenge designed to tie up the courts and cost the government money. The capricious or irresponsible detritus filed seriously handicapped those of us who had real issues. Such is life behind bars.

We suffered occasional lockdowns where we had no access to the law library from several days to a few weeks at a time. If government lawyers missed deadlines or needed extra time, the courts routinely granted the extensions. The same courtesy to inmates was seldom allowed. Again, the playing field wasn't level. Only inmates with funds for real lawyers seemed to get any court action. On February 10, 2000, my request for a COA was denied. To add insult to injury, there were three reasons articulated for the court to deny, with a check-box next to each one, and none of the boxes was exed - just a blanket denial.

February 12, 2000 brought a copy of the government's request for a 6-month extension to respond to the Fresno 2255 opening brief I sent. The extension was granted to Carl Faller, AUSA in Fresno. Faller was involved in a "major" case involving federal prosecution of California state prison guards for violating inmates civil rights. The state declined to file any charges since there was inadequate evidence so Faller's office brought federal charges. Faller's prosecution/persecution failed and the men were ultimately acquitted.

I appealed Judge Rafeedie's denial of my COA decision to the 9th Circuit on March 5, 2000. March 15 brought a 44-page California State Appeals Court decision to affirm my murder conviction. The assigned justice stated, "We conclude there was sufficient evidence from which the jury could conclude the Ole's fire was intentionally set and that the defendant did it.. Defendant makes the kinds of arguments that are of no avail where the sufficiency of the evidence is challenged; defendant's arguments are the sort best made to the jury at the time of trial..." Kessel did not desire to pursue ineffective counsel against Giannini despite my repeated pleas for her to do so. The appeals court decision as much as said Giannini should have homed in on these arguments. He didn't.

The California Appeals Court did reverse the consecutive sentencing of the 14 College Hills fire convictions. About 20-30 years was knocked off my sentence. Nobody ever sent me any documents stating exactly how many years were cut. Probably another one of those legal phantoms I'm supposed to know automatically. The affirmation was automatically appealed to the California Supreme Court and was denied for review, without comment, June 28, 2000. My next level of state appeal was a 2254 habeas petition due within one year. May 2000 brought me a copy of the 70-page government response to my Eastern District of California, Fresno, 2255 motion. Written now by Pat Hanly instead of Carl Faller (prosecution co-counsel in the 1992 Fresno trial), the reply mimicked the Los Angeles ATEDP Act cop-out: "Orr's claims are time-barred by the 1-year statute of limitations imposed by the ATEDP Act of 1996. Orr's claims fail for the additional reason that they are completely devoid of facts and, instead, are based entirely on unsupported allegations and speculation." I guess nobody told Hanly that the court did not deal in "facts" at this stage. Hanly ignored the 32 pages of his own investigation-generated documents I included as exhibits and further states, "Because Orr's motion is so poorly written the government is extrapolating somewhat on this argument in an effort to put it into some coherent form." While rambling about the 1-year limitation, Hanly surreptitiously adds, in regards to the 32 pages of exhibits(documents he withheld) "Orr does not state the nature of the evidence, how it would have affected the outcome of the trial, or how the evidence undermines the confidence in the verdict. He does not even indicate what the evidence is...therefore, his Brady claim fails for lack of showing materiality." In conclusion, Hanly lies, "The government provided full disclosure to Orr in preparation for his trial in Fresno and it is hard to imagine what documents he did not receive." I intend to get Mr. Hanly on the witness stand some day and have him explain his outright, now documented, lies about intentional withholding of exculpatory Brady material from me. By June 6, 2000, I filed my reply brief in response to Hanly's opposition to my 2255 and its being time-barred. Again, the Balazs letter is included for emphasis as well as reiteration of how the exhibits would have affected both pre-trial uncharged acts motions and trial. (As of this writing, Christmas Eve, 2001, a total of 18 months, Judge Wanger in Fresno has not examined or responded to my 2255 motion in regards to the 1992 conviction in his courtroom..) On July 24, 2000, the 9th Circuit Court of Appeals denied my ability to further appeal Judge Rafeedie's decision to not issue me a Certificate of Appeal ability on the plea bargain case. I could not withdraw my guilty plea. Ironically, as of August 2000, I have served the 84 months Rafeedie sentenced me to as a result of accepting the plea bargain in 1993 in his court On the surface, it seems fruitless to pursue withdrawal of a guilty plea after I served the sentence. Withdrawing the guilty plea would put me in jeopardy of another trial, which I gladly face with the availability of all the Brady material we now have, but there is one overall affect that can't be ignored. Since the plea bargain case and uncharged acts took up almost 30 percent of the murder trial time (calculated by transcript pages and testimony time) the successful withdrawal of the plea destroys the state case and it would reverse - in theory. No telling with the way the courts treated me so far. The overall affect of the plea bargain on the state jury was substantial. Accepting the deal was the linchpin state prosecutors needed to file the Ole's case; without it there would have been no state trial. I have to continue fighting the plea bargain. I can sympathize with defendant Sara Jane Olson and her on-again- off-again guilty plea decisions in 2001, in Los Angeles. The former SLA terrorist group member's guilty plea opened the door for the state to tie her to a Carmichael, California bank robbery where a murder went down. Admitting guilt in the L.A. case attaches her to the SLA attempted bombings securing her membership during that period when the robbery-murder occurred. I believe her lawyers saw this possibility belatedly after advising her to accept the deal, thus, her vacillation. The battle to withdraw her guilty plea just ended as I write this chapter and I'm assuming Sara Jane Olson will soon be indicted for murder after sentencing in the "deal." This scenario is similar to my indictment for the Ole's fire after pleading guilty in an unrelated arson. She, too, was forced into the "deal". Both of us faced vast amounts of circumstantial evidence, questionable witness IDs, and potentially influenced juries. Mine through hearing about my guilty plea; hers, by a trial taking place just after the 9-11 terrorist attacks. Under such conditions, a defendant is very pliable.

My appeals continue, fortunately, and my entire future hinges on Judge Wanger's decision in my Fresno 2255 motion. If he grants me relief, I believe I will prevail and get a new trial. However, there would probably be no new trial with all the Brady material we now have and I would testify as my own expert witness this time.

As an expert witness in arson, arsonists and fire investigations through my work experience in Glendale, the jury would be shown the suspects developed in Salinas and the Fresno area were good suspects for the fires I was charged with. The fires-set-as-diversion for shoplift crimes in the Fresno cases is easy to follow when explained by someone who has busted over 40 serial fire setters - me. I will no longer be muzzled by lawyers. My 2255 in the murder case is presently on hold. Technicalities in recent federal case law required me to re-submit these issues in regards to state law and once they are resolved (read denied) I will continue to the federal level. Hopefully, Judge Wanger will soon come to a favorable decision that can be included in my continuing battle with the state of California. The on-going confusion of the variety of pending appeals was kept from my family. Constant frustration with negative decisions forced me to protect my family from the courts. I now have two grandsons and the oldest, at six years of age, knows his grandfather is in jail.

The Court TV program, The System, aired recently and focused the entire hour on my case from the investigator's view. I cooperated fully with the production to the degree of having my father and mother provide photos on my early family life, and I gave them an hour-long interview. The one-hour chat was edited down to about five minutes worth of sound bites. Finally, I was able to loudly proclaim my innocence. and refute some of the "evidence" against me. The segment did little good. No information on the prosecutor's misconduct or my appeals was mentioned. The closing of the show ended with an BATF profiler stating, "Orr set hundreds, maybe thousands of fires. We may never know. He's not talking. He' s just a psychopath..." He has never asked to interview me and any studies he conducted did not come out in trial. Something else withheld that could have been considered exculpatory? I challenge the prosecutors to reveal the profiler's findings now. Despite these negative programs I will continue to talk openly, contrary to the ATF profiler's comments. I continue to offer an open interview with any authority to meet with me and go over this case. I hate it when I see a similar program and the statement is made, "...and the defendant refused to accept our offer of an interview to answer the charges." It's a lot like the general public's perception of the similar statement, "...the defendant refused to take a polygraph..." or "the defendant refused to take the stand in his own defense." I'm here. I'll talk freely. In the end, DNA may be my only salvation. The courts and public are listening; they're just not hearing.

On January 2, 2002, I was called, unexpectedly, to a parole hearing. Without mental preparation I sat before R. Haworth, the Lompoc Penitentiary Parole Hearing Officer. After a brief review of my custody level scores and comments on my clear record of conduct for the past ten years, he asked me to explain about my "crimes." I looked him straight in the eye and said, "I'm innocent. I've maintained I am innocent from the day of my arrest." We spent another ten minutes on procedural matters and I fully expected Mr. Haworth to tell me I cannot expect parole if I do not show remorse. I have heard that remorse is required before an inmate can be released. My fellow convicts had never heard of anyone being paroled under these conditions. Haworth's final statement was he would recommend parole in seven months, my first available release date. Typical of anything to do with the federal government, this parole date was counter to what I actually wanted. If I parole, the state of California throws me into one of their high-level prisons. I'd prefer staying where I am while I continue to pursue appeals and my information, from my federal overseers, has been I would be retained in federal custody until I served 2/3s of my 30-year sentence: 2012.

It is unheard of for someone convicted of the crimes I was said to have committed, to be released upon the first parole date, especially when no remorse was shown. Haworth told me, "You may have heard that remorse was a requirement for parole. I view it differently. I take your clear conduct and your appearance at this hearing and decide whether you are a risk to be released. I do not think, if you are guilty, that you would repeat these crimes. I believe you will find gainful employment and not be a parole problem at all. These are the factors I consider in my recommendations. Good luck."

The Parole Board in Washington, D.C. has to agree with Mr. Haworth's findings but I fully expect them to deny me despite Haworth's observations. My bags won't be packed for a while. The last thing I want, of course, is to be released to go to a California state prison so I imagine, in this catch-22 environment, I will be paroled. I see myself circling the drain...

EPILOGUE

I wrote this book as an memoir. After editing the work, I felt exposure of the variety of cases I investigated over the years might actually enlighten my readers; more like a textbook. Focusing *Points of Truth's* text on an audience of firefighters, police officers, and investigators, I imagined the content might inform the general reading public, too, and maybe entertain, as well. Close examination of crime scenes I evaluated, investigative techniques I developed, and overcoming fire/police professional jealousies I fought against, are typical circumstances arson and bomb investigators experience even today. Few outside these career fields know of the underlying difficulties in the public safety world. Reading like a dry police report, *Points of Truth* was not intended as a literary work; I am just a blue-collar writer, and simply want to tell a story. Despite my criminal convictions, I had an unblemished public service career for twenty-two years. Even those who feel I am guilty of arson/murder cannot argue that my career successes validate the content of this book. At least as a tool for investigators, and probably Behavioral Science enthusiasts, too.

I realize some profit from sales of my books. Son of Sam laws, used to block a prisoner from profiting from his crime, were overturned in 2002. Required now to contribute 55% of any income to a state victim's restitution fund, only a few dollars reach me here at Calipatria State Prison. The biggest portion of my 45% will be routed to pay overhead (typing/computer services, promotion, etc). a private investigator and, ultimately I hope, an attorney to assist bringing my innocence to light. Besides, what do I need money for? All my necessities are taken care of by the California Department of Corrections. How much can I spend on ramen soups and potato chips at the prison canteen.

In April 2002, the California Innocence Project accepted my case to pursue DNA issues and explore my showing of actual innocence through my time-lines. The CIP's lawyers, at least, communicated with me and took my collect phone calls. My experience with inadequate legal representation is no gauge of the entire profession. I have used several excellent advocates. Criminal defense lawyers, after all, represent guilty clients about 98 percent of the time. *Points of Truth* cannot be construed as a how-to, or how-not-to, guide for someone wrongly arrested and convicted as I was. With the pressure on, fingers pointing and trial looming, lawyer payments due and mental/physical health deteriorating, anyone could make the bad choices I did. Should I have pressed my lawyers to allow me to testify? Yes, without question; but I had little control over anything in my life during the past fifteen years. I hesitate to put myself in the company of the likes of serial killer Ted Bundy, but now I know why he fired his lawyers and attempted to defend himself in trial. I know my case better than anyone because I lived it every day and have the investigative background to pursue it and, I am innocent. Had the playing field been level, I might have had a chance at vindication. With the Innocence Project as my advocate, the possibility existed. Without funds to pay for a required private investigator, profit from this book could overcome that difficulty, but I need a lawyer to pursue this avenue. The prosecutors in my 1992 and 1998 trials cited all the coincidences in my life and case. The evidence suggested I was "always near fires when they started." I arrived before, or with, fire equipment in many fires in their "early" stages. I wrote a fictional novel about a firefighter-gone-bad and the story grew to truth, only through the efforts of overzealous prosecutors and investigators. Coincidence is not evidence of anything. As an investigator I looked closely at the events but needed more than a hypothesis to use coincidence against a suspect. Besides, such conjecture is not allowed in court; but duplicitous prosecutors find ways to slip such "evidence" in front of a jury. Even with a vigorous "objection!" from a defense attorney, sustained by the judge, you cannot unring a bell. The jury retains the "facts." An excellent example of coincidence: the best-selling non-fiction, true crime writer, Ann Rule, was commissioned in the early 1980's, to pen a book about a serial murder spree in the Washington state area. With over a dozen killings credited to the unknown suspect, Ms. Rule researched and prepared her manuscript. There were few clues to the perpetrator's identity. The novel was about the case, victims and investigative task force pursuing leads. Before she finished her manuscript, police apprehended a suspect. Ann Rule knew the now-identified killer. She actually worked with the man, dined with him on occasion, and he was in her home. He was a co-worker and friend. She, the designated chronicler of this series of murders, was acquainted with the suspect. His name, Ted Bundy, and the tale told in the fine book, *The Stranger Beside Me.* Coincidence. I wrote about a series of fires and fictionalized 80 percent of the manuscript, adding a multitude of fictitious blazes and circumstances. Coincidence is not evidence. I intentionally stopped writing this book prior to my parole from the federal prison system to the California Department of Corrections. My transition was not easy, with a touch of Post-Traumatic Stress Syndrome evident four years later. I find it difficult to relive my recent history by writing it down to update this book. The difference between doing time at a federal prison and at a state facility is like the variance of vacationing on Maui, or taking a holiday in the Kalahari Desert without shelter, water, or a weapon to protect you. I managed to get through a three-month reception center at Wasco, California without incident, but assignment to Centinela State Prison did not go as smoothly. Within weeks I was recognized by a inmate and an order for placement on a protective custody yard was made. Slammed into a segregated location (affectionately, and appropriately, called "the hole.") for three months waiting for a bed to open on the "special needs" yard, I migrated to Calipatria Prison in January 2003.

In June 2007, after five years of clandestine investigation of my case, the California Innocence Project returned about two hundred pages of documentation I provided them since 2002. There was no letter enclosed; not even a sticky-note explaining the document dumping. The package reeked rejection but I had no way of knowing without an enclosed letter. Frustrated, I wrote the Project for an explanation. Three weeks later I received a belated letter, with no apology for the dog-eared pages they forwarded without explanation, and said they no longer represented me. The obviously post-dated letter was a check-box rejection and stated further investigation of my case required expensive use of a private investigator and they do not have the funds. This letter should have been enclosed with the document return but was not.

Earlier in the year I sent a research letter to the L.A. County District Attorney's Office archives. The communication from them briefly stated "...all evidence from your case was ordered destroyed...in 2001." I assumed this included the DNA comparison material I desperately wanted tested/compared to my DNA, already in the state DNA database. I sent a copy of this letter to the Innocence Project and asked if they could verify the destruction of this critical evidence. I assumed they already made an attempt to preserve the material – wrongly. They had five years to do so. I also had provided copies of three letters I sent to the D.A.'s Office begging to preserve the DNA-testable evidence. Two letters preceded the evidence destruction date. None of the letters were ever answered by the D.A.'s Office prosecutor. Apparently, the Innocence Project prefers cases with DNA-testable materials available. Now I had none. I did, however, continue my research and examined documents available to me.

I know the Innocence Project examined my case, and the strong timeline alibis, since they requested information from me on several occasions. There were a few Project-generated margin notes on the documents I sent, and one of my caseworkers down-loaded a 10-page "Orr-case brief" from the Internet. I now thank them for that because the brief was written by L.A. Fire Department arson investigator Glen Lucero and I did not know it existed. The memoir outlined Lucero's participation in my prosecution and his involvement with "the most

435

prolific serial arsonist of the 20th century..."I now have further confirmation of the source of this insidious accusation, confirming the handwritten margin notes I found several years ago. But, what do I do with it?

Much like the withdrawal of the Innocence Project, my sources on the outside evaporated. Where my telephone book used to have 20-30 entries, in 2007 I call only three people regularly. My last partner, Joe Lopez, use to take my collect calls at the firehouse where he worked, Now I don't even know his address.

I don't fault any of my outside connections for gradually allowing this estrangement. The situation is like a failed long-term relationship. A continuing attachment, however infrequent the contacts, brings the pain of the original reason for the departure back to the surface. A clean break is necessary. One of my shift investigators died. I don't know when or the circumstances of his demise. An ex-wife had a bout with cancer. I am unaware of her condition.

Infrequently I battle depression and try to allow anger to bubble to the surface so I have something tangible to rage against. The prosecutors and overzealous investigators come to mind first but I find it more calming to slip back into a depressed state – I still feel allegiance to brother officers. Again, I find it easier to walk around the block to avoid confrontations. I find depression and anger are easily replaced by diving back into case research.

Casework is a refuge of sorts but without the resources or ability to obtain documentation or statements of confirmations, my leads remain dormant. For example, a set of 35mm negatives of pictures I took at the Ole's fire went missing prior to the 1998 murder trial. Perusing documents recently I found reference to a second set of negatives, possibly still obtainable. Without resources I cannot verify their actual existence or location. They may be the key to my door of "freedom." I also found reference to another witness to refute the only testimony against me in the 18-count College Hills fire case. His memory of events may be vital in refuting the retired pilot who says he saw me at the fire scene. I may now have three witnesses to counter that assertion.

Now I must attempt to find a defense-oriented private investigator to research my case when funds become available. He or she, in turn, can help me find an honest, reliable appeal lawyer to pursue my case. Until then, I will continue research, with my limited funds, and hope for some outside assistance.

My novel, *Points of Origin,* is available from
Infinity Publishing at:
www.buybooksontheweb.com
or
Toll-free: (877) BUY BOOK

John L. Orr P-13502
POB 5007 D1-142
Calipatria, CA 92233-5007
January 2012

Made in the USA
San Bernardino, CA
15 September 2016